SATI

A Historical Anthology

SATI

A Historical Anthology

edited by

ANDREA MAJOR

OXFORD

UNIVERSITY PRESS

OXFORD
UNIVERSITY PRESS

YMCA Library Building, Jai Singh Road, New Delhi 110 001

Oxford University Press is a department of the University of Oxford. It furthers the
University's objective of excellence in research, scholarship, and education
by publishing worldwide in

Oxford   New York

Auckland   Cape Town   Dar es Salaam   Hong Kong   Karachi   Kuala Lumpur
Madrid   Melbourne   Mexico City   Nairobi   New Delhi   Shanghai   Taipei   Toronto

With offices in

Argentina   Austria   Brazil   Chile   Czech Republic   France   Greece   Guatemala
Hungary   Italy   Japan   Poland   Portugal   Singapore   South Korea   Switzerland
Thailand   Turkey   Ukraine   Vietnam

Oxford is a registered trademark of Oxford University Press
in the UK and in certain other countries

Published in India by Oxford University Press, New Delhi

ISBN-13: 978-0-19-567895-6
ISBN-10: 0-19-567895-8

Typeset in Calisto MT 10.5/13, S.R.Enterprises, New Delhi
Printed in India by De-Unique, New Delhi 110 018
Published by Oxford University Press
YMCA Library Building, Jai Singh Road, New Delhi 110 001

For my family...

Contents

Acknowledgments

The editor and publisher are pleased to acknowledge the following individuals and organizations for their kind permission to reproduce extracts and articles included in this volume:

Ashis Nandy for 'Sati in *Kali Yuga*',
Romilla Thapar for 'In History',
Madhu Kishwar and *Manushi* for two articles, 'The Burning of Roop Kanwar' and 'Deadly Laws and Zealous Reformers',
Veena Oldenburg and Oxford University Press, New York, for 'The Roop Kanwar Case: Feminist Responses',
Hinduism Today and the Himalayan Academy for 'Uproar over Rajput Sati',
David Higham Associates for the extract from M.M. Kaye's *The Far Pavilions*,
Motilal Banarsidass for the extracts from A.S. Altekar's *The Position of Hindu Women* and Arvind Sharma's *Sati: Historical and Phenomenological Essays*,
Munshiram Manoharlal for Ananda Coomaraswamy's 'The Status of Indian Women',
The Navajivan Trust for M.K. Gandhi's 'A Twentieth Century Sati',
The Hakluyt Society for the extract from *The Travels of Ibn Battuta*.

Preface

The material contained in this anthology is just a small sample of the vast corpus of primary and secondary sources on sati that exist in archives and libraries in India and Britain. An anthologizer on this rare, but sensational, custom suffers from an embarrassment of riches when it comes to colonial and postcolonial sources on widow-burning. A different editor might produce a similar volume on the subject without replicating any of the sources here offered. The sheer volume of material available means that while many important pieces have been included, many equally significant works have perforce been left out. I do not apologize, therefore, for the omission of any particular piece, but rather proceed in the sincere hope that the reader will find interest and value in what is offered and perhaps be encouraged to explore for themselves this vast and fascinating literature. However, in order to provide the reader with a context for the choices that have been made when deciding on the contents of this anthology, it may be helpful to provide them with some background information on how this collection came about.

Many of the sources collected here were uncovered during the course of my doctoral and post-doctoral research into British and European responses to sati between 1500 and 1947. This research resulted in the recently published *Pious Flames: European Encounters with Sati 1500–1830* (New Delhi: Oxford University Press, 2006), as well as articles on sati in the Rajput States and in early twentieth-century India and a monograph, currently in preparation, on the prohibition of sati in the Princely States. While preparing

Pious Flames it was suggested to me that I might also like to produce an anthology based on the source material I had used for the monograph, an idea which I took up with enthusiasm. The resulting volume reflects these origins, for while I have endeavoured to include many Indian-authored writings on sati, much of the material from this volume comes from the colonial archive in which I have worked so extensively. In some cases reliance on colonial sources reflects the paucity of other writings on sati for a particular time and place, in others they are offered as representative of a rich body of 'Western' writing on sati that is of interest in itself. In both cases I would offer the usual caveat that, as interesting and useful as these colonial sources are, they should be read sensitively and not taken at face value. The observation and depiction of the 'other' by European writers must be understood as a political act in the colonial context and all these sources on sati, Western and Indian, tell us as much about the subjectivity of the observer as about the 'reality' of sati. Similarly, though some literary accounts are included, the anthology is primarily historical in nature, designed to make both famous and less well-known historical sources on sati more readily accessible to any with an interest in the area. The choices about what to include in this volume do not, therefore, imply a value judgment about what is important in the study of sati and what is not, but rather reflect my own interests, experience, and limitations. I hope in the future others, with different areas of expertise to myself, may take up this issue and offer other perspectives on this fascinating topic.

This anthology is so closely connected with my wider research that it is difficult to separate those who have assisted with this volume from the wider network of those who have helped and supported me in all my endeavours to date. In Edinburgh, I have received invaluable advice and encouragement from various members of the Centre for South Asian Studies, especially Markus and Umbreen Daechsel, Bashabi Fraser, Roger and Patricia Jeffery, and Crispin Bates. I cannot thank them enough for making Edinburgh such a stimulating place to carry out research on South Asia.

I would like to extend my gratitude to the staff of the various archives and libraries in which I have researched this topic, including the Oriental and India Office (British Library), the National

Library of Scotland, Bodleian Library (Oxford), Council for World Mission Archive, School of Oriental and African Studies (SOAS), Baptist Missionary Archive (Regent's Park College, Oxford), National Archives of India (Delhi), National Library of India (Calcutta), Nehru Memorial Library (Delhi), Royal Asiatic Society Library (Calcutta), and Rajasthan State Archives (Bikaner). I would also like to thank Suranjan Das, Nandini Sunder, and Sudhir Chandra for their support and advice during my time in India.

Mention must also be made of the financial support that I have received from various bodies, including full MSc and PhD studentships funded by the Arts and Humanities Research Board and a post-doctoral fellowship funded by the Economic and Social Research Council. In addition, various travel expenses have been offset in part by grants from the Society for South Asian Studies, Carnegie Foundation, and British Academy, and from the University of Edinburgh George Scott Travelling Fellowship.

I would also like to thank everybody at Oxford University Press (Delhi) who have worked so diligently on this book, particularly my editors for their invaluable help and endless hard work in the preparation of this volume.

Finally, I dedicate this book to my family—my parents Verena and Alan, my husband Garry, and my son Alex. Nobody could ask to be surrounded by more loving and supportive people and their belief in me is the foundation of everything I have achieved or hope to do.

Introduction

Sati must be one of those things that look quite different from different view-points. If we cannot see it from the orthodox Hindu's side, we cannot know what aspect it shows to him. Nor can we expect to persuade him that our view of it is clearer or truer than his.[1]

R. Hurst, 1929

For British police officer R. Hurst, as for so many Europeans before and after him, sati, the Hindu custom in which a bereaved widow burns on the funeral pyre of her deceased husband, was a profound example of the deep moral, cultural, and ideological gulf that separated 'East' and 'West'. Hurst, like many of his compatriots in the early twentieth century, assumed that there were distinct European and Indian views on sati that were both consistent within themselves and diametrically opposed to each other. Sati was a sensational and divisive issue when Hurst was writing in 1929, as it had been for centuries, and still is today, but the divisions that it evokes cannot simply be reduced to the well-worn binaries of 'East' and 'West', Indian and European, Hindu and Christian, barbarous and civilized. Rather, they cross categories of race and nationality, meaning different things to different people at different times. Not all Europeans have opposed or censured sati, and by no means all Hindus support it.

Even at the height of its occurrence sati was an exceptional act, claiming the lives of only a tiny minority of Hindu widows. Despite this, it has evoked a disproportionate level of interest among both Indian and European observers, primarily because its social and political significance goes far beyond its actual occurrence.

Generally speaking, sati is most commonly associated with two main regions in India; Bengal and Rajasthan. In Bengal, the custom's popularity seems to have peaked during the first thirty years of the nineteenth century. During the period between 1815 and 1829 the British kept a record of the immolations, which totalled between five hundred and nine hundred annually, and a vibrant debate took place in both British and Indian society about the nature and future of the rite. The scale of the immolations during this period have led some contemporary scholars, such as Ashis Nandy, to suggest that sati in Bengal was a 'colonial pathology'; an anomalous epidemic that was a direct response to the social dislocation caused by the imposition of imperial rule. [2] Although others reject this idea, most contemporary historians would now agree with Lata Mani's influential ideas about the political significance of the sati debate in nineteenth-century Bengal, which see it as an arena in which the parameters of colonial control could be tested and contested. [3]

In both these interpretations, sati in Bengal is assumed to be qualitatively different to its Rajput counterpart. Sati in Rajasthan was well known from the medieval period onwards and is often, somewhat erroneously, conflated with the warrior tradition and rites such as *jauhar*. Rajasthan has been the site of much of the contemporary debate about sati, especially in the months after September 1987 and the controversy that occurred in the wake of the much discussed burning of a young Rajput widow, Roop Kanwar. This immolation was not in itself unique—it has been estimated that there has been at least one such burning per year since independence. [4] The level of controversy it sparked was unusual however, as sati became the site of contest between those who touted a glorified version of Hindu (and specifically Rajput) tradition and culture, of which sati was a part, and those who opposed the act as another indicator of Indian women's oppression. In the process, the debate became about far more than the tragic death of a young woman; it involved crucial issues about the role of 'tradition' in Indian life and of Hindu religion in a secular state. As had been the case in the early nineteenth century and at various other points in history, sati was constructed as a site on which other, bigger issues could be played out. Debates on sati were always about far more than burning women.

The immolation of Roop Kanwar was cause for concern among feminists and liberals in India not only because of the tragic and brutal fate suffered by the young woman herself, but because the accompanying re-emergence of sati as a political issue was seen by many as reopening a debate that had been successfully concluded in 1829, when the British Governor-General Lord William Bentinck outlawed the rite. Veena Oldenburg articulates this position when she comments that for the feminists who opposed the glorification of the Deorala incident, 'sati as an issue was settled some 175 [*sic*] years ago; the question is why it is still allowed to persist'.[5] As Kamla Bhasin and Ritu Menon put it in a special number of *Seminar* devoted to the discussion of sati in the wake of the Roop Kanwar case:

One hundred and fifty years after it was banned, we find ourselves in the peculiar position of having to justify and defend our stand against the practice of sati. One hundred and fifty years later, we are having to restate the case against barbarism; exhume legal and other arguments long laid to rest; reiterate the imperative of a truly secular state and its consequent social responsibilities, and try valiantly to keep the wolves of church and state from howling at our doors. One hundred and fifty years later we are having to remind ourselves that women are not for burning.[6]

The assumption that the sati question was closed in 1829, and that its re-emergence in 1987 was a radical new departure, is not entirely accurate, however. Not only had sati attracted considerable interest and debate long before the early nineteenth century, it continued to do so long after the British prohibition. It persisted quite legally in some of the princely states until as late as 1860, and illegally in both British and 'Indian' India long after this. Indeed, far from disappearing from the equation between 1829 and 1987, the sati issue remained close to the surface of social and political life in India. Both the idea and practice of sati impinged on various nationalist and imperialist discourses throughout the colonial period. The 'abolition' of sati remained a touchstone for social reform in colonial India, although the precise nature of the precedent it set for state interference in religious/cultural issues remained the subject of debate.[7] Moreover, every illegal sati that occurred in colonial India became a site of contest to some degree. For the most part, the confrontations that accompanied individual immolations took place on a local scale, as crowds of worshippers (and sometimes native police themselves) impeded state intervention, and villages closed ranks to hamper later investigations. On some occasions, such as the sati in Barh, Bihar, in 1927, this contest broke through onto the national stage and became the site on which larger questions about the role of the colonial state in issues of religion and tradition and its right to 'speak' for a 'modern' India aspiring for independence could be addressed.

This anthology has been designed to demonstrate the diversity and significance of writing on sati, not just in the context of the well-known early nineteenth and late twentieth-century debates, but across several hundred years. It brings together a variety of disparate sources on this most controversial of customs, most of which were collected during research into changing European attitudes to the custom. They were written by men and women, Indians and Europeans, from many different backgrounds. Official documents, sacred texts, newspaper articles, personal memoirs, and works of fiction are all represented. When taken together they demonstrate the vast range of diverse and often ambivalent responses that sati has evoked among different people at different times. It includes a large number of European accounts, for while some recent discussions of sati seek to delineate modern issues and ideologies from 'the voyeuristic discourse that widow immolations have produced in colonial spectators and their contemporary progeny',[8] the fact remains that colonial representations and misrepresentations of sati have played an important part in shaping the terrain of the contemporary discourse. The debate of the early nineteenth century, which culminated in the prohibition of sati in British India in 1829, left a lasting legacy both in judicial and ideological terms, privileging as it did the question of the widow's volition, while at the same time undermining her agency and casting her as a passive victim of a 'barbaric oriental practice'. To a large extent the ideas of this period have come to represent both the normative 'Western' position on sati and a starting point for later discussions of the rite. Yet, this discourse and the prohibition that followed it was far from conclusive, either in terms of the eradication of sati in the subcontinent or the formation of colonial ideas on the subject. Far from being informed by a monolithic set of assumptions and ideas, Europeans encountered sati very differently at different times and in different contexts. The ideas about sati that came to dominate the British discourse in the early nineteenth century were quite different from those that had informed observers in the early modern and Enlightenment periods, and those that would be influential later. Rather than ending in 1829, British involvement with sati continued throughout the colonial period, and their ideas about the rite continued to change and develop throughout this time. Many of the later manifestations of the colonial discourse on sati have striking resonances with the current debate, suggesting that both indigenous and colonial interpretations of sati are implicated in the formation of the contemporary discourse.

Sati and Hindu Tradition

Literally translated, sati means 'virtuous woman'. As a term it has multiple meanings, but it is most commonly used to denote the woman who burns on her husband's funeral pyre.[9] In the colonial period the British extended the term, in its anglicized form 'suttee', to the rite itself, with the result that sati is often now used for both the practice and the practitioner. Although the application of the word to the custom suggests that sati is something that one performs, it is most correctly understood in its Hindu context as something one becomes. If a woman accumulates enough *sat* (goodness) through devotion to her husband she can become sati, usually, though not exclusively, by following him onto the pyre.[10] Although never practised by more than a small minority, and always controversial, widow immolation had, by the nineteenth century, become a socially sanctioned practice among certain communities in India.

The origins of sati remain obscure. The oldest known historical instance occurred in 316 BC when Greek observers recorded the immolation of the wife of Hindu General Keteus during Alexander's invasion of India. Archaeological and literary evidence suggest that the custom may have been known well before this, however. In the nineteenth century, British scholars and administrators initiated the search for the religious origins of sati amid the great mass of literature that makes up the corpus of the Hindu 'scriptures'. Although

there are numerous ideological and methodological problems arising from this approach, it is one that has been followed by scholars
until very recently. The results, however, are rarely conclusive. Unlike Christianity or Islam, there is no single supreme religious text
or lineal religious tradition in Hinduism from which a definitive the-
ology can be discerned. Rather, there is a heterogeneous collection of texts and edicts spanning some 4000 years, which contradict, overlap, and redefine each other, and which are cross-cut by
the infinite variations of popular practice and local custom. Even
individual texts have not been static, but have been subject to an
ongoing process of codification and evolution, with the result that
they are almost impossible to date with any degree of accuracy. In
terms of interpretation, questions exist over whether predominantly
elite, authored texts were written to reflect existing customs, or to
prescribe the correct way of future behaviour, and over the extent
the ideas expressed in them penetrated society at large.[11]

The earliest of the known Hindu scriptures, the Vedas (4000 BC–
1000 BC), do not refer to sati as an act to be practised, although
there is a verse in the *Ṛg Veda* which has been quoted by exponents
of sati to prove its Vedic origin. This verse is now widely dis-
credited and is believed to have resulted from an orthographic
mistake by which the word *agre* was replaced with *agni*, changing
the sense of the verse from 'the women advance to the altar first'
to 'let the women go into the womb of the fire'.[12] The very next
verse makes a mockery of the idea that the widow was expected
to burn. It refers to the widow lying down on the pile by the side
of her husband's body, before being called upon to return to the
land of the living, and to 'lead a prosperous life enjoying the bliss
of children and wealth'.[13] The absence of a reliable reference to
widow burning in the Vedas has led most scholars to agree that,
though it may have been known, the custom was not widely practised or enjoined during this period. The implication of this verse
and similar ones in the *Atharvaveda* and *Black Yajurveda*, however,
is that though the actual act of immolation is prevented, the faithful
wife should display the desire to accompany her deceased husband. Arguably, the ethos of wifely devotion and sacrifice, of
which sati was the ultimate expression, is evident in these verses,
even if the immolation itself is prevented.

Although the sati appears in Hindu texts as early as 400 BC, the long tradition of validating it in religious laws did not begin until the medieval period.[14] The famous passages extolling the virtue of sati, such as those found in the *Angirasa* (AD 700), which decrees '...she who follows her husband into death dwells in heaven for as many years as there are hairs on a human body, viz., three-and-a-half crores of years'[15] date from around AD 600 onwards, by which time many conservative authorities were citing sati as the preferred course for a widow. Despite growing support for sati, there was also a strong tradition of opposition to the rite, a fact often overlooked by colonial administrators. In his *Kadambari*, the poet Banabhatta (AD 600) condemned the practice as inhuman and called it 'a foolish mistake of stupendous magnitude, committed under the reckless impulse of despair and infatuation'.[16] Medhatithi (AD 900), a commentator on Manu, compares the practice to black magic and claims that as suicide it is *adharma* and forbidden to women, while the author of the *Mahanirvanatantra* condemns the act as a form of suicide which will consign the perpetrators' soul to hell.[17] Despite this persistent and vigorous tradition of protest against the rite, the custom appears to have grown in popularity from the medieval period on, and was advocated in an increasing number of texts. Mandakranta Bose suggests that '...the fact that this condemnation was silently passed over by the Hindu establishment at the time shows how active the promoters of sati were in constructing a supporting ideology from a selective reading of the sources of the Hindu belief system'.[18] As late as the eighteenth century the south Indian digest writer Tryambakayajvan could firmly advocate the practice of sati in his *Stridharmapaddhati*.[19]

The textual references to sati have been quoted and misquoted repeatedly in the scholarship on sati, and it is only in recent years that scholars have begun to move away from the debate over the specific textual origins of the custom, and begun to look more broadly at the sociocultural environment that created it. Sally Sutherland, for example, has argued that although the specific rite of sati is rare in the epics, the 'deeply ingrained...patriarchal constructions of power and misogynous attitudes'[20] that underpin it are apparent. She suggests that determination to end one's existence is a common and non-gender-specific reaction to the loss of a beloved in the epics, but that while men are prevented from realizing this intention, women are permitted to carry it through. This she attributes to the assumption that a woman who lacks her husband's protection, whether because he is dead or for any other reason, is viewed as *asati*—not virtuous. Virtue is restored through life as an ascetic or death by burning, drowning in the Ganga, etc.[21] Thus Sutherland asserts that while the specific rite of sati occurs only sporadically in the epics, the ethos which sees women's virtue and value as entirely dependent on her relationship with her husband, it is ascertainable throughout them.

Just as the precise textual origins of sati are confused and difficult to pinpoint exactly, so the social and cultural forces that lead to the adoption of the practice are obscure and a matter mainly of conjecture. Most of the information that we have on social practices in early India has been gleaned from sacred and literary texts and, as we have seen, these are far from providing us with any unproblematic explanations of the root causes of sati. Some historians, particularly in the early twentieth century, have connected the furthest origins of the custom with other similar death rites in a variety of prehistoric societies. Some go even further and suggest that the custom was brought to India by early invaders from Central Asia.[22] Others conflate sati with the Rajput custom of jauhar (by which the women of a conquered city would commit themselves to a communal pyre when defeat became inevitable) and suggest that it was adopted by martial castes to prevent the dishonouring of the widows of the defeated. Too close an identification between the two customs would be misleading, but the fact that some of the earlier textual references to sati prohibit it to Brahmin women lends support to the idea that it was originally a Kshatriya custom that was later adopted by other castes as it came to be deemed a meritorious action.[23] In Rajasthan, today, many Rajput women believe that the 'true' sati is a phenomenon unique to their caste and view the motives of satis from other castes with suspicion.[24]

Even if we accept that the original concept of sati was as an exceptional and heroic action in the warrior tradition[25] we must still explain why it was so widely adopted by other castes and gained such a broad base of societal approval across India. Some historians suggest that the dislocation caused by the numerous foreign invasions and internal conflicts of the medieval period created an environment in which rape and abduction were more common, causing the desire to protect women's chastity to reach fatal proportions. Although these factors may have exacerbated the situation to some extent, this explanation is very far from comprehensive. As Uma Chakravarti points out, the tendency to blame foreign, and especially Muslim, invasions for the various forms of oppression suffered by Hindu women is part of a wider nationalist agenda to delineate this oppression from Hinduism itself. In fact, the '…structure of institutions that ensured the subordination of women was complete in *all essentials* long before the Muslims as a religious community came into being'.[26] With reference to sati in particular, it seems unlikely that such considerations would have borne any weight had not the internal structure of gender relations already developed in a manner which supported widow immolation. To understand the growth of sati as an approved custom we must therefore consider the changing position of women within Hindu society itself.

Nationalist historians tend to view the Vedic period as a 'Golden Age' for Indian women, and most scholars now accept that their social and ritual position were relatively high during this era. Many of the practices that were to lead to the depreciation of women's status among the higher castes had their roots in the slightly later era of the Brahmanas and Upanishads.[27] The increasing complexity of Brahmanic ritual during this period prefaced a shift in the centre of education from the family home to that of the teacher, with the concomitant effect that women were increasingly alienated from education. The result of this alienation was that the Vedic ideal of man and wife as partners in the religious rituals of hospitality and worship was undermined, and woman's social role was redefined to emphasize only her reproductive function, leading to the increased popularity of early marriage for girls of higher castes. Child marriages fulfilled several social purposes: it shortened the length of time the young girl spent in the family home, thus relieving her parents both of the cost of her maintenance and responsibility for her chastity; removed the possible stigma of having an unmarried daughter; and reduced the chance of romance, making arranged matches easier to enforce and ensuring the honour and purity of the caste. From the point of view of the husband's family a young bride was more malleable and easily socialized into her new family, and, perhaps more importantly, her reproductive lifespan was maximized, increasing the chances of her producing the all-important son.[28]

The converse of these benefits was also considerable, however. The disparity in the ages between the husband, who had to complete his Vedic learning before he could marry, and his young bride, combined with the inferior care given to women generally, meant that widowhood was rendered increasingly likely, and at a younger age. As custom dictated that the widow was entitled to support for life from her husband's joint family, the surfeit of widows created by child marriage constituted a considerable economic burden on high-caste families, among whom widows were debarred from remarrying or materially contributing to the family's income. The lower castes, of course, which made up the majority of India's population, were not constrained by such considerations and among these groups widow remarriage was common, and sati relatively rare. The emphasis on women's reproductive role meant that the widow was left without a social function, although she still represented a sexual threat and an economic burden. The restrictions of austere widowhood had the result of diminishing the widow's physical attractiveness and reduced the cost of her support to a minimum. Sati, of course, represented an effective and irreversible solution to both these problems.

Closely linked to the issue of the widow's support was that of her inheritance rights. These were practically non-existent in the Vedic period, but from about AD 500 writers such as Yajnavalkya, Bṛhaspati, and Vṛdamanu began to champion widows' rights in this area. Ashini Agrawal has pointed out a chronological correlation between increasing demands for widows' inheritance and growing support for sati, and suggests that this shows that the two were interconnected.[29] She also shows that it was those writers who were most opposed to widows' inheritance rights were the most active advocates of sati, while those who supported better rights were, for obvious reasons, either against sati, or silent on the matter. It is also clear that it was the elite—the Brahmins and

Kshatriyas—who would have the most to lose from widows' inheritance, and the accompanying possibility of the alienation and partition of estates. So it does not come as a surprise that it was among these classes that sati was most prevalent.

If sati offered a practical solution to problems of inheritance and support, it also gained a political aspect, especially among the Kshatriyas. The political order of the eighteenth century had given rise to principalities—ruled over by Jats, Bhumihars, Rajputs, Rohillas, and Afghans—scattered across north India. Important Rajput lineages existed not only in what is now Rajasthan, but also in what was to become the north-western provinces of British India. Rajputs, along with other high-caste rural magnates had legal claims to land and the right to a share of its produce. Those at the very top of the social and political hierarchy were called *raja* or *rana* and were autonomous chieftains in their own right. The area of control could range from a few square miles to large independent kingdoms, such as Mewar or Marwar, where the rulers adopted the honorific *maharaja* or *maharana* meaning 'great king'. As Malavika Kasturi points out, 'to strengthen their claim to kingship, many powerful magnates linked themselves to Kshatriya genealogical "tradition" and emphasized their elite social and ritual status'.[30] This tradition included affiliation to founding *gotra*s or clans, a military ethos and specific patterns of alliance, marriage, etc. It could also include social/ritual practices such as sati. Women, marriage, and power were integrally linked; matrimonial alliances were important primarily for their ritual symbolic function, through which a ruler's power was constituted and reinforced. As Kasturi points out:

The honour of powerful brotherhoods was closely associated with that of their wives and daughters, who were viewed more as property or instruments of exchange and were largely confined to the 'female space'. Women's sexuality was controlled and they were primarily utilized by lineages to contract alliances of superior status. This devaluation of women was mirrored in elite Rajput cosmology, which reinforced Rajput caste and gender stereotypes, seeking to remove women as active agents from the arena.[31]

Among certain clans and lineages, the practice of sati became closely linked with both the ideal of female virtue and the Kshatriya tradition, and so with the honour and status of the clan.

A polygamous marriage system and the hierarchical structure of the Rajput zenana also contributed to the spread of sati. As Varsha Joshi points out, 'The maintenance of stepmothers and grandmothers in the zenana was a major problem. ...Had the widow continued to live in the zenana she could become the source of disruptive zenana 'intrigue' prompted by her need to safeguard her own interests. Against this background one can easily see how self-immolation might be encouraged as a practical solution as far as the ruling houses were concerned.'[32]

If sati was thus a practical solution to the problem of widowhood among higher castes, its desirability as an action was reinforced in ideological terms by way in which it embodied certain elite prescriptions for ideal female conduct. The perception, encouraged, as we have seen, by some authors from the medieval period on, that sati represented the ultimate expression of *stridharma* and the deification of the woman as a feminine ideal helps to explain the approval that the rite engendered even among social groups and lineages that did not themselves practise it. As Kumkum Sangari and Sudesh Vaid point out, sati has been 'mythologized precisely because of, and proportionate to, the level of violence inherent in it'.[33] This glorification of sati as the supernatural manifestation of female virtue is based on certain elite prescriptions for ideal female behaviour in which marriage and reproduction are emphasized as determining a Hindu woman's status and value. Marriage within the Hindu religion was treated as a sacrament rather than a contract, and was almost universal, especially for women.[34] An unmarried daughter was a considerable social stigma and families went to considerable lengths to provide a dowry sufficient to secure a suitable husband. The status of a married woman was deemed the highest and most auspicious to which a woman could aspire and a woman's dharma revolved almost entirely around her actions towards her husband.[35] In elite patriarchal circles, the epitome of both female virtue and of female power was embodied in the *pativrata*, literally one who makes a vow (*vrat*) for the well-being of her husband (*pati*).[36] The ultimate role models for Hindu women in this context are the triumvirate of Sita, Sati, and Savitri, for, while other less conventional women such as Mirabai and Draupadi are revered, they are not held up for emulation. In Rajasthan, court bards (*Charans*) prepared the psychological ground for sati by providing the suitable ideological rationale, making sati a strong model of female chastity and connecting it with pativratadharma. 'By valorizing the act they transformed self-immolation into a heroic sacrifice and effectively linked it to the honour and prestige of a woman's natal and conjugal clans. Through their poetry, the Charans conditioned Rajput women from their childhood to accept and even welcome immolation by glorifying it as sati.'[37] They did this by eulogizing previous satis and portraying immolation as an ideal for Rajput womanhood. Sati was not confined to Rajput castes, of course, but was practised by high and low castes, though its adoption by some communities can in part be seen as an emulation of elite ideals—what Srinivas refers to as 'Sanskritization'. Communities closely connected to the Rajput court, for example, might adopt various practices of their rulers, copying the architectural style of havelis, for example, or adopting customs such as purdah and sati.

The power of the faithful wife was believed to be formidable, and in its purest form was considered almost supernatural in nature. A pativrata through her power could 'burn the world, stop the motions of the sun and moon'.[38] That the Hindu wife protects her husband from death was an important theme in the duties of the pativrata. The devoted wife was supposed to protect her husband in three main ways—by serving him, providing him with food, care and children; by performing religious rituals, including fasts, on his behalf; and by remaining devoted and loyal to him. Indeed, the power (*sat*) created within the virtuous pativrata was believed to be so great that it could save or preserve the husband's life. This is the same *sat*, produced by her devotion and chastity during his life, which is said to give true sati the power to ignite the pyre with the heat of her inner goodness, and to bear the flames unflinchingly. In the truest sense the impetus to commit sati is not considered to be a sudden determination arrived at at the time of the husband's demise, but rather the inescapable product of the *sat* that the virtuous wife has accumulated throughout her life.[39] A woman's power to protect her husband was something of a double-edged sword, however, for as she was conceived to have this power if she was faithful, so a husband's misfortune or death could indicate that she had not lived up to the ideal. For a husband to die before the wife was considered most inauspicious, and was viewed as proof either of the wife's misdeeds of a previous life or of her failure to fulfil her duties to her husband in the present one. Either way the widow was held on some level to be responsible for her husband's death. Thus, while correct action on the part of the wife could bring her great status—indeed the good wife was viewed as Lakshmi, the bringer of wealth and progeny—so too could she be held accountable for misfortune on the part of her husband. For this reason many Hindu women will still perform weekly, monthly, and yearly *vrats* and *nompus* designed to preserve her husband's longevity.[40]

This belief in the complicity of the wife in the premature death of the husband goes some way towards explaining the dramatic drop in status suffered by a high-caste woman on the death of her husband. As Martha Alter Chen points out, many Hindu women dread widowhood not just because of the associated shock and grief, but also because of the associated guilt and blame.[41] As a wife and mother, a woman was considered the epitome of auspiciousness, her female power and sexuality (*sakti*) being channelled correctly into the conjugal union. As a widow, however, she became 'the most inauspicious of all inauspicious things',[42] 'an ogress that ate her husband with her karmic jaws',[43] polluted by the association with death and the misfortune which she had inadvertently brought upon her husband. Part of the reason that the treatment of the widow was (and in some cases still is)[44] so harsh in certain sections of Hindu society was the idea that her austerities are in part a penance for not being sufficiently devoted to a husband during his life. Other factors were at play as well, however. We have already seen that the elite patriarchal tradition had difficulty in situating uncontrolled women; the widow, however, represents a sexually experienced woman from whom the legitimating bonds of marriage have been removed and may as a result have reverted to the 'true' nature of woman—'wild, adulterous, infertile, sexual and dangerous'.[45] In the nineteenth-century Marathi, the word for widow and the word for prostitute were in some contexts interchangeable, giving some idea of the popular opinion of the widow's capacity for celibacy.

It is out of the dichotomy between the exalted married woman and the despised widow that the rationale for sati emerged among some castes and lineages, especially those that did not allow remarriage. The act of sati allowed a 'good wife' to escape widowhood and consolidate her status as pativrata, a feat which could only otherwise be achieved through a life of ascetic devotion. Katherine K. Young points out that there are many ideological similarities between sati and austere widowhood. Both are purging bad karma by performing a kind of *tapas*; the difference between them lies in their immediate reaction to the news of their husband's death. The sati thinks immediately of her husband, going with him in 'a single violent display of self-annihilating devotion'[46] and so is deemed highly auspicious. The widow thinks first of her own life and so must use the hiatus between her husband's death and her own to restore her lost *sat* through penance.[47] As a woman is not technically widowed in India until the soul has been released from the body of her husband by cremation; the woman who goes to the pyre with her husband is still a wife, and so in the eyes of the community retains her status as a pativrata. In theory, the 'true' sati is one who has accumulated so much *sat* during her husband's lifetime that on his death the accumulated heat of her inner goodness compels her to the pyre. As Paul Courtright points out, it is this 'myth' of the true sati that allows her to 'take on a supernatural persona which enables her to calmly mount the pyre and distribute blessings and curses'.[48] Varsha Joshi points to the differentiation in Rajasthani tradition between satis who 'showed their power to perform miracles, and, in a spiritual manner, were able to resolve people's social, psychological, religious and physical problems, and in this capacity were worshipped and deified' and those who did not exhibit these powers and so were not.[49] Madhu Kishwar suggests that the honour that the sati receives in death, in a culture where women are viewed as dispensable, may help explain why many women are awe-inspired by the new sati cult. They may view it as a displaced acknowledgement of the many little sacrifices ordinary women make in everyday life.[50]

Support for sati has never been universal, of course, even among the community that practises it. While many of the ideas and themes discussed above do resonate with large sections of

Indian society, there has always been a strong anti-sati discourse from early writers such as Medhatithi and Banabhatta, through Raja Rammohan Roy in the early nineteenth century, M.K. Gandhi in the early twentieth and a wide variety of feminists and liberals in the present. In the present, opinion on sati is polarized between those who believe in the potential for truly '*dharmic*' sati and support it as part of a glorious Hindu tradition and heritage and those who see even 'voluntary' sati as an act of violence against women. Pro-sati campaigners, and, indeed, perhaps a wide base of Indian popular opinion, draw distinctions between illegally coerced and divinely sanctioned voluntary sati, admitting the former as murder, but defending the legitimacy of the latter. Feminists and liberals, on the other hand, maintain that, even were it proved, a widow's complicity in the sacrifice would not legitimize the rite and argue that the suggestions of volition on the part of the widow are in themselves embedded within the discourse that attempts to justify the practice. As Kumkum Sangari and Sudesh Vaid put it:

The theories of female subjectivity which attempt to separate and reify the woman's volition—that is to represent the violence either as a product of female agency or as being anything other than violence—are in fact, methodologically speaking, working on the same model as ideological formations that structure the practice of widow immolation. Essential to both is the suppression of the materiality of the event and of the processes that inform the immolation.

In an editorial in *New Quest* in 1987, M.P. Rege argues that the key site of contestation between pro- and anti-sati groups was the former's belief in what the latter refused to acknowledge—the possibility of the truly '*dharmic*' sati in which the widow is not victim, but victorious.[51]

European Encounters with Sati

If Hindu opinion on sati is thus divided, so too were European responses to the rite. From the earliest encounters with sati in the fourth-century BC, 'Western' reactions were ambivalent, as horror at the 'barbarism' of the custom was juxtaposed against admiration for the widow's bravery and fidelity. While some European observers, such as the famous French traveller François Bernier, painted a hellish picture of sati, others, such as Francisco Pelsaert, openly expressed their admiration for the widow who preserved her chastity through death. Ideas about sati were not static and there was no absolute moral position on the rite. Rather, attitudes and images shifted over time and between observers. Reactions to sati were to some extent conditioned by attitudes towards India itself, but they also reflected ideological trends and concerns within the observers' own society. Ideas about the status and nature of women, the role of religion, suicide, family, the treatment of the human body, etc., all played a part in shaping specific images of sati at specific times.[52]

Although Europeans had been aware of sati from classical times, the first extensive body of writing on the subject appeared in the sixteenth and seventeenth centuries. During this period travellers of various nationalities, but especially the Portuguese, English, French, Dutch, and Italians, made their way to the subcontinent for purposes as diverse as trade, mission, diplomacy, and adventure. The thirst of the home audience for accounts of travels in far-off lands led many of these men to produce narratives and journals of their journeys, either at the time or after they had returned home, many of which were then published either individually or in compendiums. As one of the most 'sensational' customs of the East, sati received a considerable degree of attention. An account of widow immolation, whether personally witnessed or plagiarized from another, was almost indispensable to any account of Indian society and culture. The variety of backgrounds from which European travellers came, not to mention the nature of travel writing as a genre, allowed space for a striking heterogeneity in reactions to sati, especially when compared to the homogenization of the nineteenth-century British response. Early modern accounts reflect both condemnation and praise, as individual reactions to sati were conditioned by personal experience. In the absence of a detailed knowledge of either Indian society or 'Hinduism',[53] sixteenth- and seventeenth-century observers tended to interpret sati through experience and analogy. Unlike the eighteenth and nineteenth centuries, when increasing knowledge of 'Hinduism' led observers to contextualize the rite as part of a coherent religious and social system,[54] earlier travellers tended to understand sati through more easily observable sociological and emotional forces—honour and dishonour, love, fear of poverty, and sexuality—some of which found resonance with patriarchal Christian ideas. Thus, rather than being viewed as an act of religious sacrifice, the widow's voluntary immolation was generally understood as the result of more temporal concerns,[55] especially the fear of the indignities that accompanied ascetic widowhood. In this respect, as Kate Teltscher points out, the early modern understanding of the causes of sati was surprisingly close to the later feminist position.[56]

The eighteenth century saw both a quantitative and, more importantly, a qualitative shift in the material about sati that was available to the reading public in Europe. The most obvious locus of change occurred in the last quarter of the century, when the work of the 'orientalist' scholars in learning Sanskrit and translating ancient Hindu texts brought a new dimension to the European understanding of India, its religions and customs. Personal observation was replaced with textual authority in explaining the practices of the Hindu population and the authenticity of a particular tradition or rite came to be measured not by personal experience, but by reference to a codified body of literature believed to outline the immutable principles of the Hindu religion. Prolonged and increasing contact with the subcontinent broadened the base of knowledge available, while intellectual developments had a profound effect on the ways in which this information was processed and formulated into an image of India. The eighteenth century was a transitional period that linked the explorative impulses of the preceding centuries to the imperial imperatives of the later one, both in terms of the political and economic relationships between India and Europe and the ideological constructs that underpinned them. In terms of the European understanding of sati, it linked the individual accounts of travellers and traders to the official attitudes of administrators and rulers and saw the genesis of many of the preconceived ideas and assumptions that informed the nineteenth-century debate on sati and its abolition.

Sati continued to be an indispensable event in any narrative on India, but by the eighteenth century the openly voyeuristic nature of European attendance at immolations had been replaced by the rhetoric of scientific inquiry, as those who reported on sati increasingly explained their presence at an immolation in terms of collecting accurate information rather than attending a spectacle. Despite the widespread consensus that sati was an authentic custom, many observers felt the need to express their amazement. English merchant Abraham Caldecott, for example, wrote of sati as

...a circumstance so widely differing from the tenets of our Religion and so repugnant to human nature that had I not seen it with my own eyes, I certainly would have been apt to doubt the veracity of it, but the fact is so well established and so many instances of the like nature have occurred since writing my letter as leaves no doubt of the generality of the practice all over Bengal....[57]

Emphasizing reactions of disbelief and horror allowed the narrator to share in the projected sentiments of his reader, and to emphasize his difference in relation to the Hindu crowd. This may have been in part due to changing attitudes that made public displays of brutality less acceptable parts of everyday life for educated Europeans, but it also represented a growing tendency to divorce European experience from Indian life. Indeed, the frequency with which eighteenth-century observers prefaced their accounts with protestations of disbelief suggests a shift away from understanding sati through reference to shared or universal motivations, which had been the norm in the early modern period, and towards viewing it as part of an alien culture that had its own specific and inherent characteristics. Appreciation of the personal or immediate forces acting on the widow was submerged in a rhetoric that explained sati in terms of emerging stereotypes of Indian society.[58] As a result, sati was increasingly simplistically explained as arising out of the Indian woman's two supposedly essential characteristics—her inherent religiosity and her devotion to her husband. This duality of supposed motive is at the root of the two conflicting images of sati that emerged in the eighteenth century, for while her devotion to her husband underpinned the positive, heroic image of sati presented in some accounts and in paintings by the likes of John Zoffany and Tilly Kettle, the assumption that she was acting under the all-powerful dictates of her religion led to the emergence of the well-known image of the sati as a victim of religious fanaticism. Thus while cultural relativists like John Zephaniah Holwell could call for a sympathetic understanding of sati based on an appreciation of the 'Hindu' perspective, by the end of the century a more negative interpretation had emerged that allowed men like Charles Grant to use sati as an indicator of the backwardness and degradation of Hindu society.

The first three decades of the nineteenth century saw an exponential rise in British interest in sati. *The Times* carried its first full-length account of a sati in 1808 and the *Edinburgh Review* reported on the custom in 1824. Moreover, as the generation of 'nabobs' gave way to that of colonial rulers and the British community in India settled in for the long haul, colonial society began to develop its own organs of expression, both in terms of regional newspapers like the *Bombay Gazette* or *Bengal Hukuru* and specialist journals such as the *Asiatic Review, Oriental Observer*, and *Quarterly Oriental Magazine*. These media both disseminated knowledge about sati more widely and provided a forum in which it could be discussed. Whereas in the eighteenth century those who wrote about sati had done so primarily to supply their readers with (supposedly) objective information, by the nineteenth century much of the material produced on sati was far more personal and subjective, as authors and readers alike offered their own views and challenged the ideas and opinions of others.

The new political situation in India made the issue of sati more relevant and contentious than ever before. Previously, accounts of sati had been of interest as curiosities, one of the strange customs of a foreign land and religion that, whether admired or deplored, were outside the European sphere of action. The new role of the British as the rulers of a large part of India gave the issue new urgency. Sati was no longer solely of academic interest, but was to become a matter of politics. Rather than merely recount the spectacle of a sati, observers were increasingly likely to pass not only a moral judgment on the act, but also a political one about whether and how the rite should be prevented. This was especially the case after 1821 when the first volume of Parliamentary Papers on sati was published and several philanthropic societies adopted the issue.[59] Sati became something of a *cause célèbre*, both in India and at home, and was debated not only by the Government of India, but also by the East India Company Board of Directors, and its proprietors and stockholders, the British

Parliament, missionaries, philanthropists, and the regional and national press.

The opening of India to missionary activity indirectly helped to create one of the most copious sources of information and opinion on sati.[60] From the time of the first Baptist missionary, William Carey, sati was a cause of concern; indeed, one of Carey's earliest letters to the Baptist Missionary Society, written in 1793, discusses sati in detail and was published in the *Periodic Accounts of the Baptist Missionary Society* in 1800. Carey was soon joined by other British missionaries; first, the other members of the famous Serampore trio, Joshua Marshman and William Ward, and then, particularly after 1813, by missionaries of other denominations. Their experiences and accounts were widely available as their letters home were published in the journals of their various societies. Missionary accounts, as might be expected, tended to concentrate on the discreditable aspects of Hindu society. In many ways sati was only one of a catalogue of 'horrors' that could be used to denigrate Indian life. As in previous centuries, missionaries in particular were keen to stress the abhorrent aspects of Indian religion and culture in order to justify their own presence in the subcontinent and to gather funds for their work at home. At the same time, as the official debate on sati was going on in government circles, there was also a concerted campaign being waged by the various missionary groups and other philanthropic societies to bring the more shocking aspects of Indian life to the public's attention, both for the purpose of bringing pressure on the government to act against practices such as sati and to validate the missionary's own enterprise. In works such as the Reverend James Pegg's *India's Cries to British Humanity*[61] and William Ward's *Farewell Letters,*[62] the sacrifice of the Hindu widow was lined up alongside such 'atrocities' as infanticide, *ghat* murders (the exposing of the ill on the banks of the Ganga or other rivers), the drowning of lepers, human sacrifices (particularly before the cart at Juggernath), hook swinging, self-mortification and religious suicide in a catalogue of horrors designed to shock and motivate the God-fearing British public. These 'sensational' subjects reached a wider audience than ever before as accounts of these atrocities were distilled down into pamphlets and cheap tracts that could be distributed among the poorer sections of the community, with the aim of raising awareness of conditions in India and garnering support for the missionary enterprise.

While all of these 'barbaric practices' had their own intrinsic appeal to the charitable impulses of the evangelical community, it does seem that sati in particular caught the population's attention and concern with the rite extended far beyond the immediate sphere of missionary activity. A look at the articles on India carried by *The Times* in the nineteenth century will show that sati was by far the most extensively reported of these 'humanitarian' issues in India. In the thirty-three years between 1800 and 1833 (when the last article relating to its abolition appeared) *The Times* carried eighteen separate articles on the subject—some of considerable length. In the whole of the nineteenth century, forty-one articles on the subject appeared. Compare this to the seven articles on thuggee (all of which appeared between 1841 and 1883), four articles on human sacrifice in India (all confined to the period 1864 and 1901), or the total of sixteen articles relating to infanticide in India, and it becomes clear that sati received some of the most extensive coverage over the longest duration.[63] Indeed, the only subject to receive greater attention was the question of child marriage, which had forty-seven references in the nineteenth century. Forty-three of these, however, appeared in the period around 1891 when the Age of Consent Bill sparked controversy both in India and at home. Obviously, it would be dangerous to read too much into these figures; *The Times* was only one of many newspapers available at the time, but given its circulation and prestige in the nineteenth century, it is possible to use it as an indicator of public interest, particularly as the figures are supported by the extent of concern with sati as recorded elsewhere.

The expansion in media coverage of sati was accompanied by a marked change in attitudes towards the rite, which in the early nineteenth century was characterized by the almost universal vilification of it by all sections of the British public. As we have seen, accounts of previous centuries displayed a significant ambivalence towards sati, with the distress at the physical suffering of the widow being counterbalanced by a regard for her chastity and bravery, producing a judgment on sati that was far from entirely negative. By the early nineteenth century, however, almost all positive aspects of the sacrifice had been purged from the European understanding of it. Reactions to the rite, instead of being characterized by heterogeneity and personal subjectivity, became homogenized into a collective expression of horror. The image of the widow, once lauded for her bravery, loyalty, and conviction even to the point of being compared to the Christian martyrs, was recreated as a passive, agencyless victim, to be pitied rather than admired. Indeed, it became almost mandatory for any discussion of sati to be prefaced with an authorial expression of disapprobation. Eyewitness accounts pre-empt the moral judgment of the reader by referring to the rite from the outset as 'shocking', 'barbarous', or 'infernal' and most of the authors of the early nineteenth century conformed, outwardly at least, not only to a widely accepted intellectual assessment of the rite, but also to a preconditioned emotional response. The suggestion of admiration for the widow still existed to some extent, particularly in the romanticized rendering of sati in fiction, but increasingly this was being purged, on a superficial level at least, from the popular portrayal of the rite. Instead, eyewitnesses and editors alike sought to emphasize their moral outrage over sati and we increasingly find that accounts of sati are prefaced with comments like that of the editor of the Quarterly *Oriental Magazine* in 1825, who states that 'We have so often expressed the absolute abhorrence with which we record these abominable acts, that we can only repeat in the same terms, the sense we entertain of their atrocious wickedness.'[64]

There were several reasons for this consolidation in the moral judgment against sati. Christopher Bayly has suggested, and it has been widely accepted, that it was indicative of a wider change in attitudes towards Hinduism itself that underpinned the shift from Orientalist to Anglicist policies in the 1820s.[65] While in the eighteenth century, Enlightenment ideas about religious toleration and cultural relativism allowed space for a sympathetic approach to understanding Hinduism, the growing evangelicalism of the nineteenth century was accompanied by an impulse to denigrate rather than celebrate non-Christian religions. Increasingly, Hinduism and its accretions were seen as a malign influence on Indian society. The Baptist missionary journal *The Friend of India,* for example, claimed that 'The infelicity of [India's] inhabitants arises not from ungenerous soil, but from an unnatural system of morals; and from rites and customs, which though deemed to be sacred, are inimical to human happiness.'[66] These customs were seen to be 'hostile to reason and humanity'[67] and were used to emphasize India's lack of civilization, and to characterize her society and backward and barbaric.

Closely connected to this shifting attitude towards Hinduism was the change in the popular conception of Britain's role in India—what P.J. Marshall refers to as the 'moral swing to the East.'[68] Increasingly by the early nineteenth century, public opinion demanded that the imperial presence in India be justified not in terms of economic gain but rather in terms of the benefits it brought to the indigenous population. Public support for the empire in India, which had waned somewhat in the late eighteenth century amid damaging revelations about the East India Company's behaviour there, gave way to tacit support as the role of the British was increasingly portrayed in utilitarian or humanitarian terms. This was especially the case after 1813, when the renewal of the East India Company's charter included the lifting of the ban on proselytizing activities. This increased emphasis on the beneficence as well as the profitability of colonial rule placed issues such as sati firmly within the remit of the 'civilizing mission'. The existence of a custom such as sati in a land under British control could be considered to undermine the benevolence of colonial rule—humanitarian Fowell Buxton even went as far as to call the toleration for sati a 'disgrace to Britain'[69]—at a time when British presence in India was increasingly being rationalized in humanitarian terms.

In an article published in Francis Barker's *Europe and Its Others* (1985) and *Economic and Political Weekly* (1986) and later in her much vaunted monograph *Contentious Traditions: The Debate on Sati in Colonial India, 1780–1833,*[70] Lata Mani argued that British preoccupation with sati in the early nineteenth century was less about burning women than it was about defining the parameters of colonial control. For Mani, the debate on sati was entirely political and was concerned with testing the boundaries of legitimate interference in what had previously been the 'uncolonized' space of religion. This premise is extremely useful and her work in general has been highly influential in deconstructing the traditional image of Bentinck's regulation on sati as one of the crowning glories of the so-called 'Era of Reform'. While all these factors certainly had a huge impact on the way in which sati was represented and understood, they are not sufficient in themselves to explain Britain's obsession with it in years before 1829, however. As we have already mentioned, numerous other rites and customs elicited British criticism, but none received the same level of fascination and vilification accorded to sati. The unprecedented level of interest in it suggests that the popular obsession was about more than just Britain's changing relationship with India, or the imperatives of justifying colonial rule, although both of these certainly played a part. Rather, I would argue that sati intrigued the British in this period because it embodied certain issues that were of particular relevance in Britain itself at the time. The sati debate coalesced with concerns in Britain over religious toleration, penal reform, suicide, and changing gender ideology, and all of these played a part in firing British interest in and forming British opinion of sati. Moreover, sati itself played a significant role in defining British ideas about these and other issues.[71] Far from being a monolithic and unidirectional process tied solely to the relationship of power between Britain and India, as Edward Said might have us believe, the debate on sati was both multifaceted and multidirectional and reflected and affected Britain's own internal preoccupations as much as her relationship with India.

British involvement in the issue of sati after 1830 tended to occur in two main arenas. Within their own territories the colonial authorities were responsible for the prevention, prosecution, and punishment of illegal satis. In addition to this, between 1832 and 1861 they also involved themselves, albeit unevenly, in an attempt to eradicate the practice from the independent arena of the so-called Princely States. Much as had been the case in British India, in many of the Princely States sati became a site on which issues about influence, power, and control could be contested, as an increasingly emasculated ruling elite sought to protect the last vestments of their princely authority by protecting their autonomy in the supposedly 'uncolonized' social and religious sphere. The tale of the abolition of sati in princely India has received only a cursory treatment by historians. It appears most commonly either as a supplement to the discussion of events in British India, or as an example of social reform in works dealing with the relationship between Britain and the Indian princes more generally. A widely tolerated practice in 1830, by 1860 sati had, at least in theory, been prohibited by every state in India. This was in a considerable measure due to the pressure brought to bear on the states by the British government in India,[72] who over the course of thirty years redefined the limits of acceptable intervention in order to encourage the prohibition of sati across the subcontinent. British involvement in the sati issue, as with other social issues such as slavery, infanticide, witch-trials, mutilation, etc., helped to shape processes of social reform in these areas. Moreover, the encounter with sati in princely India had a profound effect on the way in which the British themselves perceived the practice and the women who performed it. James Tod's famous *Annals and Antiquities of Rajasthan*, for example, resurrected the image of a heroic sati in the warrior tradition that had disappeared from the discourse in early nineteenth-century Bengal. British ideas about sati, far from being entirely defined by a static paradigm that has come to characterize the discourse in early nineteenth-century British India, were in fact highly mutable and contingent on the social and political situation in which the rite was discussed. When encountering sati in the Princely States, and in particular in Rajput areas, the colonial discourse on the subject underwent subtle, but highly significant changes, which were to have important implications for the postcolonial discourse on sati.[73]

Lata Mani has represented the involvement of indigenous participants in the discourse on sati as being conditioned almost entirely by the colonial framework of debate. Although others, such as Radhika Singha,[74] have criticized this stance, arguing that indigenous involvement in fact helped to shape the terms of debate, Mani's construction has largely been left unchallenged. When transferred to the context of the Princely States, however, this position disintegrates. In this arena the British were forced to approach the eradication of sati not through legislation, but through negotiation, and as a result Indian rulers played an active role in the discourse. Moreover, they often did this not in terms dictated by the British, but through reference to their own cultural understanding of sati. Although it is perhaps arguable that in the final analysis these Indian interpolations into the discourse were silenced by the eventual triumph of British demands for abolition in the Indian states, in the process they also resulted in a subtle but important shift in British interpretations of the rite, as colonial officials and the population in general adjusted their conception of sati in response to the encounter with Indian ideas that this dialogue facilitated. Thus, although the Indian rulers were unable to completely shift the debate into their own terrains, their attempts to discuss sati within their own idiom, rather than that of the dominant colonial discourse, was to have significant ramifications.

Sati and Indian Nationalism

Despite its illegality after 1829, sati remained a contested site in late colonial India, the implications of which were not confined to the sphere of 'women's issues' or social reform agendas. Rather, the defence/discussion of sati was often subsumed into broader nationalist and imperialist discourses. As Partha Chatterjee has so influentially argued, twentieth-century Indian nationalism resolved the 'women's question' by imagining women as belonging to *ghar*, the home, a domain that was viewed as an uncolonized space and which was synonymous with the 'inner, essential, identity of the East which lay in its distinctive and superior spiritual culture.'[75] In this domestic/spiritual sphere, India remained undominated and sovereign, and it was here that women could defend their 'tradition' and identity, even while men adopted necessary Western innovations in the material sphere. As Chatterjee puts it, 'In the world, imitation of and adaption to Western norms was a necessity; at home, they were tantamount to annihilation of one's very identity.'[76] This is not to suggest, of course, that all nationalist gender ideology sought simply to relegate women to the domestic sphere and traditional roles and practices, for while some 'revivalist–nationalists' did adopt what Tanika Sarkar refers to as a 'status-quoist position on the entire question of contemporary Hindu domestic norms',[77] other, more reform-minded nationalists sought both a 'new' woman and a 'new' patriarchy that would both fulfil the needs of the modern world and preserve the essential ethos of Indian identity.[78] Thus, while all strands of nationalism adopted

elements of indigenous 'tradition' as signifiers of indigenous identity these were often chosen selectively. In the reformist discourse
elements of 'traditional' culture were reconstructed to represent
what Chatterjee calls a 'classicized' tradition that expunged the
more abhorrent aspects of local practice and looked instead to
a 'Golden Age' or Vedic ideal in which women were both virtuous and respected.[79]

An attempt to situate the question of sati within this broader framework is far from straightforward. On the surface, sati appears as
one of the abhorrent practices that nationalists sought to eliminate
from the discourse of Indian culture. The prohibition of the rite in
1829 took place with the support and encouragement of eminent
Indian ideologues such as Raja Rammohan Roy and
Dwarakanath Tagore, and though there had initially been some
orthodox opposition to this move,[80] by the twentieth century, the
prohibition of sati had generally been accepted as fact. This is
not to suggest, however, that the rite was universally censured;
both 'reformist' and 'revivalist' treatments of sati throughout this
period remained ambivalent. Many nationalists and reformers
did actively condemn the practice; Gandhi stated that he found
'nothing praiseworthy' in it and even lauded the British for outlawing it, while the Calcutta-based *Modern Review* called it an 'inhuman and barbarous practice' that could neither be commended
nor tolerated or permitted.[81] For such reformists, sati was one of
the discreditable aspects of Hindu practice that had become
incorporated into the religion as it declined in the medieval period
from its Vedic purity and as such could, and indeed should, be
purged from the religion without undermining Hinduism's essential
excellence. Even those who supported the ideal of sati could be
critical of its existence in the present. Despite maintaining that
sati in its pure voluntary form represented 'the acme of moral
perfection', even the orthodox Bihar newspaper *Searchlight* admitted that 'Over the course of time and under demoralizing
political conditions, corruption crept in and voluntariness disappeared to a very large extent' and approved the British prohibition
as preventing abuses such as forced sati. *Searchlight* maintained,
however, that in its purely voluntary form, sati was sacred to Hindus
and for it, as for other 'orthodox' Hindu groups, the 'true' sati

remained an icon for the superiority of Hindu spiritual culture. Bankimchandra, who has been seen by many as a progenitor of modern Hindutva, eulogized sati and believed that in its 'pure' form of voluntary immolation, sati was an aspect of Hinduism to be protected rather than denounced; a climactic and cathartic consummation of Hindu female/spiritual ideals.

The dichotomy between reformers who rejected sati and revivalists who defended it, while useful on a superficial level, is in fact ambivalent. The ethos of sati could be lauded as epitomizing Indian women's superior devotion and capacity for sacrifice, aspects that were at the centre of the wider nationalist construction of the 'new woman'. Even those who rejected the custom in practice could find resonances in an ideal that encouraged women to develop such female virtues as chastity, self-sacrifice, submission, devotion, kindness, and love. As such, the ideal of sati remained appealing for many less orthodox observers, even while they condemned the practice itself. Sarojini Naidu, for example, romanticized the impulse to join the beloved in death asking 'why should the blossom live when the tree is dead?' Even the *Modern Review*, which had so roundly denounced the sati in Barh, carried in a subsequent issue a short story entitled 'Suttee' in which the heroine allowed herself to be repeatedly branded with a red-hot iron in order to raise money for an unworthy and ailing husband, an action which the author lauded as the epitome of Indian women's noble capacity for sacrifice. In this idealized sense, as an icon of Hindu femininity, sati fell into the sovereign sphere of religion and domesticity, where, as Sarkar points out, were 'conceived the last traces of the vanquished Hindu nation'; nationalists could not 'permit an encroachment by the colonial power into that domain'[82] with the result that the ethos that underpinned sati was often directly or indirectly defended.

In reality, sati did not exist only in the spiritual/domestic sphere, of course. Its ideology may have been incorporated by some into a spiritual/cultural discourse of Indian identity and superiority, but as an actual practice, sati by its very nature existed within the public domain. There are two issues to consider here: the nature of sati itself and the impact of colonial intervention in it. Even prior to the criminalization of the act by the British, sati was necessarily performed within the sight and with the approval of the community. For a woman to burn herself or be burnt in private was either suicide or murder. It was the very act of making sati public and the rites and rituals that accompanied it that turned it into a meritorious act. Sati was far from the only source of violence against women in India, of course, and domestic violence, rape, and female infanticide, as well as the prevailing tendency to provide women with generally lower standards of nutrition and medical care, were all statistically more significant social problems in early twentieth-century India. Unlike other forms of violence against women, however, sati occurred with the open approval of society and was a public endorsement of the devaluation of women.[83] This made it very difficult to conceal or defend effectively the practice as belonging entirely to the domestic sphere. This difficulty in situating sati in the purely spiritual sphere was increased manifold by the prohibition and criminalization of the act, which placed it firmly, as far as the authorities were concerned, within the public domain of law and order. Police involvement, judicial proceedings, and legal wrangling were all inextricably linked to sati as it existed as a crime in British India. Thus sati, unlike many other social or 'women's' issues, represented a point at which the spiritual/domestic ideologies of the 'uncolonized' space intersected with the jurisdiction of the colonial state. As a result, it remained a contested terrain as the colonial state claimed jurisdiction over the woman's 'body', while pro-sati sections of the Hindu community claimed sovereignty over her 'spirit'.

This basic dichotomy was at the root of the controversy over the sati in Barh, Bihar in 1927. This case involved the partial immolation and eventual death of a twenty-year-old Brahmin widow, Sampati Kuer. The event itself caused a flurry of publicity due to circumstances that made it appear that the pyre had ignited spontaneously, though the longevity of public interest was primarily due the way in which the criminal case that followed was prosecuted. Sixteen people were initially arrested under Section 306 of the Indian Penal Code (abetment of suicide), of which six were acquitted at trial. The fate of the remaining ten sparked controversy, however, when the session judge referred the case to the Patna High Court, despite the fact that an Indian jury had recorded a unanimous verdict of 'not guilty' on all the remaining accused. The high court overturned their findings and sentenced the accused to up to ten years rigorous imprisonment; heavy, but not unprecedented sentences. The judgment caused a sensation, partly because of its implications for the accused, the majority of whom were respected local pandits, but mainly because the language in which Chief Justice Courtney Terrell's findings were couched was, to the say the least, inflammatory. The case provoked a strong reaction in the local and national Indian press, especially in the Bihar newspaper *Searchlight*.[84] In addition to publishing the full text of the judgment, *Searchlight* carried a series of three articles roundly criticizing the judge's findings that were so confrontational that they, along with its coverage of two other recent high court cases, led to the newspapers being charged with contempt of court. The *Searchlight* contempt case itself caused a considerable stir, although by this point the issues had moved beyond the parameters of an individual sati and had become incorporated into a wider nationalist discourse about freedom of and weight given to Indian opinion within judicial and political processes. As a result, the newspaper was championed by a number of nationalists, including Motilal Nehru himself, who, though they had little sympathy with the paper's stance on sati as a custom, saw the case as a chance to challenge the abuses of the authority vested in the high court system and in the colonial state.

As would be the case in the burning of Roop Kanwar sixty years later, orthodox Hindu groups sought to claim the Barh sati as an icon of ideal Indian femininity/spirituality, while the state sought to stamp their authority on sati as a criminal act. These contestations are to a lesser extent observable in most sati cases of the late nineteenth and early twentieth century, many of which provoked a small flurry of publicity. Even in those that were not widely reported, these tensions are visible at the micro level in the positions taken by defendants, local community, and state as the cases were prosecuted. As Kumkum Sangari and Sudesh Vaid have pointed out, ideologies surrounding sati have since the nineteenth century incorporated religious, social, and cultural beliefs into wider 'contestatory formations that address concepts such as Hinduism, tradition, nation or Indian history', situating the specific discourses that surround events of widow immolation in their historical context.[85] The treatment of all sati cases to some extent reflects the prevailing interests and expediencies of the groups involved at the time. The Barh sati case, though not unique in the issues it raised, caused an unprecedented level of controversy, because, like the Roop Kanwar sati sixty years later, a series of events and circumstances specific to that sati coalesced with a historical moment when the issues they raised were particularly poignant. In this context the *Searchlight's* response to the sati and to the high court judgment must be seen in terms of a revivalist–nationalist discourse that sought to challenge colonial intervention in Hindu society and culture by contesting the idea of 'pure' voluntary sati as a crime punishable by the courts and defending its ideological status as part of an uncolonized domestic/spiritual domain. In this respect, although the debate is to some extent about the possibility for 'authentic' sati, it is also about the right of the Hindu nation to locate its own traditions within a framework of indigenous interpretation. In this sense it is not about whether Sampati Kuer was murdered or not, but about who has the right to determine that fact. This was a particularly poignant question at this particular historical moment, as it coalesced with broader concerns about Indian right to self-determination and self-rule. The burning of Sampati Kuer took place only days after the announcement of the all-white composition of the Simon Commission, and the slight was still fresh by the time of the high court judgment and the subsequent attack on it. The question of who gets to speak for India was the central, if never directly articulated, pillar of the *Searchlight's* attack on the high court judgment with the result that the whole debate was about more than the culpability of certain men in the burning of a young woman; it was about the perimeters of colonial or indigenous control over Hindu belief, culture, and nation. As Lata Mani has pointed out in relation to the official debate about sati in the early nineteenth century, and as was so clearly the case in the politicization of Roop Kanwar's sati, the controversy that surrounded the immolation of Sampati Kuer was about far more than the burning of a young woman, it was the terrain on which issues of tradition, culture, and nationhood could be contested.

The Burning of Roop Kanwar

On 4 September 1987 in the village of Deorala in Rajasthan, an eighteen-year-old woman burnt on the funeral pyre of her husband. Roop Kanwar had been married for eight months when her husband Mal Singh died suddenly. Within hours she too was dead and thousands of onlookers were celebrating her deification and proclaiming her a *satimata*. In the wake of the sati a heated debate raged in newspapers and journals, as well as on the streets of Jaipur, as feminists and liberals clashed with orthodox, pro-sati, Hindu groups. The controversy that followed became increasingly complex and multifaceted. Initially, those who denounced the act concentrated on the question of whether Roop Kanwar had gone voluntarily to her death, or been coerced onto the pyre, but as the volume and vociferousness of the debate increased, feminists and liberals also began to publicly question the extent to which such a distinction was valid at all. Questions about the degree of agency Roop Kanwar exhibited in the sati were thus about more than the judicial distinction between suicide and homicide; they raised fundamental questions about a widow's right over her own life and about the nature of religious and societal structures that might make her wish to end it. Those who condemned the rite as murder rejected any distinction between voluntary and involuntary sati, suggesting that if Kanwar had not been forced physically onto the pyre, she had been ideologically and emotionally coerced by a series of social and religious ideals that glorified immolation and subsumed a woman's worth into that of her husband.[86] 'Pro-sati' sections of the Hindu community took a different perspective, arguing that Roop Kanwar had followed in a glorious tradition of Rajput satis and that as the ultimate expression of the ideal of pativratadharma, her sati was not only allowable, it was positively laudable. The true wife, they argued, had a moral right to end her life in this fashion; those who opposed sati were westernized liberals and degenerate women who had abandoned their religious and cultural heritage and their traditional duties to their family and society.

The nature and extent of the debate that followed Roop Kanwar's immolation was unprecedented, for though sati is seen as an exceptional act, the immolation was not a unique event.

Despite the criminalization of the act in both colonial and independent India, sati has continued to occur illegally, creating tensions between the rite's legislative prohibition and its continued social sanction. On an average one reported immolation per year had occurred in the four decades between independence and Roop Kanwar's sati in 1987;[87] well-publicized satis took place in Jhardli, Rajasthan, in 1980 and in Madya Pradesh in 2002 without provoking the same heated response. What set the Roop Kanwar sati apart was not the specifics of its performance, but, as Romila Thapar points out, the attempt by certain sections of the community to justify it at a specific historical juncture.[88] In 1987, Roop Kanwar's sati became the terrain for a highly charged and politicized debate in which an emergent and exclusivist Hindu right sought to promote a political agenda based on religious nationalism and 'traditional' Hindu values, a supposedly secular Congress government prevaricated, and feminists and liberals protested against both the rite and its glorification.

Those who opposed sati and its glorification initially represented it as highlighting the ignorance and illiteracy of India's rural masses; an example of 'how backwardness and primitivism have been preserved in India's villages'.[89] As Madhu Kishwar points out, however, Deorala was far from a rural backwater and the leaders of the pro-sati movement anything but uneducated peasants. Rather, she claims, 'they are in a large part urban-based politicians, who are not excessively religious but excessively greedy for power of a very modern kind.'[90] The politicization of the Roop Kanwar affair was evidenced by the nature of the refrains chanted at the site, the vast majority of which were based on political slogans and had not the faintest religious connection or anything to do with local Rajasthani tradition.[91] At the forefront of the conservative debate was a previously dominant Rajput elite whose political and social authority has been steadily undermined by the new political groupings and structures of power in independent India. Their support of sati can be seen as both a demonstration of group solidarity and a reaction to the threat posed to the patriarchal order by the changing status of women.[92] As Anne Hargrove has demonstrated, Marwaris, originally from the Shekhawati region of Rajasthan, have in recent years countered their geographic dispersal and emphasized their group identity as Rajputs by funding and patronizing major sati temples in Jhunjhunu, Delhi, Calcutta, and elsewhere.[93] Similarly, support and glorification of the Roop Kanwar sati acted as an arena in which orthodox Rajputs could assert their masculinity, potency and group identity. On a wider scale Hindu revivalist groups attempted to appropriate the rite as a symbol of Hindu unity, with the result that sati was turned from a 'residual quasi-religious theme into a critical political issue'.[94] As had been the case so often in the past, the sati of Roop Kanwar was imbued with multiple meanings for those who debated it, becoming the terrain on which wider questions about the role of religion and tradition in a secular state, the position of women in Indian society, and the ideals of femininity which they should aspire to could be contested.

Notes

[1]   Hurst R.J., *The Police Journal*, vol. 2, 1929, in Indian Police Collection, vol. 171 Oriental and India Office (British Library) European Manuscripts (O.I.O. Eur. Mss).

[2]   Nandy, A., *At the Edge of Psychology: Essays in Politics and Culture* (Delhi: Oxford University Press, 1980). Others connect its prevalence in this area to the Dayabhaga system of inheritance prevalent in Bengal, which allowed the widow greater inheritance rights than the traditional *Mitakshara* system common in other parts of the country.

[3]   Mani, L., *Contentious Traditions: The Debate on Sati in Colonial India, 1780–1833* (Berkeley: University of California Press, 1998).

[4]   Sangari, K. and S. Vaid, 'Institutions, Beliefs, Ideologies: Widow Immolation in Contemporary Rajasthan', in *Economic and Political Weekly* vol. 26: 17, 27 April 1991.

[5]   Oldenburg, V., 'The Roop Kanwar Case: Feminist Responses', in J. Stratton Hawley *Sati: the Blessing and the Curse* (Oxford: Oxford University Press, 1994), p. 104.

[6]   Bhasin, K. and R. Menon, 'The Problem', in *Seminar*, vol. 342, February 1988, p. 12.

[7]   References to the precedent set with regard to sati and the legislation against it were common in debates over child marriage in the late 1920s, as they had been in the question of widow remarriage in the 1840s and 1850s.

[8]   Sangari and Vaid, 'Institutions, Beliefs, Ideologies'.

[9]   Or, in some cases, on a separate pyre with an item belonging to her husband.

[10]   Not all women known as sati immolated themselves, of course; some exceptional women achieved this status by their fulfilment of the *pativrata* ideal during their lifetimes (e.g. Sati Savitri, Sati Sita, and Sati Anusuya).

[11]   Narasimhan, S., *Sati, A Study of Widow Burning in India* (Delhi: HarperCollins, 1998), p. 23.

[12]   Narasimhan, *Sati*, p. 21. When this mistake was discovered, some nineteenth-century scholars, such as Max Müller, believed it to have been a deliberate fraud perpetrated by an unscrupulous priesthood.

[13]   Thakur, U., *The History of Suicide in India* (Delhi: Munshi Ram Manohar Lal, 1963), p. 129. Interestingly, this passage also seems to contradict the practice of ascetic widowhood. It appears that it was considered better for a widow to outlive her husband in order to help increase the population through remarriage or levirate. The *niyoga* system allowed for this by advocating the cohabitation of a widow with her brother-in-law, or other close relative of her husband in order to produce a son who could offer the necessary ablutions to the dead man.

[14]   Bose, M., 'Sati: The Event and the Ideology', in M. Bose (ed.) *Faces of the Feminine in Ancient, Medieval and Modern India* (Delhi: Oxford University Press, 2000), p. 23. Stray references to sati appear in the Puranas as early as AD 400 although it does not really come to fore until much later, *c.* AD 600.

[15]   Cited in Sharma, A., *Sati: Historical and Phenomenological Essays* (Delhi: Motilal Banarsidass, 1988), p. 32. This passage also appears in the *Parasara*, the *Brahmapurana* (*Gautamimahatmya*), the *Mitaksara* and *Suddhitattva*.

[16]   Sharma, *Sati*, p. 15.

[17]   Bose, 'Sati: The Event and the Ideology', p. 27.

[18]   Ibid., p. 28.

[19]   Although this text is not in the same league as the great digests of Hindu law, it is interesting because it is the only one extant that deals solely with stridharma. Other digests contained sections relating to the right conduct of women, but only Tryambakayajvan devotes his text entirely to the subject. Julia Leslie has analysed the implications of Tryambakayajvan's work in great detail in *The Perfect Wife* (Delhi: Oxford University Press, 1989).

[20]   Sutherland, S., 'Suttee, Sati and Sahagamana: An Epic Misunderstanding?', in *Economic and Political Weekly*, vol. 29: 26, 25 June 1994, p. 1595.

[21]   For Sutherland, therefore, sati in the epic context has less to do with following the husband, and more to do with dissipating and purifying herself of the polluted state that has been incurred by the absence of her husband. Thus Sita's ordeal by fire, though not a sati in the colonial and post-colonial context, conforms to this model as it purifies Sita of perceived *asatitva* and restores her to the status of a sati.

[22]   See, for example, Ahmad, Z., 'Sati in 18th Century Bengal', in *The Journal of the Asiatic Society of Pakistan*, vol. 13: 2, 1968, p. 147. There is little

evidence to support this, and even were it true it would not explain the development of the custom in the Hindu context.

23 Thus, we find later texts admitting it to Brahmin women and suggesting that the earlier prohibition extended only to the rite of *anugamana* (burning on a separate pile with some relic of the husband) rather than to *sahagamana* (burning with the body of the husband).

24 Harlan, L., *Religion and Rajput Woman: the Ethic of Protection in Contemporary Narratives* (Berkeley: University of California Press, 1992), p. 121. Non-Rajput satis are deemed to be acting not out of pure devotion to the husband (as the true sati should be), but from considerations of caste mobility or for personal spiritual reward.

25 Catherine Weinberger-Thomas discusses the connection between sati and other forms of heroic self-sacrifice at some length in her book *Ashes of Immortality,* trans. J. Mehlman and D. Gordon White (New Delhi: Oxford University Press, 2000), pp. 13–19.

26 Chakravarti, U., 'Beyond the Altekarian Paradigm', in K. Roy (ed.) *Women in Early Indian Societies* (New Delhi: Manohar, 1999), p. 75.

27 Young, K.K., 'Hinduism', in A. Sharma, *Women in World Religions* (Albany: State University of New York Press, 1987), p. 81. The vast majority of contemporary knowledge on the position of women in ancient Indian society is gleaned from religious texts. As these were overwhelmingly authored by elite males, the assumptions that are based on them should only be accepted as patriarchal constructions of women in high castes. They tell us very little about either low-caste experiences or women's own values and opinions.

28 Young, ibid. p. 82.

29 Agrawal, A., 'The Economic Aspects of Sati', in K. Pawar (ed.) *Women in Indian History* (New Delhi: Vision and Venture, 1996), pp. 64–6.

30 Kasturi, M., *Embattled Identities: Rajput Lineages and the Colonial State in Nineteenth-Century North India* (New Delhi: Oxford University Press, 2002), p. 25.

31 Kasturi, ibid. p. 103.

32 Joshi, V., 'Deifying the Dead: The Satis of Rajasthan', in Babb, Joshi, and Meister (eds) *Multiple Histories: Culture and Society in the Study of Rajasthan* (Jaipur: Rawat, 2002), p. 201. The high number of deaths in battle among Rajput men meant that there were a disproportional number of young widows in Rajput society. As with other Hindu communities, the position of Rajput widows is very low and financially precarious.

33 Sangari and Vaid, 'Institutions, Beliefs, Ideologies', p. 383.

34 Stridharma, the rules of proper behaviour for a woman deal almost exclusively with her position as a wife. These rules are primarily laid down in the *Dharmashastras*, though mythology, legend, and folklore provide other models. The Dharmashastras are essentially Brahmin male-authored and provide perhaps the most conservative view of the position and nature

of women. Women's voices themselves are more likely to be uncovered in the 'little tradition' of popular culture and folklore, which often deals with issues of concern to women such as mother–daughter or sister–sister relationships rather than the male dominated pattern of husband–wife. Moreover, where the authoritative texts deal primarily with issues of wifely submission and devotion, oral and folk tradition also expresses ideas of romantic love, longing and loneliness. Wadley, S., 'Women and the Hindu Tradition', in R. Ghadially (ed.) *Women in Indian Society; A Reader* (New Delhi: Sage, 1988), pp. 29–32.

[35] In this respect her husband's actions, and even her own feelings for him, were to some extent irrelevant, as service and devotion to him were in her own spiritual interests and the only way she can insure a propitious rebirth.

[36] As Prem Chowdhry has shown in *The Veiled Women* (New Delhi: Oxford University Press, 2004), female ideals among lower castes, and even among higher castes in certain regions, could vary significantly from the élite paradigm discussed here. The intention of this section is thus not to provide a homogenized account of Indian ideals of femininity, which are various and contextual, but to provide an overview of the particular system of gender relations that underpinned sati.

[37] Joshi, V. 'Deifying the Dead', p. 203.

[38] In Narayan, V., 'Hindu Perceptions of Auspiciousness and Sexuality', in J. Becher (ed.) *Women, Religion and Sexuality* (Geneva: W.W.C. Publications, 1990), p. 71.

[39] For a detailed analysis of the role of *sat* in inspiring sati, see, Weinberger-Thomas, *Ashes of Immortality: Widowhood in Rural India* (New York: Oxford University Press, 2001).

[40] See, Alter Chen, *Perpetual Mourning: Widowhood in Rural India* (New York: Oxford University Press, 2000), p. 28.

[41] Ibid., p. 28.

[42] Baker Reynolds, H., 'The Auspicious Married Woman', in S. Wadley (ed), *The Powers of Tamil Women* (New York: Syracuse University Press, 1980), p. 30.

[43] Young, K.K., 'Hinduism', p. 83.

[44] The penalties associated with widowhood in most communities in India are less severe today than they were a hundred years ago, when ascetic widowhood and tonsure were still practised. Today, only very orthodox families would still impose such degradations on a widow. Generally speaking, however, widowhood is still considered inauspicious.

[45] Alter Chen, *Perpetual Mourning*, p. 24. Chen also notes that in tantric Hinduism there are ten goddess transformations called Mahavidyas, seven of which belong to the creative stages of the universe and three to the stages of withdrawal. The seventh Mahavidya is the widow Dhumavati. In tantric art she is 'tall and grim, pallid, agitated and slovenly. Her hair is tangled, her

breasts droop and her teeth are gone. Her nose is big, her body and eyes crooked; she rides a crow chariot. Horrid and quarrelsome, she is perpetually tormented by hunger and thirst' (Rawson P., *The Art of Tantra* (London: Thames and Hudson, 1973). Dhumavati is thought to represent the nadir of creation 'it is she who generates that stage of being where individuals forget their origin, lose contact with their source, and suffer continually the agonies of unsatisfied appetite and defeated hope'. The fierce, quarrelsome, powerful aspect not just of women, but of goddesses, is associated with widowhood.

46 Courtright, P., 'Sati, Sacrifice and Marriage: the Modernity of Tradition', in L. Harlan and P. Courtright (eds) *From the Margins of Hindu Marriage* (Oxford: Oxford University Press, 1995), p. 189.

47 Young, K.K., 'Hinduism', p. 84.

48 Courtright P., 'Sati, Sacrifice and Marriage', p. 189.

49 Joshi V., 'Deifying the Dead', p. 199. Actually, very few Rajput satis are worshipped in their natal or conjugal clans, most are ignored.

50 Kishwar, M., *Off the Beaten Track, Rethinking Gender Justice for Indian Women* (Delhi: Oxford University Press, 1999), p. 56.

51 Rege, M.P., 'Editorial', in *New Quest*, September–October 1987.

52 See, Major, A., *Pious Flames: European Encounters with Sati (1500–1830),* (New Delhi: Oxford University Press, 2006).

53 In fact, the term 'Hinduism' only became current in the nineteenth century. Prior to that Europeans would refer to the non-Muslim population of India as 'Gentoos' (descendents of the Gentiles of the Old Testament) or followers of the 'Pythagorean doctrine' (reincarnation), as well as by the pejorative terms 'pagans' and 'heathens'.

54 Of course, 'Hinduism' was (and is) very far from being a coherent system, but the enlightenment fixation with classification and explanatory schemata led to an image of an overarching religious structure, which informed all aspects of Indian life.

55 For more on the shift in emphasis in European understandings of sati from primarily sociological to primarily religious explanations see Major, A., *Pious Flames: European Encounters with Sati (1500–1830)* (New Delhi: Oxford University Press, 2006).

56 Teltscher, K., *India Inscribed: European and British Writing on India, 1600–1800* (Delhi: Oxford University Press, 1995).

57 Letter from Abraham Caldecott to Miss Pettet of Dartford, Kent, 14 September 1783 (Oriental and India Office Collection: European Manuscripts [O.I.O., Eur. MSS.]).

58 I am not suggesting here that eighteenth-century European ideas about India were either homogenous or static. As Lisa Lowe has demonstrated, they shifted considerably both between nationalities and over time (Lowe, *Critical Terrain: French and British Orientalisms* (Berkley, University of Cali-

fornia Press, 1991). There were some common characteristics in the European image of India, however, and as the forthcoming discussion of their interpretations of sati will show, there was a general trend towards attributing certain characteristics and 'essences' to Indian society that conditioned their reactions to individual aspects of it.

[59] Governmental interest and debate on the subject had in fact been going on since 1805, but the publication of the Parliamentary Papers was the first opportunity for the general public, and philanthropic societies, to get full access to the material.

[60] Foreign missionaries of various denominations had been working in India for centuries and had from the outset reported on the rite, but, financial sponsorship for the Lutheran missions by the Society for the Propagation of Christian Knowledge notwithstanding, British missionary involvement in India did not really take off until the nineteenth century. While sources such as the Jesuits' *Lettres Édifiantes* or individual accounts by missionaries such as Abraham Roger were sometimes available in English editions prior to 1800, these were specialist items not readily available to the general public. It was not until 1793, when the first British Baptist missionary, William Carey, arrived in India that the British evangelical community had a direct link to contemporary conditions in India.

[61] Pegg, James, *India's Cries To British Humanity* (London: Seeley and Son, 1830).

[62] Ward, W., *Farewell Letters to a Few Friends in Britain and America on Returning to Bengal in 1821* (London: 1821).

[63] This information was gathered from the entries in *Palmer's Index To The Times* (British Newspaper Library, Colindale).

[64] *Quarterly Oriental Magazine,* vol. 3, 1825, p. 10.

[65] Christopher Bayly, 'From Ritual To Ceremony: Death Ritual In Hindu North India', in J. Whaley (ed.) *Mirrors Of Mortality: Studies In The Social History Of Death* (New York: St. Martin's Press, 1981).

[66] *Friend Of India,* vol. 1: 3, (Serampore: Mission Press, 1821), p. 636.

[67] Ibid.

[68] P.J. Marshall, 'The Moral Swing To The East: British Humanitarianism, India And The West Indies', in K. Ballhatchet and J. Harrison (eds) *East India Company Studies: Papers Presented To Prof. Sir Cyril Phillips* (Hong Kong: Asian Research Service, 1986).

[69] Fowell Buxton's comment is cited by E.A. Kendall in a letter to the *Asiatic Journal,* vol. 13, 1822, p. 447.

[70] Mani, *Contentious Traditions*; Mani, L., 'Production of an Official discourse on Sati in Early 19th Century Bengal', in *Economic and Political Weekly,* 21:17, 1986; *Europe and its others: proceedings of the Essex Conference on the Sociology of Literature, July 1984* (Colchester: University of Essex, 1985).

[71] See, Major, *Pious Flames: European Encounters with Sati* (New Delhi: Oxford University Press, 2006).

[72] This generalization is in no way intended to undermine the importance of the indigenous impetus to reform, without which no progress could have been made.

[73] Most notably in the repositioning of sati as a Rajput rather than a Bengali issue.

[74] See Singha, R., *A Despotism of Law: Crime and Justice in Early Colonial India* (New Delhi: Oxford University Press, 2000).

[75] Chatterjee, P., 'The Nationalist Resolution of the Women's Question', in K. Sangari and S. Vaid (eds) *Recasting Women: Essays in Colonial History* (New Delhi: Kali for Women, 1989), pp. 238–9.

[76] Ibid., p. 239.

[77] See, Sarkar, T., *Hindu Wife, Hindu Nation* (New Delhi: Permanent Black, 2001).

[78] Chatterjee, 'The Nationalist Resolution of the Women's Question', p. 244.

[79] Ibid.

[80] In Calcutta in 1830 a *Dharma Sabha* was founded to protest the prohibition of the rite, which even took its objections to appeal before the Privy Council in London, though its case was eventually thrown out.

[81] *Modern Review,* vol. 44:1, July 1928.

[82] This for Chatterjee explains why nationalists often opposed the colonial state's proposals for effecting social reform through legislative enactment, as such a method was seen to undermine the ability of the 'nation' to act for itself even in a domain where it was sovereign. Chatterjee, 'The Nationalist Resolution of the Women's Question', p. 249.

[83] Kishwar, *Off the Beaten Track*, p. 56.

[84] *Amrita Bazar Patrika* and *Forward* also carried articles strongly denouncing the judgment.

[85] Sangari and Vaid, 'Institutions, Beliefs, Ideologies', p. 386.

[86] See, Sangari and Vaid, 'Institutions, Beliefs, Ideologies'.

[87] Sangari and Vaid, 'Institutions, Beliefs, Ideologies'.

[88] Thapar, R., 'In History', *Seminar*, V, 342, February 1988.

[89] Kishwar, *Off the Beaten Track*, p. 56.

[90] Ibid.

[91] Ibid., p. 58.

[92] Thapar, 'In History'.

[93] Hardgrove, A., 'Sati Worship and Marwari Public Identity in India', in *Journal of Asian Studies*, vol. 58: 3, August 1999.

[94] Oldenburg, 'The Roop Kanwar Case', p. 101.

I

SATI IN ANCIENT AND MEDIEVAL INDIA

1

Extracts on Sati from Hindu Texts

The process of seeking authority for sati in the Hindu scriptures began in the late eighteenth-century and was at the centre of the early nineteenth-century colonial response to the rite. The following are some of the more famous passages relating to the rite.

Ṛg Veda

'Ascend to life anticipating old age, and trying to follow due order according to your number. May Tvashtri, the well-born, being propitious, grant you prolonged life here. Let these women who are not widowed, who have good husbands, applying the collyrious butter to their eyes, enter; without tears, without disease, and full of ornaments, let these wives first enter the house. Rise up woman, thou art lying by one whose life is gone; come, come to the world of the living away from thy husband, and become the wife of him who grasps thy hand and is willing to marry thee... '[1]

The Institutes of Vishnu[2]

Now the duties of a woman (are as follows):

1. To live in harmony with her husband;
2. To show reverence (by embracing their feet and such-like attentions) to her mother-in-law, father-in-law, to Gurus (such as elders), to divinities, and to guests;
3. To keep household articles (such as the winnowing basket and the rest) in good array;

4. To maintain saving habits;

5. To be careful with her (pestle and mortar and other) domestic utensils;

6. Not to practise incantations with roots (or other kinds of witch-craft);

7. To observe auspicious customs;

8. Not to decorate herself with ornaments (or to partake of amuse-ments) while her husband is absent from home;

9. Not to resort to the houses of strangers (during the absence of her husband);

10. Not to stand near the doorway or by the windows (of her house);

11. Not to act by herself in any matter;

12. To remain subject, in her infancy, to her father; in her youth, to her husband; and in her old age, to her sons;

13. After the death of her husband, to preserve her chastity, or to ascend the pile after him;

14. No sacrifice, no penance, and no fasting is allowed to women apart from their husbands; to pay obedience to her lord is the only means for a woman to obtain bliss in heaven;

15. A woman who keeps a fast or performs a penance in the lifetime of her lord, deprives her husband of his life, and will go to hell;

16. A good wife, who perseveres in a chaste life after the death of her lord, will go to heaven like (perpetual) students, even though she has no son.

Vedavyasasmriti

...a good wife should renounce all pleasures as long as her hus-band would be about in a distant country. The widow of a Brahmana should either immolate herself in the fire with the corpse of her deceased husband or observe a lifelong vow of brahmacaryam from that date.[3]

Angirasa

...for all women there is no other duty but falling into the funeral pyre when the husband dies...she who follows her husband into death dwells in heaven for as many years as there are hairs on a human body, crores of years. Just as a snake-catcher draws a snake from a hole by force, so such a woman draws her husband from (wherever he may be) and enjoys bliss together with him in heaven, she being solely devoted to her husband and praised by bevies of heavenly damsels, sports with her husband for as long as fourteen Indras rule. Even if the husband has committed the sin of killing a Brahmana, or a friend, or be guilty of ingratitude, the wife who burns herself clasping the body on the pyre purifies him of the sin. That woman, who ascends the funeral pile when her husband dies, is equal to Arundhati in her character and is praised in heaven. And as long as a woman does not burn herself in fire on the death of her husband, she is never free from being born as a woman.[4]

The Kadambari of Bana

This path, followed by the illiterate, is a manifestation of infatuation, a course of ignorance, an act of fool-hardiness and shortsightedness, stumbling through stupidity, that life is put an end to when a parent, brother, sister, husband is dead.... If it be properly considered, this suicide has a selfish object, because it is intended to obviate the unbearable sorrow of bereavement...the custom is a foolish mistake of stupendous magnitude, committed under the reckless impulse of despair and infatuation. It does not help the dead, as he goes to heaven or hell according to his deserts. It does not ensure reunion since the wife who has uselessly sacrificed her life goes to the hell reserved for suicides. By living she can still do much good both to herself by pious works, and to the departed by offering oblations for his happiness in the other world. By dying she only adds to her misery.[5]

Mahanirvana Tantra

Every woman, O Goddess, is your very form, your body concealed within the universe; and so, if in her delusion a woman should mount her husband's funeral pyre, she would go to hell.[6]

Harita

...that woman who follows her husband in death purifies three families—that of her mother, of her father and of her husband.[7]

The Ramayana of Valmiki[8]

Sita's ordeal by fire in the Ramayana is not a sati in the strict sense, but does incorporate many of the issues that underpin the ethos of sati, such as purity, self-sacrifice, and devotion to the husband even in death. Although she did not burn on her husband's funeral pyre, she is often referred to as 'Sati Sita' because of the way in which her life fulfilled the ideals of pativratadharma.

Book XI: Rajya-abhisheka
(Rama's Return and Consecration)

1. ORDEAL BY FIRE

For she dwelt in Ravan's dwelling—rumour clouds a woman's fame—
Righteous Rama's brow was clouded, saintly Sita, spake in shame:
'Wherefore spake ye not, my Rama, if your bosom doubts my faith,
Dearer than a dark suspicion to a woman were her death!
Wherefore, Rama, with your token came your vassal o'er the wave,
To assist a fallen woman and a tainted wife to save,
Wherefore with your mighty forces crossed the ocean in your pride,
Risked your life in endless combats for a sin-polluted bride?
Hast thou, Rama, all forgotten?—Saintly Janak saw my birth,
Child of harvest-bearing furrow, Sita sprang from Mother Earth,
As a maiden true and stainless unto thee I gave my hand,
As a consort fond and faithful roved with thee from land to land!
But a woman pleadeth vainly when suspicion clouds her name,
Lakshman, if thou lov'st thy sister, light for me the funeral flame,
When the shadow of dishonour darkens o'er a woman's life,
Death alone is friend and refuge of a true and trustful wife,
When a righteous lord and husband turns his cold averted eyes,
Funeral flame dispels suspicion, honour lives when woman dies!'

Dark was Rama's gloomy visage and his lips were firmly sealed,
And his eye betrayed no weakness, word disclosed no thought
concealed,
Silent heaved his heart in anguish, silent drooped his tortured head,
Lakshman with a throbbing bosom funeral pyre for Sita made,
And Videha's sinless daughter prayed unto the Gods above,
On her lord and wedded consort cast her dying looks of love!
If in act and thought', she uttered, 'I am true unto my name,
Witness of our sins and virtues, may this Fire protect my fame!
If a false and lying scandal brings a faithful woman shame,
Witness of our sins and virtues, may this Fire protect my fame!
If in lifelong loving duty I am free from sin and blame,
Witness of our sins and virtues, may this Fire protect my fame!'
Fearless in her faith and valour Sita stepped upon the pyre,
And her form of beauty vanished circled by the clasping fire,
And an anguish shook the people like the ocean tempest-tos't,
Old and young and maid and matron wept for Sita true and lost,
For bedecked in golden splendour and in gems and rich attire,
Sita vanished in the red fire of the newly lighted pyre!
Rishis and the great Gandharvas, Gods who know each secret deed,
Witnessed Sita's high devotion and a woman's lofty creed,
And the earth by ocean girdled with its wealth of teeming life,
Witnessed deed of dauntless duty of a true and stainless wife!

2. WOMAN'S TRUTH VINDICATED

Slow the red flames rolled asunder, God of Fire incarnate came,
Holding in his radiant bosom fair Videha's sinless dame,
Not a curl upon her tresses, not a blossom on her brow,
Not a fibre of her mantle did with tarnished lustre glow!
Witness of our sins and virtues, God of Fire incarnate spake,
Bade the sorrow-stricken Rama back his sinless wife to take:
'Ravan in his impious folly forced from thee thy faithful dame,
Guarded by her changeless virtue, Sita still remains the same,
Tempted oft by female Rakshas in the dark and dismal wood,
In her woe and in her sadness true to thee hath Sita stood,
Courted oft by royal Ravan in the forest far and lone,
True to wedded troth and virtue Sita thought of thee alone,
Pure is she in thought and action, pure and stainless, true and meek,

I, the witness of all actions, thus my sacred mandate speak!'
Rama's forehead was unclouded and a radiance lit his eye,
And his bosom heaved in gladness as he spake in accents high:
'Never from the time I saw her in her maiden clays of youth,
Have I doubted Sita's virtue, Sita's fixed and changeless truth,
I have known her ever sinless,—let the world her virtue know,
For the God of Fire is witness to her truth and changeless vow!
Ravan in his pride and passion conquered not a woman's love,
For the virtuous like the bright fire in their native radiance move,
Ravan in his rage and folly conquered not a faithful wife,
For like a ray of sun unsullied is a righteous woman's life,
Be the wide world now a witness,—pure and stainless is my dame,
Rama shall not leave his consort till he leaves his righteous fame!'
In his tears the contrite Rama clasped her in a soft embrace,
And the fond forgiving Sita in his bosom hid her face!

The Mahabharata of Krishna-Dwaipayana Vyasa[9]

Sati is rare in the Mahabharata, and some argue that the few that do occur
may have been later interpolations to the epic. The following extract sees
Madri atone for having supposedly caused her husband's death by following
him onto the pyre.

Section CXXV

Vaisampayana said, 'Beholding his five handsome sons growing
up before him in that great forest on the charming mountain slope,
Pandu felt the last might of his arms revive once more. One day
in the season of spring which maddens every creature, the king
accompanied by his wife (Madri), began to rove in the woods
where every tree had put forth new blossoms. He beheld all
around Palasas and Tilakas and Mangoes and Champakas and
Parihadrakas and Karnikaras, Asokas and Kesaras and Atimuktas
and Kuruvakas with swarms of maddened bees sweetly hum-
ming about. And there were flowers of blossoming Parijatas, with
the Kokilas pouring forth their melodies from under every twig
echoing with the sweet hums of the black bees. And he beheld
also various other kinds of trees bent down with the weight of
their flowers and fruits. And there were also many fine pools of
water overgrown with hundreds of fragrant lotuses. Beholding

all these, Pandu felt the soft influence of desire. Roving like a celestial with a light heart amidst such scenery, Pandu was alone, with his wife Madri in semi-transparent attire. And beholding the youthful Madri thus attired, the king's desire flamed up like a forest-fire. And ill-able to suppress his desire thus kindled at the sight of his wife of eyes like lotus-petals, he was completely overpowered. The king then seized her against her will, but Madri trembling in fear resisted him to the best of her might. Consumed by desire, he forgot everything about his misfortune. And O thou of Kuru's race unrestrained by the fear of (the Rishi's) curse and impelled by fate, the monarch, overpowered by passion, forcibly sought the embraces of Madri, as if he wished to put an end to his own life. His reason, thus beguiled by the great Destroyer himself by intoxicating his senses, was itself lost with his life. And the Kuru king Pandu, of virtuous soul, thus succumbed to the inevitable influence of Time, while united in intercourse with his wife.

'Then Madri, clasping the body of her senseless lord, began to weep aloud. And Kunti with her sons and the twins of Madri, hearing those cries of grief, came to the spot where the king lay in that state. Then, O King, Madri addressing Kunti in a piteous voice, said, "Come hither alone, O Kunti, and let the children stay there." Hearing these words, Kunti, bidding the children stay, ran with speed, exclaiming, "Woe to me!" And beholding both Pandu and Madri lying prostrate on the ground she went in grief and affliction, saying, "Of passions under complete control, this hero, O Madri, had all along been watched by me with care. How did he then, forgetting the Rishi's curse, approach thee with enkindled desire? O Madri, this foremost of men should have been protected by thee. Why didst thou tempt him into solitude? Always melancholy at the thought of the Rishi's curse, how came he to be merry with thee in solitude? O princess of Valhika, more fortunate than myself, thou art really to be envied, for thou hast seen the face of our lord suffused with gladness and joy."

'Madri then replied, saying, "Revered sister, with tears in my eyes, I resisted the king, but he could not control himself, bent on, as it were, making the Rishi's curse true."

'Kunti then said, "I am the older of his wedded wives; the chief religious merit must be mine. Therefore, O Madri, prevent me not from achieving that which must be achieved. I must follow our lord to the region of the dead. Rise up, O Madri, and yield me his body. Rear thou these children." Madri replied, saying, "I do clasp our lord yet, and have not allowed him to depart; therefore, I shall follow him. My appetite hath not been appeased. Thou art my older sister, O let me have thy sanction. This foremost one of the Bharata princes had approached me, desiring to have intercourse. His appetite unsatiated, shall I not follow him in the region of Yama to gratify him? O revered one, if I survive thee, it is certain I shall not be able to rear thy children as if they were mine. Will not sin touch me on that account? But, thou, O Kunti, shall be able to bring my sons up as if they were thine. The king, in seeking me wishfully, hath gone to the region of spirits; therefore, my body should be burnt with his. O revered sister, withhold not thy sanction to this which is agreeable to me. Thou wilt certainly bring up the children carefully. That indeed, would be very agreeable to me. I have no other direction to give!"'

Vaisampayana continued, 'Having said this, the daughter of the king of Madras, the wedded wife of Pandu, ascended the funeral pyre of her lord, that bull among men.'

Notes

1   Quoted in Thakur, U., *The History of Suicide in India* (Delhi: Munshi Ram Manohar Lal, 1963), p.129.

2   Jolly, Julius (tr.) *The Institutes of Vishnu*, in *Sacred Books of the East*, vol. 7 (Oxford: The Clarendon Press, 1880).

3   Thakur, U., *The History of Suicide in India* (Delhi: Munshi Ram Manohar Lal, 1963), p. 134.

4   Cited in Sharma, A., *Sati: Historical and Phenomenological Essays* (Delhi: Motilal Banarsidass, 1988), p. 32. This passage also appears in the *Parasara*, the *Brahmapurana* (Gautamimahatmya), the *Mitaksara*, and *Suddhitattva*.

5   Sharma, A., *Sati: Historical and Phenomenological Essays* (Delhi: Motilal Banarsidass, 1988), p. 15.

6   Bose, M., 'Sati: The Event and the Idelogy' in M. Bose (ed.) *Faces of the Feminine in Ancient, Medieval and Modern India* (Delhi: Oxford University Press, 2000), p. 27.

7   Narasimhan, S., *Sati: A Study of Widow Burning in India* (Delhi: HarperCollins, 1998), p.28.

8   Dutt, Ramesh C. (tr.), *The Ramayana of Valmiki*, 1899.

9   Ganguli, Kisori Mohan (tr.) *The Mahabharata of Krishna-Dwaipayana Vyasa*, (1883–96).

2

Classical And Medieval Accounts

Early Greek Account[1]

The earliest historical account of a sati comes from a Greek report of an immolation observed during Alexander's campaign. The Hindu General Keteus died in 316 BC in the battle between Antigonos and Eumenes, who left two wives, both of whom were apparently eager to perform sati. The elder wife was prevented from doing so, however, on account of her pregnancy.

The elder wife went away lamenting, with the band around her head rent, and tearing her hair, as if tidings of some great disaster had been brought her; and the other departed, exalting at her victory, to the pyre, crowned with fillets by the women who belonged to her, and decked out splendidly as for a wedding. She was escorted by her kinsfolk who chanted songs in praise of her virtue. When she came near the pyre she took off her adornments and distributed them to her familiars and friends, leaving a memorial for herself, as it were, to those who had loved her.... In conclusion, she said farewell to her familiars and was helped by her brother onto the pyre, and there, to the admiration of the crowd that had gathered together for the spectacle, she ended her life in heroic fashion. Before the pyre was kindled, the whole army in battle array marched round it thrice. She meanwhile lay down beside her husband and as the fire seized her no sound of weakness escaped her lips. The spectators were moved, some to pity, and some to exuberant praise. But some of the Greeks present found fault with such customs as savage and inhuman.

Bana, *The Harsacarita of Bana*[2]

In this seventh-century Indian narrative, King Harsa's sister, bereft of his protection, determines to immolate herself to avoid dishonour. She is saved by her brother's timely reappearance. The author, Bana, was a vocal critic of the custom of sati, which he deemed a 'mistake of enormous magnitude'.

The king respectfully replied, 'Reverend Sir, you have performed everything by your zealous words which ceaselessly rain forth ambrosia-like honey to gladden my heart,—I am indeed fortunate that a venerable saint should thus consider an insignificant person like me worthy of respect. Be pleased to learn what is the cause of my being fatigued with wandering in the forest. For I have only one young sister left, who is the sole link that keeps up my life, now that I have lost all my loved kindred. Now she, while wandering fearful of outrage from her enemies in consequence of the loss of her husband, entered the thickets of this Vindhya forest, swarming with hordes of vile foresters and unnumbered troops of elephants, and terrible beyond measure with its lions and çarabhas, and having its paths infested by huge buffaloes, and impassable with sharp spear-grass, and full of pits everywhere. Night after night we have been ceaselessly exploring the wood in search of her, but we have not found her. Be pleased to tell me if any tidings of her have reached your ears from some forester.'

The holy man made answer with some agitation, 'No tidings of this nature have come to me; we are not worthy to bring to your highness such welcome narrations.' But while he was thus speaking, a mendicant of tranquil age suddenly came up in bewilderment, and folding his hands before the ascetic spoke in a compassionate tone with his eyes full of tears, 'O my lord, it is indeed a sad occurrence. A young woman overpowered by heavy misfortune, though apparently highly prosperous in former days, in helpless despair is even now mounting the funeral pile. Consider that she is not yet dead,—come to her aid with suitable topics of consolation; even a poor worm in pain which found no rest has often ere now experienced the sage's compassion.'

Fearful for his sister, melting within with grief from his fraternal affection, and having his heart greatly agitated, speaking with
difficulty in broken accents, with his voice choked and his eyes
full of tears, the king made inquiry, 'O Mendicant, how far off is
the woman whom you describe and can she be still alive? If you
asked who she was or to whom she belonged or from whence
she came or why she entered this wood or why she mounted into
the fire,—I want to know in full what she answered to each question,
and how she came into your sight and what manner of person
she was.'

The Mendicant replied, 'Listen, noble Sir. I had offered my
worship in the early morning to the sun and I was wandering on
and on by the soft sand of this river-bank. In a bower of creepers
near the mountain-stream I heard a monotonous mournful bewil-
dering sound of women's weeping like the murmur of lute-strings[3]
in a very loud note, or the hum of bees distressed at a sudden
frost cutting their lotus beds. With a sudden feeling of pity I turned
to the spot; and there I saw a woman surrounded by a troop of
other women, whose eyes were closed with the sharp pain of
the spear-points of the *Çara*-grass which had pierced their heels,
and whose feet were swollen beyond the power of moving by
the fatigue of a long journey, while their toes were bleeding with
the wounds from the jagged stones; who had birch-bark tied on
their ankles which were aching with the wounds from stakes, while
their legs were fevered and lame with blisters, and their calves
were white with dust, and their knees were torn by the matted
fibres of the date-palms, and their thighs were wounded by the
Çatāvarī shrubs; their silk skirts were torn by the *Vidārī*-plants, their
jackets rent by the sharp ends of the bambu branches; their soft
hands were pierced by the thorny *Badarī*-creepers as they pulled
them down in their wish to gather the fruit, their arms were wea-
ried by the quantities of bulbs, roots and fruits which they had dug
up with the horns of the deer; they chewed the soft myrobalans
to relieve the dryness of their mouths without their favourite betel, while they used red arsenic as an ointment for their eyes
which were swollen and bleeding with the blows of the flowers
of the *Kuça* grass, and their curls were torn by the thorny creepers;
some used boughs as umbrellas against the sun, others held

plaintain leaves as fans, others carried water in the hollow of a
lotus-leaf, others took the fibrous lotus-roots as their provisions,
others carried pine oil[4] in cocoa-nuts balanced on loops made of
strips of China silk hanging from a yoke; while the rest of the
crowd were bewildered eunuchs,[5] humpbacks, dwarfs, deaf, bar-
barians, (and all the other mis-shapen guards of the gynæceum).
The centre figure which lay prostrate in the wood, though in deep
misery, was still clothed in the grace and dignity of high birth,—
her body dyed[6] by the reflected boughs of the creepers near by,
as if it were covered with the freshly bleeding wounds of her
desperate grief,—her feet red, as with the customary lac, through
the blood pouring from the wounds made by the hard spikes of
Darbha grass, her face pale though shaded by a lotus-leaf which
one of the women held up by its stalk,—seeming to be more empty
than the desolate ether,—made as of earth in her insensibleness,
made as of air in her incessant sighing, made as of fire in her constant fever, made as of water in her streaming outflow of tears,—
like the sky in her want of all support, like the lightning in her
tremulousness, like sound in her ceaseless wailing, like the kalpa
tree of paradise,[7] dropping off her silken garments, jewels, flowers, gold, and painted decorations. She lay on the ground like
Ganges after her descent, while her limbs still shewed their inso-
lent power ready to humble imperial heads (as Ganges trampled
on Çiva's head when she fell upon it); her feet[8] were grey with
the pollen of the wood-flowers, and she herself longing for another world like the paling moon of early morning,—her long
bright eyes dimmed with the outflow of tears, and she herself fading like a lotus-bed of the Mandākinī,—passing a weary time like
a bed of night water-lilies withering beneath the fierce rays of
the sun; pale and thin like the flame of a lamp at morning, deceived by its exhausted wick;[9] like a female elephant plunged in
a lake and only rescued by the care of her companions,—lost in
the forest and in thought, bent upon death and the root of a tree,
fallen into calamity and on her nurse's bosom, parted from her
husband and happiness, exhausted by wandering and emptied of
her youth, bewildered in her dishevelled locks and in pondering
how to end her life, pale with the dust of the road and the pains
of her limbs, burned with the fierce sunshine and the woes of

widowhood, her mouth closed with silence as well as by her hand, and held fast by her companions as well as by grief. I saw her with her kindred and her graces all gone, her ears and her soul left bare, her ornaments and her aims abandoned, her bracelets and her hopes broken, her companions and the needle-like grass-spears clinging round her feet, her eye and her beloved fixed within her bosom, her sighs and her hair long, her limbs and her merits exhausted, her aged attendants and her streaming tears falling down at her feet, her band of followers and her life reduced to a scanty remnant,—languid in opening her eyes, ready only to shed tears, continuous in anxieties, broken short in hopes, wasted in her body, thick in her sighs, filled with misery, emptied of courage, dominated by fatigue, deserted by her heart, immovable in her purpose but shaken from her self-command,—herself the home of calamities, the receptacle of cares, the abode of ever varying conditions, the fixed site of want of fixity, the seat of fainting fits, the centre of calamities, the goal of misfortunes, the very dismay of dismays, the special object of pity, the ne plus ultra of helplessness. As I saw her, I reflected, "Strange! Do calamities assail even such a form as this?" But even in that destitute condition she bowed her head respectfully as I came up. I thought to myself, as, in my great compassion I wished to speak to her, "How shall I venture to address such a noble lady? If I call her 'my child' it will be too affectionate, 'mother' will be too flattering, 'sister' will be giving myself too much honour, 'your majesty' would be the address of her attendant, 'princess' will be too general, 'lay sister' will be only my hope, 'mistress' will be to accept the position of her slave, 'lady' would be suitable for other women, 'long-lived one' would be cruelty in the circumstances, 'fortunate one' would be mockery in her present plight, 'moonfaced' would be an improper idea for a *muni*, 'girl' would be disrespectful, 'venerable' would too much imply old age, 'holy' would not be borne out by the fortune which has befallen her, 'madam' would be too applicable to everybody. Moreover, 'who art thou?' would be rude, 'why dost thou weep?' would remind her of the cause of her grief, 'weep not' is not to be said unless one can remove the cause of her tears, 'be consoled' has no foundation to rest on, 'welcome' is flat and stale; 'are you well?' is false."

'While I was thus reflecting, a woman of venerable aspect but overwhelmed with sorrow, came out from that crowd of women, and laying her partially grey head on the ground, scalded my feet with her tears which expressed the vehement emotion of her bosom, and my heart with her mournful words. "Holy father, the nature of a religious mendicant is always compassionate for all beings; and the Buddhists are skilled in the self-devotion of relieving every sorrow, and the doctrine of Çākyamunī is the family-home of pity, and the Jaina saintship is ever ready to help everybody, and the religion of the Munis is a means to attain the next world, and no higher kind of merit is known in this world than saving life. Young women are naturally the objects of compassion,—still more so when they are overwhelmed in misfortune; and the good are the 'happy land' of the mourners. This our mistress, being helpless through the death of her father, the loss of her husband, the absence of her brother, and the disappearance of all her other relatives, in her excessive tenderness of heart and childless desolation, naturally wise but overwhelmed by the cruel insults of her base foes—her delicate nature tortured by her weary wandering in the forest and her heart bewildered by these continually fresh calamities inflicted by accursed fortune,— unable to bear her dreadful misery any longer,—rejecting her older friends as they tried to hinder her, whom she had never gone contrary to before even in her dreams,—and despising the friends of her youth who tried to reason with her and whose love had never known a break even in play,—and spurning away her attendants who, helplessly weeping, tried to dissuade her and whose words she had never before scorned even in thought,— she is now entering into the fire. O save her! Even a saint like thyself may employ in her case those words of thine skilled in such counsels as can remove even unendurable sorrow."As she spoke these mournful utterances, I raised her up and still more distressed myself gently addressed her, "Madam, it is as you say. This noble lady's grief is however beyond the reach of my words; but your request will not be in vain, if we can save her but for a moment. My own teacher is near at hand, who is like another holy Buddha. When I tell him this occurrence, he will certainly come, boundlessly compassionate as he is. He will guide our pious sister into the path of wisdom by the good words of Sugata which pierce the mists of sorrow, and by his own wise counsels, illustrated with apt examples and weighty with various sacred texts." When she heard this, she fell again at my feet, urging me to make haste. So I have come in haste, announcing to my teacher this startling and mournful occurrence, which threatens death to so many helpless young women.'

The king at once understood the mendicant's agitated words, which were interrupted by his tears, even though his sister's name had not been mentioned; and with his mind oppressed by grief, and with all uncertainty dissipated by the reflection that her condition so exactly agreed with every circumstance told about her, and with his ears burning at the tidings, said to the chief mendicant, 'Holy Sir, this is indeed my poor sister,—base, hard-hearted, cruel and unfortunate as I am, I have left her to fall into this condition through pitiless undeserved misfortunes,—my torn heart only too surely tells me so.' Then he turned to the inferior mendicant and said, 'Rise up, holy sir, shew me where she is; make haste,[10] we will go at once to win the merit of saving these many lives, if by any means we can imagine her to be still alive,' and as he uttered the words he himself sprang up.

Followed by the holy man who was attended by all his disciples, and followed by all his tributary kings who had alighted from their horses, which they led after them, the king made the Buddhist disciple go in front to shew the road, and went on foot after him, seeming to devour the way with his rapid strides. As he drew near, he heard from between the trees various utterances such as suited the emergency from that crowd of women all anxious to die, 'O holy Yama, come quickly,—where art thou, O goddess of our family,—O divine Earth, dost thou not support[11] thy wretched daughter?—whither is Lakṣmī gone, the matron of Puṣpabhūti's[12] house? O lord of the Mukhara family,[13] why dost thou not restore to consciousness this thy widowed wife, distracted with her various griefs? O holy Sugata, thou art asleep to thy distracted worshippers. O Royal Duty, ever fostering the house of Puṣpabhūti, why art thou become so indifferent? I raise my hands in fruitless supplication to thee also, O Vindhya, thou friend in calamity! O Mother forest, dost thou not hear the cries of this distressed daughter? O Sun, save this devoted wife, helpless in her misery. O thou, saved with difficulty, ungrateful Honour, thou utter barbarian in conduct, dost thou not save the princess? What have her royal marks secured for her? O queen Yaçovatī, devoted to thy daughter, thou hast been carried off by the robber fate! O king Pratāpaçīla, dost thou not fly to rescue thy daughter from the flames? Thy paternal love is indeed weak. O king Rājyavardhana, dost thou not hasten? Thy love for thy sister is indeed cold, the world of the dead is indeed deaf to pity! Away O fire, Art thou cruel enough to kill a woman? Art thou not ashamed of thy blaze? O brother wind, I am thy suppliant,—hasten to tell the king Harṣa that the princess is burning, he is the consoler of all who are in trouble. O pitiless barbarian, Sorrow, thou hast thy desire! O demon Separation, thou mayest well be content! In this lonely wood, whom shall I call? To whom shall I speak? to whom fly for refuge? to which direction shall I turn? What shall I do in my forlornness? O Gāndhārī,[14] this bundle of creepers is mine. O savage Mocanikā, cease that quarrelling over the gathering of boughs. O Kalahaṃsī, why do you still smite your head? O Maṅgalikā, why do you still weep so passionately? O Sundarī, your companions are all far away. O Çabarikā, how will you stay in this horrible camp of corpses? O Sutanu, will you too go into the fire? O Mālāvatī tender as a lotus-fibre, you are fainting. O mother, Mātaṅgikā, have you too accepted death! O dear Vatsikā, how will you dwell in the hated city of the dead? O Nāgarikā, you have gained glory by this loyalty to your mistress! O Virājikā, you are made famous by your resolution to die in your mistress' calamity! O pitcher-bearer, you are happy in knowing how to face the fall from a precipice! O Ketakī, how will you ever find again such a mistress even in dream? O Menakā, may the God Fire, when he burns your body, give you a service under the princess in every successive birth! O Vijayā, fan the fire! O Sānumatī,[15] Indīvarikā bows her farewell, longing to go to heaven! O Kāmadāsī, give me room to circumambulate the pile! O Vicarikā, make the fire! O Kirātikā, strew a heap of flowers! O Kurarikā, cover the pile with *Kuruvaka* buds! O chourie-bearer, clasp my neck for the last time! O Narmadā, you must fogive my excessive bursts of laughter provoked by our jests! O Subhadrā, may your journey to another world be fortunate! O Grāmeyikā, who lovest the virtues of the noble, may you rise to a happy birth! O Vasantikā, make room! O queen, thy umbrella-bearer bids thee farewell,—give me a last look! Your beloved Vijayasenā abandons life! Muktikā, the manager of your dramas, wails aloud near you! Patralatā, your loved betel-bearer, O princess, falls at your feet! O Kaliṅgasenā, this is our last embrace, press me tightly to your bosom! O Vasantasenā, my life is departing! O Mañjulikā, how often do you wipe these eyes dimmed with a thousand tears of intolerable sorrow, and how long do you weep while you embrace me? Created existence is always like this, O Yaçodhanā! O Mādhavikā, why do you still hold me fast? Is this a situation for consolations? The time is past, O Kālindī, for reverential salutations to your companions! O distracted Mattapālikā, it is a useless waste of time to fall humbly at the feet of your beloved ones! O Cakoravatī, loosen thy hold of my feet, passionate one! O Kamalinī, why these repeated reproaches against fate? The happiness of union with our friends is over only too soon! Farewell, O revered chamberlain Taraṅgasenā! O dear Saudāminī, I have at least seen you! O Kumudikā, bring the flowers with which to worship the fire! O Rohiṇī, give me your hand to support me as I climb the pyre! O mother nurse, be firm; verily such is the retribution of those who have sinned! I give my last salutation to your honoured feet! O mother, this is my last bow of farewell as I depart to the next world!—O Lavalikā,[16] at the time of death why is there this joyful shouting in my heart! With what foreboding do my limbs bristle and thrill with delight? O Vāmanikā, my left eye throbs! In vain, O friendly crow, do you keep alighting on a milky tree[17] in front of me born to ill-fortune! O Hariṇī, I hear to the north the neighing of horses! O Prabhāvatī, whose is this lofty umbrella which I see between the trees? O Kuraṅgikā, who is it that has uttered my lord's auspicious name? O queen, thou art indeed happy in the joy of the coming of King Harṣa!'

As he heard these various voices, the king hurried up and saw Rājyaçrī fainting as she prepared to enter the funeral pile, and full of agitation, he pressed her forehead with his hand as she lay with her eyes closed in her swoon. At that reviving touch of her dear brother's hand which seemed to diffuse a life-restoring power as if healing plants were fastened to his arm, and to drop a mysterious influence as of amulets in his bracelets, and to rain ambrosia from the moonbeams of his nails, and to bind on her forehead a moongem crest which dropped a cool dew like that which falls when the moon rises, and to calm her fevered heart with his fingers cold like lotus-fibres and to bring back her wandering life, Rājyaçrī instantly opened her eyes. Clasping the neck of her brother thus unexpectedly restored to her as if seen in a dream, and pouring forth a flood of tears from her eyes which were like the channels of two rivers, with the stored reservoir of grief overpowering all her soul and bursting out violently at his sudden appearance,—she cried out, 'O father, O mother, O friends.' Meanwhile her brother, as he tried to comfort her, covered her mouth with his hands, and kept calling out in a loud voice through the agitation caused by his fraternal affection, 'O my child, be firm,'—and the holy teacher exhorted her to obey the words of her elder brother, and the courtiers implored her, 'Dost thou not see, O queen, the condition of the king? Cease now to weep!' Her attendants said to her, 'O Mistress, have pity on thy brother,' and her aged relations restrained her, 'O daughter cease for the present and weep again at some future time,' and her young friends counselled her, 'Dear friend, how long will you weep? Be silent, you greatly pain the king.' Though surrounded by all these various comforters, the princess wept violently for a long time with a loud outburst of grief, her throat choked by the tears which broke forth to shew the pressure of the griefs which she had so long pondered over, and her soul filled with the weight of her distress; but when the first vehemence of her emotion was spent she allowed her brother to lead her away from the fire and sat down at the foot of a tree nearby.

Ibn Battuta, *The Travels of Ibn Battuta*[18]

One of the best medieval narratives of a sati comes from the famous Arab traveller Ibn Battuta. A contemporary of Marco Polo, Battuta gives a far more detailed account than his Italian counterpart.

Account of Indians who burn themselves to death: As I returned from visiting this sheikh, I saw people hurrying out from our camp, and some of our party along with them. I asked them what was happening and they told me that one of the Hindu infidels had died, that a fire had been kindled to burn him, and that his wife would burn herself along with him. After the burning, my companions came back and told me that she had embraced the dead man until she herself was burned with him. Later on I used often to see in that country an infidel Hindu woman, richly dressed, riding on horseback, followed by both Muslims and infidels and preceded by drums and trumpets; she was accompanied by Brahmins, who are the chiefs of the Hindus. In the Sultan's dominions they ask his permission to burn her, which he accords them and then they burn her.

Some time later I happened to be in a town inhabited by a majority of infidels, called Amjari. Its governor was a Muslim, one of the Samira of Sind. In its neighbourhood there were some unsubdued infidels, and when one day they made an attack on the road the Muslim Amir went out to engage them, together with his subjects both Muslim and infidel. There was severe fighting between them, in the course of which seven of the infidel subjects were killed, three of whom had wives, and the three widows agreed to burn themselves. The burning of a wife after her husband's death is regarded by them as a commendable act, but is not compulsory; but when a widow burns herself her family gains a certain prestige by it and gains a reputation for fidelity. A widow who does not burn herself dresses in coarse garments and lives with her own people in misery, despised for her lack of fidelity, but she is not forced to burn herself.

When these three women whom we have referred to made a compact to burn themselves, they spent three days preceding the event in concerts of music and singing and festivals of eating and drinking, as though they were bidding farewell to the world, and women from all around came to take part. On the morning of the fourth day each one of them had a horse brought to her and mounted it, richly dressed and perfumed. In her right hand she held a coconut, with which she played, and in her left a mirror, in which she could see her face. They were surrounded by Brahmins and accompanied by their own relatives, and were proceeded by drums, trumpets, and bugles. Every one of the infidels would say to one of them, 'Take greetings from me to my father, or brother, or mother, or friend', and she would say 'yes' and smile at them. I rode out with my companions to see exactly what these women did in this ceremony of burning. After travelling about three miles with them we came to a dark place with much water and trees with heavy shade, amongst which there were four pavilions, each containing a stone idol. Between the pavilions there was a basin of water over which dense shade was cast by trees so thickly set that the sun could not penetrate them. The place looked like a spot in hell—God preserve us from it! On reaching these pavilions they descended into the pool, plunged into it and divested themselves of their clothes and ornaments, which they distributed as alms. Each one was then given an unsown garment of coarse cotton and tied part of it around her waist and part of it over her head and shoulders. Meanwhile the fires had been lit near this basin in a low-lying spot, and *raughan kunjut*, that is oil of sesame, poured over them, so that the flames were increased. There were about fifteen men there with faggots of thin wood, and with them about ten others with heavy balks in their hands, while the drummers and trumpeters were there waiting for the women's coming. The fire was screened off by a blanket held by some men in their hands, so that she should not be frightened by the sight of it. I saw one of them, on coming to the blanket, pull it violently out of the men's hands, saying to them with a laugh '*mara mitarasani az atash man midanam u atash ast raha kuni mara*'; these words mean 'Is it with fire that you frighten me? I know that it is a blazing fire'. Thereupon she joined her hands above her head in salutation to the fire and cast herself into it. At the same moment the drums, trumpets, and bugles were sounded, and men threw on her the firewood they were carrying, and others put those heavy balks on top of her to prevent her moving. Cries were raised and there was a loud clamour. When I saw this I had all but fallen off my horse, if my companions had not quickly brought water to me and laved my face, after which I withdrew.

Duarte Barbosa, *A Description of the Coasts of East Africa and Malabar*[19]

The following account of sati comes from the famous Portuguese traveller and cousin to Magellan, Duarte Barbosa. The narrative was written in 1514.

'In this kingdom there are three sects of Gentiles, and each one of them is distinguished from the others, and their customs are different. In the first place the king and the grandees, and lords and chief people of the men-at-arms, can marry more than one wife, especially the grandees who can maintain them: their children are their heirs. The wives are bound to burn themselves to death and to die with their husbands when they decease, because when the people die their bodies are burned, both of men and women. And the wives burn themselves alive with them to honour them, in this manner: that is to say, if she is a poor woman of little rank, when the body of her husband is borne out to be burned in an open space outside the city, where there is a great fire, and whilst the body of the husband is being consumed, the wife casts herself, of her own will, into the fire and burns there with him. And if she is some honourable woman, and of much property, and whether she be a young woman of beautiful presence, or old, when her husband dies, the relations all go to the before-mentioned open space, and make a wide grave as deep as a man's height, and fill it with sandal and other wood, and place the dead body within and burn it; and his wife or wives weep for him, and then, should she desire to honour her husband, she asks for a term of a certain number of days to go and be burned with him. And they bid all her relations, and those of her husband, come and do her honour and give her a festal reception. And in this manner all collect together, and entertain and pay court to her, and she spends what she possesses among her relations in feasting and singing, in dances and playing on musical instruments, and amusements of jugglers. And when the term fixed has ended, she dresses herself in her richest stuffs, and adorns herself with many precious jewels, and the rest of her property she divides among her children, relations, and friends, and then mounts a horse, with a great sound of music and a large following. The horse must be grey, or very white if possible, for her to be seen better. And so they conduct her through the whole city, paying court to her as far as the place where the body of her husband was burned; and in the same grave they place much wood, with which they light a very great fire, and all around it they make a gallery with three or four steps, whither she ascends with all her jewels and robes; and when she is on top she takes three turns around it, and raises her hands to heaven, and worships towards the east three times. And having ended this, she calls her relations and friends, and to each she gives a jewel of those which she wears: and all this with a very cheerful demeanour, not as though she were about to die. And after she has given them away, and there only remains a small cloth with which she is covered from the waist downwards, she says to the men, 'See, gentlemen, how much you owe to your wives, who whilst enjoying their freedom, burn themselves alive with their husbands.' And to the women she says, 'See, ladies, how much you owe to your husbands, for in this manner you ought to accompany them even in death.' And when she had concluded uttering these words, they give her a pitcher full of oil, and she places it on her head and says her prayer, and takes three more turns and worships to the east, and casts the pitcher of oil into the pit where the fire is: and she springs into it, after the pitcher, with as much good will as though she were jumping into a pool of water. And the relatives have ready for this occasion many pitchers or pots full of oil and butter, and dry wood, which they immediately throw in, so that a great flame is at once kindled, that she is suddenly reduced to ashes. And afterwards they collect these ashes and throw them into flowing rivers. All perform this in general, and if any women do not choose to do this, their relations take them, shave their heads, and turn them out of their houses and families in disgrace. And so they wander through the world as lost ones. And those of this sort whom they may wish to show favour, are sent to the houses of prayer of the idols, to serve and gain for that temple with their bodies, if they are young women. And of these houses there are many, which contain fifty or a hundred women of this sort; and others, who being unmarried, of their own accord place themselves there. These have to play and sing, for certain hours of the day before their idols, and for the rest of the time they work for themselves.

So also when the king dies, four or five hundred women burn themselves with him in the same manner, and they throw themselves suddenly into the pit and fire where they burn with the body of the king: for the pit and fire are very large, and a great quantity can be burned in it, with a great abundance of wood, sandal, basil, eagle wood, aloes wood, and much oil of sesame and butter to make the wood burn well. So great is the haste of those who wish to burn themselves first, that it is something wonderful, and many men, confidantes to the king, burn themselves with him....There is another sect of Gentiles who are called Bramans, who are priests and directors of the houses of prayer. These do not eat meat or fish, they marry only one wife, and if she dies, they do not marry again: their children inherit their property. They wear over their shoulder three threads as a sign of their being Bramans. These do not die for any cause or crime which they may commit; they are very free and easy and are very much venerated among the people.... In this country there is another sect of people who are like Bramans: they wear around their necks hung with silken cords and wrapped in coloured cloth, a stone the size of an egg, and they say that it is their god. These people are very much venerated and honoured in this country; they do them no harm for any offence which they may commit, out of reverence for that stone, which they call tabaryne...these likewise marry only one woman, and if they die before their wives, they bury these alive in this manner. It must be said, that they make a grave for her a little deeper than she is tall, and put her in it standing, and while she is quite alive they throw in earth all around her, and press it down with their feet until she is walled in with earth much pressed down, which reaches her neck, and then they put some large stones above her, and leave her there alive covered with earth until she dies; and on this occasion they perform great ceremonies for them.

Notes

[1]   Sharma, A., *Historical and Phenomenological Essays* (Delhi: Motilal Banarsidass, 1988), p. 2.

[2]   Cowell, E.B. and Thomas, F.W. (tr.), *The Harsacarita of Bana* (London: Royal Asiatic Society, 1897).

[3]   The Kashmir text and the Comm. read *varṇatantrīṇām.*

[4]   *Saralatailena* Kashm. and MS. A.

[5]   Read -*çokavikalakalamūka-.*

[6]   Read -*pāṭalīkriyamāṅa-* (A -*pāṭalīkrita-*).

[7]   The Kalpa tree *dropped* everything which its votary desired. Note puns in Comm. in *mukta* and *rana.*

[8] With a pun in *pāda* which also means 'rays'.

[9] *Daçā* also means 'state'.

[10] The Kashmir text and A read *yatasva*.

[11] *Dhārayasi* A.

[12] An ancestor of Çrī Harṣa.

[13] Rājaçrī's slain husband was Grahavarman of the Mukhara family.

[14] These are the names of various attendants who are preparing to enter the funeral pile with their mistress.

[15] Or 'on the mountain'.

[16] This sudden change from sorrow to joy implies Çrī Harṣa's approach.

[17] This seems to be a good omen—a crow seen on one's right hand is a good omen in the Bengali poem 'Caṇḍī'.

[18] Gibb, H.A.R. (tr.) *The Travels of Ibn Battuta* AD *1325–1354*, vol. 3 (Cambridge: Hakluyt Society, 1971).

[19] Duarte, Barbosa *A Description Of The Coasts Of East Africa And Malabar In The Beginning Of The Sixteenth Century by Duart Barbosa, a Portuguese*, translated from an early Spanish manuscript by H.E.J. Stanley (London: The Hakluyt Society, 1866).

II

EARLY MODERN AND
COLONIAL ACCOUNTS

3

Early Modern Travellers

François Bernier, *Travels in the Mogul Empire*[1]

The writings of this famous seventeenth-century French traveller and physician were extremely influential, both at the time and in the eighteenth and nineteenth centuries. In particular, his depiction of devilish Brahmin priests as the instigators of sati were to become a stock image in early nineteenth-century European accounts. His travel narrative includes both accounts of actual immolations and a detailed discussion of the rite's causes.

What has been said about women burning themselves will be confirmed by so many travellers that I suppose people will cease to be sceptical upon this melancholy fact. The accounts given have certainly been exaggerated, and the number of victims is less now than formerly, the Mahometans, by whom the country is governed, doing all in their power to suppress the barbarous custom. They do not indeed forbid it by a positive law, because it is part of their policy to leave the idolatrous population, which is so much more numerous than their own, in the free exercise of their religion; but the practice is checked by indirect means. No woman can sacrifice herself without permission from the governor of the province in which she resides, and he never grants it until he has ascertained that she is not to be turned aside from her purpose; to accomplish this desirable end the governor reasons with the widow and makes her enticing promises; after which, if these methods fail, he sometimes sends her among his women, that the effect of their remonstrances may be tried. Notwithstanding these obstacles, the number of self-immolations is still very considerable, particularly in the territories of the Rajas, where no Mahometan governors are appointed. But not to tire you with the history of every woman I have ever seen perish on the funeral pile, I shall advert only two or three of those shocking spectacles at which I have been present; and first I shall give you some details concerning a female to whom I was sent for the purpose of diverting her from persevering in her dreadful intention.

One of my friends named Bendidas, Danechmend-khan's principal writer, died of a hectic fever for which I had attended him upwards of two years, and his wife immediately resolved to burn herself with the body of her husband. Her friends were in the service of my Agah, and being commanded to dissuade the widow from the commission of so frantic an act, they represented to her that although she had adopted a generous and commendable resolution, which would redound to the honour and conduce to the happiness of the family, yet she ought to consider that her children were of a tender age, that it would be cruel to abandon them, and that her anxiety for their welfare ought to exceed the affection she bore to the memory of her deceased husband. The infatuated creature attended not, however, to their reasoning, and I was requested to visit the widow, as if by my Agah's desire, and in the capacity of an old friend of the family. I complied and found on entering the apartment a regular witches' sabat of seven or eight old hags, and another four or five excited, wild, and aged Brahmins standing round the body, all of whom gave by turns a horrid yell, and beat their hands with violence. The widow was seated at the feet of her dead husband; her hair was dishevelled and her visage pale, but her eyes were tearless and sparkling with animation while she cried and screamed aloud with the rest of the company, and beat time with her hands to this horrible concert. The hurly-burly having subsided, I approached the hellish group, and addressed the woman in a gentle tone. 'I am come hither,' I said, 'by desire of Danechmend-khan, to inform you that he will settle a pension of two crowns per month on each of your two sons, provided you do not destroy your life, a life so necessary for their care and education. We have ways and means indeed of preventing you ascending the pile, and to punish those who encourage you in so unreasonable a resolution.

All your relations wish you to live for the sake of your offspring, and you will not be reputed infamous as are the childless widows who possess not the courage to burn themselves with their dead husbands.' I repeated these arguments several times without receiving any answer; but at last, fixing a determined look on me, she said, 'Well, if I am prevented from burning myself, I will dash my brains out upon a wall.' What a diabolical spirit has taken possession of you, thought I. 'Let it be so then,' I rejoined, with undissembled anger, 'but first take your children, wretched and unnatural mother! Cut their throats, and consume them on the same pile; otherwise you will leave them to die of famine, for I shall return immediately to Danechmend-khan and annul their pensions.' These words, spoken with a loud and resolute voice, made the desired impression: without uttering a syllable her head fell suddenly on her knees, and the greater part of the old women and Brahmins sneaked towards the door and left the room. I thought I might safely leave the widow now in the hands of her friends, who had accompanied me, and mounting my horse returned home. In the evening, when on my way to Danechmend-khan to inform him of what I had done, I met one of the relations who thanked me and said that the body had been burned without the widow, who had promised not to die by her own hands.

In regard to the women who actually burn themselves, I was present at so many of those shocking exhibitions that I could not persuade myself to attend any more, nor is it without a feeling of horror that I revert to the subject. I shall endeavour nevertheless, to describe what passed before my eyes; but I cannot hope to give you an adequate conception of the fortitude displayed by these infatuated victims during the whole of the frightful tragedy: it must be seen to be believed.

When travelling from Ahmedabad to Agra, through the territories of the Rajas, and while the caravan halted under the shade of a banyan tree until the cool of evening, news reached us that a widow was then on the point of burning herself with the body of her husband. I ran at once to the spot, and going to the edge of a large and nearly dry reservoir, observed at the bottom a deep pit filled with wood: the body of a dead man extended thereon; a woman seated on the same pile; four or five Brahmins setting fire to it in every part; five middle-aged women tolerably well dressed, holding one another by the hand, singing and dancing round the pit; and a great number of spectators of both sexes.

The pile, whereon large quantities of butter and oil had been thrown, was soon enveloped in flames, and I saw the fire catch the woman's garments, which were impregnated with scented oil, mixed with sandalwood powder and saffron, but I could not perceive the slightest indication of pain, or even uneasiness in the victim, and it was said that she pronounced with emphasis the words 'five, two' to signify that this being the fifth time she had burned herself with the same husband, there were wanted only two more similar sacrifices to render her perfect, according to the doctrine of the transmigration of souls; as if a certain reminiscence or prophetic spirit had been imparted to her at that moment of her dissolution.

But this was only the commencement of the infernal tragedy. I thought that the singing and dancing of the five women were nothing more than some unmeaning ceremony; great therefore was my astonishment when I saw that the flames having ignited the clothes of one of these females, she cast herself head foremost into the pit. The horrid example was followed by another woman, as soon as the flames caught her person; the three women who remained then took hold of each other by the hand, resuming the dance with perfect composure; and after a short lapse of time, they also precipitated themselves, one after the other, into the fire.

I soon learnt the meaning of these multiple sacrifices. The five women were slaves, and having witnessed the deep affliction of their mistress in consequence of the illness of her husband, whom she promised not to survive, they were so moved with compassion that they entered into an engagement to perish in the same flames that consumed their beloved mistress.

Many persons whom I then consulted on the subject would fain have persuaded me that an excess of affection was the cause why these women burn themselves with their deceased husbands; but I soon found that this abominable practice is the effect of early and deeply rooted prejudices. Every girl is taught by her mother that it is virtuous and laudable in a wife to mingle her ashes with those of her husband, and that no woman of honour will refuse compliance with the established custom. These opinions men have always inculcated as an easy mode of keeping wives in subjugation, of securing their attention in times of sickness, and of deterring them from administering poison to their husbands.

But let us proceed to another of these dreadful scenes, not witnessed indeed by myself, but selected in preference to those at which I happened to be present, on account of the remarkable incident by which it was distinguished. I have seen so many things which I should have pronounced incredible, that neither you nor I ought to reject the narrative in question merely because it contains something extraordinary. The story is in every person's mouth in the Indies, and is universally credited. Perhaps it has already reached you in Europe.

A woman, long engaged in love intrigues with a young Mahometan, her neighbour, by trade a tailor and a player of the tambourine, poisoned her husband, hoping that the young man would marry her. She then hastened to her lover, informed him of what she had done and claimed the performance of his promise to take her to wife, urged the necessity of their immediately flying, as had been previously projected, from the scene of their guilt; 'for,' added she, 'if there be the least delay, I shall be constrained by a common sense of decency to burn myself with the body of my dead spouse.' The young man, who foresaw that such a scheme would involve him in difficulty and danger, peremptorily refused, and the woman, without betraying the smallest emotion, went at that instant to her relations, informed them of the sudden death of her husband, and of her fixed resolution to die on the funeral pile. Pleased with so magnanimous an intention, and with the honour she was about to confer on the family, her friends prepared a pit, filled it with wood, lay the body upon the pile, and kindled the fire. The arrangements being completed, the woman made the round of the pit for the purpose of embracing and bidding a last farewell to her kindred, among whom stood the young tailor, invited thither with other musicians to play on the tambourine according to the custom of the country. Approaching the lover as if she intended to take a last and tender adieu, the infuriated creature seized him with a firm grasp by the collar, drew him with irresistible force to the edge of the pit and precipitated herself headlong, with the object of her resentment, into the midst of the raging fire.

As I was leaving Sourate for Persia, I witnessed the devotion and burning of another widow: several Englishmen and Dutchmen, and Monsieur Chardin of Paris were present. She was of the middle-age, and by no means uncomely. I do not expect with my limited powers of expression, to convey a full idea of the brutish boldness or ferocious gaiety depicted on this woman's countenance; of her undaunted step; of the freedom from all perturbation with which she conversed, and permitted herself to be washed; of the look of confidence, or rather insensibility, which she cast upon us; of her easy air, free from dejection; of her lofty carriage, void of embarrassment, when she was examining her little cabin, composed of dry wood and thick millet straw, with an intermixture of small wood; when she entered into that cabin and sat down upon the funeral pile, placed her deceased husband's head in her lap, took up a torch and with her own hand lighted the fire within, while I know not how many Brahmins were engaged in kindling it without. Well indeed, I may despair of representing this whole scene with proper and genuine feeling, such as I experienced at the spectacle itself, or of painting it in colours sufficiently vivid. My recollection of it is indeed so distinct that it seems only a few days since the horrid reality passed before my eyes, and with pain I persuade myself that it was anything but a frightful dream.

It is true, however, that I have seen some of these unhappy widows shrink at the sight of the piled wood; so as to leave no doubt on my mind that they would willingly have recanted, if recantation had been permitted by the merciless Brahmins; but those demons excite or astound the affrighted victims, and even thrust them into the fire. I was present when a poor young woman, who had fallen back five or six paces from the pit, was thus driven forward; and I saw another of these wretched beings struggling to leave the funeral pile when the fire increased around her person, but she was prevented from escaping by the long poles of the diabolical executioners.

But sometimes the devoted widows elude the vigilance of the murderous priests. I have often been in the company of a fair idolater, who contrived to save her life by throwing herself upon the protection of the scavengers, who assemble on these occasions in considerable numbers, when they learn that the intended victim is young and handsome, that her relations are of little note and that she is to be accompanied by only a few of her acquaintances. Yet the woman whose courage fails at the sight of the horrid apparatus of death, and who avails herself of the presence of these men to avoid the impending sacrifice, cannot hope to pass her days in happiness, or to be treated with respect or affection. Never again can she live with the Gentiles; no individual will at any time or under any circumstances associate with a creature so degraded, who is accounted utterly infamous, and execrated because of the dishonour her conduct has brought upon the religion of the country. Consequently, she is ever afterwards exposed to the ill-treatment of her low and vulgar protectors. There is no Mogul who does not dread the consequences of contributing to the preservation of a woman devoted to the burning pile, or who will offer asylum to one who escapes from the fangs of the Brahmins; but many widows have been rescued by the Portuguese, in seaports where that people happened to be in superior strength. I need scarcely say how much my own indignation has been excited, and how ardently I have wished for opportunities to exterminate those cursed Brahmins.

At Lahore I saw the most beautiful young widow sacrificed, who could not, I think, have been more than twelve years of age. The poor little creature appeared more dead than alive as she approached the dreadful pit: the agony of her mind cannot be described; she trembled and wept bitterly; but three or four of the Brahmins, assisted by an old woman, who held her under the arm, forced the unwilling victim towards the fatal spot, seated her on the wood, tied her hands and feet, lest she should run away, and in that situation the innocent creature was burned alive. I found it difficult to repress my feelings and to prevent their bursting forth into clamorous and unavailing rage; but restrained by prudential considerations, I contented myself with silently lamenting the abominable superstition of these people....

I have not yet mentioned all the barbarity and atrocity of these monsters. In some parts of the Indies, instead of burning women who determine not to survive their husbands, the Brahmins bury them alive, by slow degrees, up to the throat; then two or three of them fall suddenly upon the victim, wring her neck, and when she has been effectually and completely choked, cover over the body with earth thrown upon it from successive baskets, and tread upon the head.

Nicollao Manucci, *Storia do Mogor or Mogul India*[2]

The voluminous narrative of this famous Italian traveller, which spans over half a century, was particularly influential in the eighteenth century when it was reissued under the auspices of editor F.F. Cattrou. It includes accounts of immolations witnessed by the author himself (including one that he prevented) and a more general discussion of the rite.

I reached Qasim Bazaar, at three days' journey from Hugli.... From Qasim Bazaar I took the road to Rajmahal, and there waited to see a Hindu woman burnt, although I had already seen many. She had poisoned her husband by reason of her love for a musician, hoping to get married afterwards to this lover. But on the husband's death the musician refused to marry her. Thus finding herself deprived of a husband and her reputation gone, she resolved to be burnt. A great crowd collected to look on; among them appeared the musician, hoping to receive from her something by way of memorial. It is usual for women who go to be burnt to distribute betel leaf or jewels. The place was a large pit. As she was circumambulating this pit she came close to the young musician, and, taking from her neck a gold chain she had on as an ornament, she flung it round the young man's neck, and taking him forcibly into her arms, jumped into the pit. Everyone was taken aback by this, not anticipating such a thing. Thus did she and the youth together expiate their sin, and the murder of her husband.

During my stay in Agra, I went one day to make an excursion into the country on horseback, in the company of a young Armenian. We came to where a Hindu woman had just begun to move round her pyre, which was already blazing; she rested her eyes upon us, as if she appealed to us for help. The Armenian asked if I would join him in saving the woman from death. I said I would. Seizing our swords, and our servants doing the same, we charged with our horses into the midst of the crowd looking on, shouting 'Mata! Mata!', (Kill! Kill!), whereat the Brahmins, being frightened, all took flight and left the woman unguarded. The Armenian laid hold of her, and making her mount behind him, carried her off.

Subsequently, having had her baptized, he married her. When I passed through Surat I found her living there with her son, and she returned me many thanks for the benefit done to her. When the king returned from Kashmir, the Brahmins went to complain that the soldiers did not allow women to be burnt, in accordance with their customs. The king [Aurangzeb] issued an order that in all the lands under Mogul control, never again should the officials allow a woman to be burnt. The order endures to this day.

...If the Brahmin in question dies after binding the piece of gold on the woman's neck, which is the sign denoting the essential part of the marriage, the woman can never marry again, even though she be only four or five years of age.... After a husband's death, a widow adopts one of four courses. The most sprightly and vigorous burn alive with the corpse of the defunct husband. This is carried out as follows: Wood is heaped up to a height of about eight or nine feet, and about the same length and breadth. Upon the top, the corpse of the dead Brahmin is laid, dressed as when alive, the head to the south and the feet to the north. After he has been laid thus on the bonfire, there comes the wise man of the village and pronounces certain magic words at the five organs of sense, and anoints them with butter. The anointing done, the parents and nearest relations throw four or five grains of uncooked rice in his mouth. When these ceremonies are finished, they turn the body over on its side. As they do so the widow without tears—nay, on the contrary, all radiant and joyous—mounts to the top of the pyre, and laying down on her side, closely embraces her dead husband. At once the relations bind her feet strongly by two ropes to two posts driven into the ground for the purpose. Next, they throw some more wood and dried cow dung on the two bodies; the quantity is almost as much as that beneath them. The woman is then spoken to by her name and three times distinctly she is called on to say whether she consents to go to heaven. To this she replies in the affirmative. Her answers having been received, they apply a light, and when the bodies have been consumed, each man returns home envying the firmness and constancy which the woman has been granted the felicity of displaying.

Widows who on their husband's death lose their modesty, depart as soon as he expires, to one of the large towns and become public courtesans. Some pursue the same course in their husband's lifetime, for which crime there is no legal punishment inflicted in this country. Others, who are not filled like the first with the spirit of honour, nor like the second, give themselves over to an abandoned life, remove upon their husband's death to their parents' house and wait on them like servants. But this condition is not easy to put up with, while, on the other hand, they are keen to preserve their characters. Thus they often make complaint to those who might rescue them from this sad condition, a malady all the heavier for having no possible relief unless the Brahmins choose to relax their rules. But they are a people who cannot be reasoned with in that direction. Other women, when their husbands die and since it would be disgraceful to their caste to marry again and they cannot remain as they are, go door to door selling rice. They think nothing of this dishonour, which would be counted among Europeans as the depths of misfortune. Yet it may be said that those who adopt this plan are generally the wisest, for the work occupies them and frees them of the evils which follow in the train of laziness and idleness. For, it may be said that laziness is the mother of all the vices.

...The conduct of the Brahmins being such as I have described, I may assert that their pride is equal to their silliness, and may be justly styled that of Lucifer, for without subterfuge they claim to be gods, and as such they require all the other castes to honour and adore them. But their pretension is not justified, for in everybody else there are some evil traits while all the rest is good; whereas in the Brahmin caste, where there ought doubtless to be something good, one meets with nothing that is not entirely evil.

...Among the caste of Rajahs, it is imperative that on the husband's death the wife be burnt alive with the body, for should regard for her own honour even not force her to this act, the relations will force her to it, it being an inviolate custom of their caste. It is so whether the husband die at home of disease, or of wounds upon the battlefield. The latter death is common among the Rajahs, for all who are not princes are soldiers...no sooner has the news of a Rajah's death arrived in his country, and the wife is satisfied that he no longer lives, than she is accorded three days of grace. During those days she is permitted to adorn herself as magnificently as she can; and thus arrayed she goes about the streets with lemons tied to her head like a crown; her body is uncovered from the waist upward and rubbed with saffron, as also is her face. In this state she takes leave off all those she meets in the streets with a smiling face and free manners, and speeches repugnant to her sex and her claim to nobility. When three days have passed they prepare in an open field a circular pit, deep and wide, which is filled with wood and cowdung. Fire is then applied. On beholding this pyre, she who is to be the victim of her honour, issues, clad in new attire, covered with diverse flowers, some arranged like crowns, others like necklaces. Escorted by all her friends, male and female, she approaches the fire. Before it stands a small screen about five feet high. Over its top they throw into the fire a little saffron and some butter and other spices. After prayers have been recited the heroine retires about forty paces and returns two times, one after the other to the place she started from. At length she retires a third time some forty paces farther than before; at the last moment the screen before the fire is withdrawn. Then, with a rush, she bounds into the pit, and in a short time there is nothing left but ashes to furnish an epitaph on her constancy. The Hindus think so highly of those who are burnt in this way that they assert their reincarnation as goddesses in the heaven of Vishnu. This is done equally for the husband. They assume that men blessed with wives of such great virtue as to sacrifice their life for their honour must without fail be placed among the gods. But if any wife be found to have a greater love for life than for honour, her relations do not leave her to enjoy it for very long, for they throw her into the fire by force, where she ends by undergoing the same suffering without acquiring the same laudations. Thus it is much better for them to endure this hard penalty with firmness and equanimity than to be subjected to it by the violence of others.

Albert de Mandelslo, Voyages and Travels[3]

This account of an apparently voluntary sati comes from the German courtier Albert de Mandelslo and is a good example of the extent to which sati became a 'tourist attraction' for travelling Europeans. In his discussion of the rite's supposed origin as a deterrent to husband murdering, Mandelslo draws on an ancient Greek explanation for sati that was widely repeated in the seventeenth and early eighteenth centuries.

I was soon joined by two of the English merchants at Cambay, who obligingly reproached me with the slur I put on their nation in preferring the house of a Mahometan to their lodge.... They proffered me their company to walk and promised to carry me the next morning to a place where an Indian woman was to be burnt of her own consent. The next day the English merchants came to my lodgings, whence we went together to the riverside, outside the city, where this voluntary execution was to be done. The woman's husband was a Rajput and had been killed near Lahore, 200 leagues from Cambay. As soon as she heard of his death, she would needless do his obsequies by causing herself to be burnt alive; but whereas the Mogul and his officers are Mahometans who endeavour by degrees to abolish this heathenish and barbarous custom, the governor had a long time opposed her desires under the pretence of the news of her husband's death being uncertain, he could not consent to doing of the inhuman action, whereof afterwards there would haply be cause to repent. The governor's design was to see whether time would abate anything of her passion, and the earnestness she was in to follow her husband into the other world; but seeing that she was daily more and more insistent to do it, he permitted her to comply with the laws of her religion. She was not above twenty years of age, yet we saw her come to the place of her execution with so much confidence and a cheerfulness so extraordinary to those who go to a present and inevitable death, that I was much inclined to believe that she had dulled her senses with a dose of opium, which is as commonly used in India as in Persia. In front of the procession marched the country music, consisting of haw boys and timdrels. Then followed a great many maids and women, singing and dancing before the widow, who was dressed in her richest clothing, and had her fingers and arms and legs loaded with rings, bracelets, and carkanets. After her came a confused company of men, women, and children, and so concluded the procession. She made a stop at the funeral pile, which had been purposely erected for the ceremony. The woman has washed herself in the river that she might meet her husband in a state of purity, in regard to the body of the deceased being not upon the place she could not accompany it in its passage into the other world. The pile of wood was of apricot trees, among which they had put some sanders and cinnamon. Having looked at it with a certain contempt, she took leave of her kindred and friends, and distributed among them the rings and bracelets about her. I was somewhere near her on horseback, with two English merchants, and I think that she perceived in my countenance that I pitied her, whence it came that she cast me one of her bracelets which I had the good hap to catch and still keep in remembrance of so extraordinary an action. As soon as she was got upon the pile, they set fire to it, which she perceiving, poured on her head a vessel of perfumed oil, which the fire immediately taking hold of, she was smothered in an instant, so as she was not perceived to make the least wry face at it. Some that were present caste upon her several cruses of oil, which soon reduced the body to ashes, while the rest of the assembly filled the air with their cries and shouts, such as must needless have hindered those of the widow to be heard, if she had the time to make any in the fire which had made a sudden dispatch of her as if it had been lightning. The ashes were cast into the river. I was told that this barbarous custom had been introduced among the pagans of those parts upon this account, that polygamy occasioning much heartburning among the women, arising either from the little satisfaction they could have from a man who is obliged to divide his affections, or the jealousy which is unavoidable among rivals of that sex; it happened that women procured their husband's deaths; and 'twas found that in one year there had been four men buried for one woman; so that to oblige them to be careful of their husband's lives, it was ordered that such as were desirous to be accounted honest women should be engaged to follow their husbands at their death and be burnt together with their bodies. Certain it is that the Persians and other neighbouring nations have ever had so particular a veneration for the fire that it is not to be admired that they would rather choose to reduce their dead to ashes than bury them. I say this obligation of dying with their husband was imposed only on those women who stood upon a reputation of honesty, yet so as they were engaged thereto only by a principle of honour, there not being any punishment to be inflicted on such as refused to follow them on that dreadful journey, other than that they were not admitted to the company of persons of quality, as being looked on as infamous women. Those

who are not so scrupulous and stand not so much upon the punc-
tilio of honour, and prefer their lives to their reputation, do ordi-
narily strike in among the public dancers.

Francisco Pelsaert, *Jehangir's India*[4]

This account by the early seventeenth-century trader Francisco Pelsaert
represents sati as entirely voluntary; an example of Indian women's love for
their husband. It also provides an insight into Moghul policy on the subject.

When a Rajput dies, his wives (or rather his wife, for they marry
only one if there is genuine love) allow themselves to be burned
alive, as is the practice among the *banians* or *khettris*, and in Agra
this commonly occurs about two or three times a week. It is not
a very pleasant spectacle, but I witnessed it out of curiosity when
a woman who lived near our house declared to her friends, immediately on her husband's death, that she would be sati, which
means that she would accompany him where he had gone, making
the announcement with little lamentation, and as if her heart was
sealed with grief...when a woman has made up her mind it is
impossible for her friends or anyone in this world to dissuade her,
strive as they may, but if she persists she must be left in peace.
So she goes and bathes according to the daily custom, puts on
her finest clothes, her jewels, and the best ornaments she has,
adorning herself as if for her wedding day. The woman I have
mentioned then went, with music and songs, to the governor to
obtain his permission. The governor urged many sound arguments
to show that what she proposed to do was a sin, and merely the
inspiration of the Devil to secure her voluntary death; and because
she was a handsome young woman of about eighteen years of
age, he pressed her strongly to dissuade her if possible from her
undertaking, and even offered her 500 rupees yearly as long as
she would live. He could, however, produce no effect, but she
answered with resolute firmness that her motive was not the fear
of poverty but love of her husband, and even if she could have all
the King's treasures in this world, they would be of no use to her,
for she meant to live with her husband. This was her first and last
word throughout; she seemed to be out of her senses, and she
was taking up far too much time, so the governor, since governors

are not allowed, by the King's orders to refuse these requests, gave his consent. Then she hurried off with a light step, as if she might be too late, till she reached the place, a little outside the city, where was a small hut, built of wood, roofed with straw, and decorated with flowers. There she took off all her jewels and distributed them among her friends, and also her clothes, which she disposed of the same way, keeping only an undergarment. Then she took a handful of rice and distributed it to all the by-standers. This being done, she embraced her friends and said her last farewells; took her baby, which was only a year old, kissed it, and handed it to her nearest friends; then ran to the hut where her dead husband lay, and kissed and embraced him eagerly. Then she took the fire and applied the brand, and the friends piled wood before the door; everyone shouted out 'Ram Ram!', the shouts continuing until they supposed she was dead. When the burning was over, everyone took a little of the ash of the bones, which they regard as sacred and preserve. Surely, this is as great a love as the women of our country bear to their husbands, for the deed was done not out of compulsion but out of sheer love. At the same time there are hundreds, even thousands who do not do it, and there is no such reproach as is asserted by many who write that those who neglect it incur the reproach of their caste.

Notes

1   Bernier, François, *Travels in the Mogul Empire, AD 1656–68*, Archibald Constable (ed.) (Delhi: S.Chand and Co., 1969).

2   Manucci, Nicollao, *Storia do Mogor or Mogul India, 1653–1708*, W. Irvine (ed.) (Calcutta: Editions Indian, 1966 [1st edn 1907]). .

3   de Mandelslo, Albert, 'The Voyages and Travels of J. Albert de Mandelslo into the East Indies 1638–40', in Adam Olearius's *Voyages and Travels of the Ambassadors*, tr. by John Davies (London: John Starkey and Thomas Basset, 1969).

4   Pelsaert, Francisco, *Jehangir's India*, W.H. Moreland (tr.) (Cambridge: Heffer and Sons, 1925).

4

The Eighteenth Century

John Zephaniah Holwell, 'On the Religious Tenets of the Gentoos'[1]

John Zephaniah Holwell, born in Dublin, was a surgeon with the East India Company. This work on India, published in 1767, did not advance British knowledge greatly, but was widely read at home. His discussion of sati is important because he approaches his subject from an ideological point of view and makes a plea for cultural relativism and tolerance. His account is perhaps the most definite statement of the Enlightenment tendency to see sati as heroic when judged in its 'own' terms and contrasts well with Charles Grant's evangelical polemic against sati thirty years later.

Although we have already shown that the bloody sacrifices of the ancients was no part of the Gentoo tenets, yet there subsists amongst them at this day, a voluntary sacrifice, of too singular a nature, to pass by us unnoticed; the rather as it has been frequently mentioned by various authors, without we conceive that knowledge and perspicuity which the matter calls for; the sacrifice we allude to, is the Gentoo wives burning with the bodies of their deceased husbands. We have taken no small pains to investigate this seeming cruel custom, and hope we shall be able to throw some satisfactory lights on this very extraordinary subject, which has hitherto been hid in obscurity, in order to which we will first remove one or two obstructions that lie in our way and hinder our nearer and more perfect view of it.

The cause commonly assigned for the origin of this sacrifice (peculiar to the wives of this nation) is that it was a law constituted to put a period to a wicked practice that the Gentoo wives had of poisoning their husbands; for this assertion we cannot trace the smallest semblance of truth, and indeed the known fact, that the sacrifice must be voluntary, of its self refutes that common mistake. It also has been a received opinion that if the wife refuses to burn, she loses her caste (or tribe) and is stamped with disgrace and infamy, an opinion equally void of foundation in fact as the other. The real state of this case is thus circumstanced. The first wife (for the Gentoo laws allow bigamy, although they frequently do not benefit themselves of the indulgence, if they have issue by the first) has it in her choice to burn, but is not permitted to declare her resolution before twenty-four hours after the decease of her husband; if she refuses, the right devolves to the second, if either, after the expiration of twenty-four hours, publicly declare, before the Brahmins and witnesses, their resolution to burn, they cannot then retract. If they both refuse at the expiration of that term, the worst consequence that attends their refusal is lying under the imputation of being wanting to their own honour, purification, and the prosperity of their family, for from their infancy, they are instructed by the household Brahmin to look upon this catastrophe as most glorious to themselves, and beneficial to their children. The truth is, that the children of the wife who burns, become thereby illustrious, and are sought after in marriage by the most opulent and honourable of their caste, and sometimes received into a caste superior to their own.

That the Brahmins take unwearied pains to encourage, promote, and confirm in the minds of the Gentoo wives this spirit of burning is certain (their motives for it, the penetration of our readers may by and by probably discover), and although they seldom lose their labour, yet instances happen, where fear, or love of life, sets at naught all their preaching; for it sometimes falls out that the first wife refuses, and the second burns; at others, they both refuse; and as but one can burn, it so happens that when the second wife has issue by the deceased, and the first none, there commonly ensues a violent contention between them, which of the two shall make the sacrifice; but this dispute is generally determined by the Brahmins, in favour of the first, unless she is prevailed on by persuasion, or other motives, to waive her right in favour of the second. Having elucidated these matters, we will proceed to give our readers the best account we have been able to obtain of the origin of this remarkable custom.

At the demise of the mortal part of the Gentoos' great lawgiver and prophet Brahma, his wives, inconsolable for his loss, resolved not to survive him, and offered themselves voluntary victims on his funeral pile. The wives of the chief Rajahs, the first officers of the state, being unwilling to have it thought that they were deficient in fidelity and affection, followed the heroic example set them by the wives of Brahma; the Brahmins (a tribe then newly constituted by their great legislator) pronounced and declared that the delinquent spirits of those heroines immediately ceased from their transmigrations, and had entered the first Boboon of purification. It followed that their wives claimed a right of making the same sacrifice of their mortal forms to God, and the manes of their deceased husbands; the wives of every Gentoo caught the enthusiastic (now pious) flame. Thus the heroic acts of a few women brought about a general custom, the Brahmins had given it the stamp of religion, they foisted it into the *Chatah* and *Aughtorrah Bhades*, and instituted the forms and ceremonials that were to accompany the sacrifice, strained some obscure passages of Brahma's *Chartah Bhade* to countenance their declared sense of the action, and established it as a religious tenet throughout Indostan, subject to the restrictions before recited, which leaves it a voluntary act of glory, piety, and fortitude. Whether the Brahmins were sincere in their declared sense and consecration of this act, or had a view to securing the fidelity of their own wives, or were actuated by any other motives, we will not determine.

When people have lived together to an advanced age, in mutual acts of confidence, friendship, and affection, the sacrifice a Gentoo widow makes of her person (under such an affecting circumstance as the loss of friend and husband) seems less an object of wonder; but when we see women in the bloom of youth and beauty, in the calm possession of their reason and understanding, with astonishing fortitude set at naught the tender considerations of parents, children, friends, and the horror and torments of the death they court, we cannot resist viewing such an act, and such a victim, with tears of commiseration, awe, and reverence.

We have been present at many of these sacrifices; in some of the victims, we have observed a pitiable dread, tremor, and reluctance that strongly spoke repentance for their declared resolution; but it was now too late to retract, or retreat; Bistnoo was waiting for the spirit. If the self-doomed victim discovers want of courage and fortitude, she is with gentle force obliged to ascend the pile, where she is held down with long poles held by men on each side of the pile, until the flames reach her; her screams and cries, in the mean time, being drowned amidst the deafening noise of loud music and the acclamations of the multitude. Others we have seen go through this fiery trial with most amazing steady, calm resolution, and joyous fortitude. It will not, we hope, be unacceptable if we present our readers with an instance of the latter, which happened some years past at the East India Company's factory at Cossimbazaar in the time of Sir Francis Russell's chiefship, the author, and several other gentlemen of the factory were present, some of whom are now living. From a narrative which the author then transmitted to England, he is now enabled to give the particulars of this most remarkable proof of female fortitude, and constancy:

At five of the clock on the morning of 4th of February 1742–8, died Rhaam Chund Pundit of the Mahahrattor tribe, aged twenty-eight years; his widow (for he had but one wife) aged between seventeen and eighteen, as soon as he expired, disdaining to wait the term allowed her for reflection, immediately declared to the Brahmins and witnesses present her resolution to burn; as the family was of no small consideration, all the merchants of Cossimbazaar, and her relations, left no arguments unessayed to dissuade her, from it. Lady Russell, with the tenderest humanity, sent her several messages to the same purpose; the infant state of her children (two girls and a boy, the eldest not four years of age) and the terrors and pain of the death she sought, were painted to her in the strongest and most lively colouring; she was deaf to all, she gratefully thanked Lady Russell, and sent her word she had now nothing to live for, but recommended her children to her protection. When the torments of burning were urged in terrorem to her, she with a resolved and calm countenance, put her finger into the fire, and held it there a considerable time, she then, with one hand, put fire in the palm of the other, sprinkled incense on it, and fumigated the Brahmins. The consideration of her children left destitute of a parent was again urged to her. She replied, 'He that made them, would take care of them.' She was at last given to understand, she should not be permitted to burn. This for a short space seemed to give her deep affliction, but soon recollecting herself, she told them, death was in her power, and that if she was not allowed to burn, according to the principles of her caste, she would starve herself. Her friends, finding her thus peremptory and resolved, were obliged at last to assent.

The body of the deceased was carried down to the waterside early the following morning, the widow followed about ten o'clock, accompanied by three very principal Brahmins, her children, parents, and relations, and a numerous concourse of people. The order of leave for her burning did not arrive from Hosseyn Khan, Fouzdaar of Morshadabad, until after one, and it was then brought by one of the Soubah's own officers who had orders to see that she burnt voluntarily. The time they waited for the order was employed in praying with the Brahmins, and washing in the Ganges; as soon as it arrived, she retired and stayed for the space of half an hour in the midst of her female relations, amongst whom was her mother; she then divested herself of her bracelets, and other ornaments, and tied them in a cloth, which hung like an apron before her, and was conducted by her female relations to one corner of the pile; on the pile was an arched arbour formed of dry sticks, boughs, and leaves, open only at one end to admit her entrance; in this the body of the deceased was deposited, his head at the end opposite to the opening. At the corner of the pile, to which she had been conducted, the Brahmin had made a small fire, around which she and the three Brahmins sat for some minutes, one of them gave into her hand a leaf of the *bale* tree (the wood commonly consecrated to form part of the funeral pile) with sundry things on it, which she threw into the fire; one of the others gave her a second leaf, which she held over the flame, whilst he dropped three times some ghee on it, which melted, and fell into the fire (these two operations, were preparatory symbols of her approaching dissolution by fire), and whilst they were performing this, the third Brahmin read to her some portions of the *Aughtorrah*

Bhade, and asked her some questions, to which she answered with a steady and serene countenance; but the noise was so great, we could not understand what she said, although we were within a yard of her. These over, she was led with great solemnity three times round the pile, the Brahmins reading before her; when she came the third time to the small fire, she stopped, took her rings off her toes and fingers, and put them to her other ornaments; here she took a solemn majestic leave of her children, parents, and relations; after which, one of the Brahmins dipped a large wick of cotton in some ghee, and gave it ready lighted into her hand, and led her to the open side of the arbour; there, all the Brahmins fell at her feet; after she had blessed them, they retired weeping; by two steps, she ascended the pile and entered the arbour; on her entrance, she made a profound reverence at the feet of the deceased, and advanced and seated herself by his head; she looked, in silent meditation on his face for the space of a minute, then set fire to the arbour in three places; observing that she had set fire to leeward, and that the flames blew from her, instantly seeing her error she rose, and set fire to windward, and resumed her station; ensign Daniel with his cane, separated the grass and leaves on the windward side, by which means we had a distinct view of her as she sat. With what dignity, and undaunted a countenance, she set fire to the pile the last time and assumed her seat can only be conceived, for words cannot convey a just idea of her. The pile being of combustible matters, the supporters of the roof were presently consumed, and it tumbled upon her.

We see our fair countrywomen shudder at an action, which we fear they will look upon, as a proof of the highest infatuation in their sex. Although it is not our intention here to defend the tenets of the Brahmins, yet we may be allowed to offer some justification on behalf of the Gentoo women in the action before us. Let us view it (as we should every other action) without prejudice, and without keeping always in sight our own tenets and customs, and prepossessions that too generally result therefrom, to the injury of others; if we view these women in a just light, we shall think more candidly of them, and confess they act upon heroic, as well as rational and pious principles: in order to do this we must consider them as a race of females trained from their infancy, in 'the full

conviction of their celestial rank; and that this world, and the
corporeal form that encloses them, is destined by God, the one as
their place of punishment, the other as their prison. That their ideas
are consequently raised to a soothing degree of dignity befitting
angelic beings. They are nursed and instructed in the firm faith that
this voluntary sacrifice is the most glorious period of their lives, and
that thereby the celestial spirit is released from its transmigrations and evils of a miserable existence, and flies to join the spirit
of their departed husband in a state of purification; add to this,
the subordinate consideration of raising the lustre of their children,
and of contributing by this action to their temporal prosperity; all
these, it must be owned, are prevalent motives for cheerfully
embracing death and setting at naught every common attachment
which the weakness of humanity urges, for a longer existence in
a world of evil. Although these principles are in general so diametrically contrary to the prevailing spirit and genius of our fair
countrywomen, who (from a happy train of education), in capti-
vating amusements and dissipation, find charms sufficient in this
world to engage their wishes for a perpetual residence in it; yet
we will depend on their natural goodness of heart, generosity
and candour, that they will in future look on these their Gentoo
sisters of the creation, in a more favourable and consistent light
than probably they have hitherto done; and not deem that action
an infatuation which results from principle. Let them also recollect
that their own history affords illustrious examples in both sexes
of voluntary sacrifices by fire, because they would not subscribe
even to a different mode of professing the same faith. Besides, a
contempt of death is not peculiar to the women of India, it is the
characteristic of the nation; every Gentoo meets that moment of
dissolution, with a steady, noble, and philosophic resignation, flowing from the established principles of their faith.

Before we close this subject, we will mention one or two more
particulars relative to it. It has been already remarked in a marginal note, that the Gentoo women are not allowed to burn without an order of leave from the Mahommedan government; it is proper
also to inform our readers this privilege is never withheld from
them. There have been instances known, when the victim has, by
Europeans, been forcibly rescued from the pile; it is currently

said and believed (how true we will not aver) that the wife of Mr Job Charnock was by him snatched from this sacrifice; be this as it may, the outrage is considered by the Gentoos an atrocious and wicked violation of their sacred rites and privileges.

Durlabh Ram, 'Account of a Sati'[2]

This rare eyewitness account of a sati from an Indian observer (the Gujarati poet Durlabh Ram) emphasizes the supernatural aspects of sati, though interestingly these are confined to events leading up to the immolation. Once on the pyre the widow ignites it with a torch, rather than spontaneously combusting from the heat of her 'sat'.

In September 1741 (vs 1797 Bhadra), Shivabai, a lady of the Nagar community, came to know about the death of her husband. Thereupon she began to live on milk, having acquired 'sat'. The sensational rumour spread throughout the city and each one who heard the news went to see her. The relatives of the lady tried to dissuade her from the course. But the lady persisted and said that she would show the proofs of her bona fide. Shivabai took the letter conveying the news upon her lap and gave out that she would burn herself. She then threatened the people with curses if they refused to believe her. Thereupon Lala Sadanand, one of her kin, locked the doors of her room. But the lock broke by itself and the frenzied lady threatened to set the building ablaze [by the power of her 'sat']. Lala Sadanand came to see the sati and asked her to tell what he secretly held in his hands. The sati said, 'Lala Sadanand, take the name of Amba, you have betel nut in one hand and rupees two in the other. Look, I can also produce 'kumkum'. Being convinced by these positive proofs, Lala Sadanand rode to the darbar. There he consulted Thakore Karsandas, Mehta Manekchand, and Diwanji. Having deliberated on the matter, the four approached the Khan Sahib. The Khan Sahib, having heard the case, obtained permission from the Nabob. Lala Sadanand returned with the permit. The lady kept up self-possessed [sic] surrounded by the servants and attendants begging for gifts [as relics]. She rubbed her palms and produced live coal.

Lala Sadanand requested her if she would care to proceed riding a mare or a rath [chariot]. Satima asked to get ready a bullock rath. She then proceeded with pomp and dignity. Her sister and maternal aunt sat by her side. The rath passed through the principal streets of the city, followed by a huge crowd shouting 'Jai Ambe, Jai Ambe'.The sati alighted at Lal Darwaja and made hand impressions with kumkum on the doors. A torch was lighted on the way near Ashvani Kumar. The procession came to Gupteshwara at dusk. The sati refused to perform the ordeal after sunset and requested her relatives to wait till daybreak. The relatives being afraid lest her spirit might droop advised her not to delay. The sati confirmed her resolve to enter the fire early in the morning and expressed that the people might doubt whether the sati did not escape in the dark of night. She felt confident to keep up her spirit for five days.

Lala Sadanand sent for the Patel of the town and asked him to prepare 'Madhuli' for which he would be rewarded with gifts. The lady came to the riverbank, all elated, early in the morning. She took tulsi from the priest and went for a bath. She dipped herself one hundred and eight times all alone. Lala Sadanand stationed himself on the bank and asked the Brahmins to watch her lest she might give herself in the water. The sati came out of the water and worshipped a cow. She went round the priest and his wife and the cow. She gave her ornaments to the priest and his wife, and fed grass to the cow. She performed havan. The relatives of the lady presented seven coconuts to her and began to shed tears. But the sati forbade them to weep. Satimata had kept a platter of 'kumkum' at the havan. She took off her chuda and gave it as a gift to the wife of the priest. However, she wore the nose-ring. She once more took her bath and performed tarpan, the act of propitiating the dead. Then she put on a white sari and came to the Madhi. By that time the sun had risen hence she worshipped the sun. She took the sun's permission to burn herself. She went five times round the Madhi. She held a coconut in one of her hands and a torch in the other. She bowed to the sun and entered the Madhi. She called her relative Lala Venilal and blessed him with a gift of coconut. Lala Sadanand stood with a drawn sabre near the Madhi. The sati asked to cease beating the drums as she would not scream or shriek. She then took ghee and put it on the pyre. Finally, she entreated Lala Sadanand to approve the act as auspicious. She took the letter upon her lap and remembered her lord. The pyre was made of sandalwood, tulsi, and agaru. At first the sati set fire to her hair and then ignited the straw all around. The full blaze of the fire was revered by throwing betelnuts, coins, and almonds by the crowd. The event became memorable in the annals of the people. Thus the sati went to heaven by *Viman*.

Eliza Fay, 'Original Letters from India'[3]

In one of the earliest discussions of sati from a woman's point of view, Fay combines cultural imperialism with an incipient feminism. Her response to sati can be seen as reflective of her own experience with a husband who ran them into debt, alienated his professional friends, engaged in intrigue against the then Chief Justice of Calcutta, Elijah Impey, fathered an illegitimate child, and whom she eventually left. Her recognition of a universal subjugation of women to men, and of women to established custom, resonates strongly with her own experience, although it is interesting to note that her ideal of sacrifice is the very life of submission to the husband that she herself has rejected and which she deems far more heroic than a hypocritical sati.

I now propose, having full leisure to give you some account of the East Indian customs and ceremonies, such as I have been able to collect, but it must be considered as a mere sketch, to point your further researches. And first, for that horrible custom of widows burning themselves with the dead bodies of their husbands; the fact is indubitable, but I have never had an opportunity of witnessing the various incidental ceremonies, nor have I ever seen any European who had been present at them. I cannot suppose that the usage originated in the superior tenderness, and ardent attachment of Indian women towards their spouses, since the same tenderness and ardour would doubtless extend to his offspring and prevent them from exposing the innocent survivors to the miseries of an orphaned state, and they would see clearly that to live and cherish these pledges of affection would be the most rational and natural way of showing their regard for both husband and children. I apprehend that as personal fondness can have no part here at all, since all matches are made between the parents of the parties who are betrothed at too early a period for choice to be consulted, this practice is entirely a political scheme to ensure the care and good offices of wives to their husbands, who have not failed in most countries to invent a sufficient number of rules to render the weaker sex totally subservient to their authority. I cannot avoid smiling when I hear gentlemen bring forward the conduct of Hindoo women as a test of superior character, since I am well aware that so much are we slaves to habit everywhere, that were it necessary for a woman's reputation to burn herself in England, many a one who has accepted a husband merely for the sake of establishment, who has lived with him without affection; perhaps thwarted his views, dissipated his fortune and rendered his life uncomfortable to its close, would yet mount his funeral pile with all imaginable decency and die with heroic fortitude. The most specious sacrifices are not always the greatest, she who wages war with a naturally petulant temper, who practises rigid self-denial, endures without complaining the unkindness, infidelity, extravagance, meanness or scorn, of the man to whom she has given her tender and confiding heart, and for whose happiness and well-being in life all the powers of her mind are engaged;—is ten times more of a heroine than the slave of bigotry and superstition, who affects to scorn the life demanded of her by the laws of her country or at least by that country's custom; and many such we have in England, and I doubt not in India likewise: so indeed we ought, have we not a religion infinitely more pure than that of India?

Tryambakayajvan, 'Stridharmapaddhati'[4]

This eighteenth-century south Indian tract on the status and duties of women has been translated and discussed in detail by Julia Leslie. In the following extract she discusses Tryambakayajvan's stance on sati.

Of the nine topics discussed in this section on the duties common to all women, this is perhaps the most interesting. For in 1789, 'suttee' was officially noted by the government of Bengal. The campaign against the custom, led by Rammohan Roy (1772–1833), met with considerable hostility from the orthodox community (see Anantarāma's *Sahānumaraṇaviveka*).[5] In 1829, Suttee Regulation XVII made the practice illegal. In 1830, eight hundred Hindu conservatives appealed to the Privy Council on the grounds that the Act interfered with Indian culture and religion. In 1832, the pro-suttee appeal was rejected. In the Maratha court of Thanjavur in the mid-eighteenth century, however, the orthodox position was still maintained. Tryambaka presents it as follows.

He begins with two resounding quotations that advocate the practice of *sahagamana*. First, 'at the time of a girl's wedding, the brahmins should recite (these words): "May you be one who accompanies her husband (always,) when he is alive and even when he is dead!"'[6] Secondly, according to Śaṅkha, 'if, when her husband has died, a woman ascends with (him; *samārohe[t]*) into the fire, she is glorified in heaven as one whose conduct is equal to that of Arundhatī.'[7]

Tryambaka next considers the objection (*nanu...*) that *sahagamana* is in fact a form of suicide, and therefore prohibited (*ātmahatyārūpatvena niṣiddhatvāt*; Sdhp.42r.6–7). Of the two quotations given to support this objection, the first is the standard *pūrvapakṣa* against suicide. 'And therefore one should certainly not depart (this life) before its full length (has been lived out).'[8] The second is Īś. Up.3, together with the common misinterpretation of the phrase *ātmahano janaḥ* to mean 'people who kill themselves' instead of 'people who kill (i.e. are ignorant of) the (true) Self' (cf. Radhakrishnan 1974:570; Hume 1971:361, note 4; PVK II.ii.p.927, Vāj.S.40.3). Tryambaka argues that this objection is invalid because the prohibition on suicide is a general rule (*sāmānyavacana*) and is therefore, open to modification by supplementary rules giving the exceptions to it (*viśeṣa*). Just as the general rule that 'one should not desire to kill any living being' is modified by supplementary rules—for example, that in certain rituals an animal should be sacrificed—so the general prohibition on suicide is also modified by supplementary rules. These include rulings related to the religious suicide of the ascetic who kills himself at a sacred place in order to go directly to heaven (cf. Yatidh. 17.1–32; Olivelle 1977: 42–3, 96–8); the deliberate courting of death in battle by the heroic warrior (cf. Yatidh.17.8; Olivelle 1977: 97); and—according to Tryambaka—the self-immolation of the widow on her husband's funeral pyre (Sdhp.42r.8–42v.8).

Tryambaka's second argument in favour of the practice is that 'dying with one's husband (*bhartrānumaraṇam*) is recommended for women because it brings great rewards.'[9] Although not spelled out, the crucial issue here is whether the ritual act of *sahagamana* is *naimittika* (i.e. required by the particular 'occasion'; in this case, by the husband's death) or *kāmya* (i.e. to be performed only if one desires the rewards accruing to the action; cf. *nitya, naimittika,* and *kāmya* in the context of ritual baths, Section IIA, p. 82). If it is *naimittika*, the widow must join her husband on his pyre; if it is *kāmya*, she only needs to do so if she wants to enjoy the 'great rewards' promised by the scriptures. Tryambaka evidently admits that *sahagamana* is a *kāmya* act and therefore entirely a matter for the individual widow to decide. However, his repeated assertion that it is to be recommended (*ślāghyam, praśastaḥ*), together with his daunting descriptions of the only alternative open to the widow who remains alive, makes his own opinion on the question abundantly clear.

He proceeds to quote numerous *ślokas* describing the 'great rewards' in store for the pious widow who chooses to die. I have selected some of the more memorable examples. 'The husband is to be followed always (*sahānuyātavy[aḥ]*): like the body by its shadow, like the moon by moonlight, like a thundercloud by lightning.'[10] 'There is no doubt that the woman who follows (*anuvrajantī*) her husband gladly from his house to the cremation ground attains with every step the reward(s) of the horse-sacrifice.'[11] 'Just as the snake-catcher drags the snake from its hole by force, even so the virtuous wife (*satī*) snatches her husband from the demons of hell and takes him up to heaven.'[12] 'Yama's messengers recognize a virtuous wife (*satīm*) from afar and take to flight. Even if her husband has been an evil man, they let go of him at once, exclaiming, "When we see a devoted wife (*pativratām*) hurtling towards us (to rescue her husband), we messengers (of Death) are less afraid of fire and lightning than we are of her!"'[13] 'There are three-and-a-half crores of hairs on a person's body; she who dies with (*anugacchati*) her husband will dwell in heaven for the same length of time.'[14] '(Even in the case of) a husband who has entered into hell (itself) and who—seized by the servants of Death and bound with terrible bonds—has arrived at the very place of torment (*yātanāsthānam*); (even if he is already) standing there, helpless and wretched, quivering (with fear) because of his evil deeds;[15] even if he is a brahmin-killer or the murderer of a friend, or if he is ungrateful for some service done for him—(even then) a woman who refuses to become a widow (*avidhavā nārī*) can purify him: in dying, she takes him with her.'[16] Tryambaka concludes that 'according to established custom as shown in the eloquent statements (given above), this (act of) dying with (one's husband; *anumaraṇam*)—when put into practice by a devoted wife (*pativratayā*)—confers great blessings on both (wife and husband).'[17]

Tryambaka now considers the rewards accruing to the bad wife. 'If (this act of dying with one's husband is) put into practice by a sinful woman, it brings about the destruction of that sin.'[18] The quotation that follows is quite clear. 'Women who, due to their wicked minds, have previously (i.e. until then) despised their husbands, and who have always behaved disagreeably towards those husbands, who (though) being of that kind (yet) at the (appropriate) time perform the (ritual act of) dying with their husbands (*bhartrānumaraṇam*)—whether (they do this) of their own free will, or out of anger, or even out of fear—all of them are purified (of sin).'[19] This is the scriptural justification for forcing women to burn themselves. Whatever their reason for doing so, whatever the past deeds of either husband or wife; the sacrifice purfies both of them. 'As a result of this (ruling),' Tryambaka concludes, 'when *sahagamana* is performed by a woman who has done wrong—that is, what her husband did not like (cf. Section V)—throughout her lifetime, (then) it is said to have the quality of a *prāyaścitta*.'[20] In this sense, it is the ultimate, and only effective, *prāyaścitta* for the bad wife.

As Tryambaka admits, however, this conclusion conflicts with the special rulings relating to the *kali* age (Sdhp.43v.1–3; cf. *kalivarjya*, PVK III. p. 926–68). One of these is that the rite of atonement that culminates in death (*maraṇāntikaprāyaścitta*) is prohibited in the kali age. The quotation is unambiguous. 'These duties (i.e. those listed in the previous unquoted passages) are to be avoided in the kali age, say learned men; as is the prescribing to brahmins of any rite of atonement (*prāyaścitta*) that culminates in death.'[21] Tryambaka merely sidesteps the problem, remarking that whether or not the bad wife should perform *sahagamana* to wipe out her sins is best left to great men to decide (*kartavyaṃ na kartavyam iti mahadbhir vivecanīyam*; Sdhp.43v.3).

Tryambaka's weakness as a *mīmāṃsaka* is evident. For there are two crucial issues here: whether or not *sahagamana* is really a *prāyaścitta* for the bad wife; and, if so, whether this particular *maraṇāntikaprāyaścitta* is in fact prohibited in the kali age. Tryambaka argues neither well. Instead, he embarks on a lengthy (and poorly structured) explanation of why it is important for a wife to behave properly during her and her husband's lifetime (Sdhp.43v.3–44v.3). If there is no *maraṇāntikaprāyaścitta* for the errant wife, then she cannot escape the torments awaiting her in the next world. For— according to a variety of quotations—even if she has bathed in all the sacred places, the bad wife will go to the hell of dung and urine (*viṇmūtre narake*), or burning oil (*taptatailanarakam*); she will be a widow, or a bitch, or a sow in her next life; she will be infested with worms in this one; and so on. Since statements such as these make no reference to any other *prāyaścitta* that can wipe out the effects of a wife's bad behaviour (*prāyaścittāntarābhāvācca sarvathā*; Sdhp.44r.10–44v.1), Tryambaka suggests that there is none (that is, he implies, none other than *sahagamana*). The wife's only hope is to worship and placate her husband at every turn. The inadequacy of Tryambaka's reasoning on this point becomes clear when one compares it with, for example, that in the *Mitākṣarā* on Yājñ.III.226. Tryambaka's intention, however, is transparent. He is evidently suggesting that, despite the rulings regarding the kali age, *sahagamana* is in fact the safest course of action for the not-so-perfect wife.

Tryambaka raises one final question. 'Now the objection may be made (*nanu*) that this (practice of) dying with one's husband (*anugamanam*) is applicable to *kṣatriya* women and so on (i.e. to the lower *varṇas*), but prohibited to brahmin women.'[22] Several quotations are produced in favour of this view. For example, 'as a result of Brahmā's instruction, following one's husband when he has died (*mṛtānugamanam*) is not appropriate for brahmin women; but, for the other *varṇas*, this is held to be the supreme duty for women.'[23] Or, 'the brahmin woman who does not die with her husband, (even though she is) distracted by grief, obtains the goal of renunciation (*pravrajyā*; glossed by Tryambaka as *brahmacaryam*; i.e. *vidhavādharma*); (whereas) by dying, she becomes one who has committed suicide (*ātmaghātinī*; i.e. she incurs the sin thereof).'[24] According to Tryambaka, however, such statements in fact prohibit brahmin women from ascending a separate pyre (*pṛthakcityārohaṇaparatvāt*; Sdhp.45r.2–3). The implication here is that the chief or brahmin wife, the *patnī*, should join her husband on his pyre (*anvārohaṇa*) while the junior wives of lower *varṇa* should burn on separate ones (*anumaraṇa*). As the quotation from Uśanas explains, 'a brahmin woman should not go (i.e. die) by ascending (*samāruhya*) a separate pyre, but for other women this is the ancient duty for wives.'[25]

Tryambaka's conclusion is obvious. 'The religious duty (or practice) of dying with one's husband is commended (*praśastaḥ*) for women,' whether brahmins or not, whether good or bad.

Notes

[1] Holwell, J.Z., 'On the Religious Tenets of the Gentoos', in *Interesting Historical Events, Relative to the Provinces of Bengal, and the Empire of Indostan*, Part 2 (London: Becket and Hondt, 1767), pp. 87–101.

[2] Ram, Duralabh, 'Account of a Sati in Gujerat in 1741', trans. by S.C. Dixit, in *Journal of Anthropological Society of Bombay*, vol. 17:4, 1931.

[3] Fay, Eliza, 'Original Letters From India', Letter XX, 5 September 1781 (Calcutta s.n., 1817).

[4] Leslie, J. (trans.), 'Stridharmapaddhati', in *The Perfect Wife* (Delhi: Oxford University Press, 1989).

[5] I am indebted to J. Duncan M. Derrett for drawing my attention to this work.

[6] *atha sahagamanavidhiḥ* // Sdhp.42r.3. *kanyāvivāhasamaye vācayeyur iti dvijāḥ / bhartuḥ sahacarī bhūyaḥ jīvato 'jīvato 'pi vā / iti/* / Sdhp.42r.4-5 <Sk.P.III.2.7.52.

[7] *śaṅkho 'pi* // *mṛte bhartari yā nārī samārohed dhutāśanam / sārundhatī-samācārā svarge loke mahīyate* // Sdhp.42r.5–6 (Śaṅkh.) < Mit. on Yājñ.I.86 (*svargaloke* for *svarge loke*); Par.M.II.i.p.54 (as Mit.; śaṅkhāṅgirasau); Dh.kośa I.ii.p.1115 (as Mit.; Aṅg.). See also Sahā. I.1 (Aṅg.).

[8] *tathā ca śrutiḥ* // *tasmād u ha na purāyuṣaḥ preyāt* // *iti* //. Sdhp.42r.7 (*śrutiḥ*) < Śat.Br.X.2.6.7 (*svakāmī preyāt* for *preyāt*); Dh.kośa II.i.p.517 (as Śat.Br.). Cf. Medh. on Manu VI.32; Kull. on Manu VI.31.

[9] *mahāphalakatvād api bhartranumaraṇaṃ strīṇāṃ ślāghyam* // Sdhp. 42v.4.

[10] *tathā ca vyāsaḥ* // *strīṇām anugamanaviṣaye* // Sdhp.42v.4–5. *bhartā sahānuyātavyo dehavacchāyayā sadā / candramā jyotsnayā yadvad vidyutvān vidyutā yathā* // Sdhp.42v.5–6 (Vyāsa) < Nirṇ.438 (*sadānuyātavyo* for *sahānuyātavyo; striyā* for *sadā*). See also Saha.IV.1b (as Nirṇ.; Sk.P.).

[11] *anuvrajantī bhartāram gṛhāt pitṛvanam mudā / pade pade 'śvamedhasya phalaṃ prāpnoti asaṃśayam* // Sdhp.42v.6 (Vyāsa) < Sk.P.III.2.7.53; Nirṇ.438

(*anuvrajati* for *anuvrajantī; grhān nihsaraṇaṃ* for *grhāt pitṛvanaṃ*). See also Sahā. IV.1b (as Nirṇ.; Sk.P.).

12   vyālagrāhī yathā vyālaṃ balād uddharate bilāt / evam utkṛṣya daityebhyaḥ patiṃ svargaṃ nayet satī // Sdhp.42v.6–7 (Vyāsa) < Sk.P.III.2.7.54 (*utkramya dūtebhyaḥ* for *utkṛṣya daityebhyaḥ; vrajet* for *nayet*); Par.M.II.i. p.57 (*evaṃ strī patim uddhṛtya tenaiva saha modate*). For the first half-*śloka* only (*bilād* for *balād; balāt,* for *bilāt*), see Mit. on Yājñ.I.86 (Aṅg.); Apar. on Yājñ.I.87 (Vyāsa); Dh.kośa I.ii.pp.1111,1116,1117; Sahā.I.1.

13   *yamadūtāḥ palāyante satīm ālokya dūrataḥ / api duṣkṛtakarmāṇaṃ samutsṛjya ca tatpatim // na tathā bibhimo vahner na tathā vidyuto yathā / āpatantīṃ samālokya vayaṃ dūtāḥ pativratām //* Sdhp.42v. 7–9 (Vyāsa) <Sk. P. III. 2.7.55a (first half-*śloka* only; *tām ālokya pativratām* for *satīm alokya dūrataḥ*).

14   *parāśaro 'pi // tisraḥ koṭyo 'rdhakoṭi ca yāni romāṇi mānuṣe / tāvat kālaṃ vaset svarge bhartāraṃ yānugacchati //* Sdhp.43r.1–2 (Par.) < Par.Sm. IV.32; Mit. on Yājñ.I.86 (*lomāni* for *romāṇi; Śaṅkh., Aṅg.); Dh.kośa I.ii.p.1115 (*lomāni* for *romāṇi; tāvanty abdāni sā* for *tāvat Kāvat kālaṃ vaset;* Aṅg.). Cf. Apar.p.110.

15   *vyāsaḥ // yadi praviṣṭo narakaṃ baddhaḥ pāśaiḥ sudāruṇaiḥ / saṃ-prāpto yātanāsthānaṃ grhīto yamakiṅkaraiḥ / tiṣṭhate vivaśo dīno vepamānaḥ svakarmabhiḥ //* Sdhp.43r.4–5 (Vyāsa) < Apar. on Yājñ.I.87 (*veṣṭhamānaḥ* for *vepamānaḥ;* Vyāsa); Dh.kośa I.ii.p.1111 (as Apar.); Par.M.II.i.p.57 (as Apar.). Cf. Sahā.I.7.(*dīno 'nḍa bhujyamānaḥ* for *dīno vepamānaḥ*).

16   *brahmagno vā kṛtaghno vā mitraghno vā bhavet patiḥ / punāty avidhavā nārī tam ādāya mṛtā tu yā //* Sdhp.43r.5–6 (Vyāsa) < Mit. on Yājñ.I.86; Par.M.II.i.p.57; Dh.kośa I.ii.p.1111 (*brahmaghne vā kṛtaghne vā mitraghne yacca duṣkṛtaṃ / bhartuḥ punāty sā nārī tam ādāya mṛtā tu yā;* Vyāsa). Cf. Apar.I.87; Mit. on Yājñ.I.72; Dh.kośa I.ii.p.1116 (Aṅg.).

17   idaṃ cānumaraṇaṃ pativratayānuṣṭhitaṃ saduktarītyā ubhayoḥ śreyohetuḥ // Sdhp.43r.6–7. Cf. Par.M.II.i.p.57–8 (*cānugamanaṃ* for *cānumaraṇaṃ; dampatyorubhayoḥ* for *ubhayoḥ*).

18   *pāpīyasyānuṣṭhitaṃ cet pāpakṣayahetuḥ //* Sdhp.43r.7. Cf. Par.M.II.i. p.58 (°hetur bhavati *for hetuḥ*).

19   *tathā ca saṃgrahe //* bhārate // Sdhp.43r.7. *avamatya ca yā[ḥ] pūrvaṃ patiṃ duṣṭena cetasā / vartante yāśca satataṃ bhartṛṇāṃ pratikūlagāḥ // bhartrānumaraṇaṃ kāle yāḥ kurvanti tathāvidhāḥ / kāmāt krodhād bhayād vāpi sarvāḥ pūtā bhavanty uta //* Sdhp.43r.7–9 (Mbh.) <Sm. M.I.p. 163 (*pratikūlatāḥ* for °*gāḥ; bhayām mohāt* for *bhayād vāpi;* Vyāsaśātātapaḥ); Par.M.II. i.p.58 (as Sm.M. except *tu* for *ca; bhavanti tāḥ* for *bhavanty uta;* Mbh.); Mbh.XIII Appendix 1 no.15, 4660–3, 4665–6. Cf. Sahā.1.2 (as Par.M. except *ca* for *tu*).

20   *anena jīva[nada]śāyāṃ bhartṛvipriyaṃ pāpaṃ kṛtavatyāḥ sahagamanaṃ prāyaścittatvenoktam //* Sdhp.43r.9–10 (following the emendation of PT).

21   *kalau yugetvimān dharmān varj[y]ān āhur manīṣiṇaḥ / prāyaścitta-vidhānaṃ ca viprāṇāṃ mṛraṇāntikam //* Sdhp.43v.1–2 <Sm. A.p. 2, *ślokas* 25b, 21b.

²² *nanu idam anugamanaṃ kṣatriyāṇyādīnāṃ bhavatu / brāhmaṅyās tu niṣiddham // Sdhp.44v.3–4.*

²³ *tathā ca paiṭhīnasiḥ // mṛtānugamanaṃ nāsti brāhmaṇyā brahmaśāsanāt / itareṣāṃ tu varṇānāṃ strīdharmo 'yaṃ para[ḥ]* smṛtaḥ //Sdhp.44v.4–5 (Paiṭhīnasi; PT gives *dharmo 'yaṃ paramaḥ smṛtaḥ*) <Apar. p. 112 (Paitinasī); Mit.on Yājñ.1.86 (*itareṣu tu varṇeṣu tapaḥ paramaṃ smṛtaḥ*); Dh.kośa I.ii.p. 1115 (as Mit.: Paiṭhīnasi). Cf. Sahā.III.1.

²⁴ *vyāghrapādaḥ na mriyeta smaṃ bhartrā brāhmaṇī śokamohitā / pravrajyāgatim āpnoti maraṇād ātmaghātinī* // Sdhp.44v.9–45r.1 (Vyāghrapāda) < Apar.p.112 (Vyāghrapāda); Dh.kośa I.ii.p. 1117.

²⁵ *tathā ca uśanā // pṛthakcitiṃ samāruhya na viprā gantum arhati / anyāsāṃ caiva nārīṇāṃ strīdharmo 'yaṃ sanātanaḥ // iti //* Sdhp.45r.3–4 (Uśanas) < Par.M.II.i.p.56 (*paraḥ smṛtaḥ* for *sanātanaḥ*); Sm,M.I.p.162 (as Par.M.; Uśanas); Apar.p.112 (as Par.M.); Dh.kośa I.ii.p.1113 (Uśanas). Cf. Mit. on Yājñ.I.86; Sahā. I.8 (as Par.M.).

5

The Nineteenth Century

The Times, 'Interesting Account of A Suttee'[1]

The Times carried at least forty separate articles on sati during the nineteenth century. This eyewitness account gives graphic details of the methods used to keep the widow on the pyre and her suffering in the flames. This sort of account provided an antidote to heroic eighteenth-century treatments and illustrates the hardening of British attitudes to sati in the early nineteenth century.

Being informed that a suttee was about to take place in the vicinity of my house (in the neighbourhood of Calcutta) I repaired to the spot, in company with a friend, instigated by a strong and natural curiosity, to observe narrowly the deportment of a human being about to take a voluntary and public leave of existence, and believing from what we had read of similar cases, that our feelings would not be shocked by any open exhibition of the actual pains of dissolution. I do not recollect to have seen any account of a Suttee, which did not, upon the whole, tell rather favourably for the humanity of those whom an imperious ordinance of religion calls upon, to preside or officiate at such ceremonials. I think it therefore a duty I owe to the cause of truth, to record at least one instance on the other side of the question. With this view I beg leave to address myself to you with the hope that you will give the narration a place in your valuable newspaper, when you have nothing more interesting or novel to insert.

The Suttee in question took place at a spot by the riverside, about a quarter of a mile below Barnagore, at eleven in the morning.

We arrived about half an hour before that time, and found the widow bathing in the river, surrounded by a troop of friends, chiefly men. It was then low water, and the deep mud left by the tide prevented our approaching sufficiently near to observe the ceremonies that they were performing. Our attention was attracted to the pile, which was placed about high-water mark. It was not altogether more than about four-and-a-half to five feet long, to the best of our observation, and consisted merely of some long billets of chopped, soon dry wood, fresh and green, from the bazaar, retained in their places by four stakes driven into the ground at angles. The whole was exceeding little, if at all, longer, or broader, than one of the common cots used by the natives. The deceased was supported in a sitting posture by two men, close to the pile, and some more billets of wood, with four or five piles of dry brushwood and reeds, lay ready for use. The whole of the ceremonies observed on the occasion were such as are usually gone through, and as have been described so often in books. The widow was dressed in a robe, or sheet of bright red silk, and had her hair hanging loose and dishevelled, and stuck through with many wooden combs; her forehead was painted with yellow ochre, or orpiment, and she had no other dress or ornament whatever. From the bystanders we learned that her husband was a common washerman, and that it was not expected by anyone that she would have resolved to burn herself, especially as she had a child of three years old, and her relations had offered to maintain them both, if she would consent to live. I shall not take up your time detailing the many ceremonies that were performed. The body of her husband was placed on its right side, and in due time she ascended and lay down by its side, facing it, and literally locked in its arms. So short was the pile that the bystanders were forced to bend the legs of both very much, to enable the pile to contain them. During all this 'dreadful note of preparation' from first to last, the widow preserved the utmost, the most entire fortitude and composure, or rather apathy,—and was unmoved even at parting with her child. In her processions around the pile, she was supported and hurried through the crowd, by many men who held her arms and shoulders and made the populace give way. From this we at first concluded her to be intoxicated, but were afterwards convinced of our mistake, by seeing the steadiness of nerve, and perfect composure with which she sprinkled the corpse of her husband, and mounted the funeral pile entirely unassisted and alone. We stood within six or seven feet of the pile and could not be mistaken. The remaining billets of wood were now laid upon the bodies, with a scanty handful of dry reeds here and there. But the point to which I wish to especially draw the attention of your readers is, that thick, strong ropes, thoroughly soaked in water, were previously tied around the bodies of the living and the dead, in many places, to preclude the possibility of escape and in seeming anticipation of the dreadful scene which followed. One Brahmin only was present at the ceremony, and as soon as all was prepared, he offered the widow's child (in the arms of another) a lighted brand. The child drew back in affright, while they seized its hand by force, and applied fire to the head, and afterwards the foot of the pile. The shouting and noise from the crows had been incessant from the beginning, but at this instant it was incredibly loud. Four strong green bamboos were now laid across the whole of the pile, which were strongly held down by eight men, so as to keep down all attempts of the miserable creature within to arise; a precaution not useless if it be allowed to conjecture from what we observed from the foot of the pile near to which we stood. A quantity of ghee, not, I should imagine, a pint in all, was scattered on the pile; the scantiness of this and the brushwood, and the greenness of the billets, caused the pile to burn very slow, and rendered it necessary to apply fresh fire at one time. I scarcely know how to paint in colours that will not disgust and shock our readers, the horrible close of that scene. Suffice to say, that soon after the fire took effect, the wretched woman within, in her torment, stretched forth her leg, which now protruded from the knee, beyond the scanty pile; and by the quickness with which she attempted to withdraw it, on its touching a burning brand, it was evident that she was still too sensible of the tortures she must then have been enduring. Owing to the brushwood being scattered only at the extremities of the pile, the fire there was fiercest. In a minute or two more the scorched and mutilated limb was again thrust out, and slowly consumed before our outraged eyes, while the tremendous and convulsive motion which it exhibited to the last (for many minutes), plainly showed that sensation and life yet existed in the miserable wretch within. A kind of incredulous horror of what was passing had till now riveted us to the spot; but the scene became too shocking, and we quickly retired. I ought to observe that the utmost indifference, without any symptom of the remotest compassion, prevailed among the whole of the spectators, not excepting the mother and sister of the widow, who were pointed out to us among the crowd.

The Times, 'Suttee'[2]

This account, by a British official, of a sati at which he superintended is useful both as an example of an apparently voluntary sati and of the workings of the 1813 regulation in practice.

The following interesting account of one of those dreadful sacrifices is extracted from the letter of the English officer who superintended the ceremony he describes.

Burdwan, 18 October

In my present situation it falls to my lot to preside over the execution of criminals, and also over those horrible exhibitions peculiar to this country, of a widow burning herself on the funeral pile of her dead husband; and as the authentic account of such a scene may be interesting, I send you a short description of a suttee at which I was lately present in my new character as presiding officer. The day before it took place (as is customary) a report came from the police of the widow's intention to burn herself, if the magistrate gave his permission. On the principle of religious toleration this is always given; the magistrate is allowed to argue and endeavour to dissuade the woman from her purpose, but cannot absolutely forbid it, except under certain circumstances, such as when it is not perfectly voluntary on her part. Myself and several friends went to her house, and did all we could to turn her from her design, but she answered only by quoting her bible, in which she observed, it is written 'the widow who burns herself with her husband's body enjoys happiness with him in Heaven'. Having failed in our entreaties, which are indeed, usually to no purpose, we ordered a guard to watch, and take care that she had no opium or intoxicating drugs given to her, and that she went to her death in her senses, or at least as much so as she could be under the influence of such extraordinary fanaticism. The next morning, at daybreak, we proceeded to the ground appropriated for the ceremony, where the woman had just arrived in a rude sort of car, carried on men's shoulders and accompanied by the barbarous music of her country. She seemed quite unconcerned at the preparations for the horrid sacrifice she was about to perform. For my part, when I looked at the pile on which lay her husband's dead body, the faggots, her nearest relations with firebrands lighting the pile, the victim dressed and adorned with flowers, the whole scene appeared to me as a frightful vision: I could hardly persuade myself of its reality. I spoke to her once more (being a high-caste woman she spoke the Hindoostani language), and represented to her the horrible death she was about to suffer, and the long time that she must continue in the most dreadful agony. I urged her that this was no sudden or easy death by which she was to reach paradise, but a protracted course of torture. She heard me with calmness, and thanked me for my intentions, which she admitted were good, but again repeated her intention so decidedly as to preclude any hope of saving her. I felt her pulse, and it was far calmer than my own at the moment I am writing. Mrs E. (of whom I have often made honourable mention), thinking her own persuasion as one of her own sex, might avail, then went up to the wretched victim and in the most earnest manner tried to dissuade her. She offered her a pension for life, and an honourable asylum in the Company's territories. Among other inducement, intending it probably as an appeal to female vanity, Mrs E. said that she should be made a lady and have a palanquin to ride: she immediately answered, pointing at the pile 'ce humara palkee hy—that is my palanquin'. The victim then performed several ceremonies, and prepared herself to jump on the pile, which was blazing to receive her. The flames had arisen to a great height, and they were feeding them with tar and faggots. I then addressed her for the last time; told her no force should be used to keep her in the fire, but conjured her, if her resolution failed, to jump out and run to me; that I was surrounded by my policemen, and that I would bear her away from her cruel relations, to a place of safety where they should never see her any more. Her resolution was not to be shaken. She then distributed flowers and sweatmeats, gave me a piece of her dress, and having danced three times around the pile, threw herself in. At that moment the people shouted, the drums and native music struck up, and if she uttered any cries, I heard them not. She resolutely sat in the fire, apparently alive, for two or three minutes, but moved only her hands occasionally. Such is the description of the dreadful act that takes place every day.

Fanny Parks, *Wanderings of a Pilgrim in Search of the Picturesque*[3]

This account from Parks's well-known travelogue is of a sati prevented by the local British magistrate, accompanied by her husband. She supplements this with a summary of textual injunctions for sati and including her own comments on the custom, which she sees as an example of universal patriarchal oppression.

ALLAHABAD, 1828

A rich *buniya*, a corn chandler, whose house was near the gates of our grounds, departed this life; he was a Hindoo. On the 7th of November the natives in the bazaar were making a great noise with their tom-toms, drums and other discordant musical instruments, rejoicing that his widow had determined to perform suttee, i.e. to burn on his funeral-pile.

The magistrate sent for the woman, used every argument to dissuade her, and offered her money. Her only answer was dashing her head on the floor, and saying, 'If you will not let me burn with my husband, I will hang myself in your court of justice.' The Shastras say, 'The prayers and imprecations of the suttee are never uttered in vain; the great gods themselves cannot listen to them unmoved.'

If a widow touch either food or water from the time her husband expires until she ascends the funeral pile, she cannot, by Hindoo law, be burned with the body; therefore the magistrate kept the corpse forty-eight hours, in the hope that the hunger would compel the woman to eat. Guards were set over her, but she never touched anything. My husband accompanied the magistrate to see the suttee: about

5000 people were collected together on the banks of the Ganges: the pile was then built, and the putrid body placed upon it; the magistrate stationed guards to prevent the people from approaching it. After having bathed in the river, the widow lighted a brand, walked round the pile, set it on fire and mounted cheerfully: the flame caught and blazed up instantly; she sat down, placing the head of the corpse on her lap, and repeated several times the usual form 'Ram, Ram, suttee; Ram, Ram, suttee', i.e. 'God, God, I am chaste'.

As the wind drove the fierce fire upon her, she shook her arms and limbs as if in agony; at length she started up and approached the side to escape. A Hindoo, one of the police who had been placed near the pile to see she had fair play, and should not be burned by force, raised his sword to strike her, and the poor wretch shrank back into the flames. The magistrate seized and committed him to prison. The woman again approached the side of the blazing pile, sprang fairly out, and ran into the Ganges, which was within a few yards. When the crowd and the brothers of the dead man saw this, they called out, 'Cut her down, knock her on the head with a bamboo; tie her hands and feet and throw her back in again'; and rushed down to execute their murderous intentions, when the gentlemen and the police drove them back.

The woman drank some water, and having extinguished the fire on her red garment, said she would mount the pile again and be burned.

The magistrate placed his hand on her shoulder (which rendered her impure) and said, 'By your own law, having once quitted the pile you cannot ascend again; I forbid it. You are now an outcast from the Hindoos, but I will take charge of you, the Company will protect you and you will never want food or clothing.'

He then sent her, in a palanquin, under a guard, to the hospital. The crowd made way, shrinking from her with signs of horror, but returned peaceably to their homes; the Hindoos annoyed at her escape, the Mussulmans saying, 'It was better that she should escape, but it was a pity that we should have lost the tamasha (amusement) of seeing her burnt to death.'

Had not the magistrate and the English gentlemen been there, the Hindoos would have cut her down when she attempted to quit the fire; or had she leapt out, would have thrown her back in again, and have said, 'She performed suttee of her own accord, how could we make her? It was the will of God.' As a specimen of their religion, the woman said, 'I have transmigrated six times and have been burnt six times with six different husbands; if I do not burn the seventh time it will prove unlucky for me!' 'What good will burning do you?' asked a bystander. She replied 'The women of my husband's family have all been suttees, why should I bring disgrace upon them? I shall go to heaven, and afterwards reappear on earth, and be married to a very rich man.' She was about twenty or twenty-five years of age, and possessed of some property, for the sake of which her relatives wished to put her out of the world.

If every suttee were conducted in this way, very few would take place in India. The woman was not much burned, with the exception of some parts on her arms and legs. Had she performed suttee, they would have raised a little cenotaph, or a mound of earth by the side of the river, and every Hindoo who passed the place returning from bathing would have made a salaam to it; a high honour to the family. While we were in Calcutta many suttees took place; but as they were generally on the other side of the river, we only heard of them after they had occurred. Here the people passed in procession, flags flying, and drums beating, close by our door. I saw them from the verandah; the widow, dressed in a red garment, was walking in the midst. My servants all ran to me, begging to be allowed to go and see the tamasha, and having obtained permission, they all started off, except one man, who was pulling the pankha, and he looked greatly vexed at being obliged to remain. The sahib said, the woman appeared so perfectly determined, he did not think she would have quitted the fire. Having performed suttee according to her own account six times before, one would have thought that from her miraculous incombustibility, she had become asbestos, only purified and not consumed by fire. I was glad the poor creature was not murdered; but she will be an outcast; no Hindoo will eat with her, enter her house, or give her assistance; and when she appears they will point at her and give her abuse. Her own and her husband's family would lose caste if they were to speak to her: but, as an example, it will prevent a number of women becoming suttees, and do infinite good. And these are the people called in Europe the 'mild inoffensive Hindoos'!

The woman was mistress of a good house and about 800 rupees; the brothers of her deceased husband would, after her destruction, have inherited the property.

The burning of the widow is not commanded by the Shastras: to perform suttee is a proof of devotion to the husband. The mountain Himalaya, being personified, is represented as a powerful monarch: his wife, Mena; their daughter is called Parvuti, or mountain-born, and Doorga, or difficult of access. She is said to have been married to Shivu in a pre-existing state when she was called Suttee. After the marriage, Shivu on a certain occasion offended his father-in-law, King Dukshu, by refusing to make a salaam to him as he entered the circle in which the king was sitting.

To be revenged, the monarch refused to invite Shivu to a sacrifice that he was about to perform. Suttee, the king's daughter, however, was resolved to go, though uninvited and forbidden by her husband. On her arrival Dukshu poured a torrent of abuse on Shivu, which affected Suttee so much that she died.

In memory of this proof of great affection, a Hindoo widow burning with her husband on his funeral-pile is called a Suttee. The following passages are from the Hindu Shastras:

'There are 35,000,000 hairs on the human body. The woman who ascends the pile with her husband, will remain so many years in heaven.'

'As the snake draws the serpent from its hole, so she, rescuing her husband [from hell], rejoices with him.'

'The woman who expires on the funeral-pile of her husband, purifies the family of her mother, her father and her husband.'

'So long as a woman, in her successive transmigrations, shall decline burning herself, like a faithful wife, on the same fire with her deceased lord, so long shall she not be exempted from springing again to life in the body of some female animal.'

'There is no virtue greater than a chaste woman burning herself with her husband': the term Suttee, here rendered 'chaste' is thus explained; 'commiserating with her husband in trouble, rejoicing in his joys, neglecting herself when he is gone from home, and dying at his death.'

'By the favour of a chaste woman the universe is preserved, on which account she is to be regarded by kings and people as a goddess.'

'If the husband be out of the country when he dies, let the virtuous wife take his slippers (or anything else that belongs to his dress) and binding them, or it, on her breast, after purification, enter a separate fire.'

Mothers collect the cowrie shell strewn by a suttee as she walks around the pile, ere she fires it, and hang them around the necks of their sick children as a cure for disease.

The suttee took place on the banks of the Ganges, under the Bund between the Fort and the Raj Ghat, a spot reckoned very holy and fortunate for the performance of the rite.

Several of our friends requested me, in case another suttee occurred, to send them timely notice. Five days afterwards I was informed that a *ranee* was to be burned. Accordingly I sent word to all my friends. Eight thousand people were assembled on the suttee ground, who waited from mid-day to sunset: then a cry arose — 'The *mem sahiba* sent us here! The mem sahiba said it was to take place today! See, the sun has set, there can now be no suttee!' The people dispersed. My informant told me what he himself believed, and I mystified some 8000 people most unintentionally.

10 Oct [1830]—I see in the papers, 'A member in the House of Commons expressed his satisfaction that so abominable a practice as suttee should have been abolished without convulsion or bloodshed. Great credit was due to the noble lord at the head of the government there, and to the missionaries, to whom much of the credit was owing.'

How very absurd all this is was proved to me by what came to my knowledge at the time of the suttee at Allahabad. If the government at that time had issued the order to forbid suttee, not one word would have been said. The missionaries had nothing to do with it; the rite might have been abolished long before without danger.

Women in all countries are considered such dust in the balance when their interests are pitted against those of men, that I rejoice that no more widows are to be grilled, to ensure the whole of the property passing to the sons of the deceased.

The Government interferes with native superstition where rupees are in question—witness the tax they levy on pilgrims at the
junction of the Ganges and the Jumna. Every man, even the veriest beggar, is obliged to give one rupee for liberty to bathe at the
holy spot; and if you consider that one rupee is sufficient to keep
a man in comfort for a month, the tax is severe.

Notes

[1]   'Interesting Account of A Suttee', *The Times*, 11 June 1810.

[2]   'Suttee', *The Times*, 12 May 1823.

[3]   Parks, Fanny, *Wanderings of a Pilgrim in Search of the Picturesque* (Karachi: Oxford University Press, 1975).

III

DEBATING ABOLITION
1805–30

6

Missionaries and Philanthropists

Charles Grant, *Observations on the State of Society among the Asiatic Subjects of Great Britain*[1]

The British government published the highly influential treatise on the state of Indian society by this famous member of the Clapham Sect in 1813, though it had been written twenty years previously. Grant's evangelical standpoint foreshadowed an attitude to sati that would dominate in the early nineteenth century.

But the cruelty of the Hindu people appears in no way more evident than in the whole of the treatment to which their women are subjected in society, under the sanction and authority of the code. They are truly an unfortunate part of the community and greatly to be pitied. Receiving no education, disposed of in marriage without having their consent asked, or knowing a thing of the person to whom they are to be given, they are immured for life, and made mere servants to the family of their despotic lord. If barren or bearing only daughters, they are neglected, and not always released from oppression, even when death removes the husband; for they are then frequently reduced to the alternative of sinking into a state of infamy, or of burning themselves with his dead body.

The code expressly sanctions this inhuman and astonishing custom:

'It is proper for a woman after her husband's death to burn herself in the fire with his corpse.'

'Every woman who thus burns herself shall remain in paradise with her husband three crore and fifty lakhs of years.'

The strong recommendations and injunctions from a lawgiver believed to be divine, is of course, admitted to have the force of a religious obligation; and it is one of those institutions of which the Brahmins are very tenacious. We are naturally led to enquire what could have been the primary cause of an institution so horrid. The Hindu writings so far as they are known seem to be silent on this head; but an explanation offers itself from the principle of the perpetual separation of castes, and the manners of the people. It was essential to that principle that the castes should marry within itself. In a few permitted cases men from higher castes might take a wife from an inferior one of the original four orders, and the children were deemed of that to which the father belonged; but in no case was it allowed to a woman of a higher caste to marry with a man of a lower.

Mixed intercourses were therefore almost universally prohibited under penalties, and the offspring, which, notwithstanding prohibitions, appeared from that source, were degraded below the fourth caste. But polygamy has always been practised among the Hindoos, especially among those of higher orders; and the latter wives must infallibly, from the custom of the country, be considerably younger than the husband, and generally still young when he dies. A multitude of widows must soon arise in the community, and from the nature of the case progressively increase. Second marriages of women appear to be unknown and repugnant to the Hindu laws and usages.

When a woman's husband therefore dies, she is reckoned a useless being, and what is worse, a dangerous one. The jealousy of the Eastern people has placed their honour in the conduct of their women, as being what touches them most. Not the husband himself only, but the whole family are stained by the misbehaviour of a wife; and if she degrades herself after his death, they are still affected by her dishonour. If she should bring other children by a man of inferior caste, she would introduce, more signally than any misconduct in a man could, that disorder and confusion into the society which would tend to break down the lines of separation between castes. But seeing the number of widows must always be great, and they have no effectual superintendent or protector, there must be a proportional danger of such irregularity as would at length make the exceptions bear down on the rule; and if mothers, as in many instances might thus happen, were to rear the children of a Sooder with those left by her former noble husband, the higher caste would not be preserved, during infancy, from defilements produced by eating and drinking and touching what appertained to the other; nor could the son of a Sooder brought up in this way, afterwards regard his Brahmin brother and companion with the veneration deemed indispensably requisite to be shown to that order.

How then, might it be said, shall the evils to be apprehended from this source, notwithstanding prohibitions and disgrace, be prevented? Let an ordinance, professedly divine, recommend to widows a voluntary departure with their husbands to paradise, under an assurance of enjoying a very long succession of their felicity; honour shall stimulate them to embrace this choice, and lest the love of life should still prevail, the fear of infamy shall compel them to die. Nor would this expedient appear as shocking to the Hindu as it does to us. Admitting the separations of castes to be a sacred institution, whatever tended to subvert it might be obviated not only lawfully, but as a matter of duty.

Women there have no concern in the education of their children after infancy; they cannot go abroad; the chief, if not the only, way in which they are considered to be useful terminates with the death of the husband; the code imputes to them the most depraved, impure, unsafe nature; they are ranked in the Bhagvad with those who are 'of the womb of sin'; and it is believed they are doomed to successive transmigrations, until they are regenerated in the body of a Brahmin. Vile, therefore, in their nature, and becoming useless and dangerous, to remove them from earth would be to study the preservation of order below, and to accelerate the course they have to pass through to a happier state. And thus there is a regular progress from the first stage of a false principle to a practical consummation that is tremendous.

Our supposition that the original design of this institution was to prevent the dishonour and confusion of castes appears to be confirmed by the terms of the ordinance in which it is delivered; for after saying that 'it is proper for a woman to burn herself in the fire with her husband's corpse', it adds, 'if she cannot burn, she is to maintain an inviolable chastity'. If she remains always chaste, she goes still to paradise, and if she does not preserve her chastity, she goes to hell.

It is probable that though the ordinance speaks in general terms of any woman, the Brahmins might not mean its operation to extend beyond the higher orders, and might especially intend to preserve their own in all the distinction of purity necessary to maintain their authority. Among the lower castes it is seldom enforced. With others, what was originally, in part at least, policy, is now a superstition, or an honourable family distinction; and in this last view the practice seems to have extended to other Eastern nations, who probably adopted it from the Hindus. Expenses and domestic inconveniences attend it, which may contribute to confine it to those alone, even of the superior castes, who are in better circumstances; but among persons of that description, happiness and misery, honour and infamy, the present and the future, are all urged as motives to destruction, with great and horrid success. The number of women thus annually destroyed in Hindustan probably far exceeds the general conception of Europeans.

Reverend William Ward, *Farewell Letters*[2]

This tract by the famous Serampore missionary is a typical example of missionary writing on sati, and on the status of Hindu women more generally, and was designed for an audience in Britain. Not only is Ward trying to stir up popular opposition to sati itself; he also uses it as an example of Hindu depravity and thus as a tool in raising funds for missionary enterprise.

The anxiety of the Hindoo to obtain a son who may present the funeral offerings, upon the presentation of which he supposes his future happiness to depend, and the expenses attending the support and marriage of girls, make the birth of a female in a Hindoo family an unwelcome event: hence the sex in India come into the world frowned upon by their own parents and relations. No favourable prognostic this for future comforts!

I ought here to mention the case of the female children of the Rajpoots; for though this relation belongs only to one of the Hindoo tribes, it exhibits strong corroborative proof of the low estimation in which even the lives of females are held in India. One of the families of the Rajpoots, it is said, began this practice of butchering their female children, to prevent the fulfilment of a prediction that through a female, the succession of the crown would pass out of the family. All the tribe has since followed the royal example; and now, not one female child survives, the boys marry into the tribe next in rank to them. And does no mother interpose her tender entreaties to spare her daughter? 'Can a woman forget her sucking child, that she should not have compassion on the infant of her womb?' Oh what need of the softening and enlightening influences of the gospel, where mothers have become monsters—have sunk below the wolf and the tiger. Through what unknown, unheard of process must the female heart have passed, thus to have lost all its wonted tenderness; thus to have laid hold of a nature not found anywhere else upon the earth (see the cow butting with her horn, and threatening the person who dares approach her offspring! See woman in India, at Saugur Island, throwing her living child into the outstretched jaws of the alligator).... A Brahmin of the western provinces gave me this relation: A Rajpoot, for some unassigned reasons, spared his female child; which grew up in the father's house until the age in which girls in India are married. The sight of a girl, however, in the house of a Rajpoot was so novel, and so contrary to the customs of the tribe, that no parent sought her in marriage for his son. The father, suffering under the frowns of his tribe, and trembling for the chastity of his daughter and the honour of his family, was driven into a state of frenzy, and in this state, taking his daughter aside, he actually put an end to her existence.

To the Hindoo female all education is denied by the positive injunction of the shastru, and by the general voice of the population. Not a single school for girls, therefore, all over the country! With knitting, sewing, embroidery, painting, music and drawing, they have no more to do with than with letters: the washing is done by men of a particular tribe. The Hindoo girl, therefore, spends the first ten years of her life in sheer idleness, immured in the house of her father.

Before she has attained this age, however, she is sought after by the *ghutuks*, men employed by parents to seek wives for their sons. She is betrothed without her consent; a legal agreement that binds her for life, being made by the parents on both sides while she is yet a child.

At a time most convenient to the parents, this boy and girl are brought together for the first time, and the marriage ceremony is performed; after which she returns to the house of her father.

Before the marriage is consummated, in many instances, the boy dies, and this girl becomes a widow; and as the law prohibits the marriage of a widow, she is doomed to remain in this state for as long as she lives. The greater number of these unfortunate beings become a prey to the seducer, and a disgrace to their families. Not long since, a bride on the day the marriage ceremony was to have been performed, was burnt on the funeral pile with the dead body of the bridegroom at Chandernagore, a few miles north of Calcutta. Concubinage, to a most awful extent is the fruit of these marriages without choice. What a sum of misery is attached to the lot of a woman in India before she has attained even her fifteenth year!

In some cases as many as fifty females, daughters of so many Hindoos, are given in marriage to the same Brahmin, in order to make these families something more respectable and that the parents might be able to say, we are allied by marriage to the *kooleens*, the highest rank of Brahmins. In what kind of estimation must females be held in a country where, in numerous instances, twenty, thirty, and even fifty of them are sacrificed to promote the honour of the family? These females are doomed to a life of widowhood, and to a life of infamy, for they never live with their husbands; and there have been cases, in which several have been burnt in the same pile as this nominal husband; no doubt for the honour of the family.

Supposing, however, that the Hindoo female is happily married, she remains a prisoner and a slave in the house of her husband. She knows nothing of the advantages of liberal intercourse with mankind. She is not permitted to speak to a person of the other sex, if she belongs to a respectable family, except to old men, very nearly allied in blood: she retires at the appearance of a male guest.

She receives no benefit from books, or from society; and though Hindoos do not affirm, with some Mahometans, that females have no souls, they treat them as though this was their belief. What companions for their husbands—what mothers these! Yet it is not the females alone who are the sufferers: while such is the mental condition of the sex, of how much happiness must husbands, children, society at large, be deprived! What must be the state of that country where the female mind and the female presence (the lowest orders of females alone are seen in numbers in the streets) are things unknown?

This vacuity of thought, these habits of indolence, and this total want of information, of principles and of society, leave the Hindoo female easy prey to seduction, and the devoted slave of superstition. Faithfulness to marriage vows is almost unknown in India; and, where the manners of the East allow it, the females manifest a more enthusiastic attachment to the superstitions of the country than even the men. The religious mendicants, the priests, and the public shows preserve an overwhelming influence over the female mind. Many become mendicants, and some undertake long pilgrimages. In short, the power of superstition over the female in India has no parallel in any other country....

...But the awful state of female society in this miserable country appears in nothing so much as in dooming the female, the widow, to be burnt alive with the putrid carcass of her dead husband. The Hindoo legislators have sanctioned this immolation, showing herein, a studied determination to insult and degrade women. She is therefore, in the first instance, deluded into this act by the writings of the Brahmins; in which she is also promised, that if she will offer herself, for the benefit of her husband, on the funeral pile, she shall, by the extraordinary merit of this action, rescue her husband from misery and take him and fourteen generations of his and her family with her to heaven, where she shall enjoy with them celestial happiness until fourteen kings of the gods shall have succeeded to the throne of heaven (that is, millions of years!). Thus ensnared she embraces this dreadful death. I have seen three widows, at different times, burnt alive; and had repeated opportunities to be present at similar immolations, but my courage failed me.

The funeral pile consists of a quantity of faggots laid on the earth, rising in height about three feet from the ground, about four feet wide and six feet in length. After the female has declared her intention to 'eat fire', as the people call it, she leaves her house for the last time accompanied by her children, relations and a few neighbours. She proceeds to a river where a priest attends upon her, and where certain ceremonies are performed, accompanied with ablutions. These over, she comes up to the pile which may be ten yards from the brink of the river. She walks around the pile several times, scattering parched corn &c., and at length lays herself down on the pile by the dead body, laying her arm over it. Two cords have been laid across the pile and under the dead body, and with these cords the dead body and the living body are now tied fast together. A large quantity of faggots are now laid upon the bodies, and two levers are brought over the pile to press down the widow, and prevent her from escaping when the flames begin to scorch her. Her eldest son, averting his face, with a lighted torch in his hand then sets fire to the pile. The drums are immediately sounded which with the shouts of the mob, effectually drown out the shrieks of the widow surrounded by the flames.

There are a number of circumstances connecting themselves with these butcheries, which plainly point out to us the infamously base feelings of these people, from their rulers downwards, towards women. For instance,

1. The widow is told that there remains no higher duty to a faithful widow than to burn with her husband.
2. They next hold out to her promises of immense happiness, as well as the deliverance of her husband and all her relations from torments and elevation to the same happiness.
3. Some widows are placed under the fatal necessity of giving up their lives as their unfeeling parents have married them in families in which widows are always burnt.
4. All the motives urged for her burning meet her in the height of her first anguish for the loss of her husband: time is not allowed to deliberate.
5. In the test which these wretches sometimes demand from a widow, that she will not disappoint them by shrinking at the sight of the pile, we further see how utterly destitute the Hindoos are of all respect for the sex: They put a lamp in her hand, and demand that she shall hold her finger in the flame till it is nearly burnt to a cinder.

6. If she has an infant, and on this account is interdicted from burning, a male never fails to come forward, and rather than she shall not burn, engages to maintain the child.

7. The laws do not authorize the use of cords or levers; but the present race of Hindoos are determined to secure their victim.

8. That part of the ceremony which compels her to walk deliberately and repeatedly round the pile, appears to have been invented on purpose to aggravate her misery. One of the widows whose immolation I witnessed, was obliged to be supported as she walked around the pile.

9. It is also very remarkable that the eldest son, almost always the child to which the mother is most attached, is selected as the executioner.

10. The law allows her to recant, even at the pile; but the widow never enjoys the benefit of it; she knows that her death is determined upon, after the public avowal of her determination to burn.

11. And finally, the drums, the shouts, and the diabolical eagerness with which the natives, especially the Brahmins, go into this horrid work, bear the most decided testimony how utterly destitute these idolaters are of all proper feelings towards the sex.

It is urged that these are voluntary immolations; if it is meant that no outward brutal force is used, I allow that in this sense they are voluntary. But in what other country under heaven would they be allowed to burn? Where are men, except in India, to be found who would not use force to prevent these immolations? But has not all knowledge been denied to the Hindoo female; and have not their minds been shockingly perverted by superstition? Can a child in the same sense as an adult be called a free agent? To show, however, that a certain kind of force is sometimes used we may state the case of a female not long ago rescued from the funeral pile by Mrs Julius, then in India. The pile had already been lighted and the shoulder of the victim scorched by the flame. This widow declared, after her rescue that before she went to the pile some intoxicating drug had been administered to her, which had rendered her perfectly insensible. The Hindoo law on these immolations interdicts the application of any such drugs, a provision which would not have been made, had not Hindoos always been disposed to treat females in this manner.

The burying alive of widows manifests, if it were possible, a still more abominable state of feeling towards women than the burning them alive. The weavers bury their dead. When, therefore, a widow of this tribe is deluded into the determination not to survive her husband, she is buried alive with the dead body. In this kind of immolation the children and relations dig the grave. After certain ceremonies have been attended to, the poor widow arrives and is let down into the pit. She sits in the centre, taking the dead body on her lap and encircling it with her arms. These relations now begin to throw in the soil; and after a short space, two of them descend into the grave, and tread the earth firmly around the body of the widow. She sits a calm and unremonstrating spectator of the horrid process. She sees the earth rising higher and higher around her without upbraiding her murderers, or making the least effort to arise and make her escape. At length the earth reaches her lips—covers her head. The rest of the earth is then hastily thrown in, and these children and relations mount the grave and tread down the earth upon the head of the poor suffocating widow—the mother! Why, my dear friend, the life of the vilest brute that walks upon the earth is never taken away by a process so slow, so deliberate, so diabolical as this. And this is the state of your sex in British India! In how many situations, where we expect it not, are we reminded of the testimony of the divine word: in every part of the heathen world, in the miserable state of woman, what a confirmation to the denunciation, 'To the woman he said, I will greatly multiply thy sorrow' (Gen. iii. 16).

Ah! My dear Miss Hope! Shall I not hear, after my return to India, that the females of Britain and America have united to make the case of their sex in India a common cause—the cause of woman—but especially the cause of every Christian widow—of every Christian mother—of every Christian female? Will you not, females of Britain and America! Imitate the noble example of Col. Walker, and rescue these Rajpoot female infants? Will you not follow in the footsteps of Mrs Julius, and deliver these females, doomed to a horrible death by usages which have been long devoted to endless execration? Will you not become the guardians of these ten thousand orphans surrounding these funeral piles, and endeavouring to put out these fires with their tears? By an official statement that I brought with me from India, it appears that every year more than seven hundred women (more probably fourteen hundred) are burned or buried alive in the Presidency of Bengal alone. How many in the other parts of India? Your sex will not say that in the roasting alive of four widows every day there is not blood enough shed to call forth their exertions. Seventy-five million of females in Hindoosthan, frowned upon in their birth, denied all education, and exposed to a thousand miseries unknown among females in Christian countries, have surely a claim tender enough, powerful enough to awaken all the female sensibility of Britain and America. Let the females of the United Kingdom speak, and they must be heard. Let the females of both countries give the means of affording education to their sex in India, and these infants must be saved; these fires must be put out; these graves must be closed forever. By such an interposition, so worthy of the sex in these countries, the females in India will be blessed with all that profusion of privileges that women in Christian countries enjoy; and, being thus blessed, will become the light, the shade, and the ornament of India. One or two Hindoo females, in spite of every interdiction, have claimed the right of their sex to the cultivation of their powers; and there can be no doubt but that India will, at no distant period, speak with raptures of her female moral writers, her poets and her teachers; of her Mores and Frys, who will lay all their honours at the feet of Him who is the Desire of all nations, and in whom alone they can be blessed.

Who will say that the gospel is not wanted here to adopt and instruct these thousands of orphans, and to make the female, the widow's heart sing for joy? How sweet is that voice in my ear which says, 'Let every creature hear my gospel.'

Permit me to remain, My dear friend,

With great respect,

Your most obliged and humble servant, W. Ward

Friend of India, 'On the Burning of Widows'[3]

One of several articles carried on sati by the Baptist missionary organ, *Friend of India*, this typical example of missionary propaganda against sati is aimed at an audience in India. Rather than using sati to denigrate Hinduism directly, it emphasizes the widow's helplessness and the lack of religious motivation for sati.

Were we to hear of a nation which, on her husband's death, subjected a widow to the loss of all of her property, which she might probably have bought him as part of her dower and which she had enjoyed with him since the time of their union; and turned her onto the wide world (her protector being dead) to labour, to beg, to steal, or to perish, with what feelings of indignation should we regard such a law and such a nation! We should inquire on what principle this severity is exercised on a helpless woman at the very moment that her heart is torn with anguish at the loss of him on whom was fixed all her hope? Were imprisonment for life added to this outrage, however; were the hapless widow deprived of her liberty as well as all her property...such a procedure would excite horror and indignation in every mind. What then should we say if were we to hear for the first time that in some newly discovered land the death of the husband sealed the fate of the wife, however virtuous and exemplary in her conduct; that she was from that moment devoted to death—and to death in its most dreadful form—to be burnt to ashes! Such, however, is the case not in some lately discovered island hitherto totally cut off from the rest of mankind; but in India, famed for her literature and civilization; and above all in Bengal where Europeans are chiefly found, whose ideas the wise and candid among the natives are imbibing every day.

How then is it possible that the murder of the amiable and defenceless, attended too with such circumstances of cruelty, should have continued so long? How is it that common humanity has not overleaped every bound and constrained superstition to desist from a course so barbarous and inhuman? Among other reasons which might be mentioned this certainly has its share.

That the whole of the horrrible deed is really concealed from view. Had the deed been constantly perpetrated in the sight of all, as was formerly the case in Smithfield; had the helpless victim to superstition been bound at the stake in the open view of the multitude, as were formerly the victims to Romish bigotry; had the flames been suffered to kindle on her publicly; had the convulsions and agonies of the widow expiring in torments, often in the bloom of youth, been fully witnessed by the aged, the young, the neighbour, the near relative, humanity must have spoken out long ago; reflection must have been awakened in the public mind. At least, parents and relatives must have felt horror while anticipating the agonies which awaited a daughter or beloved sister, the moment sickness, or even accident rendered her a widow; and the voice of nature must have prevailed and abolished a practice so destructive in its anticipation to every relative whose heart was not steeled against all feelings of humanity.

But instead of this the agonies of the dying victim are completely concealed, while her shrieks are drowned in the noise and shouts of the ignorant multitude and the unfeeling ministers of death; and thus the whole is completely hidden from the public view, as though the dreadful deed was perpetrated within the most secluded cloister. The concealment indeed is far more effectual; for in that case, though the shrieks might not assail the ear without, the imagination would unavoidably paint to itself the horror of a daughter, a sister, or even an acquaintance, expiring in the flames, in a manner scarcely less vivid than the real view. But the victim's being thus brought before the multitude in a state which scarcely leaves her the power of reflection, her being hastily led through various ceremonies, and hurried to the pile by those whose countenances wear the appearance of hilarity and cheerfulness, bound to the dead body of her husband, and covered instantly with the fuel, as well as held down by a pressure which renders all resistance totally unavailing, hides all the horrors of death from the sight; while the shouts of the unthinking crowd which began to rend the air the moment the torch is applied to the fatal pile, no less effectually conceal from ear those agonizing shrieks, which it is scarce in nature to refrain at the touch of the flames. Thus completely are the multitude deluded: they think they witness all while they witness nothing; and the unnatural jocularity, which, originating with the actors in this dreadful scene, generally pervades the whole crowd, removes every feeling of pity and gives the whole rather the air of a joyous festival than a funeral scene. The agonies and shrieks and dying groans of the unhappy victim are witnessed by no-one—but by him who is the Avenger of blood. But are these agonies the less real on this account? Is the agony of this tremendous death less felt? Let reason and humanity judge.

...We wish now merely to recount some of the most obvious circumstances which attend it. Among these let us consider for a moment who those are doomed to undergo those agonies, unpitied, because never beheld. They are *the most amiable part of the Hindoo race*! In the most case they are females, possessing some degree of wealth, for the very poor seldom thus devote themselves to death: they are not worth the labour required to work up their minds to a sufficient pitch of delusion. If the term be applicable to any female in the present state of Hindoo society, they are in general persons of education; and whatever be the degree of polish and delicacy which accompany opulence, whatever the ideas included in the superior mode of living; they are in general possessed by those whom this dreadful custom marks as its victims. It follows therefore, as a matter of course, that if among the higher ranks of society in this country there be any delicacy of feeling, it is possessed by these who may be said almost from their birth to be devoted to the flames. And if there be anything to be found of conjugal fidelity, it resides among these, since an extraordinary degree of conjugal affection, either real or ascribed, is made the lure by which these unhappy victims are betrayed to death, the enjoyment for numerous ages of the highest felicity with their deceased husbands being held out as the bait to draw them on till they make the irrevocable declaration that they will commit themselves to the flames. It is probable, therefore, that those who are thus cruelly murdered year by year, are in most cases the best educated, the most amiable and the most virtuous of the Hindoo race.

By whom this crime is perpetrated is worthy of the strictest inquiry. With the victims themselves it can scarcely be said to originate, for a few days previously they are often as void of all desire to destroy themselves as to destroy others; and they are generally averse to the deed till their minds are completely deluded by fallacious representations, and their heads turned with dreams of future happiness, impossible to be realized. But whatever delusions may reign in their minds, without the concurrence of the husband's relatives, it would be perfectly harmless. The deed is constantly encouraged by the relatives of the husband; those of the wife, on the contrary, being generally on the side for which nature pleads; although her own son, if old enough, is obliged to kindle the pile prepared for his mother's destruction. It is, therefore, on the husband's relatives that the fate of every female of respectability and opulence is suspended, however young she may be, the moment her husband dies; and when it is considered that they are bound to her by none of the ties of consanguinity, it will not appear strange if some or all of the following reasons should not preponderate, as to doom to the flames one for whom they can have little or no personal feeling.

The honour of the family: This is supposed to rise in proportion to the number of unhappy victims who can be mentioned as having consigned themselves to the flames. The husband's relatives, of course, claim for themselves a certain amount of credit for having surmounted feelings of affection, which they never possessed, as they generally regard the poor unhappy relict with the same apathy with which they view a log of wood intended for the fuel; while the number of widows in their families devoting themselves to the flames, apparently from love to their husbands, gives rise to the idea that these relatives of theirs, possessed that excellence of character which rendered it impossible to survive their loss. That when the unhappy widow is regarded with the most perfect indifference, this alone should so weigh as to make them prefer her dying to her living, will create no surprise in those who are thoroughly acquainted with the native character.

The wish to get rid of a burden: A widow, though only twelve years of age, can never marry again. If her own relatives, therefore, be unwilling to support her, or not sufficiently opulent, she must live with the surviving relatives of the husband to the end of life. And although her life is far from being a plenteous and affluent one, yet a certain degree of expense is thus entailed on the family, and this possibly for a considerable number of years if she is left in the bloom of youth. The consideration of an expense therefore, though small, yet scarcely terminable in the space of their own lives, added to the trouble and vexation often arising from female relatives living together, who can scarcely be expected to have any affection for each other, may possibly make them wish to rid themselves at once of a heavy burden, when it can be done in a way, which instead of being esteemed dishonourable or any proof of the want of affection, on the contrary, reflects a high degree of lustre on the character of the family. At least, this is a temptation which humanity would not throw in the way of a Hindoo who sets so little value on human life.

This is heightened by another consideration. It has just been observed that these widows, however young, can never marry again. Now while impurity reigns among these relatives of the husband, perhaps in such a degree to attach to itself no kind of disgrace, a deviation from purity of conduct on the part of a widow, would, in the public estimation, fix an indelible stain on the family of the deceased husband. When, therefore, the hazard of this dishonour, through perhaps a long life, is present in minds, in which no natural affection towards a brother's widow is supposed to exist, it will excite little surprise that men who, if report may be credited, in some instances make no scruple of hewing into pieces a wife of their own on a mere suspicion of inconstancy, should, on the death of her husband, decide also on the death of his unhappy relict, who, should she live, instead of contributing to the support or honour of the family, would entail on it a constant burden of expense, and might possibly involve it in disgrace, when her death, while it frees them from all expense and anxiety, tends to heighten in no inconsiderable degree, its reputation.

To this may be added another circumstance which humanity will still more strongly regret. The death of the mother deprives the children of their natural guardian, their tenderest, most faithful and watchful friend, who can never see them injured with apathy, and who is ready to hazard life itself for the sake of preserving to them what is their own. It sometimes happens that a man who is opulent dies and leaves children in a state of mere infancy. That their wealth should never be desired by surviving relatives is what no-one will expect who is acquainted with the history of human nature, and much less than those who are aware with what earnestness one brother among the Hindoos will labour to supplant another, even while living. That in cases of infancy an affectionate mother, who no cunning can elude, and no sum can bribe, should stand in the way of the surviving relatives of her husband, is only what might naturally be expected. Were she removed there would be no-one—at least with her feelings—to call them to account for the expenditure of the yearly revenue of these helpless orphans; nor possibly for the dilapidation of their whole property. The history of orphans, even in Christian countries, shows how dangerous in the hands of presumptive heirs would be the power of removing, under religious pretence, the mother of rich but helpless orphans. All these are, therefore, so many temptations to the destruction of a widow, which through this dreadful practice may be accomplished without the least suspicion being excited of the real views of those interested in her death; and were these suspected, still without that public virtue being excited in the country which would urge one step forward and save the widow from death, and the orphans from oppression and poverty. Whoever considers these circumstances...will cease to wonder that so many widows are encouraged to destroy themselves; particularly as this dreadful practice is not confined to Brahmins, but extends itself to the writer caste and even as low as those who practise the trade of a barber.

Whatever be the delusive ideas which may apparently urge the widow to self-destruction, as the hope of her enjoying endless ages of felicity in company with her husband...there are other considerations which cannot but come still nearer to the mind of the unhappy widow. She cannot but be aware that those who have encouraged her in these fond hopes are either those in whose power she is completely for the rest of her life, or such as are intimate with them; for although the husband's relatives affect to dissuade her from the deed, it cannot be difficult to discern the way in which their minds really lean. From these even the slightest hint that they wish her to die must operate on a widow of delicacy and sensibility like a sentence of death pronounced

by a judge. With what feelings could she commit herself for life
to the mercy of those who had discovered this wish in the slightest degree, and felt in the least disappointed by her refusing to
precipitate herself into the flames, particularly when the laws of
the country provide her with so little relief against any unkindness
or barbarity she might hereafter experience from them? The law
itself indeed insists that while she is never to marry again, she is
also to lay aside everything like ornaments for the rest of her
days, and every sign of cheerfulness; that she is never to make a
full meal and that one day in every week she is to devote wholly
to fasting and grief to the end of her life. In these circumstances
it is almost impossible that any degree of ill-treatment which the
resentment of her husband's disappointed relatives might dispose
them to inflict on her, could interest her neighbours in her suffering so as to procure her redress; particularly when the interior of
a Hindoo house, surrounded as it often is with walls, is nearly as
impervious as an ancient castle, and the female relatives are
scarcely more in the public view than are the unhappy inmates
of its dungeons. In these circumstances therefore, it is not strange,
if at the most distant intimation of this nature from those on whose
kindness depends every future mitigation of her lot...a widow of
sensibility and reflection should feel almost distracted, and prefer
a speedy death to the unknown horrors of her future destiny.

Certain Brahmins perform the ceremonies observed at the funeral pile on which the widow sacrifices herself. These Brahmins
receive even from the most indigent families something on the
widow's actually devoting herself to the flames; and from some
wealthy families, as much as 200 rupees on these occasions.
While then, it is the obvious interest of these Brahmins that the
wife should be induced to destroy herself when the husband dies,
they have access to every family and are acquainted with the
age and circumstances of the various inhabitants, especially those
who are wealthy, that they should constantly recommend this dreadful
practice, and prepare the female mind for the perpetration of
the deed, particularly in the cases where the husband is aged or
sickly, is the natural effect of their caring for their own support.
But these Brahmins, as they are in some cases the family priests,
are in the habit of familiar acquaintance with the husband's

relatives, and have much to expect from them. In what dreadful circumstances then must a helpless female stand, who has for her spiritual adviser on the subject of her living or dying, a man who has every kindness to expect from those who are the presumptive heirs to the property of her infant son, or who may merely dread her depending on them as a burden to the end of life. Nor is it necessary to suppose that Brahmins in forwarding the views of an infirm husband's relatives, and preparing the mind of the wife for self-dstruction, should consider themselves as actual auxiliaries in the murder of a fellow-creature. They must...be supposed to be as much habituated to their employment, from which they derive their gain, as a slave captain formerly was to kidnapping and selling slaves, of whom probably a third died in the middle passage through ill-treatment and want of air. They may possibly regard the act as meritorious rather than cruel, and admire those relatives who wish to raise the reputation of their families through the death of their brother's widow. And in this case even the distant prospect of a large remuneration may urge them so to work on the mind of a simple, artless female, whose age is perhaps under twenty, that at the moment of her husband's death no persuasions shall be needed to make her make the fatal declaration—beyond the insidious dissuasions of her husband's relatives, increasing her desire by affectedly doubting her resolution and really inflaming her vanity. Were the relatives however sincere in this dissuasion, they have it always in their power to prevent the act, as both the preparation of the funeral pile and all the cost and expenses of the widow's destruction devolve wholly on them.

That other feelings than those of unconquerable affection for a husband, often twice or thrice their own age—or than any inspired by a steady belief in those wonderful tales of conjugal felicity to be enjoyed with him for boundless ages influence the minds of the greater part of these unhappy victims, might be shewn by the numerous instances wherein widows have been prevented by accident from burning....

A man of writer caste, at Kona-nugura, about four miles south of Serampore, died (in 1818) leaving two wives, one about thirteen years of age and the other about sixteen. Both of these, in the usual manner, expressed their wish to burn themselves with the body of their deceased husband. The eldest of them being pregnant, however, was advised to delay until after her confinement, and then to burn herself with something belonging to her husband. The youngest, not being prevented, was burnt with the corpse of her husband. The eldest solemnly engaged to burn herself a month after her confinement; till which period she was taken home by her own parents. She at first expressed such displeasure at being thus denied the opportunity of burning herself, as to beat herself severely and possibly accelerate the time of her confinement; but at the expiration of the month after that period, when called upon to fulfil her engagement, she had considered the subject more at leisure, and being at home in the house of her own parents, she positively refused to destroy herself, nor could all the appeals made to her feelings—all the threats and reproaches poured upon her, alter her resolution in the least degree. She was in the house of her own parents and completely independent of her husband's relatives...where she continues to this day.

As this instance is by no means a solitary one, we have little reason to conclude that the desire to destroy themselves is more firmly fixed in the minds of the multitudes besides, than it was in the mind of this young woman: the apparent wish to die, that is thus factitiously produced, is in most instances the mere effect of circumstances created by others; and therefore no more exculpatory of the guilt of deliberate murder, than would be a man's intoxicating another with wine, or any other deleterious drug, so as to deprive him of the power of resistance, that he might secure his destruction. Such then are the circumstances in which the most amiable and virtuous of the Hindoo women are constantly placed; circumstances, as already hinted, by no means confined to the sacred tribe, but extended to the lower castes among the Hindoos, as often as there is credulity enough to render the delusion sufficiently strong to become fatal.

This inhuman practice has not even those pretensions to its being a religious ceremony, which most people have been ready to imagine...it has no foundation in any particular command given in the shastras (as has been shown by Rammohan Roy).... Nor indeed is there anything in the ceremony that marks it as being peculiarly of a religious nature. The woman devotes herself to no deity; her professed object is merely that of rejoining her husband in a state of happiness. It is true that certain Brahmins officiate, and obtain a sum of money on the occasion. But this is not peculiar to this ceremony: in almost every concern of life Brahmins are called in, and there are few which are not to them a source of profit....

It is a well-known fact, that in Bengal at the present time, the Hindoos are far less tenacious of their religious tenets and ceremonies, than in almost any other part of India; that they are far less careful respecting caste, and that the Brahmins in numerous instances are guilty of actions, which according to the strictness of the law regarding caste, would degrade them completely. Yet, the number of widows who are thus put to death scarcely at all decreases. It seems to increase in the vicinity of the metropolis, where the greatest laxness is to be witnessed relative to things wholly religious. How can we account for the vast disparity in the number of these murders perpetrated in Hindoosthan, and in the lower part of Bengal without having recourse to reasons other than religious? But the moment we do recur to other reasons for the continuation of this murderous custom, they present themselves on every side. The want of feeling manifested by the natives to their own countrymen when in danger of death by accident...is known to most Europeans. The venality with which they are charged relative to oaths is not without foundation; yet these must often involve life itself as well as character and property. That they should then be peculiarly tender of the life of a brother's widow is a thing scarcely to be expected. And when we consider the circumstances in which the widow is placed together with that want of regard for human life, which is both the product of their religious system and characteristic of the nation, instead of being surprised that so many widows are every year cruelly destroyed, we shall rather wonder that any escape these fatal lures, when the husband's relatives so evidently encourage the practice.

...With almost as much justice might the slave trade have been regarded with veneration, as a sacred relict of antiquity, handed down from the earliest age; or the practice of killing all prison-

ers taken in war; or that of sacrificing hetacombs of men at the
funeral of a favourite chief; or the conduct of certain banditti in
this country, who, (from time immemorial no doubt) are said to
seize men and immolate them at the shrine of their imagined
deity. It has scarcely enough religious ceremony connected with
it to varnish it over with the name of religion.... Instead of its
being a deed of mere superstition, there is reason to fear that it is
too often the offspring of the meanest self-interest. It has not even
the features of religion. It is not binding on all. It falls only on one
sex, while the deed is perpetrated by the other, which it can
never reach; and of that sex it effects only one description of
persons, and with these it is professedly optional, were it a religious ceremony, however, it would be binding on all.

Notes

[1]   Grant, C., *Observations, on the State of Society among the Asiatic Subjects of Great
       Britain, Particularly with Respect to Morals and on the Means of Improving it,
       Written Chiefly in the Year 1792* (London: House of Commons,1813).

[2]   Ward, William Rev., 'Letter VI, to Miss Hope of Liverpool from the
       Hercules at sea, 31 March 1821', in *Farewell Letters to A Few Friends in
       Britain and America on Returning to Bengal in 1821* (London: Black, Kingsbury,
       Parbury and Allan, 1821).

[3]   'On the Burning of Widows', in *Friend of India*, October 1819.

7

Official Debate

Instruction to Magistrates, 1813, *Parliamentary Papers*[1]

Prior to the prohibition of sati in 1829, British policy was to allow the immolation to take place when performed in accordance with Hindu law. The following is the first set of instructions issued to magistrates on the subject in 1813 and outlines the basic premise of British policy. Further instructions to magistrates were issued on regular basis, updating the circumstances in which the rite was to be allowed or not.

Whereas it has appeared that during the ceremony denominated suttee (at which Hindoo women burn themselves) certain acts have been occasionally committed in direct opposition to the rules laid down in the religious institutes of the Hindoos, by which the practice is authorized and forbidden in particular cases; as for instance, at several places pregnant women and girls not yet arrived at their full age have been burnt alive; and people after having intoxicated women by administering intoxicating substances, have burnt them without their assent, whilst insensible; and inasmuch as this conduct is contrary to the Shasters, and perfectly inconsistent with every principle of humanity, (it appearing from the expositions of Hindu law, delivered by the pundits, that the burning of a woman pregnant or one having a child of tender years, or a girl not yet arrived at full age, is expressly forbidden in the Shasters; and also that intoxicating a woman for the purpose of burning her and the burning of one without her assent or against her will, is highly illegal and contrary to established usage) the police darogahs are hereby accordingly under the sanction of government, strictly enjoined to use the utmost care and make every effort to prevent the forbidden practices above mentioned from taking place within the limits of their thannahs; and they are further required on all occasions, immediately on receiving intelligence that this ceremony is likely to occur, either to proceed themselves to the spot, or send their mohurrir or jemedar, accompanied by a burkunday of Hindoo religion, to learn of the woman who is to be burnt whether she has given her assent and to ascertain the other particulars above mentioned as to her age &c. &c. In the event of the female who is going to be burnt being less than sixteen years of age, or their being any signs of her pregnancy, or on her declaring herself in that situation; or should the people proposing to burn her have intoxicated her, without her assent or against her will (the burning of a woman under any of these circumstances being in direct opposition to what is enjoined in the Shasters and manifestly an act of illegal violence) it will then be their duty to prevent the ceremony, thus forbidden and contrary to established usage, from taking place, and require those prepared to perform it to refrain from so doing; also to explain to them, that in the event of their persisting to commit any act forbidden, they would involve themselves in a crime and become subject to retribution and punishment. But in the case of the woman being of full age, and no other impediment existing, they will nevertheless, remain on the spot, and not allow the most minute particular to escape observation; and in the case of people preparing to burn a woman by compulsion, or after having made her insensible by administering spirituous liquors or narcotic drugs, it will then be their duty to exert themselves in restraining them; and at the same time to let them know that it is not the intention of government to check or forbid any act authorized by the tenets of the religion of the inhabitants of their dominions, or even to require that any express leave or permission be required, previously to the performance of the act of 'suttee;' and the police officers are not to interfere to prevent any such act taking place; and lastly, it will be their duty to transmit immediately, for the information of the magistrate, a full detail of any measures which they may have adopted on this subject; and also, on every occasion, when within the limits of their thannahs, this ceremony of 'suttee' may take place, the same being lawfully conducted, they will insert it in the monthly reports.

Walter Ewer, 1818, *Parliamentary Papers*[2]

Walter Ewer, the Acting Superintendent of Police in the Lower Provinces, was one of many East India Company officials to take up the issue of sati and write to the Government of Bengal on the matter. Ewer solicited opinions on sati from a variety of his colleagues and presented his thoughts to government.

Although the subject of the present address does not properly belong to my department, and although the subject has been taken into consideration, and instructions regarding suttees have been issued to the magistrates by the Nizamat Adalat, under the authority of the government, still I trust that I will be pardoned for intruding my opinions and observations on a matter so important to the interests of humanity.

I shall now proceed to consider the nature of the sacrifice, the expediency of abolishing the practice altogether, and the probable consequences of such proceedings.

I know it is generally supposed that a suttee takes place with the free will and consent of the widow, indeed, that she frequently persists in her intention to burn in spite of the arguments and entreaties of her relations. But I submit that there are many reasons for thinking that such an event as voluntary suttee very rarely occurs; that is that very few widows would think of sacrificing themselves, unless overpowered by force or persuasion, very little of either being sufficient to overcome the physical or mental powers of the majority of Hindu females; and a widow who would turn with natural instinctive horror from the first hint of sharing her husband's pile, will be at length gradually brought to pronounce a reluctant consent; because, distracted by grief at the event, without one friend to advise or protect her, she is little prepared to oppose the surrounding crowd of hungry Brahmins and interested relations, either by argument or by force. Accustomed to look on the former with the highest veneration, and attach implicit belief to all their assertions, she dares not, if she were able to make herself heard, deny the certainty of the various advantages which must attend the sacrifice: that by becoming a suttee she shall remain so many years in heaven, rescue her husband from hell, and purify the family of her father, mother and husband; while, on the other hand, disgrace in this life, and continued transmigration into the body of a female animal, will be the certain consequences of refusal. In this state of confusion a few hours quickly pass, and the widow is burnt before she has time even to think on the subject. Should utter indifference for her husband, and superior sense, enable her to preserve her judgment, and resist the arguments of those around her, it will avail her little—the people will not, on any account, be disappointed of their show; and the entire population of a village will turn out to assist in dragging her to the banks of the river and keeping her on the pile.

Under these circumstances nine out of ten widows are burnt to death. And having described the manner in which these sacrifices are generally performed, I shall now proceed to show that they are more frequently offered to secure the temporal good of the survivors than to ensure the spiritual welfare of the sufferer or her husband.

I have already stated that the widow is scarcely ever a free agent at the performance of a suttee, and therefore, her opinion on the subject can be of no weight, and whether she appear glad or sorry, stupid, composed or distracted, is no manner of proof of her real feelings; her relations, her attendants, and the surrounding crowd, men, women and children, will seem to wear one face of joy and delight; none of the holy exultation which formerly accompanied the departure of a martyr, but all the savage merriment which, in our days, attends a boxing match or bull bait. Nor can it be otherwise among those present: her relations are directly interested in her death; if she had a son, he might perhaps wish to be relieved from the expense of maintaining a mother, and the trouble of listening to her unreasonable advice; if she has none, her husband's male relations will take care that she stand not in their way by claiming his estate for life, which is her legal right. The Brahmins are paid for their services, and are of course interested. The crowd assemble to see a show, which, in their estimation, affords more amusement than any other public exhibition with which they are acquainted; and the sacrifice is completed, because the family is anxious to get rid of an encumbrance and the Brahmins desirous of a feast and a present.

Very properly anxious to avoid all interference with the religious prejudices and customs of the Hindoo, the government has not thought it advisable to prohibit the practice of suttee. But I submit that it has little or no connection with their religion. If the relations chance to bestow a thought of the consequences of the sacrifice, it will be directed to the benefit which will thereby accrue to themselves, in this world or the next. The future happiness of the sufferer and her deceased husband is much too disinterested a consideration to deserve one thought....

...The recommendation [of the Shaster] even is addressed to the widow; and her relations are nowhere told that they are to induce her to become a suttee, either by force or by persuasion. Now it is well known that the education of Hindoo females, of all ranks, precludes the possibility of their having, of themselves any acquaintance whatever with the contents of the Shasters; and consequently, on all subjects connected with them they are compelled to trust implicitly to the guidance of others. These are all...directly interested. It is not very probable that they will state suttee as nothing but a praiseworthy act, left to the discretion of the widow. They will of course represent it as an absolute duty; the neglect of which must be punished by disgrace, both in this world and the next.

...by tolerating sati we are not showing a proper forbearance towards the religious customs or long established prejudices of the Hindoos; but that we are virtually sanctioning the sacrifice of widow, by their relations, which is nowhere enjoined by the Shasters, and which in our own country would carry the penalty of death, and which is only tolerated because of an imposition which has transformed a recommendation into an order which the relations must carry into effect, if she should evince symptoms of disobedience. If the practice were prohibited one voluntary and legal suttee, perhaps, out of 100 murders, will be prevented; and the widow, in consequence, feel miserable for the rest of her life. But I call a voluntary and legal suttee, one in which the widow is fully aware that she is going to perform not a prescribed, but a recommended duty; and I imagine that a case of this nature will very scarcely occur.

...I meet with frequent instances of the interference of government in matters intimately connected with the prejudices of the Hindoos. The repeal of the law prohibiting the capital punishment of Brahmins at Benaras. The laws against infanticide; the rules prohibiting *dhurna*; and the sweeping clause Section 3, Reg. 8, 1799, in which even suttee may be included. And although I am aware that the exposure of infants at Saugor and at other places, and the murder of their female offspring by the *rajkoomars* are neither of them duties either directly enjoined or authorized by the Shasters; yet I submit, that the exposure of infants is in consequence of vows made by the mother, for the purpose of obtaining some favour from the gods; and that fulfilment of such is meritorious in the highest degree. The practice of the rajkoomars is, I have reason to think, but little checked by the enactment above alluded to. It is a custom founded on immemorial usage; and as such, does not require the aid of either religion or law to give it support. The practice of the widows of the jogees is not sanctioned by the shaster; yet they will undoubtedly continue to prefer burying to burning because it is the custom of their caste; and we might as well attempt to direct the mode of disposing of the husband's corpse, as prescribe rules for the conduct of the widow. I mention these facts not to suggest that prohibition would be ineffectual, but to show that interference has occurred before without exciting opposition, and that though it may be argued that this is because they are not strictly authorized by the Shasters, but I would suggest that very few actually know this and those that do must consider custom paramount as they have continued in them.

William Bentinck, 'Minute on Sati'[3]

In this famous Minute, Lord William Bentinck sets out the case for and against intervening on the sati issue and explains his reasons for deciding to outlaw the rite.

8 November 1829

Whether the question be to continue or to discontinue the practice of suttee, the decision is equally surrounded by an awful responsibility. To consent to the consignment, year after year of hundreds of innocent victims to a cruel and untimely end, when the power exists of preventing it, is a predicament which no conscience can contemplate without horror. But on the other hand, if heretofore received opinions are to be considered of any value, to put to hazard, by a contrary course, the very safety of the British empire in India, and to extinguish at once all hopes of those great improvements affecting the condition, not of hundreds and thousands, but of millions, which can only be expected from the continuance of our supremacy, is an alternative which, even in the light of humanity itself, may be considered as a still greater evil. It is upon this first and highest consideration alone, the good of mankind, that the tolerance of this inhuman and impious rite can, in my opinion, be justified on the part of the government of a civilized nation. While the solution of this question is appalling from the unparalleled magnitude of its possible results, the considerations belonging to it are such as to make even the stoutest mind distrust its decision. On the one side, religion, humanity under the most appalling form, as well as vanity and ambition, in short all the most powerful influences over the human heart, are arrayed to bias and mislead the judgement. On the other side, the sanction of countless ages, the example of all the Mussulman conquerors, the unanimous concurrence in the same policy of our own most able rulers, together with the universal veneration of the people, seem authoritatively to forbid, both to feeling and to reason, any interference on the exercise of their natural prerogative. In venturing to be the first to deviate from this practice, it becomes me to show, that nothing has been yielded to feeling, but that reason, and reason alone, has governed the decision. So far indeed from presuming to condemn the conduct of my predecessors, I am ready to say, that in the circumstances, I should have acted as they have done. So far from being chargeable with political rashness, as this departure from an established policy might infer, I hope to be able so completely to prove the safety of the measure, as even to render unnecessary any calculation of the degree of risk, which for the attainment of so great a benefit, might wisely and justly be incurred. So far also from being the sole champion of a great and dangerous innovation, I shall be able to prove that the vast preponderance of present authority has long been in favour of abolition. Past experience indeed ought to prevent me, above all men, from coming lightly to so positive a conclusion. When Governor of Madras, I saw, in the mutiny of Vellore, the dreadful consequences of a supposed violation of religious customs upon the minds of the native population and soldiery: I cannot forget that I was then the innocent victim of that unfortunate catastrophe, and I might reasonably dread, when the responsibility would justly attach to *me* in the event of a failure, a recurrence of the same fate. Prudence and self-interest would counsel me to tread in the footsteps of my predecessors. But in a case of such momentous importance to humanity and civilization, that man must be reckless of all his present or future happiness who could listen to the dictates of so wicked and selfish a policy. With the firm undoubting conviction entertained upon this question, I should be guilty of little short of the crime of multiplied murder, if I could hesitate in the performance of this solemn obligation. I have been already stung with this feeling. Every day's delays adds a victim to the dreadful list, which might perhaps have been prevented by a more early submission of the present question. But during the whole of the present year, much public agitation has been excited, and when discontent is abroad, when exaggerations of all kinds are busily circulated, and when the native army have been under a degree of alarm, lest their allowances should suffer with that of their European officers, it would have been unwise to have given a handle to artful and designing enemies to disturb the public peace. The recent measures of government for protecting the interests of the sepoys against the late reduction of companies, will have removed all apprehension of the intentions of government; and the consideration of this circumstance having been the sole cause of hesitation on my part, I will now proceed, praying the blessing of God upon our counsels, to state the grounds upon which my opinion has been formed.

We have now before us two reports of Nizamat Adalat with statements of suttees in 1827 and 1828, exhibiting a decrease of fifty-four in the latter year as compared with 1827, and a still greater proportion as compared with former years. If this diminution could be ascribed to any change of opinion upon the question, produced by the progress of education or civilization, the fact would be most satisfactory; and to disturb this sure though slow process of self-correction would be most impolitic and unwise. But I think it may be safely affirmed; that though in Calcutta truth may be said to have made a considerable advance among the higher orders; yet in respect to the population at large, no change whatever has taken place, and that from these causes at least no hope of the abandonment of the rite can be rationally entertained. The decrease, if it be real, may be the result of less sickly seasons, as the increase in 1824 and 1825 was of greater prevalence of cholera. But it is probably in a greater measure due to the more open discouragement of the practice given by the greater part of the European functionaries in the latter years; the effect of which would be to produce corresponding activity in the police officers, by which either the number would be really diminished, or would be made to appear so in the returns.

It seems to be the very general opinion that our interference has hitherto done more harm than good, by lending a sort of sanction to the ceremony, while it has undoubtedly tended to cripple the efforts of magistrates and others to prevent the practice.

I think it will clearly appear, from a perusal of the documents annexed to this minute, and from the facts which I shall have to adduce, that the passive submission of the people to the influence and power beyond the law, which in fact and practically may be and is often exercised without opposition by every public officer, is so great, that the suppression of the rite would be completely effected by a tacit sanction alone on the part of government. This mode of extinguishing it has been recommended by many of those whose advice has been asked, and no doubt this, in several respects might be a preferable course, as being equally effectual, while more silent, not exciting the alarm which might possibly come from a public enactment, and from which, in case of failure, it would be easy to retreat with less inconvenience and without any compromise of character. But this course is clearly not open to government, bound by parliament to rule by law, and not by their good pleasure. Under the present position of the British empire moreover, it may be fairly doubted, if any such underhand proceeding would be really good policy. When we had power-ful neighbours and had greater reason to doubt our own security, expediency might recommend an indirect and more cautious proceeding, but now that we are supreme, my opinion is decid-edly in favour of an open, avowed and general prohibition, resting altogether upon the moral goodness of the act, and our power to enforce it, and so decided is my feeling against any half mea-sure, that were I not convinced of the safety of total abolition, I certainly should have advised the cessation of all interference.

Of all those who have given their advice against the abolition of the rite, and have described the ill-effects likely to ensue from it, there is no one to whom I am disposed to pay greater deference than Mr Horace Wilson. I purposely select his opinion, because independently of his vast knowledge of oriental literature, it has fallen to his lot, as secretary to the Hindu College, and possessing the general esteem both of the parents and of the youth, to have more confidential intercourse with natives of all classes, than any man in India. While his opportunity of obtaining information has been great beyond all others, his talents and judgement enable him to form a just estimate of its value. I shall state the most forc-ible of his reasons, and how far I do and do not agree with him.

1st. Mr Wilson considered it to be a dangerous evasion of the real difficulties, to attempt to prove that suttees are not 'essen-tially a part of the Hindu religion'. I entirely agree in this opinion. The question is not what the rite is but what it is supposed to be; and I have no doubt that the conscientious belief of every order of Hindus, with few exceptions, regard it as sacred.

2nd. Mr Wilson thinks that the attempt to put down the practice will inspire extensive dissatisfaction. I agree also in this opinion. He thinks that success will only be partial, which I doubt. He does not imagine that the promulgated prohibition will lead to any immediate and overt act of insubordination, but that affrays and much agitation of the public mind must ensue. But he con-ceives, that, if once they suspect that it is the intention of the British government to abandon this hitherto inviolate principle of allowing the most complete toleration in matters of religion, that there will arise, in the minds of all, so deep a distrust of our ulterior designs, that they will no longer be tractable to any arrangement

intended for their improvement and that the principles of morality as well as of a more virtuous and exalted rule of action, now
actively inculcated by European education and knowledge, will
receive a fatal check. I must acknowledge that a similar opinion
as to the probable excitation of a deep distrust of our future intentions was mentioned to me in a conversation by that enlightened native, Rammohan Roy, a warm advocate for the abolition
of suttees, and of all other superstitions and corruptions, engrafted
on the Hindu religion, which he considers originally to have been a
pure deism. It was his opinion that the practice might be suppressed, quietly and unobservedly, by increasing the difficulties,
and by the indirect agency of the police. He apprehended that
any public enactment would give rise to general apprehension,
that the reasoning would be, 'While the English were contending
for power, they deemed it polite to allow universal toleration, and
to respect our religion; but having obtained the supremacy, their
first act is a violation of their professions, and the next will probably be, like the Mahomedan conquerors, to force upon us their
own religion'.

Admitting, as I am always disposed to do, that much truth is
contained in these remarks, but not at all assenting to the conclusions which though not described, bear the most unfavourable
import, I shall now enquire into the evil and the extent of danger
which may practically result from this measure.

It must first be observed, that of the 463 suttees occurring in
the whole of the presidency of Fort William, 420 took place in
Bengal, Bihar and Orissa, or what are termed the lower provinces, and of these latter, 287 in the Calcutta division alone.

It might be very difficult to make a stranger to India understand,
much less believe, that in a population of so many millions of
people, as the Calcutta division includes, and the same may be
said of all the lower provinces, so great is the want of courage
and of vigour of character, and such the habitual submission of
centuries, that insurrection or hostile opposition to the will of the
ruling power may be affirmed to be an impossible danger. I speak
of the population taken separately from the army, and I may add
for the information of the stranger, and also in support of my
assertion, that few of the natives of the lower provinces are to be
found in our military ranks. I therefore, at once deny the danger

in toto, in reference to this part of our territories, where the practice principally obtains. If, however, security were wanting against extensive popular tumult or revolution, I should say that the permanent settlement, which though a failure in many other respects and in its most important essentials, has this great advantage at least, of having created a vast body of rich landed proprietors, deeply interested in the continuance of the British dominion, and having complete command over the mass of the people, and, in respect to the apprehension of ulterior views, I cannot believe that it could last but for the moment. The same large proprietary body, connected for the most part with Calcutta, can have no fears of the kind, and through their interpretation of our intentions, and that of their numerous dependants, and agents, the public mind could not long remain in a state of deception.

Were the scene of this sad destruction of human life laid in the upper instead of the lower provinces, in the midst of a bold and manly people, I might speak with less confidence upon the question of safety. In these provinces the suttees amount to forty-three only—upon a population of nearly twenty million. It cannot be expected that any general feeling, where combination of any kind is so unusual, could be excited in defence of a rite, in which so few participate, a rite also notoriously made too often subservient to views of personal interest on the part of the other members of the family.

It is stated by Mr Wilson that interference with infanticide and the capital punishment of Brahmins offer a fallacious analogy with the prohibition now proposed. The distinction is perceptible to my judgement. The former practice, though confined to particular families, is probably viewed as a religious custom; and as for the latter, the necessity of the enactment proves the general existence of the exception, and it is impossible to conceive a more direct and open violation of the shastras, or one more at variance with the general feelings of the Hindu population. To this day, in all Hindu states, the life of Brahmins is, I believe, still held sacred.

But I have taken up too much time in giving my own opinions, when those of the greatest experience, and the highest official authority are upon our records. In the report of the Nizamat Adalat

for 1828, four out of five of the judges recommended to the Governor-General in Council the immediate abolition of the practice, and attest to its safety. The fifth judge, though not opposed
to the opinions of the rest of the bench, did not feel then prepared to give his entire assent. In the report of this year, the
measure has come up with the unanimous recommendation of
the court. The two superintendents of police for the upper and
lower provinces, Mr Walter Ewer, and Mr Charles Barwell, have
in the strongest terms expressed their opinion that the suppression might be effected without the least danger. The former officer
has urged the measure upon the attention of government in the
most forcible manner. No documents exist to shew the opinions
or the public functionaries in the interior, but I am informed that
nine-tenths are in favour of the abolition.

How again are these opinions supported by practical experience?

Within the limits of the Supreme Court at Calcutta, not a suttee
has taken place since the time of Sir John Anstruther.

In the Delhi territory, Sir Charles Metcalfe never permitted a
suttee to be performed.

In Jessore, one of the districts of the Calcutta division in 1824
there were thirty suttees, in 1825—sixteen, in 1826—three, in 1827
and 1828 there were none. To no other cause can this be assigned,
than to a power beyond the law, exercised by the acting magistrate, against which, however, no public remonstrance was made.
Mr Pigou has been since appointed to Cuttack, and has pursued
the same strong interference as in Jessore, but his course, although
most humane, was properly arrested, as being illegal, by the
commissioners. Though the case of Jessore is perhaps one of the
strongest examples of efficacious and unopposed interposition, I
really believe that there are few districts in which the same arbitrary
power is not exercised to prevent the practice. In the last week,
in the report of the acting commissioner, Mr Smith, he states that
in Gazipur in the last year, sixteen, and in the preceding years
seven suttees had been prevented by the persuasions, or rather it
should be said by the *threats* of the police.

Innumerable cases of the same kind might be obtained from
the public records.

It is stated in the letter of the collector of Gaya, Mr Trotter,
but upon what authority I have omitted to enquire, that the Peishwa

(I presume he means the ex-peishwa Baji Rao) would not allow the rite to be performed, and that in Tanjore it is equally interdicted. These facts, if true, would be positive proofs at least that no unanimity exists among the Hindus upon the point of religious obligations. Having made enquiries also how far suttees are permitted in the European foreign settlements, I find, from Dr Carey, that at Chinsurah no such sacrifices had ever been permitted by the Dutch government; that within the limits of Chandernagore itself they were also prevented, but allowed to be performed in the British territories. The Danish government of Serampore has not forbidden the rite in conformity to the example of the British government.

It is a very important fact, that though representations have been made by the disappointed party to superior authority, it does not appear that a single instance of direct opposition to the execution of the prohibitory orders of our civil functionaries has ever occurred. How then can it be reasonably feared that to the government itself, from whom all authority is derived, and whose power is now universally considered to be irresistible, anything bearing the semblance of resistance can be manifested. Mr Wilson also is of the opinion that no immediate overt act of insubordination would follow the publication of the edict. The regulations of government may be evaded, the police may be corrupted, but even here the price paid as hush money will operate as a penalty indirectly forwarding the objects of government.

I venture then to think it completely proved that, from the native population, nothing of extensive combination or even of partial opposition may be expected from the abolition.

It is, however, a very different and much more important question, how far the feelings of the native army might take alarm, how far the rite may be in general observance by them, and whether as in the case of Vellore, designing persons might not make use of the circumstance either for the purpose of immediate revolt, or of sowing the seeds of permanent disaffection. Reflecting upon the vast disproportion of numbers between our native and European troops, it was obvious that there might be, in any general combination of the former, the greatest danger to the state, and it became necessary therefore, to use every precaution to ascertain the impression likely to be made upon the minds of the native soldiery.

Before I detail to council the means I have taken to satisfy my mind upon this very important branch of the enquiry, I shall beg leave to advert to the name of Lord Hastings. It is impossible but that to this most humane, benevolent and enlightened mind, this practice must have been often the subject of deep and anxious meditation. It was consequently a circumstance of ill omen and severe disappointment not to have found, upon the records, the valuable advice and direction of his long experience and wisdom. It is true that during the greater part of his administration, he was engaged in war, when the introduction of such a measure would have been highly injudicious. To his successor, Lord Amherst, also the same obstacle was opposed. I am, however, fortunate in possessing a letter from Lord Hastings to a friend in England upon suttees, and from the following extract, dated 21 November 1825, I am induced to believe that, had he remained in India, this practice would long since have been suppressed:

The subject which you wish to discuss is one which must interest one's feeling most deeply; but it is also one of extreme nicety. When I mention that in one of the years during my administration of government in India, above eight hundred widows sacrificed themselves within the provinces comprised in the presidency of Bengal, to which number I very much suspect, that very many not notified to the magistrates should be added, I will hope to have credit for being acutely sensible to such an outrage against humanity. At the same time, I was aware how much danger might attend the endeavouring to suppress, forcibly, a practice so rooted in the religious belief of the natives. No men of low caste are admitted into the ranks of the Bengal army. Therefore, the whole of that formidable body must be regarded as blindly partial to a custom which they consider equally referable to family honour and to points of faith. To attempt the extinction of the horrid superstition, without being supported in the procedure by a real concurrence on the part of the army, would be distinctly perilous. I have no scruple to say, that I did believe, I could have carried with me the assent of the army towards such an object. That persuasion, however, arose from circumstances which gave me peculiar influence over the native troops.

Lord Hastings left India in 1823. It is quite certain that the government of that time were much more strongly impressed with the risk of the undertaking, than is now generally felt. It would have been fortunate could this measure have proceeded under the auspices of that distinguished nobleman, and that the state might have had the benefit of the influence which undoubtedly he possessed, in a peculiar degree, over the native troops. Since that period, however, six years have elapsed. Within the territories all has been peaceful and prosperous, while without, Ava and Bharatpur, to whom alone a strange sort of consequence was ascribed by public opinion, have been made to acknowledge our supremacy. In this interval, experience has enlarged our knowledge, and has given us surer data upon which to distinguish truth from illusion, and to ascertain the real circumstances of our position and power. It is upon these that the concurring opinion of the officers of the civil and military services at large having been founded, is entitled to our utmost confidence.

I have the honour to lay before council the copy of a circular addressed to forty-nine officers, pointed out to me by the secretary to government in the military department, as being from their judgement and experience the best enabled to appreciate the effect of the proposed measure upon the native army, together with their answers. For more easy reference, an abstract of each answer is annexed in a separate paper and classed with those to the same purport.

It appears—first, that of those whose opinions are directly adverse to all interference whatever with the practice, the number is only *five*. Secondly, of those who are favourable to abolition, but averse to absolute and direct prohibition under the authority of the government, the number is *twelve*. Thirdly, of those who are favourable to abolition, to be effected by the indirect interference of magistrates and other public officers, the number is *eight*. Fourthly, of those who advocate the total, immediate and public suppression of the practice, the number is *twenty-eight*.

It will be observed also, of those who are against an open and direct prohibition, few entertain any fear of immediate danger. They refer to a distant and undefined evil. I can conceive the possibility of the expression of dissatisfaction and anger being immediately manifested upon this supposed attack on their religious usages; but the distant danger seems to me altogether groundless, provided that perfect respect continues to be paid to all their innocent rites and ceremonies, and provided also, that a kind and considerate regard be continued to their worldly interests and comforts.

I trust, therefore, that the council will agree with me in the satisfactory nature of this statement, and that they will partake in the perfect confidence which it has given me of expediency and safety of the abolition.

In the answer of one of the military officers, Lieutenant-Colonel Todd, he has recommended that the tax on pilgrims should be simultaneously given up, for the purpose of affording an undoubted proof of our disinterestedness and of our desire to remove every obnoxious obstacle to the gratification of their religious duties. A very considerable revenue is raised from this head; but if it were to be the price of satisfaction and confidence to the Hindus, and of the removal of all distrust of our present and future intentions, the sacrifice might be a measure of good policy. The objections that must be entertained by all to the principle of the tax, which in England has latterly excited very great reprobation, formed an additional motive for the enquiry. I enclose the copy of a circular letter addressed to different individuals at present in charge of the districts where the tax is collected, or who had opportunities from their local knowledge of forming a judgement upon a review of the whole, my conviction is that, in connection with the present measure, it is inexpedient to repeal the tax. It is a subject upon which I shall not neglect to bestow more attention than I have been able to do. An abstract of these opinions is annexed to this minute.

I have now to submit for the consideration of council the draft of a regulation enacting the abolition of suttees. It is accompanied by a paper containing the remarks and suggestions of the judges of the Nizamat Adalat. In this paper is repeated the unanimous opinion of the court in favour of the proposed measure. The suggestions of the Nizamat Adalat are, in some measure, at variance with a principal object I had in view of preventing collision between the parties to the suttee and the officers of police. It is only in the previous processes or during the actual performance of the rite, when the feelings of all may be more or less roused to a high degree of excitement, that I apprehend the possibility of affray, or of acts of violence, through an indiscreet and injudicious exercise of authority. It seemed to me prudent, therefore, that the police in the first instance should warn and advise, but not forcibly prohibit, and if the suttee, in defiance of this notice, were performed, that a report should be made to the magistrate, who would summon the parties and proceed as in any other case of crime. The sadar court appears to think these precautions unnecessary, and I hope they may be so, but, in the beginning, we cannot, I think, proceed with too much circumspection. Upon the same principle, in order to guard against too hasty or severe a sentence, emanating from extreme zeal on the part of the local judge, I have proposed that the case should only be cognizable by the commissioner of circuit. These are, however, questions which I should wish to see discussed in council. The other recommendations of the court are well worthy of our adoption.

I have now brought this paper to a close, and I trust I have redeemed my pledge of not allowing, in the consideration of this question, passion or feeling to have any part. I trust it will appear that due weight has been given to all difficulties and objections; that facts have been stated with truth and impartiality; that the conclusion to which I have come is completely borne out, both by reason and authority. It may be justly asserted that the government, in this act, will only be following, not preceding the tide of public opinion long flowing in this direction; and when we have taken into consideration the experience and wisdom of that highest public tribunal, the Nizamat Adalat, who in unison with our wisest and ablest public functionaries, have been, year after year, almost soliciting the government to pass this act, the moral and political responsibility of not abolishing this practice far surpasses in my judgement that of the opposite course.

But discarding, as I have done, every inviting appeal from sympathy and humanity, and having given my verdict, I may now be permitted to express my anxious feelings with which I desire the success of this measure.

The first and primary object of my heart is the benefit of the Hindus. I know nothing so important to the improvement of their future conditions, as the establishment of a purer morality, whatever their belief, and a more just conception of the will of God. The first step to this better understanding will be dissociation of religious belief and practice from blood and murder. They will then, when no longer under this brutalizing excitement, view with more calmness, acknowledged truths. They will see that there can be no inconsistency in the ways of providence, that to the command received as divine by all races of men, 'No innocent blood shall be spilt', there can be no exception, and when they shall have been convinced of the error of this first and most criminal of their customs, may it not be hoped, that others which stand in the way of their improvement may likewise pass away, and that [with] this emancipation from those chains and shackles upon their minds and actions, they may no longer continue as they have done, the slaves of every foreign conqueror, but that they may assume their just places among the great families of mankind. I disavow in these remarks or in this measure any view whatever to conversion to our own faith. I write and feel as a legislator for the Hindus, and as I believe many enlightened Hindu think and feel.

Descending from these higher considerations, it cannot be a dishonest ambition that the government of which I form a part, should have the credit of an act, which is to wash out a foul stain upon British rule, and to stay the sacrifice of humanity and justice to a doubtful expediency; and finally, as a branch of the general administration of the empire, I may be permitted to feel deeply anxious, that our course shall be in accordance with the noble example set to us by the British government at home and that the adaptation, where practicable, to the circumstances of this vast Indian population, of the same enlightened principles, may promote here as well as there, the general prosperity, and may exalt the character of our nation.

Regulation against Sati

In December 1829, the British, led by Lord William Bentinck, finally decided to outlaw sati in their territories. The following is the text of the regulation by which sati was prohibited.

REGULATION XVII, AD 1829 OF THE BENGAL CODE (4 DECEMBER 1929)

A regulation for declaring the practice of suttee, or of burning or burying alive the widows of Hindus, illegal, and punishable by the criminal courts. Passed by the Governor-General in Council on the 4th December 1829, corresponding with the 20th Aughun 1236 Bengal era; the 23rd Aughun 1237 Fasli; the 21st Aughun 1237 Vilayati; the 8th Aughun 1886 Samvat; and the 6th Jamadi-us-Sani 1245 Hegira.

1. The practice of suttee, or of burning or burying alive the widows of Hindus, is revolting to the feelings of human nature; it is nowhere enjoined by the religion of the Hindus as an imperative duty; on the contrary, a life of purity and retirement on the part of the widow is more especially and preferably inculcated, and by a vast majority of that people throughout India the practice is not kept up, nor observed: in some extensive districts it does not exist; in those in which it has been most frequent it is notorious that in many instances acts of atrocity have been perpetrated which have been shocking to the Hindus themselves, and in their eyes unlawful and wicked. The measures hitherto adopted to discourage and prevent such acts have failed of success, and the Governor-General in Council is deeply impressed with the conviction that the abuses in question cannot be effectually put an end to without abolishing the practice altogether. Actuated by these considerations Governor-General in Council, without intending to depart from one of the first and most important principles of the system of British government in India, that all classes of the people be secure in the observance of their religious usages, so long as that system can be adhered to without violation of the paramount dictates of justice and humanity, has deemed it right to establish the following rules, which are hereby enacted to be in force from the time of their promulgation throughout the territories immediately subject to the presidency of Fort William.

2. The practice of suttee, or of burning or burying alive the widows of Hindus, is hereby declared illegal, and punishable by the criminal courts.

3. First. All zamindars, taluqdars, or other proprietors of land, whether malguzari or lakhiraj; all sadar farmers and under-renters of land of every description; all dependent taluqdars; all naibs and other local agents; all native officers employed in the collection of the revenue and rents of land on the part of government, or the court of wards; and all munduls or other headmen of villages are hereby declared especially accountable for the immediate

communication to the officers of the nearest police station of any intended sacrifice of the nature described in the foregoing section; and any zamindar, or other description of persons above noticed, to whom such responsibility is declared to attach, who may be convicted of wilfully neglecting or delaying to furnish the information above required, shall be liable to be fined by the magistrate or joint magistrate in any sum not exceeding two hundred rupees, and in default of payment to be confined for any period of imprisonment not exceeding—months.

Secondly. Immediately on receiving intelligence that the sacrifice declared illegal by this regulation is likely to occur, the police darogha shall either repair in person to the spot, or depute his mohurrir or jamadar, accompanied by one or more burkundazes of the Hindu religion, and it shall be the duty of the police officers to announce to the persons assembled for the performance of the ceremony, that it is illegal; and to endeavour to prevail on them to disperse, explaining to them that in the event of their persisting in it they will involve themselves in a crime, and become subject to punishment by the criminal courts. Should the parties assembled proceed in defiance of these remonstrances to carry the ceremony into effect, it shall be the duty of the police officers to use all lawful means in their power to prevent the sacrifice from taking place, and to apprehend the principal persons aiding and abetting in the performance of it, and in the event of the police officers being unable to apprehend them, they shall endeavour to ascertain their names and places of abode, and shall immediately communicate the whole of the particulars to the magistrate or joint magistrate for his orders.

Thirdly. Should intelligence of a sacrifice have been carried into effect before their arrival at the spot, they will nevertheless institute a full enquiry into the circumstances of the case, in like manner as on all other occasions of unnatural death, and report them for the information and orders of the magistrate or joint magistrate, to whom they may be subordinate.

4. First. On the receipt of the reports required to be made by the police daroghas, under the provisions of the foregoing section, the magistrate or joint magistrate of the jurisdiction in which the sacrifice may have taken place, shall enquire into the circumstances

of the case, and shall adopt the necessary measures for bringing the parties concerned in promoting it to trial before the court of circuit.

Secondly. It is hereby declared, that after the promulgation of this regulation all persons convicted of aiding and abetting in the sacrifice of a Hindu widow, by burning or burying her alive, whether the sacrifice be voluntary on her part or not, shall be deemed guilty of culpable homicide, and shall be liable to punishment by fine or by both fine and imprisonment, at the discretion of the court of circuit, according to the nature and circumstances of the case, and the degree of guilt established against the offender; nor shall it be held to be any plea of justification that he or she was desired by the party sacrificed to assist in putting her to death.

Thirdly. Persons committed to take their trial before the court of circuit for the offence above mentioned shall be admitted to bail or not, at the discretion of the magistrate or joint magistrate, subject to the general rules in force in regard to the admission of bail.

5. It is further deemed necessary to declare, that nothing contained in this regulation shall be construed to preclude the court of Nizamat Adalat from passing sentence of death on persons convicted of using violence or compulsion, or of having assisted in burning or burying alive a Hindu widow while labouring under a state of intoxication, or stupefaction, or other cause impeding the exercise of free will, when, from the aggravated nature of the offence, proved against the prisoner, the court may see no circumstances to render him or her a proper object of mercy.

Notes

1   Instructions to be issued by magistrates to the police daroghas, Extract Bengal Judicial Consultations, 17 April 1813, in *Parliamentary Papers*, vol. 18, 1821 (749), Papers relating to East Indian Affairs: viz., Hindoo Widows and Voluntary Immolations.

2   Acting Superintendent of Police in the Lower Provinces, W. Ewer, to W.B. Bayley, Secretary to the Government in the Judicial Department, 18 November 1818, in *Parliamentary Papers*, vol. 18, 1821 (749), Papers relating to East Indian Affairs: viz, Hindoo Widows and Voluntary Immolations.

3   Bentinck, W., 'Minute on Sati', in *Speeches and Documents on Indian Policy 1750–1921*, vol.1 (London: Oxford University Press, 1922).

8

Indian Opinions

Raja Rammohan Roy, 'On Concremation'[1]

In the second of two very famous and influential pamphlets, Raja Rammohan Roy asserted that sati was not enjoined by the Shastras. Roy is supposed to have been moved in his campaign against sati by his own experience at the immolation of his sister-in-law. His argument against the rite is put forward in the form of a dialogue between a supporter and an opponent of the custom.

ON CONCREMATION

A Second Conference Between An Advocate And An Opponent Of That Practice

Advocate. Under the title of Vidhayuk,[2] or Preceptor, I have offered an answer to your former arguments. That, no doubt, you have attentively perused. I now expect your reply.

Opponent. I have well considered the answer that, after the lapse of nearly twelve months, you have offered. Such parts of your answer as consist merely of a repetition of passages already quoted by us, require no further observations now. But as to what you have advanced in opposition to our arguments and to the Shastrus, you will be pleased to attend to my reply. In the first place, at the bottom of your 4th page you have given a particular interpretation to the following words of Vishnoo, the lawgiver: 'After the death of her husband a woman shall become an ascetic, or ascend the funeral pile,' implying that either alternative is optional. To this, you say, eight objections are found in the Shastrus, therefore one of the alternatives must be preferred: that is to say, the woman who is unable to ascend the flaming pile shall live as an ascetic. This you maintain is the true interpretation; and in proof you have cited the words of the *Skundu Poran* and of Ungira. I answer: In every country all persons observe this rule, that meanings are to be inferred from the words used. In this instance the text of Vishnoo is comprised in five words: *Mrite,* on death; *bhurturi,* of a husband; *bruhmuchuryum,* asceticism; *tudunwarohunum,* ascending his pile; *va,* or. That is, 'on the death of a husband, his widow should become an ascetic, or ascend his pile.' It appears, therefore, from asceticism being mentioned first in order, that this is the most pious conduct for a widow to follow. But your interpretation, that this alternative is only left for widows who are unable to ascend the flaming pile, can by no means be deduced from the words of the text; nor have any of the expounders of the Shastrus so expressed themselves.

For instance, the author of the *Metakshura,* whose authority is always to be revered, and whose words you have yourself quoted as authority in p. 27, has thus decided on the subject of Concremation: 'The widow who is not desirous of final beatitude, but who wishes only for a limited term of a small degree of future fruition, is authorized to accompany her husband.'

The Smartu Bhuttacharjyu (Rhughoo Nundun, the modern law commentator of Bengal) limited the words of Ungira, that 'besides Concremation there is no other pious course for a widow', by the authority of the foregoing text of Vishnoo; and authorized the alternative of a widow living as an ascetic, or dying with her husband; explaining the words of Ungira as conveying merely the exaggerated praise of Concremation.

Secondly, from the time that Shastrus have been written in Sungskrit, no author or man of learning has ever asserted, as you have done, that the person who, desirous of the enjoyments of heaven, is unable to perform the rites leading to fruition, may devote himself to the attainment of final beatitude. On the contrary, the Shastrus uniformly declare that those who are unable to pursue final beatitude, may perform rites, but without desire; and persons of the basest minds, who do not desire eternal beatitude, may even perform rites for the sake of their fruits.

As Vusishthu declares; 'The person who does not exert himself to acquire that knowledge of God which leads to final absorption, may perform ceremonies without expectation of reward.'

'To encourage and improve those ignorant persons, who, looking only to pleasure, cannot distinguish betwixt what is God and not God, the Srooti has promised rewards.'

Bhuguvud Geeta:

'If you are unable to acquire by degrees divine knowledge, be diligent in performing works with a view to please me, that by such works you may acquire a better state. If you are unable even to perform rites solely for my sake, then, controlling your senses, endeavour to perform rites without the desire of fruition.'

Therefore, to give the preference to self-immolation, or to the destruction of others, for the sake of future reward, over asceticism, which gives a prospect of eternal beatitude, is to treat with contempt the authorities of the *Veds,* the *Vedani,* and other *Durshuns,* as well as of the *Bhuguvud Geeta,* and many others. As the *Ved* says: 'Knowledge and rites both offer themselves to man; but he who is possessed of wisdom, taking their respective natures into serious consideration, distinguishes one from the other, and chooses faith, despising fruition; while a fool, for the sake of advantage and enjoyment, accepts the offer of rites.'

Without entirely rejecting the authority of the *Geeta,* the essence of all Shastrus, no one can praise rites performed for the sake of fruition, nor recommend them to others; for nearly half of the *Bhuguvud Geeta* is filled with the dispraise of such works, and with the praise of works performed without desire of fruition. A few of those passages have been quoted in the former conference, and a few others are here given.

'Works performed, except for the sake of God, only entangle the soul. Therefore, O Urjoon, forsaking desire, perform works with the view to please God.'

'The person who performs works without desire of fruition, directing his mind to God, obtains eternal rest. And the person who is devoted to fruition, and performs works with desire, he is indeed inextricably involved.'

'Oh, Urjoon, rites performed for the sake of fruition are degraded far below works done without desire, which lead to the acquisition of the knowledge of God. Therefore perform thou works without desire of fruition, with the view of acquiring divine knowledge. Those who perform works for the sake of fruition are most debased.'

'It is my firm opinion, that works are to be performed, forsaking their consequences, and the prospect of their fruits.'

The Geeta is not a rare work, and you are not unacquainted with it. Why then do you constantly mislead women, unacquainted with the Shastrus, to follow a debased path, by holding out to them as temptations the pleasures of futurity, in defiance of all the Shastrus, and merely to please the ignorant?

You have said, that eight objections are to be found in the Shastrus to the optional alternative deduced from the works of Vishnoo. To this I reply, Firstly, to remove an imaginary difficulty, a violation of the obvious interpretation of words, whose meaning is direct and consistent, is altogether inadmissible. Secondly, former commentators, finding no such objection to the interpretation given to the words of Vishnoo, as allowing the optional alternative of asceticism or concremation, have given the preference to asceticism. The author of the *Metakshura,* quoting this text of Vishnoo in treating of Concremation, makes no allusion to such an objection, but finally declares in favour of asceticism.

Thirdly, even allowing an optional alternative to be liable to the eight objections, former authors have on many occasions admitted such an alternative. For example:—

Srooti. 'Oblations are to be made of wheat or of barley.' But the meaning of this is not, according to your mode of interpretation, 'That if it cannot be made of barley, an offering is to be made of wheat.'

'Burnt offering is to be made at sunrise or before sunrise.' In this instance your mode of explanation may be applied; but no authors have ever given such an interpretation, but all have admitted the alternative to be optional.

Here also, according to your opinion, the meaning would be, that if you cannot worship Shivu you should worship Vishnoo. But no authors have ever given such an interpretation to those words, and to give more or less worship to Shivu than to Vishnoo is quite contrary to the decision of all the Shastrus.

Fourthly, the following text has also been quoted by you in opposition to the optional alternative in question, taken as you assert from the *Skundu Pooran:*—

'On the death of her husband, if by chance a woman is unable to perform Concremation, nevertheless she should preserve the virtue required of widows. If she cannot preserve that virtue, she must descend to hell.' To confirm this text you have quoted the words of Ungira:

'There is no other pious course for a widow besides Concremation'; which you have interpreted, that 'for a widow there is no other course so pious.'

I answer, the words of Ungira are express, that there is no other pious course for a widow than Concremation. And the Smartu commentator, having thus interpreted the text, in reconciling it with the words of Vishnoo already quoted, declares, that it conveys merely exaggerated praise of Concremation.

But you, in opposition to the true meaning of the expression and to the interpretation given by the Smartu commentator, have explained those words to suit your own argument, that there is no other course more pious than that of Concremation. Perverting thus the meaning of the Shastrus, what benefit do you propose by promoting the destruction of feeble woman, by holding up the temptation of enjoyments in a future state? This I am at a loss to understand.

If the passage you have quoted from the *Skundu Pooran* really exist, the mode in which the Smartu commentator has explained the words of Ungira ('there is no other virtuous course.') must be applied to those of the *Skundu Pooran, viz.* that the text of the *Skundu Pooran* which contradicts Munoo, Vishnu, and others, is to be understood as merely conveying exaggerated praise; because, to exalt Concremation, which leads to future enjoyments that are treated as despicable by the *Opunishuds* of the *Veds* and Smriti, and by the *Bhuguvud Geeta,* above asceticism, in which the mind may be purified by the performance of works, without desire that may lead to eternal beatitude, is every way inadmissible, and in direct opposition to the opinions maintained by ancient authors and commentators.

Section II

In the latter end of the 7th page you have admitted, that the sayings of Ungira, Vishnoo, and Hareet, on the subject of Concremation, are certainly at variance with those of Munoo; but assert, that any law given by Munoo, when contradicted by several other lawgivers, is to be considered annulled:—therefore, his authority in treating of the duties of widows is not admissible, on account of the discord existing between it and passages of Hareet, and Vishnoo, and others. With a view to establish this position you have advanced three arguments—the first of them is, that Vrihusputi says, 'whatever law is contrary to the law of Munoo, is not commendable'; in which the nominative case, 'whatever law', as being used in the singular number, signifies, that in case laws, given by a single person, stand in opposition to those of Munoo, they are not worthy of reverence; but if several persons differ from Munoo in any certain point, his authority must be set aside. I reply, it has been the invariable practice of ancient and modern authors, to explain all texts of law so as to make them coincide with the law of Munoo; they in no instance declare that the authority of Munoo is to be set aside, in order to admit that of any other lawgiver. But you have, on the contrary, set aside the authority of Munoo, on the ground of inconsistence with the words of two or three other authors. In this you not only act contrary to the practice of all commentators, but moreover, in direct opposition to the authority of the *Ved:* for the *Ved* declares, 'whatever Munoo lays down, that is commendable'; which text you have yourself quoted in p. 7. And as to what you have said respecting the words of Vrihusputi as being in the singular number, and therefore only applicable to a case in which Munoo is opposed by only one lawgiver, it is obvious that the word 'whatever', being a general term, includes every particular case falling under it; and therefore his law must be followed, whatever number of authors there may be who lay down a different direction. And the reason of this is expressed in the former part of the verse of Vrihusputi, that 'Munoo has in his work collected the meaning of the Veds'. From this it follows, that whatever law is inconsistent with the code of Munoo, which is the substance of the *Ved,* is really inconsistent with the *Ved* itself, and therefore inadmissible. Admitting the justice of your explanation of Vrihusputi's text, that the authority of any individual lawgiver, who is inconsistent with Munoo, must be set aside; but that when several authorities coincide in laying down any rule inconsistent with his law, they are to be followed; one might on the same principle give a new explanation to the following text:—

'The person who attempts to strike a Brahmun goes to the hell called Sutnuyat, or of a hundred punishments; and he who actually strikes a Brahmun, goes to the hell of Suhusruyat, or a thousand punishments.'

Here, also, the noun in the nominative case, and that in the accusative case also, are both in the singular number; therefore, according ot your exposition, where two or three persons concur in beating a Brahmun, or where a man beats two or three Brahmuns, there is no crime committed. There are many similar instances of laws, the force of which would be entirely frustrated by your mode of interpretation.

You have argued in the second place, that the practice of Concremation is authorized by a text of the *Rig Ved,* and consequently the authority of Munoo is superseded by a higher authority. I reply: in the 12th line of the 9th page of your tract, you have quoted and interpreted a text of the *Veds,* expressing that 'the mind may be purified so as to seek a knowledge of God from which absorption may accrue, by the performance of the daily and occasional ceremonies, without the desire of fruition; therefore, while life may be preserved, it ought not to be destroyed'. With this then and all similar texts, there is the most evident concord with the words of Munoo. Notwithstanding your admission to this effect, you assert that the authority of the Veds contradicts the declaration of Munoo. From the text already quoted, 'that whatever Munoo has declared is to be accepted', it follows that there can be no discrepancy between Munoo and the *Ved.* But there is certainly an apparent inconsistency between the text quoted from the ceremonial part of the *Rig Ved* authorizing Concremation, and that above quoted from the spiritual parts of the *Ved,* to which the celebrated Munoo has given the preference; well aware that such parts of the *Ved* are of more authority than the passages relating to debased ceremonies. He has accordingly directed widows to live, practising austerities. The text of the *Rig Ved,* of course, remains of force to those ignorant wretches who are fettered with the desire of fruition, which debars them from the hope of final beatitude. This too has been acknowledged by yourself, in p. 11, 1.17, and was also fully considered in the first Conference, p. 13, line 18. You cannot but be aware too, that when there is a doubt respecting the meaning of any text of the *Ved,* that interpretation which has been adopted by Munoo, is followed by both ancient and modern authors. In the *Bhuvishyu Pooran,* Muhadev gave instructions for the performance of a penance for wilfully slaying a Brahmun; but observing that this was at variance with the words of Munoo, which declare that there is no expiation for wilfully killing a Brahmun, he does not set aside the text of Munoo, founded ont the *Veds* by his own authority, but explains the sense in which it is to be accepted. 'The object of the declaration of Munoo, that there is no expiation of the wilful murder of a Brahmun, was the more absolute prohibition of the crime; or it may be considered as applicable to Kshutrees, and the other tribes.' The great Muhadev, then, did not venture to set aside the words of Munoo, but you have proposed to set up the texts of Hareet and Ungira as of superior authority.

Thirdly.—You have quoted, with the view of doing away with the authority of Munoo, the text of Juemini, signifying that if there be a diference of opinion respecting a subject, then the decision of the greater number must be adopted; and therefore, as the authority of Munoo, in the present instance, is at variance with several writers, it must yield to theirs. I reply; it is apparent that this text, as well as common sense, only dictates, that where those who differ in opinion are equal in point of authority, the majority ought to be followed; but if otherwise, this text is not applicable to the case. Thus the authority of the *Ved,* though single, cannot be set aside by the concurrent authorities of a hundred law givers; and in like manner the authority of Munoo, which is derived immediately from the *Ved,* cannot be set aside by the contradicting authorities of the others either singly or collectively. Moreover, if Ungira, Hareet, Vishnoo, and Vyas, authorized widows to choose the alternative of Concremation, or of living as ascetics; on the other hand, besides Munoo, Yugnyuvulkyu, Vusishthu, and several other lawgivers have prescribed asceticism only. Why, therefore, despising the authorities of Munoo and others, do you persist in encouraging weak women to submit to murder, by holding out to them the temptations of future pleasures in heaven?

Section III

The quotations from the *Moonduk Opunishud* and the *Bhuguvud Geeta*, which we quoted in our first conference, to shew the light in which rites should be held, you have repeated; and have also quoted some texts of the *Veds* directing the performance of certain rites, such as,

'He who desires heavenly fruition shall perform the sacrifice of a horse.' —In page 17 you have given your final conclusion on the subject to this effect: 'That rites are not prohibited, but that pious works performed without desire are preferable to works performed for the sake of fruition; and he also who performs those works without desire, is superior to him who performs works for the sake of fruition.' —If then works without desire are acknowledged by you to be superior to works with desire of fruition, why do you persuade widows to perform works for the sake of fruition, and do not recommend to them rather to follow asceticism, by which they may acquire eternal beatitude? And with respect to your assertion, that 'rites are not prohibited,' this is inconsistent with the Shastrus: for if all the texts of the *Veds* and lawgivers, prohibiting rites, were to be quoted, they would fill a large volume: (of these a few have been already quoted by me in pp.5 and 6.)— There are indeed Shastrus directing the performance of rites for the sake of fruition, but these are acknowledged to be of less authority than those which prohibit such rites; as is proved by the following text from the *Moonduk Opunishud*: 'Shastrus are of two sorts, superior and inferior; of these the superior are those by which the Eternal God is approached.'

In the *Bhuguvud Geeta* Krishnu says: 'Amongst Shastrus, I am those which treat of God.

In the *Sree Bhaguvut* is the following text: 'Ill-minded persons, not perceiving that the object of the *Ved* is to direct us to absorption, call the superficially tempting promises of rewards their principal fruit; but such as know the *Veds* thoroughly do not hold this opinion.'

The passages directing works for the sake of fruition are therefore adapted only for the most ignorant. Learned men should endeavour to withdraw all those ignorant persons from works performed with desire, but should never, for the sake of profit, attempt to drown them in the abyss of passion. Rughoo Nundun quotes and adopts the following words: 'Learned men should not persuade the ignorant to perform rites for the sake of fruition; for it is written in the Pooran, that he who knows the path to eternal happiness will not direct the ignorant to perform works with desire, as the good physician refuses to yield to the appetite of his patient for injurious food.'

Section IV

In p. 17, 1. 13, of your treatise, you have said, that the Shastru does not admit that widows, in giving up the use of oil, and betel, and sexual pleasures, & c. as ascetics, perform works without desire, and acquire absorption. And for this you advance two proofs: the first, that it appears that Munoo directs that a widow should continue till death as an ascetic, aiming to practise the incomparable rules of virtue that have been followed by such women as were devoted to only one husband. From the word aiming, it follows, that the duties of an ascetic, to be practised by widows, are of the nature of those performed with desire. Secondly, from the subsequent words of Munoo it appears, that those widows who live austere lives ascend to heaven like ascetics from their youth; therefore, from the words ascending to heaven, it is obvious that the austerities that may be performed by them are for reward. I reply; I am surprised at your assertion, that austerities practised by widows cannot be considered as performed without desire, and leading to absorption; for whether austerities or any other kind of act be performed with desire or without desire, must depend on the mind of the agent. Some may follow asceticism or other practices for the sake of heavenly enjoyments, while others, forsaking desire of fruition, may perform them, and at length acquire final beatitude. Therefore, if a widow practise austerities without the desire of fruition, and yet her acts are asserted to be with desire of fruition, this amounts to a setting at defiance both experience and the Shastrus, in a manner unworthy of a man of learning like yourself. As to what you have observed respecting the word aiming in the text of Munoo, it never can be inferred from the use of that word, that the asceticism of widows must necessarily be with desire; for with the object of final beatitude, we practise the acquisition of the knowledge of God, which no Shastru not any of the learned has ever classed amongst works performed with desire of fruition. For no man possessed of understanding performs any movement of mind or body without an object: it is those works only, therefore, that are performed for the sake of corporeal enjoyments, either in the present or in a future state of existence, that are said to be with desire, and that are, as such, prohibited, as Munoo defines: 'Whatever act is performed for the sake of gratifications in this world or the next is called Pruberttuk; and those which are performed according to the knowledge of God are called Niburttuk.'

As to your second argument, that widows leading an ascetic life are rewarded by a mansion in heaven, I reply; that from these words it does not appear that austerities should necessarily be reckoned amongst works performed for reward; for a mansion in heaven is not granted to those alone who perform works with desire, but also to those who endeavour to acquire a knowledge of God, but come short of attaining it in this life. They must after death remain for a long time in the heaven called the Brumhulok, and again assume a human form, until they have, by perfecting themselves in divine knowledge, at length obtained absorption. The *Bhuguvud Geeta* says distinctly:

'A man whose devotions have been broken off by death, having enjoyed for an immensity of years the rewards of his virtues in the regions above, at length is born again in some holy and respectable family.' Koo-look Bhuttu, the commentator on Munoo, says expressly, in his observations on the text of his author, that those ascetic widows ascend to heaven like Sunuk Balukhilyu and other devotees from their youth. By this, it is clearly shewn, that those widows ascend to heaven in the same way as those pious devotees who have already acquired final beatitude, which can only be attained by works performed without desire. And hence the austerities of widows must be reckoned amongst works without desire.

Section V

In page 18, you have asserted that a widow who undergoes Concremation has a higher reward than she who lives as a devotee; for the husband of the woman who performs Concremation, though guilty of the murder of a Brahmun, or of ingratitude or treachery towards a friend, has his sins, by her act, expiated, and is saved from hell, and her husband's, her father's, and her mother's progenitors, are all beatified, and she herself is delivered from female form. —I reply, you have stated, in page 27, commencing at the third line, that works without desire are preferable to those performed for the sake of fruition; while here again you say, that Concremation is preferable to asceticism. You have, however, assigned as a reason for your new doctrine, that Concremation saves progenitors as well as the husband. I have already shewn, that such promises of reward are merely held out to the most ignorant, in order to induce them to follow some kind of religious observance, and to withdraw from evil conduct. Therefore, to prefer works performed with a desire of fruition, to works without desire, merely on the ground of such exaggerated promises, is contrary to all the Shastrus. If, in defiance of all the Shastrus, you maintain that such promises of reward are to be understood literally, and not merely as incitements, still there can be no occasion for so harsh a sacrifice, so painful to mind and body, as burning a person to death in order to save their lines of progenitors; for, by making an offering of one ripe plantain to Shivu, or a single flower of Kurubeer, either to Shivu or to Vishnoo, thirty millions of lines of progenitors may be saved.

'He, who maketh an oblation of a single ripe plantain to Shivu, shall with thirty millions of races of progenitors ascend to the heaven of Shivu.'

'By presenting a single Kurubeer, white or not white, to Vishnoo or Shivu, thirty millions of races of progenitors are exalted to heaven.'

Nor is there any want of promise of reward to those who perform works without desire. In fact, rather more abundant rewards are held out for such works than those you can quote for the opposite practice. 'Those who have acquired knowledge in the prescribed mode can, by mere volition, save any number of progenitors; and all the gods offer worship to the devotees of the Supreme Being.' A volume filled with texts of this kind might be easily written. Moreover, should even the least part of any ceremony performed for reward be omitted or mistaken, the fruits are destroyed, and evil is produced. But there is no bad consequence from a failure in works performed without desire, for the completion of these, even in part, is advantageous. In proof I quote the *Bhuguvud Geeta*: 'Works without desire, if only commenced, are never without advantage; and if any member be defective, evil consequences do not ensue, as in works performed with desire. And the performance of even a small portion of work without desire brings safety.'

There is evidently a possibility of a failure in some portion of the rites of Concremation or Postcremation, particularly in the mode in which you perform the ceremony contrary to the directions of the Shastrus. What connection is there betwixt that mode and the enjoyment of temporary heavenly gratification—a mode which only subjects the widow to the consequences of a violent death!

Section VI

Again in p. 17, 1. 3, you admit it to be more commendable for a widow to attend to the acquisition of knowledge than to die by Concremation; but afterwards, in order to persuade them to the practice of Concremation, and to prevent them from pursuing the acquisition of knowledge, you observe, that women are naturally prone to pleasure, are extremely devoted to works productive of fruits, and are always subject to their passions. To persuade such persons to forsake Concremation, in order to attempt the acquisition of knowledge, is to destroy their hopes in both ways. In support of your opinion you have quoted the *Geeta*: 'Those ignorant persons who are devoted to works ought not to be dissuaded from performing them:'

I reply; your object in persuading women to burn themselves may now be distinctly perceived; you consider women, even of respectable classes, as prone to pleasure, and always subject to their passions; and therefore you are apprehensive lest they should lose both prospects of hope, by giving up Concremation, and attempting to acquire knowledge. For this reason you lead them to the destruction of their lives, by holding out to them the temptation of future reward. It is very certain that all mankind, whether male or female, are endowed with a mixture of passions; but by study of the Shastrus, and frequenting the society of respectable persons, those passions may be gradually subdued, and the capability of enjoying an exalted state may be attained. We ought, therefore, to endeavour to withdraw both men and women from debased sensual pleasures, and not to persuade them to die with the hope of thereby obtaining sensual enjoyments, by which, after a certain period of gratification, they are again immersed in the pollutions of the womb, and subjected to affliction. The Shastrus have directed those men or women, who seek after a knowledge of God, to hear and reflect upon his doctrine, that they may escape from the grievous pain of this world; and they have also prescribed daily and occasional rites to be performed without the hope of reward by those who do not seek after divine knowledge, in order that their minds may be purified, and prepared to receive that knowledge. We, therefore, in conformity with the Shastru, make it our endeavour to dissuade widows from desiring future base and fleeting enjoyments, and encourage them to the acquisition of that divine knowledge which leads to final beatitude. Widows, therefore, by leading an ascetic life in the performance of duties without desire, may purify their minds and acquire divine knowledge, which may procure for them final beatitude. And consequently there is no reason why they should lose both objects of future hope by forsaking Concremation.

'Oh, Urjoon, by placing their reliance on me, women and those of the lower classes of Vueishyu and Soodru may obtain the highest exaltation.'

You, however, considering women devoted to their passions, and consequently incapable of acquiring divine knowledge, direct them to perform Concremation; and maintain that, if any amongst them should not burn with their husbands, according to your final decision from the Shastrus, they must lose the hopes that belong to both practices; because, according to your opinion, they are entirely incapable of acquiring divine knowledge, and by not adopting Concremation, they give up the prospect of future gratifications. As to your quotation from the *Geeta*, to show that persons devoted to works ought not to be dissuaded from the performance of them, it may be observed that this text applies only to rites offered without desire of reward, though applied by you to works performed for the sake of future enjoyment, in direct inconsistency with the authority of the *Geeta*. The object of this, as well as of all texts of the Geeta, is to dissuade men from works performed with desire. The *Geeta* and its Commentaries are both accessible to all. Let the learned decide the point

You have quoted the following text of Vusishthu: 'He who, being devoted to worldly pleasures, boasts, saying, "I am a knower of God," can neither obtain the consequences procurable from works, nor attain final beatitude, the fruit of divine knowledge.'

I admit the force of this text. For whether a man be devoted to worldly pleasures or not, if he be a boaster, either of divine knowledge or of any other acquirement, he is indeed most despicable; but I am unable to see how this text, which forbids vain-glory, is applicable to the question before us, which relates to the Concremation of widows.

Section VII

In your 20th page, you have stated for us, that we do not object to the practice of Concremation, but to the tying down of the widow to the pile before setting it on fire. I reply; this is very incorrect, for it is a gross misrepresentation of our argument; because Concremation or Postcremation is a work performed for the sake of future reward, which the *Opunishud* and the *Geeta*, and other Shastrus, have declared to be most contemptible. Consequently, relying on those Shastrus, it has been always our object to dissuade widows from the act of Concremation or Postcremation, that they might not, for the sake of the debased enjoyment of corporeal pleasures, renounce the attainment of divine knowledge. As to the mode in which you murder widows by tying them to the pile, we do exert ourselves to prevent such deeds, for those who are witnesses to an act of murder, and neglect to do any thing towards its prevention, are accomplices in the crime.

In justification of the crime of burning widows by force, you have stated, towards the foot of the same page, that in those countries where it is the custom for widows to ascend the flaming pile, there cannot be any dispute as to the propriety of following that mode: but where that is not the mode followed, and it is the practice for those that burn the corpse to place a portion of fire contiguous to the pile, so that it may gradually make its way to the pile, and at that time the widow, according to the prescribed form, ascends the pile; in this mode also there is nothing contrary to the Shastrus. You have at the same time quoted two or three authorities to show, that rites should be performed according to the custom of the country. I reply, female murder, murder of a Brahmun, parricide, and similar heinous crimes, cannot be reckoned amongst pious acts by alleging the custom of a country in their behalf; by such customs rather the country in which they exist is itself condemned. I shall write more at large to this purpose in the conclusion. The practice, therefore, of forcibly tying down women to the pile, and burning them to death, is inconsistent with the Shastrus, and highly sinful. It is of no consequence to affirm, that this is customary in any particular country—if it were universally practised, the murders would still be criminal. The pretence that many are united in the commission of such murder will not secure them from divine vengeance. The customs of a country or of a race may be followed in matters where no particular rules are prescribed in the Shastrus; but the wilful murder of widows, prohibited by all Shastrus, is not to be justified by the practice of a few. From the *Skundu Pooran*: 'In those matters in which neither the *Veds* nor lawgivers give either direct sanction or prohibition, the customs of a country or of a race may be observed.' If you insist that the practice of a country or of a race, though directly contrary to the directions of the Shastrus, is still proper to be observed, and to be reckoned amongst lawful acts, I reply, that in Shivukanchee and Vishnookanchee it is the custom for the people of all classes of one of those places, whether learned or ignorant, mutually to revile the good peculiarly worshipped by the people of the other—those of Vishnookanchee despising Shivu, and of Shivukanchee in the same manner holding Vishnoo in contempt. Are the inhabitants of those places, whose custom it is thus to revile Shivu and Vishnoo, not guilty of sin? For each of those tribes may assert, in their own defence, that it is the practice of their country and race to revile the god of the other. But no learned Hindoo will pretend to say, that this excuse saves them from sin. The Rajpoots, also, in the neighbourhood of the Dooab, are accustomed to destroy their infant daughters; they also must not be considered guilty of the crime of child-murder, as they act according to the custom of their country and race. There are many instances of the same kind. No Pundits, then, would consider a heinous crime, directly contrary to the Shastrus, as righteous, by whatever length of practice it may appear to be sanctioned.

You have at first alleged, that to burn a widow after tying her down on the pile, is one of the acts of piety, and have then quoted our argument for the opposite opinion, that 'the inhabitants of forests and mountains are accustomed to robbery and murder: but must these be considered as faultless, because they follow only the custom of their country?' To this you have again replied, that respectable people are not to be guided by the example of mountaineers and foresters. But the custom of burning widows, you say, 'has been sanctioned by the most exemplary Pundits for a length of time. It is the custom, then, of respectable people that is to be followed, and not that of men of no principles'. I answer; respectability, and want of respectability, depend upon the acts of men. If the people of this province, who have been constantly guilty of the wilful murder of women by tying them to the pile in which they are burnt, are to be reckoned amongst the respectable, then why should not the inhabitants of mountains and forests be also reckoned good, who perpetrate murder for the sake of their livelihood, or to propitiate their cruel deities? To show that the custom of a country should be followed, you have quoted a text of the *Ved*, signifying that the example of Brahmuns well versed in the Shastrus, of good understanding, and whose practice is in conformity with reason and the Shastrus, not subject to passion, and accustomed to perform good works, should be followed. And you have also quoted the words of Vyas, signifying that the authorities of the *Veds* and Shastrus, as well as of reason, being various, the practice pointed out by illustrious men should be adopted. I reply; you have shown that the example of men versed in the Shastrus, and who act in conformity with reason and the Shastrus, should be followed; but can you call those who, in defiance of the Shastrus, wilfully put women to death by tying them down to the pile on which they are burned, illustrious, acquainted with the *Veds*, and devoted to acts prescribed by the Shastrus and by reason? If not, their example is to be disregarded. If you can call those, who wilfully tie down women to put them to death, righteous and illustrious, then there is no instance of unrighteousness and depravity. I have already said, that when any act is neither directly authorized nor prohibited by the Shastrus, the custom of the country, or of the race, should be the rule of conduct; but in the present case, the words are express in prescribing that the widow shall enter the flaming pile. But those who, in direct defiance of the authority of the Shastrus, act the part of woman-murderers, in tying down the widow to the pile, and, subsequently applying the flame, burn her to death, can never exculpate themselves from the sin of woman-murder. As to the words you have quoted from the *Skundu Pooran*, signifying that the arguments of one who has no faith in Shivu and Vishnoo can have no weight in the discussion of the legality of facts, I reply, this text is applicable to those who worship images. Those who worship forms under any name, and have no faith in Shivu and Vishnoo, their worship is vain, and their words to be disregarded. In the same way the words of the *Koolarnuv*: 'He whose mouth does not give out the smell of wine and flesh, should perform a penance and be avoided, and is as an inferior animal. This is undoubted.' These words are applicable only to those who follow the Tuntrus; and if all such texts are considered otherwise applicable than in relation to the sects to whom they are directed, there is no possibility of reconciling the variances betwixt the different Shastrus. The Shastru, treating of God, contains the following words: 'Acts and rites that originate in movements of the hands, and other members of the body, being perishable, cannot effect beatitude that is eternal.'

'Those that worship forms under appellations, continue subject to form and appellation; for no perishable means can effect the acquisition of an imperishable end.'

'That man who considers the Being that is infinite, incomprehensible, pure, extending as far as space, and time, and vacuity, to be finite, perceptible by the senses, limited by time and place, subject to passion and anger, what crime is such a robber of Divine Majesty not guilty of?' That is, he is guilty of those that are considered as the most heinous, as well as of those that are considered ordinary sins. Therefore the words of so sinful a person can have no weight in the discussion of the legality of rites.

Section VIII

You have stated in p. 2, that in the same manner as when part of a village or of a piece of cloth has been burnt, the village or piece of cloth is said to be burnt, so if a portion of the pile is inflamed, the whole pile may be said to be flaming. Therefore, it may with propriety be affirmed, that widows do in this country ascend the flaming pile.

I reply; you may afford gratification to those who take delight in woman-murder by such a quibble, but how can you avoid divine punishment by thus playing upon words?—for we find in the text of Hareet and of Vishnoo, the phrase 'pruvivesh hootasunum,' which means entering into flames, and the term 'Sumaroheddhootasunum, signifying ascending the flames. You have interpreted these directions in this way;—that, at a considerable distance from the pile, fire may be placed, and a piece of grass or rope may connect the fire with the pile; and that thus, by ascending the pile, which has not been in the smallest degree affected by the fire, the widow may fulfil the direction of ascending and entering the flaming pile. But I beg to remark, that both in the vulgar dialect and in Sungskrit, the word 'Pruvesh' express only the introgression of one substance into another; as for example, 'Grihu pruvesh koriachhilam.' I entered the house; the word entered cannot be used unless I actually passed into the house. If a long bamboo be attached to the house and a rope be fastened to that bamboo, no one can in any language say, that in merely touching that rope or bamboo he has entered that house. If a single billet of wood belonging to the pile were indeed inflamed, then you might say, according to your quibble regarding the burning of the cloth and of the village, that the pile was inflamed, and the flaming pile entered; but even this is by no means the case, in the mode in which your pile is used. Unless, however, the pile is so completely in fire that the flames may surround the whole of her body, the woman cannot be said to enter into flame. You must then, before you can justify your murder of helpless women, prepare a new dictionary; but there is no great probability of its interpretations being adopted by men of knowledge.

Towards the end of the 28th page you assert, that those who tie down the woman to the pile according to the custom of the country, are not guilty of violation of the Shastrus: for it is to be understood from the words of Hareet before quoted, that until her body be burnt, the widow cannot be delivered from female form, which implies that her body ought to be completely consumed; and that it is on this account that those who burn her make her fast to the pile, lest by accident any part of the dead body should fall out of the pile, and fail of being consumed, and in that case the burning be incomplete. This practice of tying down, therefore, is also conformable to the Shastru; and those who, in burning the woman, make her fast to the pile, are not therein guilty of any sin, but rather perform a pious act. In support of this assertion you have quoted the words of Apustumbu, signifying that he who performs an act prescribed by the Shastrus, or he who persuades or permits another to perform a prescribed act, ascends to heaven; and he who commits an act forbidden by the Shastru, or who persuades or permits another to perform a prohibited action, sinks to hell.

I reply; you mean to say, that it is not in order to avoid the danger of the widow's flying from the pile from fear of the flames, or from pain, that she is made fast—but merely, lest any fragments of the body should fall from the pile unburnt, that she is tied down to the pile while alive. I ask, is it with an iron chain that the woman is made fast, or with a common rope? For by securing the body by means of iron, the danger of portions of it being scattered from the pile may undoubtedly be avoided. But if, on the contrary, the body is bound with a common rope, the rope will be consumed before life has altogether quitted the body, and the rope, when so burned, can be of no use in retaining within the pile the members of the body. So far have Pundits been infatuated, in attempting to give the appearance of propriety to improper actions, that they have even attempted to make people believe, that a rope may remain unconsumed amidst a flaming fire, and prevent the members of a body from being dispersed from the pile. Men of sense may now judge of the truth of the reason to which you ascribe the practice of tying down widows. All people in the world are not blind, and those who will go and behold the mode in which you tie down women to the pile, will readily perceive the truth or falsehood of the motives you assign for the practice. A little reflection ought to have convinced you of the light in which such an argument must be viewed, even by those of your friends who have the smallest regard for truth. As for the text you have quoted from Apustumbu, it might have, with more propriety, been cited by us, because it is established by that passage, that those who commit, persuade to, or permit an improper action, descend to hell; for those that are guilty of wilful woman-murder, by tying women down with ropes, and burning them to death, a practice unauthorized by the Shastrus, and considered as most heinous, and those who persuade or permit others to do so, are certainly obnoxious to the denunciation of Apustumbu. The pretext of custom of the country, or of the object of preventing portions of the body from being scattered, will not exculpate them.

You have written, in page 29, that those who, by the permission of the widow, increase the flames by throwing wood or straw on the pile, are meritorious: for he who without reward assists another in a pious act, is to be esteemed most meritorious. In confirmation, you have quoted an anecdote of the *Mutshyu Pooran*, that a goldsmith, by affording his gratuitous assistance in a pious act, obtained a great reward. To this I have already replied: for if those who voluntarily commit woman-murder, by tying down a widow to the pile, and holding her down with bamboos to be burnt to death, are to be reckoned as performers of a pious act, those who assist them in so doing must be esteemed meritorious: but if this be a most heinous and debased crime, the promoters of it must certainly reap the fruits of woman-murder.

In your concluding paragraph you have quoted three texts, to prove the continual observance of this practice during all ages.

The first recounting, that a dove entered into the flaming pile of her deceased husband. The second, that when Dhriturashtru was burning in the flames of his hermitage, his wife, Gandharee, threw herself into the fire. The wives of Busoodev (the father of Krishnu), of Buluram, of Prudyoomnu, and of others, entered the flaming piles of their respective husbands. These three instances occurred, as narrated by the Pooran writers, within intervals of a few years towards the close of the Dwapur Yoog. You ought then to have quoted other instances, to show the continual observance of this practice throughout all ages. Let that be as it may, you yourself cannot fail to know, that in former ages there were, as in later times, some who devoted themselves to the attainment of final beatitude, and others to the acquisition of future pleasure. Some too were virtuous, and some sinful; some believers, some sceptics. Amongst those, both men and women, who performed rites for reward, after enjoying pleasures in heaven, have again fallen to earth. Those Shastrus themselves declare this fact; but in the Shastrus that teach the path to final beatitude, the performance of rites for the sake of reward is positively forbidden. According to these Shastrus, numberless women, in all ages, who were desirous of final beatitude, by living as ascetics, attained their object. Evidence of this is to be found in the *Muhabharut* and other works: 'The widows of the heroic Kooroos, who fell valiantly with their faces to the foe, and were translated to the heaven of Bruhma, performed only the prescribed ceremonies with water,' and did not burn themselves on the piles of their husbands. I have moreover to request your attention to the fact, that in the three instances you have quoted, the very words 'entered into fire' are used. In those three cases, then, it appears that the widows actually entered the flames, and therefore, whatever widow in the present time does not enter the fire, but is burnt to death by others tying her down to the pile, has not performed the ceremony according to the ancient practice you have instanced; and from rites so performed she cannot even be entitled to the temporary enjoyment of heavenly pleasures; and those who tie her down, and, pressing on her with bamboos, kill her, must, according to all Shastrus, be considered guilty of the heinous crime of woman-murder.

Section IX

Advocate.—I alluded, in p. 18, 1. 18, to the real reason for our anxiety to persuade widows to follow their husbands, and for our endeavours to burn them, pressed down with ropes: *viz.* that women are by nature of inferior understanding, without resolution, unworthy of trust, subject to passions, and void of virtuous knowledge; they, according to the precepts of the Shastrus, are not allowed to marry again after the demise of their husbands, and consequently despair at once of all worldly pleasure: hence it is evident, that death to these unfortunate widows is preferable to existence; for the great difficulty which a widow may experience by living a purely ascetic life, as prescribed by the Shastrus, is obvious; therefore, if she do not perform Concremation, it is probable that she may be guilty of such acts as may bring disgrace upon her paternal and maternal relations, and those that may be connected with her husband. Under these circumstances, we instruct them from their early life in the idea of Concremation, holding out to them heavenly enjoyments in company with their husbands, as well as the beatitude of their relations, both by birth and marriage, and their husbands, become desirous of accompanying them; but to remove every chance of their trying to escape from the blazing fire, in burning them we first tie them down to the pile.

Opponent.—The reason you have now assigned for burning widows alive is indeed your true motive, as we are well aware; but the faults which you have imputed to women are not planted in their constitution by nature; it would be, therefore, grossly criminal to condemn that sex to death merely from precaution. By ascribing to them all sorts of improper conduct, you have indeed successfully persuaded the Hindoo community to look down upon them as contemptible and mischievous creatures, whence they have been subjected to constant miseries. I have, therefore, to offer a few remarks on this head.

Women are in general inferior to men in bodily strength and energy; consequently the male part of the community, taking advantage of their corporeal weakness, have denied to them those excellent merits that they are entitled to by nature, and afterwards they are apt to say that women are naturally incapable of acquiring those merits. But if we give the subject consideration, we may easily ascertain whether or not your accusation against them is consistent with justice. As to their inferiority in point of understanding, when did you ever afford them a fair opportunity of exhibiting their natural capacity? How then can you accuse them of want of understanding? If, after instruction in knowledge and wisdom, a person cannot comprehend or retain what has been taught him, we may consider him as deficient; but as you keep women generally void of education and acquirements, you cannot, therefore, in justice pronounce on their inferiority. On the contrary, Leelavutee, Bhanoomutee (the wife of the prince of Kurnat), and that of Kalidas, are celebrated for their thorough knowledge of all the Shastrus: moreover in the *Vribudarunyuk Opunishud* of the *Ujoor Ved* it is clearly stated, that Yagnuvulkyu imparted divine knowledge of the most difficult nature to his wife Muitreyee, who was able to follow and completely attain it!

Secondly, you charge them with want of resolution, at which I feel exceedingly surprised: for we constantly perceive, in a country where the name of death makes the male shudder, that the female, from her firmness of mind, offers to burn with the corpse of her deceased husband; and yet you accuse those women of deficiency in point of resolution.

Thirdly, with regard to their trustworthiness, let us look minutely into the conduct of both sexes, and we may be enabled to ascertain which of them is the most frequently guilty of betraying friends. If we enumerate such women in each village or town as have been deceived by men, and such men as have been betrayed by women, I presume that the number of the deceived women would be found ten times greater than that of the betrayed men. Men are, in general, able to read and write, and manage public affairs, by which means they easily promulgate such faults as women occasionally commit, but never consider as criminal the misconduct of men towards women. One fault they have, it must be acknowledged; which is, by considering others equally void of duplicity as themselves, to give their confidence too readily, from which they suffer much misery, even so far that some of them are misled to suffer themselves to be burnt to death.

In the fourth place, with respect to their subjection to the passions, this may be judged of by the custom of marriage as to the respective sexes; for one man may marry two or three, sometimes even ten wives and upwards; while a woman, who marries but one husband, desires at his death to follow him, forsaking all worldly enjoyments, or to remain leading the austere life of an ascetic.

Fifthly, the accusation of their want of virtuous knowledge is an injustice. Observe what pain, what slighting, what contempt, and what afflictions their virtue enables them to support! How many Kooleen Brahmuns are there who marry ten or fifteen wives for the sake of money, that never see the greater number of them after the day of marriage, and visit others only three or four times in the course of their life. Still amongst those women, most even without seeing or receiving any support from their husbands, living dependent on their fathers or brothers, and suffering much distress, continue to preserve their virtue: and when Brahmans, or those of other tribes, bring their wives to live with them, what misery do the women not suffer? At marriage the wife is recognised as half of her husband, but in after-conduct they are treated worse than inferior animals. For the woman is employed to do the work of a slave in the house, such as, in her turn, to clean the place very early in the morning, whether cold or wet, to scour the dishes, to wash the floor, to cook night and day, to prepare and serve food for her husband, father and mother-in-law, sisters-in-law, brothers-in-law, and friends and connections! (For amongst Hindoos more than in other tribes relations long reside together, and on this account quarrels are more common amongst brothers respecting their worldly affairs.) If in the preparation or serving up of the victuals they commit the smallest fault, what insult do they not receive from their husband, their mother-in-law, and the younger brothers of their husband! After all the male parts of the family have satisfied themselves, the women content themselves with what may be left, whether sufficient in quantity or not. Where Brahmuns or Kayustus are not wealthy, their women are obliged to attend to their cows, and to prepare the cow-dung for firing. In the afternoon they fetch water from the river or tank; and at night perform the office of menial servants in making the beds. In case of any fault or omission in the performance of those labours, they receive injurious treatment. Should the husband acquire wealth, he indulges in criminal amours to her perfect knowledge, and almost under her eyes, and does not see her perhaps once a month. As long as the husband is poor, she suffers every kind of trouble, and when he becomes rich she is altogether heart-broken. All this pain and affliction their virtue alone enables them to support. Where a husband takes two or three wives to live with him, they are subjected to mental miseries and constant quarrels. Even this distressed situation they virtuously endure. Sometimes it happens that the husband, from a preference for one of his wives, behaves cruelly to another. Amongst the lower classes, and those even of the better class who have not associated with good company, the wife, on the slightest fault, or even on bare suspicion of her misconduct, is chastised as a thief. Respect to virtue and their reputation generally makes them forgive even this treatment. If, unable to bear such cruel usage, a wife leaves her husband's house to live separately from him, then the influence of the husband with the magisterial authority is generally sufficient to place her again in his hands; when in revenge for her quitting him, he seizes every pretext to torment her in various ways, and sometimes even puts her privately to death. These are facts occurring every day, and not to be denied. What I lament is, that seeing the women thus dependent and exposed to every misery, you feel for them no compassion, that might exempt them from being tied down and burnt to death.

East India Magazine, Congratulatory Address[2]

This petition thanking the Government of India for outlawing sati was presented to Lord William Bentinck by eminent Hindus (primarily Brahmos) of Calcutta, and was orchestrated by Raja Rammohan Roy and Dwarakanath Tagore.

'My Lord—With hearts filled with the deepest gratitude and impressed with the utmost reverence, we the undersigned native inhabitants of Calcutta and its vicinity, beg to be allowed to approach your Lordship to offer personally our humblest but warmest acknowledgements for the invaluable protection which your

Lordship's government has recently afforded to the lives of the
Hindoo female part of your subjects, and for your humane and
successful exertions in rescuing us forever from the gross stigma
hitherto attached to our character as wilful murderers of females
and zealous promoters of the practice of suicide. Excessive jealousy of their female connections operating in the breasts of
Hindoo princes rendered those despots, regardless of the common bonds of society and of their incumbent duty as protectors
of the weaker sex, insomuch that with a view to prevent every
possibility of their widows forming subsequent attachments, they
availed themselves of the arbitrary power, and under cloak of
religion introduced the practice of burning widows alive, under
the first impressions of sorrow or despair, immediately after the
demise of their husbands. This system of female destruction, being
admirably suited to the selfish and servile disposition of the populace, has been eagerly followed by them in defiance of the most
sacred authorities, such as the Oopanishads or the principal parts
of the Veds or the Bhagvud Geeta, as well as of the direct com-
mandment of Manu the first and greatest of all the legislators
conveyed in the following words 'Let a widow continue till death,
forgiving all injuries....' While in fact fulfilling the suggestions of
their jealousy, they pretend to justify this hideous practice by
quoting some passages of authorities of evidently inferior weight,
sanctioning the wilful ascent of a widow on the flaming pile of
her husband, as if they were offering such female sacrifices in
obedience to the dictates of the Shastras, and not from the influence of jealousy. It is, however, very fortunate that the British
Government, under whose protection the lives of both the males
and females of India have been happily placed by Providence,
has, after diligent inquiry, ascertained that even those inferior
authorities permitting wilful ascent by a widow to the flaming
pile, have been practically set aside, and that in gross violation
of their language and spirit, the relatives of widows have, in the
burning of those infatuated females, almost invariably used ropes
to fasten them down on the pile, and heap over them vast quantities of wood and other materials adequate to the prevention of their
escape; an outrage on humanity, which has been frequently perpetrated under the indiscreet sanction of native officers, undeservedly

employed for the security of life and preservation of peace and tranquillity. In many instances in which the vigilance of the magistrate has deterred the native officers of police from indulging their own inclination, widows have either made their escape from the pile after being partially burnt, or retracted their resolution to burn when brought to the awful task, to the mortifying disappointment of the instigators; while in some instances the resolution to die has been retracted on pointing out to the widows the impropriety of their intended undertaking, and on promising them safety and maintenance during life, notwithstanding the severe reproaches liable thereby to be heaped upon them by their relatives and friends. In consideration of circumstances so disgraceful in themselves and so incompatible with the principles of British rule, your Lordship in council, fully impressed with the duties required of you by justice and humanity, has deemed it incumbent on you for the honour of the British name to come to the resolution that the lives of your Hindoo female subjects should be henceforth more efficiently protected; that the heinous sin of cruelty to females shall no longer be committed and that the most ancient and purest of the system of the Hindoo religion should not any longer be set at nought by the Hindoos themselves. The magistrates in consequence are, we understand, positively ordered to execute the resolution of government by all possible means. We are, my Lord, reluctantly constrained by the consideration of the nature of your exalted situation from indicating our inward feelings by presenting any valuable offering as commonly adopted on such occasions, but we should consider ourselves highly guilty of insincerity and ingratitude, if we remained negligently silent, when urgently called upon by our feelings and conscience to express publicly the gratitude that we feel for the everlasting obligation which you have graciously conferred on the Hindoo community at large. We are, however, at a loss to find language sufficiently indicative even of a small portion of the sentiments we are desirous of expressing on this occasion. We must, therefore, conclude this address with entreating that your Lordship will condescendingly accept our most grateful acknowledgements for this act of benevolence towards us, and will pardon the silence of those who, though equally partaking of the blessing bestowed by your

Lordship, have through ignorance or prejudice omitted to join in this common cause.

We have the honour to be, My Lord, your Lordship's most humble and obedient servants. Callynauth Roy Choudhury, Rammohan Roy, Dwarkanauth Tagore, Prussunu Comar Tagore &co, &co.

'Petition of the Orthodox Community against the Sati Regulation'[3]

This address opposing the suppression of sati and giving religious arguments for its continuance was presented to Lord Bentinck in January 1830 by orthodox Calcutta groups. Opposition to the prohibition of sati was taken as far as the Privy Council, where the case against the regulation was eventually dismissed.

We the undersigned beg leave respectfully to submit the following petition to your Lordship in Council in consequence of having heard that certain persons taking upon themselves to represent the opinions and feelings of the Hindu inhabitants of Calcutta have misrepresented those opinions and feelings and that your Lordship in Council is about to pass a resolution founded on such erroneous statements to put a stop to the practice of performing suttees, an interference with the religion and customs of the Hindus which we most earnestly deprecate and cannot view without the most serious alarm.

With the most profound respect for your Lordship in Council we the undersigned Hindu inhabitants of the city of Calcutta beg leave to approach you in order to state such circumstances as appear to us necessary to draw the attention of government fully to the measure in contemplation and the light in which it will be regarded by the greater part of the more respectable Hindu population of the Company's territories who are earnest in the belief as well as in the profession of their religion.

From time immemorial the Hindu religion has been established and in proportion to its antiquity has been its influence over the minds of its followers. In no religion has apostasy been more rare and none has resisted more successfully the fierce spirit of proselytism which animated the first Mahomedan conquerors.

That the Hindu religion is founded like all religions on usage as well as precept and one when immemorial is held equally sacred with the other. Under the sanction of immemorial usage as well as precept Hindu widows perform of their own accord and pleasure and for the benefit of their husbands' souls and for their own the sacrifice of self-immolation called suttee—which is not merely a sacred duty but a high privilege to her who sincerely believes in the doctrine of her religion—and we humbly submit that any interference with a persuasion of so high and self-annihilating a nature is not only an unjust and intolerant dictation in matters of conscience but is likely wholly to fail in procuring the end proposed.

Even under the first Mussalman conquerors of Hindustan and certainly since this country came under the Mogul government, notwithstanding the fanaticism and intolerance of their religion, no interference with the practice of suttee was ever attempted. Since that period and for nearly a century the power of the British government has been established in Bengal, Bihar and Orissa and none of the Governors General or their Council have hitherto interfered in any manner to the prejudice of the Hindu religion or customs and we submit that by various acts of the parliament of Great Britain under the authority of which the honourable Company itself exists, our religion and laws, usages and customs such as they have existed from time immemorial are inviolably secured to us.

We learned with surprise and grief that while this is confessed on all hands the abolition of the practice of suttee is attempted to be defended on the ground that there is no positive law or precept enjoining it. A doctrine derived from a number of Hindus who have apostatized from the religion of their forefathers and who have defiled themselves by eating and drinking forbidden things in the society of Europeans are endeavouring to deceive your Lordship in Council by assertions that there is no law regarding suttee practices and that all Hindus of intelligence and education are ready to assent to the abolition (of them) on the ground that the practice of suttee is not authorized by the laws fundamentally established and acknowledged by all Hindus as sacred. But we humbly submit, (on) a question so delicate as the interpretation of our sacred books and the authority of our religious usages none but pandits and brahmins and teachers of holy lives and known learning and authority ought to be consulted and we are satisfied and flatter ourselves with the hope that your Lordship in Council will not regard the assertion of men who have neither any faith nor care for the memory of their ancestors or their religion; and that if your Lordship in Council will assume to yourself the difficult and delicate task of regulating the conscience of a whole people and deciding what it ought to believe and what it ought to reject on the authority of its own sacred writers that such a task will be undertaken only after anxious and strict enquiry and patient consultation with men known and reverenced for their attachment to the Hindu religion, the authority of their lives and their knowledge of the sacred books which contain its doctrines. And if such a satisfactory examination should be made we are confident that your Lordship in Council will find our statements to be correct and will learn that the measure will be regarded with horror and dismay throughout the Company's dominions as the signal of a universal attack upon all we revere.

We further beg leave to represent that the enquiry in question has been already made by some of the most learned and virtuous of the Company's servants whose memory is still reverenced by the nations who were under their rule and that Mr Warren Hastings late Governor General at the request of Mr Nathaniel Smith the then chairman of the Court of Directors (the former being well versed in many parts of the Hindu religion) having instituted the enquiry was satisfied as to the validity of the laws respecting suttees—that a further and similar enquiry was made by Mr Wilkins who was deputed to and accordingly did proceed to Benares and remain there a considerable time in order to be acquainted with the religion and customs in question, that his opinion was similar to that of Mr Warren Hastings and that this opinion was since confirmed by Mr Jonathan Duncan whose zealous and excellent administration Benares and other parts of Hindustan will long be remembered by the nations with gratitude.

In the time of Lord Cornwallis some of the Christian missionaries who then first appeared in this country secretly conveyed to the Council some false and exaggerated accounts of the suttee practice and first advanced the assertion that it was not lawful. His Lordship in Council after enquiry and by the assistance of Mr

Duncan was satisfied of its lawfulness and was contented to permit us to follow our customs as before.

In the time of Lord Moira and Amherst a number of European missionaries who came out to convert Hindus and others renewed their attack upon this custom and by clamour and falsely affirming that by compulsive measures Hindu women were thrown into the fire procured the notice of government and an order was issued requiring magistrates to take steps that suttees might perform their sacrifice at their pleasure and that no one should be allowed to persuade or use any compulsion. On the concurrent reports of various gentlemen then cognizant, the widows went to the funeral pyres of their deceased husbands cheerfully, these Governors-General were satisfied and no farther interference was attempted.

The ratified measure last adverted to did not answer the object proposed and it proved (as we humbly submit) the unpolicy of interference in any degree with matters of conscience.

The fact was that the number of suttees in Bengal considerably increased in consequence within a short time—and in order to ascertain the cause a reference was made to the Sadar Diwani Adalat who could assign no satisfactory cause to account for it. Though it might perhaps have occurred to gentlemen of so much experience that the interference of government even to this extent with the practice was likely, by drawing to it the attention of the native community in a greater degree than formerly, to increase the number of votaries.

From a celebrated instance relating to suttees that we immediately hereafter beg leave to cite, your Lordship in Council will find that on the occasion alluded to, no other good was obtained by an attempt to prevent the widow burning with her deceased husband than that religion was violated and to no purpose. In the time of Lord Clive his Diwanraja Nobkissen endeavoured to prevent a widow performing the sacrifice by making her believe that her husband had been already burnt and when she discovered that she had been deceived offering her any sum of money that might be required for her support as a recompense but nothing would satisfy her and she starved herself to death. His Lordship then gave orders that no one should be allowed to interfere with the Hindu religion or customs.

Independent of the foregoing statement, your Lordship in Council will see that your predecessors, after long residences in India, having a complete knowledge of the laws and customs of Hindus were satisfied as to such laws and never came to a resolution by which devout and conscientious Hindus must be placed in the most painful of all predicaments and either forego in some degree their loyalty to government and disobey its injunctions or violate the precepts of their religion.

Before we conclude we beg to request your impartial consideration of the various acts of parliament passed from time to time since the reign of His Majesty George the Third and which have ever since been strictly preserved. The substance and spirit of which may be thus summed up, viz., that no one is to interfere in any shape in the religion or the customs of Hindu subjects. These acts conceived in the spirit of trust, wisdom, and toleration, were passed by men as well acquainted at least as anyone in existence with our laws. Our language, our customs, and our religion have never been infringed by the wisest of those who have here administered the powers of government and we trust will be preserved far in the future as far in the past, inviolate as they are a most solemn pledge and charter from our rulers to ourselves, on the preservation of which depend rights more sacred in our eyes than those of property or life itself—and sure we are that when this most important subject has been well and maturely weighed by your Lordship in Council the resolution will be abandoned and that we shall obtain a permanent security through your Lordship's wisdom against the renewal of similar attempts.

Notes

1   Roy, Rammohan, 'On Concremation: A Second Conference between an Advocate and an Opponent of that Practice (1818)', in Robertson B.C., (ed), *The Essential Writings of Raja Rammohan Roy* (Delhi: Oxford University Press, 1999).

2   'From the Hindus of Calcutta to Lord William Bentinck', reprinted in *Alexander's East India Magazine*, vol. 1, December 1830–June 1831.

3   'Petition of the Orthodox Community against the Sati Regulation, 14 January 1830', in Majumdar, J.K. (ed.), *Raja Rammohan Roy and Progressive Movement in India* (Calcutta: Art Press, 1941, reprint).

IV

SATI IN THE PRINCELY STATES

9

Accounts

James Tod, *Annals and Antiquities of Rajasthan*[1]

This famous work by the British political agent James Tod became the unofficial handbook on all things Rajput for both East India Company servants and the general public. This section deals with the Rajput customs of sati, infanticide, and jauhar, which Tod sees as synonymous with the Rajput character. Although Tod ostensibly denounces sati, his heroic treatment of the subject in the rest of the annals belies this stance.

We now procced to consider another trait of Rajput character, exemplified in the practice of female immolation, and to inquire whether religion, custom, or affection, has most share in such sacrifice. To arrive at the origin of this rite, we must trace it to the recesses of mythology, where we shall discover the precedent in the example of *Sati*, who to avenge an insult to Iswara, in her own father's omission to ask her lord to an entertainment, consumed herself in the presence of the assembled gods. With this act of fealty (*sati*) the name of Dacsh's daughter has been identified; and her regeneration and reunion to her husband, as the mountain-nymph *Mérá*, or 'Párvati', furnishes the incentive to similar acts. In the history of these celestial beings, the Rajpootni has a memorable lesson before her, that no domestic differences can afford exemption from this proof of faith: for Jupiter and Juno were not more eminent examples of connubial discord than Mérá and Siva, who was not only alike unfaithful, but more cruel, driving Mérá from his Olympus (Kylas), and forcing her to seek refuge in the murky caverns of Caucasus. Female immolation, therefore, originated with the sun-worshipping *Saivas*, and was common to all those nations who adored this the most splendid object of the visible creation. Witness the Scythic Gete or Jut warrior of the Jaxartes, who devoted his wife, horse, arms, and slaves, to the flames; the 'giant Gete' of Scandinavia, who forgot not on the shores of the Baltic his Transoxianian habits; and the Frisian Frank and Saxon descended from him, who ages after omitted only the female. Could we assign the primary cause of a custom so opposed to the first law of nature with the same certainty that we can prove its high antiquity, we might be enabled to devise some means for its abolition. The chief characteristic of *satiism* is its expiating quality: for by this act of *faith*, the Sati not only makes atonement for the sins of her husband, and secures the remission of her own, but has the joyful assurance of reunion to the object whose beatitude she procures. Having once imbibed this doctrine, its fulfilment is powerfully aided by that heroism of character inherent to the Rajpootni; though we see that the stimulant of religion requires no aid even in the timid female of Bengal, who, relying on the promise of regeneration, lays her head on the pyre with the most philosophical composure.

Nothing short of the abrogation of the doctrines which pronounce such sacrifices exculpatory can be effectual in preventing them; but this would be to overturn the fundamental article of their creed, the notion of metempsychosis. Further research may disclose means more attainable, and the sacred Sastras are at once the surest and the safest. Whoever has examined these, is aware of the conflict of authorities for and against cremation; but a proper application of them (and they are the highest who give it not their sanction) has, I believe, never been resorted to. Vyasu, the chronicler of the Yadus, a race whose manners were decidedly Scythic, is the great advocate for female sacrifice: he (in the *Mahabharat*) pronounces the expiation perfect. But Menu inculcates no such doctrine; and although the state of widowhood he recommends might be deemed onerous by the fair sex of the west, it would be considered little hardship in the east. 'Let her emaciate her body, by living voluntarily on pure flowers, roots, and fruit; but let her not, when her lord is deceased, even pronounce the name of another man.' Again he says, 'A virtuous wife ascends to heaven, if, after the decease of her lord, she devote herself to pious austerity; but a widow, who slights her deceased husband by marrying again, brings disgrace on herself here below, and shall be excluded from the seat of her lord.'[2]

These and many other texts, enjoining purity of life and manners to the widow, are to be found in this first authority, but none demanding such a cruel pledge of affection. Abstinence from the common pursuits of life, and entire self-denial, are rewarded by 'high renown in this world, and in the next the abode of her husband'; and procure for her the title of '*sáddwi*, or the virtuous'. These are deemed sufficient pledges of affection by the first of sages.[3] So much has been written on this subject, that we shall not pursue it further in this place; but proceed to consider a still more inhuman practice, infanticide.

Although custom sanctions, and religion rewards, a Sati, the victim to marital selfishness, yet, to the honour of humanity, neither traditionary adage nor religious text can be quoted in support of a practice so revolting as infanticide. Man alone, of the whole animal creation, is equal to the task of destroying his offspring: for instinct preserves what reason destroys. The wife is the sacrifice to his egotism, and the progeny of her own sex to his pride; and if the unconscious infant should escape the influence of the latter, she is only reserved to become the victim of the former at the period when life is most desirous of extension. If the female reasoned on her destiny, its hardships are sufficient to stifle all sense of joy, and produce indifference to life. When a female is born, no anxious inquiries await the mother—no greetings welcome the new-comer, who appears an intruder on the scene, which often closes in the hour of its birth. But the very silence with which a female birth is accompanied, forcibly expresses sorrow; and we dare not say that many compunctious visitings do not obtrude themselves on those who, in accordance with custom and imagined necessity, are thus compelled to violate the sentiments of nature. Families may exult in the Satis which their cenotaphs portray, but none ever heard a Rajpoot boast of the destruction of his infant progeny.

What are the causes, we may ask, sufficiently powerful to induce the suppression of a feeling which every sentient being has in common for its offspring? To suppose the Rajpoot devoid of this sentiment would argue his deficiency in the ordinary attributes of humanity: often is he heard to exclaim, 'Accursed the day when a woman child was born to me!' The same motive which studded Europe with convents, in which youth and beauty were immured until liberated by death, first prompted the Rajpoot to infanticide: and, however revolting the policy, it is perhaps kindness compared to incarceration. There can be no doubt that monastic seclusion, practised by the Frisians in France, the Langobardi in Italy, and the Visigoths in Spain, was brought from Central Asia, the cradle of the Goths.[4] It is, in fact, a modification of the same feeling, which characterises the Rajpoot and the ancient German warrior,— the dread of dishonour to the fair: the former raises the poniard to the breast of his wife rather than witness her captivity, and he gives the opiate to the infant, whom, if he cannot portion and marry to her equal, he dare not see degraded.

Although religion nowhere authorises this barbarity, the laws which regulate marriage amongst the Rajpoots powerfully promote infanticide. Not only is intermarriage prohibited between families of the same clan (*campa*), but between those of the same tribe (*gote*); and though centuries may have intervened since their separation, and branches thus transplanted may have lost their original patronymic, they can never be regrafted on the original stem: for instance, though eight centuries have separated the two grand subdivisions of the Gehlotes, and the younger, the Seesodia, has superseded the elder, the Aharya, each ruling distinct states, a marriage between any of the branches would be deemed incestuous: the Seesodia is yet brother to the Aharya, and regards every female of the race as his sister. Every tribe has therefore to look abroad, to a race distinct from its own, for suitors for the females. Foreign war, international feuds, or other calamities affect tribes the most remote from each other; nor can war or famine thin the clans of Marwar, without diminishing the female population of Amber: thus both suffer in a twofold degree. Many virtuous and humane princes have endeavoured to check or mitigate an evil, in the eradication of which every parental feeling would cooperate. Sumptuary edicts alone can control it; and the Rajpoots were never sufficiently enamoured of despotism to permit it to rule within their private dwellings. The plan proposed, and in some degree followed by the great Jey Sing of Amber, might with caution be pursued, and with great probability of success. He submitted to the prince of every Rajpoot state a decree, which was laid before a convocation of their respective vassals, in which he regulated the *daeja* or dower, and other marriage expenditure, with reference to the property of the vassal, limiting it to one year's income of the estate. This plan was, however, frustrated by the vanity of the Chondawut of Saloombra, who expended on the marriage of his daughter a sum even greater than his sovereign could have afforded; and to have his name blazoned by the bards and genealogists, he sacrificed the beneficent views of one of the wisest of the Rajpoot race. Until vanity suffers itself to be controlled, and the aristocratic Rajpoot submit to republican simplicity,[5] the evils arising from nuptial profusion will not cease. Unfortunately, those who could check it, find their interest in stimulating it, namely, the whole class of *mangtas* (mendicants), bards, minstrels, jugglers, Brahmins who assemble on these occasions, and pour forth their epithalamiums in praise of the virtue of liberality. The *bardais* are the grand recorders of fame, and the volume of *precedent* is always recurred to, in citing the liberality of former chiefs; while the dread of their satire (*viserva*, literally 'poison') shuts the eyes of the chiefs to consequences, and they are only anxious to maintain the reputation of their ancestors, though fraught with future ruin. 'The Dahima emptied his coffers' (says Chund, the polestar of the Rajpoots) 'on the marriage of his daughter with Pirthiraj; but he filled them with the praises of mankind.' The same bard retails every article of these *daejas* or 'dowers', which thus become precedents for future ages; and the '*lakh passao*', then established for the chief bardai, has become a model to posterity. Even now the Rana of Oodipoor, in his season of poverty, at the recent marriage of his daughters bestowed 'the gift of a lakh' on the chief bard; though the articles of gold, horses, clothes, etc., were included in the estimate, and at an undue valuation, which rendered the gift not quite so precious as in the days of the Chohan. Were bonds taken from all the feudal chiefs, and a penal clause inserted, of forfeiture of their fief by all who exceeded a fixed nuptial expenditure, the axe would be laid to the root, the evil would be checked, and the heart of many a mother (and we may add father) be gladdened, by preserving at once the point of honour and their child. When ignorance declaims against the gratuitous love of murder amongst these brave men, our contempt is excited equally by its short-sighted conclusions, and the affected philanthropy which overlooks all remedy but the 'sic volo'. Sir John Shore, when acting on the suggestions of the benevolent Duncan for the suppression of this practice amongst the Rajkumars, judged more wisely as a politician, and more charitably in his estimate of human motives. 'A prohibition,' says he, 'enforced by the denunciation of the severest temporal penalties, would have had little efficacy in abolishing a custom which existed in opposition to the feelings of humanity and natural affection;' but 'the sanction of that religion which the Rajkoomars professed was appealed to in aid of the ordinances of civil authority; and an engagement binding themselves to desist from the barbarous practice was prepared, and circulated for signature amongst the Rajkoomars.' It may well be doubted how far this influence could extend, when the root of the evil remained untouched, though not unseen, as the philanthropic Duncan pointed out in the confession of the Rajkoomars: 'all unequivocally admitted it, but all did not fully acknowledge its atrocity; and the only reason they assigned for the inhuman practice was the great expense of procuring suitable matches for their daughters, if they allowed them to grow up.' The Rajkoomar is one of Chohan sachœ, chief of the Agnicúlas, and in proportion to its high and well-deserved pretensions on the score of honour, it has more infanticides than any other of the 'thirty-six royal races'. Amongst those of this race out of the pale of feudalism, and subjected to powers not Rajpoot, the practice is fourfold greater, from the increased pressure of the cause which gave it birth, and the difficulty of establishing their daughters in wedlock. Raja Jey Sing's enactment went far to remedy this. Conjoin his plan with Mr Duncan's, provide dowers, and infanticide will cease. It is only by removing the cause that the consequences can be averted.

As to the almost universality of this practice amongst the Jarejas, the leading cause, which will also operate to its continuance, has been entirely overlooked. The Jarejas were Rajpoots, a subdivision of the Yadus; but by intermarriage with the Mahomedans, to whose faith they became proselytes, they lost their caste. Political causes have disunited them from the Mahomedans, and they desire again to be considered as pure Rājpoots; but having been contaminated, no Rajpoot will intermarry with them. The owner of a *hyde* of land, whether Seesodia, Ráhtore, or Chohan, would scorn the hand of a Jareja princess. Can the '*sic volo*' be applied to men who think in this fashion?

Having thus pointed out the causes of the sacrifice of widows and of infants, I shall touch on the yet more awful rite of *Johur*, when a whole tribe may become extinct, of which several instances have been recorded in the annals of Méwar. To the fair of other lands the fate of the Rajpootni must appear one of appalling hardship. In each stage of life, death is ready to claim her; by the poppy at its dawn, by the flames in riper years; while the safety of the interval depending on the uncertainty of war, at no period is her existence worth a twelvemonth's purchase. The loss of a battle, or the capture of a city, is a signal to avoid captivity and its horrors, which to the Rajpootni are worse than death. To the doctrines of Christianity Europe owes the boon of protection to the helpless and the fair, who are comparatively safe amidst the vicissitudes of war; to which security the chivalry of the Middle Ages doubtless contributed. But it is singular that a nation so refined, so scrupulous in its ideas with regard to females, as the Rajpoot, should not have entered into some national compact to abandon such proof of success as the bondage[6] of the sex. We can enter into the feeling, and applaud the deed, which ensured the preservation of their honour by the fatal *johur*, when the foe was the brutalised Tatar. But the practice was common in the international wars of the Rajpoots; and I possess numerous inscriptions (on stone and on brass) which record as the first token of victory the captive wives of the foeman. When 'the mother of Sisera looked out of the window, and cried through the lattice, Why tarry the wheels of his chariot—have they not sped? Have they not divided the prey; to every man a damsel or two?'[7] We have a perfect picture of the Rajpoot mother expecting her son from the foray.

The Jewish law with regard to female captives was perfectly analogous to that of Menu; both declare them 'lawful prize', and both Moses and Menu establish rules sanctioning the marriage of such captives with the captors. 'When a girl is made captive by her lover, after a victory over her kinsman,' marriage 'is permitted by law.'[8] That forcible marriage in the Hindu law termed *Rachasa*, namely, 'the seizure of a maiden by force from her house while she weeps and calls for assistance, after her kinsman and friends have been slain in battle',[9] is the counterpart of the ordinance regarding the usage of a captive in the *Pentateuch*,[10] excepting the '*shaving of the head*', which is the sign of complete slavery with the Hindu. When Hector, anticipating his fall, predicts the fate which awaits Andromache, he draws a forcible picture of the misery of the Rajpoot; but the latter, instead of a lachrymose and enervating harangue as he prepared for the battle with the same chance of defeat, would have spared her the pain of plying the 'Argive loom' by her death. To prevent such degradation, the brave Rajpoot has recourse to the *johur*, or immolation of every female of the family: nor can we doubt that, educated as are the females of that country, they gladly embrace such a refuge from pollution. Who would not be a Rajpoot in such a case? The very term widow (*rand*) is used in common parlance as one of reproach.[11]

Menu commands that whoever accosts a woman shall do so by the title of 'sister'[12] and that 'way must be made for her, even as for the aged, for a priest, a prince, or a bridegroom'; and in the admirable text on the laws of hospitality, he ordains that 'pregnant women, brides, and damsels shall have food[13] before all the other guests'; which, with various other texts, appears to indicate a time when women were less than now objects of restraint; a custom attributable to the paramount dominion of the Mahomedans, from whose rigid system the Hindus have borrowed. But so many conflicting texts are to be found in the pages of Menu, that we may pronounce the compilation never to have been the work of the same legislator: from whose dicta we may select with equal facility texts tending to degrade as to exalt the sex. For the following he would meet with many plaudits: 'Let women be constantly supplied with ornaments at festivals and jubilees, for if the wife be not elegantly attired, she will not exhilarate her husband. A wife gaily adorned, the whole house is embellished.'[14] In the following text he pays an unequivocal compliment to her power: 'A female is able to draw from the right path in this life, not a fool only, but even a sage, and can lead him in subjection to desire or to wrath.'

With this acknowledgment from the very fountain of authority, we have some ground for asserting that *les femmes font les mœurs*, even in Rajpootana; and that though immured and invisible, their influence *on* society is not less certain than if they moved in the glare of open day.

Most erroneous ideas have been formed of the Hindu female from the pictures drawn by those who never left the banks of the Ganges. They are represented as degraded beings, and that not one in many thousands can even read. I would ask such travellers whether they know the name of Rajpoot, for there are few of the lowest chieftains whose daughters are not instructed both to read and write; though the customs of the country requiring much form in epistolary writing, only the signature is made to letters. But of their intellect, and knowledge of mankind, whoever has had to converse with a Rajpootni guardian of her son's rights, must draw a very different conclusion.[15] Though excluded by the Salic law of India from governing, they are declared to be fit regents during minority; and the history of India is filled with anecdotes of able and valiant females in this capacity.[16]

The Times, 'Sati at Edur'[17]

This account of a sati at Edur, in the Mahi Canta, in which seven wives of the deceased monarch were immolated, is interesting both as an example of mass royal sati and of the palace politics that might underlie immolations. Although the British ordered an inquiry into the sati nobody was ever held to account for it.

HORRIBLE SUTTEE—(from the *Bombay Courier*, 28 September 1833)—The Rajah of Edur, a small independent state beyond the British frontier in Guzerat, died on the afternoon of the 12th August last, and when the event, which was for some time concealed, became known to his household, seven of the Ranees (his wives) rushed into the apartment where the dead body lay. The mother of the present young Rajah was alone ignorant of the fact of the death, being detained in her room by the Karbarees, or native ministers. On the morning of the 5th, the above seven Ranees, two concubines of a different caste to the Rajah, one personal man servant, and four female slaves were taken with the corpse and burnt with it, before the whole assembled population of Edur. Everybody of influence is said to have aided in the horrid tragedy, and not a single person, either connected with the Rajah's family, or otherwise, seems to have interposed a solitary effort, by word or deed, to prevent these fourteen unfortunate people from taking the fatal step and burning with their chief's body. On the contrary, the greatest alacrity was shown on all sides to complete this infamous outrage. One of the Ranees was several months advanced in pregnancy; another, who had throughout shown disinclination to sacrifice herself, had only been married nineteen months to the Rajah, and was under twenty years of age. Just before lighting the funeral pile the eldest Ranee (sixty years of age) addressed the Karabees, saying that 'she herself had always determined to die with the Rajah, and no expostulation would have turned her from her purpose, but that it was strange that she had not heard one word of dissuasion or compassion from anyone.' She concluded her remarks by desiring them to go and live on the plunder they were securing themselves by the destruction of their chief's family. The Karabees were influenced, it is understood, in sparing the life of the surviving Ranee, as she is the mother of the late Rajah's only son, and her loss might have been injurious to their interest. An extensive pillage in the Rajah's personal property, consisting of various valuables and jewels etc. is stated to have taken place for the benefit of the Karabees.

J. Erskine, Letter to J. Williams, Sati in Ahmednuggar[18]

In this official letter the local political agent gives his account of the apparently forcible immolation of the five widows of the late Raja of Ahmednuggar and the ruckus that ensued when the British tried to intervene to prevent it. In the wake of the sati, Prithee Singh and some of his retainers escaped into the hills, where they remained for some weeks before being persuaded to come in. Despite the opinion of the local political agent that the state should be sequestered, the Government of India decided that such a penalty would be unfair as a previous sati in Edur had gone unpunished.

On arriving in Ahmednuggar on the 6th Feb I was told that the Rajah Kurn Singh was not expected to live out the day. Prithee Singh, who I sent for about 12 p.m. on another matter, told me there was no hope and on his return to the palace sent word that his father was dead. Before this had taken place I had sent to ascertain whether a forcible suttee with his widows who were seven in number was contemplated, as in Edur in August 1833. I was informed that until the actual decease of the Rajah nothing on that head could be known, but immediately [after] Prithee Singh sent word of his father's decease it became generally known that five out of the seven ranees were to be sacrificed. I afterwards learnt that Kurn Singh had died late on the evening of the 5th but that it had been concealed in order to complete the preparation for the destruction of the widows. There were several large wagon loads of wood waiting outside the gate of the town as early as the morning of the 6th when I arrived, which strengthens this supposition. Early on the morning of the 7th I sent for Prithee Singh and Amir Singh, the son of Kurn Singh's first cousin, when they acquainted me that it was the intention that 5 of the 7 widows should be killed. I explained to them the horror entertained for such practices by the British government, and my intention, if possible, to prevent it on this occasion. Such an occurrence taking place at a time when a British force was on the spot, and in a country subject to British jurisdiction, rendered it in my opinion more imperative for me to exert my utmost efforts to put a stop to this ceremony formerly tolerated as a prejudice, but now rightly enacted to be a crime. At first both Prithee Singh and Amir Singh considered my persuasion to be for purposes of effect, and that I was not sincere in my desire to prevent the suttee, and the whole day was spent in representations on their part stating the necessity of the ceremony and on mine earnestly entreating them to do everything in their power to prevent it, and in stating that I should do the same. I was perfectly unconscious that this was merely to gain time, and that emissaries had been sent to every village in the Ahmednuggar zillah to send in every armed Bheel and matchlock man they could procure in order to proceed with the suttee by main force. Towards the evening large bodies of these men were pouring in from every direction in sight of our camp, on which I requested the officer commanding to insist that no more armed men should enter the town. As I conceived that there could be no occasion for that kind of force for the purpose of burning the Rajah, I was apprehensive that accidents might occur. One or two parties were disarmed and allowed to go on, being told that they should get their arms back next day. Towards evening it was reported that an immense body of armed men was assembled in the fort and a party of about fifty or sixty Coolies headed by a man said to be the Kotwal of Kurn Singh, with lit matches and strung bows passed by Lt. Lewis, who was on parade close under the walls of the town. He addressed the Kotwal, who was on horseback and told him the orders and asked him to disarm the men, on which he was menaced by one of the matchlock men, and immediately afterwards a fire of arrows and matchlock balls was opened upon him by order of the Kotwal, and one of the latter struck him in the side. This was the signal of fire, and the man made of for the gate of the fort, which was immediately closed, and fire opened on the detachment, which was not more than 200 paces from the walls from the top of the ramparts, which continued till dark. I am happy to say that Lt. Lewis's wound does not appear at present serious.... As night had set in there was no alternative but to retire to the lines, and Capt. Lardner thought necessary to remove the camp a few hundred paces from the walls, as there were known to be guns in the town, which if mounted might have done much damage to the troops. I sent immediately to the officers commanding at Ahmedabad and Husole as nothing could be done without reinforcements. The camp was removed about 8 p.m. and all was quiet until 2.30 a.m., when the alarm was given that the pile was on fire. The Guicowar Horse were encamped between the ground we formerly occupied and the river, on the banks of which the pile had been erected, and I have been informed this morning that the cries and supplications of the woman were so vociferous that every man who was asleep started from his bed. Enough people to perpetrate the violence were taken but no more, and the women were dragged over a broken part of the wall on the river side by these ruffians, attended by Kurn Singh's two sons, and with the utmost haste hurried into the pile, which, saturated with oil and clarified butter, was set fire to and the abomination completed. The Rajah's two sons, attended by a band of Rajputs, the instigators of the murder, and others, escaped from the town, and I have been able to gain no intelligence where they have gone. Any attempt to prevent the suttee must have been too late as when I was informed of the fire

I beheld the extensive blaze and knew all was over. In the morning no attempt was made to molest us from the fort except a few shots fired at the water carriers going and coming to and from the river, and most of the Bheels and Coolies had made their escape from the fort during the night.... I have since been informed that the whole of the case of suttee at this place was one of compulsion, both towards the women and towards Prithee Singh, who was disposed to take my advice on that subject, and I am happy to say that one of the principle instigators of the violence fell into our hands on the occasion of the attack on Lt. Lewis, and that he is in confinement. I have omitted to state that I went to the funeral pile which was erected, accompanied by Mr Lewis, and that it was built on such a principle that the escape of the women was quite impossible, had they showed any disposition to have effected it, and that from the statement of some of the Guicowar Horse men who happened to be awake at the time that the pile was set fire to, it appears that great violence was made use of before the abominable rite was carried into execution. Severe punishment by the British government of the perpetrators of this enormity is absolutely necessary in this instance, which will have the happy effect of putting at once an end to this repeated deluge of blood carried on in these petty states of Ahmednuggar and Edur, and unless immediate and effectual measures are adopted against these refractory chiefs the state of this part of the country will assume a most alarming appearance.

Punjabee Akhbar, Death of Maharaja Ranjit Singh[19]

This account from a Punjabi newspaper recounts the events that took place on the death of Ranjit Singh, Lion of the Punjab. It is interesting to note that as well as the four ranees and seven slave girls, a male minister also declared his intention to immolate himself, but unlike his female counterparts he was prevented from burning.

The death of the Maharaja being known, the Ranees, Koonwar Khurruck Singh, Raja Dhian Singh, Jemedar Khooshal Singh, and others raised their cries and lamentations, tearing their hair, casting earth upon their heads, throwing themselves on the ground, and striking their heads against bricks and stones. This continued during the night by the side of the corpse. Every now and then looking towards the corpse their shrieks were shriller. The gates of the fort were shut, but Koonwar Khurruck Singh ordered the shops in the city to be open and business to be carried on. Koonwar Khurruck Singh, Raja Dhian Singh and others had a bier of sandalwood prepared and embroidered with golden flowers. Raja Dhian Singh prepared to burn himself with the Maharaja, but the Koondar and the Sirdars threw their turbans at his feet to dissuade him, alleging that without him the affairs of the state would be deranged. It was not until after some hours passed in their beseeching that they could prevail on him. Then the Raja proposed to go to Benaras after a year, which was complied with. Ranee Koondan, called 'Guddhan' daughter of Raja Sunsar Chund of Kuttack, Ranee Hurderie, daughter of Meehan Pudum being of Noorpore, Ranee Raj Koonwar, daughter of Sunder Jysing of Chynpore, a village about seven miles from Amritsar and the Ranee Baewallee came and approached the corpse weeping and resolved to burn themselves with their husband. Koonwar Khurruck Singh did his utmost to dissuade them, he pointed out to them the dignity and the affluence they were possessed of and promised that in future he would be with all his heart and soul most devoted to them would they only relinquish their intention, but they would not for a moment listen either to the appeals of the Koonwar or the other chiefs. Ranee 'Guddhan' taking Raja Dhian Singh by the hand and placing it on the breast of the corpse made him swear never to be a traitor to Koonwar Khurruck Singh and Nowuihal Singh or to be inattentive to the welfare of the state. Koonwar Khurruck Singh was in like manner made to swear to be led away by no misrepresentations of interested parties to renounce Raja Dhian Singh; and the torment due for the slaughter of a thousand cows was imprecated on him who should violate his oath. The corpse was then washed by the Koonwar with the waters of the Ganges and placed on the splendid bier. Raja Dhian Singh and Herah Singh, Khooshal Singh Ajeet Singh Sundhanwalla, the Vakeels of Alloowalla of Ladoak of Jehara Hursundas and others threw flowers on the bier and it was carried in procession in the garden at Dhoolkote, situated in the fort near the Huzlgoree Gate adjoining to Gooroo Higin's residence. The four Ranees clad in the richest apparel and jewels worth many lakh of rupees accompanied the procession, bestowing every now and then some portion of their jewels and ornaments to the singers and the Brahmins. Having arrived at the funeral pile made of sandalwood the corpse was placed upon it. Ranee Khoondun sat down by its side and placed the head of the deceased on her lap while the other three Ranees with seven slave girls seated themselves around with every mark of satisfaction on their countenances. At ten o'clock, nearly the time set by the Brahmins, Koonwar Khurruck Singh set fire to the pile and the ruler of the Punjab with four Ranees and seven slave girls was reduced to ashes. A small cloud appeared in the sky over the burning pile and having shed a few drops cleared away. No one saw a hope of relief but in resignation. Raja Dhian Singh attempted four times to jump into the burning pile but was withheld by the multitude. After the ceremony was over Koonwar Khurruck Singh and the other chiefs bathed themselves in the Ravee and returned to the Huzgooree Garden. Fifteen lakh shawls and twenty ducats were given to the singers of the holy Hymns of Baba Nanuk and 1000 rupees were distributed among the poor. The Koonwar sat lamenting. The heart is rent in attempting a description of the distress and lamentations in the Palace amongst the Ranees and among the citizens of every age, sex and religion.

Notes

1   Tod, James, *Annals and Antiquities of Rajasthan*, vol.2, W. Crooke (ed.) (London: Oxford University Press, 1920)

2   Menu, *On Women*, chap. v. text 157, 160, 161.

3   Were all Menu's maxims on this head collected, and with other good authorities, printed, circulated, and supported by Hindu missionaries, who might be brought to advocate the abolition of Satiism, some good might be effected. Let every text tending to the respectability of widowhood be made prominent, and degrade the opponents by enumerating the weak points they abound in. Instance the polyandrism which prevailed among the Pandus, whose high priest Vyasu was an illegitimate branch; though above all would be the efficacy of the abolition of polygamy, which in the lower classes leaves women destitute, and in the higher

condemns them to mortification and neglect. Whatever result such a course might produce, there can be no danger in the experiment. Such sacrifices must operate powerfully on manners; and, barbarous as is the custom, yet while it springs from the same principle, it ought to improve the condition of women, from the fear that harsh treatment of them might defeat the atonement hereafter. Let the advocate for the abolition of this practice by the hand of power, read attentively Mr Colebrooke's essay, 'On the Duties of a faithful Hindu Widow', in the fourth volume of the *Asiatic Researches*, to correct the notion that there is no adequate religious ordinance for the horrid sacrifice. Mr C. observes (p. 220): 'Though an alternative be allowed, the Hindu legislators have shown themselves disposed to encourage widows to burn themselves with their husband's corpse.' In this paper he will find too many authorities deemed sacred for its support; but it is only by knowing the full extent of the prejudices and carefully collecting the conflicting authorities, that we can provide the means to overcome it. Jehangir legislated for the abolition of this prac-tice by successive ordinances. At first he commanded that no woman, being mother of a family, should under any circumstances be permitted, however willing, to immolate herself; and subsequently the prohibition was made entire when the slightest compulsion was required, 'whatever the assurances of the people might be'. The royal commentator records no reaction. We might imitate Jehangir, and adopting the partially prohibi-tive ordinance, forbid the sacrifice where there was a family to rear.

4   The Ghikers, a Scythic race inhabiting the banks of the Indus, at an early period of history were given to infanticide. 'It was a custom,' says Ferishta, 'as soon as a female child was born, to carry her to the marketplace and there proclaim aloud, holding the child in one hand and a knife in the other, that any one wanting a wife might have her; otherwise she was immolated.' By this means they had more men than women, which occa-sioned the custom of several husbands to one wife. When any one husband visited her, she set up a mark at the door, which being observed by the others, they withdrew till the signal was removed.

5   Could they be induced to adopt the custom of the ancient Marsellois, infanticide might cease: 'Marseille fut la plus sage des républiques de son temps: les dots ne pourraient passer cents écus en argent, et cinq en habits, dit Strabon.' —*De l'Esprit des Loix*, chap. xv. liv. v. 21.

6   *Bunda* is 'a bondsman' in Persian; *Bandi*, 'a female slave' in Hindi.

7   Jud. v. 28–30.

8   Menu, on Marriage, art. 26.

9   Menu, on Marriage, art. 33.

10   'When thou goest forth to war against thine enemies, and the Lord thy God hath delivered them into thine hands, and thou hast taken them cap-tive, and seest among the captives a beautiful woman, and hast a desire unto her, that thou wouldest have her to thy wife; then thou shalt bring her

home to thine house, and she shall shave her head, and pare her nails; and she shall put the raiment of her captivity from off her, and shall remain in thine house, and bewail her father and her mother a full month: and after that thou shalt go in unto her, and be her husband, and she shall be thy wife.'—Deut. xxi. 10, 11, 12, 13.

11   I remember in my subaltern days, and wanderings through countries then little known, one of my Rajpoot soldiers at the well, impatient for water, asked a woman for the rope and bucket by the uncivil term of *rand*: 'Myn Rajpútni ché,' 'I am a Rajputni,' she replied in the Hara dialect, to which tribe she belonged, '*aur Rajpoot ca ma cho*,' 'and the mother of Rajpoots'. At the indignant reply the hands of the brave Kulian were folded, and he asked her forgiveness by the endearing and respectful epithet of 'mother'. It was soon granted, and filling his brass vessel, she dismissed him with the epithet of 'son', and a gentle reproof. Kulian was himself a Rajpoot, and a bolder lives not, if he still exists; this was in 1807, and in 1817 he gained his sergeant's knot, as one of the thirty-two firelocks of my guard, who led the attack, and defeated a camp of fifteen hundred Pindarries.

12   On Education, art. 129.

13   On Marriage, art. 114.

14   On Marriage, arts. 57, 60, 61, 62, 63.

15   I have conversed for hours with the Boondi queen-mother on the affairs of her government and welfare of her infant son, to whom I was left guardian by his dying father. She had adopted me as her brother; but the conversation was always in the presence of a third person in her confidence, and a curtain separated us. Her sentiments showed invariably a correct and extensive knowledge, which was equally apparent in her letters, of which I had many. I could give many similar instances.

16   Ferishta in his history gives an animated picture of Durgavati, queen of Gurrah, defending the rights of her infant son against Akber's ambition. Like another Boadicea, she headed her army, and fought a desperate battle with Asoph Khan, in which she was wounded and defeated; but scorning flight, or to survive the loss of independence, she, like the antique Roman in such a predicament, slew herself on the field of battle.

Whoever desires to judge of the comparative fidelity of the translations of this writer, by Dow and Briggs, cannot do better than refer to this very passage. The former has clothed it in all the trappings of Ossianic decoration: the latter gives 'a plain unvarnished tale', which ought to be the aim of every translator.

17   'Sati at Edur', in *The Times*, 17 March 1834.

18   Letter from J. Erskine (Assistant Police Commissioner of Gujerat) to J. Williams, the Commissioner of Gujerat, 9 February 1835, Oriental and India Office, Board's Collections, vol. 1540, 1835–6, 61224.

19   Account from *Punjabee Akhbar*, 27 June 1839.

10

Official Policy

Bombay Despatches, East India Company Board of Control[1]

In this letter the Board of Control passed judgment on the Bombay government's handling of the Ahmednuggar affair in 1835 and discussed possible ways of proceeding with relation to this case and to sati more generally.

We now reply to your Political Letter dated 17th September (No. 34) and 15th October (No. 36) of 1835, the former reporting to us the occurrence of a compulsory suttee at Ahmednuggar on the death of Kurn Sing, the Raja of that petty state; the latter relating the disturbed state of the Myhee Caunta generally. We have perused these dispatches with much concern; both on account of the painful nature of the events reported in them, and the new evidence they afford of that mismanagement of the affairs of the Myhee Caunta which we have on several occasions had to deplore; but which our admonitions have not yet caused to be remedied. When the death of Kurn Sing, Raja of Ahmednuggar took place, Mr Erskine, the assistant to the Political Commissioner happened to be at that town with a detachment of 300 men. On learning from common report that a suttee was in contemplation, Mr Erskine endeavoured by representations to the late Raja's eldest son Prithee Sing, a youth of seventeen years of age, and other members of the family to avert the catastrophe. That his attempts should have been unsuccessful can excite no surprise when it is remembered that less than two years ago a compulsory suttee had taken place at Edur on the death of Raja Gumbhere Sing, of so sanguinary a kind as to have excited, according to Mr Erskine 'a universal feeling of horror and disgust' notwithstanding which, although an enquiry and the punishment of the delinquents was threatened by your government, the threat was never carried into effect, but on the contrary, one of the principal authors of the crime was found some months after in the full possession of the favours of government. Considering the strong feelings of family pride in which these barbarous ceremonies on the part of Rajpoot families originate, and the fact that Edur and Ahmednuggar are the two principal Rajpoot principalities of the Myhee Caunta, it is probable that nothing but the most decided measures against the authors of the suttee at Edur could have prevented the example set on that occasion from being followed by the rival family. And if the events at Edur really excited the general horror mentioned by Mr Erskine, decided measures might on that occasion have been taken without offending the prejudices of the people. But when by overlooking the transaction you had held out to all other persons in similar circumstances the expectation that they would be allowed to follow the example, there would have been gross injustice in your punishing the Ahmednuggar family for acting upon that; and the only ground on which any measures against that family can be justified, is the fact that the British troops were fired upon by the coolies who had been assembled to protect the suttee. For this act of hostility an ample reparation was indispensable; and that reparation would have been afforded by a fine, and the punishment of Nackjee, the Kotwal who ordered the men to fire upon the British troops, and of the man who wounded Lt Lewis. Instead, however, of proceeding to Ahmednuggar and entering into communication with Prithee Sing, who does not appear to have been personally implicated in the transaction, and on whom there seems little doubt that by conciliatory means the desirable impression might have been made; Mr Williams, immediately upon receiving Mr Erskine's report, forwarded it to your government with the following recommendation. 'I beg leave strongly to recommend to Government the necessity of taking possession of Ahmednuggar and its dependencies in the name of the British

Government, as such an outrage as the present cannot be suffered to pass with impunity, and the conduct of the Government of that state has never been such as to deserve any consideration. Even if it could be proved that Prithee Sing had been compelled to these acts, it must be considered that his inability to prevent the disturbance clearly proves his unfitness to have the nominal control over so turbulent a race. I beg, therefore earnestly, to press on the consideration of Government the propriety of this measure.'

You pointed out to Mr Williams that the state of Ahmednuggar was not under British jurisdiction; that we were connected with it solely as collectors of the Guicowar's dues, and that our assuming the country and governing it in our own name, was therefore out of the question. You, however, ordered Mr Williams to proceed to Ahmednuggar and to assume the temporary administration of the country. The town of Ahmednuggar was consequently occupied with our troops; Prithee Sing and the Carbarrees and other persons implicated in the late transactions, having in the meantime retired to the hills. After considerable delay Prithee Sing was induced to come in and deliver up the Carbarree Roopram and Nackjee Kotwal, who gave the order to fire upon our troops; but you were at the date of the last advices awaiting the instructions of the Government of India both as to the treatment of the prisoners, the settlement of the Government, and measures to be adopted to abolish the peculiarly atrocious form of suttee which prevails among the Rajpoot families of the Myhee Caunta. Until we are apprised of the sentiments of the Supreme Government we are not prepared to decide upon the suggestion of your President with a view to the abolition of suttee in the Myhee Caunta. We, however, do not hesitate to express our agreement in the opinion that has already been intimated to you by the Supreme Government; that this object, like the suppression of infanticide, should be sought by negotiation rather than by authoritative imposition. And in regard to the particular case, we are distinctly of the opinion that to deprive the reigning Ahmednuggar of their inheritance in consequence of the suttee, or to punish the perpetrators of it with anything more severe than exclusion from power, would have the hardship and injustice of an ex-post-facto law. For the defiance of our authority manifested by firing on our troops, adequate but not vindictive punishment must of course be inflicted, both upon the immediate agents and upon all persons in authority may be proved to have been their instigators.

Major Thoresby to the Rajput Chiefs[2]

Prior to 1844, the official policy of the Government of India towards sati in the Rajput States was one of non-interference. It was feared that any attempt by the British to intervene on the issue would only cause greater attachment to the custom. In 1844, however, prompted by the success of unilateral discussion held by Capt. John Ludlow with the Jaipur court, the Board of Directors relaxed their view and allowed individual political agents to use their own judgment on the matter. The result was this circular from the chief political agent for Rajputana to the Indian rulers, stating British abhorrence of sati and suggesting the pleasure which prohibition of the rite would be viewed by the British Government.

The act of suttee is still performed in some parts of Rajasthan, though this practice, like that of seeking death by leaping off the summit of precipices or jumping into a well etc. etc. is forbidden and improper. Referring to the well-known Munnoo Smriti, Yag-Balika Dhurm Shastera, agreeable to the doctrines of which it is incumbent that the conduct should be regulated in the present Kal Yoong age of the world, there is no mention to be found of the rite of suttee by burning, which custom must therefore have had its origin and its currency in the unaided device of the human mind and in self-will and the force of example; but the denounced sin of self-destruction appears obviously to attach to it. Wherefore it is the wish of the British government that guilt involved in this species of self-destruction may not continue to pervade Rajasthan, from which consideration, I now address you to express my sentiments as to the urgent propriety of your endeavouring to bring about that this practice shall become extinct in your territories. Should anyone contemplate such a deed, let it be fully explained on the occasion that the prescribed and authorised life of purity and devotion must necessarily be infinitely preferable to the act of concremation, and more beneficial to the departed husband. And should the individual unhappily, from want of enlightenment, not listen to reason, then it would be expedient that she receive no assistance from relatives and others in the way of collecting fuel and setting fire to the pile etc. etc. In this manner the practice will of itself, as a matter of course cease to exist, which event will redound to the honour of all Rajasthan throughout the world.

Lt. Col. Sir Henry Lawrence to the States of Rajputana[3]

In the letter from which the following extract is taken, Sir Henry Lawrence, then the Agent to the Governor-General for Rajputana, detailed the progress made so far in the abolition of sati and discussed possibility of more stringent action against those states who had not yet fallen into line with British requests for prohibition, especially Udaipur. Lawrence's tone is in keeping with the more authoritarian stance of the British Government at this point, but his suggestions were never implemented as the Uprising of 1857 soon broke out and after this the Government was more cautious in its treatment of the Princes.

As I have told the Political Agent these crimes [satis] and the slight punishments inflicted, prove not only that Maharaja Tuckt Singh [of Jodhpur] is not in earnest in trying to put down the crimes, but that he can hardly be earnest about desiring to please the British Government. He has less excuse in that he was born and brought up a petty chief in Goojrat, where these crime [sic] have for many years been prohibited. He is also well acquainted with British manners and customs and I have little doubt that countenanced by us he has the power, if he chooses, of suppressing the crimes. I have no doubt at all that if he had exerted himself in the least, not one half of the recent atrocities would have occurred. The Maharana of Meywar [Udaipur] has acted a more open part. He justifies suttee as a holy and ancient rite, obtaining from the earliest times, and as having so strong a hold on the so-called religious feeling of the people as to render it difficult for him to forbid and impossible to prevent. He says, however, that he will do what he can but that no-one obeys him. His tone is altogether objective. I am, however, quite satisfied that he could have prevented every one of the four suttees that have occurred, or rather that have been reported, in the past year in Meywar. Not one was in the family of a chief. The parties concerned were all more or less directly dependent on the Durbar.... For forty years British power alone has supported the several princes of Meywar. The sovereignty hardly existed at the beginning of British connection. It has ever since been propped up by us, yet the prince will not do, in the cause of humanity, what every other sovereign throughout India has done. It is all nonsense his saying that nobody obeys him. He has power enough to do mischief; half his chiefs are obedient and he has three regiments with some guns at command. Assertions of weakness are put forward for evading unpleasant requisitions. If the Maharana is to be an exception to the rest of India in one great question of humanity, he ought in other matters to be similarly isolated, and left to manage his territory in his own way. The very threat, coming from Government would probably bring him to reason; it has failed coming from myself and the Political Agent. He has been too long accustomed to undeserved favours to be now easily moved in any matter contrary to his own views and prejudices. I have never dealt with so impracticable a prince.... After much consideration and consultation with many natives and Europeans in this Province I consider it quite safe to forbid by proclamation throughout Foreign States, as has been done in British territory, suttee and sumadh. I am not sure that the Maharana of Meywar will not in his heart prefer such an order (and the political agent in Meywar says he will) to voluntarily following the example of his brother Princes. Meywar alone stood out against matrimonial alliances with the Moguls and similarly her pride prevents her voluntarily joining the throng in prohibiting suttee. Possibly, the fact of successful resistance on former occasions influences present conduct. An order on our part would save the Maharana's honour...as Paramount in India I believe we are fully justified in issuing such an order. The Kings of Delhi, when strong enough to enforce their orders, issued them throughout the Hindoo Principalities.... I do not at all agree in the present prevailing opinions regarding annexation, but on some other points I hold that we have not done our duty. It seems to me as incumbent upon us to put down suttee as thuggee and dacoity, even if it be done by the sword. Nowhere in India have judiciously carried out honest measures occasioned disturbance. I see no reason why an order such as I suggest should occasion difficulties in Rajpootana. Still less do I see why we should support a people who before our eyes commit or permit murder.... If Meywar would even agree to do what other states have done and exert itself some, there would be excuse for further parley, but the Maharana, at a juncture when…he is most anxious to conciliate us, defends the rite and declares his inability even if he possessed the will, to put it down, the plea being true to some extent in the estates of half a dozen of his nobles. There therefore, seems to me no remedy but to act imperatively.

Henry Bushby, *Widow-Burning*[4]

This account of the British campaign to abolish sati in princely India, published in the form of a short tract, was written by ex-political agent Henry Bushby. Like many other officials, Bushby gave the credit for suppressing the rite almost entirely to the British, and in particular to Captain John Ludlow, the political agent at Jaipur.

On 30th August 1838, the princely city of Oodeypore was the scene of a terrible solemnity. About midday, a prolonged discharge of artillery from the fort announced the unexpected decease of Maharana Juwan Singh; and, as is usual in tropical climates, preparations for his obsequies immediately commenced. The palace gate was thronged with an expectant populace. Something, however, in the excitement of their voices and gestures, boded the approach of a spectacle even more thrilling than mere pomp could render even a royal funeral. It was not the dead alone that the eager crowd was waiting to see pass from among them. Sculptured in startling abundance on the tombs of their rulers, the well-known effigies of women's feet (the distinctive memorial of a suttee) gave ghastly assurance that a prince of Oodeypore would not that day be gathered to his fathers without a wife, or concubine, sharing his pyre. The only question was— how many? It was known that the younger of the two queens came of a family in which the rite was rarely practised; while the suddenness of the Maharana's death had given but scanty time for any of his inferior women to mature so tremendous a resolution. Great therefore was the admiration of the multitude when they learnt that immediately on the fatal tidings reaching the zenana, both queens and six out of seven concubines determined to burn. The seventh, a favourite, had excused herself on the plea—which, characteristically enough, was at once admitted—that 'she felt none of the inspiration deemed necessary to the sanctity of the sacrifice'.

It next became the duty of the nobles to address the ladies with the forms of dissuasion. But to these they quickly put an end by an act that rendered retreat impossible; loosening their hair and unveiling their faces, they went to the gates of the zenana, and presented themselves before the assembled populace. All opposition to their wishes now ceased. They were regarded as sacred to the departed monarch. Devout ejaculations poured incessantly from their lips. Their movements became invested with a mysterious significance, and their words were treasured as prophetic.

Meantime the pile had been prepared. The eight victims, dressed in their finest attire, and mounted on horseback, moved with the procession to the cemetery. There they were stripped of their ornaments and jewels, distributed gifts to the bystanders, and lastly, mounting the pile, took their places beside the corpse. As the Maharana had left no son, his nephew, the present sovereign, applied the torch. The crash of music, the chanting of the priests, and the cries of the multitude arose simultaneously, and the tragedy was consummated. 'The father of one of the queens' (concludes the native report) 'was present during the whole. He is here immersed in contemplation and grief, and his companions are comforting him.'

Perhaps at this point, some of our readers may feel puzzled by the recollection that Lord William Bentinck is celebrated in numberless works as having put down all atrocities of this kind more than twenty years ago. And true that he did so as far as his authority extended; but within that limit the operation was necessarily confined. In other words, out of about seventy-seven million souls, this prohibition reached directly only the thirty-seven million who were British subjects, indirectly perhaps some nineteen million more, consisting of the subjects of princes in whose internal management we had some voice; while there remained not less than twenty-one million, the subjects of states which, though our allies, could in no degree be reached by the legislation of 1829. The kingdom of Oodeypore, or Meywar was of the last class. The only notice, therefore, that the Governor-General of 1838 (Lord Auckland) could take of the horrors above detailed, was by way of private communication. The Resident of Oodeypore was instructed to explain unofficially displeasure with which the British government had heard of the tragedy, and the prominent part played in it by the new sovereign himself. The Resident's opinion was then asked as to the most suitable compliment to be paid to those nobles who had sought to dissuade the ladies from their resolution; and the answer was noteworthy. Lord Auckland was apprised that the personages in question would simply feel 'disgraced' by any tribute which should imply that their dissuasions had been meant for aught but decorous forms!

Such was the veneration in which, up to a date so recent, the sacrifice of suttee was held by a vast proportion of our allies, and such the acquiescence with which the British government perforce regarded its celebration. Within the last seven years [this piece was written in 1851], however, the rite has occasioned one of the most remarkable movements recorded in eastern annals. Never before, within historical memory, had the Hindoos exhibited the phenomenon of religious change. During that brief period, an agitation has sprung up, which has led more than half the great independent states to repudiate a sacrifice regarded by their forefathers, not only as sacred, but as a standing miracle in attestation of their faith. So extraordinary an exception to the tyranny of tradition would demand investigation were it only as a psychological problem; but how much more is this the case when the wonder is known to be the work of a single British officer!

Strange to say, the movement originated in the very stronghold of the rite. Among the states which gloried in the readiness of their women to brave this supreme test of conjugal devotion, none exercised a wider influence over Hindu opinion than the small knot of powers on the North-West frontier, who occupy the provinces collectively known as Rajputana. The respect paid throughout India to the blood of the Rajputs—*Anglice*, 'the progeny of Princes'— is well known.

Matrimonial alliances with their chiefs are eagerly sought by potentates of thrice their territorial importance. A race of soldiers and hunters, their figures and faces are eminently handsome and martial, their voices loud; and when they laugh it is with a hearty burst, like Europeans, in broad contrast to the stealthy chuckle of the Bengali, or to the silent reserved smile of the Mussalman. Unlike those too they scorn the pursuits of the desk; and even agriculture has only become common among them since the tranquilisation of the frontier has diminished their opportunities of obtaining military service among their feudal lords. Whatever a Hindu knows of chivalry and nationality, he deems to be exemplified in this model race. Since, therefore, Rajputs were renowned for the frequency of their suttees, the great independent states thought it beneath their orthodoxy to return any other answer to the remonstrances of the British government against the rite than that 'it would be time enough to prohibit it when Rajputana lead the way'.

This, they doubtless thought, was to postpone the change indefinitely. Many in truth and pitiful were the instances, which seemed to forbid hope that the Rajputs would ever take the lead in such a course. One of these had already been given. A second—the last with which we shall pain our readers—must be added because it illustrates the chief difficulty with which the friends of abolition had to contend. It was the belief of those officers who had acquired the longest experience in Rajput affairs that every attempt on the part of the British government to remonstrate against suttee had been followed by an increase in the number of the sacrifices. This opinion, which whether right or wrong, naturally carried weight with the government, and had caused the active discouragement of any active interference in the matter, was supposed to receive further corroboration in the occurrence we are about to narrate. Early in 1840 the political agent, or chargé d'affaires, at the Rajput court of Kotah had ventured, on his own responsibility, to break through the cautious reserve thus prescribed by apprising the chief of that state that the British government would be gratified to hear that His Highness had abolished suttee throughout his dominions. 'My friend,' replied the prince, 'the customs alluded to have been handed down from the first fathers of mankind. They have obtained in every nation of India, and more especially in Rajputana; for whenever a sovereign of these states has bidden farewell to life, the queens, through the yearnings of the inward spirit have become suttees, notwithstanding that the relatives were adverse to the sacrifice and would fain have prevented it altogether.

It is not in the power of a mortal to nullify a divine, though myste-rious ordinance!' With true Oriental complaisance, however, His Highness promised his best efforts to undertake the impossibility. 'Since,' he concludes, 'it will afford the English government pe-culiar pleasure, I shall take such measures as lie in my power to prohibit the practice.'

It appears that nobody except the officer to whom it was ad-dressed attached any value to this plausible assurance. The veteran diplomatist who at the time superintended our relations with the Rajput states, was even led to augur from it some fresh outbreak of religious zeal in favour of the rite. An example was not long wanting. About 3 p.m. on 29 October 1840, a Brahmin, by name Luchman, died at Kotah and his widow declared her intention of burning with the corpse. The permission of the reigning prince had in the first instance to be obtained. Now therefore, was the time for testing the pledge which he had given to the chargé d'affaires. His Highness absolutely declined to use his authority. The chief constable was indeed sent to address the ordinary dis-suasions to the woman and to promise her a livelihood in case she survived, but the victim, as usual, was resolute. To the offer of maintenance she is said to have answered, 'There are a hundred people related to me, and I have no such thoughts to annoy me. I am about to obey the influence of God.'

The sight of her infant son did not shake her. All the marvels which the arts of the priesthood could conjure up on such occasions were employed to convince the populace that it was the will of heaven that the sacrifice should proceed. 'It has been usual,' naively wrote the Kotah minister in his exculpatory account of the catastrophe to the chargé d'affaires, 'it has been usual on a disposition to burn being evinced, to confine the individual in a room under lock and key; and if these efforts should be frustrated by the voluntary bursting of the locks and doors, it was a sure sign that her intention was pure and sincere and that it was useless to oppose it. This test was applied on the present occasion, and both locks and doors flew open! Moreover, it was known that a Suttee's words, for good or evil, would assuredly come true; which of itself deterred any spectator from interfering. Your agency messenger brought her to the palace, and took her by the hand;

though, as she was regarded as dead to the world and all its creatures, this ought not to have been done. He was told to take a guard and dissuade her if he could, but he did not succeed.'

The chief constable soon obtained sufficient warranty on the strength of the woman's determination to satisfy himself of the propriety of ordering the pyre...the funeral procession was on the point of commencing when the resident sent a servant of his own to make a final effort to dissuade the victim. The messenger found the Brahmins plying her with camphor, and was wholly unable to overcome the natural and artificial exaltation she exhibited. Moreover, the crowd was impatient at what they deemed so pernicious an opposition to divine will, and bore the woman off to the palace in order to obtain the chief's prohibition of any further attempts of the kind. The messenger had the courage to accompany them. On being admitted to the presence, he reminded His Highness of his late promise to the resident; but his remonstrances were quickly neutralized by an adroit hint to the prince from a native courtier that 'if the widow's purpose were thwarted, she might utter some imprecations fatal to the state!'

On this His Highness declared that he would stand neutral on the matter 'he would neither assent nor dissent—the messenger might do his best'. The Brahmin crowd of course, interpreted this as it was meant; they jostled the emissaries of the chargé d'affaires, and even threw out threats against that officer himself, in case of further interference. Musicians now came out from the palace to assist at the ceremony; a sumptuous dress and ornaments were presented to the woman; and thus decorated and attended she was escorted to the place of sacrifice. Secret orders to use dispatch had in the meantime been sent by the prince, and so well were these obeyed, that within three hours of Luchman Brahmin's death, his widow had shared his obsequies.

It is true that cases have occurred more horrible than those above related. Instances are on record in which, at the supreme moment, women have lost courage and starting up from the pile have torn off their sacrificial garlands and cried out for mercy! Unhappily too, it is not improbable that, on some of these occasions, the fatal belief that a suttee's resolution, once voluntarily taken is irrevocable, may have caused the bystanders to thrust the victim remorselessly back into the flames; or if, from British interposition, a rescue has been effected, the woman has, it may be, survived only to curse the pity which, to save her from a few moments of pain, has deprived her, as she deems, of ages of happiness. These things have been but with rare exceptions, the suttee is a voluntary victim. Resolute, undismayed, confident in her own inspiration, but betraying by the tone of her prophecies which are almost always auspicious—and by the gracious acts by which she takes leave of her household, and by the gifts which she lavishes on the bystanders, that her tender woman's heart is the true source from which that inspiration flows, the child widow barely has time to bewail her husband before she makes ready to rejoin him.

She is dressed like a bride, but it is a bride who has been received within the zenana of her bridegroom. Her veil is put off, her hair unbound; and so adorned, and so exposed, she goes forth to gaze on the world for the first time face to face, ere she leaves it. She does not blush nor quail. She scarcely regards the bearded crowd who press so eagerly towards her. Her lips move in momentary prayer. Paradise is in her view. She sees her husband awaiting with approbation the sacrifice which shall restore her to him, dowered with the expiation of their sins, and enobled with a martyr's crown. What wonder if, dazzled with these visionary glories, she heeds not the shouting throng, the ominous pile? Exultingly she mounts the last earthly couch she shall share with her lord. His head she places fondly on her lap. The priests set up their chant—it is a strange hymeneal—and her firstborn son, walking thrice round the pile, lights the flame. If the impulse which can suffice to steel a woman's nerve to encounter so painful a death, and to overpower the yearnings of her heart to the children she may leave behind her—if such an impulse is, even to the eye of philosophy, a strange evidence of the power of faith and of the depth and strength of tenderness. Surely we may well conceive how the superstitious Hindu should trace in it more directly the finger of God himself. They, we are persuaded, will best cope with this superstition—for they alone will comprehend the grounds on which it rests—who, content with the weapons of truth, will own, that love, and beauty, and death—terror, wonder, pity—

never conspired to form a rite more solemn and affecting to the untutored heart of man.[5]

The confirmation that the Kotah case seemed to give to the current opinion on the danger of interference, had naturally caused an official neutrality on the subject to be prescribed more strictly than ever to our residents at the native courts; and complete inaction was the order of the day. Not to multiply instances of this policy, we may mention that in 1842 Lord Ellenborough expressly declined to sanction an offer made by the chargé d'affaires at Hyderabad, to procure from its Mohammedan ruler a prohibition of the rite.

It was in the midst of this general despondency that Major (now Lt. Col.) Ludlow, chargé d'affaires at Jyepore, conceived the idea of assailing the superstition in its stronghold. His scheme was simple, and not new—qualities which are the best evidence of the difficulties that had hitherto prevented its execution. Long ago, Oriental scholars, both native and European, had shown that the rite was not only unsanctioned, but inferentially forbidden, by the earliest and most influential Hindu scriptures. Nay, Col. Tod, in his book on Rajputana had actually indicated this anomaly in the Hindu doctrine as the best point of attack for abolitionists to select.

Yet, though that valuable work was published in 1829, and though the author, from the position he long held as chief diplomatic officer in the country he so well describes, had the amplest opportunities for carrying out his own suggestion, it was reserved for Major Ludlow in 1844, to put it to the test of practice and vanquish the obstacles that had hitherto confined it to the dreamland of speculative benevolence. The explanation for this previous inaction is not difficult. Scholars, it is true, had proved suttee to be an innovation and a heresy; but it was an innovation of 2000 years standing and a heresy abetted by the priesthood since the days of Alexander. Though unnoticed by Menu, the supplementary writings which the Hindus, like the Jews, have overlaid their primitive books are profuse in its praise. Above all, let the force of appeal from the more recent to the primitive code be what it might—it could not but be attended with suspicion when proceeding from religionists who equally repudiated both one and the other. It is not a matter for surprise that Englishmen should have hesitated long to assail with the delicate weapon of theological criticism a rite thus strong in remote antiquity, in venerated records, in a hierarchy at once ignorant and unscrupulous, and in the associations with which innumerable traditions of womanly courage and constancy had ennobled it in the eyes of the Hindu people.

His resolution once taken, however, there were circumstances in Major Ludlow's position not unfavourable to the enterprise. He enjoyed peculiar opportunities of intercourse with the nobles of the court to which he was accredited. The prince of Jyepore was a minor and the government was carried out by a council of regency, over which the Major presided. Not only did he thus possess a more direct voice in the administration than his post as charge d'affaires would have given him, but he had already used this vantage ground to dissipate to an extraordinary degree, the jealousies likely to be excited by his native colleagues by any interference in their native customs. He had even contrived to bring the other Rajput states to combine with Jyepore for an object not wholly alien from that which he had at present in view.

Then, as now, the abuse that he had undertaken to assail concerned their zenanas; and his bitterest opponents were likely to be found among their priests. Old maids, as our readers have probably heard, are sadly depreciated in the East. A Rajput girl who remains long unwedded is a disgrace to her house but that was not the only danger that but a few years ago her father had to fear. Should he succeed in finding her a husband, the chances were that the family estate would be hopelessly encumbered in providing the gratuities claimed by the priests and minstrels who were certain to flock to the nuptials. No Rajput is above the dead of satire and imprecations; and those worthies notoriously dispensed their blessings and applauses, or their curses and lampoons according to the price at which their services were retained. The result was that their favour was purchased at almost any cost. 'The Dahima emptied his coffers at the marriage of his daughter', ran a favourite distich of these venal bards, 'but he filled them up with the praises of mankind!'

The Rajputs at large were not disposed to be Dahimas, nor yet to brave the scandal of housing marriageable daughters. They found refuge from the dilemma in infanticide. Parents reared just so many girls as they could afford to marry off, and destroyed the rest. The criminality of the practice was indeed acknowledged. Rajput decorum demanded that it should be veiled in secrecy but that was all. A trifling penance absolved the perpetrator. Nobody dreamed of dragging such affairs into publicity. If a son was born the fact was announced to enquirers with exaltation; if a daughter, the answer was 'Nothing!' and those who came to congratulate went silently away. At the same time it must not be supposed that this system had grown up to such monstrous maturity without some degree of resistance on the part of the native rulers. It appears that here and there, and at various periods, a Rajput prince had sought to reach the evil by sumptuary enactments in restraint of nuptial gratuities; but that fear of reproach of their kinsmen in neighbouring communities had invariably deterred the subjects from taking advantage of the remedy.

Major Ludlow conceived that he saw his way to improving on these precedents. He conjectured that, if the various states of Rajputana could be brought to agree on a common scale of such largesse, apportioned to the revenue of the bride's parents, and with uniform penalties for all demands in excess, the problem might be solved. Nothing, however, is harder than to bring these tenacious principalities to act together on any subject. What could seem more so than to bring them to work in concert on a question involving points so delicate as the largesse to be dispensed on their daughters' weddings, and the comparative claims of their minstrels and priests? It was certain that failing this agreement, no measure of the kind could be demanded of them by the British government without a breach of the treaties that secured the freedom of their internal administrations.

In spite of these obstacles, Major Ludlow obtained permission to do his best, on the single condition of using no direct solicitations towards the chiefs. His first efforts were thus confined to his fellow diplomatists, and to such native deputies as resided at Jyepore for the purpose of communicating on plunder cases. The latter, gradually coming into the idea, promulgated it among their respective governments; by this indirect process, he at length succeeded in obtaining the enactment of an international sumptuary law which had rid Rajputana of its most frightful scourge and stigma. Never probably before, since the origin of the Rajput states, had their jealousies and divisions been even temporarily suspended. But the advantage of their tardiness was at once rendered palpable to them by their delivery from the ruinous system of extortions; and thus between him and themselves there sprung up a relation on such subjects, which the antipathies of race and religion very seldom allowed among Englishmen and Hindus. What then if he could avail himself of these aids to accomplish an infinitely harder undertaking? He had rid the Rajputs of a practice which their consciences condemned. Could he rid them of one to the full as terrible, which they revered?

He had rescued her child for the mother. Could he rescue the mother for the child? It was, doubtless, much for an Englishman to hope to tear aside the prescriptive sanctions which, for twenty centuries, had elevated Indian widows' cruel martyrdom into the holiest of mysteries; but if the shock was ever to be given, it was now, and at Jyepore. The resident Vakeels would communicate it to all the Rajput states, and whenever Rajputana should lead the way in breaking through the 'traditions of the elders' Hindustan at large was tolerably certain to follow.

The hour, the place and the man all favoured the design. One lion there was, however, in the path. Major Ludlow could not hope that the permission given to him to use his personal influence with the convention of Vakeels to promote measures against female infanticide, would be extended to any similar undertaking against suttee. The acknowledged criminality of the one practice, and the reputed sanctity of the other, made here all the difference; and we have already alluded to the belief on the part of the British authorities, which so many facts had seemed to substantiate, that the efforts of our diplomatists to check the rite had tended only to the opposite effect. As an essential condition therefore to success, and on pain of having his operations summarily suspended, Major Ludlow was compelled to work unseen. He determined, if possible, to induce two or three trustworthy and influential natives to unertake the cause; to ply them with the critical objection drawn from the older scriptures; and, by declaring his own intention to remain neutral till public opinion had declared itself, to excite in them the ambition of taking the lead. He found a person admirably adapted for this purpose in the financial minister of the court at which he was accredited. Seth Manick Chund belonged to a sect whose distaste for destruction in all its forms was singular even in the East. The Oswal tribe do not wilfully slay the meanest animal. Carrying out the doctrine of the transmigration of souls to its logical result—viewing in every insect a possible human intelligence, and as yet blissfully ignorant of the revelations of the oxy-hydrogen microscope—their priests carry besoms to sweep the ground on which they tread, and cover their mouths with gauze, to avoid the scandal of inhaling their ancestors, or crushing them wholesale under foot! One result of this tenderness for life in every shape is that they disapprove of suttees. To the financial minister, therefore, and to his own head munshi, Major Ludlow communicated all the arguments he thought likely to be of use; and thus charged they betook themselves to the High Priest of Jyepore.

Warily and as if on their own accord, he pressed this important dignitary with the omission of all mention of sati in the Code of Menu; with the inferential prohibition of that rite in the denunciations in that work against suicide; and with its promise to widows living chastely of eternal felicity with their husbands. Whereas even the writings which countenanced the sacrifice, limited the duration of its recompense to the comparative bagatelle of thirty-five million years!

In addition to these objections, already familiar to oriental scholars, Major Ludlow supplied his emissaries with two others, at least as efficacious. Pope's Universal Prayer embodied, it appears, a favourite sentiment of the Hindu moralists: 'What conscience dictates to be done, or warns me not to do; This teach me more than Hell to shun, That more than Heaven pursue.' But the Hindu divines assert, not only that the love of goodness for its own sake ought to prevail over the hopes of posthumous reward, but that the slightest intrusion of an interested motive is fatal. What more easy than to apply this dogma to the poor widow bent on earning by a cruel death her own and her husband's salvation? Her devotion was represented as a mercenary calculation of profit and loss. She did but mock the deity with the unclean sacrifice of a selfish bargain. Was the martyr's crown her aim? She had for-feited it by that very aspiration!

Major Ludlow wound up these arguments by a shrewd appeal to national pride. Suttee (urged his emissaries), unwarranted by Menu, was the evident invention of some degenerate race whose women were worthless, and whose widows, if they survived, would bring reproach to the memory of their lords. To such it might be left. The honour of the Rajput husband was in safer keeping; and the fair fame of their daughters was aspersed by the mere retention of so disgraceful a security!

The High Priest received these representations with surprising candour. In less than six months he was induced to put forth a document, in which he adopted all the theological arguments and declared authoritatively that the self-immolation of widows was less meritorious than their practising 'the living suttee of chastity and devotion'! This was evidently half the battle. Major Ludlow now personally entered into the contest, so far as to cause the manifesto to be shown at his residence to various Vakeels who came there to transact business; and these in turn communi-cated its contents to their masters. A religious agitation sprung up and spread widely. At the same time there could be little doubt that, let the impression produced by the High Priest's decision be what it might, no man of rank, least of all a Rajput Sovereign, would be anxious to proclaim himself the first convert.

To iterate day by day the same arguments, to be ever on the stretch to discover methods of rendering them more efficient, to confirm the wavering, to encourage those who were already com-promised as abolitionists. Above all to keep within the delicate line that severed his private advocacy of the High Priest's dictum from his official adhesion to it. Here was an arduous combination of aims; and the major knew that if he failed in any one of them, a quick and mischievous reaction of public opinion would render the object of his toil more distant than ever, and expose him to the censure of his own government. But what then? It was the old alternative of every man wiser and braver than his fellows—the criterion would be success. If he did not win the palm of benefactor of his race, he must be content to be reproached as a meddler whose untimely zeal had but injured a noble cause.

Within a few months of the issue of the High Priest's manifesto, that personage died. Never, not even in his last sickness did he receive the slightest message or civility from Major Ludlow. So important was it deemed to give no ground for the imputation of a secret understanding between them. While therefore it was part of the good fortune attending his enterprise that the High Priest should have left the scene in the odour of sanctity before he had leisure to retract or modify his opinion, it was probably due to Major Ludlow's caution, that the public faith in the honesty of the manifesto remained to the last unshaken.

And now the fruit of all this untiring energy began to appear. One by one the members of the Council of Regency declared themselves in favour of the legal prohibition of suttee; though they did not as yet think proper to pledge the infant sovereign to so critical a measure. Most of the nobles connected with the court were avowed abolitionists, and three of the tributary provinces of Jyepore actually issued enactments against the rite. Their example was followed by several neighbouring petty states.

Major Ludlow believed that the time had come for bolder measures. Everything depended on the utmost publicity being given to the adhesions he had already received. Great as was the general respect for the deceased High Priest's authority, the timid were not likely to be converted except in good company, and, as has been said, the timidest of all in matters of Rajput orthodoxy would be the Rajput sovereigns. He was aware, indeed, that rumour had already befriended him in this respect. The resident Vakeels had, as a matter of course, kept their masters throughout Rajputana well acquainted with the progress of the strange agitation at Jyepore. But these functionaries had no access to the letter which, in his capacity as President of the Council of Regency, he had from time to time received from leading abolitionists; and such documents, forming collectively a very imposing record of opinion in high places, had now accumulated in his hands. These he resolved to turn to account. He sent copies of the whole body of correspondence to two or three of his fellow diplomatists in Rajputana, in order that they might communicate it to the courts to which they were attached.

The result was his first and only check. His official superior, apprised of the circulation of these documents, took alarm and arrested the whole proceeding. The mortification of Ludlow must have been great; but there remained so much to be done and by means so foreign to the routine of official experience, that we can scarcely be astonished that the first impression inspired by the promulgation of the plan should have been one of distrust. When, however, a year had passed without any evil resulting from the agitation of the subject, the able officer who had thus felt it his duty to interpose his authority, so far withdrew his opposition as to issue a circular to the chiefs, urging on the grounds already taken, not indeed the prohibition of suttee, but the imposition of penalties on all persons abetting the widow in the rite.

Happily, the event surpassed these cautious advances and proved how little Major Ludlow had overrated the strength of the movement. In eight months' time from the issuing of the circular (23 August 1846) the Council of Regency at Jyepore led the way among the great independent Rajput states in declaring suttee penal on all parties engaged in it, principals as well as accessories. Lord Hardinge, then at Simla, at once caused a notification of this event, coupled with an expression of thanks to Major Ludlow, to be published in the Government Gazette (22 September 1846); and so vast and so swift was the effect of this example and of the prominence thus judiciously assigned it that, before Christmas, his Lordship was able to announce the prohibition of suttee in eleven out of the eighteen Rajput Principalities and by five out of the remaining sixteen free states of India! Of the territory then exempt from internal control, more than two-thirds were gained over to the cause of abolition within four months of the Jyepore proclamation.

Abolitionist – Rajputana	Non-abolitionist – Rajputana
Jyepore – 13,427 sm	Meywar – 11, 784
Kotah – 3102 sm	Ulwar – 3235
Jahalawar – 1287 sm	Bikaneer – 18, 060
Boondee – 2291 sm	Kishengurh – 724
Jessulmere – 9779	Bhurtpore (Jat) – 1946
Banswarra – 1440	
Pertabgurh – 1457	
Doongurpore – 2005	

Kerowlee – 1870

Serohi – 3024

Dholepore – 1626

Ameer Khan (Mohamedan) – 1633

Jodhpore – 34,132

Abolitionist – not Rajputana

Hyderabad (Mahomedan) – 88,887

Indore (Mahratta) – 4245

Rewah (Rajput) – 10,310

Bundlehund – 16,173

Gwalior (Mahratta) – 32,944

Cashmere – 1500

Non-abolitionist – out of Rajputana

Baroda (Mahratta) – 5525

Katteewar (Rajput) – 19, 424

Bhopal (Mahomedan) – 6772

Cutch (Rajput) – 7396

Dhar (Rajput) – 1465

Sawuntwaree (Mahratta) – 935

Four protected Sikh states – 16,602

To persons unacquainted with the influence of Rajputana on Hindustan, so sudden an interruption of the torpor of ages might well have appeared too momentous to be ascribed to the seemingly simple measures at Jyepore which it immediately followed. It was as though Major Ludlow had thrown a pebble from the shore, and the ice of the Arctic Sea had riven before him. Yet never did a train of events less deserve to be ranked as coincidences. If any further proof were necessary we might point to the fact that the state of Gwalior, in proclaiming suttee penal, expressly cited as its authority the edict from Jyepore; while nearly every abolitionist sovereign assigned as the grounds of his adhesion, the very arguments that had obtained the Jyepore High Priest's sanction. The recognition of Major Ludlow's services by his own superior was immediate and hearty:—'the last political agent,' wrote Col. Sutherland to Government, 'was as little prepared for the abolition of suttee at Jyepore as I was on my return to that capital in May 1846; and it is almost exclusively to Major Ludlow's influence that we are indebted for the first promulgation of a law prohibiting suttee in a Hindu principality.' Major Ludlow's aids were, a superior utterly incapable of petty jealousies, and ready to abandon his own anti-abolitionist views directly abolition appeared possible; a variety of British officers residing at other courts, eager to forward the good work when once begun; a Governor-General capable of appreciating the lustre such an achievement would cast upon an administration already bright with military glories; and last, not least, a court of directors ever prompt in the recognition of great services. Our narrative is concluded. It would be a strangely superficial view that saw in it nothing but a skilful series of measures by which a certain annual saving of female life has been effected, to the gain of Eastern morality, and the credit of the chief actor. The great fact it teaches is that *the Hindu mind is capable of advance even in the department where its immobility has been deemed most absolute—traditionary faith.*

Notes

[1]   Letter from the East India Company Board of Control to the Government of Bombay, 15 June, no. 4 of 1836, *Bombay Depatches*, vol. 65, 6 April 1836 to 25 April 1837.

[2]   Translation of a letter from Major Thoresby (Agent to the Governor-General for Rajputana) to the chiefs of Jaipur, Jodhpur, Udaipur, Bikaner, Jaisalmer, Kota, Bundi, Jhallowar, Dholepur, Serohi, Banswarra and Pertaubgurh-Dungapur. N.A.I., Foreign Department, Political: No. 118–21, 25 April 1846.

[3]   Letter from Lt Col. Sir H. Lawrence, Agent of the Governer-General to the States of Rajputana, to the Government of India, 5 February 1857. N.A.I., Foreign Department, Political: No. 232–3, April 1859.

[4]   Bushby, Henry.,' *Widow-Burning: A Narrative* (London: Longman, Brown, Green and Longman, 1855).

[5]   'I have heard,' says Mountstuart Elphinstone, 'that in Guzerat women about to be burnt are often stupefied with opium. In most other parts this is certainly not the case. Women go through all the ceremonies with astonishing compousure and presence of mind, and have been seen seated, unconfined amidst the flames, apparently praying, and raising their joint hands to their heads with as little agitation as at their ordinary devotions. The sight of a widow burning is a most painful one but it is hard to say whether the spectator is most affected by pity or admiration. The more than human serenity of the victim, and the respect that she receives from all around her, are heightened by her gentle demeanour and her care to omit nothing in distributing her last presents, and paying the usual marks of courtesy to the bystanders; while the cruel death that awaits her is doubly felt from her apparent insensibility to its terrors'[*History of India*, i. 361].

11

Indian Responses

Jaipur[1]

In August 1846 Jaipur became the first state of Rajputana to prohibit sati. The custom's abolition was due in part to the influence of Major John Ludlow, who entered into correspondence with many local nobles in order to solicit their support for its suppression. It should be noted, however, that sati had always been rare in Jaipur, especially when compared to its prevalence in Mewar and Marwar. Significantly, it is the region of Shekhawat, previously part of the Jaipur state, which is most closely associated with sati in the present.

Throughout a lengthened period and by the force of example, on the demise of an individual among the tribe of Hindus, the wife possessed of a strong feeling of love and affection burns in the fire and is said to have become a suttee. This practice having fallen under reflection and discussion, it has been ascertained that it is improper, nay, that it is an evil, a wickedness for a living woman of her own choice to burn in the flames, and it is therefore proclaimed for general information that no woman calling herself a suttee shall henceforth be permitted to burn within the limits of this territory. This practice is strictly prohibited and must be provided against. Wherefore all Sirdars, Jageerdars, Zamindars, Bhoomeas, Zillahdars, thanadars, jemadars, tehseldars, talooqdars and others belonging to the Raj or in its service shall securely provide against any living woman being suffered to burn as a suttee. Should any living woman burn in anyone's *Ilagu* it will be considered a grave offence attaching alike to the proprietor the relatives of the deceased, to those who reside near the spot, to those who bring firewood, etc., and to those who willingly shall neglect to use exertions for preventing the sacrifice. All such persons shall be summoned here to the capital and whoever among them shall be convicted of the offence of failing to exert themselves to prevent the act of burning or bringing firewood, etc., shall be regarded as criminal offenders according to the proofs which may be exhibited against them and will be punished accordingly. It therefore behoves all persons to consider well the purport of this proclamation and to effect arrangements whereby no living woman may burn in this Ilagu.

Bundi[2]

James Tod is said in 1821 to have used his personal influence with Rao Raja Bishan Singh of Bundi to persuade him to forbid satis at his own funeral, but it was not until 1847 that this state, along with several others, formally prohibited the custom. The following is the letter sent by the Maha Rao Raja to the British political agent explaining his decision to outlaw the custom and the official proclamation so doing.

[You stated that] the practice of suttee was still prevalent in Rajputana, and like the practice of suicide by persons casting themselves off precipices or drowning themselves in wells, was forbidden as criminal, and in the same manner so was this of suttee. That it is nowhere alluded to in the Smritis or law books of Manu and Yagnavalkya and other Dharmashasters now chiefly respected, that it appeared to have been gradually introduced by force of example, that it seems to involve the perpetration of the sin of suicide, and that for this reason the British government was desirous that the stigma of this crime should no longer attach to Rajasthan, but that means should be adopted to abolish the practice and enjoin in its stead that of the living suttee of a devoted life, and where this was unattended to that the relations of the widow should be forbidden to afford any assistance in the way of furnishing wood or other requisites for the sacrifice, measures such as these that would redound to the credit of the Rajput states. By the perusal of these observations of such excellent meanings the bud of desire in my heart was expanded into full flower, and I have now likewise received intimation through my

Vakeels of the efforts you are making and the advice you have given to fulfil the dictum of the Shasters on this subject. Praise be to God, and gratitude towards those benefactors of the world whose regards are so full of mercy to mankind, who are desirous of promoting the temporal and spiritual interests of Rajasthan and maintaining the principles of the Hindoo faith agreeably with its own books of revelations and traditions, or Dharmashasters and increasing the good fame and reputation of Rajasthan. May god ever more increase the high fortune of the honourable and exalted Sirkar. I am also desirous by the aid of the Sirkar to secure a share of these temporal and spiritual benefits, and indeed, in the increased population of my country, have already obtained by its means some worldly, and in the privilege of pilgrimage some spiritual advantage. I have myself entertained opinions similar to those contained in Major Thoresby's letter, and accordingly, in full reliance on the precepts of my own faith, as far as lay in my power I have required obedience to its injunctions in all that related to the sin of suicide and infanticide and other subjects forbidden in the Shasters, and ordered that throughout my territory the indignity to which the body of the suicide is to be subjected by way of fine, and the atonement required by the Shaster to be made for it, shall be enforced, and now with compliance with the same Shasters of my faith which it is so incumbent to act up to, having made enquiry, I have issued a proclamation prohibiting the burning of women under the name suttee as an act contrary to the Shasters.... My friend, the only reason for the delay which has occurred in making this reply has been the necessity for examining and studying the Shasters, for the question was one of great delicacy, a question of religion involving the worldly interests of the state, but by your favour I trust that the interests of my faith and of my worldly prospects both be promoted.

PROCLAMATION PROHIBITING SATI BY THE
BUNDI GOVERNMENT.[3]

Several improper and unworthy practices, such as the destroying of female children, the inhumation of jogees, the voluntary suicides of individuals in fits of passion, by poison, by weapons of violence, by casting themselves off precipices or other means,

the burning or mutilating of women upon charges of witchcraft—
for these and other unworthy acts in violation of the Shasters, and
occasioning injury on this life and the next, preventative measures have previous to this been enacted in conjunction with your-
selves. It is now further enacted that with regard to those loving
women who retain their affection towards their Lords, when these
have been removed by death, the Dhurm Shaster have prescribed
two modes of proceeding, viz., that they should accompany them
in death, or else perform the living suttee of a devout life. But
many now from motives of vainglory or reputation, regarding
only their own fancies and not the conditions of the Shasters,
take no care to dissuade a woman from at that moment of her
anguish, but on the contrary, giving her all the adventitious aids
of camphor and other intoxicating drugs, make thus a suttee sacrifice of her. Such are their impressions, and they are entirely
erroneous and censurable, and surely compared with this, the
suttee of a devoted life is much more becoming and preferable.
Therefore, everyone of you make arrangements in your respective
jurisdictions, and know that in whatever district so improper and
so contrary to the Shaster shall occur and a woman be burnt as a
suttee, the chief of that district and all those whose concern in
the burning shall be established by evidence, shall be punished in
such a manner as the Dharm Shaster as administered in Boondee
prescribes for criminals who have been guilty of acts of blood.

Kota[4]

Not all Indian rulers were willing to go along with British requests to outlaw
sati. In the early 1840s the Maharao of Kota supported the rite and on more
than one occasion lent practical assistance to widows in committing it, against
the wishes of the British. The following is his response to the suggestion
that he suppress the custom, in which he defends it as a divine ordinance.
Although he ostensibly agreed to do what he could to prevent it, in practice
he continued to allow satis to occur unabated.

My friend, the customs alluded to have been handed down since
time immemorial, even from the first fathers of mankind. They
have obtained in every nation of India, and especially in the provinces of Rajwarra such as Joudpore, Oodeepore &c. for whenever

the sovereign of those states has bid farewell to life, then queens, through the yearning of the inward spirit have become suttee, notwithstanding that their relatives were adverse to the sacrifice and would have prevented it altogether. It has even happened that when they have been imprisoned in barred chambers the bolts and bars have, by the power afforded of themselves flown open. Hence, it appears that it is not in the power of mortals to nullify by opposition the divine yet mysterious ordinance. Since however, it will afford the British government particular pleasure, I will take such measures as be in my power for the prohibition of the practice. The custom of burying alive is confined to the sect of jogis and is enjoined by their laws. That also shall be put a stop to.

Notes

[1]   Proclamation by the Raj of Jeypore, 23 August 1846, *Board's Collections*, vol. 2240, 1847–8, 112476.

[2]   Khureeta from Maha Rao Raja of Bundi to Major Ludlow, Political Agent Jeypore and in charge of the Harauti Agency, 6 May 1847, *Board's Collections*, vol. 2240, 1847–8, 112476.

[3]   Translation of Proclamation Issued by the Bundi Government, 6 May 1847, *Board's Collections*, vol. 2240, 1847–8, 112476.

[4]   Translation of a letter from the Maha Rao of Kota to Capt. Richards, 9 May 1840, *Board's Collections*, vol. 1925, 1841–2, 82602.

V

SATI IN THE ERA OF NATIONALISM

12

The Barh Sati, 1927

Sati at Barh, Police Report[1]

The following is the official police report of a sati that occurred in Barh in November 1927. Although by no means the only sati to occur in the early twentieth century, this case is significant for the way it caught public attention. The police report contains a detailed account of the actions of all parties (the widow, Brahmins, crowds, and police) and provides an interesting insight into the problems facing the authorities in policing and prosecuting sati. Interesting comparisons can be drawn between this and revivalist reporting of it (see next extract) and with the sati of Roop Kanwar.

On the evening of the 21st November the young widow of an indigent Brahmin started with the dead body of her husband to the burning ghat on the bank of the Ganges at Barh in the district of Patna, some fifteen miles from her home. Whether or no preparations were made before she left the village for her committing sati is not clear as the villagers, including the Dafadar and chowkidar, have combined to suppress all evidence on the subject. At any rate, on the way it became known that this was her intention and a large crowd assembled at Barh on the following morning. One of the local Sub-inspectors and other police subordinates attempted to reason with her, and the Sub-inspector alleges that she had agreed to give the idea and go away quietly, when he left for the railway station to go to the district headquarters on other business. The woman, however, proceeded to the ghat, where she bathed and changed her clothes and took her seat on the pyre holding the dead body of her husband. At this stage the officiating Inspector of Police, a Hindu himself, forced his way through the crowd and started reasoning with her. He also placed a cordon of constables around the pyre. Suddenly, the woman's clothes were found to be on fire—the origin of which is still unexplained, but is believed even by educated men of the locality to be supernatural. Unable to bear the agony she jumped, or fell, into the water, her husband's body falling with her. A constable threw out a cloth to draw her into the bank, though some of the crowd warned the police not to interfere. The woman, however, succeeded in swimming back by herself to the bank, and proceeded to an open enclosure nearby where she remained till she was removed by the Subdivisional Officer on the afternoon of 24th November, more than forty-eight hours later.

The local Assistant Surgeon was sent for to render medical aid, but some of the bystanders again interfered, and the Assistant Surgeon did not carry out his intention of injecting morphia to relieve the unfortunate woman's pain, which must have been acute as the Subdivisional Officer reports that almost the whole of her back, and her legs and thighs had been burnt, exposing the raw flesh below. At this stage, apparently, the Hindu Sub-Deputy Magistrate, who was in charge in the absence of the Subdivisional Officer on tour, came to the bank ostensibly to record a dying declaration, but went back without doing so or taking any further action. In the meantime the woman, or the abettors of the 'sati', sent for the sandals of her husband's, which are apparently an orthodox substitute for the husband's body, with a view to a further attempt at 'sati'. On the 23rd the sandals were brought, their arrival having been, it is reported, expedited by the action of certain railway subordinates at Bakhtiarpur railway station who specially stopped a goods train for the purpose.

The local government has asked for verification of this report and are taking the matter up with the railway authorities.

The Inspector of Police addressed a report on the evening of the 22nd to the Subdivisional Officer, in camp, but it was kept back by an orderly to be sent out next day with the office mail, and it reached the hands of the Second Officer at midday on the 23rd. Both this report, and another by the Second Officer, only reached the Subdivisional Officer on the 23rd evening, and he at once started back from camp, arriving at Barh at 6 a.m. the next morning.

Meanwhile, the woman had remained on the bank, guarded by police, but even after the arrival of the sandals on the 23rd she seems to have made no further attempt on her life, though a pyre was reconstructed in the early morning of the 24th. By this time the crowd had increased to very large dimensions and the site had taken on the appearance of 'a place of pilgrimage', many of the sightseers having come from considerable distances.

The Subdivisional Officer on arrival consulted the Inspector of Police, who advised him that the crowd were likely to resist the removal of the woman. He thereupon telegraphed the Superintendent of Police and the District Magistrate for thirty armed police, in addition to the force of ten unarmed constables for which the Inspector sent a request to the Superintendent of Police on the previous evening, and going to the spot, ordered the woman's relatives to remove the woman to the hospital at once, and the crowd to disperse. He explained the orders personally, and when the half an hour allowed by him had elapsed, finding his orders disregarded, he marched off three of the woman's relatives under arrest, in the hope that this step, coupled with the request of the arrested men themselves that the woman should be removed to the hospital, might prove effective. At twelve o'clock the ten unarmed constables arrived and were sent to the spot, and about two hours later fifteen armed constables arrived in a bus which the Subdivisional Officer had sent for them to the railway station, the second batch of fifteen being left at the railway station to wait for the return of the bus.

The Subdivisional Officer decided to take action without waiting for the full reinforcement. A stretcher was accordingly provided, the Assistant Surgeon was sent to the sub-jail to be ready to give medical treatment, and amidst continuous shouts of 'sati ki jai' the Subdivisional Officer instructed the local police to remove the woman. As they showed reluctance, he ordered some of the armed police to lend a hand, and he himself set an example by taking hold of one of the corners of her bedding. The stretcher was then quickly carried to the bus, which had been left about hundred yards away, and was driven rapidly to the sub-jail, followed by the Subdivisional Officer in his car and pursued by a large crowd on foot. The woman reached the hospital at 3 p.m., where the Subdivisional Officer had also brought the local Lady Doctor. At this juncture the District Magistrate also arrived.

The woman died at 11.30 p.m. on the night of the 25th and the Subdivisional Officer made arrangements for the removal of her body as quickly as possible to the river for the last rites. When the news of her death became public, a local committee demanded the body for a public procession to the ghat and a public cremation. This the Sub-divisional Officer refused, and ultimately succeeded in getting the body driven away quickly on a motor bus which had been decorated with flowers, and disposed of in the river. This operation was carried out quickly in spite of the protests that the arrival of the pandits and photographers from Patna should be awaited.

Ten persons have already been sent up under Section 306 of the Indian Penal Code, but action against them has been postponed as it is proposed to add some six more accused, including those who brought the woman in a palki with her husband's body. The Subdivisional Officer is doing his best to prevent the perpetuation of this revolting episode by erecting a memorial, though he reports that certain Marwaris at Patna City are anxious to erect one.

With the exception of the Subdivisional Officer, Mr M.S. Mazumdar, I.C.S., who appears to have handled a situation full of difficulties with credit, and possibly the Inspector of Police, the local officers all came out of the affair very badly indeed. In particular the inaction of the Sub-Deputy Magistrate was amazing, and suggests either sympathy with the woman's intentions or cowardice. His explanation has already been called for with a view to departmental action. Enquiry into the conduct of other officers and if necessary proceedings against them will be taken up immediately after the conclusion of the prosecution of those who abetted the sati.

His Excellency in Council regrets to report that the local Hindu community appears enthusiastic at the revival of an abominable custom, and the only disapproval shown is at the Subdivisional Officer in ordering the woman's removal and hastening her funeral arrangements after her death.

Sati at Barh, *Amrita Bazar Patrika*[2]

The two articles reporting the Barh sati carried by this Indian newspaper painted a very different picture of the sati from the official report. Instead of a criminal act of violence, the *Amrita Bazar Patrika* represented the immolation as a miraculous 'true' sati, and criticized the authorities' refusal to allow its glorification.

MIRACULOUS SATI. ENTHUSIASTIC SCENES WITNESSED AT BARH.[2]

From our own correspondent:

A remarkable case of sati recent took place at a village near Barh amid scenes of great enthusiasm and sensation. It is said that people from far off places such as Calcutta and Benares came to witness the incident, which was an attempt to revive a custom which over a hundred years ago the British prohibited but found great difficulty suppressing. One Siddheswar Sharma, son of Pundit Bisweswar Sharma, of Sartha Behadurpur, age twenty-one years, was suffering from phthisis for the last eight months. He was married to the daughter of one Kesho Pandy. On the 20th November last, seeing that her husband was about to die, the young wife of Siddheswar, who was only eighteen, expressed her desire to become 'sati' during the lifetime of her husband. She retired to a room in the house reserved for the family deity, where she read religious books and offered her prayer. As she was coming out of the room fire suddenly caught her clothes, which however was soon extinguished by the members of the family. In the meanwhile her husband died. She hired a *khatooli*, sat in it with the dead body and proceeded towards Barh with a view to taking permission of the S.D.O. The police authorities, her relatives and the public reasoned with her not to sacrifice her life in that way, but all persuasion proved to no avail. A funeral pyre was erected on the banks of the Ganges in the presence of the police officers. The religious ceremonies over, she was seated on the pyre with the head of her husband on her thigh. Then a very miraculous incident happened. It might be mentioned here that the police gave her permission to become sati if the fire breaks out from her person itself. The officers were strictly watching that no fire be set from outside. She was reading the Gita and other religious books when all of a sudden, to the infinite surprise of thousands of spectators present on the spot, fire gushed out of her sari and she was seen in flames. When she was almost half-burned a great rush of bystanders ensued, which came upon the burning lady with the result that the lady fell into the river together with the corpse of her husband. The corpse was drowned, but the lady came ashore alive. The lady was removed to a temple, where she was kept under police guard. Her position is precarious and she has now been removed by the S.D.O. to the Barh sub-jail with the help of the military. The spectators, although overwhelming in number, were quite peaceful and did not interfere with the police in any way. The District Magistrate was also present. It is understood that police officers have instituted a criminal case against the lady and seven of her relatives. Bail petition has been moved, but she has not been released as yet. It has been reported that Pandit Malaviya of Patna came here and moved the S.D.O. for bail and release of the sati, which was also refused. It is reported the girl died two or three days after the occurrence.

SEQUEL TO THE BARH SUTTEE. LADY EXPIRES IN JAIL. BODY IMMERSED IN GANGES: S.D.O.'s CONDUCT[3]

From our own correspondent:

Shrimati Sampati Devi, who as an accused under Section 309 I.P.C. was removed to the Barh sub-jail under police escort in a motor lorry on Thursday last, breathed her last within the jail premises about 11.15 p.m. on Friday 25th instant. The news of her death spread early next morning. The leaders of the town, the President and Secretary Satee Relief Committee, approached the S.D.O. and prayed him make over the body of the satee to her relations. The permission was granted and the dead body made over to the near relations. The police practically did not give up charge of the body and kept it under their strict control. The leaders and relations then prayed to the S.D.O. for permission to take the dead body to the cremation ghat on a Biman with procession. The S.D.O. decided that the Biman should be placed on a motor lorry. Babus Parameswamy and Jageshwary Prasads' motor lorries were then very tastefully decorated with flowers, flags and festoons. There was a huge gathering of spectators standing on the roads from the jail up to the cremation ghat, an area covering about two miles. The gathering consisted of men, women and children of all ages, castes and creeds. Numerous pitembari coffins were offered by the public and officials. The motor lorry then started, at first very slowly, but the S.D.O. who in his own car was proceeding ahead, warned the driver of the lorry to follow his car otherwise his licence would be cancelled. The S.D.O. drove his car at full speed. The satee's lorry accordingly moved with full speed. Thousands of people who were standing along the road could not offer their coffins or wreaths as the lorry moved very fast. Consequently the procession broke hopelessly. The music and the musicians, flags, were all left behind. The bhajan party could not sing. A third car belonging to Sahib Bansi Lal, which was conveying the leaders and was running behind the motor lorry carrying the dead body, knocked down a spectator, who died in hospital. At the ghat there was a short discussion about whether the body of the satee should be burnt, immersed in the Ganges or put in a samadhi, but it was decided that the body should be immersed in the Ganges. Thereupon the S.D.O. wanted that the dead body should be immersed at once, but the leaders and the Secretary Satee Relief Committee wanted time till the Patna leaders and photographer from Patna arrived. This was disallowed. However, Havan commenced, but the Pandits were warned from time to time to finish the Havan as quickly as possible. Here the question arises, what business or right had the S.D.O. or the police to interfere in the discharge of religious rites and ceremonies? It was the main and only duty of police officers to make proper arrangements to regulate the traffic on the roads in such a way that everyone might have a good view of the satee. This was not done. The people were left to move disorderly. Numerous respectable gentlemen and ladies with photographers and Pandits came from Patna and they were very much disappointed as the immersion of the dead body had taken place before they arrived.

Sati at Barh, Judgment of Chief Justice Courtney Terrell[4]

The findings of the Patna High Court in the Barh sati case were hugely controversial. Chief Justice Terrell overturned the verdict of the Sessions Court and presented the sati as a premeditated murder on the part of the Brahmin associates of Sampati. He sentenced the accused, who had originally been acquitted by an Indian jury, to terms ranging from one to ten years' hard labour. However, it was the tone as much as the content of his judgment that caused a furore among the Indian elite.

The following is the full text of the judgment delivered by Courtney Terrell, C.J., and Adami J. in the sensational Barh Sati case sentencing the accused to undergo heavy terms of imprisonment ranging from one to ten years.

Courtney Terrell C.J. and Adami J.: This is the judgment of the Court in a reference under Section 307 of the Code of Criminal Procedure by the Sessions Judge of Patna. There are ten persons accused to which the reference relates and there were in trial with them six others. They were all charged under Sections 149 and 307 of the Indian Penal code with being members of an unlawful assembly whose common object was to abet the suicide of Sampati Kuer at Barh and with abetting the woman's suicide. Six of the accused were acquitted by the Jury and the Sessions Judge sees no reason to dissent from their view. As to the others the Judge dissents from the verdict of the Jury and refers the case to the High Court.

The accused persons, to which the reference applies, consist of two separate groups and may I say that yesterday I took advantage of a visit of inspection to the jail to see these accused persons. I had them examined by the Medical Superintendent who gave me his views upon their ages and my inspection of the prisoners confirms the opinion that has been arrived at by him.

The first group is that which comes from Berhna, a village two miles south of Barh. It consists of one Muralidhar Pande, a Brahmin, who is the brother of the deceased girl. His age is seventeen years. Then there is one Jagdeo Pande who is also a Brahmin and a distant relative of the deceased woman. His age is twenty years. Then there is one Raghu Singh, who is a Bhumihar Brahmin, who is no relation to the others. He is a religious enthusiast and is aged forty. There was also a Brahmin named Gaya Pande who was acquitted with the concurrence of the Judge.

The next group is that which comes from a village named Sartha, twenty miles south-west of Barh, which consists of Vidyasagar Pande, a Brahmin who is the brother of the deceased woman's deceased husband, whose age is sixteen, Lachman Pande, whose age is forty-eight, Sahdeo Pande whose age is twenty-five and Herdeo Pande aged twenty-six (these last two Sahdeo and Herdeo are relatives). There is also Kesho Pande who is a Brahmin aged forty-two. Then there is a woman Mosst. Lakhia, a Kaharain, who was the deceased woman's servant. Her age is thirty-five.

There are thus seven Pandey Brahmins, a Bhumihar Brahmin, a woman Kahar and a Dusadh and there were also a Brahmin and four Kahars or bearers who were acquitted by the Jury with the approval of the judge.

The deceased woman Sampati Kuer was the daughter of one Kesho Pande of Berhna who died ten or twelve years ago. At the time of her death in November last she was aged about twenty years. Ten or twelve years ago she was married to one Sidheshwar Pande of Sartha, but she continued to live at her father's house. In August last Sidheshwar fell ill. Sampati went to his house to nurse him and she nursed him until his death on the 21st November last. It would appear that the marriage was never consummated. The young widow was a pious, gentle Hindu girl of high caste. She was a pardanashin and was possessed of such rudiments of education as that condition permits. She had no father, she had no efficient male protection. Her only male relative, who was of age, was a man named Kuldip, her uncle, who has not appeared in these proceedings at all, and would appear to take no interest in them. And she was left, therefore, with only the weak-minded, superstitious boy brother. What a victim she presented to those who were to profit by her death!

The story of the crime we are now investigating begins on the early morning of 22 November when a party of persons who arrived late the night before were found resting in a shed in the compound of the Subdivisional Officer's Court at Barh. This party carried with them a khatoli on which they rested the body of the deceased Sidheshwar. They were taking it to the burning ghat on the banks of the Ganges, about two miles further to the north. At five o'clock in the morning on the 22nd a Rajput constable Ramayan Singh found the party consisting of fifteen or sixteen persons in all. He identified all of the accused, save Raghu Singh and the driver Ramautar, among them. The corpse was lying on the khatoli and sitting by the side of the corpse was the widow Sampati. The constable was told of the intention that the woman should become sati. Knowing that this was contrary to the law he went to the police station about a mile away and half way on the journey to the ghat, and there he told the Writer Head Constable Nurul Haq of what he had seen. He and the Writer Head Constable and constable Mukh Lal Singh returned to the shed to expostulate with the woman and her companions. By that time it was getting light. The persons were all there and they were all identified and their names were taken. The woman was still sitting on the khatoli and the three constables reasoned with them. They pointed out that the proposed sati was unlawful but these men declined to listen. Then the Writer Head Constable fetched the treasury Jamadar, Mahabir Tewari, who was a Brahmin, and the constable Lachmi Singh and they also further reasoned with the party, but the party refused to listen to reason. Then the head Daroga Lal Behari Lal arrived. He joined in the attempts at persuasion and the police threatened to detain the body and prosecute the party. They said they would detain the body until it was putrid. Thereupon, the poor, brave, weak-minded lady was convinced of the foolishness of the whole proceeding and got off the khatoli and the corpse was sent off to the ghat carried by the four Kahars and accompanied by all the Pandes, save Sampati's brother Murlidhar, the youthful relation Jagdeo, and it appears also the man who was acquitted, Gaya Pande. The funeral party vanished along the bund road towards the ghat. The lady was now left alone with her maid, her feeble-minded brother Murlidhar, and the youth Jagdeo and she was willing to go to Berhna. Then men then called an ekka and the ekka was conducted by the accused Ramautar Dusadh whose position in this case is peculiar and I shall have further occasion to refer to it. She thought, we have no doubt that she was going back to her dead father's house and the police thought that they had saved the situation. They did not reckon on the malignant ingenuity of the Pandes who had gone off with the body. In a few minutes back came the miserable boy Vidyasagar, undoubtedly sent by the older members of the party. The three youth got Sampati and her maid into the ekka, ostensibly to take her to Berhna. The police followed with a gradually increasing crowd and the crowd was shouting the familiar cry of 'sati-mata-ki-jai'. Some 100 yards north-east of the shed in which the body had rested the Bakhtiarpur Road is crossed by a road which leads from the bund road south-east to Berhna and at this point the ekka should have turned down towards Berhna. But this would have spoiled the Pandes' plan. So leaving the corpse to pursue its unresisting way to the ghat along the bund road, carried by the docile Kahars, they came down by the crossroads further north and joined the crowd and recaptured their victim. About a mile from the shed the bund road and the Bakhtiarpur Road converge at the thana and here the crowd had increased until it numbered about four or five thousand persons and all the Pandes were present and close to the ekka. Again, the police endeavoured to reason with them. They consisted now of the Inspector Harnandan Singh, two Jamadars and fifteen constables and they tried for half an hour to persuade Sampati to return to her home and the Pandes to allow her to return to her home. Sampati said that she was about to become a true sati, that is to say, she believed that when she reached the funeral pyre miraculous fire would appear to destroy her and the body of her husband on the pyre. That she believed in or had been told of the physical agony she was to endure, we do not merely doubt, we disbelieve. However, the Pandes, in pursuance of their scheme said that they would take her to Berhna and they succeeded in deceiving the police into the idea that this was their intention and Ramayan Singh and Mukhlal were told to escort the ekka to Berhna. Sampati, the maid and Sampati's brother Murlidhar were on the ekka: Vidyasagar and the other six Pandes followed on foot. The driver led the ekka and the party now went south again, retracing their steps. At about 400 or 500 yards from the thana it came to where the road has a fork back to the north-east towards Gulab Bagh and the ghat, and here the Pandes intervened and forced the driver to lead it up the fork. The police were pushed aside. They felt that they were helpless against the Pandes and the fanatical mob and the two policemen went back to the thana and informed the Inspector. The alarm bell was rung and the Inspector and the Writer Head Constable and sixteen or seventeen constables were hurriedly mobilised and they went to the ghat, whither the scene now changes.

The body had arrived before the Pandes and the girl who was to be sacrificed. It was carried by the four Kahars and accompanied by the Bhumihar Brahmin, Raghu Singh, who was doubtless defferentially obeying his revered masters, the Pandes, and the Inspector and the town Jamadar Kedar Nath Pande tried to get Raghu Singh to burn the corpse before the rest of the party arrived. It was clear that he was in the plot because he refused to do anything of the kind. When the ekka arrived the widow alighted. She bathed in the Ganges and made her pathetic toilet with the assistance of the maid, supervised by Murlidhar and the old Pande Lachman. They held up the screen for her, Lachman took her ornaments, Lachman supervised the cutting of her nails and dying of her feet. She seated herself on the pyre prepared by the three boys and Lachman. Then Raghu and the young Pande Hardeo performed the easy and relatively unimportant duty of putting the corpse upon the pyre.

Now, note the situation. If the Pandes themselves set fire to the pyre, they were under the observation of the police and they knew perfectly well that their necks would be in the hangman's noose. Moreover, if they themselves set fire to the pyre there would have been no miracle of heaven-sent fire. All the merit would have belonged to Sampati alone and not to her religious assistants at the supernatural phenomenon. To satisfy the Pandes and their dupes, the crowd, fire must appear as though by magic. Moreover, the poor girl herself expected the fire to be miraculous and the Pandes were prepared for the emergency. It is true that her toilet was performed by Lakhia, but it was supervised by Lachman and the boy Murlidhar or under his directions. When she took her seat her left hand was concealed in her draperies. She took the corpse on her lap and its head lay on her left thigh near the concealed hand. Did the poor girl know what was to happen? She only expected the divine fire to appear. A moment later flames burst from her clothing and the cause of those flames is no matter of surmise as we are asked to believe. We are not fools. Not for one moment at the ghat had she been left alone. She had been closely surrounded. The trick was simpler than any conjuror's trick at a country fair and it was the Pandes that performed it. At the torture of the flames the poor creature leapt from the pyre and rushed into the river. Now the Pandes were in a very serious difficulty. If the woman was rescued the trick was revealed and the hangman's noose again dangled in front of them. They could not start the fire again; they could not repeat the trick. The apparatus was gone and therefore Sampati must drown. They threw her the corpse, which slipped out of her hands and went to the Ganges crocodiles, but no such merciful fate attended Sampati. They shouted to her to drown herself. Some police put out in a boat and attempted to rescue her. They were threatened and told that they were not to stop her. She was told to drown herself.

However, with the assistance of the police she was ultimately helped ashore in a shocking condition. She went to lie down under a tree by a temple sixty paces away and then began that which was the first fruits for which the Pandes had been waiting—a stream of coins began to flow which they greedily picked up. After some hours a doctor came. He tried to give the poor suffering woman an injection to relieve her agony; he was driven away. The police endeavoured to take her away to the hospital; they were driven away. For two days and two nights she lay there in agony. On the 24th the Subdivisional Officer, who had been away on tour, arrived with his armed police and swept the rabble aside and took the poor girl to the jail. On the 25th her sufferings came to an end. We are told that on the banks of the Ganges there is a little shrine to perpetuate her memory.

What are the defences of these people? First it is said that we should respect the verdict of the Jury because they were learned men. Learning connotes neither wisdom nor courage and, in our opinion, these jury men were deficient in both these qualities, the qualities which are necessary to a jury, the qualities which are necessary to citizenship. We now turn to certain matters of law. Mr Pugh rightly quoted from the judgment of Mr Justice Macpherson in Queen v. Sham Bagdi (1873:–13. B.L.R. App. 19) which was quoted and followed in Emperor v. Swarnamoyee Biswas (I.L.R. 41 Cal. 621) and it is true that the verdict of a jury has more weight than the opinion of the assessors and should not be set aside unless no sensible man could have arrived at their verdict, particularly in the case of a verdict of acquittal. In the light of this principle we approach the defences as offered. The first defence offered is a general defence of law, it is said that these people were expecting a miracle and that there is no evidence to show that anyone in particular fired the pyre, and with that state of mind the pyre having caught fire and the woman having been burned they cannot convict under Section 107. It is difficult to treat this defence seriously, but the answer is that they are charged with assisting the woman in her acts to meet a voluntary death. The method of destruction resolved on by the suicide was fire, and the method of ignition of the fire, whether miraculous, whether self-applied or whether applied by others is totally im- material. The contention is not worthy of further consideration and we follow the judgment in the case of Emperor v. Ram Dayal (I.L.R. 36 All. 26) which is conclusive on this point.

On the facts and the identity of the accused, Mr Pugh, on behalf of Vidyasagar, Lachman and Hardeo, all of the Sartha party, could offer no defence beyond the general observations above. Mr Manohar Lal, on behalf of Kesho Pande and Sahdeo Pande, urged some points on the identification. Of these two, Sahdeo is an agnate of Hardeo as he himself admits and he comes from Sartha. The denial of his presence is supported by no evidence whatsoever. Kesho says he arrived after the burning of the body. Mr Manohar Lal did not attempt to deny that both were at the ghat: indeed he says because they were there they were accused. On the question of mere probability they come from the same village of Sartha twenty miles away and there is no satisfactory reason except for this incident to account for their presence. The constable Ramayan Singh (P.W.5) identified them at the shed as also did Mahabir Tewari (P.W.14), the head con- stable of the treasury guard. Numerous witnesses identified them at the thana. Then followed some weak criticism to the effect that no mention is made of their names in the station diary on the 22nd. But it mentions none of the accused. Then it was said that there were discrepancies in the evidence of the Writer Head Constable as to whether he followed the ekka from the shed the whole way to the thana. It is said that as these two men had been sent with the corpse they could not have joined the party with the ekka which they undoubtedly did accompany to the thana. The answer is that there was a huge crowd and they had plenty of opportunity to join up by the two crossroads and the Writer Head Constable undoubtedly accompanied the ekka in the final part of its journey to the thana. Sub-Inspector Lal Behari Lal (P.W.20) identified all of them and took their names at the ghat.

Then a whole list of observations was made to show that the entire story up to the incidents at the ghat was invented by the police. That is not worthy of one moment's attention. However lacking in judgment the police may have been in neglecting to take steps at an earlier stage which might have stopped this deplorable incident, not one word can be said against the evidence which they have given, which, in our opinion, was given with conspicuous honesty and courage and reflects credit on their service.

By the learned, moving and interesting address of Mr Jayaswal, whose knowledge of Hinduism in unrivalled in this province and is acknowledged all over the world, we were reassured in our view that sati has long been discarded by all pious Hindus with any pretence to the respect of their fellows, and Mr Nandkeolyar frankly described it as a relic of brutal barbarism. We must now consider what punishment should be awarded to these people. I will first deal with the driver Ramautar Dusadh. His case requires special attention because his defence was greatly hampered. The main objects perhaps—I can only speculate—of those who were responsible for financing the defence was to provide for the safety of those Pandes. This man was a Dusadh and perhaps of no particular account. He should have been separately defended, but the provision of a separate defence for him would have involved serious difficulty for the other accused persons, because his defence, if properly put—as I shall indicate by the evidence—is that he was under the impression that he was called upon to drive the ekka back to Berhna. The actual owner of the ekka distinctly states in his evidence that he was approached by a party of Hindus, including Ramautar Dusadh, who said that they wished him to conduct a party to Berhna. For some reason he did not wish to do that and so he was thrust off his vehicle. Ramautar Dusadh seized his whip and he took the ekka to the shed and we know that it was the intention of the party at that stage, the intention at any rate of the poor woman, to go to Berhna. He says himself in his examination that in the crowd a constable seized him and told him to drive up to the ghat. The last part of his story is not true, but such part as is believable is entirely consistent with the evidence of one of the men who really owned the ekka. In our view Ramautar Dusadh believed he was going to drive the ekka to Berhna and he was compelled by the Pandes to drive to the ghat. It would have been difficult, and it was difficult, as I pointed out to Mr Nandkeolyer, to set up that defence in view of the fact that his defence was conducted jointly with those who said there was no plan to go to Berhna at all. As I say, he should have been defended separately. It is right that he should be convicted because he should have refused, when he learned the real nature of the trick, to conduct the ekka further. The justice of the case will be met by sentencing him to rigorous imprisonment for one year. The period of imprisonment already undergone by Ramautar will be included in this period of one year. As to the woman Lakhia, her condition mentally is hopeless. She was entirely dominated by the situation, by her superstition, by her ignorance and it is conceivable that she believed and had been made to believe in this lie about the miraculous fire. The justice of her case will be met by sentencing her to rigorous imprisonment for the term of one year. The period of imprisonment already undergone by Lakhia will be included in this period of one year. As to the boys Murlidhar and Vidyasagar, they are of an age when it is still possible that in better surrounding they may be freed from the grossness of the superstition in which they were reared. We intend to protect them for a considerable period so that at the time when they arrive at an age when they can think for themselves they may become men and may discard these beliefs of savages. They will be sentenced to rigorous imprisonment for five years. As to Jagdeo, he is an older youth and he should have exercised more intelligence. We believe, but we are not certain, that he was in the plot also, but we consider that the justice of his case will be met by sentencing him to rigorous imprisonment for seven years. As to the Pandes, Lachman, Hardea, Sahdeo and Kesho and the Bhumihar Raghu Singh, they are sentenced to rigorous imprisonment for ten years. This is our judgment, firstly that such evil-doers may be punished, secondly that an innocent girl may be avenged so far as we may avenge her, and thirdly, in order that those who will not learn by reason may be taught by fear. We can only punish the body. I do not pretend to know if there be any survival after this life is finished, but if so and if God be just and merciful in the sense that we very imperfectly understand justice and mercy, then such of these men as survive their earthly punishment may well go on humble pilgrimage to Sampati's flower-decked shrine, and with ashes on their heads, cast themselves down and invoke her gentle spirit to intercede with the Almighty to save their guilty souls from everlasting damnation.

Patna,   Sd. Courtney Terrell,
The 13th June 1928.   Sd. L.C. Adami

Searchlight, 'The Sati Case'[5]

The conservative Bihar newspaper *Searchlight*, which like the *Amrita Bazar Patrika* had eulogized the Barh sati as miraculous when it took place in 1927, reacted angrily to Terrell's judgment. It printed three articles responding to it in June 1928, which were so vitriolic that the paper was eventually charged with contempt of court on account of them. The following is the first of these three articles.

Sunday, 24 June 1928.

One cannot rise from a perusal of the judgment in the Sati case, which we reproduced in our last issue, without a feeling of profound depression. The judgment consists of a series of impressions which the learned Chief Justice formed in his mind and is conspicuously devoid of any reasons for his findings or of any reference to the evidence in respect of those findings. And His Lordship's impressions, it is quite obvious, were influenced by a wholly misconceived notion about the institution of Sati. Not only is His Lordship yet a stranger in the country and, therefore, naturally not able to appreciate the psychology behind this institution, but it seems, if the statement in the judgment be correct, he was influenced to a certain extent by the remarks of the counsel appearing for some of the accused. One of them is said to have described it as 'a relic of brutal barbarism' and another appears to have said that Sati has long been discarded by all pious Hindus with any pretence to the respect of his fellows. Knowing as we do these learned gentlemen, we believe such statements were probably made under the exigency of the case of their respective clients, but these statements are, we have no doubt, but half-truths. None who even pretends to know the culture and tradition of the Hindus, can accuse a Hindu, pious or not, of the cannibalistic tendency of revelling in human sacrifice for supposed religious merit. Sati is essentially a human institution and not divine. It represents the acme of moral perfection, and its whole merit is based upon its pure *voluntariness*. This is the only reason why it has received the homage of Hindus, cultured and uncultured, pious or otherwise, throughout ages. It is a typically oriental institution, which regards life as but a step or a means in realisation of an ideal. Even during the Mahammadan period, it was the great Mahammadan poet Faizi who sang:

'Hamchu hinduzan kase dar ashqi mardane neest; Sokhtan bar shama kushta kar har parwane neest;' (There is none so brave in love as a Hindu woman. It is not every moth that can burn on an extinguished flame.)

In course of time, however, under demoralizing political conditions, corruption crept in and 'voluntariness' disappeared to a very large extent. Against such abuse Raja Rammohan Roy raised his voice of protest, and under his inspiration Lord Bentinck passed his famous regulation interdicting the institution. But with all this, a pure Sati—pure in the sense of voluntariness—yet invokes the profound reverence of all Hindus who have not divested themselves of their age-long culture. We have emphasised this aspect of the case because it is impossible not to hold that His Lordship's conception of Sati, his horror of what he regards as a brutal crime, had a very great deal to do not merely with the impressions he formed from the facts of the case but with the sentences passed by him on the accused persons. We should like to emphasise once again that Sati in the sense of a woman being forcibly sacrificed with the body of the husband was and has always been regarded as a crime. It is not Sati—but a brutal murder. But Sati in the sense of a woman immolating herself on the funeral pyre with her dead husband, under an irresistible impulse of devotion, must be a different affair and, as a matter of fact, does invoke, as we have said, the admiration and respect of all Hindus. We very much wish His Lordship had kept this in mind when he chose to declaim against the institution as a 'belief of savages'—an observation which we respectfully think was clearly unwarranted. As a matter of fact, His Lordship went beyond his province in indulging in this sweeping generalization which his lordship failed to see involved an attack on one of the most cherished sentiments of Hindus.

But apart from this aspect of the question, it seems to us that the Hon'ble Chief Justice has approached the case from an erroneous standpoint, which has led him into a perspective not warranted by commonsense appreciation of the trend of events and facts of the case. Not being able to conceive the possibility of a purely voluntary Sati, instances of which are daily sung in eyery Hindu home and belief about which is ingrained in every fibre of a Hindu woman, it is scarcely suprising that His Lordship should form the idea that the girl Sampati was deliberately victimized by her relations and some others who were complete strangers to her, except that they belonged to the village with which she was connected. These relations, both from her father's and husband's sides, have been lumped together as the Pandeys and there is frequent suggestion to the effect that it is they who had together planned to encompass the death of Sampati. This is the basic standpoint from which the Chief Justice has surveyed the case—a fatal mistake which has, we suggest, effected the conclusions at which he has arrived. It is evident that the theory of some people profiting by the death of Sampati was uppermost in His Lordship's mind. At the very outset, referring to the defenceless condition of the girl after the death of her husband, His Lordship asks 'what a victim she presented to those who were to profit by her death?' That he was obviously referring to the Pandeys is the impression indelibly left on the mind by subsequent references to them. Referring to the progress of the two parties, one with the corpse

heading towards the ghat and the other with Sampati towards
Berhna, he says:—'At this point the ekka should have turned down
towards Berhna. *But this would have spoiled the Pandeys' plan. So leaving
the corpse to pursue its unresisting way to the ghat along the bund road,
carried by the docile kahars, they came down by the crossroad further north
and joined the crowd and recaptured their victim.* (Italics ours.) Later on
he refers to them as being 'present in the crowd and close to the
ekka conveying the lady'. Later still he says: 'here the Pandeys
intervened and forced the driver to lead it (the ekka) up to the
fork'. Next there is the distinct suggestion that these self-same
Pandeys hoodwinked the police who were surrounding the pyre
by planting a 'trick for ignition of Sampati's body. These suggestions have a purpose there is no mistaking—that the Pandeys were
out to encompass her death.

Now, the question is, with what end? Motive, we are told, guides
all human actions, and yet curiously enough there is no suggestion anywhere, either inferential or as a deduction from a single
piece of evidence, to explain what inspired this murderous instinct in the Pandeys, nor is there an iota of evidence to show that
the Pandeys were persons with any abnormal criminal propensi-
ties. What is more, anyone familiar with Indian life, could have
enlightened the Chief Justice that joint action with a murderous
intent, developed so suddenly between members of the husband's
family and that of the father's, is as improbable a possibility as anything could be. Moreover, the fact that these Pandeys comprised
both the groups is likewise a clear repudiation of the suggestion
that there could be any conspiracy between them for material
gain as anyone familiar with Indian social life could easily en-
lighten the Chief Justice. As for spiritual merit, even the veriest
school boy in the village is aware that forced victimization of a
widow with her husband is murder pure and simple and the end
of it is damnation. It is obvious therefore that there is no explanation
whatever of the motive that could have inspired the Pandeys in
intriguing the brutal crime imputed to them. More than this, the
fact is significant that the very first place to which the party resorted to in the night after their arrival at Barh was the Magistrate's
court. If this is so, can it be seriously suggested that persons with
the fixed determination of the Pandeys, out to manipulate the

sacrifice of a lady, would do anything of the kind? Indeed, clever men such as the Pandeys are suggested to be would put as much distance between themselves and the thana or the court as they could possibly do and hasten to the ghat by some circuitous route avoiding as far as possible the danger of detection. But they go straight to and rest for the night in the Magistrate's court. In the light of these, the utter absence of any common motive and the behaviour of the Pandeys, the theory about the Pandeys' machination and determination is unsustainable even if there be any basis for it in the evidence. His Lordship relying on the circumstance that the Pandeys kept surrounding the lady and supervised her toilet has deduced the finding that Sampati's body was ignited by a 'trick simpler than any seen at a country fair'. This is obviously an assumption, and it is unfortunate that we have not been told what the trick was that these unsophisticated rustics from the interior of Barh successfully resorted to despite the vigilant watch kept by a whole army of police officers and constables who upon oath told the court that they kept a careful lookout, to see that no outside agency helped Sampati with means of ignition. But the learned Chief Justice after coming to a finding which should convict them not of mere abetment of suicide but of cold-blooded murder, comes to another finding which, we respectfully suggest, involves him in an obvious contradiction. Let us examine the point.

After the woman jumped into the river tortured evidently by the flames, His Lordship says, 'The Pandeys were in very serious difficulty. If the woman were rescued, the trick was revealed and the hangman's rope again dangled in front of them. They could not start the fire again; they could not repeat the trick. The apparatus was gone and therefore Sampati must drown. They threw her corpse etc.' Obviously according to His Lordship, they were deter-mined that the woman should die. And yet the learned Chief Justice proceeds, 'However with the help of the police she was ultimately helped ashore in a shocking condition. She went to lie down under a tree by a temple sixty paces away and *then began that which was the first fruit for which the Pandeys had been waiting—a stream of coins began to flow which they greedily picked up*' (Italics ours). We confess we find it difficult to reconcile the two theories—the one of Pandeys' encompassing the death of Sampati and the other of their waiting for the coins they had calculated would pour in in case Sampati came out of the water half-burnt, exciting the sympathy, pity or piety of the audience. Either the Pandeys were out to consume her by fire or they were out to earn the coins that they hoped would pour in in case the girl shook herself out of the river after jumping into it under the stress of agony. Both, we respectfully suggest, cannot be possible, for if the former was the truth the latter eventuality could not have been foreseen and awaited with the diabolical fiendishness displayed by the Pandeys according to the Chief Justice. Evidently in His Lordship's view the Pandeys were not only conjurors but also astrologers who knew accurately what would happen and had made their calculations accordingly.

Now we know that as the law stands at present 'Sati', whether voluntary, or involuntary, is a crime, and the abetment of the same is equally criminal. But we do apprehend that the judging of the case from a wrong perspective may have led to a grave injustice being done to individual accused. That this seems to have been very probably the case is more than apparent from the nature and the terms of the findings in respect of the accused Lakhia, Ramautar, and also Jagdeo. We propose to deal with this aspect of the case in a subsequent issue. The police, upon the finding of His Lordship have come out with flying colours in the case. Yet, people of Barh, who witnessed the tragic sight, have a different story to tell. It is true, and to us it seems to have been a grievous misfortune, that they did not come to give evidence in the case. No one can condemn their lack of public spirit in this matter more than we do. Yet it is but right to say that promiscuous issue of notices under Section 144 Cr. P. C. by the S. D. O. of Barh upon a very large number of people, who exhibited even in the slight degree any sympathy with the Sati, was responsible to a great deal for general demoralization in that subdivision. And the record itself is more than eloquent of the fact that the police themselves deliberately avoided collecting evidence from the general public upon the specious plea that none would come forward to give evidence. His Lordship has thought it fit to condemn the jurors who brought in a verdict of 'not guilty' in very severe terms. Knowing as we do Professors Ashutosh Chatterji, Hazari and Ganguli, no one in this province will believe that they were such moral cowards as to sacrifice their conscience at the altar of popular applause or religious prejudice. They know the true character of the Sati, and the value of police evidence. To say the least, their experience of police and knowledge of local customs are certainly greater than those of His Lordship. So far as their integrity, character, and intellectual equipment are concerned, they can bear comparison with any. But whatever it be, the pious exhortation with which the learned Chief Justice eloquently concludes his judgment is not only out of place in a judicial pronouncement, but must further lose its force because of the wrong viewpoint from which the case has been adjudged. However unpleasant it be, we feel it our duty to point it out to His Lordship that the severe sentence which he has passed is absolutely unprecedented in such cases and has sent a thrill of horror throughout the province and will have a tendency to defeat the very object which His Lordship has been anxious to serve. We understand steps are being taken to take the case to the Privy Council. This, however, should not deter the members of the Council to take such steps as they can to move the Local Government for a proper mitigation of the sentences.

Stri Dharma, 'Sati'[6]

Not all Indians shared the Searchlight's view of events, of course. The following attack on the Searchlight's glorification of the Barh sati is from Stri Dharma, an organ of the women's movement.

A young girl of Bihar committed sati. When the flames became intolerable she jumped into the Ganges, but was rescued. After two days and nights of agony she died. Sufferings such as these, which gave a thrill of horror to all civilized sensibilities elicits the following remark from the Searchlight of Bihar: 'Sati represents the acme of moral perfection and its whole merit is based on its voluntariness. In course of time, however, under demoralizing political conditions corruption crept in and voluntariness disappeared to a very large extent. But for all this a pure sati—pure in the sense of voluntariness yet invokes the profound reverence of all Hindus who have not divested themselves of their age-long culture.' There is no voluntariness in conduct to the extent that it is wrought in deception. It is deception to tell uneducated young girls that their husbands are their gods however devoid of merit, and that to mount their funeral pyre is the surest way to heaven. There is no voluntariness in action to the extent it is induced by pressure. Public opinion is a mighty pressure, and in olden days there were millions like the writers to the *Searchlight* who pointed to widows the funeral flames of their husbands as the best place for them. There is no voluntariness in deeds to the extent they are inspired by fear. The fear inspiring is the suffering and humiliation which Hindu society has reserved for widows who elect to live. One may also consider how many men have followed 'the acme of moral perfection' which they so easily preach to women, and mounted the flames of their wives. 'Voluntary' self-torture seems never popular with those who have the liberty to do what they please. Do women have that liberty? 'No liberty for women,' says the Code of Manu. Spirituality is often distinct from the practice of religion and ceremonials. The history of religion and crime have therefore many coinciding points—Sati is one. Also, religious men are often the worst criminals. When wickedness stoops to cruelty, cowardice seeks exculpation in ceremonies and religion.

Notes

1　Home Department Records, Government of Bihar and Orissa, Political Department, H.K. Briscoe, Chief Secretary to Government, to the Secretary to the Government of India, Home Department, Patna, 15 December 1927.

2　*Amrita Bazar Patrika*, 29 November 1927.

3　*Amrita Bazar Patrika*, 30 November 1927.

4　Chief Justice Courtney Terrell and Justice Adami, Judgment in the Barh Sati Case, Patna High Court, 13th June 1928 (as reproduced in full in *Searchlight*, 22 June 1928)

5　'The Sati Case', *Searchlight*, 24 June 1928.

6　'Sati', from *Stri Dharma*, an organ of the women's movement, August 1928.

13

British Ideas

The Times, 'The Abolition of Suttee'[1]

The Times marked the centenary of the abolition of sati with this homily to Lord William Bentinck. It is typical of the British attitudes towards the reform of Indian society, for although it mentions the role of Rammohan Roy and Dwarakanath Tagore, it claims that reform would not have happened without the benign influence of the British.

Exactly a hundred years have passed today since the British Governor-General of India struck a decisive blow against one of the cruellest rites ever practised by superstitious men. Suttee, the practice of burning a widow alive on her husband's funeral pyre, had been established among Hindus for many centuries. It may have reached India with the Aryans. It certainly flourished on the Russian steppes—the cradle, so philologists aver, of Indo-European speech—from the days of the Scythians to the tenth century of our era, when Masudi described its horrors. But its modern prevalence in parts of Hindu India arose from the revival by Brahmins of a custom that was called 'ancient' in the earliest sacred books and was not prescribed by Manu. Some of the women who perished on the pyre desired this fate; many were forced into the flames by their kin; and it is significant that Lady Amherst, in the diary she kept while her husband was Governor-General, recorded that the rite had become a degrading entertainment, a spectacle witnessed by curious crowds. Defended by many Brahmins, admired by members of lower castes who did not practise it, suttee survived the disapproval of Akbar, and of a series of British

Governors-General. The honour of its suppression was left to Lord William Bentinck, whose regulation of 4 December 1829, declaring the practice to be illegal and punishable by the criminal courts as culpable homicide, put an immediate end to it in Bengal and was extended to the rest of British India the following year.

It is possible that Hinduism might have repudiated a custom not universal in India, confined to a few castes and condemned by enlightened Hindus, such as Rammohan Roy and Dwarakanath Tagore. But without any disparagement to their efforts, it must be admitted that the long resistance to such social reforms as the abolition of child marriage suggests that generations might have passed before the entrenchments of suttee were carried by the Hindu reformers alone. In this case, the British Governor-General, undeterred either by the charge that he was interfering with the religious observances of Hinduism or by the prophecies of the dangers of that interference, took the lead on the ground that 'to abstain from taking action would be making oneself guilty of the crime of multiple murder'. He knew that most of the Hindu who applauded suttee were as blind devotees of custom as the Englishman of his own generation who defended Negro slavery: he risked their displeasure, and the event proved that his confidence was justified. The result of his courageous decision may be profitably studied. Hinduism is gradually freeing itself of many of the accretions and superstitions unknown to the authors of the Vedic hymns and attacked by later reformers. The recent passage of the Sarda Bill against child marriage through the legislative assembly, and the movement for the abolition of the most serious caste disabilities, are among the proofs of an increasing desire for reform. But is it unfair to ask how the social progress of India would have faired without contact with Europe and without the religious and social ideas of the West?

Edward Thompson, *Suttee*[2]

Edward Thompson's book on sati was hailed as authoritative by British critics at the time of its publication and is typical of imperial attitudes to the rite in the early twentieth century. Thompson's treatment of the subject provoked an angry response from the nationalist journal the *Modern Review* which saw it as akin to Katherine Mayo's *Mother India*. The following is the conclusion of Thompson's well-known work.

CONCLUDING CONSIDERATIONS

I have not conducted this enquiry into an obscure subject from any love for the gruesome or the cruel, or only because in India the stories and traditions of suttee stirred profound pity in my mind and made me wish to win for its victims at least this posthumous justice, that their fate should not be misunderstood. I believe that the history of the rite sheds light on dark passages of Indian and British relations, and on certain periods and personalities of the last century; also that conclusions of value for today can be drawn.

Effect of Suttee on Europeans

Suttee, as Sir Vernon Lovett remarked to me, by arousing the disgust and abhorrence of Englishmen who saw it or were contemporary with it, caused them to do injustice to Indian thought. It was impossible to think of Indian civilization as anything but a barbarian civilization. Macaulay's often-abused Minute about the relative value of Sanskrit literature and of 'a single shelf' of modern European books had this background of barbarities shadowing his mind. If it was a mistake to set Indian education on solely Western lines, it was a mistake for which Indians had themselves to thank, for the fruits of Hinduism a century ago were bad. As an Indian student of mine, a fervent Hindu, said to me, 'A hundred years ago, not only Christian missionaries, but the early Brahmos also, thought that Hinduism was idolatrous.' That is so; they also thought it cruel. There is a simple explanation of both beliefs, strange as they seem to neo-Hindus and theosophists today. Hinduism was what it seemed to be.

There were many other barbarities practised in India a century ago; but some might be dismissed as mere superstition, or as the crimes of backward tribes and perverted sects of Hinduism, such as those who practised human sacrifice. Infanticide had an economic cause. But suttee cut to the very roots of social morality, and the society which practised it and gloried in it made itself an outcast from the civilized comity of nations. It is often made a reproach against the British that, after a century and a half of predominance in India, they have not advanced the people any further along the road of fitness for self-government. I am not, I think, likely to ignore or forget the mistakes and shortcomings of our administration. But India's primary need today is fair judgment—from us to it and from it to us. And if we have written Indian history with unfairness, Indians have with equal unfairness put upon us the blame for many things for which they have been responsible. I have no doubt whatever that such things as suttee kept back Indian political progress by many years; until the rite was abolished, even a beginning in self-government was impossible.

To put the matter in a lower but a very practical light, we say that advancement of natives to high posts of emolument or responsibility was simply impossible while such relics of dark ages and dark superstitions were fostered or endured. The most grotesque and horrible incongruities would arise had suttee kept pace with our avowed and earnest desire to see natives taking a larger share in the government of the country. Imagine a native gentleman dying who was a member of the Governor-General's Council for making laws, and the Viceroy, on sending a message of condolence to his family, being quietly told that his wives had all burnt themselves the day before; or the native Justices of the Peace for the town of Calcutta stating their inability to attend a discussion on the waterworks of the metropolis because they wished to follow the widow of one of their number to her husband's pile at Chitpore or Garden Reach; or a Bengalee member of the Civil Service, for such there may be, refusing to subscribe to the civil fund because he would, under the shastras, be only survived by his widow for the space of twelve hours. It was in one sense truly said that such practices were incompatible with the spread of education, but the sound rule, we submit, for our guidance would have been to put down violent crimes first and then educate and refine afterwards. The demoralization of the survivors entailed by the rite of suttee was palpably spreading, and was a worse feature than even the cruel tortures of the dying wife, which is saying a good deal.[3]

But India paid an immeasurable price, in other than practical ways, for the practice of suttee. The rite aroused in foreigners a contempt, especially in Bengal, where the men were—and always had been—exempt from risk of death and maiming in battle, which is not yet eradicated. Its apologists and hymnists today are the large body of sentimentalists who are unteachably inaccurate,

Europeans and Americans incapable of any intellectual process higher than unthinking ecstasy in the presence of what they imperfectly understand and wholly misrepresent, Indians incapable of any statement that is not tilted by some nationalist bias. India has been damned by the mental slackness of its exponents: we who love it are most of us people entitled to very little respect on intellectual grounds.

It may seem unjust and illogical that the Moguls, who freely impaled and flayed alive, or nationals of Europe, whose countries had such ferocious penal codes and had known, scarcely a century before suttee began to shock the English conscience, orgies of witch-burning and religious persecution, should have felt as they did about suttee. But the difference seemed to them this— the victims of their cruelties were tortured by a law which considered them offenders, whereas the victims of suttee were punished for no offence but the physical weakness which had placed them at man's mercy. The rite seemed to prove a depravity and arrogance such as no other human offence had brought to light.

Something may be urged in support of every kind of custom, show, or amusement of a national character, however barbarous and demoralizing in many respects. In gladiatorial exhibitions, the old Romans, who, amidst all their fine qualities, had no sentiments of chivalry or generosity to the vanquished, learnt to admire the skill of the exhibitors, as well as the calm determination with which they passed by the Chief Magistrate, saluting him as dying men. In the bull-fights of Spain the adroitness of the matador sometimes half-drowns the pity felt for the mangled and disembowelled horses. Even at a prize-fight, gentlemen of taste and education have dwelt on the artistic position, the muscular, well-shaped, and healthy frame, and the exquisite skill in attack and defence manifested by the pugilists. Yet, in spite of skill and activity and heroic resolution, the almost universal consent of civilized nations now pronounces such spectacles to be barbarous and demoralizing. But in these cases the actors, anyhow, are men, strong and independent, and capable of judging for themselves. Suttees were made out of the weakest part of the creation. Illiterate women, preyed on by relatives, cowed by priests, morally if not physically drugged, were urged to continue to their husband after death that servile obedience to which they had been condemned in their lifetimes, or to encounter a state of dull and dreary widowhood to which death was almost preferable. Suttee appears to have sprung from, as well as to have perpetuated, some of the vilest feelings of our human nature. It began in selfishness, it was supported by falsehood, and it ended in cruelty such as might give support to fiends. No language is too strong for it.

When we read the long record of human lives sacrificed to what was called our national good faith, the vacillating minutes, the elaborate reports, the indignant remonstrances which the subject excited, and the inactivity of a Government presided over at least by one able statesman, we can but sigh, as we read the blood-stained page, for one hour of either Bentinck or Dalhousie.[4]

Contemporary accounts of Bengal suttees a century ago, and the cases that, for one irregularity or another, reached the courts, show that the rite was a huge public *tāmāshā*,[5] in which the lowest Mahommadans joined actively with the dregs of the Hindu populace.

Bentinck and Dalhousie

We have seen that we cannot claim the abolition of suttee as a triumph of 'British justice' or an example of the righteous and fearless character of our administration. The garland belongs to one man almost alone, and no praise is too high for him.

Another thing that has become clear is the underlying motive of Dalhousie's annexations, some of them carried out against the strong disapproval of such men as Sir Henry Lawrence. His humanitarianism, reinforced and sharpened by his experience of the unwillingness of native states to set their houses in order in matters of elementary decency, was responsible for his anxiety to annex whenever possible. I believe that there was no 'earth-hunger' behind his doctrine of 'lapse'; and while criticizing him we should remember the exasperating refusal of many states to abolish suttee and female infanticide.

'A saying of his quoted by Hunter has, as that author observes, 'the ring of a great soul'.
'I circulate these papers,' he wrote hastily on one case in which he had successfully insisted on justice being done at the risk of a tumult; 'they are an instance of the principle that we should do what is right without fear of consequences. To fear God and to have no other fear is a maxim of religion, but the truth of it and the wisdom of it are proved day by day in politics.'[6]

1829 to 1857

We have further seen that the 1829 Regulation opened a period of intensive warfare against violent and cruel crime: British officers fought against dacoity, suttee, human sacrifice, thuggee, female infanticide. It was not kid-glove work: even the rites of the Aztecs were not more depraved and ferocious than those which marked the 'meriah' human sacrifices of Orissa, and the officers who extirpated them were dealing with subhuman beings. Thuggee was stamped out by a ruthlessness that was unavoidable and well deserved.

During the years 1831–1837, 3,266 thugs were disposed of in one way or another, 412 out of that number being hanged and 483 admitted as approvers. The approvers and their descendants were detained for many years in a special institution at Jubbulpore (Jabalpur).[7]

The work of these years was largely summary: it necessarily developed the summary outlook and method. The period was marked also by four hard-fought wars—those with Sind, Gwalior, and the two Sikh wars—as well as two outside India, with Afghanistan and Burma. The summary mind was working in the aggression which forced Afghanistan and Sind to fight us, and in the annexations that made the period one of growing exasperation against the foreigner. The summary mind, when it is an individual dealing with unwilling and wild subjects, becomes the gamekeeper mind. These years, which saw province after province added to British India—Sind, the cis-Sutlej lands, and the Jullunder Doab, Kashmir, Hazara, the Panjab itself, Oudh—saw the improvization of a loose and mainly personal system of administration for the vast tracts and fierce frontier where Nicholson and his compeers won their reputations and formed their characters. If we remember that the men who served in India during these years often felt that they were exterminating vermin, and that they were flung widely over newly conquered territory where their authority was almost entirely personal and their power enormous, the ruthlessness and spiritual arrogance with which our people confronted the Mutiny become explicable, and there is the less reason for the whitewashing of our textbooks and their extraordinary moral judgements. The Panjab administration, before and after, as well as during, the Mutiny, was terribly stern. These years of suppression of inhumanities and of conquest and subjugation, after the explosion of 1857 threw a wild storm-light over all our thinking, produced the hard, unattractive English life in India which our novelists, consciously and unconsciously, have so successfully made us realize. That life was perhaps the most cynical (and yet confidently righteous) and least humorous phase in all our history as a people.

I am not justifying anything that happened; I am trying to explain; and I do not believe that to explain is to justify. Between 1830 and 1880 a beneficial ruthlessness was busy, and a self-satisfaction and an isolation from the people of India reigned. If I would see the writing of Indian history a franker, less cautious thing, and salted with a magnanimous and less narrowly political philosophy, it is because this would go far towards winning the interest of my people, who are weary both of the querulous plaints of Indians and of the angry pompousness of our own satraps and apologists. I believe, too, that another long step towards winning interest will be taken if we can arrest some of the excessive attention that has been given to the men prominent in 1857 and later years and turn it towards the able and generous men who worked in India in the period immediately before the great annexations and the great rebellion—towards Munro, Malcolm, Elphinstone, Tod.

The Psychology of the 'Satīs'

I had intended to try to examine this; but the truth is, it has ceased to seem a puzzle to me. Obviously, the mental state of the women who were sacrificed varied infinitely, as that of martyrs for religion or patriotism. The Rajput lady who died when a foe girdled in her city and her whole sex was swept away, or who ascended the pyre with her lord newly slain in battle, was in a mood that had no contact or resemblance with the mood of the cowed and unwilling slave girl. Yet, even Rajput queens ultimately refused to go to the pyre.

Indians cherish with a rapture of exultation their many stories of *satīs* who died calmly or with lofty ecstasy. Those who saw Dip Kunwar, 'the last distinguished *satī* in Bikanir', go to her death in 1825 spoke of her radiant heroism as long as they lived. Yet, after all, even such cases as this are only examples of what the history of every country has shown—that men and women, not only separately but in the mass, can be disciplined and trained to an extent to which no limit can be set. Soldiers, members of communities dedicated to destruction—as some warrior tribes and sects have been in times of national despair—slaves, the labouring classes during the long industrial depression now slowly lifting—all these have been trained to accept without question a fate that to sober thought is horrible. It is but a few years since men of almost every nation in Europe were disciplined to the point that they would accept a command to go to inevitable death with resignation or even joy. Women especially have shown a power of passive acceptance of a drab and colourless plane of existence in which their personality was crushed out of even a claim for recognition, that may be to their credit—I am by no means sure that it is—but is certainly not to that of man. That large sections of Indian society trained their women to look forward to the funeral pyre of their lord as the crown and glory of their lives is true. It is true also that to this day many Indian women cherish a sentimental worship of that mood, in which their menfolk encourage them, and that the writer who lays the facts in sunlight and thereby slays the ignoble and slavish folly that has given them so much satisfaction will receive only resentment. Nevertheless, the discipline that made suttee possible was a discipline of slaves; and the civilization that hounded widows, in the first moments of grief or surprise, into a declaration that they would die, and then forbade any withdrawal, was a barbarous one.

Would Suttee Revive if the British left India?

Not as an established custom—at any rate, not where the nationalist movement connected with the name of Mr Gandhi has been strong. For that movement has been a cleansing one, since it has brought with it the deepest and most radical criticism to which Indians have ever submitted themselves; it has loosened a great many things, besides the British hold on India.

But there would undoubtedly be instances of suttee, especially where Brahman or Rajput influence is strong; and in some districts the rite might become not uncommon. The disquieting thing is, suttee has troubled the Hindu conscience hardly at all. Even a saint such as Kabir mentions it with detachment, as an illustration of his theme, the extent to which love, whether of a husband or of God, can move those it possesses.

Yet, as European history has shown, it is not fair to expect even saints to be in all ethical questions in advance of their age. What we *are* entitled to consider strange is that, while some Indian writers whom the West has deeply influenced—for example, Romesh Dutt and Rajendralal Mitra—have condemned suttee uncompromisingly, it is common—indeed, usual—for Hindu writers to glorify it today, and there is a widespread belief that it proved the superior chastity of their women. Suttee and nationalism are the two subjects on which the irony-loving Bengali is nearly always heavily and solemnly serious. The courage of the *satīs* appeals to something in even the most 'advanced' Hindu that is absent from the normal-thinking person in the West, and that courage is the only thing that Indians have fixed their eyes on. It is at last worth while trying to draw attention to other aspects of the rite. The last few years have brought to the younger generation of Indians, especially those studying in the West, such a feeling of weakness and humiliation that they are anxious to be *right* in their thinking, and are ceasing to be sensitive lest a confession that they were mistaken in some matter lower their dignity with foreigners. The free man can face the opinion of others, for their condemnation is nothing to him unless his own conscience go along with it.

Indians are with reason resentful of much that is said on missionary platforms in Europe and America and in missionary journals. Missionary apologetics have stressed the weak points in Hinduism, and have brought to the comparison only the strength of Christianity, ignoring such matters as its stormy and poetic but chaotic and mistaken eschatology. India has a right to point out to her critics the materialism of Western civilization and Europe's record of aggression outside herself. The weakest thing in Hinduism is its ethical record, which is a shocking one. There is no single instance of a cruelty or an injustice which the religion or the people have shaken off from within. Reform has always come by forcible interposition from without, and without that forcible interposition would never have come. If the positive programme of Mr Gandhi is followed, in such matters as the removal of untouchability, this record of Hinduism will be for the first time broken.

The refusal to glorify the past where it was vile is the only course consistent with self-respect. It is also the only way to win the respect of the world and, I believe, the help of English men and women in the struggle for Indian self-determination. For it is one thing to recognize the abstract justice of a cause, and quite another to move to its assistance. Greece and Italy have been trumpet-calls to civilized men everywhere; India is usually only a *Ducdame*, and will be until more sense is talked by us who love her. It is possible for a civilization to spoil its women by adulation and by attaching importance to their silliest and most trivial opinions. But Indian civilization has spoiled its men, a fact written large on Indian literature, making much of its finest poetry and fiction unreadable outside India without contempt mingling with admiration. I am sure that in India generally, and in certain parts especially, the men have for millenniums accepted and commanded from the women more than they could afford to take. As a result, the thinking and imagination of peoples second to none intellectually have been largely sterile.

I believe the time is come for a much more radical sifting of Hindu tradition by Indians themselves; and they will be wise if they adjust their attitude to the past by one consideration only— that of truth, and if while doing this they forget that they are a dependent people and exposed to a galling criticism from outside. The criticism that matters is their own; and on this question, of woman's position in society and her duties towards man, that criticism has not been searching or brave enough. I have tried to make it as impossible for an educated Indian to defend suttee as it is now impossible for an educated Englishman to defend execution by torture; and when the defence is abandoned, the contempt that the defending inspires will pass away. What is more important, once the light of honest thinking is let in on this sacrifice of woman, other ideas that have sheltered behind this idol will be dragged out to question. The nonsense about the wonderful purity and spirituality of the Hindu marriage ideal cannot survive examination; still less can the sex-obsession of the civilization and the social system which, in making one sex the unpitied servant to the other, drains and destroys both. If the matter is brought to the political test, which— not unnaturally—is what appeals most to educated Indians today, then we may say this: they have friends who gladly acknowledge their right to complete self-determination, yet cannot see what *use* freedom can be to them until the whole of their sex-thinking has been ruthlessly overhauled and the plain conclusions of reason and justice put in practice. Suttee has gone, but its background remains. Children are married and ravished, their bodies maimed, their minds mutilated. If a generation could arise with the physical and mental vigour that in nearly every other land is a normal possession, much that is now thought admirable in Hindu literature and religion would be seen as a revolting nightmare. There are communities free from man-worship and sex-obsession, such as the Brahmo Samaj and kindred Churches; but even these are dishonoured, and their humiliating sense of impotence deepened, by the inability of the vast majority of their fellow-countrymen to see anything amiss in Hindu civilization or anything that needs to be done in India except political agitation. If there is any 'gulf' between East and West, it is where sex and the family are in question, and woman's function and her relation to man. India cherishes some exquisite stories of wedded love. But if even the tales of Sita and Savitri and Damayanti, or—to bring the matter on to the plane of history—those of Dip Kunwar and the gallant ladies who burned for Prithviraj and Sardar Shan Singh, represent the whole or the best of what they can conceive of the comradeship of man and woman, then there is a gulf between East and West indeed.

Notes

1   'The Abolition of Suttee', *The Times*, 4 December 1929, p.15.
2   Thompson, E., *Suttee* (London: George Allen and Unwin, 1928).
3   *Calcutta Review*, 1867, 'Suttee'.
4   *Calcutta Review*, 1867, 'Suttee'.
5   Show.
6   *Oxford History of India*, p. 709.
7   Ibid., p. 668.

14

Indian Attitudes

Bankimchandra Chattopadhyay[1]

Bankimchandra, seen by many as the progenitor of modern Hindutva, depicted sati as epitomizing ideal Hindu womanhood—part of a glorious Hindu past.

When I think of elevated sections of women, the vision that rises is of the sati, determined to be cremated along with her dead husband. I picture the burning pyre and in the midst of rising flames, the virtuous woman lovingly holding to her bosom her husband's feet. Opening out slowly, the fire embraces one portion of her body and moves towards the other. The fire-gripped woman thinks of her master's feet, and, in between, exhorts the assemblage to chant the name of Hari. She betrays no trace of physical pain. Her face is joyous. Gradually, the sacred flame flies up, life is left behind, and the body reduced to ashes. Blessed is her tolerance! Blessed her love! Blessed her devotion! When I think that, until a while back, the delicate women of my country could court death in this manner, a new hope courses through my mind. I am convinced that the seeds of greatness are in us. Shall we not be able to witness this greatness tomorrow?

Mohandas Karamchand Gandhi[2]

Gandhiji strongly opposed sati as a custom, even going as far as to suggest that the British should be lauded for putting a stop to it. It is arguable, however, that his emphasis on women's capacity for sacrifice drew on the very ethos of femininity that underpinned the rite. The following is a translation of a letter written by Gandhi to a lady correspondent, from Ghatkopar, who had asked his opinion of a recent sati case.

I hope that the incident, as reported in the press, is not true, and that the lady in question died through illness or through accident, not by suicide. A sati has been described by our ancients, and the description holds good today, as one who, ever fixed in her love and devotion to her husband, signalizes herself by her selfless service during her husband's lifetime as well as after, and remains absolutely chaste in thought, word and deed. Self-immolation on the death of the husband is a sign not of enlightenment but of gross ignorance as to the nature of the soul. The soul is immortal, unchangeable, and immanent. It does not perish with the physical body, but journeys on from one mortal frame to another till it completely emancipates itself from earthly bondage. The truth of it has been attested to by the experience of countless sages and seers, and can be realized by anyone who may wish to even today. How can suicide be then justified in the light of these facts?

Again, true marriage means not merely union of bodies. It connotes the union of the souls, too. If marriage meant more than a physical relationship, the bereaved wife should be satisfied with a portrait or a waxen image of her husband. But self-destruction is worse than futile. It cannot help to restore the dead to life; on the contrary it only takes away one more from the world of the living.

The ideal that marriage aims at is that of spiritual union through the physical. The human love that it incarnates is intended to serve as a stepping stone to the divine or universal love. That is why immortal Mira sang: 'God alone is my husband—none else.' It follows from this that a sati would regard marriage not as a means of satisfying the animal appetite but as a means of realizing the ideal of selfless and self-effacing service by completely merging her individuality in her husband's. She would prove her satihood not by mounting the funeral pyre at her husband's death, but she would prove it with every breath that she breathes from the moment that she plighted her troth to him at the *saptapadi* ceremony, by her renunciation, sacrifice, self-abnegation and dedication to the service of her husband, his family and the country.

She would shun creature comforts and delights of the senses. She would refuse to be enslaved by the narrow domestic cares and interests of the family, but would utilize every opportunity to add to her stock of knowledge and increase her capacity for service by more and more cultivating renunciation and self-discipline, and by completely identifying herself with her husband, learn to identify herself with the whole world.

Such a sati would refuse to give way to wild grief at the death of her husband, but would ever strive to make her late husband's ideals and virtues live again in her actions and thereby win for him the crown of immortality. Knowing that the soul of him whom she married is not dead but still lives, she will never think of remarrying.

The reader will here be perhaps tempted to ask, 'The sati that you have pictured is a being untouched by passion or animal appetite. She can have no desire for offspring. Why should she marry at all?' The reply is that in our present-day Hindu society marriage, in a vast majority of cases, is not a matter of choice. Again, there are some who believe that in our ramshackle age marriage is necessary as a shield to virtue and as an aid to self-restraint. And as a matter of fact I personally know several instances of persons, who, though at the time of the marriage were not free from animal passion, later on became imbued with the ideal of absolute chastity and found in their married life a powerful means for realizing their ideal. I have cited these instances to show that the ideal of sati that I have depicted is not merely a counsel of perfection that has no place outside the world of theory but something that has to be lived up to and realized in this very matter-of-fact world of ours.

But I readily concede that the average wife who strives to attain the ideal of sati will be a mother, too. She must, therefore, add to her various other qualities mentioned above—a knowledge of rearing and bringing up children so that they might live to be true servants of their country.

All that I have said about the wife applies equally to the husband. If the wife has to prove her loyalty and undivided devotion to her husband, so has the husband to prove his allegiance and devotion to his wife. You cannot have one set of weights and measures for the one and a different one for the other. Yet, we have never heard of a husband mounting the funeral pyre of his deceased wife. It may, therefore, be taken for granted that the practice of the widow immolating herself on the death of her husband had its origin in superstitious ignorance and the blind egotism of man. Even if it could be proved that at one time the practice had a meaning, it can only be regarded as barbarous in the present age. The wife is not the slave of the husband but his comrade, otherwise known as his better half, his colleague and friend. She is a co-sharer with him, of equal rights and of equal duties. Their obligations towards each other and towards the world must, therefore, be the same and reciprocal.

I, therefore, regard the alleged self-immolation of this sister as vain. It certainly cannot be set up as an example to be copied. Don't I appreciate at least her courage to die, I may perhaps be asked. My reply is 'no' in all conscience. Have we not seen even evil-doers display this sort of courage? Yet, no one has ever thought of complementing them on it. Why should I take upon me the sin of even unconsciously leading astray some ignorant sister by my injudicious praise of suicide? Satihood is the acme of purity. This purity cannot be attained or realized by dying. It can be attained only through constant striving, constant immolation of the spirit from day to day.

Ananda Coomaraswamy, 'The Status of Indian Women'[3]

In this well-known essay the famous Boston-based Indian art historian defended 'traditional' Indian womanhood against the deprecations of the Western observers. He discusses sati a practice, but also uses the term to designate a certain type of Hindu woman, whose morality, status, and treatment he contrasts favourably with her American and European counterparts.

In the Mahabharata there is reported a conversation between Shiva and Uma. The Great God asks her to describe the duties of women, addressing her, in so doing, in terms which acknowledge her perfect attainment of the highest wisdom possible to man or god—terms which it would be hard to parallel anywhere in Western literature. He says:

Thou that dost know the Self and the not-Self, expert in every work: endowed with self-restraint and perfect same-sightedness towards every creature: free from the sense of I and my—thy power and energy are equal to my own, and thou hast practised the most severe discipline. O Daughter of Himalaya, of fairest eyebrows, and whose hair ends in the fairest curls, expound to me the duties of women in full.

Then She, who is queen of heaven, and yet so sweetly human, answers:

The duties of woman are created in the rites of wedding, when in presence of the nuptial fire she becomes the associate of her Lord, for the performance of all righteous deeds. She should be beautiful and gentle, considering her husband as her god and serving him as such in fortune and misfortune, health and sickness, obedient even if commanded to unrighteous deeds or acts that may lead to her own destruction. She should rise early, serving the gods, always keeping her house clean, tending to the domestic sacred fire, eating only after the needs of gods and guests and servants have been satisfied, devoted to her father and mother and the father and mother of her husband. Devotion to her Lord is woman's honour, it is her eternal heaven; and O Maheshvara,

she adds, with a most touching human cry,

I desire not paradise itself if thou are not satisfied with me!

'She is a true wife who gladdens her husband,' says Rajashekhara in the *Karpura Manjari*. The extract following is from the Laws of Manu:

Though destitute of virtue, or seeking pleasure elsewhere, or devoid of good qualities, a husband must be constantly worshipped as a god by a faithful wife.... If a wife obeys her husband, she will for that reason alone be exalted in heaven. The production of children, the nurture of those born, and the daily life of men, of these matters woman is visibly the cause.
She who controlling her thoughts, speech and acts, violates not her duty to her Lord, dwells with him after death in heaven, and in this world is called by the virtuous a faithful wife.

Similar texts from a variety of Indian sources could be indefinitely multiplied.

If such are the duties of women, women are accorded corresponding honour, and exert a corresponding influence upon society. This power and influence do not so much belong to the merely young and beautiful, nor to the wealthy, as to those who have lived— mothers and grandmothers—or who follow a religious discipline—

widows or nuns. According to Manu: 'A master exceedeth ten tutors in claim to honour; the father a hundred masters; but the mother a thousand fathers in right to reverence and in the function of teacher.' When Rama accepted Kaikeyi's decree of banishment, it was because 'a mother should be as much regarded by a son as is a father.' Even at the present day it would be impossible to overemphasize the influence of Indian mothers not only upon their children and in all household affairs, but upon their grown-up sons to whom their word is law. According to my observation, it is only those sons who have received an 'English' education in India who no longer honour their fathers *and* mothers.

No story is more appropriate than that of Madalasa and her son Vikranta to illustrate the position of the Indian mother as teacher. As Vikranta grew up day by day, the *Markandeya Purana* relates, Madalasa 'taught him knowledge of the Self by ministering to him in sickness; and as he grew in strength and there waxed in him his father's heart, he attained to knowledge of the Self by his mother's words'. And these were Madalasa's words, spoken to the baby crying on her lap:

My child, thou art without a name or form, and it is but in fantasy that thou hast been given a name. This thy body, framed of the five elements, is not thine in sooth, nor art thou of it. Why dost thou weep? Or, maybe, thou weepest not; it is a sound self-born that cometh forth from the king's. ...In the body dwells another self, and therewith abideth not the thought that 'This is mine,' which appertaineth to the flesh. Shame that man is so deceived!

Even in recent times, in families where the men have received an English education unrelated to Indian life and thought, the inheritance of Indian modes of thought and feeling rests in the main with women; for a definite philosophy of life is bound up with household ritual and traditional etiquette and finds expression equally in folk tale and cradle song and popular poetry, and in those Puranic and epic stories which constitute the household Bible literature of India. Under these conditions it is often the case that Indian women, with all their faults of sentimentality and ignorance, have remained the guardians of a spiritual culture which is of greater worth than the efficiency and information of the educated.

It is according to the Tantrik scriptures, devoted to the cult of the Mother of the World, that women, who partake of her nature more essentially than other living beings, are especially honoured; here the woman may be a spiritual teacher (*guru*), and the initiation of a son by a mother is more fruitful than any other. One doubts how far this may be of universal application, believing with Paracelsus that woman is nearer to the world than man, of which the evidence appears in her always more personal point of view. But all things are possible to women such as Madalasa.

The claim of the Buddhist nun—'How should the woman's nature hinder us?'—has never been systematically denied in India. It would have been contrary to the spirit of Indian culture to deny to individual women the opportunity of saintship or learning in the sense of closing to them the schools of divinity or science after the fashion of the Western academies in the nineteenth century. But where the social norm is found in marriage and parenthood for men and women alike, it could only have been in exceptional cases and under exceptional circumstances that the latter specialized, whether in divinity, like Auvvai, Mira Bai, or the Buddhist nuns, in science, like Lilavati, or in war, like Chand Bibi or the Rani of Jhansi. Those set free to cultivate expert knowledge of science or to follow with undivided allegiance either religion or any art, could only be the *sannyasini* or devotee, the widow, and the courtesan. A majority of women have always, and naturally, preferred marriage and motherhood to either of these conditions. But those who felt the call of religion, those from whom a husband's death removed the central motif of their life, and those trained from childhood as expert artists, have always maintained a great tradition in various branches of cultural activity, such as social service or music. What we have to observe is that Hindu sociologists have always regarded these specializations as more or less incompatible with wifehood and motherhood; life is not long enough for the achievement of many different things.

Hinduism justifies no cult of ego-expression, but aims consistently at spiritual freedom. Those who are conscious of a sufficient inner life become the more indifferent to outward expression of their own or any changing personality. The ultimate purposes of Hindu social discipline are that men should unify their individuality with

a wider and deeper than individual life, should fulfil appointed
tasks regardless of failure or success, distinguish the timeless
from its shifting forms, and escape the all-too-narrow prison of
the 'I and mine'.

Anonymity is thus in accordance with the truth; and it is one
of the proudest distinctions of the Hindu culture. The names of
the 'authors' of the epics are but shadows, and in later ages it
was a constant practise of writers to suppress their own names
and ascribe their work to a mythical or famous poet, thereby to
gain a better attention for the truth that they would rather claim
to have 'heard' than to have 'made'. Similarly, scarcely a single
Hindu painter or sculptor is known by name; and the entire range
of Sanskrit literature cannot exhibit a single autobiography and
but little history. Why should women have sought for modes of
self-advertisement that held no lure even for men? The governing
concept of Hindu ethics is vocation (*dharma*); the highest merit
consists in the fulfilment of 'one's own duty', in other words, in
dedication to one's calling. Indian society was highly organized;
and where it was considered wrong for a man to fulfil the duties
of another man rather than his own, how much more must a confusion of function as between woman and man have seemed
wrong, where differentiation is so much more evident. In the words
of Manu: 'To be mothers were women created, and to be fathers
men'; and he added significantly, 'therefore are religious sacraments
ordained in the Veda to be observed by the husband together
with the wife.'

The Asiatic theory of marriage, which would have been perfectly comprehensible in the Middle Ages, before the European
woman had become an economic parasite, and which is still very little
removed from that of Roman or Greek Christianity, is not readily
intelligible to the industrial democratic consciousness of Europe
and America, which is so much more concerned for rights than
for duties, and desires more than anything else to be released from
responsibilities—regarding such release as freedom. It is thus that
Western reformers would awaken a divine discontent in the hearts
of Oriental women, forgetting that the way of ego-assertion cannot be a royal road to realization of the Self. The industrial mind is
primarily sentimental, and therefore cannot reason clearly upon

love and marriage; but the Asiatic analysis is philosophic, religious, and practical.

Current Western theory seeks to establish marriage on a basis of romantic love and free choice; marriage thus depends on the accident of 'falling in love'. Those who are 'crossed in love' or do not love are not required to marry. This individualistic position, however, is only logically defensible if at the same time it is recognized that to fall out of love must end the marriage. It is a high and religious ideal which justifies sexual relations only as the outward expression demanded by passionate love and regards an intimacy continued or begun for mere pleasure, or for reasons of prudence, or even as a duty, as essentially immoral; it is an ideal which isolated individuals and groups have constantly upheld; and it may be that the ultimate development of idealistic individualism will tend to a nearer realization of it. But do not let us deceive ourselves that because the Western marriage is nominally founded upon free choice, it therefore secures a permanent unity of spiritual and physical passion. On the contrary, perhaps in a majority of cases, it holds together those who are no longer 'in love'; habit, considerations of prudence, or, if there are children, a sense of duty often compel the passionless continuance of a marriage for the initiation of which romantic love was felt to be a *sine qua non*. Those who now live side by side upon a basis of affection and common interest would not have entered upon marriage on this basis alone.

If the home is worth preserving under modern conditions—and in India at any rate, the family is still the central element of social organization, then probably the 'best solution' will always be found in some such compromise as is implied in a more or less permanent marriage; though greater tolerance than is now usual must be accorded to exceptions above and below the norm. What are we going to regard as the constructive basis of the normal marriage?

For Hindu sociologists marriage is a social and ethical relationship, and the begetting of children the payment of a debt. Romantic love is a brief experience of timeless freedom, essentially religious and ecstatic, in itself as purely antisocial as every glimpse of Union is a denial of the Relative; it is the way of Mary.

It is true the glamour of this experience may persist for weeks and months, when the whole of life is illumined by the partial merging of the consciousness of the lover and beloved; but sooner or later in almost every case there must follow a return to the world of unreality, and that insight which once endowed the beloved with innumerable perfections fades in the light of commonsense. The lovers are fortunate if there remains to them a basis of common interest and common duty and a mutuality of temperament adequate for friendship, affection, and forbearance; upon this chance depends the possibility of happiness during the greater part of almost every married life. The Hindu marriage differs from the marriage of sentiment mainly in putting these considerations first. Here, as elsewhere, happiness will arise from the fulfilment of vocation, far more than when immediate satisfaction is made the primary end. I use the term vocation advisedly; for the Oriental marriage, like the Oriental actor's art, is the fulfilment of a traditional design, and does not depend upon the accidents of sensibility. To be such a man as Rama, such a wife as Sita, rather than to express 'oneself', is the aim. The formula is predetermined; husband and wife alike have parts to play; and it is from this point of view that we can best understand the meaning of Manu's law, that a wife should look on her husband as a god, regardless of his personal merit or demerits—it would be beneath her dignity to deviate from a woman's norm merely because of the failure of a man. It is for her own sake and for the sake of the community, rather than for his alone, that life must be attuned to the eternal unity of Purusha and Prakriti.

Whatever the ultimate possibilities of Western individualism, Hindu society was established on a basis of group morality. It is true that no absolute ethic is held binding on all classes alike; but within a given class the freedom of the individual is subordinated to the interest of the group, the concept of duty is paramount. How far this concept of duty trenches on the liberty of the individual may be seen in Rama's repudiation of Sita, subsequent to the victory in Lanka and the coronation at Ayodhya; although convinced of her perfect fidelity, Rama, who stands in epic history as the mirror of social ethics, consents to banish his wife, because the people murmur against her. The argument is that if the king should receive back a wife who had been living in another man's house, albeit faithful, popular morality would be endangered, since others might be moved by love and partiality to a like rehabilitation but with less justification. Thus the social order is placed before the happiness of the individual, whether man or woman. This is the explanation of the greater peace which distinguishes the arranged marriage of the East from the self-chosen marriage of the West; where there is no deception there can be no disappointment. And since the conditions on which it is founded do not change, it is logical that Hindu marriage should be indissoluble; only when social duties have been fulfilled and social debts paid, is it permissible for the householder to relinquish simultaneously the duties and the rights of the social individual. It is also logical that when the marriage is childless, it is permissible to take a second wife with the consent—and often at the wish— of the first.

It is sometimes asked, what opportunities are open to the Oriental woman? How can she express herself? The answer is that life is so designed that she is given the opportunity to be a woman—in other words, to realize, rather than to express herself. It is possible that modern Europe errs in the opposite direction. We must also remember that very much which passes for education nowadays is superficial; some of it amounts to little more than parlour tricks, and nothing is gained by communicating this condition to Asia, where I have heard of modern parents who desired that their daughters should be taught 'a little French' or 'a few strokes on the violin'. The arts in India are professional and vocational, demanding undivided service; nothing is taught to the amateur by way of social accomplishment or studied superficially. And woman represents the continuity of the racial life, an energy which cannot be divided or diverted without a corresponding loss of racial vitality; she can no more desire to be something other than herself, than the Vaishya could wish to be known as a Kshattriya, or the Kshattriya, as a Brahman.

It has been shown in fact, some seventy-five per cent of Western graduate women do not marry; and apart from these, if it be true that five-sixths of a child's tendencies and activities are already determined before it reaches school age, and that the habits then deeply rooted cannot be greatly modified, if it be true that so much depends on deliberate training while the instincts of the child are still potential and habits unformed, can we say that women whose social duties or pleasures, or self-elected careers or unavoidable wage slavery draws them into the outer world are fulfilling their duty to the race, or as we should say, the debt of the ancestors? The modern suffragist declares that the state has no right to demand of woman, whether directly or indirectly, by bribe or pressure of opinion, that she consider herself under any obligation, in return for the protection afforded her, to produce its future citizens. But we are hardly likely to see this point of view accepted in these days when the right of society to conscript the bodies of men is almost universally conceded. It is true that many who do not acquiesce in the existing industrial order are prepared to resist conscription in the military sense, that is to say, conscription for destruction; but we are becoming accustomed to the idea of another kind of conscription, or rather cooperation, based on service, and indeed, according to either of the two dynamic theories of a future society—the syndicalist and the individualistic—it must appear that without the fulfilment of function there can exist no *rights*. From the cooperative point of view society has an absolute right to compel its members to fulfil the functions that are necessary to it; and only those who, like the anchorite, voluntarily and entirely renounce the advantages of society and the protection of law have a right to ignore the claims of society. From the individualist point of view, on the other hand, the fulfilment of function is regarded as a spontaneous activity, as is even now true in the cases of the thinker and the artist; but even the individualist does not expect to get something for nothing, and the last idea he has is to compel the service of others.

I doubt if anyone will deny that it is the function or nature of women, as a group—not necessarily in every individual case—in general, to be mothers, alike in spiritual and physical senses. What we have to do then, is not to assert the liberty of women to deny the duty or right of motherhood, however we regard it, but to accord this function a higher protection and honour than it now receives. And here, perhaps, there is still something to be learnt in Asia. There the pregnant woman is auspicious, and receives the highest respect; whereas in many industrial and secular Western societies she is an object of more or less open ridicule, she is ashamed to be seen abroad, and tries to conceal her condition, sometimes even by means that are injurious to her own and the child's health. That this was not the case in a more vital period of European civilization may be seen in all the literature and art of the Middle Ages, and particularly in the status of the Virgin Mary, whose motherhood endeared her to the folk so much more nearly than her virginity.

To avoid misunderstanding, let me say in passing, that in depicting the life of Hindu women as fulfilling a great ideal, I do not mean to indicate the Hindu social formula as a thing to be repeated or imitated. This would be a view as futile as that of the Gothic revival in architecture; the reproduction of period furniture does not belong to life. A perfection that has been can never be a perfection for us.

Marriage was made for man, not man for marriage. One would gladly accept for Europe very soon, and for Asia in due time, temporary marriage, the endowment of motherhood, and matriarchal succession, or whatever other forms our own spiritual and economic necessity may determine for us—not because such forms may be absolutely better than the Asiatic or mediaeval European institutions, but because they correspond more nearly to *our* inner life. In comparing one social order with another, I have no faith in any millennium past or future, but only in the best attainable adaptation of means to ends; and, 'let the ends determine the means' should be the evidence of our idealism.

Let us now return to the Indian Sati and try to understand her better. The root meaning of the word is essential being, and we have so far taken it only in the wide sense. But she who refuses to live when her husband is dead is called Sati in a more special sense, and it is only so that the word (suttee) is well known to Europeans. This last proof of the perfect unity of body and soul, this devotion beyond the grave, has been chosen by many Western critics as our reproach; we differ from them in thinking of our 'suttees' not with pity, but with understanding, respect, and love. So far from being ashamed of our 'suttees' we take a pride in them; that is even true of the most 'progressive' amongst us. It is very much like the tenderness which our children's children may some day feel for those of their race who were willing to throw away their lives for 'their country right or wrong', though the point of view may seem to us then, as it seems to so many already, evidence rather of generosity than balanced judgment.

The criticism we make on the institution of Sati and woman's blind devotion is similar to the final judgment we are about to pass on patriotism. We do not, as pragmatists may, resent the denial of the ego for the sake of an absolute, or attach an undue importance to mere life; on the contrary we see clearly that the reckless and useless sacrifice of the 'suttee' and the patriot is spiritually significant. And what remains perpetually clear is the superiority of the reckless sacrifice to the calculating assertion of rights. Criticism of the position of the Indian woman from the ground of assertive feminism, therefore, leaves us entirely unmoved: precisely as the patriot must be unmoved by an appeal to self-interest or a merely utilitarian demonstration of futility. We do not object to dying for an idea as 'suttees' and patriots have died; but we see that there may be other and greater ideas we can better serve by living for them.

For some reason it has come to be believed that Sati must have been a man-made institution imposed on women by men for reasons of their own, that it is associated with feminine servility, and that it is peculiar to India. We shall see that these views are historically unsound. It is true that in aristocratic circles Sati became to some degree a social convention, and pressure was put on unwilling individuals, precisely as conscripts are even now forced to suffer or die for other people's ideas; and from this point of view we cannot but be glad that it was prohibited by law in 1829 on the initiative of Raja Rammohan Roy. But now that nearly a century has passed it should not be difficult to review the history and significance of Sati more dispassionately than was possible in the hour of controversy and the atmosphere of religious prejudice.

It is not surprising that the idea of Sati occupies a considerable place in Indian literature. Parvati herself, who could not endure the insults levelled against her husband by her father, is the prototype of all others. In the early Tamil lyrics we read of an earthly bride whom the Brahmans seek to dissuade from the sacrifice; but she answers that since her lord is dead, the cool waters of the lotus pool and the flames of the funeral pyre are alike to her. Another pleads to share her hero's grave, telling the potter that she had fared with her lord over many a desert plain, and asking him to make the funeral urn large enough for both. Later in history we read of the widowed mother of Harsha that she replied to her son's remonstrances: 'I am the lady of a great house; have you forgotten that I am the lioness-mate of a great spirit, who, like a lion, had his delight in a hundred battles?'

A man of such towering genius and spirituality as Kabir so takes for granted the authenticity of the impulse to Sati that he constantly uses it as an image of surrender of the ego to God; and indeed, in all Indian mystical literature the love relation of woman to man is taken unhesitatingly as an immediate reflection of spiritual experience. This is most conspicuous in all the Radha–Krishna literature. But here let us notice more particularly the beautiful and very interesting poem of Muhammad Riza Nau'i, written in the reign of Akbar upon the 'suttee' of a Hindu girl whose betrothed was killed on the very day of the marriage. This Musulman poet, to whom the Hindus were 'idolaters', does not relate his story in any spirit of religious intolerance or ethical condescension; he is simply amazed 'that after the death of men, the woman shows forth her marvellous passion.' He does not wonder at the wickedness of men, but at the generosity of women; how different from the modern critic who can see no motive but self-interest behind a social phenomenon that passes his comprehension!

This Hindu bride refused to be comforted and wished to be burnt on the pyre of her dead betrothed. When Akbar was informed of this, he called the girl before him and offered wealth and protection, but she rejected all his persuasion as well as the counsel of the Brahmans, and would neither speak nor hear of anything but the Fire.

Akbar was forced, though reluctantly, to give his consent to the sacrifice, but sent with her his son Prince Daniyal who continued to dissuade her. Even from amidst the flames, she replied to his remonstrances, 'Do not annoy, do not annoy, do not annoy.'

'Ah,' exclaims the poet:

> Let those whose hearts are ablaze with the Fire of Love learn courage from this pure may!
> Teach me, O God, the Way of Love, and enflame my heart with this maiden's Fire.

Thus he prays for himself; and for her:

> Do Thou, O God, exalt the head of that rare hidden virgin, whose purity exceeded that of the Houris,
> Do Thou endear her to the first kissing of her King, and graciously accept her sacrifice.

Matter-of-fact accounts of more modern 'suttees' are given by Englishmen who have witnessed them. One which took place in Baroda in 1825 is described by R. Hartley Kennedy, the widow persisting in her intention in spite of 'several fruitless endeavours to dissuade her'. A more remarkable case is described by Sir Frederick Halliday. Here also a widow resisted all dissuasion, and finally proved her determination by asking for a lamp, and holding her finger in the flame until it was burnt and twisted like a quill pen held in the flame of a candle; all this time she gave no sign of fear or pain whatever. Sir F. Halliday had therefore to grant her wish, even as Akbar had had to do three centuries earlier.

It is sometimes said by Indian apologists that at certain times or places in India—amongst the Buddhists, or the Marathas, or in the epics—there was no purdah; or that certain historic or mythic individual women were not secluded. Such statements ignore the fact that there are other kinds of seclusion than those afforded by palace walls. For example, though Rama, Lakshman, and Sita had lived together in forest exile for many years in closest affection, it is expressly stated that Lakshman had never raised his eyes above his brother's wife's feet, so that he did not even know her appearance. To speak more generally, it is customary for Hindus, when occasion arises for them to address an unknown woman, to call her 'mother' irrespective of her age or condition. These unseen walls are a seclusion equally absolute with any purdah. One result is that the streets of an Indian city by night are safer for a woman than those of any city in Europe. I have known more than one European woman, acquainted with India, express her strong conviction of this. Western critics have often asserted that the Oriental woman is a slave, and that we have made her what she is. We can only reply that we do not identify freedom with self-assertion, and that the Oriental woman is what she is, only because our social and religious culture has permitted her to be and to remain essentially feminine. Exquisite as she may be in literature and art, we dare not claim for ourselves as men the whole honour of creating such a type, however persistently the industrious industrial critic would thrust it upon us.

The Eastern woman is not, at least we do not claim that she is, superior to other women in her innermost nature; she is perhaps an older, purer, and more specialized type, but certainly an universal type, and it is precisely here that the industrial woman departs from type. Nobility in women does not depend upon race, but upon ideals; it is the outcome of a certain view of life.

Savitri, Padmavati, Sita, Radha, Uma, Lilavati, Tara—our divine and human heroines—have an universal fellowship, for everything feminine is of the Mother. Who could have been more wholly devoted than Alcestis, more patient than Griselda, more loving than Deirdre, more soldier than Joan of Arc, more Amazon than Brynhild?

When the Titanic sank, there were many women who refused—perhaps mistakenly, perhaps quite rightly—that was their own affair—to be rescued without their husbands, or were only torn from them by force; dramatic confirmation of the conviction that love-heroism is always and everywhere the same, and not only in India, nor only in ages past, may be stronger than death.

I do not think that the Indian ideal has ever been the exclusive treasure of any one race or time, but rather, it reappears wherever woman is set free to be truly herself, that is wherever a sufficiently religious, heroic, and aesthetic culture has afforded her the necessary protection. Even the freedom which she seeks in modern self-assertion—which I would grant from the standpoint of one who will not govern—is merely an inverted concept of protection, and it may be that the more she is freed the more she will reveal the very type we have most adored in those who seemed to be slaves. Either way would be happier for men than the necessity of protecting women from themselves, and the tyranny of those who are not capable of friendship, being neither bound nor free.

The cry of our Indian Sati, 'Do not annoy, do not annoy,' and 'No one has any right over the life of another; is not that my own affair?' is no cry for protection from a fate she does not seek; it is individualistic, and has been uttered by every woman in the world who has followed love beyond the grave. Deirdre refused every offer of care and protection from Conchubar: 'It is not land or earth or food I am wanting,' she said, 'or gold or silver or horses, but leave to go to the grave where the sons of Usnach are lying.' Emer called to Cuchullain slain: 'Love of my life, my friend, my sweetheart, my one choice of the men of the world, many is the women [sic], wed or unwed, envied me until today, and now I will not stay living after you.'

Irish women were free, but we are used even more to look on the old Teutonic type as representative of free and even Amazonian womanhood. We do not think of Brynhild, Shield-may and Victory-wafter, as compelled by men to any action against her will, or as weakly submissive. Yet, when Sigurd was slain she became 'suttee'; the prayers of Gunnar availed as little as those of Conchubar with Deirdre. He 'laid his arms about her neck, and besought her to live and have wealth from him; and all others in like wise letted her from dying; but she thrust them all from her, and said that it was not the part of any to let her in that which was her will.' And the second heroic woman figured in the saga, wedded to Sigurd, though she did not die, yet cried when he was betrayed:

> Now am I as little
> As the leaf may be
> Amid wind-swept wood,
> Now when dead he lieth.

'She who is courteous in her mind,' says the *Shacktafelsk*, 'with shyness shall her face be bright; of all the beauties of the body, none is more shining than shyness.' This theory of courtesy, of supreme gentleness—'full sweetly bowing down her head,' says the English Merlin, 'as she that was shamefast,' runs also through all medieval chivalry. Yet, it is about this shy quiet being, a mystery to men, that the whole medieval world turns; 'first reserve the honour to God,' says Malory, 'and secondly, the quarrel must come of thy lady.' Like Uma and Sita, Virgin Mary is the image of a perfect being—

> For in this rose conteined was
> Heaven and earth in litel space—

and for a little while, in poetry and architecture, we glimpse an idealization of woman and woman's love akin to the praise of Radha in the contemporary songs of Chandidas and Vidyapati.

But for our purpose even more significant than the religious and knightly culture, the product of less quickly changing conditions, and impressive too in its naiveté, is the picture of the woman of the people which we can gather from folk song and lyric. Here was a being obviously strong and sensible, not without knowledge of life, and by no means economically a parasite. If we study the folk speech anywhere in the world we shall see that it reveals woman, and not the man, as typically the lover; when her shyness allows, it is she who would pray for man's love, and will serve him to the utmost. Industrialism reverses this relation, making man the suppliant and the servant, a condition as unnatural as any other of its characteristic perversions.

The woman of the folk does not bear resentment. Fair Helen, who followed Child Waters on foot, and bore his child in a stable, is overheard singing:

> Lullaby, my owne deere child!
> I wold thy father were a king,
> Thy mother layd on a beere.

Is she not like the Bengali Malanchamala, whose husband had married a second wife, and left her unloved and forgotten—who says, 'though I die now, and become a bird or a lesser creature or whatever befall me, I care not, for I have seen my darling happy?'

If woman under industrialism is unsatisfied, it would be difficult to say how much man also loses. For woman is naturally the lover, the bestower of life:

Conjunction with me renders life long.
I give youth when I enter upon amorousness.

Her complaint is not that man demands too much, but that he will accept too little.

Long time have I been waiting for the coming of my dear;
Sometimes I am uneasy and troubled in my mind,
Sometimes I think I'll go to my lover and tell him my mind.
But if I should go to my lover, my lover he will say me nay,
If I show to him my boldness, he'll ne'er love me again.

And it is to serve him, not to seek service from him that she desires:

In the cold stormy weather, when the winds are a-blowing, My dear, I shall be willing to wait on you then.

The Oriental woman, perhaps is not Oriental at all, but simply woman. If the modern woman could accept this thought, perhaps she would seek a new way of escape, not an escape from love, but a way out of industrialism. Could we not undertake this quest together?

It is true that the modern woman is justified in her discontent. For of what has she not been robbed? The organization of society for competition and exploitation has made possible for the few, and only the very few, more physical comfort and greater security of life; but even these it has robbed of all poise, of the power to walk or to dress or to marry wisely, or to desire children or lovers, or to believe in any power not legally exteriorized. From faith in herself to a belief in votes, what a descent!

Decade after decade since the fourteenth century has seen her influence reduced. It was paramount in religion, in poetry, in music, in architecture and in all life. But men, when they reformed the church and taught you that love was not a sacrament without the seal of clerical approval; when they forced your music into modes of equal temperament; when they substituted knowledge for feeling and wisdom in education, when they asked you to pinch your shoes and your waists, and persuaded you to think this a refinement, and the language of Elizabethan poetry coarse;

when at last they taught you to become imperialists, and went away alone to colonize and civilize the rest of the world, leaving you in England with nothing particular to do; when, if you have the chance to marry at all, it is ten or fifteen years too late—who can wonder that you are dissatisfied, and claim the right to a career of your own 'not merely to earn your livelihood, but to provide yourself with an object in life?' How many women have only discovered an object in life since the energies of men have been employed in activities of pure destruction? What a confession! To receive the franchise would be but a small compensation for all you have suffered, if it did not happen that we have now seen enough of representative government and the tyranny of majorities to understand their futility. Let women as well as men, turn away their eyes from the delusions of government, and begin to understand direct action, finding enough to do in solving the problems of their own lives, without attempting to regulate those of other people. No man of real power has either time or strength for any other man's work than his own, and this should be equally true for women. Aside from all questions of mere lust for power or demand for rights, untold evils have resulted from the conviction that it is our God-given duty to regulate other people's lives—the effects of the current theories of 'uplift', and of the 'white man's burden' are only single examples of this; and even if the intentions are good, we need not overlook the fact that the way to hell is often paved with good intentions.'

Meanwhile, there lies an essential weakness in the propaganda of emancipation, inasmuch as the argument is based on an unquestioning acceptance of male values. The so-called feminist is as much enslaved by masculine ideals as the so-called Indian nationalist is enslaved by European ideals. Like industrial man, the modern woman values industry more than leisure, she seeks in every way to externalize her life, to achieve success in men's professions, she feigns to be ashamed of her sexual nature, she claims to be as reasonable, as learned, as expert as any man, and her best men friends make the same claims on her behalf. But just in proportion as she lacks a genuine feminine idealism, inasmuch as she wishes to be something other than herself, she lacks power.

The claim of women to share the loaves and fishes with industrial man may be as just as those of Indian politicians. But the argument that women can do what men can do ('we take all labour for our province,' says Olive Schreiner) like the argument that Indians can be prepared to govern themselves by a course of studies in democracy, implies a profound self-distrust. The claim to equality with men, or with Englishmen—what an honour! That men, or Englishmen, as the case may be, should grant the claim—what a condescension!

If there is one profound intuition of the non-industrial consciousness, it is that the qualities of men and women are incommensurable. 'The sexes are differently entertained,' says Novalis, 'Man demands the sensational in intellectual form, woman the intellectual in sensational form. What is secondary to the man is paramount to the woman. Do they not resemble the Infinite, since it is impossible to square (*quadriren*) them, and they can only be approached through approximation?' Is not the Hindu point of view possibly right; not that men and woman should approach an identity of temperament and function, but that for the greatest abundance of life, there is requisite the greatest possible sexual differentiation?

What is it that great men—poets and creators, not men of analysis—demand of women? It is, surely, the requirements of the prolific, rather than of the devourers, which are of most significance for the human race, which advances under the guidance of leaders, and not by accident. The one thing they have demanded of women is Life.

To one thing at least the greatest men have been always indifferent, that is, the amount of knowledge a woman may possess. It was not by her learning that Beatrice inspired Dante, or the washerwoman Chandidas. When Cuchullain chose a wife, it was Emer, because she had the six gifts of beauty, voice, sweet speech, needlework, wisdom, and charity. We know only of Helen that 'strangely like she was to some immortal spirit'; in other words, she was radiant. Radha's shining made the ground she stood on bright as gold. The old English poet wrote of one like her:

Her luve lumes liht
As a launterne a nyht.

It is this radiance in women, more than any other quality, that urges men to every sort of heroism, be it martial or poetic. Everyone understands the heroism of war; we are not surprised at Lady Hamilton's adoration of Nelson. But the activity of war is atavistic, and highly civilized people such as the Chinese regard it with open contempt. What nevertheless we do not yet understand is the heroism of art, that exhausting and perpetual demand which all creative labour makes alike on body and soul. The artist must fight a continual battle for mastery of himself and his environment; his work must usually be achieved in the teeth of violent, ignorant, and often well-organized opposition, or against still more wearing apathy, and in any case, even at the best, against the intense resistance which matter opposes to the moulding force of ideas, the tamasic quality in things. The ardent love of women is not too great a reward for those who are faithful. But it is far more than the reward of action, it is the energy without which action may be impossible. As pure male, the Great God is inert, and his 'power' is always feminine, and it is she who leads the hosts of heaven against the demons.

When man of necessity spent his life in war or in hunting when women needed a personal physical as well as a spiritual protection, then she could not do enough for him in personal service; we have seen in the record of folksong and epic how it is part of woman's innermost nature to worship man. In the words of another Indian scripture, her husband is for her a place of pilgrimage, the giving of alms, the performance of vows, and he is her spiritual teacher—this according to the same school which makes the initiation of son by mother eight times more efficacious than any other. What we have not yet learnt is that like relations are needed for the finest quality of life, even under conditions of perpetual peace; the tenderness of women is as necessary to man now, as ever it was when his first duty was that of physical warfare, and few men can achieve greatness, and then scarcely without the danger of a one-sided development, whose environment lacks this atmosphere of tenderness. Woman possesses the power of perpetually creating in man the qualities she desires, and this is for her an infinitely greater power than the possession of those special qualities could ever confer upon her directly.

Far be it from us, however, to suggest the forcing of any pre-conceived development upon the modern individualist. We shall accomplish nothing by pressing anything in moulds. What I have tried to explain is that notwithstanding that the formula of woman's status in Oriental society may have ere now crystallized—as the formulae of classic art have become academic—nevertheless, this formula represented once, and still essentially represents, al-though 'unfelt' in realization, a veritable expression of woman's own nature. If not so, then the formula stands self-condemned. I do not know if through our modern idealistic individualism it may be possible to renounce all forms and formulae for ever—I fear that it is only in heaven that there shall be neither marrying nor giving in marriage—but were that the case, and every creature free to find itself, and to behave according to its own nature, then it is possible, at least, that the 'natural' relation of woman to man would after all involve the same conditions of magic that are implied in the soon-to-be-discarded conventional and calculated forms of medieval art and Oriental society. If not, we must accept things as they really are—however they may be.

Meanwhile, it would be worthwhile to pause before we make haste to emancipate, that is to say, reform and industrialize the Oriental woman. For it is not for Asia alone that she preserves a great tradition, in an age that is otherwise preoccupied. If she too should be persuaded to expend her power upon externals, there might come a time on earth when it could not be believed that such women had ever lived, as the ancient poets describe; it would be forgotten that woman had ever been unselfish, sensu-ous and shy. Deirdre, Brynhild, Alcestis, Sita, Radha, would then be empty names. And that would be a loss, for already it has been felt in Western schools that we 'are not furnished with adequate womanly ideals in history and literature'.

The industrial revolution in India is of external and very re-cent origin; there is no lack of men, and it is the sacred duty of parents to arrange a marriage for every daughter: there is no divergence of what is spiritual and what is sensuous: Indian women do not deform their bodies in the interests of fashion: they are more concerned about service than rights: they consider barrenness the greatest possible misfortune, after widowhood. In a word, it has never happened in India that women have been judged by or have accepted purely male standards. What possible service then, except in a few externals, can the Western world render to Eastern women? Though it may be able to teach us much of the means of life, it has everything yet to relearn about life itself. And what we still remember there, we would not forget before we must.

A.S. Altekar, *The Position of Women in Hindu Society*[4]

In his seminal account of the position of Hindu women, Altekar provides a detailed textual and historical background to sati. His understanding of the rite is influenced both by the popular nationalist paradigm of popular Hinduism's fall from the 'Golden Age' of the Vedas, and his own personal experience of reverence for a sister-in-law who performed sati.

THE POSITION OF THE WIDOW

The position of the widow in society is one of the most important topics which the historian of woman has to discuss and elucidate. The treatment which she receives is often an index to the attitude of society towards women as a class. What was the general lot of the widow? Was she allowed to survive her husband, or was she compelled to die with him? If permitted to survive, could she marry again if she so desired? Did she receive a humane and considerate treatment from the family and society? Could she hold or inherit property, so that she could lead an honourable and independent life after her husband's death? These are the main topics which we have to discuss in connection with the position of the widow.... Here we shall take up the problems of Satī, levirate, remarriage, and tonsure. Of these, the question of the Satī custom will engage us in this chapter and the rest will be discussed in the next, which will close with a general survey of the position of the widow from age to age.

THE CUSTOM OF SATĪ (SUTTEE)

In prehistoric times there prevailed a belief in several societies that the life and needs of the dead in the next world are more or less similar to those in this life. It, therefore, became a pious duty of surviving relations to provide a dead person with all the things that he usually needed when alive. Especially, when an important personage like a king, a nobleman or a warrior died, it was felt that his usual paraphernalia should be 'sent' with him. He would of course, require his wives, horses, and servants in the next world, and it would therefore be necessary and desirable to kill these all, and burn or bury them with him. Such a belief should have given rise to the custom of burning or burying the husband also along with the wife. Man, however, wielded supreme power in society almost everywhere and was not prepared to sanction a custom adverse to his own interest and comfort. It may, however, be pointed out that in Ashanti, kings' sisters were allowed to marry handsome youth among commoners, but they were compelled to commit suicide on the death of their royal consorts.

The custom of the sacrifice of the widow at the funeral of her husband was widely prevailing in ancient times. There is no direct evidence to show that it prevailed in the Indo-European age, but the fact that it was practised among the Gauls, the Goths, the Norwegians, the Celts, the Slavs, and the Thracians would justify the inference that it was probably well established among the Indo-Europeans. It was quite common among the Scythians. In China if a widow killed herself in order to follow her husband to heaven, her corpse was taken out in a great procession.[5]

The general prevalence of this custom among the primitive warlike tribes is not difficult to understand. Fighting races are very jealous of their women and often prefer to kill them, rather than take the risk of their going astray after their husbands' death. There was also the general belief already referred to, that the warrior will require in his next life all those things that were near and dear to him in this existence. It was, therefore, as reasonable to bury his clothes, bows, arrows, and horses as to inter his wife. The wife is usually the dearest relation of a man, and the visitations of a chief's ghost were popularly attributed to his desire to be united with his quondam queen. Why not lessen these dreaded visitations by burning or burying her along with his remains? This custom also made the life of the patriarch very safe; it practically eliminated all possibility of any one among his numerous mutually envious wives intriguing against his life. They all knew that even if successful, they had no chance of surviving him. They were, therefore, all care and attention to see that no preventable accident intervened to shorten the husband's life.

Whatever the real reasons may have been, we find, as shown already, that the custom of sacrificing the wife at the husband's death existed among the Aryans in the Indo-European period. By the time they entered India, it had, however, gone out of vogue. We do not find it mentioned in the *Avesta*. Nor is it referred to in the funeral hymns of the *Ṛigveda*, where it would certainly have been mentioned if it had been in existence. It is true that in the great controversy that raged at the time of the legal prohibition of the Satī custom by Lord William Bentick, it was argued that the custom had a Vedic sanction. It was maintained that the funeral hymn in the *Ṛigveda* refers to widows ascending the funeral pyre. The case, however, could be rendered plausible only by fraudulently changing the last word of the stanza from *agre* into *agneh*: The verse in question refers to women with their husbands living coming forward to anoint the corpse before it was consigned to flames, and contains no reference whatsoever to any widow immolating herself on her husband's funeral pyre.[6]

It was also argued that a passage in the Aukhya Śākhā of the *Saṁhitā* quoted in the 84th *anuvāka* of the *Nārāyaṇīya Taittirīya Upanishad* refers to a prayer by a widow to god Fire that she was about to follow the *anugamana-vrata* or the Satī custom and that she may be able to bear the ordeal and reap the promised reward.[7] The *Nārāyaṇīya-upnishad* is however, a late work; the passage from the Aukhya Śākhā quoted in it is otherwise not known to us from any other source. We cannot, therefore, conclude from it that the Satī custom was recognized as a ritual in the Vedic period.

The *Artharvaveda*, however, shows that the funeral ritual of the Vedic age preserved some formalities reminiscent of the archaic custom of Satī. It shows that it was still customary for the widow to lie by the side of her husband's corpse on the funeral pyre; she was, however, asked to come down, and a prayer was offered that she should lead a prosperous life enjoying the bliss of children and wealth.[8] It is, therefore, clear that the Vedic age expected the widow rather to remarry than to immolate herself.

The reasons that led to the discontinuation of the Satī custom in the Vedic age can only be inferred. Probably the finer cultural outlook, that the Vedic Aryans had developed by this time, had convinced them that the custom was a barbarous one; probably they found themselves in minority in India and felt the compelling necessity to increase their population in order to ensure their political domination. Instead of allowing widows to be burnt, they thought that it would be better to encourage them to live and increase the population by levirate or remarriage.

Whatever the reasons may have been, it is undisputed that the Satī custom had gone out of vogue among the Aryans at the time they had entered India. We find no traces of it whatsoever down to *c.* 400 BC The Brāhmaṇa literature (*c.* 1500 BC to *c.* 700 BC) is silent about it. The Gṛihyasūtras (*c.* 600 to *c.* 300 BC) describe numerous rituals and Sanskāras, but the custom of Satī does not figure among them. From the details of the funeral ritual and procedure given in them, we find that the widow was to be brought back from the funeral pyre, either by her husband's brother or disciple, or by an old trusted servant.[9] From the *Taittirīya Āraṇyaka* we find that while returning from the funeral pyre, the widow took away from her husband's hand objects like bow, gold, jewels, etc., which were burnt along with the widow in an earlier age. A hope was then expressed that the widow and her relatives would lead a happy and prosperous life.[10] It is clear that the custom of Satī had died down long ago.

The Buddhist literature also is unaware of the custom of Satī. If it had existed in the days of the Buddha, one feels certain that the great Śākya sage would have started a vehement crusade against it. He who opposed sacrifices to gods, because dumb animals were immolated therein, would certainly have been exasperated by a custom which entailed the burning of human beings alive. So we may well conclude that even in Kshatriya circles the custom was not prevalent in *c.* 500 BC Megasthenes and Kauṭilya both do not mention the custom. The authors of the Dharmasūtras (*c.* 400 BC to *c.* AD 100) and the writers of the early Smritis like those of Manu and Yājñavalkya (*c.* AD 100 to *c.* AD 300) have laid down detailed rules about the duties of women and widows. None of them, however, even hints that it would be commendable for a widow to burn herself alive with her dead husband on his funeral pyre.

We begin to get stray references to the custom of Satī from about 300 BC The *Mahābhārata*, a major portion of which was composed at about this time, records only a few cases of Satī. The most important among them is that of Mādrī. But in her case, it is interesting to note that the assembled sages try their best to dissuade her from her resolve. Mādrī, however, is unmoved by their arguments. She says that she is determined to die with her husband, firstly because she was the cause of his death, secondly because she would be unable to control her passions, and thirdly because she might find it difficult to treat evenly her sons and stepsons. No argument of any religious merit is assigned by her or by anybody else.[11]

In the Mausala-parva of the *Mahābhārata* we find that four wives of Vasudeva, Devakī, Bhadrā, Rohiṇī, and Madirā, ascend his funeral pyre.[12] When the news of Kṛishṇa's death reaches Hastināpura, five of his wives, Rukmiṇī, Gāndhārī, Sahyā, Haimavatī, and Jambavatī ascend the funeral pyre, of course, without their husband's body. Satyabhāmā retires to forest for practising penance.[13]

As against the above few cases of Satī, we have scores of instances of widows surviving their husbands. The wives of Abhimanyu,[14] Ghaṭotkacha, and Droṇa do not become Satīs. There is a talk of Draupadī being consigned to flames along with Kīchaka, but that was merely for the sake of revenge.[15] If four wives of Vasudeva became Satī, there were thousands of Yādava widows who survived their husbands and accompanied Arjuna to Hastināpura. In the eleventh book of the epic we have the spectacle of hundreds and thousands of dead heroes being burnt along with their costumes, weapons, and chariots; in not a single case, however, do we find a widow burning herself along with the remains of her husband (Chapters 31–3). The *Veṇīsaṃhāra* no doubt refers to the case of a Satī on the Kaurava battlefield (Act IV), but it is quite clear that it is due to the anachronism of its author. The epic itself states that all the widows of the fallen heroes remained behind and offered them funeral oblations.[16]

In the original portion of the *Rāmāyaṇa* there is no case of Satī. In the Uttarakāṇḍa (17, 14) we find Vedavatī's mother becoming a

Satī; but this story is more legendary than historical and the book where it occurs is admittedly a later addition, being as modern as about AD 500. In the original kernel of the epic, we find that when Rāvaṇa by means of his magic raised before the eyes of Sītā the illusion of the fall of Rāma, she expressed the wish to be burnt along with her husband (VI, 32, 32). This passage also is probably a later interpolation, for none of the wives of Daśaratha or Rāvaṇa are represented in the epic as accompanying their husbands on the funeral pyre.

Purāṅas refer only to a few cases of Satī. This shows that by about AD 400 when the Purāṇas were given their present form, the custom was gradually coming into general vogue. It does not prove its antiquity. It is interesting to note that some of the Satī cases in Purāṇas are the imaginary creations of a later age, and go against the earlier tradition. Thus the Mahābhārata is unaware of any Yādava widows having burnt themselves on their husband's funeral pyres; according to the Padmapurāṇa, however, all of them became Satīs (Uttarakāṇḍa, chap. 279). The vast majority of the widows that figure in Purāṇas survive their husbands.

The earliest historical instance of Satī is that of the wife of the Hindu general Keteus, who died in 316 BC while fighting against Antigonos. Both the wives of the general were very anxious to accompany their husband on the funeral pyre, but as the elder one was with child, the younger one alone was allowed to carry out her wish. Greek writers tell us that she was led to the pyre by her brother, and that she was all gleeful even when the flames enveloped her person. Some Greek historians tell us that the custom was prevalent among the Kathians (Kaṭhas) of the Punjab. It was, however, still confined only to a few Kshatriya circles, for it is not noticed by Greek writers in connection with other fighting tribes, which stubbornly opposed Alexander and many members of which died while fighting with the invader.

The custom was gradually struggling into existence in the early centuries of the Christian era. Hence, as shown above, we get stray references to it in the later portions of the Rāmāyaṇa and the Mahābhārata, and in the present version of some Purāṇas. Vishṇusmṛti (c. AD 100) thinks the custom to be not illogical; it advanced the view that in spite of diversity of Karman, a widow can, though other relations cannot, go the way of the departed soul by dying after him.[17] The custom, however, was not yet regarded as a religious duty. Vishṇu himself does not recommend it; he merely mentions it. He is in fact one of the earliest writers to recognize the widow as an heir to her husband; he allows her to remarry also (17, 43). The custom began to become gradually popular from c. AD 100. It is known to Vātsyāyana, Bhāsa, Kālidāsa, and Sūdraka. Vātsyāyana points out (VI, 2, 53) how clever dancing girls gain ascendancy over the mind of their lovers by swearing that they would burn themselves on their funeral pyres. From the *Dūtaghaṭotkacha* and *Ūrubhaṅga* of Bhāsa, it appears that the dramatist differed from the *Mahābhārata* in holding that Uttarā, Duśśalā, and Pauravī died on the funeral pyres of their husbands, Abhimanyu, Jayadratha, and Duryodhana respectively. In the *Kumārasambhava* (Canto IV) Ratī is about to burn herself after her husband's death; it is only a voice from the heaven that dissuades her from her resolve. In the *Mṛichchhakaṭika* the wife of Chārudatta wants to burn herself before the arrival of the expected news of her husband's execution (Act X). To turn to historic cases of the period, we find that the wife of general Goparāja, who fell in AD 510 while fighting for his country against the Hūṇas, immolated herself on her husband's funeral pyre.[18] In AD 606 the mother of king Harsha chose to predecease her husband by committing herself to flames, when it was declared that there was no chance of her husband's recovery. At about this time a Nepalese queen, named Rājyavatī, is also seen becoming a Satī.

Some Smṛiti writers of the period now begin to refer to the practice. They do not, however, hold it as an ideal for the widow; they allow it only as a second alternative and regard ascetic life as preferrable to it. Such is the case with Bṛihaspati, Parāśara (IV, 26–8) and the author of *Agnipurāṇa*.[19]

There were, however, several thinkers, who were altogether opposed to the idea of giving even a qualified recognition to the custom. Thus Medhātithi admits that the custom has been mentioned by *Aṅgirassmṛiti*, but maintains that it has no authoritative value, for it is opposed to an express Vedic text which prohibits suicide to all.[20] Virāṭa takes a more decisive stand and positively prohibits the custom. He points out that the widow can do some good to her husband, if she survives and offers him the prescribed oblations at the Śrāddha; if she ascends the funeral pyre, she will be only incurring the sin of suicide.[21] Devaṇabhaṭṭa, a twelfth-century writer from south India, maintains that the Satī custom is only a very inferior variety of Dharma and is not to be recommended at all.[22] To the poet Bāṇa (c. AD 625), however, belongs the credit of offering the most vehement, determined and rational opposition to this inhuman custom. 'To die after one's beloved,' says he, 'is most fruitless. It is a custom followed by the foolish. It is a mistake committed under infatuation. It is a reckless course followed only on account of hot haste. It is a mistake of stupendous magnitude. It does no good whatsoever to the dead person. It does not help him in ascending to heaven; it does not prevent him from sinking into hell. It does not all ensure union after death; the person who has died goes to the place determined by his own Karman, the person who accompanies him on the funeral pyre goes to the hell reserved for those who are guilty of the sin of suicide. On the other hand, by surviving the deceased, one can do much good both to oneself and to the departed by offering prescribed oblations for his happiness in the other world. By dying with him one can do good to neither.'[23]

It is clear that Bāṇa was struck with horror by the tendency to eulogize the Satī custom, shown in some quarters in his days, and was anxious to offer the most determined opposition to it. Tantra writers also joined him in the crusade. They pointed out that woman was the embodiment of Supreme Goddess, and boldly declared that if a person burnt her with her husband, he would be condemned to eternal hell.[24]

Unfortunately, this crusade sponsored by wise thinkers failed to have any effect. The custom continued to gain in popularity mainly among fighting classes. Ascetic ideals were gaining the upper hand in society; the conduct of a widow boldly burning herself with the remains of her husband appeared to it as the most glorious example of supreme self-sacrifice. The theory of Karman also was modified so as to support the Satī custom. There was no doubt that normally a relation could not join a dead person in the other world by dying after him, as the Karman of the two persons would lead them to different destinations. The Satī, however, was an exception; the merit of her self-sacrifice was more than sufficient to annihilate her husband's sins and raise him to heaven to live in eternal union with his wife. From about AD 700 fiery advocates began to come forward to extol the custom of Satī in increasing numbers. Aṅgiras argued that the only course which religion has prescribed for a widow is that of Satī.[25] Hārīta maintained that the wife can purify her husband from the deadliest of sins, if she burns herself with his remains. The two will then happily reside in heaven for three-and-a-half crores of years.[26] A passage interpolated in *Parāśarasmṛiti* observes that just as a snake-charmer forcibly drags out a snake from a hole by force, in the same manner the Satī takes out her husband from hell and enjoys heaven with him for three-and-a-half crores of years.[27] Even if the wife had led a dissolute life, it would not matter; her immolation, even if not voluntary, will ensure a permanent seat in heaven both to her and her husband.[28]

The views advocated by these writers gradually began to produce some effect on society. During the period AD 700–1100 Satīs became more frequent in northern India and quite common in Kashmir. The history of Kashmir during this period teems with the cases of Satīs in royal families. Kalhaṇa, the historian of the province, is surprised to find that even notoriously unchaste queens like Jayamatī, the wife of King Uchchala, should be seen immolating themselves on their husband's funeral pyres.[29] The custom of Satī was so deep-rooted in the ruling families of Kashmir, that not only regularly married wives, but even concubines used to follow it. Kings Kalaśa and Utkarsha were, for instance, followed both by their wives and concubines (*Rājataraṅgiṇī*, VII, 858). It seems that the principle of dying after a beloved relative was extended to relations other than the husband as well; we sometimes come across mothers, sisters and sisters-in-law burning themselves with the dead relation (*Ibid*, VI, 1380; VIII, 448; VII, 1486). Cases are also on record of ministers, servants and nurses burning themselves with their masters (*Ibid*, V, 206; VII, 481; VII, 490; VIII, 1447). This reminds us of the *harikari* custom of Japan. Kalhaṇa records the case even of a cat, which out of affection for its royal master Sussala, voluntarily threw itself on his funeral pyre (VII, 2441). In the stories of the *Kathāsaritsāgara* (which was written in *c.* AD 1100 in Kashmir,) the custom of Satī is quite common. Its great prevalence in the valley of Kashmir is probably due to its proximity to Central Asia, which was the home of the Scythians, among whom the custom was quite common.

There is evidence to show that outside Kashmir also the custom of Satī and *Anumaraṇa* was getting gradually more popular in northern India. The mother of Harsha, queen Yaśomatī, did not care to wait till the death of her husband; when his case was pronounced to be hopeless, she gave away her ornaments, took a sacred bath, put on all the marks of a lady with her husband living (*avidhavāmaraṇachihnamudi ahantī*) and entered the funeral pyre. When her husband Prabhākaravardhana died, some of the royal officers, including the physician, entered the fire.[30] In the 4th Act of the *Veṇīsaṁhāra* we find the mother of a dead hero coming on the battlefield to enter his funeral pyre along with her daughter-in-law.[31]

Down to *c.* AD 1000 Satīs were rare in the Deccan. Sulaiman, an Arabian merchant who had spent some time on the western coast of India at the beginning of the tenth century, states that it was only sometimes that queens used to mount the funeral pyres of their consorts; there was no compulsion; it was entirely left to them to choose (Elliot and Dowson, Vol. I, p. 6).

As far as the extreme south of India is concerned; Satī was more an exception than a rule down to *c.* AD 1000. The queen of only King Bhūta Pāṇḍya of the Saṅgam age is known to have followed the custom (*Puram*, 246–7). Her historicity is, however, a matter of uncertainty. Among the members of the Pallava, the Chola, and the Pāṇḍya ruling families, so well known to us from numerous inscriptions, we do not come across any cases of Satī down to *c.* AD 900. It is, therefore, clear that the custom was yet to obtain a footing in south India.

We have already observed that Satī was originally a Kshatriya custom. The accounts of the Greek historians make it clear that it was confined only to fighting classes in the fourth century BC. The *Bṛihaddaivata*, while recognizing the validity of the custom among the Kshatriyas, doubts whether it could be permissible for other castes to follow it.[32] The *Padmapurāṇa* extols the custom to the sky, but expressly prohibits it to Brāhmaṇa women. It declares that any person, who will be guilty of helping a Brāhmaṇa widow to the funeral pyre, will be guilty of the dreadful and unatonable sin of the murder of a Brāhmaṇa[33] (*brahmahatyā*).

The Brāhmaṇa community, however, was accustomed to pride itself on following the most ascetic and self-denying code of life; eventually it began to feel that it should not allow itself to be outdistanced by the Kshatriyas in the custom of Satī. The custom therefore began to be followed by a few Brāhmaṇa families soon after AD 1000. We have seen already how there are express commands in earlier texts prohibiting a Brāhmaṇa widow from following the new fashion of suicide, but commentators of this period began to explain them away with their proverbial ingenuity. It was argued that when death by mounting the funeral pyre of the husband was apparently prohibited to a Brāhmaṇa widow, what was meant was that she should not take the step merely under a temporary sense of overwhelming grief. It should be the result of full and mature deliberation.[34] Or, the intention may be to interdict death by mounting a separate funeral pyre; a Brāhmaṇa widow must be always burnt along with her husband's remains on the same pyre.[35] These arguments are advanced by south Indian commentators of the twelfth and fourteenth centuries; it is, therefore, clear that the custom had by this time spread to south India and penetrated into the Brāhmaṇa community as well.

We have shown above how the literary evidence from the works of Bhāsa, Kālidāsa, Bāṇa, Śūdraka and Kalhaṇa tends to show that the Satī custom was getting gradually popular in the royal families of northern India during the period AD 200 to 1000. It is, however, rather strange that only a few epigraphical records from northern India of this period should be referring to the actual cases of Satī. Negative evidence is never conclusive, but it is only reasonable to expect that the court panegyrists would not have failed to mention the cases of Satī, when they were eulogizing the kings and queens of their royal families. As it is, only a few epigraphs refer to the Satī cases even in Rajputana, which later became a stronghold of the Satī custom. The earliest among these is that of the mother of the Chāhamāna King Chaṇḍamahāsena, who became a Satī in AD 842. The next case is that of Sampalladevī, who became a Satī at Ghaṭiyāla in Rajputana in AD

890. We have no other recorded cases of Satī in Rajputana records prior to AD 1000. The Chedi King Gāṅgeyadeva is stated to have obtained salvation at Prayāga at the root of the holy Vaṭa tree along with his 100 wives in c. AD 1020. The language of the record however suggests that the old king and his hundred queens simultaneously drowned themselves at the confluence of the Gaṅgā and the Yamunā[36]; it was not the case of the Satī custom. It may be, therefore, doubted whether the Satī custom had become common even in the Rajput royal families of northern India before the tenth century. Kashmir is of course, an exception.

The Satī custom had however, obtained the status of a well-recognized but optional practice in Hinduism; for we find it travelling to the islands of Java, Sumatra, and Bali along with the Hindu emigrants.

The enthusiastic advocacy of the Satī custom by medieval commentators began to have an appreciable effect on society only after about AD 1300. About twenty cases of Satīs are referred to by records in Rajputana between the period 1200 and 1600;[37] most of these are of ladies belonging to the royal or Kshatriya families. In Mahākośala, the Satī stones near Saugar show that widows belonging to the weaver, barber, and mason classes were often becoming Satīs during AD 1500–1800.[38] Among the Karnatak inscriptions published in the *Epigraphia Carnatica* there are only eleven cases of Satīs during the period AD 1000–1400, but forty-one during the period AD 1400–1600. Most of these Satīs, however, belonged to the Nāyaka and the Gauḍa classes, which formed the main fighting community of southern India. Two of them belonged to the Jain sect;[39] it is clear that some Jains had also begun to feel that they ought not to lag behind Hindus in the matter. Inscriptions, however, record only very few cases of Brāhmaṇa widows becoming Satīs; it is obvious that the lifting of the canonical ban had not yet succeeded in popularizing the custom in the priestly order.

Among the ruling Rajput families of northern India the custom became firmly established by this time. The average Rajput princess welcomed the opportunity to become a Satī and would not allow her husband to be cremated alone. Bards, ministers and relatives would often expostulate, but without any success. So, generally at the death of almost every Rajput king or nobleman, those among his widows, who were not with child or who were not required to direct the government as regents, used to ascend the funeral pyre. Their number was sometimes appallingly large. When Raja Ajit Singh of Marwar died in 1724, sixty-four women mounted his funeral pyre. When Raja Budh Singh of Bundi was drowned, eighty-four women became Satīs.[40] The example of Rajputs was emulated by the Nāyakas of Madura. When two rulers of this family died in 1611 and 1620, we are told that as many as 400 and 700 women ascended the funeral pyres. These numbers are probably exaggerated by missionary reporters; it is, however, clear that a large number of women used to become Satīs at the death of each member of the Nāyaka family.

Amaradas, the third Sikh Guru (AD 1552–74) had condemned the Satī custom, and it was not followed by the Sikhs for a long time. When, however, they developed into a fighting community, they did not like to lag behind the Rajputs in following time-honoured martial traditions, which enjoined Satī as a matter of course. The Satī custom became common in Sikh aristocracy in spite of its prohibition by the Gurus. Thus when Ranjit Singh died, four queens and seven concubines of his ascended the funeral pyre. During the troublesome period following his death, princes and generals fell in quick succession and almost everyone of them was accompanied by his wives and concubines. Three women died with Maharaja Kharag Singh, five with Basant Singh, eleven with Kishori Singh, twenty-four with Hira Singh and 310 with Suchet Singh.

The Maratha ruling families claimed Rajput descent and so could not remain immune from the influence of the custom. Satī, however, was rather an exception than a rule with them. When Shivaji died, only one of his wives became a Satī. The same was the case with Rajaram. The queen of Shahu was compelled to burn herself owing to the political machinations of her mother-in-law, Tarabai. There are very few other cases of Satīs recorded among the annals of the Maratha ruling families at Satara, Nagpur, Gwalior, Indore, and Baroda. Among the members of the Peshwa family, only Ramābai, the widow of Madhavarao I, became a Satī. It is clear that the custom did not become popular among them, as it did among the Sikh princes and generals.

Numerous Satī stones that are to be seen in almost all parts of India belonging to the seventeenth and the eighteenth centuries, show that the Satī custom was frequently followed by the commoners as well. There are, for instance, fifty-one Satī stones in the Saugar district ranging in date from *c.* AD 1450 to 1824, attesting to the women of all classes including weavers, barbers and masons becoming Satīs.[41] It would appear that about two per cent widows used to become Satīs at this time.

Muslim rulers as a general rule did not like the custom. Humayun wanted to prohibit it in the case of the widows who had passed the child-bearing age (*J.A.S.B.*, 1935, p. 76). He, however, could not take any adequate steps in the matter. In the twenty-second year of his reign Akbar translated his opposition to the custom into action by appointing inspectors to see that no force was used to compel widows to burn themselves against their will. As a consequence, Satīs became rare in the territories contiguous to Agra. Many Muslim administrators had made it a rule that no widow should be allowed to mount the funeral pyre without the permission of the local government officer. This provision did not materially check the custom, as the prescribed permission could be usually obtained without much difficulty.

That the practice of Satī was mainly a medieval development is also proved by the circumstance that its detailed procedure has not been described even by those few late Smṛitis, which recommend the practice. We get detailed information on the point only from some late medieval Purāṇas and foreign merchants and travellers. The ritual is described in detail only in very late digests like the *Nirṇayasindhu*[42] and the *Dharmasindhu*[43] written after the seventeenth century.

The Satī was an object of the highest veneration, and so was taken out to the accompaniment of music in a grand procession through the town to the cremation grounds. She was given a bath, and then she put on her person all the insignia of saubhāgya or married bliss.[44] She used to carry with her *kumkuma*, mirror, comb and betel leaves which were the insignia of saubhāgya. Very often, she used to give away her ornaments and belongings to her friends and relations, who used to keep them as sacred mementos. Then she used to take final leave of her relations. Some travellers have narrated that people used to entrust to her messages to their dead relations in heaven; whether such was really the case may well be doubted. Ascending the funeral pyre, she used to place her husband's head on her lap. Then the pyre was lighted.

Usually there was *sahamaraṇa,* i.e. the widow mounted the same pyre that was prepared for her husband. If there were several widows, the practice differed. Sometimes the favourite wife was selected for the honour of sahamaraṇa, others being burnt on separate pyres; sometimes all were placed on the same pyre, their petty jealousies if any, being reconciled during the last fateful moments of their life.

If the husband had died on a distant battlefield, joint cremation was impossible. In such cases the widow used to mount a separate pyre, along with her husband's turban or shoes as a substitute for his body.

Even widows intensely anxious to follow their husbands were likely to recoil and jump out under the agony of the flames of fire. So special funeral arrangements were made in the case of a Satī. The funeral pyre was piled in a deep pit in many parts of the country, especially in the Deccan and western India. This rendered an escape impossible. A Mysore inscription refers to a lady going out to become a Satī as going forth to the fire pit to die (*E.C.,* vol. IV, 2, Hg. No. 18). Barbosa and Linschoten have also referred to this method. In Gujarat and northern U.P., a wooden house, about twelve feet square, was constructed and the widow was tied to one of its pillars. In Bengal the widow's feet were tied to posts fixed into the ground; she was thrice asked whether she really wished to go to heaven, and then the pyre was lighted. Where burial was practised, the widow was interred along with her husband. This was the case in Andhra province in the sixteenth century.

Was any force exercised to compel unwilling widows to mount the funeral pyre? A straight reply like 'yes' or 'no' cannot be given to this question. There can be no doubt that in some cases unwilling widows were forced to burn themselves. Kalhaṇa has recorded the cases of two Kashmir queens bribing their ministers in order to induce them to come to the cremation ground for dissuading them from their apparently voluntary resolution to accompany their departed husbands. Queen Diddā adopted this strategem and was saved by her minister Naravāhana (VI, 195). Garga, the wily minister of queen Jayamatī, had fiendish heart; he took the bribe alright but deliberately delayed going to the cremation ground. The poor queen had to allow herself to be burnt in pursuance of her so-called voluntary resolve (VIII, 363). Medieval travellers record many cases of force being exercised, and their accounts must be true at least in some cases. Manucci tells us that Kshatriya women were burnt even against their wishes (III, p. 65); he himself rescued one such woman, who was eventually married to a European friend of his. Nicoli Conti informs us that financial pressure was often exercised, the widow being informed that she would lose her right to Strīdhana, if she decided to survive (J.A.S.B., 1935, p. 256). Bernier has narrated the pathetic case of a child widow of twelve being burnt against her will at Lahore (pp. 363–4). In the case of Jaimall, one of Akbar's officers, his son wanted to forcibly immolate his mother; she was eventually saved only by the intervention of Akbar (Akbarnāmā, 28th year). Sometimes the unfortunate widows, who were forced to become Satīs, used to recoil and run away from the funeral pyre. They were then regarded as untouchables and were not accepted back by their castes and families. They had to throw themselves on the mercy of low-caste men, who used to assemble at the funeral when they suspected that the widow was likely to recoil at the eleventh hour. Sometimes they were rescued by European traders, who used to marry them. It is a pity that in spite of such instances society should not have realized the enormous inequity of the custom.

The failure of society in this respect is partly attributable to the fact that in the vast majority of cases widows were willing parties to their immolation. A Karnatak inscription, belonging to the eleventh century, tells us how a lady named Dekabbe would not listen to the earnest entreaties of her parents not to mount her husband's pyre (E.C., IV, Hg. No. 18). Muktabai, the daughter of Rani Ahalyabai of Indore, became a Satī in 1792 in spite of the weeping and heart-rending entreaties of her old and saintly mother. Tavernier, a seventeenth century traveller, narrates how a widow of twenty-two went to the governor of Patna to get his permission, and how she held her hand in the flame of a torch till it was burnt to cinders in order to convince the officer that she was a willing party, and was not afraid of fire (pp. 414–7). Ibn Battuta, a fourteenth-century traveller, tells us how he fainted to see the unbelievable courage of a dauntless widow, who gleefully embraced the devouring flames of the funeral fire (p.191). Bernier, while describing a case of which he was an eye witness, states that it is impossible to describe the brutish boldness or the ferocious gaity depicted on the woman's countenance; her step was undaunted, her conversation was free from all perturbation; her easy air was free from all dejection, her lofty courage was void of all embarrassment. She took a torch and with her own hand lighted the fire. It appeared to be a dream, but it was a stern reality (pp. 312–13). Pietro della Valle was also impressed by the courage of the average Satī. 'If I knew (of a lady about to become a Satī), I will not fail to go and see her and honour by my presence her funeral with that compassionate affection, which such a great conjugal fidelity and love seem to deserve' (Travels, II, p. 266).

That it is a religious duty for a woman of sufficient courage and resolution to accompany her husband was so deep-rooted a conviction in medieval times, that we sometimes come across cases of betrothed but unmarried women insisting to mount the funeral pyres of their would-be husbands. Mustaqui has recorded one such case; the betrothed husband died in trying to save his sweetheart from a serpent, which eventually bit him with fatal effects. Though not yet married, the girl insisted on becoming a Satī and burnt herself on the funeral pyre of her lover (J. A. S. B., 1935, p. 259).

The present writer is not inclined to disbelieve the above accounts of foreign travellers. For his own sister Mrs Indirabai Madhav Udgaonkar showed an indescribable fortitude in carrying out her long-formed and oft-announced resolution not to survive her husband when on 17 January 1946 she committed herself to flames within twenty-four hours of her husband's death, in spite of the pressing entreaties of all her relations. Nothing, not even the presence of a suckling child, would dissuade her from taking a step which she believed to be dictated by her duty and Dharma as a pativratā.

The available evidence shows that, barring a few exceptions, most of the widows, who used to become Satīs, were free agents in their choice. The average Rajput or Kshatriya lady ascended the funeral pyre with the same reckless courage with which her husband used to embrace death on the battlefield, when leading a forlorn hope against very heavy odds. It is probable, however, that in some cases the force of public opinion may have been felt to be too strong. It is equally clear that young and childless widows in particular may have in some cases decided to terminate their life with their husbands, because they feared that it would be too dreary for them. Remarriage was out of question, and even for their maintenance they had to depend upon not very sympathetic relations.[45] Grown up widows like the mother of King Harsha would feel that the purpose of their life was over, that they had nothing more to achieve or enjoy, and that it was, therefore, in the fitness of things that they should accompany their beloved spouses. The vast majority of widows, who terminated their life on their husband's funeral pyres, did so out of genuine love and devotion to their husbands whom they also revered as God. They believed that the course they were following was in the best spiritual interest both of themselves and their husbands. A stern sense of duty, a stoical contempt of physical pain, and the hope of an eternal union with their beloved husbands in heaven sustained them through the terrible ordeal on the burning pyre. Naturally, society held them in reverence and immortalized their memory by suitable memorials, as it does in the case of heroes who deliberately and cheerfully sacrifice their lives in the cause of their religion or motherland out of a sense of duty and patriotism, often after undergoing long and excruciating pain on the dismal and desolate battlefield.

What was the percentage of widows who ascended the funeral pyre, when the course came to be fervently recommended by later Purāṇas? It is difficult to answer this question for the period 1300–1800, as there are no statistics for it. We have no doubt numerous Satī stones scattered throughout the country, but it is difficult to utilize them for determining the percentage. There is no doubt that it was high in the warrior families of Rajputana. It may have been as high as ten per cent.

As far as the general population is concerned, perhaps one widow in a thousand became a Satī, when the custom was in its greatest vogue. Public opinion and government had not begun to assert themselves against the custom in the first quarter of the nineteenth century; we may therefore well presume that the prevalence of the custom at this time was more or less the same as it was during the preceding four or five centuries. Government records of this period show that in the presidencies of Bombay and Madras, the average annual number of Satīs was well below fifty. In the Poona dominion of the Peshwa the annual average was about twelve during the period 1800 to 1812. Tanjore district had the worst reputation for Satīs, but its record was of only twenty-four cases during the eighteen months preceding 1817. In Central India only three or four cases of Satīs used to take place annually.[43] It is quite possible that these statistics may be incomplete. But even if we suppose that the actual number of Satīs was twice the number officially recorded, the conclusion becomes inevitable that only an infinitesimal number of widows in the general population were immolating themselves. It is clear that not more than one widow in a thousand used to mount the funeral pyre in the Deccan and Central India.

In Bengal the Satī custom was more prevalent; this would clearly appear from the following table of Satī statistics, prepared by the British government:

Name of the Division	Number of Satīs during the years 1815–28.
Calcutta Division, predominantly Hindu	5099
Dacca Division, predominantly Muslim	610
Murshidabad Division, predominantly Muslim	260
Patna Division, predominantly Hindu	709
Bareily Division, predominantly Hindu	193
Benares Division, predominantly orthodox	1165

The above table will show that the percentage of Satīs in the Hindu population of Bengal was much larger than what obtained in the presidencies of Bombay and Madras, or even in the division of Benares, which was the greatest stronghold of orthodoxy.[47] There is therefore, some force in the view that undue advantage was taken in Bengal of the helpless and grief-stricken condition of the widow in order to induce her to become a Satī by some coparceners, who stood to gain by her elimination as an heir. The Dāyabhāga law, which permitted even the childless widow to become an heir to her husband, was thus not an unmixed blessing to the weak-minded section of the women of Bengal. The cases of force or undue influence, however, could not have been many. The annual average of Satīs in the Calcutta Division was about 370. This Division was at that time probably having a population equal to the whole of the then Bombay Presidency, and its statistics also were very probably compiled much more accurately. It would, therefore, appear that Satīs were only twice as common in Bengal as they were in Bombay or Madras. In the latter provinces usually one widow in a thousand became a Satī. In Bengal the ratio was probably double, but not higher. Most of the Satīs in Bengal and U.P. were from the Brāhmaṇa caste. It is clear that the lifting of the canonical ban on the Brāhmaṇa widows to become Satīs had greatest effect in the Gangetic Plain.

We have already observed that the Satī custom could not have been in much greater vogue in the Hindu and Muslim periods than it was in the first quarter of the nineteenth century. Available statistics clearly show that outside ruling and priestly families the custom did not make a wide appeal. The fact was that the advocacy of the custom in later Smṛitis and Purāṇas failed to make a wide appeal to the Hindu community. Though it admired and even deified the Satī as an example of supreme devotion and sacrifice, it really disliked the custom. It had not, however, the moral courage at this time to start a crusade against the custom, as Bāṇa had done in the seventh century. Its religious leaders believed implicitly in the authority of later Smṛitis and Purāṇas and would not countenance any open agitation against a custom sanctioned by them. Society, therefore, tried to check the custom by individual persuasion. Usually, relations would try their best in dissuading a widow from becoming a Satī. Thus when the father-in-law of Narayanrao Peshwa died, his wife desired to follow him on the pyre. She was, however, dissuaded by her relations. Ahalyabai Holkar, who embodied the orthodox Hindu culture of the age, did not herself become a Satī, and tried her best, though without

success, to dissuade her daughter from becoming one. Towards
the beginning of the nineteenth century, the Brāhmaṇa government of Poona and the Maratha government of Savantwadi had
issued official orders, definitely disapproving and discouraging
the custom.

When therefore, Lord William Bentinck issued his famous regulation in December 1829, making the custom illegal in British
India, there was not much opposition to the proposal. It undoubtedly created a stir in the orthodox community, and its journal the
Chandrikā wrote vehemently against the step. But the appeal to
the Privy Council to annual the new regulation could get only 800
signatures. The new regulation was welcomed by the enlightened
Hindu public opinion, and its mouthpiece the *Kaumudī* went on
defending the action of the government. A memorial was presented to the Governor-General thanking him for his humane regulation. Raja Rammohan Roy, the Morning Star of Asian Renais-
sance, went to England and pleaded before the members of the
parliament and Privy Council that the new regulation should not
be annulled. Strengthened by this advocacy, the authorities in
England rejected the memorial of the pro-Satī party in 1832.

The credit for the suppression of the Satī custom belongs, however, undoubtedly to Lord Bentinck, who resolved to take the
step in spite of the almost general opposition of his subordinate
English officers. Enlightened Hindu opinion came to support him
only when he had promulgated the regulation. Left to itself, it would
certainly have taken a few decades more to stamp out the custom.

Though the custom of Satī was prohibited in British India in
1829, it continued to linger in Rajputana, its greatest stronghold,
for about thirty years more. At the deaths of Maharana Jivan
Singh of Udaipur in 1838 and of Maharaja Man Singh of Jodhpur
in 1843, several women mounted the funeral pyre. Jaipur first
agreed to prohibit the custom in 1846 and other Rajput states
gradually followed. Udaipur was the greatest stronghold of the
orthodox Rajput tradition and the last public case of a legal Satī
took place there in 1861 at the death of Maharana Sarup Singh in
1861. But even the Rajput public opinion had by this time so
strongly ranged itself against the custom that not a single one among
the legal wives of the Maharana felt it necessary to accompany

her husband. Frantic efforts were made to induce at least one of them to become a Satī in order to 'preserve the honour of the Sisodias by preventing its chief being burnt all alone'. All of them however flatly refused to mount the funeral pyre. Eventually, a slave girl was induced to become a Satī and was burnt with the remains of the Maharana. The incident will show how firmly even the Rajput public opinion had ranged itself against the custom by this time.

Since AD 1861, no case has occurred of a public legal Satī. During the subsequent years some Hindu widows, who intensely believed that it was their bounden religious duty to accompany their husbands, have tried to ascend their funeral pyres, but have been usually prevented from achieving their object by the public and the Police. Foiled in this attempt, some of them often shut themselves in a room and put an end to their lives by igniting their saris.

Notes

1.   Bankimchandra, 'Bankim Rachanabali', in S. Chandra, *The Oppressive Present: Literature and Social Consciousness in Colonial India* (Delhi: Oxford University Press, 1992).

2.   Gandhi, M.K., 'A Twentieth-Century Sati', *Young India*, 21 May 1931, repr. in *Women and Social Justice* (Ahmedabad: Navajivan Publications, 1947).

3.   Coomaraswamy, A.K., 'The status of Indian Women' (1913) in *The Dance of Shiva: Fourteen Indian Essays* (Delhi: Munshiram Manoharlal, 1984).

4.   Altekar, A.S., *The Position of Woman in Hindu Society* (Delhi: Motilal Banarsidass, 1959).

5.   Tawney: *Kathāsaritsāgara*, vol. IV, Terminal Essay on Suttee by Penzer.

6.   इमा नारीरविधवाः सपत्नीरांजनेन सर्पिषा संविशन्तु ।

     अनश्रवोऽनमीवाः सुरत्ना आरोहन्तु जनयो योनिमग्रे ।।

R. V., x,18,7.

Even when the last word is changed into *agneh*, it is only a forced construction that can detect in this stanza a reference to the widow immolation.

7.   अग्ने व्रतानां व्रतपतिरसि पत्न्यनुगमनव्रतं करिष्यामि तच्छकेयं तन्मे राध्यताम् ।

     इह त्वाऽग्ने नमसा विधेम सुवर्गस्य लोकस्य समेत्यै ।

     जुषाणोऽद्य हविषा जातवेदो विशामित्वा सत्वतो नय मां पत्युरन्ते ।

Wilson's Collected Works, II, pp. 295–6.

[8] इयं नारी पतिलोकं वृणाना निपद्यते उप त्वा मर्त्य प्रेतम् ।

धर्मं पुराणमनुपालयन्ती तस्य प्रजां द्रविणं चह धत्त ।।

xviii, 2, I

[9] तामुत्यापयेद्देवरः पतिस्यानीयोऽन्तेवासी जरद्दासो वा 'उदीर्ष्व नारि अभि जीवलोकम्' इति ।

A. G. S., IV, 2, 18.

[10] धनुर्हस्तादाददाना मृतस्य श्रियै ब्रह्मणे तेजसे बलाय ।

अत्रैव त्वमिह वयं सुशेवा विश्वाः स्पृधोऽभिजातीर्जयेम ।।

VI

The verse is repeated twice more with the change of the first word into मणिम् and सुदर्णम् ।

[11] अहमेवानुयास्यामि भर्तारमपलापिनम् ।

न हि तृप्तास्मि कामनां ज्येष्ठा मामनुमन्यताम् ।।

वर्तेयं न समां वृत्तिं जात्वहं न सुतेषु ते ।

I, 138, 71–2.

[12] *Mbh*, XVI, 7. 18.

[13] *Ibid*, XVI, 7. 73–4.

[14] In the *Kādambarī*, Bāṇa expressly refers to the case of Uttarā in justification of the conduct of Mahāśvetā in deciding to survive her lover. We, however, find Uttarā represented as burning herself with her husband Abhimanyu in the Bali island version of the *Māhabhārata*. The reason of the discrepancy is obvious; the Bali island version belongs to a time when the custom of Satī had become popular.

[15] दृदृशुस्तु ततः कृष्णां सूतपुत्राः समागताः ।

हन्यतां शीघ्रमसतो यत्कृते कीचको हतः ।

अथवा नैव हन्तव्या दह्यतां कामिना सह ।

मृतस्यापि प्रियं कार्यं सूतपुत्रस्य सर्वथा ।।

IV, 23, 4 ff.

[16] Later on they are represented as plunging into the Gaṅgā and being reunited with their husbands in heaven. At best, this would be a case of suicide. The procedure has no affinity with the custom of Satī.

[17] मृतोऽपि बान्धवः शक्तो नानुगन्तुं प्रियं जनम् ।

जायावर्जं हि सर्वस्य याम्यः पन्था विरुध्यते ।।

20, 36.

[18] भक्तानुरक्ता च प्रिया च कान्ता भार्यावलग्नानुगताग्निराशिम् ।।

C. I. I. Vol. III, p. 93.

[19] भर्त्राग्नि या विशेन्नारी सापि स्वर्गमवाप्नुनात् ।

221, 23.

²⁰ पुंवत्स्त्रीणामपि प्रतिषिद्ध आत्मयागः । यथैव 'श्येनेन हिंस्याद्भूतानि' इति अधिकारस्य
अतिप्रवृद्धद्धेषान्धतया सत्यामपि प्रवृत्तौ न धर्मत्वम् एवमिहापि (अनुमरणस्य) न
शास्त्रीयत्वम् । किं चतस्मादु ह न पुरायुषः प्रेयादिति प्रत्यक्षश्रुतिविरोधोऽयम् अतोऽस्त्येव
पतिमनुमरणे स्त्रियाः प्रतिषेधः ।

On *Manu*, V, 157.

²¹ अनुवर्तेत जीवन्तं न तु यायान्मृतं पतिम् ।
जीवद्भर्तृ हितं कुर्यान्मरणादात्मघातिनी । ।

Quoted by Aparārka on *Yaj.*, I, 87.

²² तद्धर्मान्तरमपि ब्रह्मचर्यधर्माज्जधन्यं निकृष्टफलत्वात् ।

Vyavahārakāṇḍa, p. 598.

²³ यदेतदनुमरणं नाम तदतितिनिष्फलम् । अविद्वज्जनाचरित एष मार्गः ।
मोहविलसितमेतद्वरभसाचरितमिदं यदुपरते पितरि भर्तरि भ्रातरि वा प्राणाः परित्यज्यन्ते ।
स्वयं चेन्न जहित न परित्याज्याः । उपरतस्य तु न कमपि गुणमावहति । न तावदुस्यायं
शुभलोकोपार्जनहेतुः, न निरयपातप्रतिकारः, न परस्परसमागमनिमित्तम् । अन्यामेव
स्वकर्मफलपाकोपचितामसौ अवशो नीयते भूमिम् । असावपि आत्मघातिनः केवलमेनसा
संयुज्यते । जीवंस्तु जलाञ्जलिदानादिना बहूपकरात्युपरतस्यात्मनश्च मृतस्तु नोभयस्यापि ।

Kādambarī, Pūrvārdha, p. 308

²⁴ भर्त्रा सह कुलेशानि न दहेत्कुलकामिनीम् ।
तव स्वरूपा रमणी जगत्याच्छन्नविग्रहा ।
मोहाद्भर्तुश्चितारोहाद् भवेन्निरयगामिनी । ।

Mahānirvāṇatantra, X, 79–80.

²⁵ साध्वीनामिह नारीणामग्निप्रपतनादृते ।
नान्यो धर्मोऽस्ति भूते भर्तरि कुत्रचित् । ।

Quoted by Aparārka on *rāj*, I, 87.

²⁶ तिस्रः कोट्यर्धकोटी च यानि रोमाणि मानुषे ।
तावत्कालं वसेत्स्वर्गे भतीरं यानुगच्छति । ।
व्यालग्राही यथा व्यालं बिलादुद्धरते बलात् ।
एवमुद्धृत्य भतीरं तेनैव सह मोदते । ।

IV, 31–2.

This passage is an interpolation, because two verses earlier, Parāśara
permits a widow to remarry.

²⁷ ब्रह्मघ्नं वा सुरापं वा कृतघ्नं वापि मानवम् ।
यमादाय मृता नारी सा भतीरं पुनाति हि । ।

Vṛddhāhārīta 201.

²⁸ अवमत्य तु याः पूर्व पतिं दुष्टेन चेतसा ।
वर्तन्ते याश्च सततं भर्तृणां प्रतिकूलतः । ।

भर्तानुमरणं काले याः कुर्वन्ति तथाविधाः ।

कामोक्रोधादुमयान्मोहात्सर्वाः पूता भवन्ति ह । ।

Mādhava attributes these verses to the *Mahābhārata* at Parāśara, IV, 33; they, however, do not occur in the epic.

29 दौश्शील्यमप्याचरन्तयो घातयन्त्योऽपि बल्लभान् ।

हेलया प्रविशन्त्यग्निं न स्त्रीषु प्रत्ययः क्वचित् । ।

Rājalaraṅginī, VIII, 366.

30 *Harshacharit*, Book V.

31 हा अतिकरूणं वर्तते । एषा वीरमाता समरविनिहतं पुत्रं श्रुत्वा रक्तांशुकनिरसनया समग्रभूषणया वध्वा सहानुप्रिय वा ।

32 वर्णानामितरेषां तु स्त्रीधर्मोऽयं भवन्न वा ।

VII, 15.

33 न म्रियेत समं भर्त्रा ब्राह्मणी ब्रह्मशासनात् । प्रब्रज्यागतिमाप्नोति मरणादात्मघातिनी । । नरोत्तम उवाचः-सर्वासामेव जातीनां ब्राह्मणः श्रेष्य   उच्यते । पुण्यं च द्विजमुख्यान अत्र किं वा विपर्यवः । । भगवानुवाचः--ब्राह्मण्या साहसं कर्म नैव कार्य कदाचन । निश्शेषेऽस्यां वधं कृत्वा स नरो ब्रह्महा भवेत् । ।

Srishṭikhaṅḍa, 49, 72–3.

34 तद्विधितः प्रवर्तमानाया ब्राह्मस्माः अनुगमनान्निषेधो न विधते । शोकादिप्रवृण्यायास्तु विद्यते एव ।

Aparārka on *Yaj.*, I, 87.

35 अस्य निषेधस्य पृथक् चितिनिषेधत्वात् । अत एवोशनाः । पृथक्चितं समारूह्या न विप्रा गन्तुमर्हति ।

Mādhava on *Parāśara* IV, 31.

36 प्राप्ते प्रयागवटमूलनिवेशबन्धौ सार्ध शतेन गृहिणीभिरमुत्र मुक्तिम् । ।

E.I., XII, p. 211, V. 12.

37 *Bhandarkara's List*, No. 227, 394, 407, 413, 423, 615, 616, 713, 935, 980, 1009 and 1242.

38 Hiralal, *Inscriptions from C. P.*, p. 53.

39 *Ep. Car.*, Vol. VIII, Sorab Nos. 106 and 261, dated 1376 and 1408 respectively.

40 Tod : *Annals*, vol. II, p. 837.

41 Hiralal, *Inscriptions from C. P.*, p. 51.

42 Part III, Uttarārdha, p. 623.

43 Pp. 483–4.

44 स्नानं मंगलसंस्कारो भूषणाञ्जनधारणम् ।

गन्धपुष्पं तथा धूपं हरिद्राक्षतधारणम् । ।

मंगलं च तथा सूत्रं पादालक्तकमेव च ।

शक्तया दानं प्रियोक्तिश्च प्रसन्नास्त्वमेव च ।।
नानामंगलवाद्यानां श्रवणं गीतकस्य च ।
कुर्यादथ स्वकां भूषां विप्राय प्रतिपादयेत् ।।

Padmapurāṇa, Pātālakhaṇḍa, 102, 67 ff.

[45] Compare, for instance, the following extract from a thirteenth-century Tamil inscription which contains the passionate outpourings of the heart of a young widow, afraid of the woes and ill-treatment in store for her: 'If she lived after her husband, she would be the slave of her cowives (who apparently had sons and were therefore going to be de facto owners of the family property). Whosoever said that she ought not to die,...those, who did not bind her, and throw her into fire, and kill her would get the sin of prostituting their wives. *S. I. E. R.*, 1907, p. 77.

[46] The statistics in this and subsequent paragraphs are taken from Edward Thomson's *Suttee*, London (1926).

[47] The annual number of Satīs in Bengal, during the years 1815 to 1828, is as follows:

Year	Number	Year	Number	Year	Number
1815	378	1820	598	1825	639
1816	442	1821	654	1826	518
1817	707	1822	583	1827	517
1818	839	1823	575	1828	463
1819	650	1824	572		

Bengal, however, then included U.P., Bihar, Orissa, and Assam.

Mill and Wilson, *History of British India*, IX, p. 271.

VI

LITERARY REPRESENTATIONS

15

Early Modern and Eighteenth-Century Fiction

John Dryden, *Aureng-Zebe*[1]

Dryden's play of 1675 includes a short scene in Act Five in which the heroine, Melesinda, declares her intention to perform sati. The piece is somewhat quixotic in that Dryden has a Muslim princess performing sati. Also included below is an extract from the author's dedicatory epistle, in which the playwright commends the sati's devotion and compares it favourably to the morality of European women.

DEDICATORY EPISTLE

That which was not pleasing to some of the fair ladies in the last act of it, as I dare not vindicate, so neither can I wholly condemn, till I find more reason for their censures. The procedure of Indamora and Melesinda seems yet in my judgment natural, and not unbecoming of their characters. If they that arraign them fail not more, the world will never blame their conduct; and I shall be glad for the honour of my country to find better images of virtue drawn to the life in their behaviour than any I could feign to adorn the theatre. I confess I have only represented a practicable virtue, mixed with the frailties and imperfections of human life. I have made my heroine fearful of death, which neither Cassandra nor Cleopatra would have been; and they themselves, I doubt it not, would have outdone romance in that particular...I have made my Melesinda...a woman passionately loving of her

husband, patient of injuries and contempt, and constant in her
kindness to the last; and in this, perhaps, I may have erred, because it is not a virtue much in use. Those Indian wives are loving fools, and may do well to keep themselves in their own country, or at least to keep company with the Arrias and Portias of
old Rome; some of our ladies know better things.

Act 5

Enter a procession of priests, slaves following, and last Melesinda,
in white.

Indamora   : Alas, what means this pomp?

Aureng-zebe: 'Tis the procession of a funeral vow,
Which cruel laws to Indian wives allow,
When fatally they their virtue approve;
Cheerful in flames and martyrs of their love.

Indamora   : Oh my foreboding heart! Th'event I fear.
And see! Sad Melesinda does appear.

Melesinda   : You wrong my love; what grief do I betray?
This is the triumph of my nuptial day.
My better nuptials, which in spite of fate,
Forever join me to my dear Morat.
Now I am pleased, my jealousies are o'er;
He is mine and I can lose him now no more.

Emperor   : Let no false show of fame your reason blind.

Indamora   : You have no right to die; he was not kind.

Melesinda   : Had he been kind I could no love have shown;
Each vulgar virtue would as much have done.
My love was such it needed no return,
But could, though he supplied no fuel, burn.
Rich in itself, like elemental fire,
Whose pureness does no aliment require.
In vain you would bereave me of my lord,
for I will die. Die is too base a word;

I'll seek his breast, and kindling by his side,
Adorned in flames I'll mount a glorious bride.

(*Exit*)

Marianna Starke, *The Widow of Malabar*²

This play, based on a French piece of the same name, was performed in London in the 1790s. In it an unwilling sati is eventually rescued from the pyre by her British paramour—a classic variation of the rescue trope. The prologue makes much of the horror of the widow's fate, but also emphasizes the duty of the British to intervene and use their position in India for social good.

When fate cuts short the Hindoo's thread of life,
One tomb engulfs the husband and the wife:
The widow, warm in youth, must yield her breath,
And self-devoted seek her lord in death:
In gay attire she mounts the awful pile,
Nor dares with tears the horrid rites defile;
Her heaving bosom must repress the sigh,
And learn with stoic apathy to die:
For should she yield to nature's powerful sway,
And not with smiles this Brahmin law obey,
Should she with horror shun the scorching flame,
Eternal infamy awaits her name!
Driven from her caste she wanders on the earth,
Disowned by those to whom she owes her birth;
Life grows a burden which she cannot bear,
And death the only refuge from despair!
Unhappy race, by double chains confined,
Oppressed in body and enslaved in mind;
Ever doomed some tyrant to obey,
The priest's, the despot's or the stranger's prey!
How blessed the natives of this happier land,
Where freedom has long made her glorious stand!
Where neighbouring kingdoms may with envy see
The monarch great because the subjects free!
A nation famed in arms, in arms renown'd,
By laws themselves created only bound;

Who boast what history can seldom prove,
A prince enthroned upon his people's love!
Would Europe's sons, who visit Asia's shore,
Where plundered millions can afford no more,
To nobler ends direct their future aim,
And wipe from India's annals Europe's shame;
Let them, with reason's power subdue the breast,
Inform the erring and relieve the oppressed;
By laws benign a general bliss impart,
And fix an empire in the grateful heart!
There are pursuits more worthy of their care
Than realms obtained by all devouring war.

Note

1   Dryden, J., *Aureng-Zebe* (London: Edward Arnold, 1972).

2   Starke, Mariana, *The Widow of Malabar: A Tragedy in Three Acts* (London: William Lane, 1791).

16

Early Nineteenth-Century Fiction

Alexander's East India Magazine, 'The Suttee'[1]

The following short story, in which a young British officer falls in love with a beautiful widow who he has saved from the funeral pyre, is typical of the romanticized rescue fantasy genre.

Lt. Albert Morrison was a young man of tall stature and exceedingly handsome proportions; his cheek still bloomed with the healthy hues of a northern climate, and his nose was formed according to the purest models of Rome, but even these qualifications did not, perhaps, so much recommend him to the special favour of the fair as the lustre of his fine dark eyes, rich with an expression of manly good nature, and his raven black hair which fell in ringlets over his high forehead. No man practised less those insinuating attentions and unmeaning compliments which have such a magic influence over the soft hearts of maidens from fifteen to forty-five, but even amidst the eternal lispings of fashionable nothings from the exquisites of the regiment, many a tender heart sighed for that manly unadorned form in its careless bearing and disregard for artificial movements. Albert was the idol of the ladies, and happy was she whom he selected for his partner in the dance, although to tell the truth he was but an awkward hand at the quadrille, and would have been much more at home dancing the highland fling with some rustic maiden on the village green. One cold November morning he was out riding with an ensign of the same regiment. They had their swords with them as the area was troubled by dacoits.

After about a mile they heard the sounds of native music, indicating some ceremony, and cantered over to the spot. They found themselves on the banks of the Ganges. A little further on, the shouts of an assembled multitude pealed through the sky. On inquiry they ascertained that a suttee was about to take place, a pile of firewood and various combustibles had already been erected, over which were methodically arranged a couple of heavy billets and some bamboos. Roses and jessamines were scattered over the ground, and several fakirs disposed in attitudes of humility and prayer. Some vented their religious feeling in horrid yells, accompanied by unnatural and disgusting contortions of the body, others viewed the preparations for the sacrifice with immovable apathy. Many minutes had not elapsed when the intended victim was seen slowly egressing from the village, followed by a disorderly crowd, and supported by two lusty young men and an old woman, the brothers and mother of the deceased Brahmin. No symptom of pity or sorrow could be traced in their countenances; on the contrary, they exhibited a wild fanatical expression of savage joy. The victim was dressed in a loose robe of thin white muslin, fancifully decked with flowers which completely concealed her features, her whole person enveloped in its pliant folds, save her right arm which stood partially exposed.

Albert gazed on its elegantly turned symmetry with feelings of extraordinary interest and excitement; he had never seen anything so taperingly beautiful. His romantic heart warmed with an intense emotion, such as he had never before experienced, and he determined to have a nearer view of the interesting object whose arm alone had stirred such a tumult in his bosom. He dismounted and gave his horse to his syce, and with a bold step regardless of all opposition, made good his way to the spot where the young woman stood surrounded by a crowd of fanatical Brahmins. With what mingled feelings did his heart beat when on a nearer view he beheld a face of surpassing loveliness, receiving its expression from eyes of the darkest lustre, now subdued into languid eloquence by overwhelming sorrow. She could not be more than fourteen as her charms were just budding into the rounded beauties of womanhood.

Albert's heart was smitten and he felt he could easily throw his own life away than witness the immolation of that lovely

Hindoo. He used all his eloquence of speech, and looks to dissuade her from the purpose; she answered not, but her eyes gave
expression to the feelings which her tongue dared not utter. It
was evident that she was about to become an unwilling sacrifice
to the interested views of others. Independent of the common
feelings of humanity, there was a degree of romantic glory, quite
congenial to his spirit, in the rescue of a lovely young woman
from so cruel a fate, and he determined to try it at all hazards,
should she show the least symptom of reluctance, and the slightest inclination to prevail herself of his proffered protection. He
fondly hoped that when she reached the pile and witness the
dreadful preparations, her resolution would waver; and all force
he boldly resolved to prevent with his sword, if necessary. With
this gallant intention he stationed himself close to the pile and
ordered his syce to be at hand with his horse.

Her savage executioners now led her on to the combustible
mass—she shrank back with horror, but it was only momentary,
she recovered resolution, and laid herself down by the side of
her deceased husband, deaf to all Albert's offers of protection.
The work of death was now commenced; the heavy billets were
carefully placed over her, and the two brothers employed themselves in securing the unfortunate victim with the two bamboos—
this Albert would not allow, he explained that it was entirely a
ceremony of choice, and called upon the most learned of their
pundits to expound their own law. It would be vain to attempt any
description of the mingled feelings which raged in Albert's bosom when he beheld the fiery faggots being placed under the
combustible mass amidst the simultaneous shouts of assembled
thousands, which fell like a death knell on his heart. He, too, was
a Briton, descended from a race of men renowned in arms, the
passive witness of so cruel a spectacle. 'Twas better to die the
death of a hero than to cast a stain on the name of those who now
mouldered in the dust. Full of this noble resolution he was about
to rush into the pile, through which volumes of smoke now ascended,
determined to rescue her or meet his death in the attempt, when an
agonizing shriek of such piercing shrillness arose from the fiery
mass that for a moment the voice of the assembled multitude sank
into silence; the pile was evidently in motion.

Albert caught a glimpse of her form, struggling with the weight which had been placed over her. The flames had already begun to burst forth, 'twas the work of an instant—he sprung forward with supernatural energy, his bright battle blade in his right hand, gleaming amidst the flames, while with the other he grasped her waist with irresistible strength, cut his way through the paralysed crowd, sprung on his gallant Arab, with his prize firm in his grasp, and ere the astonished Brahmins had recovered from their surprise, he was galloping across the country at a rate which made it hopeless for them to pursue. It was a proud day for Albert; with one hand he supported his half-fainting charge, and with the other reined in his fleet Arab, which galloped on at a rapid pace, as if conscious of the nature of his burden.

It was considered an extraordinary and scandalous sight to see Albert Morrison riding through the military lines in open day, with a beautiful native girl placed before him, for he had always been considered the most exemplary young man in his corps. The ladies considered it a direct insult to themselves, and felt the more offended on the account that most of them had at some time or other conferred on him marks of their especial esteem. Some positively asserted that he was intoxicated, and others, of a very nice sense of honour, considered it absolutely necessary that such conduct should not be overlooked, that justice demanded that he should be brought before a court martial, for conduct disgraceful for an officer and a gentleman, in riding through the lines at nine o'clock in the forenoon, in a state of intoxication, with a female placed before him in the saddle. The voice of scandal, however, was soon stilled by the circulation of facts, and those who made themselves most busy in its propagation, wondered how they could so easily have been led into a belief of what was so directly opposed to Morrison's general principles and conduct.

It was some time before the poor widow recovered from the state of langour, exhaustion, and partial derangements of mind occasioned by the horrors of her late situation. It was not an easy matter to impress upon her mind a perfect confidence of security; at length her eye gradually regained its lustre. Albert watched every symptom of improvement with boundless satisfaction, her spirits recovered their elasticity, and instead of the enfeebled languid being he had first seen her, stupefied with opium, she became as light, as bright, and as playful as Albert could wish, and the charms of her person called back to new life, opening daily into a more interesting maturity, woke new feelings in his bosom, which those alone who have experienced the ecstatic glow of impassioned love can comprehend.

An Assistant, *Calcutta Literary Gazette*

Mrs Phelps, 'The Suttee'—A Poem²

This highly romanticized poem was written for an Oxford poetry competition in 1830, the theme of which was 'Suttee'. It is typical of British evangelical literature on sati at the time, including the usual comparisons between Christian and Hindu morality, an emphasis on the benefits of spreading Christianity, and the requisite rescue—in this case by Bishop Heber himself!

> ...Yet sad the thought, that in this fertile land,
> Where plenty springs spontaneous to the hand,
> Where generous nature yields a full supply,
> Of all to please the taste and charm the eye,
> Where luscious fruits in rich profusion glow,
> And spicy groves and crystal waters flow,
> Where the rich mine displays a dazzling store,
> And heaven with blessings make the cup run o'er.
> Yet here alas! A God is little known,
> And the poor Indian worships wood and stone;
> A willing victim to his priest's control,
> He wounds his body to secure his soul;
> And taught his idol takes delight in blood,
> From his own veins bestows the crimson flood;
> Bears on his head the heat of noontide ray,
> Nor seeks a shelter from the scorching ray;
> Distorts his limbs and crawls on hands and feet
> To visit Juggernaut's imperial seat.
> There wrought to frenzy—happiness he feels,
> To cast his body 'neath the Chariot wheels;
> Nor deems these tortures extreme to win
> An expiation for some deadly sin.
> From such sad scenes the Christian turns his eye,

And bends his inmost thoughts on Calvary;
Beholds his bleeding Saviour on the tree,
And marks his patient suffering agony;
...Dying to save the sinner from his doom,
And to redeem them entering the tomb.

...O could these heathens, now so dark in night,
Receive the glories of the Gospel light!—
Could they behold the sacrifice complete,
And throw their burdens at their Saviour's feet!
Could they but hear the joyful news from far,
And like the Magi see the dazzling star!—
Then would Christian notes of gladness raise,
And Eastern nations join the hymn of praise.

...In God's appointed time the veil shall fall,
And India's sons obey their Father's call;
...Shall raise the suppliant eye, and bend the knee,
Breath forth contrite prayer, and quit idolatry.

As yet far other scenes this land engage,
And superstition vents its deadly rage;
Reigning triumphant, like a magic spell,
It deals horrors worse than tongue can tell.
Mark my sad tale and bless the mighty hand,
Which fixed your birthplace in a Christian land.

Beneath the Peepul's wide extended shade,
In soft luxuriance see Abdallah laid;—
Wafted around him what rich perfumes rise!
What vivid colours charm th'admiring eyes.—
And O! how lovely robed in virgin white
The grand Dhature burst upon the sight;
Her stately flowers expanding far and wide,
Proclaim her Empress, clad in regal pride:
While gay attendants decked in varied hues,
Enchanting odours o'er the plain diffuse;
But hers the richest by far—each sense confess,
And all must own her peerless excellence!

Must own her lovely as a virgin Queen,
And truly formed to grace so fair a scene,
To yield a shade, expand the silken flower,
And waft her perfume o'er Abdallah's bower.

In this cool bower had beauty fixed her seat,
And virtuous Zoe graced the calm retreat;
What tho' her cheeks assumed a brighter glow,
And richer tints than Northern beauties know!
Her graceful form with every clime could vie,
For Zoe's form was perfect symmetry!

...How blessed was Abdallah such a heart to win,
And could we find a mortal free from sin,
Such was his Zoe's pure and spotless nature,
Perfect alike in form and mind and feature.

Oh happy they, the happiest of their kind,
Whom tender love in close affection bind;
...Such was the tender, close endearing tie,
The virtuous love, the perfect harmony,
Which shed lustre o'er Abdallah's hours,
And strewed his path with never fading flowers.
While to increase his bliss and crown his joy,
Close by his side he viewed his darling boy,
And on his Zoe's fond maternal breast,
A smiling girl was tenderly caressed.

...Alas! Poor Zoe, little did she dream
Her happiness was fading like the beam
Of day's declining orb,—which sunk to rest
In streams of glory down the crimson west;
How little did she dread the coming blow,
Which crushed at once her happiness below!
For who could gaze on a scene so fair,
And fancy cruel death was lurking there?

...Poor Abdallah thought the scene so bright,
He lingered careless of the coming night.

Remaining long upon the dewy ground,
A sudden chillness wrapped his limbs around;
Which baffling every art and every care,
Reduced the wretched Zoe to despair:
Who, like a ministering Angel, now
Wipes the cold damp collecting on his brow;
...And as his sufferings hourly increase,
Bends fondly o'er him whispering sounds of peace;
Till, faintly struggling, he resigns his breath,
And her Abdallah sleeps the sleep of death.

Language is weak, and powerless and faint,
The bitter anguish of such woe to paint;
...Stunned by the weight of such a sudden blow,
She sank beneath the pressure of her woe.
...Ere she had felt the luxury of grief,
And ere her soft tears had come to her relief,
Careless of all her widowed agony,
The cold stern Priest demands the dread Suttee.

In India's sultry clime brief space is given,
To weep o'er those whom cruel death has riven:
And while her mind was like a troubled sea,
Which almost doubted the reality
Of the sad change a few short hours had brought,
As yet too dreadful to admit the thought.
Bewildered—stunned—the wretched Wife complies
To share her Husband's funeral obsequies.

Behold her now so lately loved—caressed,
A passive victim for the Suttee dressed.
In all her bridal robes once more attired,
When last put on alas! How much admired,
Then her Abdallah claimed her for his own,
And vowed her beauty might adorn a throne:
...Gay youth was hers—her lover by her side—
And she his beautiful and happy bride.

...And what she was—and what she now possessed—
A change from bliss to perfect wretchedness;

Abdallah gone and she his widowed wife,
Compelled to bid farewell to light and life:
Ere seventeen summers had passed quickly by,
Her race was run, and she alas! must die.
The dread horror of so sad a death,
Blanched her pale cheek and stopped her heaving breath.
Her very heart seemed to change to a stone,
And her brain maddened as such thoughts came on.
And then a sickening sense of all her woe,
Which none can paint and few are doomed to know,
Seemed to congeal her very frame to ice;
And the priests dreaded lest the sacrifice
Should yet escape them and the spirit fly
Before the time appointed her to die.

O had poor Zoe felt in that dread hour,
The aid and comfort of religion's power;
Had her young mind been early taught to know,
What streams of tender love and mercy flow
From Christianity's all-cheering tide,
And a beloved redeemer crucified;
Then might she fearlessly have met the flame,
And died exalting in a Saviour's name.

But no such cheering news had met her ear,
The God she worshipped was a God of fear;
A horrid monster, made by human hands,
And dealing terrors by the Priest's commands;
In blood delighting, and denouncing woe,
And Zoe viewed him as her deadly foe:
For he had robbed her life of all its charms,
And torn her loved Abdallah from her arms:
And now to satisfy his vengeance dire,
She too must die the torturing death of fire!

The time draws nigh alas! there's no retreating,
The cymbals clang, the hollow drums are beating;
While guided by the Priest she moves along,
Almost unconsciously, amidst the throng;

Who raise a horrid din of wild applause,
And drown her sobbing by their brutal noise.

Is there no hope? She has almost reached the spot,
And soon must consummate her dreadful lot!

But what arrests her steps with that dread start,
What sudden anguish rends her broken heart?
...She feels a little hand within her own,
And hears her tender infant's plaintive moan;
'Tis more than human nature can withstand,
The tender pressure of that little hand;
And the poor baby's weak and mournful cry,
Awakes the mother's bitterest agony.
She wildly turns, and on each cherub face
Imprints, in frenzy, one farewell embrace;
While the stern Priests her kind attendance chide,
And bid them take the babes and quickly hide
Them from her gaze; as none may dare to stay
The wretched suttee on her destined way.

On, on they hurry the distracted wife,
Careless of all her woe and mental strife;
Eager alone the horrid sight to view,
The assembled multitude their shouts renew;
And to increase the horror of the sight,
Her little son the deadly pile must light!

Behold her feet that fatal pile ascend,—
O gracious heaven! Has she not one friend!
In all that concourse is there not one hand
To turn aside the death-inflicting brand?
Not one kind heart her agony to share,
And snatch the passive victim from despair?
No! all are anxious to behold her die,
And chide the moments as they linger by.
On that raised pile see every eye is bent,
The wretched Zoe all exhausted—spent—
Gives one last look on her Abdallah dead,

Closes her eyes and droops her aching head.
And now the expected signal must be given,
And music's clangour rends the vaults of heaven.
But hush! What voice is heard amongst the throng?
What sounds of mercy falter on that tongue?
'Tis England's Bishop—Heber's self appears—
And dashing from his cheek the manly tears,
Bids the attendants raise the wretched Wife,
And stops the fiery brand and quells the murderous strife.
Gives to her arms her helpless tender babes,
And from the fire the destined Suttee saves.
May we not hope that when time has mellowed o'er
Her deep regret, and shed its softening power
O'er her sad bosom, mild religion's sway
May guide her future path and point the way
To realms above; and the benignant voice
Which saved her life—may soon direct her choice
To better things,—and teach her how to know
A God from whom all tender mercies flow.
And may the Gospel's light, the glorious news
Which Heber spread, through every heart diffuse;
And like the leaven hidden in the meal,
With silent influence—powerfully steal,
Till scenes like these no more offend the sight,
But pure religion glows with radiant light;
Through this wide land an idol cease to sway,
And heathen darkness brighten into day.

H.L.V. Derozio, 'On the Abolition of Suttee'[3]

In the 'The Fakir of Jungheera' the young Anglo-Indian poet, Henry Louis Vivian Derozio, provided an alternate view of sati in which the heroine is seen worrying as to whether her secret lover will rescue her from the pyre in time. In this poem, he praises Bentinck for intervening to prevent the custom.

ON THE ABOLITION OF SATTEE

'The practice of Sattee, or of burning or burying alive the widows of Hindoos is hereby declared illegal, and punishable by the Criminal Courts'—Regulation XVII, 1829.

Red from his chambers came the morning sun
    And frowned, dark Ganges, on thy fatal shore,
Journeying on high; but when the day was done
    He set in smiles, to rise in blood no more,
Hark! heard ye not? the widow's wail is over;
    No more the flames from impious pyres
                       ascend,
See Mercy, now primeval peace restore,
    While pagans glad the arch ethereal rend,
For India hails at last, her father and her friend.

Back to its cavern ebbs the tide of crime,
    There fettered, locked, and powerless it sleeps;
And History bending o'er the page of time,
    Where many a mournful record still she keeps,
The widowed Hindoo's fate no longer weeps;
    The priestly tyrant's cruel charm is broken,
And to his den alarmed the monster creeps;
    The charm that mars his mystic spell is broken,
O'er all the land 'tis spread he trembles at the to-
ken.

Bentinck, be thine the everlasting mead!
    The heart's full homage still is virtues' claim,
And 'tis the good man's ever honoured deed
    Which gives an immortality to fame;
Transcient and fierce, though dazzling is the flame
    That glory lights upon the wastes of war;
Nations unborn shall venerate thy name,
    A truimph than the conqueror's mightier far,
Thy memory shall be blessed as is the morning star.

He is the friend of man who breaks the seal
    The despot custom sets in deed and thought,
He labours generously for human weal
    Who holds the omnipotence of fear as naught;
The winged mind will not to earth be brought,
    'Twill sink to clay if it imprisoned be;
For 'tis with high immortal longings fraught,

And these are dimmed or quenched eternally,
Until it feels the hand that sets its pinions free.

And woman hath endured, and still endures
  Wrong, which her weakness and her woes should
                                              shield,
The slave and victim of the treacherous lures
  Which wily arts, to man, the tyrant yield:
And *here* the sight of star, or flower, or field,
  Or bird that journeys through the sunny air,
Or social bliss from woman has been sealed,
  To her, the sky is dark the earth is bare,
And Heaven's most hallowed breath pronounced
                                      forbidden fare.

Nurtured in darkness, born to many woes
  Words, the mind's instrument but ill-supplied,
Delight, even as a name she scarcely knows,
  And while an infant sold to be a bride,
To be a mother, her exalted pride,
  And yet not her's a mother's sigh or smile
Oft doomed in youth, to stern the icy tide
  Of rude neglect, caused by some wonton's wile
And forced at last to grace her lord's funeral pile.

Daughters of Europe! by our Ganges side
  Which wept and murmured as it flowed along
Have wives, yet virgins, nay, yet infants died,
  While priestly fiends have yelled a dismal song
'Mid deafening clamours of the drum and gong
  And mothers on their pyres have seen, the hands
Which clung around them when those hands were
                                              young
  Lighting around them such unholy brands
As demons kindle when they rave through hell in
  bands.

But with prophetic ken, dispelling fears
  Which haunt the mind that dwells on nature's plan

The Bard beholds through mists of coming years
A rising spirit speaking peace to man,
The storm is passing, and the Rainbow's span
Stretcheth from North to South: the ebon car
Of darkness rolls away: the breezes fan
The infant down, and morning's herald star
Comes trembling into day: O! can the Sun be far?

INDIA.

NOTE

[1] 'The Suttee', from *Alexander's East India Magazine*, vol. 3, January–June 1832.

[2] Mrs Phelps, 'The Suttee'—A Poem (Thame: H. Bradford, 1831).

[3] Derozio, H.L.V., 'On the Abolition of Suttee', in *Poetic Works of H.L.V. Derozio*, vol. 1, B.B. Shah (ed.) (Calcutta: Santo, 1907).

17

Raj Fiction

Rudyard Kipling, 'The Last Suttee'[1]

Kipling, like Verne and Kaye, sets his poem in the Princely States, reflecting British ideas about the 'heroic' tradition of the Rajput sati, rather than reproducing the 'victim' image, which dominated representations of sati in Bengal.

Not many years ago a King died in one of the Rajpoot States. His wives, disregarding the orders of the English against Suttee, would have broken out of the palace had not the gates been barred. But one of them, disguised as the King's favourite dancing-girl, passed through the line of guards and reached the pyre. There, her courage failing, she prayed her cousin, a baron of the court, to kill her. This he did, not knowing who she was.

> Udai Chand lay sick to death
> In his hold by Gungra hill.
> All night we heard the death-gongs ring
> For the soul of the dying Rajpoot King,
> All night beat up from the women's wing
> A cry that we could not still.
>
> All night the barons came and went,
> The lords of the outer guard:
> All night the cressets glimmered pale
> On Ulwar sabre and Tonk jezail,
> Mewar headstall and Marwar mail,
> That clinked in the palace yard.

In the Golden room on the palace roof
All night he fought for air:
And there was sobbing behind the screen,
Rustle and whisper of women unseen,
And the hungry eyes of the Boondi Queen
On the death she might not share.

He passed at dawn-the death-fire leaped
From ridge to river-head,
From the Malwa plains to the Abu scars:
And wail upon wail went up to the stars
Behind the grim zenana-bars,
When they knew that the King was dead.

The dumb priest knelt to tie his mouth
And robe him for the pyre.
The Boondi Queen beneath us cried:
'See, now, that we die as our mothers died
In the bridal-bed by our master's side!'
Out, women!—to the fire!'

We drove the great gates home apace:
White hands were on the sill:
But ere the rush of the unseen feet
Had reached the turn to the open street,
The bars shot down, the guard-drum beat—
We held the dovecot still.

A face looked down in the gathering day,
And laughing spoke from the wall:
'Ohe', they mourn here: let me by—
Azizun, the Lucknow nautch-girl, I!
When the house is rotten, the rats must fly,
And I seek another thrall.

'For I ruled the King as ne'er did Queen,—
Tonight the Queens rule me!
Guard them safely, but let me go,
Or, ever they pay the debt they owe
In scourge and torture!' She leaped below,
And the grim guard watched her flee.

They knew that the King had spent his soul
On a North-bred dancing-girl:
That he prayed to a flat-nosed Lucknow god,
And kissed the ground where her feet had trod,
And doomed to death at her drunken nod,
And swore by her lightest curl.

We bore the King to his fathers' place,
Where the tombs of the Sun-born stand:
Where the gray apes swing, and the peacocks preen
On fretted pillar and jewelled screen,
And the wild boar couch in the house of the Queen
On the drift of the desert sand.

The herald read his titles forth,
We set the logs aglow:
'Friend of the English, free from fear,
Baron of Luni to Jeysulmeer,
Lord of the Desert of Bikaneer,
King of the Jungle,—go!'

All night the red flame stabbed the sky
With wavering wind-tossed spears:
And out of a shattered temple crept
A woman who veiled her head and wept,
And called on the King—but the great King slept,
And turned not for her tears.

Small thought had he to mark the strife—
Cold fear with hot desire—
When thrice she leaped from the leaping flame,
And thrice she beat her breast for shame,
And thrice like a wounded dove she came
And moaned about the fire.

One watched, a bow-shot from the blaze,
The silent streets between,
Who had stood by the King in sport and fray,
To blade in ambush or boar at bay,
And he was a baron old and gray,
And kin to the Boondi Queen.

He said: 'O shameless, put aside
The veil upon thy brow!
Who held the King and all his land
To the wanton will of a harlot's hand!
Will the white ash rise from the blistered brand?
Stoop down, and call him now!'

Then she: 'By the faith of my tarnished soul,
All things I did not well,
I had hoped to clear ere the fire died,
And lay me down by my master's side
To rule in Heaven his only bride,
While the others howl in Hell.

'But I have felt the fire's breath,
And hard it is to die!
Yet if I may pray a Rajpoot lord
To sully the steel of a Thakur's sword
With base-born blood of a trade abhorred,'—
And the Thakur answered, 'Ay.'

He drew and struck: the straight blade drank
The life beneath the breast.
'I had looked for the Queen to face the flame,
But the harlot dies for the Rajpoot dame—
Sister of mine, pass, free from shame,
Pass with thy King to rest!'

The black log crashed above the white:
The little flames and lean,
Red as slaughter and blue as steel,
That whistled and fluttered from head to heel,
Leaped up anew, for they found their meal
On the heart of—the Boondi Queen!

Jules Verne, *Around the World in Eighty Days*[2]

Although written more than fifty years after the abolition of sati in British India, the subcontinental portion of Phileas Fogg's journey included the requisite rescue of a sati. The action occurs in Bundelkhund, a region made

up of petty Indian states. By setting it here Verne can include an immolation—
by this point an iconic image of Indian society in the British imagination—
without undermining the effectiveness of British legislation on the subject.
Sati had in fact been prohibited by the rulers of Bundelkhund since 1847.

At two o'clock the guide entered a thick forest which extended
several miles; he preferred to travel under cover of the woods.
They had not as yet had any unpleasant encounters, and the journey seemed on the point of being successfully accomplished,
when the elephant, becoming restless, suddenly stopped.

It was then four o'clock.

'What's the matter?' asked Sir Francis, putting out his head.

'I don't know, officer,' replied the Parsee, listening attentively
to a confused murmur which came through the thick branches.

The murmur soon became more distinct; it now seemed like a
distant concert of human voices accompanied by brass instruments.
Passepartout was all eyes and ears. Mr Fogg patiently waited
without a word. The Parsee jumped to the ground, fastened the
elephant to a tree, and plunged into the thicket.

He soon returned, saying: 'A procession of Brahmins is coming
this way. We must prevent their seeing us, if possible.'

The guide unloosed the elephant and led him into a thicket, at
the same time asking the travellers not to stir. He held himself
ready to bestride the animal at a moment's notice, should flight
become necessary; but he evidently thought that the procession
of the faithful would pass without perceiving them amid the thick
foliage, in which they were wholly concealed.

The discordant tones of the voices and instruments drew nearer,
and now droning songs mingled with the sound of the tambourines and cymbals. The head of the procession soon appeared
beneath the trees, a hundred paces away; and the strange figures
who performed the religious ceremony were easily distinguished
through the branches. First came the priests, with mitres on their
heads, and clothed in long lace robes. They were surrounded by
men, women, and children, who sang a kind of lugubrious psalm,
interrupted at regular intervals by the tambourines and cymbals;
while behind them was drawn a car with large wheels, the spokes
of which represented serpents entwined with each other. Upon
the car, which was drawn by four richly caparisoned zebus, stood

a hideous statue with four arms, the body coloured a dull red, with haggard eyes, dishevelled hair, protruding tongue, and lips tinted with betel. It stood upright upon the figure of a prostrate and headless giant.

Sir Francis, recognizing the statue, whispered, 'The goddess Kali; the goddess of love and death.'

'Of death, perhaps,' muttered back Passepartout, 'but of love— that ugly old hag? Never!'

The Parsee made a motion to keep silence.

A group of old fakirs were capering and making a wild ado round the statue; these were striped with ochre, and covered with cuts whence their blood issued drop by drop—stupid fanatics, who, in the great Indian ceremonies, still throw themselves under the wheels of Juggernaut. Some Brahmins, clad in all the sumptuousness of Oriental apparel, and leading a woman who faltered at every step, followed. This woman was young, and as fair as a European. Her head and neck, shoulders, ears, arms, hands, and toes were loaded down with jewels and gems with bracelets, earrings, and rings; while a tunic bordered with gold, and covered with a light muslin robe, betrayed the outline of her form.

The guards who followed the young woman presented a violent contrast to her, armed as they were with naked sabres hung at their waists, and long damascened pistols, and bearing a corpse on a palanquin. It was the body of an old man, gorgeously arrayed in the habiliments of a rajah, wearing, as in life, a turban embroidered with pearls, a robe of tissue of silk and gold, a scarf of cashmere sewed with diamonds, and the magnificent weapons of a Hindoo prince. Next came the musicians and a rearguard of capering fakirs, whose cries sometimes drowned the noise of the instruments; these closed the procession.

Sir Francis watched the procession with a sad countenance, and, turning to the guide, said, 'A suttee.'

The Parsee nodded, and put his finger to his lips. The procession slowly wound under the trees, and soon its last ranks disappeared in the depths of the wood. The songs gradually died away; occasionally cries were heard in the distance, until at last all was silence again.

Phileas Fogg had heard what Sir Francis said, and, as soon as the procession had disappeared, asked: 'What is a suttee?'

'A suttee,' returned the general, 'is a human sacrifice, but a voluntary one. The woman you have just seen will be burned to-morrow at the dawn of day.'

'Oh, the scoundrels!' cried Passepartout, who could not repress his indignation.

'And the corpse?' asked Mr Fogg.

'Is that of the prince, her husband,' said the guide, 'an independent rajah of Bundelcund.'

'Is it possible,' resumed Phileas Fogg, his voice betraying not the least emotion, 'that these barbarous customs still exist in India, and that the English have been unable to put a stop to them?'

'These sacrifices do not occur in the larger portion of India,' replied Sir Francis, 'but we have no power over these savage territories, and especially here in Bundelcund. The whole district north of the Vindhias is the theatre of incessant murders and pillage.'

'The poor wretch!' exclaimed Passepartout, 'to be burned alive!'

'Yes,' returned Sir Francis, 'burned alive. And, if she were not, you cannot conceive what treatment she would be obliged to submit to from her relatives. They would shave off her hair, feed her on a scanty allowance of rice, treat her with contempt; she would be looked upon as an unclean creature, and would die in some corner, like a scurvy dog. The prospect of so frightful an existence drives these poor creatures to the sacrifice much more than love or religious fanaticism. Sometimes, however, the sacrifice is really voluntary, and it requires the active interference of the government to prevent it. Several years ago, when I was living at Bombay, a young widow asked permission of the governor to be burned along with her husband's body; but, as you may imagine, he refused. The woman left the town, took refuge with an independent rajah, and there carried out her self-devoted purpose.'

While Sir Francis was speaking, the guide shook his head several times, and now said: 'The sacrifice which will take place tomorrow at dawn is not a voluntary one.'

'How do you know?'

'Everybody knows about this affair in Bundelcund.'

'But the wretched creature did not seem to be making any resistance,' observed Sir Francis.

'That was because they had intoxicated her with fumes of hemp and opium.'

'But where are they taking her?'

'To the pagoda of Pillaji, two miles from here; she will pass the night there.'

'And the sacrifice will take place—'

'Tomorrow, at the first light of dawn.'

The guide now led the elephant out of the thicket, and leaped upon his neck.

Just at the moment that he was about to urge Kiouni forward with a peculiar whistle, Mr Fogg stopped him, and, turning to Sir Francis Cromarty, said, 'Suppose, we save this woman.'

'Save the woman, Mr Fogg!'

'I have yet twelve hours to spare; I can devote them to that.'

'Why, you are a man of heart!'

'Sometimes,' replied Phileas Fogg, quietly; 'when I have the time.'

IN WHICH PASSEPARTOUT RECEIVES A NEW PROOF THAT FORTUNE FAVOURS THE BRAVE

The project was a bold one, full of difficulty, perhaps impracticable. Mr Fogg was going to risk life, or at least liberty, and therefore the success of his tour. But he did not hesitate, and he found in Sir Francis Cromarty an enthusiastic ally. As for Passepartout, he was ready for anything that might be proposed. His master's idea charmed him; he perceived a heart, a soul, under that icy exterior. He began to love Phileas Fogg.

There remained the guide: what course would he adopt? Would he not take part with the Indians? In default of his assistance, it was necessary to be assured of his neutrality.

Sir Francis frankly put the question to him.

'Officers,' replied the guide, 'I am a Parsee, and this woman is a Parsee. Command me as you will.'

'Excellent!' said Mr. Fogg.

'However,' resumed the guide, 'it is certain, not only that we shall risk our lives, but horrible tortures, if we are taken.'

'That is foreseen,' replied Mr Fogg. 'I think we must wait till night before acting.'

'I think so,' said the guide.

The worthy Indian then gave some account of the victim, who, he said, was a celebrated beauty of the Parsee race, and the daughter of a wealthy Bombay merchant. She had received a thoroughly English education in that city, and, from her manners and intelligence, would be thought a European. Her name was Aouda. Left an orphan, she was married against her will to the old rajah of Bundelcund; and, knowing the fate that awaited her, she escaped, was retaken, and devoted by the rajah's relatives, who had an interest in her death, to the sacrifice from which it seemed she could not escape.

The Parsee's narrative only confirmed Mr Fogg and his companions in their generous design. It was decided that the guide should direct the elephant towards the pagoda of Pillaji, which he accordingly approached as quickly as possible. They halted, half an hour afterwards, in a copse, some five hundred feet from the pagoda, where they were well concealed; but they could hear the groans and cries of the fakirs distinctly.

They then discussed the means of getting at the victim. The guide was familiar with the pagoda of Pillaji, in which, as he declared, the young woman was imprisoned. Could they enter any of its doors while the whole party of Indians was plunged in a drunken sleep, or was it safer to attempt to make a hole in the walls? This could only be determined at the moment and the place themselves; but it was certain that the abduction must be made that night, and not when, at break of day, the victim was led to her funeral pyre. Then no human intervention could save her.

As soon as night fell, about six o'clock, they decided to make a reconnaissance around the pagoda. The cries of the fakirs were just ceasing; the Indians were in the act of plunging themselves into the drunkenness caused by liquid opium mingled with hemp, and it might be possible to slip between them to the temple itself.

The Parsee, leading the others, noiselessly crept through the wood, and in ten minutes they found themselves on the banks of a small stream, whence, by the light of the rosin torches, they perceived a pyre of wood, on the top of which lay the embalmed body of the rajah, which was to be burned with his wife. The pagoda, whose minarets loomed above the trees in the deepening dusk, stood a hundred steps away.

'Come!' whispered the guide.

He slipped more cautiously than ever through the brush, followed by his companions; the silence around was only broken by the low murmuring of the wind among the branches. Soon the Parsee stopped on the borders of the glade, which was lit up by the torches. The ground was covered by groups of the Indians, motionless in their drunken sleep; it seemed a battlefield strewn with the dead. Men, women, and children lay together. In the background, among the trees, the pagoda of Pillaji loomed distinctly. Much to the guide's disappointment, the guards of the rajah, lighted by torches, were watching at the doors and marching to and fro with naked sabres; probably the priests, too, were watching within.

The Parsee, now convinced that it was impossible to force an entrance to the temple, advanced no farther, but led his companions back again. Phileas Fogg and Sir Francis Cromarty also saw that nothing could be attempted in that direction. They stopped, and engaged in a whispered colloquy.

'It is only eight now,' said the brigadier, 'and these guards may also go to sleep.'

'It is not impossible,' returned the Parsee.

They lay down at the foot of a tree, and waited.

The time seemed long; the guide ever and anon left them to take an observation on the edge of the wood, but the guards watched steadily by the glare of the torches, and a dim light crept through the windows of the pagoda.

They waited till midnight; but no change took place among the guards, and it became apparent that their yielding to sleep could not be counted on. The other plan must be carried out; an opening in the walls of the pagoda must be made. It remained to ascertain whether the priests were watching by the side of their victim as assiduously as were the soldiers at the door.

After a last consultation, the guide announced that he was ready for the attempt, and advanced, followed by the others. They took a roundabout way, so as to get at the pagoda on the rear. They reached the walls about half-past twelve, without having met anyone; here there was no guard, nor were there either windows or doors. The night was dark. The moon, on the wane, scarcely left the horizon, and was covered with heavy clouds; the height of the trees deepened the darkness.

It was not enough to reach the walls; an opening in them must be accomplished, and to attain this purpose the party only had their pocket-knives. Happily the temple walls were built of brick and wood, which could be penetrated with little difficulty; after one brick had been taken out, the rest would yield easily.

They set noiselessly to work, and the Parsee on one side and Passepartout on the other began to loosen the bricks so as to make an aperture two feet wide. They were getting on rapidly, when suddenly a cry was heard in the interior of the temple, followed almost instantly by other cries replying from the outside. Passepartout and the guide stopped. Had they been heard? Was the alarm being given? Common prudence urged them to retire, and they did so, followed by Phileas Fogg and Sir Francis. They again hid themselves in the wood, and waited till the disturbance, whatever it might be, ceased, holding themselves ready to resume their attempt without delay. But, awkwardly enough, the guards now appeared at the rear of the temple, and there installed themselves, in readiness to prevent a surprise.

It would be difficult to describe the disappointment of the party, thus interrupted in their work. They could not now reach the victim; how, then, could they save her? Sir Francis shook his fists, Passepartout was beside himself, and the guide gnashed his teeth with rage. The tranquil Fogg waited, without betraying any emotion.

'We have nothing to do but to go away,' whispered Sir Francis.

'Nothing but to go away,' echoed the guide.

'Stop,' said Fogg. 'I am only due at Allahabad tomorrow before noon.'

'But what can you hope to do?' asked Sir Francis. 'In a few hours it will be daylight, and—'

'The chance which now seems lost may present itself at the last moment.'

Sir Francis would have liked to read Phileas Fogg's eyes. What was this cool Englishman thinking of? Was he planning to make a rush for the young woman at the very moment of the sacrifice, and boldly snatch her from her executioners?

This would be utter folly, and it was hard to admit that Fogg was such a fool. Sir Francis consented, however, to remain to the end of this terrible drama. The guide led them to the rear of the glade, where they were able to observe the sleeping groups.

Meanwhile Passepartout, who had perched himself on the lower branches of a tree, was resolving an idea which had at first struck him like a flash, and which was now firmly lodged in his brain. He had commenced by saying to himself, 'What folly!' and then he repeated, 'Why not, after all? It's a chance, perhaps the only one; and with such sots!' Thinking thus, he slipped, with the suppleness of a serpent, to the lowest branches, the ends of which bent almost to the ground.

The hours passed, and the lighter shades now announced the approach of day, though it was not yet light. This was the moment. The slumbering multitude became animated, the tambourines sounded, songs and cries arose; the hour of the sacrifice had come. The doors of the pagoda swung open, and a bright light escaped from its interior, in the midst of which Mr Fogg and Sir Francis espied the victim. She seemed, having shaken off the stupor of intoxication, to be striving to escape from her executioner. Sir Francis's heart throbbed; and, convulsively seizing Mr Fogg's hand, found in it an open knife. Just at this moment the crowd began to move. The young woman had again fallen into a stupor caused by the fumes of hemp, and passed among the fakirs, who escorted her with their wild, religious cries.

Phileas Fogg and his companions, mingling in the rear ranks of the crowd, followed; and in two minutes they reached the banks of the stream, and stopped fifty paces from the pyre, upon which still lay the rajah's corpse. In the semi-obscurity they saw the victim, quite senseless, stretched out beside her husband's body. Then a torch was brought, and the wood, heavily soaked with oil, instantly took fire.

At this moment Sir Francis and the guide seized Phileas Fogg, who, in an instant of mad generosity, was about to rush upon the pyre. But he had quickly pushed them aside, when the whole scene suddenly changed. A cry of terror arose. The whole multitude prostrated themselves, terror-stricken, on the ground.

The old rajah was not dead, then, since he rose of a sudden, like a spectre, took up his wife in his arms, and descended from the pyre in the midst of the clouds of smoke, which only heightened his ghostly appearance.

Fakirs and soldiers and priests, seized with instant terror, lay there, with their faces on the ground, not daring to lift their eyes and behold such a prodigy.

The inanimate victim was borne along by the vigorous arms which supported her, and which she did not seem in the least to burden. Mr Fogg and Sir Francis stood erect, the Parsee bowed his head, and Passepartout was, no doubt, scarcely less stupefied.

The resuscitated rajah approached Sir Francis and Mr Fogg, and, in an abrupt tone, said, 'Let us be off!'

It was Passepartout himself, who had slipped upon the pyre in the midst of the smoke and, profiting by the still overhanging darkness, had delivered the young woman from death! It was Passepartout who, playing his part with a happy audacity, had passed through the crowd amid the general terror.

A moment after all four of the party had disappeared in the woods, and the elephant was bearing them away at a rapid pace. But the cries and noise, and a ball which whizzed through Phileas Fogg's hat, apprised them that the trick had been discovered.

The old rajah's body, indeed, now appeared upon the burning pyre; and the priests, recovered from their terror, perceived that an abduction had taken place. They hastened into the forest, followed by the soldiers, who fired a volley after the fugitives; but the latter rapidly increased the distance between them, and ere long found themselves beyond the reach of the bullets and arrows.

M.M. Kaye, *The Far Pavilions*[3]

This account of a sati in a fictional Indian state from Kaye's well-known novel of 1963 displays all the hallmarks of the author's imperialist standpoint, but does provide some interesting perspectives on the issue of sati. In this extract, the hero is prevailed upon to shoot the intended sati before the flames reach her, but is later seen agonizing over whether by sparing her from pain he has also deprived her of sainthood.

'Well, come on,' said Ash, the curtness of his voice betraying the extent of his inner tensions. 'We cannot afford to wait. The head of the procession will be here any moment now and raising enough noise to cover any moaning these creatures in here will make. Besides, we must be well clear of the valley before dark, and the later we leave the sooner someone is going to come in here and find the Rani gone. We must go at once.'

But still no one moved, and he glanced quickly from one face to the next, and was baffled by the mixture of exasperation, embarrassment and unease that he saw there: and the fact that they were not looking at him, but at Anjuli. He turned swiftly to follow the direction of their gaze, and saw that her back was still towards them and that she too had not moved. She could not have avoided hearing those last words he had spoken, for he had not lowered his voice. Yet she had not even turned her head.

He said sharply: 'What is it? What is the matter?'

His question had been addressed to Anjuli rather than to the three men, but it was Sarji who answered it:

'The Rani-Sahiba will not leave,' said Sarji, exasperated. 'We had decided that if our plan succeeded, the Hakim-Sahib and Manilal would take her away as soon as she had donned the disguise, leaving me to find you and follow after them. That would have been best for us all, and at first she agreed to it. But then suddenly she said she must wait and see her sister become suttee, and that she would not leave before then. See if you can make her change her mind. We cannot—though the gods know we have tried hard enough.'

Anger blazed up in Ash, and heedless of the watching eyes, he strode across the room, and grasping Anjuli's shoulders, jerked her round to face him:

'Is this true?'

The harshness in his voice was only a small measure of the fury that possessed him, and when she did not answer he shook her savagely: *'Answer me!'*

'She...Shushila...does not understand,' whispered Anjuli, her eyes still frozen with horror. 'She does not realize what...what it will be like. And when she does—'

'Shushila!' Ash spat out the name as though it were an obscenity. 'Always Shushila—and selfish to the end. I suppose she made you promise to do this? She would! Oh, I know she saved you from burning with her, but if she'd really wanted to repay you for all you have done for her, she could have saved you from reprisals at the hands of the Diwan by having you smuggled out of the state, instead of begging you to come here and watch her die.'

'You don't understand,' whispered Anjuli numbly.

'Oh, yes I do. That's where you are wrong. I understand only too well. You are still hypnotized by that selfish, hysterical little egotist, and you are perfectly prepared to jeopardize your chances of escaping from Bhithor and a horrible form of mutilation—and risk all our lives into the bargain, Gobind's, Sarji's, Manilal's and my own, just so that you can carry out your darling little sister's last wishes and watch her commit suicide. Well, I don't care what she made you promise. You are not keeping it. You are going to leave now if I have to carry you.'

His rage was real; yet even as he spoke, a part of his brain was saying, 'This is Juli, whom I love more than anything else in the world, and whom I was afraid I should never see again. She is here at last—and all I can do is to be angry with her....' It didn't make sense. But then nor did his threat to carry her, for if anything were to draw attention to them, that would. He could not do it, and she would have to walk; and to go with them willingly. There was no other way. But if she would not...?

The funeral cortège must be very near by new. The discordant braying of the conches and the shouts of '*Khaman Kher!*' and '*Haribol!*' were growing louder every minute, and already isolated voices in the crowd below had begun to take up the cries.

Anjuli turned her head to listen, and the movement was so slow and vague that Ash recognized suddenly that in her present state of shock, his anger had not reached her. He drew a long breath and steadied himself, and his hands on her shoulders relaxed to tenderness. He said gently, coaxing her as though she were a child: 'Don't you see, dear, as long as Shu-shu thinks you are here, watching her and praying for her, she will be satisfied. Listen to me, Juli. She will never know that you are not, for though you and I can see out through this *chik*, no one out there can see us, so you cannot even signal to her. And if you called out to her, she could not possibly hear you.'

'Yes, I know, But....'

'Juli, all you can do is to hurt yourself cruelly by watching a sight that may haunt you for the rest of your life; and that is not going to help her.'

'Yes, I know...but you could. *You* could help her.'

'I? No, dear. There is nothing that I or any of us can do for her now. I'm sorry, Juli, but that is the truth and you must face it.'

'It isn't. It isn't true.' Anjuli's hands came up to his wrists, and her eyes were no longer frozen but wide and imploring, and at last he saw her face, for the turban-end had become loose when he shook her, and now it fell down about her throat.

The change in that face was like a knife in Ash's heart, because it was terribly altered—more so than he could have dreamed possible. The flesh had wasted from it leaving it thin and drawn and desperate, and as drained of colour as though she had spent the last two years penned up in a dungeon where no gleam of light ever penetrated. There were lines and deep hollows in it that had not been there before, and the dark shadows that circled her eyes owed nothing to the artful use of *kohl* or antimony, but told of fear and intolerable strain; and tears—an ocean of tears...

There were tears in her eyes now, and in her breathless, pleading voice, and Ash would have given anything in the world to take her in his arms and kiss them away. But he knew that he must not.

'I *would* have left,' sobbed Anjuli. 'I would have gone at once with your friends, for I could not bear to see what I had been brought here to see, and had they not come I would have shut my eyes and ears to it. But then they—the Hakim-Sahib and your friend—told me why you were not with them, and what you had meant to do for me so that I should not burn to death but die quickly and without pain. You can do that for her.'

Ash took a quick step back and would have snatched his hands away, but now it was Anjuli who held him by the wrists and would not let him go.

'Please—*please*, Ashok! It is not much to ask only that you will do for her what you would have done for me. She could never endure pain, and when...when the flames...I cannot bear to think of it. You can save her from that, and then I will go with you gladly—gladly.'

Her voice broke on the word and Ash said huskily: 'You don't know what you are asking. It isn't as easy as that. It would have been different with you, because—because I had meant to go with you; and Sarji and Gobind and Manilal would all have got safely away, for they would have been a long way from here when our time came. But now it would mean that we would all be here; and if the shot were heard and anyone saw where it had come from, we should all die a far worse death than Shushila's.'

'But it will not be heard. Not above all that noise outside. And who will be looking this way? No one—no one, I tell you. Do this for me. On my knees, I beg of you—'

She let go his wrists, and before he could prevent it she was at his feet with the orange and scarlet turban that she wore touching the ground. Ash bent quickly and pulled her upright, and Sarji, from behind them, said tersely: 'Let her have her way. We cannot carry her, so if she will not come with us unless you do as she asks, you have no choice.'

'None,' agreed Ash. 'Very well, since I must, I will do it. But only if you four will go now. I will follow later, when it is done, and meet you in the valley.'

'No!' There was pure panic in Anjuli's voice, and she brushed past him and addressed Gobind, who averted his eyes from her unveiled face: 'Hakim-Sahib, tell him that he must not stay here alone—it is madness. There would be no one to watch for other men who may come up here, or help to overpower them as you three did to these others. Tell him we must stay together.'

Gobind was silent for a moment. Then he nodded, though with obvious reluctance, and said to Ash: 'I fear that the Rani-Sahiba is right. We must stay together, for one man alone, looking out through the *chik* into the sunlight and choosing his moment, could not guard his back or listen for steps on the stair at the same time.'

Sarji and Manilal murmured agreement, and Ash shrugged and capitulated. It was, after all, the least he could do for poor little Shu-shu, whom he had brought from her home in the north to this remote and medieval backwater among the arid hills and scorching sands of Rajputana, and handed over to an evil and dissolute husband whose unlamented end had proved to be her death-warrant. And perhaps the least that Juli too could do for her, because although it was only Shu-shu's hysterical refusal to be parted from her half-sister that had brought her to this pass, at the end the little Rani had done what she could to make amends. But for her intervention, Juli would even now be out there in the dust and the glare, walking behind her husband's bier towards the moment when a bullet from her lover's revolver would give her a swift and merciful death: and if he had been prepared to do that for Juli, it was not fair to refuse the same mercy to her little sister....Yet the very idea of doing so appalled him.

Because he loved Juli—because he loved her more than life and because she was so much a part of him that without her life would have no meaning he could have shot her without a tremor, and never felt that her blood was upon his head; but to put a bullet through Shushila's head was a very different matter, because pity, however strong, did not provide the terrible incentive that love had done. And then, too, his own life would not be involved. The next bullet would not be for himself, and that alone would make him feel like a murderer—or at best, an executioner, which was absurd when he knew that Juli would have faced the flames with far less terror and endured the pain with more fortitude than poor Shu-shu would ever do, and yet he had resolved to save her from that agony...and was now sickened by the thought of doing the same for Shu-shu.

Sarji broke in on the confusion of his thoughts by remarking in a matter-of-fact voice that the range would be greater from up here than it had been from the edge of the terrace below, and that as Ash would be aiming downwards, and from at least twelve to fifteen feet higher, it was not going to be easy. He might have been discussing a difficult shot from a *machan* on one of their hunting trips in the Gir Forest, and strangely enough it seemed to take some of the horror out of this supremely horrible situation. For he was talking sense.

If the thing must be done, it must be done well; and at the last possible moment, so that it might be thought that Shushila, having taken her place on the pyre, had fainted. To bungle it would be a disaster, not only for Shushila, but for them all; because though there was every chance that the crack of a single shot would be lost in the noise of the crowd, a second or third could not fail to attract attention, or to pin-point the spot from where it had been fired.

'Do you think you can do it?' asked Sarji, coming to stand beside him.

'I must. I can't afford not to. Have you a knife?'

'You mean for the *chik*. No, but I can cut you a gap in it with this thing—' Sarji set to work with the short spear that all members of the Rana's bodyguard carried, and sliced a small oblong out of the split cane. 'There. That should serve. I do not think the cane would deflect a shot, but it might; and there is no need to take chances.'

He watched Ash take out the service revolver and sight along the barrel, and said in an undertone: 'It is all of forty paces. I have never handled one of those things. Will it reach as far?'

'Yes. But I don't know how accurately. It was never intended for such distances, and I—' He swung round abruptly: 'It's no good, Sarji. I daren't risk it from here. I shall have to get closer. Listen, if I go down there again, will you and the others—Yes, that's it. Why didn't we think of it before? We will all leave now, at once, and when we reach the terrace you three can go on ahead with the Rani-Sahiba, and I will get back to my place near the parapet and—'

Sarji cut brusquely across the sentence: 'You could not get there. The crowds are too thick. It was all I could do to get to you before; and even wearing this livery they would never make room for you now. Besides, it is too late. Listen—they come.'

The conches sounded again. But now the mournful and discordant bray was deafeningly loud, while the roar that followed it came from the crowd lining the last short stretch of pathway that lay within the grove itself. In another minute or so the funeral cortège would be here, and there was no longer time to make for the terrace and try to force a way to the front of the close-packed and half-hysterical multitude that thronged it. It was too late for that.

The crowds on the ground below were swaying backwards and forwards as a flood-tide surges between the supports of a pier, pushing, jostling, craning to see over the heads of those in front, or striving to dodge the indiscriminate blows of men who laid about them with *lathis* in order to keep a way clear for the slow-moving procession. And now the advance guard were emerging from the tree shadows into the golden blaze of the afternoon sun, a phalanx of shaven-headed Brahmins from the city's temples, clad in white loin-cloths, with ropes of *tulsi* beads adorning their naked chests and the trident mark that is the fork of Vishnu splashed upon their foreheads.

The leaders blew on conches while the rear rank whirled strips of brass bells above the heads of those who walked between, and behind these came a motley company of other holy men, a score or more of them: saints, sadhus and ascetics, jangling bells and chanting; naked and ash-smeared or soberly dressed in flowing robes of saffron or orange, dull red or white; some with their heads shaved and others whose matted hair and beards, having never been cut, reached half-way to their knees. As wild a crew as Ash had ever seen, they had gathered here like kites who can see death from a great distance away, converging together from every corner of the State to attend the suttee. Behind them came the bier, borne high above the crowd and rocking and dipping to the pace of its bearers like a boat on a choppy sea.

The body that it bore was swathed in white and heaped about with garlands, and Ash was astonished to see how small it looked. The Rana had not been a big man, but then he had always been magnificently dressed and glittering with jewels, and always the centre of a subservient court; all of which had tended to make him seem a good deal larger than he was. But the spare, white-shrouded corpse on the bier looked no larger than an under-nourished child of ten. An insignificant object; and a very lonely one, for it was not the focus of the crowd's attention. They had not come here to see a dead man, but a still living woman. And now at last she was here, walking behind the bier; and at the sight of her, pandemonium broke loose, until even the solid fabric of the *chattri* seemed to tremble at the impact of that roar of sound.

Ash had not seen her at first. His gaze had been fixed on the shrunken thing that had once been his enemy. But a movement near him made him turn his head and he saw that Anjuli had come to stand beside him, and that she was staring through the *chik* with an expression of shrinking horror, as though she could not bear to look and yet could not keep herself from looking. And following the direction of that agonized gaze, he saw Shushila. Not the Shushila he had expected to see—bowed, weeping and half-crazed by terror, but a queen...a Rani of Bhithor.

Had he been asked, Ash would have insisted that Shu-shu would never be able to walk to burning-ground unassisted, and that if she walked at all and did not have to be brought in a litter, it would only be because she had been stupefied by drugs and then half dragged and half carried there. But the small, brilliant figure walking behind the Rana's bier was not only alone, but walking upright and unfaltering; and there was pride and dignity in every line of her slender body.

Her small head was erect and the little unshod feet that had never before stepped on anything harsher than Persian carpets and cool polished marble trod slowly and steadily, marking the burning dust with small neat footprints that the adoring crowds behind her pressed forward to obliterate with kisses.

She was dressed as Ash had seen her at the marriage ceremony, in the scarlet and gold wedding dress, and decked with the same jewels as she had worn that day. Pigeon's-blood rubies circled her throat and wrists, glowed on her forehead and her fingers, and swung from her ears. There were rubies too on the chinking golden anklets, and the hard sunlight glittered on the gold embroidery of the full-skirted Rajputani dress and flashed on the little jewelled bodice. But this time she wore no sari, and her long hair was unbound as though for her bridal night. It rippled about her in a silky black curtain that was more beautiful than any sari made by man, and Ash could not drag his gaze from her, though his body cringed from that tragic sight.

She seemed wholly unconscious of the jostling crowds who applauded her, calling on her to bless them and struggling to touch the hem of her skirt as she passed, or of the sea of eyes that stared avidly at her unveiled face. Ash saw that her lips were moving in the age-old invocation that accompanies the last journey of the dead: *Ram, Ram...Ram, Ram...Ram, Ram....*

He said aloud and incredulously: 'You were wrong. She is not afraid.'

The clamour from below almost drowned his words, but Anjuli heard them, and imagining that they had been addressed to her instead of to himself, she said: 'Not yet. It is still only a game to her. No, not a game—I don't mean that. But something that is only happening in her mind. A part she is playing.'

'You mean she is drugged? I don't believe it.'

'Not in the way you mean, but with emotion and desperation and shock. And—and perhaps...triumph....'

'*Triumph!*' thought Ash. Yes. The whole parade smacked more of a triumphal progress than a funeral. A procession in honour of a goddess who has deigned to show herself, for this time only, to accept the homage of her shouting, exultant and adoring worshippers. He remembered then that Shushila's mother, in the days before her beauty captured the heart of a Rajah, had been one of a troupe of entertainers: men and women whose livelihood depended upon their ability to capture the attention and applause of an audience—as her daughter was doing now. Shushila, Goddess of Bhithor, beautiful as the dawn and glittering with gold and jewels. Yes, it was a triumph. And even if she was only playing a part, at least she was playing it superbly.

'Well done!' whispered Ash, in a heartfelt endorsement of all those outside who were hailing her with the same words. 'Oh, well done—!'

Beside him, Anjuli too was murmuring to herself, repeating the same invocation as Shushila: '*Ram, Ram—Ram, Ram....*' It was only a breath of sound and barely audible in that tumult, but it distracted Ash's attention, and though he knew that the prayer was not for the dead man but for her sister, he told her sharply to be quiet.

His mind was once again in a turmoil and torn with doubts. For watching the unfaltering advance of that graceful scarlet and gold figure, it seemed to him that he had no right to play providence. It would have been excusable if she had been dragged here weeping and terrified, or dazed with drugs. But not when she showed no sign of fear.

She must know by now what lay ahead; and if so, either the stories that Gobind had heard were true and she had come to love the dead man—and loving him, preferred to die cradling his body in her arms rather than live without him—or else, having steeled herself to it, she was glorying in the manner of her death and the prospect of sainthood and veneration. In either case, what right had he to interfere? Besides, her agony would be very quickly over; he had watched the pyre being built and seen the priests heap cotton between the logs and pour oils and clarified butter on it, and had thought even then that once it was lit the smoke alone would probably suffocate poor little Shu-shu before a flame touched her.

'I can't do it,' decided Ash. 'And even if I do, it won't be all that much quicker: Juli ought to know that.... Oh, God, why don't they hurry up. Why can't they get it over, instead of dragging it out like this.'

His whole being was suddenly flooded with hatred for everyone out there: the presiding priests, the excited onlookers, the mourners in the funeral procession and even the dead man and Shushila herself. Shushila most of all, because—

No, that was not fair, thought Ash; she couldn't help being herself. This was the way she was made, and she could not help battening upon Juli any more than Juli could keep from allowing herself to be battened upon. People were what they were, and they did not change. Yet despite all her selfishness and egotism, at the last Shu-shu had spared a thought for her sister, and instead of insisting on her support to the end, had let her go—at what cost to herself, no one would ever know. He must not let himself forget that again....

The red haze of rage that had momentarily blinded him cleared away, and he saw that Shushila had moved on, and that where she had been there was another small, lonely figure. But this time it was a child: a boy of about five or six years old, walking alone a little way behind her. 'The heir, I suppose,' thought Ash, grateful for something else to think about. 'No, not the heir— the new Rana, of course. Poor little beggar. He looks done up.'

The child was stumbling with weariness and plainly bewildered by the strangeness of his surroundings and his sudden elevation in rank, a rank that was clearly shown by the fact that he walked directly behind the widowed Rani and several paces ahead of the hundred or so men who followed—the nobles, councillors and chiefs of Bhithor who brought up the end of the procession. Prominent among these was the Diwan, who carried a lighted torch that had been lit at the sacred flame in the city temple.

By now the noise had risen to a crescendo as those nearest to her fought to touch the Rani and beg her blessing, and others took up the cry of *Hari-bol* or *Khaman Kher*, or shrieked with pain as the guards rained blows upon them, forcing them back. 'At least the shot will not be heard,' observed Sarji.

'There is that to be thankful for. How much longer do you mean to wait?'

Ash made no reply, and presently Sarji muttered in an undertone that now would have been the time to leave — if they had any
sense left in their thick heads. He had not intended his words to
carry, but the end of the sentence was startlingly audible; for the
crowds outside had suddenly fallen silent, and all at once it was
possible to hear the hard breathing of the gagged prisoners and
the cooing of doves from somewhere overhead under the eaves
of the dome.

The cortège had reached the pyre and the bier was placed on
it. And now Shushila began to divest herself of her jewels, taking
them off one by one and handing them to the child, who gave
them in turn to the Diwan. She stripped them off quickly, almost
gaily, as though they were no more than withered flowers or
valueless trinkets of which she had tired and was impatient to be
rid of, and the silence was so complete that all could hear the
clink of them as the new Rana received them and the late Rana's
Prime Minister stowed them away in an embroidered bag.

Even Ash in the curtained enclosure heard it, and wondered
incuriously if the Diwan would ever relinquish them. Probably
not; though they had come from Karidkote, and being part of
Shushila's dowry should have been returned there. But he thought
it unlikely that either Shu-shu's relatives or the new Rana would
ever see them again once the Diwan had got his hands on them.

When all her ornaments had been removed except for a neck-
lace of sacred *tulsi* seeds, Shushila held out her slender ringless
hands to a priest, who poured Ganges water over them. The water
sparkled in the low sunlight as she shook the bright drops from her
fingers, and the assembled priests began to intone in chorus....

To the sound of that chanting, she began to walk round the
pyre, circling it three times as once, on her wedding day and
wearing this same dress, she had circled the sacred fire, tied by
her veil to the shrunken thing that now lay waiting for her on a
bridal bed of cedar-logs and spices.

The hymn ended and once again the only sound in the grove
was the cooing of doves: that soft monotonous sound that together
with the throb of a tom-tom and the creak of a well-wheel is the
voice of India. The silent crowds stood motionless, and none
stirred as the suttee mounted the pyre and seated herself in the

lotus posture. She arranged the wide folds of her scarlet dress so as to show it to its best advantage, and then gently lifted the dead man's head onto her lap, settling it with infinite care, as though he were asleep and she did not wish to wake him.

'*Now*,' breathed Anjuli in a whisper that broke in a sob—'Do it now...*quickly*, before—before she starts to be afraid.'

'Don't be a fool!' The retort cracked like a whip in the quiet room. 'It would make as much noise as a cannon and bring them all down on us like hornets. Besides—'

He had meant to say 'I'm not going to fire', but he did not do so. There was no point in making things worse for Juli than they were already. But the way in which Shu-shu had cradled that awful head in her lap had made up his mind for him at last, and he had no intention of firing. Juli took too much upon herself: she forgot that her half-sister was no longer a sickly infant or a frail and highly strung little girl who must be protected and cosseted—or that she herself was no longer responsible for her. Shu-shu was a grown woman who knew what she was doing. She was also a wife and a queen—and proving that she could behave as one. This time, for good or ill, she should be allowed to make her own decision.

The crowd outside was still silent, but now a priest began to swing a heavy temple bell that had been carried out from the city, and its harsh notes reverberated through the grove and awoke echoes from the walls and domes of the many *chattris*. One of the Brahmins was sprinkling the dead man and his widow with water brought from the sacred river Ganges—'Mother Gunga'—while others poured more *ghee* and scented oil upon the logs of cedar and sandalwood and over the feet of the Rana.

But Shushila did not move. She sat composed and still, looking down at the grey, skull-like face on her lap. A graven image in scarlet and gold: remote, passionless and strangely unreal. The Diwan took the torch again and gave it into the trembling hands of the boy-Rana, who seemed about to burst into tears. It wavered dangerously in the child's grasp, being over-heavy for such small hands to hold, and one of the Brahmins came to his assistance and helped to support it.

The brightness of that flame was a sharp reminder that evening was already drawing near. Only a short time ago it had been almost invisible in the glaring sunlight, but now the sun was no longer fierce enough to dim that plume of light. The shadows had begun to lengthen and the day that had once seemed as though it would never end would soon be over—and with it, Shushila's short life.

She had lost father and mother, and the brother who, for his own ends, had given her in marriage to a man who lived so far away that it had taken months and not weeks to reach her new home. She had been a wife and a queen, had miscarried two children and borne a third who had lived only a few days; and now she had been widowed, and must die.... 'She is only sixteen—' thought Ash. 'It isn't fair. It isn't *fair* !'

He could hear Sarji's quickened breathing and the thump of his own heart-beats, and though Anjuli was not touching him he knew, without knowing how he knew, that she was shivering violently as though she was very cold or stricken with fever. He thought suddenly that provided he fired a shot she would not know if the bullet had done its work or not, and that he had only to aim over the heads of the crowd. If it comforted Juli to think that her sister had been spared the flames, then all he needed to do was pull the trigger—

But the trees on the far side of the clearing were full of men and boys who clung like monkeys to the boughs, while every *chattri* within range swarmed with spectators, and even a spent bullet or a ricochet could cause death. It would have to be the pyre itself; that was the only safe target. He lifted the revolver and steadied the barrel on the crook of his left arm, and said curtly and without turning his head: 'We leave as soon as I have fired. Are you ready to go?'

'We men are,' said Gobind very softly. 'And if the Rani-Sahiba—'

He hesitated, and Ash finished the sentence for him: '—will cover her face—it will save time. Besides, she has already seen more than enough of this and there is no need for her to stand staring any longer.'

He spoke with deliberate harshness in the hope that Juli would be forced to busy herself rewinding the free end of her turban across her face and so miss the last act of the tragedy. But she made no move to cover her face or turn away. She stayed as though rooted to the spot: wide-eyed, shivering and unable to stir hand or foot, and seemingly unaware that he had spoken.

All of forty paces, Sarji had said. It did not look as far as that, for now that there was no movement in the vast crowd the dust had settled; and with the sun-glare no longer dazzling his sight, the faces of the chief actors in the tragedy could be seen as clearly as though they were only twenty feet away instead of thirty-five to forty paces.

The little Rana was crying. Tears poured down the pallid, childish features that were crumpled with fear and bewilderment and sheer physical exhaustion, and if the Brahmin beside him had not held his small hands firmly about the torch, he would have dropped it. The Brahmin was evidently exhorting him in an undertone, while the Diwan looked scornful and the nobles exchanged glances that varied according to their temperaments— and the degree of their disappointment over the selection of the next ruler. And then Shushila looked up...and suddenly her face changed.

Perhaps it was the brightness of the torch, or the sound of it as the flames streamed up on the still air, that woke her from the dream-world in which she had been moving. Her head came up sharply and Ash could see her eyes widen until they looked enormous in her small, pale face. She started about her, no longer calmly, but with the terrified gaze of a hunted animal, and he could tell the exact moment when reality broke through illusion and she realized, fully, what that flaming brand signalled....

The boy's hands, guided by the Brahmin's, lowered the torch until it touched the pyre near the feet of the dead man. Bright flowers of fire sprang up from the wood and blossomed in orange and green and violet, and the new Rana having performed his duty to the old one—his father by adoption—the priest took the brand from him and went quickly to the other end of the pyre and touched it to the logs at the suttee's back. A brilliant tongue of flame shot skyward, and simultaneously the crowd found its voice and once again roared its homage and approval. But the goddess of their worship thrust aside the head on her lap, and now, suddenly, she was on her feet, staring at those flames and screaming—screaming....

The sound of those screams cut through the clamour as the shriek of violin strings cuts through the full tempest of drums and wind-instruments and brass. It drew a gasping echo from Anjuli, and Ash lifted his aim and fired.

The screams stopped short and the slender scarlet and gold figure stretched out one hand gropingly as though searching for support, and then crumpled at the knees and pitched forward across the corpse at her feet. And as she fell the Brahmin flung the torch on the pyre, and flames gushed up from the oil-drenched wood and threw a shimmering veil of heat and smoke between the watchers and the recumbent figure of the girl who now wore a glittering wedding-dress of fire.

The crash of the shot had sounded appallingly loud in that small confined space, and Ash thrust the revolver into the breast of his robe and turning, said savagely: 'Well, what are you waiting for? Get on—go on Sarji—you first.' Anjuli still seemed dazed, and he pulled the cloth roughly across her nose and mouth and made sure that it was secure, and having adjusted his own, caught her by the shoulders and said: 'Listen to me, Juli—and stop looking like that. You've done all you can for Shushila. She's gone. She has escaped; and if we hope to, we must stop thinking of her and think of ourselves. We come first now. All of us. Do you understand?'

Anjuli nodded dumbly.

'Good. Then turn around and go with Gobind, and don't look back. I shall be behind you. *Walk*—!'

He turned her about and pushed her ahead of him towards the heavy purdah that Manilal was holding open for them, and she followed Sarji through it and down the marble stairway that led to the terrace and the crowds below.

Notes

[1] Kipling, Rudyard, 'The Last Suttee', in *Barrack-room Ballads and Other Verses* (London: Methuen, 1899).

[2] Verne, J., *Around the World in Eighty Days*, Chapters 12 and 13 (The Rescue of Aouda), (Oxford: Oxford University Press, 1995).

[3] Kaye, M.M., *The Far Pavilions* (London: Allen Lane, 1978).

18

Indian Fiction

Sita Devi, *The Modern Review*, 'The Suttee'[1]

In order to support her no-good, ailing husband, the heroine of this short story poses for a painting of a sati, pressing hot irons against her skin to achieve the expression of agony. Though not about an actual immolation, the author uses the sati motif to praise the courage and self-sacrifice of Indian women, indicating the ambivalent attitude among nationalists to sati and the ethos of sacrifice that underpinned it.

Abani and Surendra were old friends. They belonged to the same village and afterwards had belonged to the same college. But now they lived far apart owing to their work. Surendra had settled in Behar, while Abani still clung to good old Calcutta.

But they had kept up the habit of being together during the Pujah vacation. This time Surendra had come down to Calcutta. His wife had gone home to her father with the children. So he was at liberty to enjoy his friend's company, as long as he liked.

They were having their morning tea. A couple of newspapers lay in front on the table.

Abani took a good sip at the cup and said, 'So long as a man does not feel the inner urge to reform, the law can never reform him. They are enacting various laws for making intercaste marriage valid, for raising the age of marriage, etc. Do you think it will do a bit of good? Nobody will pay heed to these.'

'They will have to,' said Surendra. 'The law may not be of positive use, but it will stop abuse, to a certain extent. You must never expect a whole nation to feel the urge to reform all at once. But the few, who have already felt it, may now give effect to their convictions. The law will make it safe for them. And others may follow their good example. All reforms take place gradually in this manner.'

'But child-marriage, etc., were gradually disappearing of themselves,' said Abani. 'Within a few years, they would have gone completely. Our countrymen need not have made such a row over them, thereby publishing our own disgrace to the whole world. It is we who give the Katharine Mayo's their cues.'

'I beg to differ,' said Surendra. 'These evils are too deep-rooted in our nature, to be easily forsaken. And why should we wait, even a few years, if we could remove them now? If we could have got the reforms ten years earlier, we would have saved ten thousand girls' needless sufferings thereby. A human life is a priceless thing. You cannot go on sacrificing it endlessly for the sake of a theory.'

'Tell you what,' said Abani, 'I don't like the law interfering in social matters, especially as the making and unmaking of laws lie with foreigners now. We have no political rights and if we allow them to dictate even our social laws, we should be worse than slaves.'

Surendra lighted a cigarette and threw away the match. 'We must choose the lesser evil,' he said. 'Slavery is bad, but suicide is worse. Do you mean to say that we should not enact laws against even Suttee or the sacrifice of children in the name of religion?'

'I would not go so far,' said Abani. 'Where human life is concerned everything else must be subordinated.'

'But is it less horrible to suffer lifelong agony than to burn oneself in a fit of sorrow?' asked Surendra.

Abani remained silent for a few minutes. Then he said, 'I don't support Suttee or child sacrifice. But one thing I should like to say regarding them. These things proved how much love and religious fervour can effect. But the law has stopped all that now. Nobody can even think of Suttee or child sacrifice now. Don't you think we have thereby laid a limit to the power of voluntary sacrifice which every human heart possesses?'

'Don't speak like an idiot,' said Surendra. 'Law can never change human nature. Do you think that none of the women who lose their husbands nowadays, love them or can sacrifice as much for them as the women of yore did?'

'I have grave doubts,' Abani said. 'They would not dare to think of what those heroic women did.'

'Certainly they can,' Surendra said. 'If you have leisure, I should like to tell you of an incident of which I have first-hand knowledge.'

'I am at your service,' said Abani.

'Why don't you call your missus too?' asked Surendra jestingly. 'It may teach her a lesson in wifely devotion.'

'She had better supervise the cooking.' Abani said, 'It is much the better form of devotion.'

'As you please,' Surendra said, 'so here goes....'

I have altered all the names, as the persons concerned are still living. They may not like it. You may remember that I was in dreadful financial difficulties when I first began to practise here. I made next to nothing and I had no patrimony to fall back upon. So I had no other option than to go away somewhere else.

But where to go? I was nearly at my wit's end, when I received a letter from Manoranjan. You remember him, don't you? He was a few years my senior but we were good friends once. I had heard that after passing the law examination, he had gone to Behar, and was doing well there. After that, for a few years, I heard nothing more about him.

I was rather surprised at his writing to me. Why had he remembered me all of a sudden? I went through the letter and found that he had invited me to go there and take up his practice. It had been a good one, but he had fallen ill and was in much trouble. He was too ill to do anything and was deeply in debt. If I went there, I could take up his practice, and I could give him a bit of friendly help too.

I found nothing to object to in the plan. I packed in a hurry, borrowed some money with great difficulty and started. I sent on a wire to Manoranjan. But I did not expect him to meet me at the station, since he was so ill.

After a long and dusty journey in one of the passenger trains of the EIR, I arrived at my destination rather sick of my experience.

I saw no sign of my friend at the station. I decided to try my luck at finding his residence.

I called a porter and putting all my luggage on his head, walked out of the platform. I was just going to get into a hackney carriage, when a boy ran up to me. I think I was the only Bengali traveller, so he had no hesitation in picking me out.

'Are you Surendra Babu?' he asked.

'Yes,' I said. 'But who may you be, my boy? I don't think I have seen you before.'

'No, you have not,' he said, 'I live near the house of Manoranjan Babu. As he could not come, his wife has sent me.'

'Come, get in then,' I said. It took us nearly half an hour to reach Manoranjan's house. He had given up his old house and had removed to a dirty little hole, in a far-off quarter of the town. The whole street could not boast of a new or a fair-sized house. The open drains on both sides made one positively sick. I fervently hoped I would not have to remain here long. Even starvation at home was better than this.

The boy ordered the coachman to stop and got down. He knocked at a door which was cracked in many places and shouted, 'Auntie !' The door opened with a grating noise. I could discern a veiled female figure standing within the doorway. I guessed rightly that there were no servants; so I ordered the coachman to take down the luggage and carried them inside with his help. The boy took a rupee from me and went outside and paid off the man.

The lady had retreated inside. I stood hesitating, not knowing exactly what to do, when I heard Manoranjan's voice. 'Come right in,' he cried out. 'I am too weak to go out and welcome you.'

I went in. There was only one wooden bedstead in the room and a man was lying on it. I took him to be Manoranjan. Not that I recognized him but because it could not be anyone else. He bore no resemblance whatever to the Manoranjan I knew. I sat down by his side, as there was nothing else on which I could sit.

'So, you have come after all,' he said. 'I hope you had a pleasant journey.'

'Only so so,' I said, 'But I am surprised at your condition. How did things become so bad? We always understood that you were doing pretty well here.'

'I was,' he said. 'A year ago I could never have dreamt of such a state of affairs. Then I fell ill. I don't know what's the matter with me, but the fever never leaves me. It may be malaria, or kala-azar or consumption.'

'But, are not you being treated by any doctor?' I interrupted.

'As long as I had money,' he said, 'I called in every doctor, homeopath and *kaviraj* the town had. But now I can scarcely pay for food. So I have no money to spare for doctors.'

'Why didn't you return home?', I asked. 'At least you would never have starved there.'

'I had thought of that,' he replied. 'But who was there to take charge of me? Both my parents are dead, and I have no brother, I have relatives of course, but none so loving on whom I can hang on in this state. My wife's father is living, but her mother is dead. So relations are rather strained in that direction. Besides, they are poor people. So I stayed on where I was.'

'But we must arrange for medical treatment,' I said. 'We cannot leave you like this.'

'All right, all right,' he said, 'there's no hurry. First have some refreshments yourself, I say.' He called out to his wife, 'Where have you gone and hidden yourself? This won't do now. We have not got a dozen servants. Surendra is like a younger brother to me. So you need not veil yourself before him.'

Manoranjan's wife came back slowly into the room. She had lifted the veil off her face. I looked at her. It was a wonderful face. Not only was it exquisitely beautiful but it held something indescribable. I tried to think out what it was, but could not.

'This is my wife,' said Manoranjan. I got up and bowing down to her took the dust of her feet, though she must have been years younger than myself. But I felt I wanted to show my reverence for her. 'Don't be shy to come before me,' I said. 'Regard me as your younger brother-in-law.'

She smiled slightly. 'What about breakfast, Saroja?' asked Manoranjan.

'It is nearly ready,' she said. 'As soon as he has finished bathing, I shall serve it.'

'Is there any fish today?' he asked. What an ass! He should not have asked her this in my presence. Lest she should feel embarrassed, I put in quickly, 'It does not matter a bit, if she has not got fish. I would rather have vegetable dishes than fish or flesh any day.'

'But I have got fish', Saroja said, 'please go and have your bath.'

I took out a change of clothing, a towel and soap and started to have a bath. The house did not boast a bathroom. So, I had to finish my ablutions in the yard.

Manoranjan was an invalid. So, I had to take my breakfast alone in the kitchen. The fare was exceedingly simple, still I don't think I had ever eaten with greater relish. Saroja was serving me. I looked at her face and seemed to know it. I must have seen her somewhere before. After a few minutes I understood my feeling. I had never seen Saroja before, but I had seen exactly this expression on the face of our goddesses, Annapurna, Lakshmi, and others. This girl belonged to the modern age but her appearance, manners, everything about her belonged to the Vedic or the Epic ages. She could easily have been a Savitri or a Damayanti. She never seemed to be fully living this life. Half of her lived in some forgotten past existence. She was a being one could worship, one could revere, but one dared not love. I wondered how a creature like Manoranjan could think of her as his wife.

After finishing my meal, I began to feel rather drowsy and, spreading a mat in the outer room; I fell fast asleep. I got up after sunset and went out for a stroll. Five minutes, inside that stuffy and dark house made my head reel. Next day I began work. I could not afford to sit idle, but I saw that Manoranjan could afford it still less. The house he used to live in before was fortunately vacant. I went and rented it trusting to luck. I put a big signboard in front, and furnished the office room pretty decently, though the inner apartments remained bare like a desert. Manoranjan had quite a good number of law books getting moth-eaten. I rescued them and put them in my room. He gave me letters of introduction to all his wealthy clients and I went and saw them all.

My luck had turned. So I was not unsuccessful in my efforts. I began to get clients from the very beginning. I don't mean to say that I became a millionaire, but I could pay my way and help Manoranjan too. I called in his old doctor. I would pay for the medicines, I told him, for the present. But if my luck held he would be paid in full for his services, I promised him. The doctor was not a bad sort. He agreed.

Everyday I used to go to Manoranjan's house once to see him. I took fruits or rusks, or some such things with me. And I always managed to pay their bazaar money.

He felt no scruples about accepting these. He had put me in the way of earning money. So he was entitled to a fair commission. He was too ill besides, to have much sensitiveness left. But Saroja's face expressed her mortification clearly. She hated to be the recipient of charity.

One day she suddenly asked, 'Won't you bring over your wife and child here?'

'I am in no hurry,' I replied, 'they are getting on quite well there. Till I am fairly well established here, I won't send for them.'

'Then why did you take such a big house?' she asked. 'Most of the rooms are empty, I suppose? Why don't you sublet half of it to us? We have to pay some rent here, small though it is. If I am there you won't have to keep that cook of yours.'

'If you be kind enough to come,' I said warmly, 'I cannot say how glad I shall feel. The house is like a desert, it gives me the creeps. But don't talk about paying rent or you will spoil everything. If I am exempted from tasting the delicacies produced by Maharaj, I shall deem myself fortunate.'

I don't think Saroja found this arrangement much to her liking, but Manoranjan became so enthusiastic over it that she had to remain silent perforce. Two days later they moved to my house.

The house presented a better sight no doubt, and the cooking improved vastly. But I cannot say, that it gained much in the way of cheerfulness. Manoranjan was too ill to be cheerful. He groaned and moaned all the time. And Saroja drudged like a slave the whole day. She scarcely had the time to talk. She seemed even more depressed here, than she had been before. She ceased to smile even.

I could not understand the reason. True, her husband was ill, but that was nothing new. They were far more comfortable here. So why this increase of depression?

The cause, I found out only accidentally, or so I thought then. I paid little attention to my neighbour, who lived in the house next to mine. I sometimes saw him coming out or going in. He was a young man. I did not know who he was, or what he did. There was something peculiar in his appearance and dress. Afterwards I heard that he was an artist and was earning a good deal of money. Nobody knew much about him. He seemed to live alone in that house. He never went into society, perhaps he did not think anyone here good enough to associate with.

Through the window of Manoranjan's bedroom, if he left his window open, we could see a portion of the artist's studio. I had not noticed it to remain open before, but nowadays whenever I went by to see Manoranjan I found the artist's window open. Saroja was too beautiful a woman to pass unnoticed by a man, especially by an artist. So, I could find it in my heart to be lenient to the fellow. More so, as I knew Saroja to be the incarnation of virtue and faithfulness. So I never bothered about this perpetually gaping window.

One day, I had returned rather earlier than usual from the court. I had brought a bottle of medicine for Manoranjan. I walked into his bedroom with it. I found Manoranjan sleeping and his wife standing before the open window. The window of the artist's studio was open too, and he was standing there. I don't know whether they were talking; at any rate I heard nothing. But I seemed to turn into stone with surprise.

Saroja stood with her back to me. So the artist chap was the first to catch sight of me. He gave a start and moved off instantly. Saroja too turned round. She became pale as death and hurried out of the room without a single word. Their behaviour served to confirm my suspicion. Looking at a man through the window cannot be considered a sin, even for a Hindu woman. I would not have been much surprised, if I had seen anyone else doing it. But for Saroja, it was rather strange. Besides, if they were not guilty, why did both of them run away like that? They stood self-convicted.

After this incident Saroja ceased to talk to me. I understood the whole affair in a way. But what was I to do? I had no definite proof, so I could not go and accuse the artist. He would be justified in kicking me out. I could not say anything to Saroja out of diffidence. To speak to her husband would mean murder. So I remained dumb.

Manoranjan had collected quite a large number of creditors during the course of his long illness. They were getting restive. First came abusive letters, then Durwans, then the gentlemen themselves began to appear on the scene, one by one. The house now belonged to me, and Manoranjan was too ill to come out. So they could not have it out with him as they desired. But their voices penetrated within and filled the mind of their victims with helpless rage and sorrow.

Lawyers' notices began to arrive. Saroja used to open all their letters, before passing them on to Manoranjan. She opened one of those letters and seeing that it was written in English, she brought it over to me. 'Please see,' she said, 'who has written it.'

This was the first time she had spoken to me, after that deplorable incident. I felt too uncomfortable even to look at her. I managed to make her acquainted with the contents of the letter. She stood like one turned to stone, with the letter in her hand.

This woman was becoming an enigma to me. I could not mistrust my own eyes. But I could hardly believe her to be guilty, after seeing her wholehearted devotion to her husband. She nursed him with untiring zeal, day and night. The world struck at Manoranjan, but she received the blows midway, thus shielding him from pain and insult. Could such a wife be faithless? Perhaps she was really innocent. Being a lawyer, I knew that appearance of guilt was not always guilt. I could not convict her even in my own mind, before obtaining further and stronger proofs.

But we are as pawns in the hands of fate. The affair made rapid progress within the next few days and its tragic climax too loomed into sight.

My *chokra* used to come to my rooms in the evening, with a table lamp. This evening, he came as usual, but instead of going away after depositing the lamp, he remained standing near the door.

'What do you want, Raghua?' I asked.

'Master, I want to tell you something,' the boy said with folded hands. 'You are like a father to me, and I cannot bear calumny to touch you.'

'What on earth are you hinting at?' I asked. 'Speak plainly.'

'When you go out and the sick gentleman falls asleep, the mistress goes away to the house next to us. She returns after an hour or so,' said Raghua.

I felt inclined to clout his head. But I restrained myself. After all the boy was not to blame. He had only reported what he had seen.

It was a mercy that others had not done so yet. But could a human being's face bear such false witness? Saroja looked like Sati herself, the spouse of the great god Shiva. Could she be faithless?

'How do you know it?' I asked the boy.

'Every afternoon, the mistress lets me off for an hour to go out. The other day, I had a headache and did not like to go out. Instead I came out here and had a good nap. The mistress did not know that. Afterwards, I felt very thirsty and went into the kitchen to have a glass of water. I found the back door open, which rather surprised me. Just as I was going to close it, I saw the mistress coming out of that house, through their back door. Before she could see me, I made my escape.'

'Was this the only time you noticed her going there?' I asked.

'No, I noticed her yesterday, and the day before,' the boy said. 'She goes out at one o'clock and returns at two.'

I dismissed him, saying I would look into the matter. I ordered him to keep his mouth shut about this affair. But I could not determine what to do. I had no right over Saroja. I could not go and have it out with her. Her husband was the right person to interfere, but he was near death. To tell him would be to deliver the death blow. Still I determined to ask Saroja about it. But I must not trust entirely to a servant's words. I was going to catch her myself. Then I shall go and horsewhip that dandy of an artist, even if I could do nothing else.

Next day, I did not go to court, though I went out at ten o'clock as usual. I told the boy to keep the front door unlocked as I was going to come back after an hour. He agreed, saying that he would remain concealed within the house, after he had received permission to go. I felt heartily ashamed of myself for laying this trap, but cruel fate had left me no option.

I returned at about half past one. Raghua met me with the news that Saroja had gone out a little while ago and was due to return very soon. I took up my post at a spot from where I would be able to do my watching undetected.

Very soon after, the back door of the artist's house opened and Saroja came out. She entered the house by the kitchen door. I was about to come out of my hiding place to give her a good piece of my mind, when I stopped amazed at the sight of her face. It expressed such agony as I had never before seen on any human face. Her whole face was distorted.

I was puzzled. What could it mean? After she had gone in, I came out of my hiding place and went to my office room. I sat thinking and thinking. I decided to go to the artist at last. Tomorrow, when Saroja would go to her tryst I too would follow her and confront the guilty pair. I would make an end of this.

But my plans were all upset. I thought of returning at one o'clock but got unavoidably detained. Just as I entered the house, I heard a terrible shout from Manoranjan's room. I ran into it and found him holding Saroja by the hand and shrieking like one possessed. The stream of foul abuse pouring out of his lips scared my ears.

I caught hold of him and dragged him back to bed. 'What are you doing?' I asked. 'Do you want to kill yourself? What do you mean by getting so excited in your present state of health?'

'What's the use of living any longer?' he gasped. 'I am better dead now. Do you know where my faithful wife had been this while, leaving me dying? She went to that house to meet her lover. Take her away from before my eyes. Or I will kill her. I have strength enough left for that. My brain is on fire, my heart is full of poison. I trusted that woman more than God.'

'Come away,' I said to Saroja. 'Your presence only excites him. It is fatal for him.'

'Get out,' screamed the wretched husband. 'Get out of the world, if you can. Don't show your face any more before man. Death is the only way out for you now.'

Saroja wrapped herself in a heavy sheet and walked out of the room. I followed her, leaving Manoranjan shouting imprecations.

I saw that Saroja was really bent on leaving the house. I barred her way saying, 'What are you doing? Your husband is mad, you need not mind him so much.'

'Let me go, please,' she said. 'It...is useless keeping me now.'

My heart ached for her. With what joy had I invited her here, and now she was to be driven out like an unclean creature. 'Remain in this room,' I told her, pointing to one of the outer rooms. 'Your husband need not know. Though appearances are bad, still I cannot believe you guilty.'

She smiled rather wanly. 'Why cannot you?' she asked. 'A woman's guilt is very easily proved and believed in in our country.'

'Be that as it may,' I said, 'I request you not to go now. Let Manoranjan calm down a bit, then give your explanation. I am sure, you have got a good one.'

'I have no explanation to give,' was her strange reply. 'You have done much for me. Even my own brother could not have done more. Do me this last service. Let me go. I cannot stay here a moment longer.'

'At least tell me where you are going,' I pleaded. 'If by God's grace this terrible muddle is cleared up any time, I shall go and bring you back at once.'

'Very well,' she said. 'You remember the boy who went to meet you at the station? He will know my whereabouts.' Slowly she passed out of the front door. I saw her getting into a hackney carriage, which soon drove out of sight.

Manoranjan refused to be pacified. He went on shouting and abusing. I told Raghua to look after him and started for the house next door. One had got away but the other was still there to pay for the affair. I took a stout cane with me.

I found the front door closed. After repeated knockings and blows, an old man opened the door.

'Where is your master?' I asked. The master had gone out. He did not know when the master would return, or if he would return at all. Sometimes he would stay out for days. I asked whether he had taken any luggage with him. Nothing much, the old fellow replied.

So this one too had escaped me. I called myself a fool for having delayed too long. If I had come yesterday, I could have beaten him to jelly for wrecking another's home like this. I could not do anything by staying at the fellow's house, so I returned home.

Manoranjan drove me nearly crazy. He refused to eat, drink, or sleep. If I tried to give him medicine, he ran for me with a stick. The boy Raghua was too frightened to go near him. I could not afford to sit at home all day, taking care of a lunatic. I had my practice to think of. So, I had to write to his relatives at home. I lied coolly and told them that his wife was dead. I told Manoranjan to keep his mouth shut. There was no use publishing one's disgrace. Perhaps time would explain everything. I could not have given up such a wife, even if she had sinned once. She had been a staunch and faithful helpmate all these years, and one slip should be forgiven. But my friend was very orthodox on this point. All the same he agreed to remain silent, and a few days later one of his cousins came and took him away.

After I had disposed of Manoranjan, I began my search for Saroja. I went to the boy Saroja had referred me to. But they refused to say anything. They did not know, they pretended. Their faces belied their statement, but I could not compel them to tell the truth. I told them again and again that I was a sincere friend of the poor woman, and all I wanted was to help her to regain her home. But they remained adamant.

I went on searching. I advertised, I employed detectives, all to no purpose. After a while, I gave up in despair. I tried to drown myself in my work, so as to forget everything. But whenever I looked at the now deserted rooms, my heart ached terribly. Within this short space, I had come to look upon Saroja as my own sister.

Nearly a month had gone by. I had begun to forget. Suddenly, a small incident served to remind me of the whole tragic history. A few letters addressed to Manoranjan arrived by the morning post. I was about to redirect them, when something prompted me to open the letters. He was an invalid and should not be troubled with bills or lawyers' notices.

But imagine my surprise, when I found the envelopes containing no bills, but receipts. Somebody had paid them off on the quiet!

A horrible suspicion stole into my mind. Was it Saroja by any chance? Who else would bother so much about that good-for-nothing Manoranjan? Had she sacrificed herself to pay her husband's debts? Could any honest woman do that? Perhaps she could. I wondered whether to call it sacrifice or sin. Still she should not have sold her honour, even to save her husband. I remembered the agony I had seen depicted on her face. Was that the result of inner conflict? Nobody knew besides God.

Anyway, I redirected the letters. Manoranjan would enjoy some peace of mind now. He, too, would wonder about the generous helper. Perhaps, he would think that I myself had given it. Days passed on. The courts closed for the October holidays. My friends, who lived with their families, stayed at home, enjoying the society of their wives and children. I had no incentive for staying at home. I wandered about the whole day. Many meetings and conferences were held at this time. So I did not have any trouble about spending my time.

There was also an art exhibition going on. I started for it, one afternoon, with one of my friends. The hall where the exhibition was held stood at a considerable distance from my house. So we got a taxi, and started.

There was not much of a crowd there. So we wandered about at leisure, inspecting the paintings. Gradually we got separated from each other. Suddenly, I heard my friend calling me. I went over to him quickly and asked, 'What's up?'

'Look at this painting,' he said, pointing to a large canvas, hanging in front. 'Didn't you say the other day that Indian artists were no good at oil paintings? Isn't it simply grand? If this had been painted in England, say, there would have been a rush for it.'

I scarcely listened to him. I stared thunderstruck at the painting. It was called 'The Suttee'. A huge funeral pyre, burning, on the desolate and frightful bank of a dried-up river. A woman sat in the midst of the burning pile, clasping the corpse of her husband in her arms. The face of the woman was the face of Saroja! The agony I had seen on her face was painted even more intensely on the canvas. Still she looked divine as if glorying in the torture. The name of the painter, too, was familiar. It was that of my erstwhile neighbour.

'You seem rooted to the spot,' my friend remarked. 'Is it not just superb? If I had the money, I would buy it. But it has already been sold to some Maharaja for four thousand.'

'Yes, it is excellent,' I said. 'You don't mind, if I leave you now? I am feeling rather unwell.' Without waiting for his reply, I left the hall.

I knew the authorities of the Exhibition. With their help, I traced the artist Anukul Mallik very easily. I rehearsed a very sharp speech in my mind and started for his house.

The man had just finished his tea and was lighting a cigarette, when the unexpected and unwelcome sight of myself upset him. He forgot his cigarette and remained staring at me.

I bowed to him and asked, 'Don't you recognize me? You used to be my neighbour.'

He had pulled himself together somehow and replied, 'Oh, was that you, who lived in No. 15? To what do I owe this pleasure?'

'I saw your canvas at the exhibition, "The Suttee",' I said. 'It is superb. I could not refrain from giving myself the pleasure of calling on you.'

He cast a look of suspicion at me, but remained silent. 'But couldn't you secure another model for it?' I asked. 'Why did you break up the home of a poor man?'

The artist had regained control of himself. 'Yes, I could have got another model, but not for a picture of the "Suttee",' he said boldly. 'But how did I break up a home? What do you accuse me of? I hope she did not tell you that I have not paid her adequately for her services?'

'Don't pretend to be so innocent,' I said angrily, 'Money does not make up for lost honour.'

'Don't you, on your part, pretend to be silly,' he said heatedly. 'Because she had to sit before me for an hour, daily, you think she had lost her honour? Did she tell you that?'

'You know very well she cannot tell us anything as she is not with us,' I said sarcastically. .

The man got fed up. 'Look here,' he cried, 'I have no time to waste listening to nonsense. If you can prove that I had treated her with any lack of respect or that I had not paid her the promised money, then I will listen to you. It is true I had to inflict suffering on her, but she agreed to undergo it.'

'Suffering?' I asked rather mystified. 'What was the nature of it?'

'Well, if you want to hear it, I have no objection to tell,' he said, with forced indifference. 'I wanted the expression of intense suffering on her face. So I had to brand her with hot iron on the back.'

I nearly fainted with horror. I could not have imagined such cruelty existed amongst civilized men. Poor martyred Saroja! We were not fit to take the dust of her feet. And we had sat in judgement on her, and condemned her.

I felt too disgusted to stay there any longer. I got up, saying, 'The law does not empower me to exact retribution. Otherwise I would have cracked your fine artistic head with this stick. I would do it even if it landed me in jail; only I have far more urgent business upon my hand. So, goodbye; but don't try this game again.'

He essayed a sickly smile. I rushed out of the house.

Surendra stopped. After a while, he asked, 'Can you say that this girl could not have become a suttee?'

'No, I cannot,' said Abani. 'But the tale sounds too strange to be true.'

'Yes, it is rather,' said Surendra.

'But it is unmitigated tragedy so far,' Abani said. 'Did you not find her again?'

'You are fond of happy endings, aren't you?' asked Surendra. 'A schoolgirl mentality. Yes, we traced her. There are pearls that are destined to be cast before swine. Not that I call poor Manoranjan a swine.'

Sarojini Naidu, 'The Suttee'[2]

In this poem, 'Gandhi's poetess' glorifies the ethos, if not the actual practice of sati by romanticizing the desire to join the beloved in death. Naidu's poem is indicative of an elite attitude that, while not condoning burning women, still saw something praiseworthy in the ideology that underpinned sati.

SUTTEE

Lamp of my life, the lips of Death
Have blown thee out with their sudden breath;
Naught shall revive thy vanished spark...
Love, must I dwell in the living dark?

Tree of my life, Death's cruel foot
Hath crushed thee down to thy hidden root;
Naught shall restore thy glory sped...
Shall the blossom live when the tree is dead?

Life of my life, Death's bitter sword
Hath severed us like a broken word,
Rent us in twain who are but one...
Shall the flesh survive when the soul is gone?

Notes

[1]   Sita Devi, 'The Suttee', *The Modern Review*, vol. 44: 3, September 1928.

[2]   Naidu, Sarojini, 'The Suttee', in *The Golden Threshold* (London: William Heinemann, 1905).

VII

SATI IN CONTEMPORARY INDIA, ROOP KANWAR, AND BEYOND

19

Roop Kanwar

Manushi, 'The Burning of Roop Kanwar'[1]

This article by feminist scholars Madhu Kishwar and Ruth Vanita first appeared in the Delhi-based feminist journal *Manushi* in September 1987. It views the immolation of Roop Kanwar as a political rather than religious issue and discusses ways to prevent such events from occurring in the future.

On 4 September 1987, eighteen-year-old Roop Kanwar was burnt to death on her husband's pyre in village Deorala, Sikar district, Rajasthan. In one sense, there is not much difference between the death of Roop Kanwar and the deaths of thousands of women burnt alive in their own homes in many parts of the country. But her death was significantly different in its social and cultural resonance.

Wife-burning, like many other acts of violence, occurs with the tacit consent of society, but it incurs public disapproval. Therefore, it is perpetrated secretively, behind locked doors. The woman's husband and in-laws invariably claim that her death was a regrettable suicide or accident, and that they made every attempt to save her.

Modern day sati, on the other hand, though rare, is a public spectacle, conducted with the approval and applause of the local community. It is this aspect that is particularly alarming. If the widespread implicit acceptance of wife-murder in our society today expresses the low value set on women's lives, the public burning to death of a woman is an open endorsement of that devaluation.

When parents advise their daughters to endure maltreatment by a husband and in-laws, and to 'adjust' at all costs in the marital home, they too are endorsing the norm that a woman's life is worthless except as an object of use or abuse by her husband. In this context, the reaction of Roop Kanwar's natal family to her death is not very surprising. When we met her brother in Jaipur, he said that though their family was mourning her death, they had no complaints regarding the manner of her death. Although Roop Kanwar was burnt in the presence of thousands of people from around Deorala, her family, who live in Jaipur, a mere two-hour drive away, were not informed that she was about to become a sati. Yet, they condoned her being burnt alive and say she has brought honour to them.

In most ordinary wife-murder cases, the husband and in-laws of the woman try to defame her after her death as an unstable woman with suicidal tendencies or a bad character. But Roop Kanwar's past is being recreated to mythologize her as an embodiment of the best womanly and wifely virtues. In a culture where a woman is considered a burden, easily dispensable and replaceable, it is a rare woman who is honoured in her death. No wonder, then, that so many women are awe-inspired by the new sati cult. Roop Kanwar's glorification may even appear as some sort of acknowledgement, however bizarre, of the many unrewarded sacrifices women make in everyday life for the husband and family.

The Roop Kanwar case has sharply polarized public opinion. Those who are glorifying her death are trying to project it as part of a 'glorious tradition' of Rajput and Hindu culture. Unfortunately, those opposed to it have inadvertently strengthened this myth by their inaccurate descriptions of the phenomenon and the forces behind it.

Most reformers have attributed the Deorala episode to the 'ignorance and illiteracy' of the rural masses that they describe prone to 'blind superstitiousness and excessive religiosity'. The phenomenon is seen as an indication of 'how backwardness and primitiveness has been preserved in India's villages'.

This kind of characterization of the Deorala episode assumes that it is a tradition of the masses to which the modern and the educated, supposedly stand opposed. But the fact of the matter is that Deorala is not a neglected village, nor are its inhabitants illiterate rustics. Nor are leaders of the pro-sati campaign mainly rural-based people. They are in large part urban-based politicians who are not excessively religious but excessively greedy for power of a very modern kind.

Thus, what was essentially a women's rights issue has been distorted into an issue of 'tradition' versus 'modernity'. A struggle of the religious majority against an irreligious minority.

THE PEOPLE OF DEORALA

In failing to recognize that Roop Kanwar's sati is a thoroughly 'modern' phenomenon in its political, economic, and social moorings, the reformers have played into the hands of the pro-sati camp. The Roop Kanwar case has as little to do with tradition as Ramanand Sagar's Sita has to do with Valmiki's Sita.

In an attempt to understand the context of Roop Kanwar's death and the forces behind its subsequent glorification, we visited Deorala and Jaipur in the last week of October, 1987.

Deorala is about two hours drive from Jaipur, the capital of Rajasthan, and about five hours drive from Delhi, by another route. It is an advanced prosperous village by Rajasthani and even by all-India standards. Its initial prosperity may have been based on agriculture because this part of the state is well-irrigated by private tubewells.

But, today, its prosperity is entrenched in its intimate connections with employment in the urban sector. Almost every family in Deorala has one or more male members who has a job in nearby towns. Most of these men are in government employment. A large majority of them are in the police or the army.

Deorala has many schools, a very high literacy rate (about 70 per cent) and has produced many matriculates and graduates. Roop Kanwar was a city-educated girl, her husband a science graduate, her father-in-law a school teacher and her brothers well-educated men, running a prosperous transport business in Jaipur.

The village has a population of about 10,000, the dominant castes being Rajputs and Brahmins. Almost all the houses are brick and cement structures. There is a market where a wide variety of consumer goods are available; the village has electricity and tap water. Many people own TV sets, cycles and motorcycles.

We saw hardly any visibly poverty-stricken people. The villagers looked well-fed. Most of the young people were dressed in fashionably tailored outfits of mill-made cloth. The men all wore Western dress—trousers and shirts. The young women wore Punjabi or Rajasthani dress, tailored in an urban style, clearly influenced by Hindi films.

The Sati Sthal

The Sati Sthal (the sati site) is situated at one end of the village, in an open ground. It is a temporary structure, a platform topped by a pavilion. When we reached there, four schoolboys, who appeared as aged between seven and fifteen years old, were walking round and round it, with sticks in their hands, chanting slogans. They wore shirts and shorts with outsize turbans perched incongruously on their heads.

Nearby, a group of young men were selling coconuts and other offerings, and distributing *prasad*. At a little distance, another group of young men were selling reprints of the now famous photo-collage showing a beatific Roop Kanwar on the pyre with her husband's head on her lap.

Clusters of women sat around talking, among them a number of schoolgirls. They were very different from the filmy stereotype of the village woman, as a shy secluded belle. They assumed that we were journalists and kept staring at us with overt hostility for about forty-five minutes. Since we refrained from asking any journalistic questions or taking photos, they finally called us and began cross-examining us with great confidence. Their hostility melted into the warmth and hospitality characteristic of an Indian village only after they were somewhat assured that we were not seeking to extract any statements from them. None of the women was veiled and they talked, joked, teased, and laughed unabashedly in the presence of men.

Religion or Politics?

Most of the slogans being shouted at the Sati Sthal were clearly modelled on electoral slogans and had not the remotest connection to any kind of religious chant. One boy would shout the first line and the others would then shout the second line, in the manner that slogans are raised at political rallies.

> *Sati ho to kaisi ho?*
> *Roop Kanwar ke jaisi ho.*
> Model: *Desh ka neta kaisa ho*
> *Rajiv Gandhi (X, Y, Z) jaisa ho.*

> *Jab tak suraj chand rahega*
> *Roop Kanwar tera naam rahega.*
> Model: *Jab tak suraj chand rahega*
> *Indira tera naam rahega.*

Others were victory chants of an inappropriate, even meaningless kind:

> *Ek do teen char*
> *Sati Mata ki jai jaikar*
> *Sati Mata ki jai*
> *Deorala Gaon ki jai*
> *Sati ke pati ki jai.*

A couple of slogans had a pretence of religiosity but were linked to a generalized term denoting God, not to any specific cult associated with sati:

> *Hari Om nam karega par*
> *Sati Mata ki jai jaikar.*

The most interesting slogan, clearly an offshoot of cow protection slogans popularized by political organizations like the Vishwa Hindu Parishad, was:

> *Desh dharam ka nata hai*
> *Sati hamari mata hai.*

The entire exercise had the flavour of a political rally, a show of strength vis-à-vis a political adversary rather than devotion to a deity.

We also attended the daily evening worship. The ground was floodlit. The schoolboys were replaced by young men with naked swords in hand. The *arti* sung was *Om Jai Jagdish Hare*, an arti of recent origin in modern Hindi which has been popularized by Bombay cinema to the extent that it has now assumed the status of a sort of national arti, sung indiscriminately on all occasions. It has nothing at all to do with sati, and certainly is not of Rajput or Rajasthani origin.

A majority of those gathered at the worship were young men and women, most of them educated. That the arti was a recent imposition on village culture was evident from the fact that most of those who sang it had no notion of the tune and only a few of them knew the words, with the result that the rendering was ragged and unintelligible. The arti was performed by educated youth whose idea of religious ritual seemed more influenced by Hindi films than by any local religious tradition.

The fascination with the sati cult has been attributed to the superstitious ignorance of illiterate village women, but it is noteworthy that the entire cult being created at Deorala is in the hands of educated men. Women participate by standing at a respectable distance, and joining in the singing.

URBAN-BASED CAMPAIGN

The pro-sati campaign is not an indigenous product of Deorala. It is based in Jaipur. Its leaders are urban, educated men in their twenties and thirties. These men have landed property and family connections in rural areas so their influence extends over both urban and rural areas. Some of them have government jobs, others have political power. The two networks are closely connected through kinship ties and with contacts in New Delhi also.

Thus, they constitute a powerful regional elite. They project themselves as representatives of rural India. In fact, they have no more claim to such a position than most urban dwellers, including many anti-sati campaigners, who have an ancestral village that they visit from time to time.

The secretary of the newly founded Dharm Raksha Samiti (original name Sati Dharm Raksha Samiti, changed after the ordinance was passed forbidding glorification of sati), Mr Narendra Singh Rajawat, is an educated man in his thirties, running a prosperous leather export business. His wife seemed in most ways to go along with the politics of the Samiti, although she has no official post in it. She is in her late twenties, a product of Lady Shri Ram College, one of Delhi's leading elite colleges for women. Even though she admitted being habituated to wearing modern Western clothes as also the fashionable salwar kameez, the day she met us she was wearing traditional Rajasthani *ghagra choli*, as though ready to go to fancy dress party or a ceremonial occasion like a wedding. By contrast, none of the village women we met wore anything as exotic as that.

We met a well-educated, young Rajput man in Deorala, who said he had rushed there from Delhi as soon as he had heard of the sati, and had been camping in Deorala ever since, helping organize the pro-sati campaign. He admitted to having played a prominent part in organizing the pro-sati rally in Jaipur. It was this man and his ilk who kept claiming that miraculous cures had been effected by the Sati Mata's powers.

The lifestyle of this urban-based elite is far removed from any traditional rustic lifestyle. It has little understanding of tradition. This was evident from the phoney ritualism that surrounds the Sati Sthal in Deorala. Several Rajputs from traditional families told us that satis in the past were never worshipped in the fashion that is being institutionalized at Deorala today. There was no tradition of offering *prasad* and singing artis to worship a sati. People would silently fold their hands before a Sati Sthal. Families, who had a sati in their ancestry would invoke her blessings but there was no big ceremonial cult around the satis.

CHUNRI MAHOTSAV—A VICTORY CELEBRATION

Another example of how a newfangled cult is being created today is the *chunri mahotsav* held after Roop Kanwar's death, which we saw notified in handbills on the walls at Deorala. The leaders of the Sati Dharm Raksha Samiti and Roop Kanwar's brother pointed out that the *chunri rasam* is a ceremony performed for any deceased woman and is the counterpart of the *pagri rasam* for men. It is a solemn ritual, held in the days of mourning. They were trying to say that ordinary ceremonies like this one should not have been objected to even by opponents of sati. But they could not explain why the ceremony had been termed a chunri mahotsav when no one would traditionally hold a mahotsav (festival) after a death, or why the ceremony became a militant celebration, a show of strength.

The pro-sati rally in Jaipur was another example of departure from tradition. It totally lacked the solemnity that would befit a procession connected with a death. The bulk of the demonstrators were young, educated men. Contingents of Rajput young men had come from many cities all over India. They shouted slogans in a militant fashion, posturing and dancing as if they were part of a victory celebration. In contrast, the anti-sati rally by women in Jaipur was an absolutely silent procession.

The sati cult in its present-day form is primarily the product of a phoney religiosity that is the accompaniment of new-found prosperity, harnessed by political leaders for their own vested interests. This religio-political combine is being imported into villages from cities. It is not really a traditional residue from the rural backwaters of the country.

It is commonly found in many parts of the world that as groups become more prosperous, they become more institutionally and ostentatiously religious and begin to spend money on building temples and promoting rituals. It is no coincidence that the largest number of new temples are springing up in cities, built by big businessmen. The dozen or so big sati temples in urban and semi-urban areas that have become centres of a cult have been built in the last decade by the rich Marwari businessmen and not the Rajput community.

Hindu Custom?

Proponents and opponents of sati have embarked on an examination of ancient texts to establish whether or not these texts 'sanction' sati. This search for a sanction or prohibition of various practices is an empty exercise that nineteenth-century British administrators began and that Indian social reformers picked up.

The British assumed that every religion, like Christianity, would have one book which all believers would accept as the 'gospel truth', and began a search for such a book for Hinduism. The search is a futile one because Hinduism is not a closed body of doctrines nor does it treat any text or set of texts as the final truth.

In different times and places, different Hindu communities follow widely different social and religious practices. Many of these practices are not mentioned in any text, but are nonetheless rigorously followed. Many practices sanctioned in texts are never practised and would be viewed with horror if proposed— for example, the practice of *niyoga* whereby unmarried persons may, at prescribed times, cohabit for the purpose of bearing children and satisfying their desires.

No society has one, single-track tradition. A whole range of ideas and beliefs, many of them contradictory, coexist and are handed down by each generation. In the process, they are continually transformed. Particular sections of community leadership pick up and glorify different traditions at different times. Therefore, we must enquire what forces are at work at a particular time and place to create an aura of legitimacy around an event, and why they choose to do so?

In Rajasthan, women who became satis were not the only ones traditionally glorified and revered by Rajputs or by Rajasthanis in general. Mirabai, too, was a Rajput woman (born *c.* AD 1512) who has been deeply revered over the centuries and whose songs continue to be sung today with love and devotion by Rajput and other Rajasthani women and men. She did not spend her life serving her husband, let alone giving up her life for him. Her songs openly proclaim her determination to undertake a spiritual quest, resisting the opposition of her husband and in-laws. In one song, she addresses her husband thus:

> Ranaji, you cannot stop me now
> I love to be among the wise
> I throw off the veil of modesty...
> Take your necklaces and jewels
> I tear and fling your finery...
> Mira wanders, a mad woman,
> Her hair flies free.
> (*Ranaji, Ab no rahoongi tori hatki*)

She lived a highly unconventional life, breaking out of seclusion, travelling widely with a following of women, and singing and dancing in temples. In many songs, she stressed her defiance of social opinion:

> Mira dances with bells on her feet...
> 'Mira is mad' people say
> 'Destroyer of family' kindred call me
> Mira dances with bells on her feet...
> (*Pag ghungroo bandh...*)

In one song she even states:

> I will sing of Girdhar
> I will not be a Sati
> (*Girdhar gasya, Sati na hosya*)

Mira continues to have a powerful grip over people's imagination in Rajasthan. One evidence of this is that over the centuries, more and more songs have been added to the body of her work, and scholars have difficulty sifting them. Women add to and change the songs as they sing them. Her songs are in Rajasthani, the people's own language, unlike the songs being sung in worship of Roop Kanwar today.

The urge towards self-definition and freedom that Mira represents is more integrally a part of Rajasthani traditions relating to women than is the cult being created around Roop Kanwar today. That the new self-proclaimed leaders should choose a Roop Kanwar rather than a Mira as a symbol of Rajasthani womanhood indicates what they believe of woman's place, but it is not evidence that a major section of Rajasthani women have chosen that ideal for themselves.

Many politicians used the Deorala episode as a pretext to attempt to unite the internally divided Rajput community and capture it as a vote bank. Many other leaders of Hindu revivalist organizations are trying to use the issue as a symbol of Hindu unity.

The call to boycott Diwali celebrations if government did not release those arrested at Deorala was first issued to Rajputs, but later extended to 'all Hindus'. At the rally organized by the Dharm Raksha Samiti in Jaipur, the call to save religion was issued in nasty, communal terms. What this portends can be gauged from the fact that burning a woman to death has become the symbol of this unity.

A number of saffron-robed religious figures were collected, and seated on the platform at the pro-sati rally. However, they were not the organizers of the campaign. The campaign was not led by religious leaders, but by politicians under the façade of newly floated organizations like the Dharm Raksha Samiti. These politicians pretend to be ordinary non-political religious Rajputs. For instance, we met Rajendra Singh Rathore, an ex-Yuva Janata student leader. Asked about his affiliations, he said, 'Here, I am just a member of the Dharm Raksha Samiti. I am not a political person.' But, a little later, he gloatingly remarked that V.P. Singh had lost Rajput hearts and votes by issuing a statement against the Deorala sati. It was clear that he was enjoying his new-found power as a Rajput leader able to mobilize the votes of sections of his community.

Fortunately, the diversity of Hindu society still lends it strength and sanity. The sati symbol is not likely to carry much weight beyond certain parts of the Hindi belt. In fact, the symbol has further divided Hindu opinion. For example, the Shankaracharya of Puri's pro-sati pronouncements have not convinced even Hindus in south India, let alone in Bengal or Gujarat, the North-east or the Arya Samaji, Radhaswami, and other Hindu sects in the north.

It is important to remember that many Rajputs are also totally opposed to sati. Several Rajput women and men were active in the protests against Roop Kanwar's death. A Rajput man was one of the advocates involved in filing petitions against the proponents of sati. Those who took a public stand had to face considerable hostility. Rani Chuhrawat, a well-known public figure, expressed her opposition to sati on public platforms. She was gheraoed and abused and is being defamed by many pro-sati elements in an attempt to silence her.

She pointed out that sati cannot be equated with the right to suicide because even where the right to suicide exists in law, suicide is not a socially encouraged act. One's family members would try their best to dissuade one from committing suicide and would certainly not help in any way. If one still wanted to commit suicide, one would do it privately, in solitude, not as a public spectacle. Even technically, sati is not suicide since someone else lights the pyre, not the woman herself.

Second, and most important, she asked how many women have the right to decide anything voluntarily?

If a woman does not have the right to decide whether she wants to marry, and when, and whom, how far she wants to take a particular job or not—how is it that she suddenly gets the right to take such a major decision as to whether she wants to die? Why is it that her family meekly acquiesces in her decision, when in the normal course, they would not scruple to overrule decisions she made of which they did not approve? Given women's general powerlessness, lack of control over their own lives, and definition of their status by their relationship to men (as daughters, wives, widows, mothers), can any decision of theirs, particularly such a momentous decision, really be called voluntary and self-chosen?

Women's groups in Rajasthan made an effort to work as a concerted lobby. They conducted a public debate on the issue, and mobilized women from different strata of society to protest the Deorala incident. A large rally was held in Jaipur. Many organizations from outside Rajasthan supported these efforts in various ways. These were positive developments.

State Action

However, it is unfortunate that opposition to sati took mainly the form of seeking government intervention. Our government, by its skilful use of progressive rhetoric, has convinced reformers that even though it has a consistent track record of being both dishonest and ineffective, it is ultimately on the side of progress. Reformers seem to accept the government's own evaluation of itself rather than going by its abysmally poor record.

In fact, our government machinery, far from being progressive, is not even neutral. It is controlled by politicians, for whom considerations of power and profit are far more important than human rights. The machinery is not only corrupt but often outright murderous. Witness the Indian police record of atrocities, ranging from the Arwal massacre, to innumerable rapes in custody, to the recent PAC killings in cold blood of arrested Muslims in Meerut.

In Deorala, too, the police is living up to its own traditions. The village has become a police camp. The police is actively obstructing journalists and anti-sati campaigners from investigating the case.

It is likely that the facts of the case—whether it was murder or suicide—would have come out, were it not for the heavy police presence in the village. Under the Ordinance, anyone who admits to having witnessed the sati is liable to prosecution. Most villagers are afraid to say anything for fear of being implicated by the police. Those who are determinedly pro-sati are camping at the Sati Sthal under police protection.

Any attempts to challenge the cult are prevented by the police. The march by anti-sati Hindu religious leaders, led by Swami Agnivesh, from Delhi to Deorala, was prevented from entering Deorala, and the marchers arrested. Women activists of Jaipur also say they are not allowed to enter the village in groups. The facts of the case are being suppressed and the cult built up under police protection.

About two kilometres from the village, a police picket stopped us, saying no journalist was allowed further. In Deorala, most of the policemen were in plainclothes. They mingled with the local people in a very friendly manner. It was hard to know who was a villager and who a policeman. When we tried to take photographs, some men aggressively forbade us. We thought they were villagers but they turned out to be plainclothes policemen. We were told there were 'orders' forbidding photography at the site but no one could explain why.

The ostensible reason for the police being there was to implement the Ordinance forbidding the glorification of sati. But they were making no attempt at all to do so. They were quite as involved in the worship as other villagers. One policeman reminded us to take off our shoes when approaching the Sati Sthal, and another cheerfully advised us to attend the arti at 7 p.m. We saw many jeeps and matadors (vans) full of worshippers from other areas coming to the village. Not one was stopped by the police.

Yet, the villagers claim the police victimized them. They claim that press publicity has led to police repression and that indiscriminate arrests have been made. Scores of persons had been arrested from Deorala, most of whom have been released in subsequent months. The villagers we met claimed most of those arrested were innocent bystanders.

The people of Deorala, whom we met, young and old alike, were highly suspicious and hostile towards the press and anyone who looked like a journalist. The police seemed to share this hostility. Whenever we began talking to any one villager, many others would immediately gather around and suspiciously demand: 'What are they asking? What are you telling them?' So effective was this mutual policing of each other by the villagers that we ended up answering more questions than they did.

This mutual policing within the community, hostility to outsiders, particularly journalists, and the mingling of the police with the people they are accused of repressing, was highly reminiscent of the situation we encountered in those parts of Meerut, which had witnessed mass burnings and the death of Muslims during the recent riots.

ROLE OF GOVERNMENT

The government and the police failed to prevent Roop Kanwar's death in an area that is teeming with government servants and police personnel. There was no way local government and police personnel could have been unaware of what was about to occur. There was a two-hour gap between the announcement that Roop was to become a sati and the actual immolation. People gathered from surrounding areas to witness it, and it took place in broad daylight.

No special anti-sati law was needed to prevent Roop Kanwar's death. The existing law was perfectly adequate. Both murder and suicide are illegal, punishable offences under the Indian Penal Code. The police is duty-bound to prevent their commission. A policeman who knows that a murder or suicide is about to occur, and neglects to intervene, also commits a serious offence.

Where a whole community chose to collude in a woman being murdered or pressured to submit to immolation, the local government and police, which are not after all a separate species but a part of the same society, also colluded in the crime. The upper levels of government, at the state and central levels, reacted with delaying and evasive tactics, succumbing to different pressure groups, and did not investigate the crucial question of why the local police had not intervened. Instead, that same local police was posted in the village to create an intimidating atmosphere to prevent proper investigation. It remains to be seen whether Roop Kanwar's in-laws' prosecution actually proceeds effectively.

It was the lack of will on the government's part, not the lack of a law, that resulted in its failure to intervene. Yet, the anti-sati campaigners assumed that a stringent law was all that was needed to solve the problem. If sati is just a cover used to get away with hounding a woman to death why is a special law needed to deal with such incidents? Does this not amount to conceding to the view that sati constitutes a special category distinct from murder or suicide?

Our government has perfected the art of passing draconian laws which it then uses not to solve problems but to acquire additional arbitrary powers and then uses these powers to intimidate the citizenry even further. For example, the Anti Terrorist Act[2] has not resulted in an end to terrorism but is used as a new weapon by policemen to threaten ordinary people and petty offenders and extract even larger bribes.

The anti-sati Ordinance passed by the Rajasthan government, with its vague definition of 'abetment of sati' as including presence at the site as a participant, has ample scope for misuse. The police can easily pick up any person from the area whom they wish to harass. It is alleged that they have already arrested several innocent people from Deorala. A person has to prove that he or she was not present at the site since the Ordinance, in violation of the principle that a person is innocent until proven guilty, lays the burden of poof on the accused.

The Ordinance also prescribes the death sentence for abetment of sati. At a time when most countries are considering abolition of the death sentence, as it has proven futile as a way of reducing the murder rate, that we should be introducing it for more offences is a singular irony. The Ordinance also has a ridiculous provision for punishing the victim. A woman who attempts sati is to be imprisoned for one to five years and fined Rs 5,000 to Rs 20,000. Central legislation along the same lines is now being drafted.

WHAT WENT WRONG?

Somewhere along the way, the anti-sati campaign became somewhat counter-productive. The campaigners became characterized as a handful of anti-Hindu, anti-Rajput, anti-religion, pro-government, anti-masses, urban, educated, Westernized people, and the pro-sati lobby as those sensitive to the sentiments of the rural, traditional poor. This completely false polarization occurred because:

1. The reformers wrongly characterized the Deorala episode as the product of illiteracy and backwardness among the rural poor, whereas it was the product of a modernized, developed, prosperous combine of local people.
2. The reformers saw the Deorala episode as the product of an old tradition, whereas in its present form it is a newly created cult, organized primarily by political, not by religious leaders.
3. The reformers entered into a debate on the religiosity or otherwise of the Deorala sati. It is important that we demystify it and see it as a case of a woman being hounded to death under a specious religious cover, and of her death being made a symbol by certain power groups to demonstrate their clout.
4. The main thrust of the anti-sati campaign took the form of petitions to government authorities asking for more stringent laws. This gave government the opportunity to pose as progressive by introducing a repressive law, and let the government off the hook for its complicity in Roop Kanwar's death.
5. The reformers asked that the police be used as an agent of social reform, forgetting that the police is incapable of performing this role. The police acquired more powers which it used to aid and abet pro-sati forces and to prevent the reformers and the press from purveying information about the case. In addition, it made a lot of money on the side.

WHAT MIGHT HELP

We have to consider what course of action could create a state of affairs wherein people would not be able to justify and escape retribution for burning a woman to death in public. To prevent any more such incidents from occurring must be our main concern. Any course of action that has the negative, unintended consequence of heightening the aura around the Deorala episode and of arming with more arbitrary powers those who colluded in Roop Kanwar's death—namely, the local government and police—should be avoided.

When we consider the question of what is to be done, we have to bear in mind that not everyone in every part of the country can be equally effective in acting on every issue. Where we are placed inevitably affects our sphere of influence and effective activity. Alternative courses of action that are being pursued, but unfortunately, with much less vigour than the course of demanding more legislation and more police, are:

1. Indicting the local police for not having intervened to save Roop Kanwar. All the local officers who failed to stop the burning should be treated as abettors of Roop Kanwar's murder, immediately suspended, and tried under the Indian Penal Code. This is one way to ensure that other policemen know what the consequences will be of condoning any other such deaths.

2. Monitoring the case against Roop Kanwar's in-laws to see that all the facts are uncovered, that it is not quietly dropped for 'lack of evidence' as too many wife-murder cases routinely are; following it up consistently to see that the accused are exposed, prosecuted, and convicted.

3. Instead of relying on ordinances, stay orders, and the police to prevent the glorification of the Deorala episode and the construction of a temple, it would be better if local human rights and women's organizations mobilized all persons concerned to offer indefinite satyagraha at Deorala to facilitate a dialogue and debate with those involved in the sati cult. Outside activists might be permitted to join in on a relay basis. This could have been done better if Deorala had not been converted into a police camp. But it should still be possible, though it will now involve fighting the government for the citizens' right to protest the murder and its subsequent glorification.

4. Some laudable attempts have been made to engage the wider public in a debate that goes beyond the newspaper pages. One such attempt was a yatra from Delhi to Deorala, led by Arya Samaj sanyasis. This is an important symbolic statement that anti-women forces do not have a monopoly on defining Hindu traditions and do not represent all Hindus.

The Women's Development Programme and other social work organizations in Ajmer district, Rajasthan, have organized a padyatra through villages, with plays and songs that raise questions of concern to people including the drought, women's issues, and sati.

More such efforts could mobilize a broader social consensus in Rajasthan against maltreatment of women, and provide an atmosphere conducive to expression of dissent from amongst local communities themselves.

That a woman could be burnt to death in public is a stark indication of women's vulnerability in our social system. Roop Kanwar's death was only one expression of the general devaluation of women's lives. Unless the consensus within our society changes in favour of a more dignified and self-sustaining life for women, any number of repressive laws and policemen are not likely to preserve women's lives.

UPDATE ON ROOP KANWAR, 1998

After a great deal of pressure and agitation by women's organizations and human rights groups all over the country, the Government of Rajasthan filed a case in the court of additional district judge, Neem ka Thana. The case dragged on for years at the level of the lower court. In the meantime, all the witnesses had turned hostile, further weakening the case. Finally on 11 October 1996, a judgment was delivered acquitting all the accused.

There were a number of protest demonstrations in Rajasthan against this judgment, including a siege of the secretariat. All this to pressure the Rajasthan government to file an appeal in the high court—something it should have done on its own initiative. The case has not even been listed for hearing since then. It is noteworthy that the anti-sati Ordinance passed in response to Roop Kanwar's sati, cannot be appealed to in this case (except for preventing glorification of sati) since the law came into effect after her death.

Hinduism Today, 'Uproar over Rajput Sati'[3]

In the wake of the Roop Kanwar sati, this online magazine dedicated to Sanatana Dharma carried the following defence of women's right to perform sati.

A pretty, young bride of eight months, Roop Kanwar gained universal fame on 4 September at Rajasthan's Deorala village in north-west India. She became a sati—burning herself to death on her husband's funeral pyre. The reaction in India was an unresolved mixture of shock, admiration, outrage, reverence, and embarrassment over the young girl's action. Local police failed to stop the sati. The Indian press called the act 'a pagan sacrifice' and 'a barbaric incident which blackened India's image in the world'. Women's groups demonstrated against the sati all across India, prompting belated government action against Roop's relatives. Yet private opinions, even of prominent politicians, were ambivalent.

Roop's people, the martial Rajputs (who have inspired fear in every invader of India from the Muslims to the British), claim sati as their custom and religious right—the free choice of the widow. Groups of Rajput women marched last month in favour of sati and burned copies of the anti-sati ordinance. The situation remains a stand-off, the Rajputs proceeding with plans to build a temple on the site (they have collected over $230,000), despite a government ban and demanding that those arrested be freed.

Many newspaper reports say the widow was forced into the deed; in a word, murdered. According to all available first-hand reports, however, it was Roop Kanwar's personal decision to commit this form of ritual suicide. 'Roop did not weep [upon seeing her husband's body], but she kept saying, "I will not let you go alone, I am also coming",' recalled eyewitness and neighbour Meenakshi Khandelwal. When Roop's relatives tried to talk her out of it, she threatened them with *sati shraap*—a curse put upon those who would oppose a sati and thought to bring ruin to not only the person but his entire village. The last sati of Deorala—sixty-nine years ago—in fact cursed and ruined a man who sought to dissuade her.

Contrary to many press reports, her intentions were not only known before the funeral, but several village elders and holy men came to test her resolve, according to their tradition. Convinced that she had received the power to become a sati from the Goddess, the elders and her in-laws gave their blessings.

Meenakshi Khandelwal said, 'I saw Roop dressed in bridal make-up walking along with her husband's body with a coconut in hand. There were about 900 people when the body was taken to the cremation ground. Later, the crowd swelled. It took about an hour for the preparation of the pyre. The girl stood like a rock chanting the Gayatri. Once the pyre was ready, she entered it and sat holding her husband's head in her lap. She ordered Pushpendra Singh, her brother-in-law, to light the pyre. As the fire engulfed her, Roop sat serenely talking to her relatives, not showing any sign of pain.'

Many newspapers discounted this as incredible, saying she must have been heavily sedated or pushed in. But courageous willingness is, in fact, a common aspect of satis. A seventeenth-century traveller, François Bernier, witnessed a sati where he 'could not perceive the slightest indication of pain or even uneasiness in the victim'. One witness to Roop's sati, Tej Singh, is quoted in *India Today* as saying, 'She is from a well-educated family. Could this kind of woman have been forced? And there are hundreds of widows here whose husbands died even before there were pension schemes. Why were they not forced? She was a woman who believed her husband was a god and there could be no life for her without him.'

Grief at the death of a loved one is one of the most common reasons for suicide in all societies. In America the suicide rate is very high, 1 in 2,000 for persons aged fifteen to thirty-four whose spouses die. Rejecting the concept that suicide is a sin, most westerners have accepted the idea, according to scholars, that man has a right to take his own life. In the last twenty years, nearly all countries have removed suicide from the law books; aiding a suicide remains a crime.

'Ritual suicide' is done in matters of injustice, honour, and love. It is tied to belief in reincarnation and viewed as a sacrifice of the body, not a mortal sin against the soul. East or West, ritual suicide is regarded with respect and reverence. Will anyone forget the Buddhist priests who, in protest of the Vietnam War, burnt themselves to death in the Saigon town square? The Japanese *samurai* commits *hari kari* when his honour is lost.

Western reaction to sati—outside of missionary reports—has often been one of awe. The early Portugese traveller Pietro della Valle said, 'If I knew [of a lady about to become a sati], I will not fail to go and see her and honour by my presence her funeral with that compassionate affection, which such a great conjugal fidelity and love seem to deserve.'

From its first instances in India, sati has been a practice of the warrior class, or Kshatriyas. Later, other castes picked it up. Similar practices are found in the history of other peoples, e.g. American Indian, African, Chinese, Egyptian, and Greek.

The first historical mention of sati in India is in the Mahabharata, composed around 300 BC. There the wives of Lord Krishna— Rukumini, Gandhari, Sahya, Haimavati, and Jambavati—ascended the funeral pyre upon his death. Sati is not mentioned in Hindu scriptures until the first century AD when the minor scripture Vishnusmriti commends it. This scripture claims a sati will be freed from rebirth as a woman. Other commentators reject this logic. The hard life of a widow contributed to the occurrence of sati among those who did not feel they could live the required life of renunciation. Sati was formally outlawed in India in 1829 as a result of numerous reports of coercion on the part of relatives who sought to steal the widow's inheritance or avoid supporting her.

Without question, it is the duty of the police to make every effort to stop a sati from occurring. Yet, it is doubtful whether such a determined person as Roop Kanwar could be thwarted. It may be impossible to dissuade fighting people such as the Rajputs from their ideals of self-sacrifice—either of their men in battle or their women in the love of their husbands. Western societies are embroiled in the ethical issues of terminal patients seeking 'a conscious, dignified death'. The customs of sati raise equally perplexing problems.

Veena Oldenburg, 'The Roop Kanwar Case: Feminist Responses'[4]

In the following article, Veena Oldenburg outlines the various responses of feminist groups to the immolation of Roop Kanwar and discusses the social and political implications of this controversial sati.

On 5 September, 1987, in Jaipur, Bal Singh Rathore and Sneh Kanwar discovered that their eighteen-year-old daughter Roop Kanwar—married only eight months before—had suddenly been

widowed and then cremated along with the corpse of her husband in the manner of a sati in the village of Deorala, a two-hour
drive away. They read this piece of information in the local Hindi
language daily; they had not been informed either of the death
of their son-in-law in a hospital in the district headquarters in Sikar,
nor of their daughter's wish to die as a sati on her husband's funeral
pyre. They were later persuaded by Roop Kanwar's in-laws that
their daughter had, over efforts to dissuade her, chosen this way
to die.

Under usual circumstances, this brief newspaper report would
have caused little stir, not unlike the forty other cases of sati-style
deaths recorded since 1947, when India became an independent
and secular republic. Some twenty-eight of these have occurred
in Rajasthan, mainly in and around Sikar district. What made the
profound difference this time was the activism and concern of
women. Arguably, the Roop Kanwar case has converted the idea
that a woman can become (an alleged) sati—and be glorified
for it—from a residual quasi-religious theme into a critical political
issue on which women's voices were heard for the very first time.

In the colonial period it was chiefly men—Hindu reformers
and British officials who debated, and the East India Company
that eventually legislated, to abolish the practice in 1829. The
Maharaja of Amber and Jaipur followed the company's lead in
1846. He banned the practice in his kingdom, as did eighteen
other princely states in the Rajputana Agency. The Indian Penal
Code, as revised in the early 1950s, did not incorporate the East
India Company regulation. The presumption was that its sections
on murder and abetment to suicide (Sections 302 and 306, respectively) would be enough to deal with such a happening, and
therefore no explicit reference to the custom of sati was made.

This implicit redefinition of sati as a crime is accepted by
women opposed to the custom—they deem it to be murder or
abetted suicide—and sati has, quite properly, no separate place
in the penal code of a secular state. The redefinition also ought to
have eliminated the possibility of further debate on the authenticity
of such an event and on whether or not it enjoys scriptural sanction,
issues much discussed and presumably settled before legislation
was hammered out in 1829. With the law in place and enforced,

the act of committing sati—whether the widow's participation was voluntary or coerced—was shorn of all mystification, glory, glamour, and ritual significance, and adjudged to be simply a crime. Those implicated in it would be equally punished by death or life imprisonment. After its abolition and an initial upsurge of incidents, the practice of sati faded into a very rare crime; and statistically speaking, today it is rarer still. Nonetheless, satis did still occur. The Roop Kanwar death mobilized feminists and liberals to ensure that the present crime and all others like it be punished, so that even a single sati would become unthinkable in the future in Rajasthan or anywhere else in India. On the other end of the spectrum of opinion are conservatives who believe that Roop Kanwar heroically sacrificed her own life, in keeping with the ideology of sati, which finds honour and pride in the most painful and brutal of deaths—the burning of a woman on her deceased husband's funeral pyre.

The purpose of this essay is to summarize the Indian feminists' response to Roop Kanwar's death[5]. This response has come in the shape of active protests, detailed reports of the knowable facts, and a stream of analytical articles. I expect to tell the story of the event as it emerges from this literature, which is published in English, and to distil its substantive and interpretive points. Before proceeding, however, a caveat is in order, and a word of preparation.

First the caveat: I use the word *feminist* advisedly, although I am more than aware that it is not accepted by some of the women activists and scholars whose work is reviewed in this essay. It is rejected by these women on the grounds that the term has specific meanings that grew out of the experience of women activists in the West, and that it is therefore unsuitable in the Indian context. I believe this is mistaken. Feminism has a long history and is no longer monolithic; multiple feminisms abound, and *feminism* is capable of the same kinds of distinctions one would expect in any analysis of the word *patriarchy*. I define the word *feminist* in its simplest political sense, as a person (and not necessarily a woman) whose analytical perspective is informed by an understanding of the relationship between power and gender in any historical, social, or cultural context. To me, the argument against using the word *feminist* is weakened by the fact that terms and theories of equally Western provenance—*Marxist, socialist, Freudian,* or *post-structuralist*—do not arouse similar indignation and are in fact (over) used as standard frameworks for analyses of Indian society by Indian scholars. I rather suspect that gender analysis will one day trip off the scholarly tongue with the same panache as class analysis does now in Indian academic and activist circles; in the meantime, I will take my chances.

My second preliminary comment has to do with background. Historians are indispensable when a custom or tradition is being bruited about as a timeless phenomenon, and sati is clearly believed by many to be a Hindu tradition with such credentials. Therefore, before launching into my review of contemporary feminist reactions to the Roop Kanwar episode, I urge the reader to consult the account that has been provided by the leading historian of India, Romila Thapar. Her essay, entitled 'In History', appears in the excellent issue of the journal *Seminar* which is devoted to sati (February 1988). This essay was prompted by Roop Kanwar's death; and although it does not deal directly with the event, it puts us in a position to appreciate both the discursive and material aspects of the response to it, providing a solid background to frame the contemporary event and gently but firmly clearing away the historical misinformation and misinterpretations that non-historians have produced in their own attempts to put the Roop Kanwar case into perspective.[6] Authoritative, rigorous, and elegant, Thapar's essay may be read in conjunction with my own historical construction of 'The Continuing Invention of the Sati Tradition'.[7] As one moves closer in time and space to the Roop Kanwar case, one should consult the work of Sudesh Vaid, whose detailed historical analysis of sati in the Shekhavati region provides the tools for best understanding the Roop Kanwar sati and the larger pattern to which her immolation belongs.[8]

After reading many reports of Roop Kanwar's death, it is possible to conclude that gender-sensitive scholars and activists in India—whatever their disagreements on a wide range of issues that concern women—are of one mind about the tragic end of Roop Kanwar. The consensus is profound; the analyses differ only in the method or details they choose to emphasize.

Feminists are united, first and foremost, in denouncing the event as one among many crimes against women. They do not admit any obfuscating rhetoric about whether this event was or was not an 'authentic' sati; coercion or consent is not really relevant to their formulations of the problem. Their concern is about the women involved—their lives, the pain they endure, the cruelty and barbarity they experience, and the resultant negation of the meaning of their separate existence. It is not far-fetched to say that feminists would be steadfast in their view of sati even if Roop Kanwar's volition could be established without doubt, by some magical replay of linear time. For them, sati as an issue was settled 175-odd years ago; the question is why it is still allowed to persist. Feminists unanimously reject the glorification that follows an alleged sati, what with the endowment of commemorative shrines and temples and the holding of festivals and anniversaries. They also continue to work hard to counter the propaganda in the media that represented Roop Kanwar as a symbol of an alleged ideal of Hindu womanhood—chaste, devoted, and able to sacrifice her very life for her husband. This propaganda is part of the agenda of the Bharatiya Janata Party, which has become the leading opposition party in the Indian Parliament by touting an essentialized and homogenized Hinduism while projecting itself as the defender of a beleaguered faith.

Another common strand is feminists' anger at the reactions of governments at the state and federal levels. Rajiv Gandhi's Congress government in New Delhi is sharply criticized, first for its apathy towards or tacit approval of the event, then for its ineptitude in trying to prevent the site of the sati from becoming a shrine for the offerings of the multitudes that converged on Deorala, and finally for its pernicious policy of giving in to demands by religious extremists to destroy the secular foundations of the Constitution of India. All the reports also see caste more than class as the decisive factor behind the incident. They allege a conspiracy among the three dominant castes, which moved in swiftly to capitalize on the alleged sati. They blame Rajput men for using women's lives as the means of propping up old chivalric traditions in a time when they are otherwise disenfranchised. They censure the Marwari businessmen for imitating and supporting these traditions in their quest for status and power and for contributing their wealth and commercial acumen to perpetuate this custom. And they hold Brahmins responsible for lending an air of legitimacy to the ethos of sati as a way to bolster their own dwindling importance in the modern world. Through the efforts of these three castes, a combination of patriarchal values and opportunistic greed approves the event and orchestrates its aftermath by converting the site of the cremation into a shrine, inventing a chunri (veil) festival to glorify the painful death of a woman, and assisting a prosperous but undistinguished village to become a pilgrimage site. Finally, most feminists are agreed that, although each sati is projected as a rare and spontaneous happening, nonetheless all satis share a common plot or script, as well as the costuming and dramatization necessary to make sati a riveting spectacle for those who withness it. Witnesses affirm the nature of the event as religious; their gaze makes it sati. I would add that the event also reinforces the base appetites of the male members of the audience to see women suffer, while in women sati confirms the ideology that women's strength lies in the act of sacrifice and the endurance of untold pain.

Feminists have pointed out that, as the news media lost interest in the issue, the battle of words finally narrowed into a duel between pro- and anti-sati scholars, unwittingly mimicking the tradition-versus-modernity debate on what British bureaucrats termed 'social evils' in India in the colonial period. That debate pitted orthodox Hindu religionists against Hindu liberal reformers and British utilitarian evangelicals.[9] The former, who were temporarily eclipsed by the secular thrust of the Nehruvian era, have forcefully reappeared and been joined by scholars who defend sati as a widow's unique act of sacrifice incomprehensible to modern women. The latter groups have been replaced by feminists and secularists who are irate to see such a practice make a comeback, albeit in a modernized form.

All this has finally moved the sati debate from its familiar rut of profit and patriarchy onto new ground, where questions about women's subjectivity, about pain and suffering, and about culturally constructed and gendered notions of volition and sacrifice are explicitly asked. This last twist in the feminist argument has rescued the debate from being a mere replay of its nineteenth-century predecessor. The fact that women are now speaking for their sisters, who could not, may finally unmake the tradition of sati.

Feminists in Jaipur were alerted to the death of Roop Kanwar by the report of the first journalist who arrived in Deorala, Tej Pal Saini of the *Rashtradoot*, a newspaper that covers Sikar district.[10] He probably did not realize that he had fired the opening salvo of a debate that was going to rage in the print media for years. Interpreting his mission as the need to establish whether or not Roop Kanwar's death was a 'voluntary' or 'authentic' sati, he visited Deorala for a week, interviewing all the relatives, friends, and other inhabitants of the village, and firmly concluded that the act was indeed voluntary. *India Today*, a major fortnightly newsmagazine, sent out its hounds, who later confirmed this view. An early editorial in the Hindi daily *Jansatta*, widely distributed in north India, wrote a ringing approval of the live burning:

Roop Kanwar did not become a sati because someone threatened her. ...[S]he purposely followed the tradition of sati which is found in the Rajput families of Rajasthan. Even among Rajasthan's Rajputs sati is no ordinary event. Out of hundreds of thousands of widows perhaps one would resolve on a sati. It is quite natural that her self-sacrifice should become the centre of reverence and worship. This therefore cannot be called a question of women's civil rights or sexual discrimination. It is a matter of a society's religious and social beliefs...

People who accept that this life is the beginning and the end, and see the greatest happiness in their own individual happiness and pleasure, will never understand the practice of sati. ...The practice of sati should now be totally reexamined. But this is not the right of people who neither know nor understand the faith and belief of the masses of India.[11]

This editorial summed up the general pro-sati, anti-woman, conservative position. The day after its publication, about fifty angry women stormed into the offices of *Jansatta*, besieged the author of the article, and obtained the right to publish a rebuttal in the same paper. The ensuing debate was defined by these reports, and a nation of historical amnesiacs ardently resumed the old arguments about voluntary versus coerced sati.

Among the first feminists to respond to the event was Dr Sharada Jain, an activist, scholar, and teacher based in Jaipur. She was part of the delegation representing three women's organizations that called on Hardeo Joshi, the chief minister of Rajasthan, two days after the event. They reminded him that sati was a crime and urged prompt and stern action against the culprits, but were coolly and quickly dismissed. They did not fail to press the view that, as Sharada Jain put it, 'Roop Kanwar's death could not have been an act of free will. She was murdered.'[12] In a chronology of the first few weeks after the event (including feminist responses to it), published in Bombay's *Economic and Political Weekly*, Sharada Jain and two colleagues pose what was to become the central question for feminists regarding the issue of sati:

Why was the burning of a girl [sic] described as 'sati' and not as 'murder' even in the first press reporting? Even if the overt 'form' of a widow being dressed up and being taken to the funeral pyre with ostentatious celebration camouflaged the crime for the simple-minded, tradition-oriented villagers, why was the official perception not that of a violation of a law? ...[T]he episode cannot be viewed as emerging out of an 'illiterate', backward situation. Ironically, not only are Roop Kanwar's family and Maal Singh's father educated (in the conventional sense of the word), but she too had received formal education up to class ten. ...This exposes the hollowness of the entire educational engagement, which leaves basic attitudes untouched.

The climax of the horror story in fact lies not in Deorala, or even in other parts of Rajasthan. It lies in the elitist 'distanced' quarters. It is from the urban-educated elite that the oft repeated question came: 'Did Roop Kanwar commit sati of her own will or was she forced?' If, even at this level, the utter irrelevance of the question is not clear and if, even here, the condemnation or approval of the event depends on an answer to this question, then the focus of action has to be deliberated on with great care.[13]

These were the issues Jain and her delegation brought before the Rajasthan chief minister as well. They culminated in two unambiguous demands: one, that the alleged sati be named and booked as murder, and not abetment to suicide; and two, that the public celebrations planned for the chunri mahotsav (a ritual held on the thirteenth day after the cremation, when a red veil is placed on a trident at the site) be prevented. Both demands were ignored; but a case for abetment to suicide was registered the next day, and Roop Kanwar's fifteen-year-old brother-in-law was arrested. Yet, the excitement over the planned chunri ceremony ballooned unchecked as news of the now 'miraculous' sati, with burgeoning anecdotal evidence, spread from the village to the district, the state, New Delhi, and beyond. Several newspapers carried daily descriptions of the feverish anticipation of the chunri ceremony that probably served as unwitting advertisement for the action to come. Approximately 10,000 pilgrims were debouched daily from trucks, buses, and camel carts, and many travelled miles on foot to gather in the village of Deorala for the forthcoming ceremony, while the state government did nothing. The event also became a commercial opportunity, as crudely cut and pasted photographs of Roop Kanwar, often with her husband Mal Singh, were reprinted as lurid posters and icons for sale. Her marital home, particularly the bedroom she had shared with her husband, became consecrated as a site for pilgrims to view. Stalls selling sati memorabilia and snacks mushroomed, while thousands of handbills informing the visitors of the chunri ceremony were systematically distributed. An obscure village was ready for an obscurantists' carnival.

Four days before the chunri ceremony was to take place, seven women's groups in Rajasthan serving rural and urban constituencies came together for the first time to plan joint action. They agreed to condemn the barbaric murder of Roop Kanwar publicly and to appeal to citizens at large to demand immediate and appropriate action against the crime. They also planned to hold a public demonstration on 14 September to demand that the chief minister enforce the law and stop the planned celebrations on 16 September. They sent telegrams to the prime minister, Rajiv Gandhi, and to Margaret Alva, the minister of state for women's welfare, since the state government had virtually abetted the glorification of sati by its silence and inaction. According to Rajasthan state's own standard procedures, the offenders should have been charged under the Indian Penal Code, and the worship of the sati and the collection of donations should have been prohibited. By allowing thousands to congregate in Deorala, by sending messages to permit restricted numbers to worship at the site, and by failing to forestall the chunri ceremony, the chief minister proved his credentials as a puppet of Rajiv Gandhi's Central government, which was unwilling to offend the powerful Rajput lobby in Rajasthan.

The anti-sati demonstration in Jaipur on 14 September was a small affair in contrast to the milling, jostling crowds in Deorala.

About 350 people, including members of thirteen women's organization, journalists, scholars, college and university teachers, students, actors, and other professionals—people of all castes and creeds—marched in silence under a relentless midday sun to the state legislature. Their memorandum was finally accepted by a bureaucrat, because the elected leaders of the state (the chief minister and his cabinet) were curiously unavailable; even the women ministers showed little courage and did not meet the protestors, who waited for hours for them to appear. And while the government displayed 'a total absence of political will' and disowned all responsibility to enforce the law, a 'culture of silence emerged among the prominent citizens and intellectuals (barring the few who had joined the march)'.[14] This deliberate occlusion forced the next step: the feminist leaders decided to make a last-ditch appeal to the Jaipur High Court, before it closed at five o'clock that evening, to direct the state government to prohibit the glorification ceremonies to be held two days later in Deorala, on the grounds that they were illegal. The next day, 15 September, the advocate for the women's groups persuaded the bench to admit the petition and to direct the state government to ensure that no public function be held in Deorala.

This injunction finally elicited a statement from the chief minister. He conceded that the act in Deorala had been 'unlawful and improper'.[15] But this statement failed to spur a resolutely inert government to take any steps to prevent the chunri ceremony; indeed, to the contrary, many members of the Rajasthan Legislative Assembly proceeded to join the throng that had gathered in Deorala. This provoked hitherto uncommitted scholars and teachers to join the discussions that the women's groups were holding on the subject of sati the same evening. Their indignation was compounded by the fact that the state had accepted this murder as a matter of religious and communal pride for the Rajputs. Rajput youth were out in force, brandishing swords, to protect the site of the cremation. That the event in Deorala was not a religious matter but a question of women's social identity and status was the crux of the deliberations by the women's groups.

Margaret Alva chose to express her belated anguish in a telegram to the Women's Studies Centre at Jaipur University after the festivities were safely over, and Rajiv Gandhi despatched his minister of state for home affairs, P. Chidambaram, to 'inquire into the matter' on 19 September. Chidambaram delivered the government's assurances that the situation was now under control, since the main culprits—Roop Kanwar's father-in-law and his three sons—had been arrested, and that no temple would be permitted to be built on the site to glorify the alleged sati. Later that afternoon he met with 500 or so young Rajput men, who had driven recklessly through the streets of Jaipur in triumph and demanded an audience, uninhibited by the police. The meeting was an angry one, since the minister held firm in his position against the event, and the youths went away swearing to protect sati dharma. Public opinion seemed to polarize along gender lines. Women activists abhorred the event as the murder of a young and helpless widow; and men saw it as a mark of Rajput high society. As activists, the latter formed the overwhelming majority. The Congress party is often thought of as a bulwark protecting secular values in India, but it was Atal Bihari Vajpayee, the nationally important leader of the Bharatiya Janata Party, who called a public meeting and roundly and unequivocally denounced the glorification of the Deorala incident. The Congress party acted only when embarrassed by reminders from feminist groups.

Sikar, where the district headquarters governing Deorala are located, lacked any women's organization that could raise consciousness and determine to prevent such acts in future; and indeed, only a few representatives of women's groups in Jaipur visited Deorala after the event. These were glaring omissions. Finally on 25 September, a select group of women from the various women's organizations in Jaipur went to Sikar to help form a women's organization in that district. Local women who responded to this initiative 'were very clear that the religious cover given to the entire episode was false. It was a clear case of murder and needed to be condemned in unmixed terms.'[16] Meanwhile women's groups from other parts of the country began to call and express their solidarity with the women in Rajasthan; women journalists working for national dailies had also convened in Jaipur, meeting with the women's group to ensure better coverage of the steps taken to protest the event.

Unfortunate as Roop Kanwar's death had been, it seemed to have given women's organizations fresh impetus to come together and forge new alliances and put into place better networking procedures and strategies for mobilization. On 29 September, the disparate women's groups in Jaipur formed a joint action committee. It formally condemned 'all atrocities committed on women in the name of religion or community' and stated that 'the basic issue in our struggle was that of women's identity and status.' It also decided that signatures should be collected from those who supported the groups' stand, particularly among Rajputs. Further, it resolved to produce a pamphlet that would unambiguously spell out the groups' position on the issue of sati. This pamphlet would be distributed to the national media and to women's groups in other parts of India who were also in the process of forming anti-sati committees.[17]

These deliberations and exchanges resulted in plans for a large anti-sati rally on 6 October, for which strict ground rules were laid down. It was agreed that the march would be silent, no political party or institutional banner would be allowed, and nobody would be paid even for transport; it had to be an entirely voluntary commitment. Selected people would speak, including a rural woman, a woman from an urban slum (basti), two men who had proved very supportive, and two Rajput women. It was also decided that no political party or outside person would be given a platform.[18] An open discussion at a local girls' high school on the eve of the rally attracted droves of new supporters, particularly male faculty from Rajasthan University and representatives of women's groups from Ahmedabad, New Delhi, Nagpur, and Pune. The decision to march without party banners and in silence is a recent departure for women's groups; from such small but significant strategic moves, a coherent feminist platform was built and shared by all groups, including male participants.

On 6 October, 3,000 people marched through the streets of Jaipur. They represented some twenty-five organizations from Rajasthan and thirty-one from other cities. At the public meeting that followed, sati was proclaimed to be not just an issue that concerned women but a crime against women; it was seen as a move to manipulate religion and caste to exploit women. The state government was strongly indicted for its failure to enforce the law. Laxmi Kumari Chundawat, a Rajput writer and former member of the Legislative Assembly of Rajasthan, asserted that the burning of widows was a barbaric act and that no religion gave sanction to it; a Sanskrit scholar challenged anyone to prove that the Shastras, the cultural repositories of Hindu legal wisdom, advocated sati. The feminist agenda for further thought and action on the matter of widow-burning emerged with clarity and force:

A systematic and sustained dialogue on this issue of widows (should they always be described as widows?) and their status needs to be carried on at all levels just as much as the even more sensitive issue of religious sanction. Unless the matter is brought out in the open and talked about, its supercharged emotive character will not wear off and rational decision making will always stand in danger of being swept away by the mere chanting of a few words.[19]

When reminded by an interviewer that the women who participated in the march had been accused by Rajput critics of being overly westernized, Sharada Jain spoke passionately. 'It is totally false to say that we are westernized women. The Rajputs have taken to Western ways much more than any other community. The sati was not a question of tradition against modernity.' In some ways, she went on to say, it was just the reverse. The glorification of sati was to be seen as the sly revival of a shameful custom by the three most powerful castes in Rajasthan, whose investment in the process of modernization was the greatest: Rajputs, Brahmins, and Marwaris. Jain charged that these three had promoted the murder as sati for their own gain:

Take the family that committed this murder. They are Rajputs. They pride themselves on their tradition of chivalry and valour. In villages throughout Rajasthan, the Rajputs were once the main landowners. Now there is little opportunity for deeds of chivalry, the government has taken away much of their land, and so the Rajputs are in search of an identity. A sati by a woman of the Rajput caste was a tremendous boost to their morale and image. ...[The Brahmin priests'] approval was necessary before Roop Kanwar's sati could be accepted. Brahmins' prestige still depends on their priestly role. ...They would certainly want to dip into something so unusual as a so-called sati. ...The banias [merchants, especially Marwaris] are a very rich and powerful caste. You could say that they are commercially very daring, but they are basically very superstitious. They are religious-minded but their religion is based on luck. They would want to touch the ground where a sati was committed because they would believe it would bring them luck. The banias have the economic power, the Rajputs the political power and the Brahmins the power of religious knowledge. Is it right that a woman's identity should be controlled by these vested interests?[20]

Sharada Jain's argument—albeit an oversimplification, because it attributes greater homogeneity of opinion to members of a caste than actually exists—contains the nucleus of the analysis that would be couched in more sophisticated language in several later articles by other scholars. Her question puts the central issue of woman's identity, autonomy, volition, and agency squarely into place: even if Roop Kanwar was willing, she would only have been responding to an internalized ideology. In that case she should be seen more as a puppet than as an agent. This line of argument, by no means new, finds its most detailed treatment in the work of Kumkum Sangari and Sudesh Vaid. These scholars have been investigating sati in the Shekhavati region for well over a decade; the Roop Kanwar sati spurred them to write a comprehensive article that collects and updates previous research and culminates in the Roop Kanwar case. They systematically expose the long collaboration between Rajputs and Banias in inventing a formula with an appealing blend of ideological, ritual, and commemorative elements for these periodic spectacles of sati. This formula judiciously borrows features from many traditions of goddess worship already prevalent in Rajasthan. They recount the earlier brutal murder of the young widow Om Kanwar, on 30 August 1980, ill-disguised by her in-laws as a sati and glorified through the erection of a shrine that has become a popular pilgrimage site in Jhardli, Rajasthan. From the details, they abstract what emerges as a model and horrifying inspiration for subsequent instances of sati. A chilling replay of this plot can be seen in the Roop Kanwar murder seven years later.[21]

In the weeks and months that followed the death of Roop Kanwar, a flood of articles on the subject appeared in newspapers, special numbers of journals, and independently produced reports and analyses. Every piece that lamented the event was matched by another that approved it. These pro-sati attacks, articulated by men who postured as keepers of a timeless Hindu tradition, such as the Shankaracharya of Puri, challenged the right of feminists to act as spokespersons on behalf of the alleged satis, and served to focus the feminist position sharply. Nationally known women's groups such as the Women and Media Committee of the Bombay Union of Journalists and the editors of the leading women's journal *Manushi* were provoked to conduct their own fact-finding missions to reconstruct a clear narrative of events in Deorala. Both groups' reports are worth examining at some length.

Three members of the Women and Media Committee visited Deorala in the last week of September 1987.[22] A part of their stated brief was to 'examine the sequence of events that led to the sati and obtain a clear perspective on the debate on whether or not there was an element of coercion in the act.' This may sound somewhat regressive, considering what has already been said about implicit coercion, but the Committee, nevertheless, unearthed some very startling facts. Its members had other purposes as well. They wanted to document the impact of the event on the village— 'the communal overtones the incident had assumed' and the 'socio-cultural influence of *sati* in the region, especially among the Rajputs'—and they wanted to analyse how this incident was reported in the mainstream press.[23] Their report, *Trial by Fire*, deals systematically with each item on their agenda, although much of the reportage contains no new analytical perspective. They faithfully catalogue the doings of the women's organizations and analyse the sensational way the English-language press in India reported the event, with journalists feeling free to make the most obvious and insensitive puns and jokes about fire and burning.

But the real value of *Trial by Fire* lies in the nuggets of information it reports that appear to have been overlooked by the rest of the media. At first the authors seem dispirited at finding 'a conspiracy of silence in Deorala'.[24] Yet, it was not quite silence, judging from the text that follows, although some residents refused to confirm that they had witnessed the event. This, of course, may be explained by the fact that a women's investigative team would be greeted with suspicion even if there had been no controversial event in the village.

Despite that 'conspiracy of silence', the Bombay team amassed a wealth of amazing details showing how legends are made and how myths are perpetuated—the sorts of things Sangari and Vaid had assiduously tracked in other locations earlier, especially in the village of Jhardli.[25] The team also found some medical and material evidence in the police files that could eventually be used to cut through the mystique and solve the criminal case. The visual details recreate the scene. The now canopied sati sthal (cremation site) was raised into a brick platform, beside which was embedded a trident covered with Roop Kanwar's red chunri, which, they write, ominously resembled the figure of a woman. Seven youth bearing swords and chanting slogans circumambulated the site; two-hour shifts had been organized to make this round-the-clock vigil. The Women and Media Committee team also noted the odd little artifacts on sale: wedding pictures of the couple; the sati photomontage; ribbons; toys; and all the paraphernalia needed to offer prayers at the site, such as coconuts and incense sticks. The alliance of religion, commerce, and patriarchy was evident everywhere.

The Women and Media Committee members also recorded the stories circulating in Deorala about Roop, her marriage, her character, and the miraculous nature of the event. They went to Roop Kanwar's home and peered into the lamp-lit room, adorned with large framed photos of various gods and a colour television set. This room now served as a new version of a shrine for a modern sati. They could not meet the mother-in-law, who was in the house, obstructed in their intent by a male relative; her husband and two sons had by now been arrested, and she, understandably, was not feeling too well. Elsewhere in the village they heard, from women who claimed to have heard it from others, an account of the sati itself. Immediately before the event

The girl, they say, acquired *sat*—a supernatural power which is akin to a trance-like state where the woman's body burns to the touch and her eyes redden and glow. No one dared dissuade her for fear of being cursed by *sati mata*. She is said to have led the procession, chanted the *gayatri mantra* and blessed people. Roop Kanwar, they say, had only raised her hands and the pyre lit itself.

This miraculous rendering of the event was not only believed by the villagers but also 'shared by powerful Rajput politicians, her family and even the police'.[26] Government investigations, tardy and inadequate as they were, were perceived as meddlesome and intrusive by most people in Deorala. Reporters and cameramen were treated with hostility.

The Bombay team also interviewed the parents of Roop Kanwar. While the couple appeared 'disturbed', they seemed reassured that the in-laws' delay in informing them of their daughter's decision to die was understandable, considering that they were devastated by the loss of their eldest son. This telling excuse was made by Sneh Kanwar, Roop Kanwar's mother; she betrays the view that a son's death is more serious than that of a daughter-in-law or a daughter. In normal circumstances in any Hindu household, the parents would have been instantly informed of the death of their son-in-law, no matter how upset the bereaved family might be. In this case they would have rushed to the funeral, being only two hours away and having a car at their disposal. Instead of questioning this serious failure to notify them of their daughter's intentions, Roop Kanwar's parents gave the team a well-rehearsed summary of the pious character of their dead daughter: she was very religious, an indifferent student, a girl who preferred to play with idols rather than with toys, and a frequent visitor to the sati temple in Jhunjhunu. This evidently was intended to establish her predisposition to make the decision to commit sati.[27]

A counter-narrative, which was also somewhat problematic, emerged from the 'bits and pieces' in 'eyewitness accounts' provided to the same team. A Congress party worker (who had not witnessed the event, but whose relatives confirmed the account) claimed that Roop had actually hidden herself in a nearby' barn as she 'got an inkling' of the planned immolation.[28] She was found and forcibly put on the pyre at 1:30 p.m. 'She screamed and struggled to get out when the pyre was lit, but Rajput youth with swords surrounding her made escape impossible.' Her flailing arms, seen by the crowd, were 'interpreted by the villagers, not as a sign of her struggling to get out, but of her showering blessings on them'.[29] One witness claimed that she 'was frothing at the mouth'; another, that she had been swaying all the way from her home to the cremation site while ringed by Rajput sword bearers. Because the scene was obscured by the plumes of smoke, clouds of red

powder (*gulal*) flung on such auspicious occasions, and the pressing throng, few witnesses had a clear view of the cremation site
itself; but there is no doubt that the younger brother of the dead
man lit the pyre, because that is the ritual procedure in the case
of a man who has no son. Given these circumstances, the team
concluded that the crime committed was murder.[30]

The Women and Media Committee's report also contained a
detailed study of what the police had done until then, and the
group's members seem to have had very easy access to all levels of police officers and their documents on this case. The only
variance between the police view and the team's own assessment of the event was that the police seemed to be making one
crucial distinction: sati, in their minds and in the minds of the
population they were dealing with, was something other than
murder or suicide. While they had booked the offenders—the
deceased man's father and brothers—under Sections 302 and 306
of the criminal code, they expressed a clear wish that a law specifically banning sati should be promptly enacted to strengthen
their hand. The police did not explain their own bumbling incom-
petence in failing to cordon off the site so as to prevent the chunri
ceremony planned for the thirteenth day. Through sins of careful
omission such as these, sati rites found new legitimacy in Deorala.
Of the hundred or more people who were alleged to have witnessed
the cremation, not one was willing to provide testimony for the
police. Given the widespread fear of policemen and their tactics,
and considering the danger of becoming embroiled in a matter
that was being billed as a miracle, it was by no means easy to step
forward and attest to the nature of the occurrence under oath. This
explains the silence, the rumours, the myths, and the snippets of
detail only heard from equally vague 'others' who could not be
named.

The police files yielded some intriguing material that other
investigators seem not to have found, and it is surprising that the
team did not work some of this into their conclusions or pursue a
lead that might have answered the very first question on their list.
These facts emerged from interviews with M.M. Meherishi of
the Criminal Investigation Department (Vigilance Branch) and
pertain to the medical history of Roop Kanwar's husband Mal

Singh and the particulars of the dowry that she brought into his family at the time of their marriage. Meherishi spoke on the basis of information recorded in the police report.

Let us consider the medical history first. The circumstances of Mal Singh's death are even cloudier than those surrounding the death of Roop Kanwar. Meherishi asserted that the opportunity to collect valuable forensic information was lost because the police had not troubled to investigate the case after registering it. All they did was hand it over to the Criminal Investigation Department eighteen days after the event, when sufficient political pressure had been applied by women's groups. The Bombay team actually examined the police records, including the first information report (written on 4 September 1987), and took the trouble to verify the medical information in the police records directly from the medical personnel involved in treating Mal Singh.

Meherishi raised a brand new issue. He felt he had some facts and leads strongly indicating that the death of Mal Singh 'appears to be suspicious'. The evidence in support of this claim is as follows. Unaccountably Mal Singh, the acutely sick man, was taken to a hospital in Sikar instead of to one in Jaipur, which is not only closer to Deorala but has far better medical facilities. The doctors at Sikar were equivocal about the cause of the death. The initial diagnosis of gastroenteritis was later dismissed, since it was supported by symptoms recorded only as 'acute abdominal pain' at the Sikar hospital. It was claimed that the patient arrived in a state of shock and with low blood pressure. The chief medical officer at Sikar, who later diagnosed Mal Singh's condition as pancreatitis, 'felt that there was no need for a post mortem', and no autopsy was ever performed.[31]

To compound the gravity of such evidence, it was established that the patient had been suffering 'from shock and depression' and had been under the care of a Jaipur neuropsychiatrist, Dr K.G. Thanvi, only a few months before his death. Mal Singh, Dr Thanvi said, had twice failed to pass the pre-medical examination to enter medical school; the news of the results of his second attempt at the examination reached him only two weeks before his death. Dr Thanvi told the team that Mal Singh had been under his care from 5 June to 1 July in 1987. He 'had complained of having lost interest in life and was suffering from androgynous depression. An outpatient, he had been prescribed the usual antidepressants'.[32] The doctor felt that the patient was 'fully cured' but admitted the high possibility of a relapse. He added that he had not followed up the case and was only reminded of it when he was called up by some journalists in connection with the sati. A local doctor who was summoned to treat Mal Singh in Deorala and accompanied the patient to Sikar had in the meantime absconded, and the police were trying to locate him. He is also suspected by the police of having administered a strong drug to tranquilize Roop Kanwar prior to undergoing the live cremation ordeal so that she would go to her death without too much pain or obvious resistance.[33] This body of evidence would smell foul even to the most credulous of sati-watchers. One suspicious death seems to have made the second one possible.

Now let us scrutinize the facts about the dowry. The police discovered that Roop Kanwar's dowry consisted of 40 *tola*s (a tola is approximately 11.6 grams) of gold, 30,000 rupees in fixed-deposit receipts in her own name, a colour television, a cooking range, a refrigerator, and household furniture, apart from her personal wardrobe and other gifts. The police officers saw more significance in this dowry than did the Bombay investigative team, who merely saw it as '[a]nother aspect to be borne in mind'.[34] The police officers were right. This is a very substantial dowry by Indian middle-class standards, a tola of gold being roughly worth 210 dollars in 1987. It was a fortune far beyond the dreams of a village schoolteacher such as Roop Kanwar's father-in-law. The team confirmed that the custom in the area was for a young, childless widow to return to her parents with all her dowry. The team saw the television set and the furniture that Roop Kanwar had brought, and the fact that her parents were very affluent is reported in several places. Yet, none of the feminist reporters or scholars—not even the editors of *Manushi*—pursued this matter. The parents of Roop Kanwar would probably have been open to questions about how this marriage was arranged and what the wedding and alliance cost them in material terms.

It is incomprehensible that this very suggestive and potentially incriminating published information has been ignored or treated as insignificant by other feminists who reported on the case sub-sequently. Instead, implausible speculation about a supposed secret romantic past for Roop Kanwar and allegations of em-barrassing ailments suffered by Mal Singh appeared in the press, eroding the possibility of ever getting close to what might have truly ailed Mal Singh and how he died. A story by a woman journalist in the Delhi paper, the *Hindustan Times*, published three-and-a-half weeks after Roop Kanwar's death, claimed that Mal Singh was being treated for impotency and that Roop Kanwar was having an affair with a man from a lower caste presumably to explain why her in-laws forced her onto the funeral pyre.[35] Such unsubstantiated and irresponsible stories justifiably outraged the villagers at Deorala and increased their mistrust of women reporters, which may account for much of the hostility that various feminist investigative teams report they encountered.

It has been impossible for me, as a feminist historian, to read the evidence gathered by the Women and Media Committee without speculating about what might really have happened. My own research over the past several years for a book on dowry murders, in connection with which I have read innumerable police reports, not to mention case files in a women's resource centre, intensify my urge to help clarify some of the mystery shrouding Roop Kanwar's death. So, here is how I read it.

$\sim$

The village schoolteacher and his wife find that their eldest son is not particularly bright, is unemployed, and is prone to depression. He has already failed his entrance examination to medical school—a serious matter, since one can only take the test a few times—and the prospects for achieving his family's ambitions for him to be-come a doctor seem dim. Yet, the situation is not hopeless: his failure can be shielded from public view for a while. To give the boy a sense of purpose and responsibility, and possibly to help him get over his depression, it might be best to find him a suitable bride while he still appears to have at least the potential of be-coming a physician. Marriage is often proposed to cure young men who have strayed from the socially acceptable path and begin to gamble, drink, womanize, or show sexually 'deviant' interest;

depression, as in Mal Singh's case, probably invited such intervention even sooner. Hindu wives are famous for their endurance of lacklustre husbands and for their therapeutic and nurturing qualities. A good match is found in Roop Kanwar, an attractive and educated girl (but only up to the tenth grade) from Jaipur.

They probably did not need to demand a dowry, but they are delighted that their future daughter-in-law is from a wealthy family. As for Roop's parents, they regard this young man as a respectable, highly educated son-in-law with the potential to earn a high income as a doctor.

The young man's condition, however, does not improve; nor do his prospects for a job. He makes another attempt at the medical entrance examination, but that only confirms for him the doubts he has about his own worth. His marriage to this hopeful and beautiful eighteen-year-old heightens his chagrin and possibly his frustration at his own inadequacy. When he failed the examination for the first time, he may have been depressed enough to want to end his life. Failure in examinations prompts many young students to take their lives in India. Waiting for the dreaded results for a second time might bring him to the brink of a nervous collapse. The seriousness of the situation—possibly even a failed suicide attempt?—now compels the family to seek the services of a 'neuropsychiatrist' in Jaipur to treat their hapless eldest son. It is well known that resort to any kind of psychological help in India is seen as a drastic recourse and would be taken only in extreme circumstances. For a village family to go to the big city and seek this particular kind of help suggests that plenty more might have been wrong with the lad than even the Criminal Investigation Department knows.

In the meantime, Roop Kanwar spends most of her time with her parents in Jaipur. The Women and Media Committee team discovered that she had spent only twenty days with her husband after the wedding; she rejoined him only a few days before their deaths.[36] It is even conceivable that Mal Singh's psychiatric treatment was kept from his wife and in-laws so as not to alarm them. Another crisis might have forced them to send for Roop Kanwar. Perhaps, he tried to take his life (again?) when the results of his failure came out, two weeks before he was to die. On the eve of his death, he is first treated by a local doctor—the one who later absconded and so could not be questioned by the police. Then he is inexplicably rushed to a hospital in Sikar, or so it is claimed. Mark Tully, incidentally, found a serious discrepancy in the story told to him by Mal Singh's family about this event: he personally checked and found that there was no record of Mal Singh's admission to the Sikar hospital.[37] So the role of the local doctor, who is alleged to have treated him at home, is a vital—and missing—piece of the puzzle.

Whatever may have actually transpired the night before, we do know for certain that Mal Singh was dead and cremated in Deorala shortly after midday on 4 September, along with his wife. Mal Singh's death was probably a fate to which his parents were in some way already reconciled. Their problem suddenly was Roop Kanwar. She must have known what happened to her husband on the days just before he died. When death actually came, Roop Kanwar—as a young, attractive widow—would have presented them with two awkward possibilities. Either she could return to her parents' home, taking back her dowry and dwelling sorrowfully there (because widows find it impossible to marry in the class and circles to which she belonged), or she could opt to remain with her parents-in-law in Deorala. Either way, as time went on, her sexuality would pose problems and be perceived as a threat to the honour of both families; a sati would convert impending shame into glory. Therefore, persuading her to commit sati seemed an attractive expedient and a culturally acceptable solution. Young women are presumed to be vulnerable and obedient. In this instance, persuasion may have meant anything from brainwashing an already religious and sati-temple-visiting teenager to drugging her into compliance. The same local doctor would administer a drug if needed. The doctor's sudden disappearance from the village suggests culpability on his part: he may even have suggested the latter course to the distraught parents. Deorala, it is reported, had already been the site for two earlier satis. Whatever was done was done with speed, and Roop Kanwar took the story of her brief marriage to a troubled young man with her to her death. It was murder.

~

The above scenario, speculative and unspeakably evil as it may sound, would make sense of why Roop Kanwar's parents were not informed until too late. There really was no good reason for keeping Mal Singh's death and her resolve from them unless Roop Kanwar was not entirely persuaded and could not be relied on to go through with it. The presence of her own family—parents, brothers, possibly friends—would have made this act difficult, if not impossible. So the in-laws hastily decided that it would be best to inform the parents *after* the cremation; surely, they would understand how grief and pain keep people from their worldly obligations. This, however, was also the case in all the preceding sati-style deaths in the Jhunjhunu–Shekhavati region: no parents were informed until after the cremation.[38] Prominent people in the village, who nostalgically approve of women's sacrifice and purity, came to the cremation ground in every case. They certainly would have done so this time, since the schoolteacher commands some respect in the village, and his circle of acquaintances certainly would have exceeded the hundred or more who did come. And so they stood there and watched and approved, with their chants and slogans, and added coconuts and buckets of ghee to the flames, as they beheld the spectacle of Roop Kanwar's flailing limbs showering blessings on them amid the smoke and gulal. This was not just a dowry murder but a doubly cynical and criminal act committed, not with the help of kerosene in the kitchen, but in the full gaze of an applauding and credulous multitude. As for Roop Kanwar's parents, they not only believed the story of their daughter's sacrifice, they donated 100,000 rupees towards its commemoration on its first anniversary. Are people capable of such self-serving evil? Yes, everywhere and in all cultures.

Madhu Kishwar and Ruth Vanita, editors of *Manushi*, were the next major team of women to visit Deorala. They arrived in the last week of October; by then, all the possible interpretive angles on the event were already in print, and a heated 'modernity-versus-tradition' debate was in full swing. While they rightly condemned the sterility of this controversy, they ironically furthered it by arguing that this so-called traditional event is a thoroughly modern phenomenon. By preserving the binary opposition of traditional versus modern in their analysis, they unwittingly proved that sati has resurfaced on the scene in modern-day India with inevitable modern-day political (instead of religious) trappings. In their subsequent report, Kishwar and Vanita insist on calling the Deorala happening a 'modern-day Sati', conceding thereby that it *was* a sati.[39] They reinforce this impression by carefully explaining the distinctions between a dowry death and a sati. Interestingly, in their analysis of the ensuing debate on sati, they criticize the argument made by 'most reformers' that the Deorala event was a product of 'blind superstitiousness and excessive religiosity' and 'backwardness and primitiveness...preserved in our rural vastness', because this unwittingly supports the position of the pro-sati camp, which sees modernity as the enemy of traditional values.[40] In distancing themselves from the anti-sati campaign, the editors write that 'Somewhere along the way' it became 'counterproductive,' and the campaigners 'became characterized as a handful of anti-Hindu, anti-Rajput, anti-religion, pro-government, anti-masses, urban, educated, westernized people, and the pro-sati lobby as those sensitive to the sentiments of the rural, traditional poor.' The 'reformers', they feel, saw the Roop Kanwar case as a 'product of an old tradition, whereas in its present form it is a new created cult [*sic*], organized by political, not by religious, leaders'. They go on to say that it was also a mistake to enter into the debate 'on the religiosity or otherwise of the Deorala Sati'. It should have been demystified and seen as 'a case of a woman being hounded to death under a specious religious cover, and of her death being made a symbol by certain power groups to demonstrate their clout'. Petitioning the government, they say, only let the government 'off the hook for its complicity in Roop Kanwar's death' and gave it the opportunity 'to pose as progressive by introducing a repressive law'.[41] They suggest that human rights and women's organizations should use Mahatma Gandhi's weapon; satyagraha, non-violent civil disobedience, to protest 'the murder and its subsequent glorification'.[42]

This sati was indubitably the creation of modern economic, political, and social forces. Deorala, the *Manushi* team points out, is a modern village of 10,000 inhabitants with a 70 per cent literacy rate, electricity, and tap water—a relatively prosperous place dominated by Brahmins and Rajputs. It has brick houses, a large market well stocked with consumer goods, and inhabitants who dress as fashionably as their counterparts in the cities and who are not uninfluenced by the ubiquitous Hindi film manners and mores. Roop Kanwar's family is educated, as was she. Her father-in-law was a schoolteacher, her husband a science graduate, her brothers the owners of a thriving transport business in Jaipur. As for the sati event itself, Kishwar and Vanita show that it was no less modern than the setting in which it occurred. They list many crass adaptations from Hindi films, political rhetoric, and other aspects of popular culture that had been incorporated to valorize the sati. The slogans they heard voiced by youth near the cremation site were emended political slogans, shouted in a cheerleading fashion rather than in the manner of chants at a religious ritual. The inspiration for the lurid photomontage on sale in the village was traced to a publicity poster for the film, *Sati Sulochana*, 'The Sati with the Beautiful Eyes'. The arti sung at what had now been instituted as a daily evening worship at the sati sthal was a generic modern Hindi hymn popularized via the Hindi cinema.[43] And the chunri rasam, a solemn ritual performed for any deceased woman, was converted into a chunri mahotsav, a carnival with slogan-shouting, sword-wielding young men as the major attraction.

Kishwar and Vanita attempt to show—and largely succeed in doing so—that the environment of the Deorala sati is not only modern but primarily male. In their view, men created the cult, although women would seem complicit since they join in the singing. The power wielders of the newly formed Sati Dharma Raksha Samiti ('Committee for the Defence of the Religion of Sati': the word *sati* in the name was dropped after the government passed an ordinance that forbids the glorification of sati) are Jaipur-based men in their twenties and thirties; its secretary, Narendra Singh Rajawat, is educated, affluent, the owner of a leather export business, and married to a graduate of one of Delhi's leading women's colleges. The sati rally they organized in Jaipur drew hundreds of young Rajput men from all over India. They danced, postured, and screamed slogans 'as if part of a victory celebration'.[44]

Another dismaying part of this new trend is the construction and patronage of sati temples in the cities and hamlets of Rajasthan and elsewhere by Marwari businessmen. But all is not lost for women in Rajasthan. Kishwar and Vanita offer us a heartening counter-example to the sati ideal in the life and songs of the much loved Mirabai, a sixteenth-century bhakti saint who is revered by men and women alike in north India. Her

urge towards self-definition and freedom...is much more integrally a part of Rajasthani traditions relating to women than is the cult being created around Roop Kanwar today. That the new self-proclaimed leaders should choose a Roop Kanwar rather than a Mira as a symbol of Rajasthani womanhood indicates what they believe is woman's place, but is no evidence that a major section of Rajasthani women have chosen that ideal for themselves.[45]

This last statement is more than amply bolstered in a very rich article based on interviews with thirty rural women of Bhilwara district published in *Seminar*. These outspoken village women remain unimpressed with attempts at reviving the sati cult in Rajasthan, and see right through the vested interests involved in the Deorala episode.[46]

The Kishwar and Vanita analysis of the actions and inaction of the state largely conforms with those already discussed. Briefly, they assert that 'our government machinery, far from being progressive, is not even neutral. It is controlled by politicians for whom considerations of power and profit are far more important than human rights.'[47] Few would disagree with the spirit of that generalization. Particular accusations by the *Manushi* team against the police, however, seem to be totally contradicted by the experience of other journalists—notably the encounter of the Women and Media team with the Deorala police discussed earlier. Kishwar and Vanita claim that '[a]ny attempts to challenge the cult are prevented by the police. ...The facts of the case are being suppressed and the cult built up, under police protection.'[48] They seem unaware of the fact that the police have foiled several satis in the last decade, and that only four or five have been successfully carried out.[49] The *Manushi* editors appear to have made no attempt to interview the police and Criminal Investigation Department officers in charge of the case; instead they claim that Deorala was sprinkled with plainclothes policemen, making it difficult for them to distinguish villagers from policemen. Be that as it may, it explains why the *Manushi* team had nothing to say about Mal Singh's illness or Roop Kanwar's dowry.

A more trenchant critique of the state and its involvement in the Deorala episode was published in the *Economic and Political Weekly* in November 1987.[50] Using a broader perspective, the authors, both women professors at Jawaharlal Nehru University in New Delhi, reflect on the Roop Kanwar death as one more dramatic example of the recent upsurge of communalism by both Hindu and Muslim obscurantist forces. However, 'this particular incident has happened,' they write, 'just as communal violence happens because the government is not willing to enforce the norms and laws of a modern and civilized state.'[51] In treating the Deorala episode neither as an isolated event nor as exclusively a women's issue explainable in terms of local Rajashthani patriarchal pride and prejudice, they illumine the interconnected complexity of recent communal reactions and violence in India. 'In sharp contrast to the past when Gandhi and Nehru forged a secular consensus,' write Imrana Qadeer and Zoya Hasan, 'now, these backward social forces have entered the centre state with direct and indirect backing of the state.'[52]

Imrana Qadeer goes further in a marxist–feminist critique entitled 'Roop Kanwar and Shah Bano' (*Seminar*, February 1988), in which she explains how the prevarication of the Congress party government, then headed by Rajiv Gandhi, led tacitly to the arousal of fundamentalist passions. In 1986, Rajiv Gandhi's capitulations to Muslim fundamentalists in the Shah Bano case and to Hindu fundamentalists in the Babari Mosque–Ramjanmabhumi dispute progressively frayed secular liberalism in India. Briefly, Shah Bano, a seventy-five-year-old Muslim woman abruptly divorced by her very affluent lawyer husband, petitioned the Supreme Court for maintenance, which was granted. This judgment was perceived by fundamentalist Muslims as undermining Muslim family law, which does not recognize a divorcee's right to maintenance. A prolonged and bitter fight of Muslim women, Indian liberals of all religions, and women's organizations ended in their defeat when Rajiv Gandhi's government overturned the Supreme Court's judgment by an Act of Parliament. The fundamentalist mullahs then cornered the powerless old woman and made her retract her demand for maintenance as a grave religious 'error' and made her flout the judgment of the highest court in the land.[53] The Act of Parliament shredded the secular constitution of the country in the same way as did the government's irresponsible opening of the locked doors of the Babari Mosque while the dispute over its proprietorship was awaiting judgment in the local courts. In each case either Muslim or Hindu extremists were given an extrajudicial arena to play out the dispute, transforming what might have remained long-standing grumbling matches into a make-or-break deal for the opposition Bharatiya Janata Party.[54]

Qadeer describes the triumph of religious fundamentalists and militants who have brazenly exploited the tragic circumstances of powerless women in both Hindu and Muslim communities. She delineates the emerging trends as follows:

1. That fundamentalist forces are capitalizing not upon an event or two but on a persistent feature of the social system: the position of women as second-class citizens. This...strengthens their alliance with the ruling classes.
2. That fundamentalists have not only succeeded in capturing the imagination of the majority in their respective communities but also succeeded in confusing a section of their intelligentsia.
3. That the state not only gives in to their anti-secular demands but also justifies them—and its [own] actions—by changing the very definition of secularism. Then in the name of democratic practice it supports the majority view within religious communities.
4. That as a consequence of the above, the liberal democratic sections are becoming increasingly paralysed and marginal.[55]

This was said in 1987; the situation of late has grown far grimmer, and Qadeer's verdict holds more true than ever before.

Now we can return to the issue of women's identity and autonomy in the context of sati. In a thought-provoking recent article, Rajeswari Sunder Rajan expressly addresses the question of pain and agency in an effort to counter the absence or transcendence of pain that is claimed as reality by those who argue in defence of sati. While the results of her attempt to theorize female subjectivity as agency in this particular situation remain tentative, one cannot gainsay her observation that 'in the discourse of the anti-sati position, however, while pain is undeniably everywhere present, it is nowhere represented.'[56] She looks for signs of pain in a large assortment of 'social texts' produced by this event, such as newspapers, photographs, and documentary films, as well as in the law itself, and finds it only in a single feminist poster and in a consciousness-raising documentary. In the popular posters and commercial mementos of the Roop Kanwar sati, the woman's face and body show no marks of the experience of burning; the aforementioned photomontage shows her smiling as she sits serenely on the pyre in all her bridal finery while a small figure of a goddess beams down the magic ray to ignite it.[57] Sunder Rajan argues that the subjectivity of pain is important to stress because it

needs to be conceptualized as a dynamic rather than a passive condition, on the premise that the subject in pain will be definitionally in transit towards a state of no-pain (even if this state is no more than a reflexivity. ...[T]he effect produced by a body in pain—pity, anger, sympathy, identification—is an important consideration in formulating the politics of intervention.[58]

While Sunder Rajan has made the most valiant attempt yet, in the Indian context, to articulate the idea that a woman's pain is to be apprehended as subject-constitutive, the idea of a woman's agency in sati remains problematic at several levels. First the belief in a woman's volition, her special power of *sat*—a 'miraculous' driving force that enables her to shower blessings, heal the sick, and order the funeral pyre to ignite itself yet feel no pain—makes her the agent of her own destiny in the ideology and biographical narratives of sati. Sangari and Vaid point out the difficulties that arise in 'squaring widow immolation as a product of the woman's own volition with the necessarily public and participatory nature of the funeral', in whose absence the miraculous nature of the event cannot be established.[59] In fact, one could go further and add that it makes female agency a very dangerous idea—one that sati perpetrators would be happy to appropriate in Deorala and elsewhere. Deeper still, even when agency can be forensically established, can the woman's act of self-immolation be judged to be a product of her own will, or must it be judged as a product of the very studious socialization and indoctrination of women (particularly for the role of wife) that shape her attitudes and actions from girlhood? At yet a fourth level, as Lata Mani points out, the current legislation on sati, by making a woman who escapes or otherwise survives the burning liable for attempting sati, implicitly conceives of her as 'free agent'. The law is self-contradictory, in that case, for it cannot logically claim to locate coercion and agency in the same act. So the question of agency is delicate, complex, even contradictory, and it certainly cannot be conceptualized as neatly as it has been in liberal feminist theories in the West. In fact, it might be better to settle for a provisional view of woman as victim until some way is found to resolve the question of woman's agency in this particular setting. As Lata Mani says,

The example of women's agency is a particularly good instance of the dilemmas confronted in simultaneously attempting to speak within different historical moments and to discrepant audiences. What might be a valuable pushing of the limits of the current rethinking of agency in Anglo-American feminism, may, if not done with extreme care, be an unhelpful, if not disastrous move in the Indian context.[60]

Perhaps the last word on 'agency' should belong to a Rajput woman, Rani Chundawat, who has spoken eloquently against sati and is a prominent Rajasthani public figure. In commenting to the editors of *Manushi* on what Mal Singh's family maintains was Roop Kanwar's decision to commit sati, she poses a series of rhetorical questions that challenge the notion of woman's agency very profoundly in the context of sati: 'How many women have the right to decide anything voluntarily?' If a woman does not choose her husband and does not decide matters such as her own education or career, how can she choose in a matter as imperative as that of life and death? Given that a women's status is generally determined by her relationship to men (as daughter, wife, widow, mother), 'can any decision...particularly such a momentous decision, really be called voluntary and self-chosen?'[61] The answer to the last question is, of course, no. Therefore, it may be ill-advised to seek female agency in the act of committing sati.

The question that has not come up anywhere in the literature and remains a silent subtext in other equally harrowing situations, whether dowry murders or other widow immolations in the Shekhavati region, is the question of the fear of a young woman's sexuality. If we see few images of her pain, we see even fewer images of her desire; and in the concept of sati, both the pain and the desire that arise in a woman's body are erased. Sati is about transcendent states, not embodied ones. For feminists it has been enough to invoke patriarchy, that umbrella term that serves as an explanatory backdrop for all crimes against women, including the punitive control of female sexuality. Like the wordless language of pain—flailing arms, screams, tears—desire is smothered at the source in the body language of modesty and in silence. It is easier to trot out the material reasons for sati and other violent crimes against women than to venture into the psychosexual realm of human motivations. The idea of a desirable and desiring widow whom no one will marry and whom many will want to exploit remains unexpressed—oddly, even more so than in the case of pain. This is true both with respect to the perpetrators of sati and with respect to its critics, opponents, and analysts. The need for a more forthright discussion of this issue is urgent. Feminists will have to take the lead in demolishing this blank wall.

But what of feminists' achievements so far? What have been the results of feminist intervention in Roop Kanwar's case? A law, called the Commission of Sati (Prevention) Act of 1987, has been inserted into the statute book. Vasudha Dhagamwar, a professor of law and an activist, offers a capsule history of the legislation that has attended the custom from the earliest legal debates of 1805 to the present.[62] She recounts that the clamour for fresh and separate anti-sati legislation (which in her view was redundant with the existing Indian Penal Code) came entirely from anti-sati activists who were drawn into the debate on whether or not this event could have been voluntary. She pleaded, along with others, that there was no such thing as 'voluntary sati' and that a law against murder already existed and simply needed to be enforced. After a fractious interlude, which Dhagamwar describes with zest, Parliament enacted comprehensive anti-sati legislation outlawing not only sati but its glorification in any way, shape, or form. Yet, this piece of legislation was not drafted by feminists, and a close inspection of its many sections would please them little. It has replicated, in some parts verbatim, many of the prejudices, caveats, and ambiguities of the East India Company Regulation of 1829, and it adds a few complications of its own by attempting to define sati. In fact, if I may put a gloss on it, instead of making a law that prohibits an incontestable crime against women, the framers of the new law succeeded in defining sati as a woman's crime. Dhagamwar points out that, in refusing to distinguish between voluntary and involuntary sati, they have in effect managed to 'treat all sati as voluntary. That is why the woman is punished and that is why those who kill her are punished for abetment, and not for murder.'[63] So, should a woman by some chance manage to escape the pyre, she would be culpable first and foremost. This is not exactly a giant step forward for womankind, and it can be lamented as yet another inroad into the secular terrain of the Indian Penal Code.[64]

What did this law achieve in the case of Roop Kanwar's death? Before it was promulgated the police had arrested her father-in-law and her two brothers-in-law; the village doctor had absconded. Then the law was enacted, but even so the culprits were eventually released without bail. The case against them is pending, but the frustrating reality is that they will not come up for trial; and no one quite knows or cares to determine the whereabouts of the doctor. Thus the case has effectively stalled; and as far as I am able to find out, no one plans to reactivate the charges. On the other side of the ledger, the glorification of sati has been curtailed to the extent that some sati temples find worship interrupted on occasion by a policeman on duty. Yet, we shall have to wait until the next festival season—or the next—to see what impact the anti-glorification legislation really has on popular reverence for sati. In the meantime, the silence is deafening. When in January 1993 a foreign traveller asked how he could get to Deorala, he was told, 'Why do you want to go to Deorala? There is nothing to see.'

ACKNOWLEDGMENTS

I wish to thank Arati Rao for our many discussions on feminism and for the bibliographic suggestions she made while work on this article was in progress. Philip Oldenburg, my captive editor and critic, helped in his usual manner with careful and constructive comments.

Ashis Nandy, 'Sati in *Kali Yuga*'[65]

Feminists were not the only ones to respond to Roop Kanwar's immolation. The following is Ashis Nandy's well-known response the event.

The peculiar mix of fascination, fear, theatrics, self-righteousness, and anger with which India's westernized middle classes reacted to the sati committed by Roop Kanwar at Deorala in Rajasthan in 1987 would have delighted a psychologist. Evidently, the very idea of suicide on the funeral pyre of one's husband—or the possibility that this ancient rite could be exploited to hide the murder of a young widow—had its own strange fascination for the modern mind. However, for a small minority, the reactions to the sati only deepened the tragedy of the death of a teenage widow.

The minority could not forget that during the previous decade, a number of such instances of sati had taken place in Rajasthan without arousing the same passions in urban India. Some remembered their discomfort at the unconcern with which most social activists and journalists had greeted instances of sati only a few years earlier. Such events were almost invariably reported in the inside pages of the English-language dailies, usually as a form of esoterica that had survived the juggernaut of progress. A large majority of those who were ready to throw epileptic fits at the mention of the word 'sati' after Roop's death, did not care to write even a few standard letters to the editor when, for instance, the last-known sati took place only a year earlier, even though that case, too, was duly mentioned in the English-language press.[66]

Were the passions aroused at Roop's death caused by a sharply heightened moral awareness or was there something more to it? Why did this instance of sati at this point of time so inflame the urban intelligentsia?

Both questions relate to the politics of public consciousness in contemporary urban India. To that extent, one would think, journalists, social scientists, and activists should find them relatively easy to handle. Other important questions about the incident demand answers that have to be teased out of a mass of tangled data and from a world that is more unfamiliar to modern India. What motivated those who organized, witnessed, or applauded the rite?

What is the symbolic meaning of sati in contemporary times? And what structure of self-interests fuelled it?

Strangely, while answers to the latter questions have been attempted, the first two questions about the role of the Deorala sati in the politics of public consciousness have been little discussed either in India's English press or in scholarly journals. Does this tell us, urban, westernized Indians, something about ourselves? This is the first question to which we must give an answer, however imperfect, before proceeding any further.

My tentative answer to the question would be: I suspect that two contradictory social–psychological forces are operating in India's middle-class culture of politics. On one side is the growing political power of the mass culture through which the urban, middle-class Indian has begun to influence the political process. This pan-Indian mass culture, now closely linked to the global mass culture, is strengthened by a number of social forces, among which are the growing reach of the media, urbanization, industrialization, physical mobility brought about by changing occupational patterns, and technological growth. On the other side is the democratic process, threatening to consolidate further the political presence of non-modern India in the public sphere. In an open system, in however distorted a form, numbers count.

In such a system, the only way the 'moderns' can retain the legitimacy of their social and political dominance is by setting themselves up as the bastions of rationality and in the vanguard of social change. They have to seek a sanction for their disproportionate political power from what they regard as the symbols of their superior knowledge and morality. Thus it is not surprising that in recent years, the westernized and semi-westernized middle classes have tended to justify their political power by playing up in the media the spectacular technological and organizational achievements of the Indian state and the modern sector—or the equally spectacular evidence of backwardness and irrationality in non-modern India and its status in the higher reaches of Indian public life. Hence the feigned panic and hyperbole that followed the Deorala sati; they are an attempt to confirm the status of this sati as the clinching evidence of the need to give modern India a disproportionate access to political power, even if it meant bypassing the democratic process. Hence also the remarkable claim, as part of the same hyperbole, made by India's Harvard-trained minister of state for home affairs at the time, that hundreds and thousands of Roop Kanwars have been killed in India. In so claiming, P. Chidambaram ignored the fact that in the last fifty years cases of sati have been confined mainly to one state, and within that state to one region. Naturally, he neglected to point out that the figures involved do not match the rate of homicide in even the smallest Indian town.[67]

One suspects that it is this search for grand spectacles of evil that has shaped much of the middle classes' response to Roop's sati and caused them to avoid some of the basic issues raised by her death. For only this search for evidence of the inferiority of the other India can explain the paradox in the public debate on the subject: those who declared the Deorala sati to be a 'pure case of murder' attacked, in the same breath, Indian traditions, village superstitions, even the Mahabharata and the Ramayana. As if a pure case of murder could not involve greed, pure and simple, and could not be handled under the existing Indian penal code, without reference to the larger cultural factors.[68]

This ambivalent response, depicting sati as simple murder, yet as something more than murder, has already created strange anomalies in Indian public life. First, thanks to the supposed legal reforms brought about by anti-sati activists—the new statute relating to the glorification of sati and prosecution of those involved in a sati—there can now be systematic attempts to pass off cases of sati as cases of murder, since cases of murder now give the accused and the police more room for manoeuvring than cases of sati.[69] For instance, abetment to murder does not invite the death penalty, but abetment to sati now does.[70] Second, this draconian law, rushed through Parliament as a public gesture against a social pathology, is now available to the state for misuse against political opponents, or even for the simpler purpose of extorting money by the lower levels of the law-enforcing agencies.

In the following pages, I shall try to rescue four such 'undiscussable' issues that have fallen victim to the new mystifications produced by the public debate on sati in metropolitan India. The issues I have chosen to reproblematize are: the nature of coercion in sati, the glorification of sati, the roots of sati in the traditional role of women, and the use of the state to stop the practice of sati.

II

First, the matter of coercion. The earliest reports on the Deorala sati did not mention any coercion. Some people, including Roop Kanwar's parents and their relatives staying at Deorala, seemed sure that none was used. (As one knows from cases of wives killed by their in-laws for failure to bring satisfactory amounts of dowry from their parents, the victim's parental family is usually the first to challenge the suicide theory floated by the in-laws.) In the second week stray reports of coercion came in, but the majority still did not mention force.[71] By the end of the third week the large majority of journalists were fully convinced that Roop's death was a clear case of cold-blooded murder. One newspaper gave lurid details of how she had run away and hidden in a barn and was pulled out from there to be burnt.[72] Nine months later, coercion was so obvious an element that at least one reporter in a major national newspaper—and some policemen—had reached the point of lamenting that torture could not be used to extract information from some of the witnesses.[73]

I believe that the possibility of coercion having been exercised exists in all cases of sati. I say so not merely because I am a sceptic in such matters, but also because I once studied the epidemic of sati in eastern India in the early years of British rule.[74] Nearly all the cases of sati for which there were data suggested direct or indirect coercion; something that is difficult to forget. For the moment, however, I am concerned not with the empirical reality of the sati at Deorala but with the certitudes of middle-class commentators on that reality.

I believe it was naïve on the part of journalists and social workers to assume at the beginning that there had been no coercion. In the main, their information came from the same villagers who had applauded the rite in the first place. It was equally naïve for others, who later came to believe that the Deorala sati was a clear case of homicide, to trust the same villagers who had earlier denied any coercion. In both cases, there being no outside observers when the sati took place, a little healthy scepticism about the constructions of the villagers would have done no harm. Villagers, when dealing with their urban compatriots, can be remarkably devious, cautious, and secretive, and display a sharp sense of survival. Many of the same Rajput youth who bared their swords at Deorala in 1987 to defend the sacred place of sati against its opponents were later seen hedging their bets, after the state had reaffirmed the illegality of sati. To depend upon such defenders of the faith as informants may reveal one's trust in human nature, but is no indication of one's political acuity.

In any event, direct physical coercion was hardly the central issue—unless those claiming that Roop's death was a case of murder really meant that had force not been used, the rite would have been justified. If they did, theirs was essentially the position of the Shankaracharya of Puri and local politicians such as the Janata Party chieftain in Rajasthan, Kalyan Singh Kalvi. They too said that sati was unjustified when force was used, but concluded that since force had not been used in this instance, Roop's sati was justifiable. There may have been disagreement about the fact of coercion but, at least in the public debate, there was perfect agreement between most supporters and opponents of sati as to the principle involved. Few raised the crucial question: could sati be justified if no direct physical coercion was used?

The answer to this question must be based on an awareness that no religious event of this kind can any more remain uncontaminated by our times. Nothing is safe from the secular cost calculations and market morality which have now entered the interstices of Indian society. (Many Rajputs protesting against the new anti-sati legislation refuse to acknowledge that triumph of secularism and modernity. Some of them are convinced that the rest of society is merely trying to get them. In reaction, they are trying to defend a rite which now only theoretically remains part of the traditional religious world view. In practice, that rite is already outside the compass of tradition and has become part of the modern business culture that has already engulfed most religious spectacles, festivals, pilgrimages, and religious family endowments and trusts.)

Thus it is possible to argue that today, even when a widow independently decides to commit suicide, her independence in doing so cannot but be imperfect. One can never be sure that her family, her village, and her caste, motivated by common greed and the hunt for higher status, have not pushed her into it. They need not even be self-consciously greedy or status-hungry. It is possible to push a person to self-destruction by creating the right atmosphere, often without being aware of doing so.

In any case, even if no force was used in Roop's case, it is clear that the family and village did nothing to persuade her against her 'impetuous' decision. Nor did they help her come out of the depression caused by her husband's death; rather, they colluded with her self-destructive impulses. The sati was organized within a few hours, before Roop's parents could even talk to her, and there is no record of any serious effort by her in-laws to dissuade her from self-immolation. Roop's own family behaved no better: after being confronted with a fait accompli they evidently decided not to create a fuss. But this proves their pragmatism, not the authenticity of the sati. Both sides of the family knew that they did not know beforehand the full extent to which they would profit. Living in the kali yuga—the final, fallen age in the Indian version of the human time cycle—they should have known.

The second question is: how far can or should glorification of sati go? A recent act proscribing all glorification of sati may seem prima facie justified to many but cannot stand up to critical scrutiny. Does the new law mean that children will not read about or admire Queen Padmini's self-chosen death in medieval times? Does it mean that that part of the Mahabharata which describes Mādrī's sati will now be censored? What about Rabindranath Tagore's awe-inspiring, respectful depiction of sati and Abanindranath Tagore's brilliant invocation of the courage, idealism, and tragedy of sati in medieval Rajasthan?[75] Do we proscribe their works, too, forgetting that the Tagores had been in the forefront of the movement against sati during the colonial period? What about Kabir, who, over the last four centuries, has remained the ultimate symbol of spiritual achievement and inter-religious tolerance in this country? After all, as Coomaraswamy points out, Kabir constantly uses 'the impulse to sati' as an image of surrendering one's ego to God.[76]

Finally, what does one do with the original Sati? Does one ban the celebration of Durgā Pujā or, for that matter, the reading of Kālidāsa's *Kumārasambhava,* because both celebrate the goddess who committed sati? Do we follow the logic of the two young activists who were keen to get the Ramayana declared unconstitutional, so that the epic could not be shown on India's state-owned television? What does one do with the faith of millions of Indians that the soil that received the divided body of Sati constitutes the sacred land of India? That these questions may not in the future remain merely theoretical or hypothetical is made obvious by the fact that the Indian History Congress felt obliged to adopt a statement critical of the TV Ramayana in its 1988 convention.[77]

One possible response to such questions is to *presume* that in the mythical past sati was a rare, fearsome, but moving ritual which symbolized the reaffirmation of the purity, self-sacrifice, power, and dignity of women and the superiority of the feminine principle in the cosmos. Those decultured, ill-informed Indians who view classical or mythological instances of sati as instances of the degradation of women would do well to read what is probably the twentieth century's most spirited defence of the philosophy of sati, the one offered by Ananda K. Coomaraswamy. It questions the artificial line drawn between self-immolation for trendy, secular causes like revolution and nationalism, and self-immolation for low-brow, old-fashioned religious or cultural causes:

The criticism we make on the institution of Sati and woman's blind devotion is similar to the final judgment we are about to pass on patriotism. We do not, as pragmatists may, resent the denial of the ego for the sake of an absolute, or attach an undue importance to mere life; on the contrary we see clearly that the reckless and useless sacrifice of the 'suttee' and the patriot is spiritually significant. And what remains perpetually clear is the superiority of the reckless sacrifice to the calculating assertion of rights.[78]

This asymmetric public perception of sacrifices for secular and non-secular causes, to which Coomaraswamy drew our attention, persists. It is now being systematically propagated through the Indian media as the last word on the subject. In the third week of November 1987, when the debate on sati was at its height, the self-immolationof a DMK party worker in Tamil Nadu for the cause of Sri Lankan Tamils was mentioned without any fanfare in the inside pages of virtually all the national dailies. It is no surprise that there was not even a murmur of discomfiture from the newspaper-reading public.[79]

However, whatever one may presume about the nobility of sati in the mythic past, its status now—in deep kali yuga—is a different story. In practice the rite has been corrupted by modern market forces and by the idea of negotiable social status. In historic times, as opposed to the mythic, it is safer to presume that sati is a perverted form of sacrifice, if not homicide. Therefore, to borrow a phrase from criminal law, it is better to prevent a hundred authentic satis than to allow one inauthentic sati to occur.

This differentiation between sati in mythical times and sati in historical times, between sati as an event (*ghatanā*) and sati as a system (*pratha*), between the authentic sati and its inauthentic offspring, between those who respect it and those who organize it in our times, is not my contribution to the understanding of the rite. These distinctions were already implicit, for instance, in the writings of Rabindranath Tagore, who was an aggressive opponent of sati as practised in contemporary times, yet respectful towards the ideas behind it. It is implicit in folk culture in many parts of India. It is also implicit in the difference between the simple faith of the pilgrims who thronged to Deorala after the sati of Roop Kanwar, and the actions of the organizers of the event, who profited from it.[80] And certainly it is implicit in the contrast between the monuments that have attended some of the satis in west and south India and the absence of such monuments in the wake of the largest epidemic of sati ever witnessed, namely the one that occurred in eighteenth- and and nineteenth-century Bengal.

While there are more than a hundred sati temples and hundreds of *chhatri*s spread over large parts of India, to the best of my knowledge there is no such temple or chhatri in honour of any one of the thousands of women who committed sati in the eastern Indian epidemic. There are a few sati temples in Bengal, set up mainly by Rajasthanis, and someone may discover one or two of them to have developed a connection with mythologized satis from the early years of colonialism. Yet the paucity of temples commemorating late eighteenth- and early nineteenth-century satis and the inability of Bengalis to find even a few satis to honour among the five per day or so that took place at the height of the epidemic, tell us something. As does the comment of the priest in one of the few existing sati temples in Bengal that true sati is impossible in our times. Evidently, at some level, there is an awareness that the satis in colonial Bengal were not authentic and therefore did not deserve to be honoured. It is not all a matter of superstition and blind faith. Traditional Indians do discriminate; they do make moral choices.

However, one acquires the right to talk of the inauthenticity of satis in the kali yuga only after respectfully admitting the authenticity of the values that speak through the acts of sati recorded in epic and myth or through mythologized accounts of satis in historical times, such as those recounted by the balladeers and folk-singers of Rajasthan. The two Tagores, Rabindranath and Abanindranath, showed us how to do it, by writing with great sensitivity and a touch of tragedy about sati in mythologized history, even though they were proud that their own family had been at the forefront of the struggle for the abolition of sati in their own time.

If such discrimination is not shown, modernist criticisms of sati are likely to have the same impact that criticism of child marriage has had so far on village India—none at all. For obviously, the ideas represented in the myth of the original sati, as reaffirmed in epics, folk tales, and ballads, continue to live in the hearts of millions of Indians. These ideas constitute part of the basic substratum of Indian culture. They cannot be wiped away by angry letters to newspapers.

Once one shows respect for the idea of sati at the mythological level, one paradoxically acquires the right to criticize all individual instances of sati, even those put forward in the myths themselves. One can even say Mādrī in the Mahabharata or, for that matter, Pārvatī should not have committed sati, and that what took place at Deorala was not sati but murder. Such criticism will make sense to many of the 300,000 pilgrims to Deorala, in the same way that similar criticism by reformers made sense to earlier generations. After all, the criticism of sati that began many centuries ago in a traditional context has continued to resonate up to now, even if not in a tone audible to modernists.[81]

In this respect sati is part of a larger picture. Rammohan Roy was listened to when he ridiculed Kṛṣṇa for killing Putanā; and

Tagore when he criticized the way Sumitrā was treated in the Ramayana or when he made Karṇa, not Arjuna, the hero of a verse-play based on part of the Mahabharata. Both had precedents in pre-modern times. Madhusudan Dutt made Rama the villain of his epic and Meghnād the hero, and he too was said to have been inspired by lesser-known, earlier texts: a Tamil and a Jain Ramayana. These great Indians viciously attacked aspects of traditions that did not fit in with their concept of *yugadharma*, ethics appropriate to their age, and few challenged their right to do so. Because they understood and respected the values enshrined in tradition, they were listened to with respect when they attacked or reinterpreted certain figures in the Indian epics or even made fun of them. Only a few illegitimate children of the British Raj— the comic-strip warlords of Hindutva—whose feelings of cultural inferiority made them semiticize and masculinize Hinduism— have challenged this traditional right to dissent in recent years, and got away with it. And only in metropolitan India at that.

Third, there is the question of the alleged degradation of women in the ideology of sati. The existing literature on sati in some Indic traditions—sati was not endemic to them all nor was it unknown in non-Indic traditions—indicates that the traditional concept of sati was associated with ideas of the sacred and magical powers of woman, of both the straightforward right-handed and potentially sinister left-handed kinds. These associations went with fear of woman, her power, and her special status in the cosmos. As the carrier of the ultimate principle of nature and representative of the cosmic feminine principle, a woman was thought to be the natural protector of her man. It was taken for granted that a man could not match her in piety, power, and will. To moderns, the mythology of the rite seems an insult to women mainly because these meanings are lost to us. While we blame traditional India for being organized around religion we claim in the same breath that the sacred power women enjoyed in Indian society was meaningless.

What has happened in recent times is that these non-economic powers of women have both declined and been devalued. Like men, women in India, too, are assessed more and more in terms of their productive capacity and the market value of that capacity.

Wherever that market value is low and market morality enters social relationships, the chances of sati—now more appropriately called widow-burning—increase.[82] They also increase when women have access to economic power within families in which social relationships become brittle or interest-based due to cultural changes.

It was such a combination of circumstances—and the one-dimensional valuation of women that it produced—that precipitated the one large-scale epidemic of sati we have witnessed in the last three hundred years. The Bengal epidemic of sati was the logical culmination of rational, secular cost calculation in a society convulsed by massive disruption of traditional values.

Fourth and finally, there is the question of social intervention through the state. V.N. Datta in a recent book has tried to sum up the attitudes of the Muslim rulers of India, specially the Mughal emperors, towards sati.[83] The Mughals were hostile to sati and some of them saw it as a by-product of Hindu idolatry. But they did not use the might of the state to suppress it. Instead, they insisted on prior government permission for the performance of sati as an insurance against coercion. By delaying such permission, supposedly to screen the genuine sati from the inauthentic one, they placed obstacles in the way of the prospective sati. The aim, Bernier says, was to tire out the patience of the widows. That this usually worked is surely indicated by Jean de Thevenot's remark that the relatives of prospective satis sometimes sought to bribe Mughal officers. Women with children were in any case not allowed by the Mughals to burn themselves, because they were expected to look after and educate their children. One emperor, Jahangir, required those wishing to commit sati in regions near the capital to appear before him personally to obtain permission. Promises of gifts and land were made to them to dissuade them from the act.

Such tactics probably worked because, paradoxically, the Mughal hostility to sati accompanied the deep respect of the Mughal state towards the values represented by the rite. Coomaraswamy reminds his modern readers of the poem of Muhammad Riza Nau'i, written in the reign of Akbar, upon the sati of a Hindu girl whose betrothed was killed on the day of their marriage.

This Musulman poet, to whom the Hindus were 'idolaters', does not relate his story in any spirit of religious intolerance or ethical condescension. ...He does not wonder at the wickedness of men, but at the generosity of women. ... This Hindu bride refused to be comforted and wished to be burnt on the pyre of her dead betrothed. When Akbar was informed of this, he called the girl before him and offered wealth and protection, but she rejected all his persuasion.... .

Akbar was forced, though reluctantly, to give his consent to the sacrifice, but sent with her his son Prince Daniyal who continued to dissuade her. Even from within the flames, she replied to his remonstrances, 'Do not annoy, do not annoy, do not annoy.'[84]

The last word of Nau'i on the subject is:

Teach me, O God, the Way of Love,
and enflame my heart with this maiden's Fire.[85]

As for the colonial period, it is not widely known that Rammohan Roy (1772–1833), the social reformer whose name is most closely associated with the struggle against sati in historical times, was himself ambivalent towards a legal ban on sati; according to some, he opposed such a ban.[86] Moreover, he showed respect to the values underlying the mythology of sati by pointing out that the rite presumed the superiority in the cosmos of the feminine principle over the masculine, and recognized the woman's greater firmness of spirit, loyalty, and courage.[87] Perhaps he wanted the reform movement he had initiated from within the society, and not the colonial state, to be the main instrument of social change. Given that he also saw the values constituting the philosophy of sati to be an endorsement of the superiority of the feminine principle over the masculine, it could even be hypothesized that he saw his society as perfectly capable of handling the pathology of sati with the help of its own cultural resources. He had certainly sensed that the epidemic of sati all around him was a product of colonialism, not of India's own traditions; and that the epidemic affected exactly that section of society—the westernizing, culturally uprooted, urban and semi-urban Indians—which was often dismissive towards the rest of the society, regarding it as a swamp of superstition and atavism.[88]

Interestingly, many contemporaries of Rammohan Roy acknowledged the modern, colonial links with sati. Some of them were aggressively anti-Hindu and would have loved to blame Indian tradition for the outbreak of sati in Bengal—for instance, the Baptist missionary Joshua Marshman. Even those who were unable to see the direct colonial connection often identified the distorted remnant of tradition as the main culprit, and saw that sati became a social problem only when such traditions were under attack.[89]

One can end by saying that, even if one takes a consistently modernist view, sati, when it was a ghatanā or an event, was an instance of individual pathology and thus remained primarily in the domain of clinical psychology and psychiatry; when it became a prathā or system, it became primarily a social problem and entered the domain of social psychology and social psychiatry. The state comes in as an important actor mainly in the second case.

Blurring the two categories—sati as an event and sati as a custom or epidemic—is an essential device for those who seek to adapt the colonial discourse on sati for internal use, both as a political strategy and as a psychological defence. It is remarkable how since the Deorala event there has been a revival of efforts by Anglophile, psychologically uprooted Indians (exactly the sector which produced the last epidemic of sati in eastern India) to vend sati as a stigma primarily of Hinduism, and not as one of the by-products of the entry of modern values—especially the absolutization of impersonal human relationships, the productivity principle, and market morality—into the interstices of Indian society. At one time, most of these efforts were closely associated with attempts to justify British rule in India. Now, as the cultural projection of a new form of internal colonialism, such efforts are primarily associated with the rootless, westernized, Indian bourgeoisie that controls the media, either directly or through the state. Only one scholar has so far expressed her distress that the criticisms of sati since the Deorala event have borrowed so heavily from colonial discourse.[90]

Actually, such borrowing is to be expected. Colonialism has to try to discredit the culture of the colonized to validate the colonial or quasi-colonial social relationships that it itself creates. The persistence of culture is a form of resistance, and those seeking hegemony in the realm of political economy cannot afford to leave culture alone. Those who see themselves as social engineers in the southern world and their supporters within the Western knowledge industry know this fully. It is an indicator of that awareness in India today that Roop's tragically unnecessary death has become for the urban, uprooted, Indian bourgeoisie another marker of the backwardness of the traditional Indian, even though responsibility for the death should be shared by the social forces that these westernized Indians have supported handsomely. These forces constitute the kind of attack on traditional lifestyles that has resulted in epidemics of sati in the past.

Middle-class progressivism reveals itself most clearly in its intolerance towards the values that prompted Indians to venerate the remembered pre-modern satis that took place over the centuries. These values cut across Indian society, across the barriers of caste, class, gender, age, and even religion. Available data show that the veneration of sati continues to be a characteristic of the society as a whole.[91] Many middle-class social critics and radicals call such respect 'glorification of sati' and want it to be banned. They believe it contributes directly to the practice of sati in contemporary times. Many who hold this view style themselves historical materialists; yet when it comes to sati and village India, they conveniently forget the socio-economic determination of social pathologies. They speak as if the ideology of sati itself produced sati.[92]

III

Let me conclude by admitting a central problem that every critic of modernity must face. Every culture has a dark side. Sati in the kali yuga is an actualization of some of the possibilities inherent in the darker side of India's traditional culture, even if this actualization has been made possible by the forces of modernity impinging on and seeking to subvert the culture. After all, the tradition of sati exists only in some cultures, not in all; the kind of pathological self-expression displayed by some cultures in South Asia is not found in other parts of the world.

It is not easy to acknowledge the complicity of either the underside of traditions or of South Asian modernity. For modern academics it is the reference group of professional colleagues

and the fear of being shamed in the metropolitan centres of intellectual life; for non-moderns, there are the loyalties to one community and the pathetic attempts to reaffirm a faith that has become
shaky within. Particularly in Roop's case, the moderns suspect
that it was a matter not only of blind superstition but of rational
cost calculation superimposed on non-rational faith. They are
horrified by villagers using secular, instrumental rationality to
profit from their traditions. Many angry interpreters of the case
probably see their own faces, distorted by the 'strange customs'
of village India, in those of Roop's in-laws. It is perhaps the absence of that particular mix of the rational and non-rational which
makes the middle classes relatively indifferent towards dowry
deaths in urban India. Dowry deaths—in which a young wife is
torched, usually by her in-laws because she has brought them
less dowry than they expected—are the result of rational cost
calculation and profiteering through and through. Though the
greed for dowry does hang on the peg of what is allegedly a
pan-Indian custom—I say allegedly because it is known that bride
price was more widespread in India than dowry until the earlier
decades of this century—no scope for mystery is left by the practice. That is why the hundreds of dowry deaths (the average for
New Delhi in the mid-1980s was roughly 150 deaths per year)
cannot match the impact of one sati. As a letter to the editor of
The Times of India pointed out soon after the Deorala event:

On November 1, *The Times of India* reported the death of five women by
burning. All the incidents were from Delhi. What is shocking is that it is
almost a daily feature now, with only the numbers varying.
The sati incident at Deorala pales into insignificance before this phenomenon. ...These are not mishaps; these are planned deaths. ...When will women's
welfare organisations and the Central and State governments wake up?[93]

The letter draws attention to the asymmetry which is not obvious
to many urban westernized Indians but was all too obvious to
some of the Deorala women, who sarcastically pointed out to
visiting women journalists that burning to death in a West Delhi
lower-middle-class concrete slum was no less painful than burning to death in a Rajasthani village; that they, the Deorala women,
were not accustomed to burning their daughters-in-law to death
the way urban women did.[94]

In sociological terms, dowry deaths are clear cases of murder, for no one justifies them, not even the neighbours. Sati is different. It arouses anxieties which moderns—Indians as well as non-Indians—are unable to cope with. The very idea of self-immolation is deeply disturbing in a world where self-interest is the ultimate currency of public life. That is why, after saying that sati is nothing but unalloyed murder, moderns worry not about the nearly three thousand people getting murdered every year in Bihar's countryside in land-related disputes but about the few cases of sati in Rajasthan. Moderns can understand the use of sati for profit, but they nervously remember the 300,000 people who went to Deorala on pilgrimage after Roop's death, with no interest in profit at all. Their faith was real and not feigned; that faith tells something to modern Indians they do not like to hear.

For modern societies do not lack their own rituals of self-imposed or forced self-immolation. Why is it not troubling to see teen-aged soldiers goose-stepping to their death in war? Or seeing one's own country getting increasingly militarized? Instead of opium, soldiers are given alcohol; instead of fears of the widow going back on her decision to commit sati, in their case there is fear of desertion. Modern Indians have even argued that any mention of conjugal loyalty in the context of sati is sexist, because men do not immolate themselves at the death of their wives. But just because self-immolation in war is largely a male preserve, does that mean that women are incapable of loyalty to the nation? As in sati, so in war, there is the charged atmosphere and ritual fervour that makes all self-immolation seem justified; there are even the priests, secular and non-secular, to ease one's journey to the other world. Above all, there is profit to be made from the self-immolations of wars; in fact the magnitude of the profits made through modern warfare could put to shame both Roop's in-laws and their political supporters. Is the comic anti-hero in *Monsieur Verdoux* correct when he insists that if one kills a few one is a murderer, but if one kills a million, one is a hero, for number sanctifies? Can it be that war is acceptable because it does not prove the superstitions of the defeated cultures of Asia and Africa but is a respectable instrument of diplomacy and a profession on which the modern world is built?[95]

What is the sickness of soul that numbs social sensitivities thus? Is it the same that blinded the apologists of sati to Roop

Kanwar being an eighteen-year-old girl, traumatized by her husband's death and unable to take responsible decisions? Is it the same that prevented 'her people' from helping her out of her depression and made them push her into self-immolation even before her parents could meet her?

Notes

1   Kishwar, Madhu and Ruth Vanita, 'The Burning of Roop Kanwar', in Kishwar, M.(ed.) *Off the Beaten Track* (New Delhi: Oxford University Press, 1999). First published in *Manushi,* Nos 42–3, September–December 1987.

2   It is assumed that the author is referring to the Terrorist and Disruptive Activities (Prevention) Act (1985, amended 1987).

3   Uproar Over Rajput Sati', *Hinduism Today,* December 1987.

4   Oldenburg, Veena, 'The Roop Kanwar Case: Feminist Responses', in J.S. Hawley (ed.) *Sati: The Blessing and the Curse* (New York. Oxford University Press, 1994).

5   This is not the entire range of responses. Ashis Nandy represents quite a different side of the debate. For brief feminist analyses of the various political positions—liberal, conservative, and feminist—see Lata Mani, 'Multiple Mediations: Feminist Scholarship in the Age of Multinational Reception', *Feminist Review* 35 (Summer 1990), pp. 24–41, and Rajeswari Sunder Rajan, 'The Subject of Sati: Pain and Death in the Contemporary Discourse on Sati', *Yale Journal of Criticism* 3:2 (1990), pp. 1–23.

6   Romila Thapar, 'In History', *Seminar* 342 (February 1988), pp. 14–19. For example, Ashis Nandy had claimed, in the *Indian Express* on 5 October 1987, that there had been only three historical periods when sati had become an epidemic. Without fuss, without even mentioning his name, Thapar offers a well-documented explanation for Nandy's misperception in the case of Vijayanagara in the sixteenth century (p.17).

7   In Hawley, J.S., *Sati: The Blessing and the Curse* (New York: Oxford University Press, 1994), pp. 159–74.

8   Sudesh Vaid, 'Politics of Widow Immolation', in *Seminar* 342 (February 1988), pp. 20–3. This essay remains the clearest statement of the historicity and world view of sati in the Shekhavati region.

9   Lata Mani has written extensively on the colonial discourses on sati. Her observations on the discursive continuities between the colonial and the present debates on Roop Kanwar in her 'Multiple Mediations' are exceptionally pertinent here.

10   The information in the following paragraph is based on Mark Tully's chapter entitled 'The Deorala Sati' in his book, *No Full Stops in India* (New Delhi: Viking Penguin India, 1991), pp. 210–36; also published in *The Defeat of a*

Congressman and Other Parables of Modern India (New York: Knopf, 1992), pp. 191–215. His interview with Sharada Jain, the sociologist and women's rights activist who spearheaded the women's protest against the valorization of the sati, captures both her anger at and her analysis of Roop Kanwar's murder very well.

11   Prabhash Joshi, *Jansatta,* 18 September 1987, as translated in Tully, *No Full Stops,* p. 228.

12   Tully, *No Full Stops,* p. 222.

13   Sharada Jain, Nirja Misra, and Kavita Srivastava, 'Deorala Episode: Women's Protest in Rajasthan', *'Economic and Political Weekly* 22:45 (7 November 1987), p. 1894. The following account is abstracted from this chronology, pp. 1891–4.

14   Jain et al., 'Deorala Episode,' p. 1891.

15   Jain et al., 'Deorala Episode,' p. 1893.

16   Ibid.

17   Ibid.

18   Jain et al., 'Deorala Episode,' p. 1894. The entire chronology is taken from this source and checked against other newspaper reports.

19   Ibid.

20   Tully, *No Full Stops,* p. 223.

21   The article referred to here is their most recent piece, 'Institutions, Beliefs, Ideologies: Widow Immolation in Contemporary Rajasthan', *Economic and Political Weekly* 26:17 (27 April 1991), pp. WS-2–18, which subsumes earlier publications.

22   These three were Meena Menon, Geeta Seshu, and Sujata Anandan, and they produced a thirty-three page report entitled *Trial by Fire: A Report on Roop Kanwar's Death,* published in Bombay by the Bombay Union of Journalists. It has no date of publication but states that the authors visited Deorala, Sikar, and Jaipur between 24 and 30 September 1987, after the chunri mahotsav had already taken place. They must have written their report not long afterwards.

23   Menon et al., *Trial by Fire,* p. 1.

24   Menon et al., *Trial by Fire,* p. 2

25   Sangari and Vaid, 'Institutions, Beliefs, Ideologies,' pp. WS-3–6.

26   Menon et al., *Trial by Fire,* p. 3.

27   Menon et al., *Trial by Fire,* p. 4.

28   Menon et al., *Trial by Fire,* pp. 4–5.

29   Menon et al., *Trial by Fire,* p. 5.

30   Ibid.

31   Menon et al., *Trial by Fire,* pp. 6–7.

[32] Menon et al., *Trial by Fire*, p. 7. The term 'androgynous depression' is unusual but not explained. It may be a euphemism for repressed homosexual desire or for impotence caused by a lack of enthusiasm for heterosexual activity, such as Mal Singh might have experienced after marriage; it certainly merits further investigation.

[33] Ibid.

[34] Ibid.

[35] Tully, *No Full Stops*, p. 215.

[36] Menon et al., *Trial by Fire*, p. 1.

[37] Tully, *No Full Stops*, p. 216.

[38] This fact raises questions about the conventional view of the natal family's callousness towards daughters in India, especially after marriage—a view that has wide currency among feminists in the West.

[39] Madhu Kishwar and Ruth Vanita, 'The Burning of Roop Kanwar', *Manushi* 42–3 (1987), p. 15.

[40] Ibid., p. 16. These 'reformers'—a puzzling usage at best—are not named, nor are the direct quotes used in the article attributed to any particular 'reformer'. The editors' report makes no mention of the other fact-finding teams' analyses of political slogans, although these had been published long before the *Manushi* team visited the site, and although these had argued in much the same way. *Manushi* is a leading feminist journal and carries many scholarly articles, yet its editors seldom practice the art of scholarly attribution of borrowed ideas. Their report develops the sati-as-a-modern-phenomenon argument more fully than did Sharada Jain et al. or the Women and Media Committee report, among others, but the editors waste no space on acknowledgment to suggest the provenance of the many themes they bring to a fullness in their own much later report.

[41] Kishwar and Vanita, 'Burning', p. 24.

[42] Kishwar and Vanita, 'Burning', p. 25.

[43] Kishwar and Vanita, 'Burning', pp. 16–18, 24.

[44] Kishwar and Vanita, 'Burning', p. 18.

[45] Kishwar and Vanita, 'Burning', p. 20.

[46] Kavita, Shobha, Shobita, Kanchan, and Sharada, 'Rural Women Speak', *Seminar* 342 (February 1988), pp. 40–4. The authors of this piece (who, like most feminist activists, do not use their family names) are affiliated with the Women's Development Programme in Rajasthan.

[47] Kishwar and Vanita, 'Burning', p. 21.

[48] Kishwar and Vanita, 'Burning', p. 22.

[49] Rajeswari Sunder Rajan, 'The Subject of Sati', p.3.

[50] Imrana Qadeer and Zoya Hasan, 'Deadly Politics of the State and Its Apologists', *Economic and Political Weekly* 22:46 (14 November 1987), pp. 1946–9.

51 Qadeer and Hasan, 'Deadly Politics,' p. 1947.

52 Ibid.

53 Considering that Shah Bano succumbed to religious pressure to recant in the full glare of national multimedia publicity, one can imagine how easy it might have been to convince an eighteen-year-old widow in the privacy of her marital home in an obscure village in Rajasthan to immolate herself.

54 Briefly, Hindu militants claimed the soil as their god Rama's birthplace and wished to build a temple to him on the site where a Rama temple is believed to have once stood. This alleged space was since 1528 occupied by a mosque built by the Mughal Emperor Babar's general. The critique is even more pertinent if we consider the habit of dangerous vacillation inherited by Narasimha Rao's government. The same apparent inertia overwhelmed it when throngs of hoodlums destroyed the Babari Mosque in Ayodhya on 6 December 1992, and an eminently preventable act became the signal for thousands to go berserk and bloody the face of a secular republic.

55 Imrana Qadeer, 'Shah Bano and Roop Kanwar', *Seminar* 342 (February 1988), p. 33. In this essay Qadeer incorporates some of the points discussed in her other cited piece, but she goes much farther in producing a cogent and gender-sensitive analysis.

56 Sunder Rajan, 'The Subject of Sati', p. 7.

57 Sunder Rajan, 'The Subject of Sati', pp. 14–15. She discusses the very important ideas of Elaine Scarry, *The Body in Pain: The Making and Unmaking of the World* (New York: Oxford University Press, 1985) and in the process has stimulated discussions among Indian feminists about the inadequacy of current theory on the subjectivity and identity of women.

58 Sunder Rajan, 'The Subject of Sati', p.9.

59 Sangari and Vaid, 'Institutions, Beliefs, Ideologies', p. WS-10.

60 Lata Mani, 'Multiple Mediations', p. 38.

61 Kishwar and Vanita, 'Burning', p. 21.

62 Vasudha Dhagamwar, 'Saint, Victim or Criminal', *Seminar* 342 (February 1988), pp. 34–9. Apart from being a compact piece of legal history, this essay is valuable for its very careful comparative analysis of the Rajasthan and Central government statutes on sati occasioned by the Roop Kanwar incident.

63 Dhagamwar, 'Saint, Victim or Criminal', p. 38.

64 The first was made in 1986 when the Shah Bano case led to the exemption of Muslim husbands from the requirement to pay maintenance for their abandoned or divorced wives under the Penal Code section designed to prevent vagrancy. This exemption, for Muslims only, was enacted separately as the Muslim Women's (Protection of Rights on Divorce) Act.

65 Nandy, Ashis, 'Sati in *Kali Yuga*: The Public Debate on Roop Kanwar's Death', in *Return from Exile* (Delhi: Oxford University Press, reprint 2005), pp. 32–52.

66 For instance, Chinu Panchal, '1,500 Witness "Sati" Ritual', *The Times of India*, 6 October 1986.

67 P. Chidambaram, quoted in Tavleen Singh, *Indian Express*, 29 May 1988. On the broad sociology and 'epidemiology' of sati, see the special issue of *Seminar*, February 1988 (342).

68 In the context of Deorala, only one paper comes close to recognizing the nature of this problem. See Madhu Kishwar and Ruth Vanita, 'The Burning of Roop Kanwar', *Race and Class*, July–September 1988, 30(1), pp. 59–67, esp. pp. 66–7.

69 See the case of Shakuntala Yadav, reported in Rahul Pathak, 'Confess to Murder, Cops Tell Family', *Indian Express*, 13 January 1988; Minu Jain, 'Sati or Murder', *The Sunday Observer*, 18 January 1988; also 'Sati or Suicide', *Indian Express*, 12 January 1988; and 'Another Sati Reported in U.P. Village', *The Statesman*, 12 January 1988.

70 Maja Daruwala, 'Overkill of Sati Bill', *The Statesman*, 21 January 1988. For the text of the new sati legislation, see *The Commission of Sati (Prevention) Act, 1987 [Act No. 3 of 1988] with Short Notes* (Lucknow: Eastern Book Co., n. d.).

71 For instance, Shabnam Virmani, 'The Spirit of Sati Lives On', *The Times of India*, 12 September 1987. According to her, it was 'unlikely that Roop Kunwar was coerced into it by relatives', and that the villagers were 'tight-lipped and wary of press reporters and the public'. Within two weeks the same newspaper published Sunil Menon's 'Roop Kanwar's Act was not voluntary', *The Times of India*, 25 September 1987. Roop Kanwar's parents have till now maintained that she was not coerced. See Sanjeev Srivastava, 'Deorala Revisited', *The Illustrated Weekly of India*, 22 May 1988, pp. 20–3.

72 'Dragged to Pyre for Sati', *The Statesman*, 21 October 1988.

73 Sanjeev Srivastava, 'Doctor Elusive about Deorala Incident', *The Times of India*, 4 June 1988. Srivastava wrote wistfully, 'Some of the police officials associated with the investigation of the case also feel handicapped in their efforts to extract more information as no 'third degree methods' could be used during the interrogation of Dr Singh'.

74 Ashis Nandy, 'Sati: A Nineteenth Century Tale of Women, Violence and Protest', *At the Edge of Psychology: Essays in Politics and Culture* (New Delhi: Oxford University Press, 1980, reprint 1989), pp. 1–31.

75 For instance, Rabindranath Tagore, 'Vivāha', *Kathā o Kāhini*, in *Racanābalī* (Calcutta: Vishwabharati, 1987), 4, pp. 71–3; and 'Mā Bhaih', *Racanābalī*, 3, pp. 676–9; Abanindranath Tagore, *Rājkāhinī* (Calcutta: Signet Press, 1956).

76 Ananda K. Coomaraswamy, 'Status of Indian Women', *The Dance of Shiva: Fourteen Indian Essays* (Delhi: Munshiram Manoharlal, 1982), pp. 115–39. See p. 128.

[77] Only one scholar has critically assessed the modern discomfort with the TV Ramayana, arguing that the discomfort comes from the moderns' lack of access to the epics and inability to use them creatively. See G.P. Deshpande, 'The Riddle of the Sagar Ramayana', *Economic and Political Weekly*, 22 October 1988, pp. 2215–16.

[78] Coomaraswamy, 'Status of Indian Women', p. 127.

[79] The reaction of modern India to the self-immolation of a Jain man of religion at about the same time was also minimal. The death was viewed as the foolish self-destruction of a slightly senile religious enthusiast. The reaction to the self-chosen death of Vinoba Bhave some years earlier did not differ greatly.

[80] When I first made a distinction between sati as a ghatanā (event) and sati as a pratha (system or practice) in this and an earlier essay ('Sati in Kaliyuga', *Indian Express*, November 1987), there were howls of protest in some journals and news weeklies. It was read as directly supporting sati and some, not knowing that I was not a Hindu, even found in it indicators of Hindu fanaticism. One called it a *dhārmic* support to sati (Sudhir Chandra, 'Sati: The *Dhārmic* Fallacy', *New Quest*, March–April 1988 (68), pp. 111–14). Another found in the use of the 'Hindu' fourfold division of yugas itself clinching evidence of my real self (Kumkum Sangari, 'Perpetuating the Myth', *Seminar*, February 1988 (342), pp. 24–30). It restored my faith in the practical wisdom imposed by involvement in the politics of social reform when two women activists, troubled by the sati bill, subsequently wrote: 'The bill assumes sati is a practice, whereas it could be described as a kind of rare and frightful event which reveals, in a flash, several of the problems of our time. In other words, we might do well to consider whether it is now being given the sanctity of tradition and practice, and if so by whom and with what motives. In order to do this, we must first distinguish between sati as an act, sati as an ideology, and sati as a source of political and financial profit.

'There is...a difference between those who organise the event of sati,...those who eulogise the principle of sati underlying one particular incident hundreds of years ago but repudiate the act of sati today,...and those who glorify the act in self-interest, be it practical or financial' (Latika Sarkar and Radha Kumar, 'Flaws in New Sati Bill', *The Times of India*, 15 December 1987).

The only thing I might add is that Sarkar and Kumar do not seem to be aware here that sati is being associated with 'the sanctity of tradition and practice' not merely by religious fanatics but also by a large section of India's modern literati, with a different set of motives and interests. Cf. S. Sahay, 'Perspective on Sati', *The Telegraph*, 26 January 1988.

[81] Cf. Arvind Sharma, *Sati* (Delhi: Motilal Banarsidass, 1988), pp. 15–17; and Romila Thapar, 'In History', *Seminar*, February 1988, (342), pp. 14–19.

[82] Nandy, 'Sati'.

[83] V.N. Datta, *Sati: Widow Burning in India* (New Delhi: Manohar, 1987), esp. pp. 13–14.

84   Coomaraswamy, 'The Status of Indian Women', pp. 128–9.

85   Ibid., p. 129.

86   Ramesh Chandra Majumdar, *Glimpses of Bengal in the Nineteenth Century* (Calcutta: Firma K.L. Mukhopadhyay, 1960).

87   Nandy, 'Sati'.

88   Ibid.

89   Ibid.

90   Veena Das, 'Strange Response', *The Illustrated Weekly of India*, 8 February 1988.

91   'Roop Kanwar did the Right Thing', *The Times of India*, 11 December 1987. This survey showed that 63.4 per cent of the respondents (63 per cent of women and 41.5 per cent in the age group 25–40) supported sati and 50.8 per cent refused to accept it as a crime. This is 160 years after sati was legally banned.

92   In much that I have said, I have compared contemporary middle-class and earlier colonial reactions to sati. There is an even closer comparison in the reaction of the urban bourgeoisie to the Muslim Women's Bill of 1986—the Shah Bano affair—and in a not-so-widely-known plea that some well-known Bengali intellectuals made to the West Bengal government at about the same time to suppress Santhal witch doctors. As the agitation against the Muslim Women's Bill is likely to be better known than the Santhal case to my readers, I shall confine my comments to it.

       The protest against the Muslim Women's Bill, like that against sati, too, was meant to resist the victimization of women and was justified as such. But those who made a public issue out of the victimization of the likes of Shah Bano (who had been divorced and left in penury by her well-to-do Muslim husband) ignored or tried to whitewash the larger victimization of the community involved. They pretended that the Shah Bano case which triggered the Bill, and the Bill itself, could be discussed without taking into account the fact that a sizeable proportion of the Muslims had been discriminated against, subjected to violence, and pushed increasingly into urban ghettos by a series of riots. They behaved as if one could ignore that in this discrimination and violence, the Indian state and its law-enforcing agencies—two main actors in the Shah Bano case and professed agents of social change within Muslim society—had played a growing role, both deliberately and by default. (Cf. Bhikhu Parekh, 'Between Holy Text and Moral Void', *The New Statesman*, 24 March 1989, pp. 29–33.)

       In their insecurity, fear, and sense of being cornered, a large section of Muslims were bound to see the Supreme Court's decision in favour of Shah Bano, especially in view of the homilies on Islam included in the judgment, as another attack by the same state machinery on their identity and culture, which had already become their last line of defence. No wonder they closed ranks, supporting even the more obscurantist and fanatic elements among them. This closing of ranks perfectly suited the westernized middle-class Indians who opposed the Bill; as if they were waiting for just that. The moment some of the more atavistic elements in Muslim society joined the protest, it was interpreted by a drove of excited social analysts as the final proof of the moral and cultural decadence of the Muslims—in fact, as another of the stigmata of Islam itself. Notorious Muslim-baiters shed copious tears over the plight of Muslim women in much the same way that some well-furnished drawing rooms in urban India later reverberated with lamentations about the plight of rural Rajasthani women after the Deorala event.

[93] Satish Gogia, Letter to the Editor, *The Times of India*, 5 November 1987. Also see Pradeep S. Mehta, Letter to the Editor, *The Times of India*, 5 December 1988.

[94] Perhaps I should also add here that if Roop's death was a case of murder through burning, there is no dearth of modern Indians who either kept silent or colluded with the burning of thousands of Sikhs on the streets of Delhi in 1984. Some national dailies, which published the most strident condemnations of the Deorala sati, were then busy censoring news of the anti-Sikh pogrom lest the role of the Indian state and the ruling Congress party in it became apparent.

[95] In the entire debate on sati during 1987–8 in the English press, probably only Bill Aitken in his 'Abomination (Private) Limited', *The Statesman*, 30 March 1988, had the honesty to confront the issue of priorities, which was first raised by Ananda Coomaraswamy in the 1930s. Aitken, being a mere intellectual and not an academic, raised the issue in response to the shallow, crypto-racist, bogus anthropology of George L. Hart in 'Sati Just a Form of Human Sacrifice', *The Statesman*, 29 March 1988. There have been more human sacrifices in this century, Aitken says in response to Hart, than in the 2000 years leading up to it.

Aitken also recognized that Hart's article was a crude attempt to placate India's westernized elite, provoked by his protégé Patrick D. Harrigan's two articles: 'Tyranny of the Elect?' (*The Statesman*, 5 November 1987) and 'Is Tradition Ridiculed by Western Values?' (*The Statesman*, 5 March 1988). Both dissented from the views popular among India's modern elites, though the dissent was steeped in innocence about the political sociology of traditions in contemporary India.

20

Charan Shah

Manushi, 'Deadly Laws and Zealous Reformers'[1]

Although by far the most notorious, the immolation of Roop Kanwar is not the only sati to have taken place in india in recent years. The following is the text of an article which appeared in the feminist journal *Manushi* following the immolation of Charan Shah in 1999.

THE CONFLICTING INTERPRETATIONS AND POLITICS OF SATI

In large parts of the world people are busy making preparations to celebrate the end of the second millennium and the beginning of the third. This millennium has not been a particularly happy one for India. Throughout the past thousand years, this subcontinent witnessed a series of invasions with certain regions experiencing repeated plunder and political subjugation by rule of the conquerors. In some instances, however, instead of returning to their homelands after collecting enough loot, the invaders settled down in India giving impetus to a new cultural mix and thereby creating a need for building bridges of communication between the conflicting groups. But nothing disrupted and damaged this country as much as British colonization, which lasted nearly two centuries.

Unlike earlier conquerors, the British didn't just stop at pillage and appropriation of wealth. They attempted to destroy almost all indigenous institutions, knowledge, notion of ethics, and most importantly, the sense of self-worth among the people of South Asia. The modern education system they imposed on us created an elite trained to look at their own society through colonial eyes, and to treat their own people as colonial subjects—especially if they happen to be poor and uneducated.

Our erstwhile colonial rulers who needed the pretence of being on a civilizing mission here to justify their brutal reign had a vested interest in identifying select criminal acts and projecting them as Indian traditions in need of reform. They began this cultural invasion by deliberately targeting a few cases of young widows in Bengal who were forcibly burnt on their husband's pyres, calling those murders sati and banning it by law, so they could appear as agents of a superior civilization rescuing victims from a savage culture. They even called their mission the White Man's Burden! Thereafter, the supposedly miserable plight of a newly invented creature called the Indian women became emblematic of the inferior civilization and culture of the Indian people.

There is absolutely no evidence that any of our vast array of religious texts sanctified such murders as sati. The word 'sati' derives from the word 'sat' which means 'truth'. So sati means a woman who is true—not a woman who spontaneously combusts.[2] In this context, it is noteworthy that none of the mythological heroines revered as *mahasatis*—Sati (Shiva's wife), Draupadi, Mandodari, Tara, Ahalya, and Sita—burned on their husband's pyre. Though some references to women committing voluntary self-immolation along with their dead husbands can be found in the Mahabharata and Puranas, the practice never received much sanctity or popularity. It is only in nineteenth-century British discourse that forced immolation of women on the husband's pyre came to be regarded as 'sati'.

It is understandable that the British should resort to such distortion and defamation as part of the imperial game of convincing Indians that they were 'uncivilized' and hence unfit for self-governance. When reformers in post-Independence India operate with the same colonial mindset while dealing with the customs of their own people, it only goes to prove that the brown sahibs of India have learnt to treat the people of this country with the same contempt as did our colonial masters.

The recent debate on sati, following Charan Shah's self-immolation on 11 November 1999 in Satpura village located in Uttar Pradesh's Mahoba district illustrates this attitude very well.

MISINFORMED VERDICT

Without as much as conducting a preliminary investigation into the circumstances under which the immolation took place, several activists passed a verdict solely on the basis of some sensational and misleading media reports that Charan Shah's in-laws and other relatives are guilty of abetting her suicide.[3] They, along with some powerful voices in the media, demanded that the family along with other villagers should be arrested and charged under the Sati Prevention Act.[4] This was even before they checked to find out if her in-laws were indeed alive and/or living in that village. As it turned out, Charan Shah lived with her grown-up son and was surrounded by her own natal family at the time of her husband's death. Some had decided in advance that there must have been a property angle to it, without finding out whether this poor Dalit family had any land worth its name.

Among others, Charan Shah's own sister, brother, and son have repeatedly stated that they had no idea she was contemplating such an act. She quietly walked out of the house and rushed to the burning pyre while other women attended to post-cremation ceremonies and the men had left for the ritual bath. By the time people realized what had happened, Charan Shah was already in flames. Despite such repeated clarifications, some zealots are still insisting that the draconian provisions of the Sati Prevention Act must be invoked against the people of Satpura. Thanks to this concerted pressure, the police felt compelled to save their skin by arresting Charan Shah's son and maternal uncle. These two were kept in police custody for two days and pressured into stating that Charan Shah was mentally deranged.

One section of reformers is also demanding that all those who witnessed the event ought to be arrested and punished sternly. In addition, they demand action against all those who interpret her immolation as a case of sati, under the Sati Prevention Act. It is shocking that several responsible and respected people and even some human rights organizations should respond in such a high handed manner to the death of fifty-five-year-old Charan Shah.

FORCED INTO STEREOTYPES

No one actually knows whether Charan Shah killed herself on the spur of the moment, or if it was a premeditated act. One thing is certain: there was no ceremony, no ritual preparation, no ideological statement made before she flung herself on the pyre. Yet, it is assumed that Charan Shah acted out of an obscurantist belief that her life as a widow was useless and that she would gain religious merit by following her husband in death.

Why is she considered incapable of other motives or sentiments? Could she not have acted out of love? After all, by all accounts, she nursed her husband for thirty long years with total dedication. Maybe, they had a tender loving relationship. Some villagers were reported to have remarked: 'She has been a sati for thirty years. This was only the culminating act.' Or maybe she became so worn out from her life of poverty that she thought there would be no purpose in living on any further. Could it be that she killed herself in a mood of quiet rage and protest, because her son reportedly turned down her request for carrying Man Shah's dead body in a decorated *doli*, and cremating him with ceremonial *band-baaja*? Could it be that Charan Shah felt hurt at this refusal and burnt herself on her husbands pyre—as though to say 'I save you the expense of my funeral as well?'

CALLING FOR REPEAL OF ANTI-SATI LAW

The Sati Prevention Act of 1987 was added to the statute book under pressure from women's organizations and other progressive activists following Roop Kanwar's sati in Deorala village. Even at that time *Manushi* had protested against this ill-conceived and draconian piece of legislation (see issue 42–3). Unfortunately our voice went unheeded by obsessed reformers who campaigned for a stringent law to deal with sati. Recently, when the debate was revived following Charan Shah's immolation, we were surprised to find that not many people who vigorously demand its implementation are aware of its actual provisions—which are not only draconian but also just plain stupid.

To begin with, the Act states that if any person commits sati, all those accused of abetting sati, directly or indirectly, 'shall be punishable with death, or imprisonment for life and shall also be liable to a fine'. Those accused of abetting any attempt to commit sati 'shall be punishable with imprisonment for life and also be liable to fine'. A woman accused of attempting sati is also liable to a prison term of up to six months plus a fine—the same as for attempted suicide.

How does the Act define 'abetment'? Apart from inducing or encouraging a widow, 'directly or indirectly', to commit sati, abetment includes 'being present at the place where sati is committed as an active participant to such commission or to any ceremony connected with it'. In addition, whoever performs any act for the 'glorification' of sati is also punishable with a fine and jail term of not less than one year, but extendable to seven years.

Most important of all, when the state accuses any person of 'abetting' sati, the burden of proving that he/she has not committed the offence shall be on the accused. That is, you are assumed guilty until you can prove, to the court's satisfaction, that you are innocent.

What would this mean in actual practice? That the police can arrest, as it did in Deorala, any number of people in an area where a woman, either voluntarily or through family pressure, ends up immolating herself. They can all be accused of 'abetting' sati by having witnessed the act. Those accused will have to corroborate they were nowhere at the scene of crime. It is not enough for them to establish that they did not encourage the woman to die along with her husband. The accused have to convince the authorities that they tried to actively prevent her from committing suicide in order to certify innocence.

Here, it is necessary to point out that no such onus falls on those who may perchance witness a murder. They are not expected to offer proof of their innocence by demonstrating they tried to save the murdered person. Thus, the anti-sati law is very similar to anti-terrorist laws like TADA, where the burden of proof also rests with the accused. It is noteworthy that numerous civil liberties groups all over the country worked hard to have TADA repealed, dubbing it a 'Black Act' because its draconian provisions allow for gross misuse. Many innocents have been implicated under TADA, and consequently are kept rotting in jail without trial. If a person is falsely charged by the police, it is as difficult for him/her to prove that he/she did not 'actively' assist in disruptive or terrorist activities, as it is to prove that he/she was not present at an immolation site or that he/she did not 'actively participate' in the event. Granting the state agencies the right to execute any number of people who are accused of 'witnessing' one woman's immolation and thereby being declared guilty of abetting sati can by no stretch of imagination be called an exercise in dispensing justice, or an exemplary instance of judicious law-making.

It is absurd to have a law which threatens to punish people with a death sentence, if they admit to having witnessed the voluntary or coerced immolation of a woman, because their presence at the site makes them guilty of having participated in sati. Would anyone in their right mind want to give evidence in court in such a case? Does the law not force people into lying out of sheer self-defence? Is a death sentence the appropriate response to such an event?

Given the ways of our police, it can well be imagined how opportunities for abuse are built into the anti-sati law, which gives the authorities arbitrary powers to arrest and implicate anyone they choose to target?

This is exactly what happened in Deorala. Is it any surprise, then, that all the witnesses turned 'hostile', that is, denied having any knowledge of circumstances under which Roop Kanwar died? Consequently, all of the accused were acquitted by the lower courts and even today we don't know whether Roop Kanwar killed herself voluntarily, or if she was forced into the act. For a change, the police have not shown much interest in arresting all and sundry in the Charan Shah matter, as they did previously in Deorala. One reason could be that there are some exceptionally decent officials overseeing this case. But a more likely (or at least additional) reason could be that seeing the community's abject poverty, they don't see any possibility of being able to extort money by arresting and harassing the villagers of Satpura and neighbouring regions. Deorala, by contrast, has many well-off families because a large number of men from the village are in government jobs, notably the police.

Yet leading civil rights activists and other reformers want to see such a vicious law invoked on the villagers of Satpura. It is worth noting that these organizations have earlier valiantly fought for the democratic rights of even known terrorists because their treatment under TADA violated the whole idea of due process and fair trial. But when it comes to poor illiterate villagers of India, our fervour for social engineering makes us overlook the illegal and undemocratic nature of the enactments meant for the apparent reform of those we have unilaterally and presumptuously dubbed 'backward'.

All those who have campaigned for the right to a fair trial of those accused of terrorism have not cared to raise similar objections against the inherently abusive provisions of the Sati Prevention Act. The fear of being 'politically incorrect' has silenced the most courageous human rights campaigners, allowing extremely punitive provisions to receive enshrinement as pro-women laws in our statute books.

It is time to regain courage and demand the repeal, or at least improvement, of such a patently anti-people law. *Manushi* intends to do exactly that and invites others interested to join us.

I am not suggesting that my speculations are correct. This is only to point out that no one really knows what transpired in Charan Shah's mind, what motivated her to take her own life in such a painful way. Yet, the social reformers both in the media and in some NGOs have chosen to dub her act 'medieval madness', a symptom of her cultural backwardness. Why? Because she was a poor, illiterate, rural Indian woman who is only permitted to live up to the stereotypes the so-called culturally advanced people have of her.

AN ATTACK ON THE DEFENCELESS

There is something macabre about the fact that the torchbearers of modern civilization who wish to cure Satpura villagers of their 'cultural backwardness', 'superstitious beliefs', and 'obscurantism' are paying little attention to the fact that people of this region live in abject poverty. Situated in a chronically drought-afflicted, neglected region of Uttar Pradesh, this particular village is located 7–8 kilometres away from the main road, accessible only through a dirt track. Satpura lacks even a primary health centre. One located in a nearby village exists only in name and does not provide even minimal services as is the case with most PHCs in north India.

Charan Shah's own family has a small plot of unirrigated land which does not provide year-round subsistence for them. Therefore, they work as labourers on other people's fields as well. Even landowning families in this drought-stricken region are pathetically poor. Thus, wage rates are also abysmally low. The family is so poor that they could not afford medical treatment for either Charan Shah's tuberculosis-infected husband, or her elder son, who died earlier from the same disease. People succumbing in the prime of their lives to a curable disease like TB speaks volumes about the failure of our health care system.

What is the wonderful gesture of concern our reformers have to offer to all these people living such impoverished lives? Vigorous demands that the police should be sent to arrest them and criminal cases should be instituted for 'murdering' Charan Shah, or at least, 'abetting' her suicide, since they did not or could not prevent her death. Thus, they are to be taught their mandatory lessons in modern cultural values through the agency of our notoriously corrupt and tyrannical police.

Despite the fact that no one has been able to provide any evidence of coercion in this case, Charan Shah's family and community are still considered liable for action because they effectively did nothing to prevent her from killing herself. The facts, as given in several reports, suggest otherwise. A shepherd boy did raise an alarm as soon he saw her moving towards the pyre. Women did come running after her as soon as they realized she had left for the cremation ground. Men who had left to bathe also rushed to the scene upon hearing this. But they all say she was already burning by then. At this point they are held guilty for failing to pull her out of the fire. I find this expectation unreasonable. Firstly, pulling someone out of a raging pyre amounts to running the risk of getting burnt yourself—the kind of courage even those recommending such action for Satpura villagers are not likely to have.

More important, who in their sane mind would want to pull out a half-burnt person in a village which lacks treatment facilities even for ordinary diseases, leave alone for life-threatening injuries? If this family could not access TB treatment, could they possibly handle a case of severe burns without proper medical help? Charan Shah would have died a far more painful and slower death. Do we have to insist on interventions that make things worse for the victims?

CONFLICTING VERSIONS

Much is being made of the supposedly conflicting versions coming from villagers now. In the article, 'Countering Earlier Reports: Charan Shah's Immolation', the versions of some neighbouring villagers in Imaliya is counterposed against those of Satpura's inhabitants to build a case that the latter's story cannot be trusted even with regard to the timing of Man Shah's death. By turning the village into a police camp and starting an aggressive campaign against a whole community through the national and international press to label them criminals, aren't we creating conditions for them to protect themselves by doctoring their story according to police requirements? However, even in these circumstances, the Satpura villagers have by and large given one consistent story. Narratives of nearby villagers are bound to vary with ones from Satpura, because those people are likely to depend on hearsay, rather than first-hand eyewitness accounts. Charan Shah's son's plea says it all: 'I shall call it whatever you want me to. If you want to call it a suicide then so be it. Equally, if you say it was a sati, then I shall follow suit.'

In this context, it is noteworthy that Satpura does not seem to have a very repressive code for widows. Several reports have told us that when Charan Shah's eldest son died, his widow was remarried to the younger brother, with whom she has raised a family. If a young widow in that family was not treated as an inauspicious pariah or forced to immolate herself, it is far-fetched to believe that Charan Shah's sons would have pushed their fifty-five-year-old mother to commit such an extreme act—especially when she was an earner, an authority figure, and an effective head of the family, rather than a hapless dependent.

Moreover, as the AIDWA report points out, members of this family are followers of a progressive sect, the Charan Data Panth. Charan Shah's son let it be known in all the interviews that among their community, they did not encourage practices such as sati. Had the family any intention of building a sati cult and temple around her, they would not have chosen the common cremation ground of the village for the last rites because according to traditional beliefs a temple cannot be built on such a site. They would have chosen a special spot as happened in the Roop Kanwar's case. But once

Charan Shah committed the act, it was not within their control to stop others from treating it with awe and reverence. Dramatic acts of self-sacrifice in any society evoke such sentiments.

Even after it was grudgingly acknowledged after more careful investigations that Charan Shah was not impelled to burn at her husband's pyre, many social justice advocates are convinced that the Sati Prevention Act must be invoked against the people of Mahoba region. They are upset at 'the local people who refuse to regard the incident as a crime'. Their reasoning: irrespective of whether she died voluntarily or whether she was pressured into the act, the very fact of her deification by villagers, and evidence indicating the existence of a whole sati cult centring her, consolidate and propagate injurious traditions against women. The reformers insist that anyone from a neighbouring village who comes to pay respects at Charan Shah's cremation site should also be arrested and tried for the crime of glorifying sati.

Zeal without Compassion

The truth is, despite a highly draconian law, that provides for death penalty for anyone accused of participating in sati, and life imprisonment for anyone glorifying sati, several million people in this country refuse to be 'modernized' into believing that voluntary self-immolation is a crime. Just as most people don't believe that suicide is a crime though many modern states in the world (even India) have declared it to be so. The question is, how do we wish to deal with people who hold different values? How many millions do we want to imprison for life and put to death for subscribing to cultural norms which somehow do not meet the approval of 'modernists' like us?

I personally abhor the practice of sati and would do everything in my power to persuade or prevent a woman from killing herself in such a gruesome fashion. Similarly, I abhor killings in the name of national wars and do all I can to build opinion against warmongering. However, I would not suggest 'ruthless action' against those who refuse to heed me.

Responsible societies lay down certain limits of conduct even during war, such as the principle of not attacking unarmed populations. The fervour of self-appointed reformers knows no limits.

They are not bothered with mundane details like confirming if even one family in that entire village has the means and money to secure bail, or to hire lawyers for fighting the prolonged litigation that would follow such a case. In all likelihood, the accused would rot in jail till death do them release from the benevolent concern of our social activists. The Charan Shah episode only underscores how reforming zeal without respect for facts, empathic understanding and compassion can easily degenerate into *Khomeinivaad*.

Why doesn't anyone demand the arrest and conviction of health ministry officials of the UP government for criminal negligence and dereliction of duty, since they failed to provide a decent health centre in Satpura? Or that public works department officials face trial and also to link this village by road, for failing to provide basic public transport in five decades of independence— so that it would have been easier for Charan Shah to take her spouse to a city hospital? If both her eldest son and her husband did not have easily avoidable premature deaths, she may not have felt the need to end her own life in such a way.

AN UNFASHIONABLE DEATH

Let's face the question squarely: what is it about her death that bothers us? That she did not want to outlive her husband? Or that she chose a politically incorrect form of death? Is it conceivable that Charan Shah's death would have evoked similar outrage, had she popped a few dozen sleeping pills along with a few pegs of liquor in Marilyn Monroe style, and let it be known through a poetic suicide note that she was ending her life because she felt jilted by a lover? Then she might have qualified as a subject for many a bestseller, as well as Hollywood romance. Monroe continues to be one of the most celebrated icons of femininity in the Western world. But Charan Shah was foolish enough to be born poor in a country which is the favourite object of contempt and flagellation for twentieth-century modernists, and so she becomes a symbol of Indian primitivism. Would we be as outraged if, out of grief, she stopped eating and slowly starved herself to death?

The sad truth is that the educated elite express horror mostly about those things which the West looks down upon. People who cremate their dead instead of giving them a decent Christian burial are already somewhat uncivilized in the eyes of many westerners. Therefore, a Charan Shah who jumps onto her husband's pyre instead of swallowing sleeping pills becomes ten times more uncivilized. When women demean themselves in ways currently approved by the West, nobody is particularly upset.

There is some validity in the argument that by idealizing such sacrificial acts, women are conditioned into believing that their lives are essentially worthless after their husband's death. But is it fair that people whose value system meets our disapproval, or whose deities we don't judge worthy of respect, should be treated as criminals simply because we have the privilege and power to implement any kind of legislation against them? Do the reformers give others similar rights to impose restrictions on their practices, values, and objects of worship?

Some others taking a more benign approach argue that the poor villagers of Satpura take to extolling sati because they have been denied the benefits of modern, liberal education. Hence they retain 'primitive' cultural practices. Reformers are convinced it is 'a lethal combination of superstition and prejudice that accounts for the veneration elicited by Charan Shah'. They tell us that 'apart from stern official measures, it will take years of educational effort with a pronounced bias in favour of the cultivation of a rational and scientific temper', and 'a genuine campaign for the empowerment of women through a sustained liberal education' to combat the culture which valorizes anti-women traditions like sati.

ICONS OF 'MODERN' TIMES

However, the beneficiaries of liberal and rational education often worship and deify far more harmful varieties of icons on a much grander scale—and that too proudly—without granting others the right to protest or condemnation.

A good example of a lavish glorification cult constructed around a negative role model is that of Princess Diana, a woman who led a very self-destructive existence. She began her public life by willingly offering a virginity test to prove herself worthy of marrying a known philanderer—all because he belonged to a rich and royal family. Despite that, she failed to win either his respect or love. Diana herself admitted to constant humiliation and neglect by her husband while he had a merry time with his mistress. Yet, she desperately kept trying to be sexually attractive for him. In the process, she developed severe eating disorders, starved herself until she became a mental, emotional, and physical wreck—all so that she could stay fashionably trim and beautiful for her uncaring prince. She spent a good part of her life shopping, buying designer clothes and jewellery in order to mesmerize people with her glamour and charm. When all those tactics failed with her prince, she got into a series of exploitative clandestine relationships—including one with her riding instructor, who literally auctioned their love story for millions of pounds. Finally, she died a perfectly unheroic death with yet another clandestine lover.

Ms Diana had everything going for her—a rich family, good, modern, 'liberal' education, beauty, health, social status, and powerful connections. Yet, what a sorry mess she made of her life. She lent a bit of glamour to a few good causes by occasional forays into social work, but the bulk of her energy seems to have been channelled into looking pretty, engaging in unsatisfactory romantic alliances, and coping with the resultant emotional melodramas.

ONLY APPROVED MODES OF WORSHIP ALLOWED!

It has been a long-standing demand of feminist reformers that ancient sati temples must be declared illegal and shut down because they glorify the sati cult, thus beckoning women to follow suit.

First, for all the so-called glorification of sati in certain regions, we have not witnessed anything resembling a sati epidemic. For all the sati temples in Rajasthan, not many women offer themselves for immolation, including those who might bow in reverence before a sati shrine. After Roop Kanwar's immolation in 1987, there have been no more than three cases of attempted self-immolations by widows in India. Each of these was easily averted by timely intervention. Even before the anti-sati act was passed, a very small number of women killed themselves on their husband's pyres within the last several decades.

Trying to close sati temples by force has the potential of setting into motion a very dangerous dynamic. Taking an authoritarian route to social reform is mostly counterproductive. Today, one group demands the closure of sati temples because they violate the values of one community. Tomorrow, another group might demand the closure of all Kali temples because they might see her worship as idealizing vengeful aspects of femininity. Some others might want Krishna temples declared illegal because he was a known philanderer and polygamist. Still others might want Ram temples banned because he subjected his wife to a cruel *agnipariksha*. Then there will be some group of 'rationalists' who might want all churches closed down because Jesus Christ claimed to be the son of God without offering any 'scientific' evidence for the same. There is indeed no end to this game of any self-declared group of social reformers seeking to discipline others into 'approved' behaviour and making them worship only certain 'approved' deities.

One of the great strengths of our civilization is that people are free to choose their own gods, their own modes of worship. New icons are constantly invented without need for sanction from any hierarchical authority. Each village has its own preferred pantheon of gods and goddesses, with varied sets of qualities for which they are deified. For instance, Ram is valued because he was supposedly perfection incarnate. Likewise, Krishna is revered despite the fact that he deceived and played tricks on everyone—including his mother, lovers, wives, friends, and enemies as part of an elaborate *leela*. There are goddesses like Parvati who are approached as benign mothers, symbols of happy conjugality, and wifely devotion. However, that does not come in the way of the same people celebrating Radha's 'illicit', extramarital love for Krishna. In Mahoba itself, a Radha Krishna temple coexists with a sati mandir in the same complex. Then, there are ferocious Chandi–Durga-type of goddesses who strike fear in the hearts of devotees because any man who tried taming or desecrating them invited death in the most brutal manner.

Even Mahoba region has very recently created such an icon. To quote Smeeta Mishra Pandey: '...It was in March last year that I had visited Mahoba chasing yet another tale: the story of Ram Shree, the village woman who along with her brother and father killed her relatives. Shree was the first woman to have been given a death sentence after Independence. ...It was no different last year [in Shree's Tingra *gaon* in Mahoba district].

'Villagers then spent their evening narrating tales about Ram Shree. They often debated whether Ram Shree did the right thing. Shree had apparently killed her relatives because they had tortured her and beaten her up mercilessly. Women wondered...why the court had anything to do with happenings in their village. In no time, Ram Shree became a living legend. When the Supreme Court swapped her death sentence for life imprisonment, taking pity on her one-and-a-half-year-old daughter, the villagers believed the Goddess had come to her rescue' (*The Indian Express*, 16 November 1999).

The coexistence of Ram Shree legends along with Charan Shah's shows that the culture of this region allows for diverse ideals and icons to be celebrated simultaneously. The same people who worship Sita or Charan Shah as symbols of wifely devotion are also capable of valorising Durga-like behaviour by ordinary village women.

Moreover, there is no sharp divide between divine and human in the Hindu tradition. On the one hand, gods come to earth in varied human avatars to share the trials and tribulations of ordinary human beings. On the other, human beings can easily achieve divine status by living extraordinary lives and displaying inspiring qualities. Numerous village gods and goddesses in India are creations of this latter process. What is best, deification is not confined to the human form of creation. We sanctify various living and non-living beings—cows, trees, elephants, snakes, mice, monkeys, and even rivers, stones, mountains, earth, sun, moon, and winds. At the same time in some states like Tamil Nadu there are temples where popular film stars are enshrined as deities.

Those who have tried to cure us of polytheism and become subservient to the dictates of monotheistic faiths have inflicted a great deal of violence on our people throughout this millennium. Let us not become willing agents for carrying that legacy forward.

As long as sati shrines coexist with Durga and Yogini temples, as long as Parvati is not forced to repress her Kali-*roop*, as long as none of our gods dare claim perfection and demand the banishment of others, we will continue to value tolerance, dissent, diversity, respect for different ways of doing and living—to have regard for the diverse species that inhabit this earth and life forces that coexist in this universe. As long as our people feel free and empowered to choose their own gods and goddesses, they will respect the choices of others as well.

Those who wish to arrogate to themselves the right to subject other people's modes of worship to an arbitrarily determined qualifying criteria—no matter how well intended—can easily veer towards Stalinist forms of repression or trigger off counter-demands for more censorship. If I demand a ban on sati worship through coercive means, others can very well demand a ban on *Manushi* because it advocates easy and stigma-free divorce. To safeguard my own freedom, I have to respect that of others.

However, as emphasized earlier, the call for state intervention is valid when there is evidence of force being used to make someone adopt a pernicious tradition, or when violence is committed in the name of religion and social custom. Invoking laws to deal with crime is perfectly legitimate, but using the *danda* of the police, and threatening imprisonment to force a change in cultural values, inevitably leads to backlash.

Real reform lies in creating viable options which are easily accessible and help women move out of dependence. We have to have faith that the vast majority of people tend to act in self-affirming ways when circumstances don't constrict their choices. But nihilistic acts come easily to defeated people whose life is a long, arduous struggle without hope.

Not just the royalty-stricken Brits, but millions all over Europe, America, Australia, and other parts of the world have remained star-struck, obsessively following the shenanigans of this foolish woman. When Diana died, thousands of people—all beneficiaries of modern, liberal education—queued up to offer tributes to her. Even today they buy tickets to have a darshan of her grave, which is crowded with mounds of flowers, trinkets, love epistles, and much more. Dresses worn by her are auctioned at astronomical prices. A whole industry has emerged around the myth and legend of Lady Diana. Even the saintly Mother Teresa's demise was overshadowed by the mass mourning and hysteria evoked by Diana's filmy death.

Now, many of us do find this whole drama and glorification not just silly but also damaging. Diana's life holds up a very negative role model for women. It teaches women to be self-pitying, hungry, and desperate for male attention, and to give in to feelings of worthlessness if men don't respond as desired. Yet would I have the right to propose that the crowds thronging Diana's grave should be declared criminals, lathi-charged by police (as was done at Charan Shah's immolation site), arrested on charges of idealizing this woman, and then sentenced to life imprisonment or death?

Since I don't believe in authoritarian, statist measures for reforming or curing people out of their mental kinks or personal values, I wouldn't actually suggest death sentences or prison terms for the crazies who went into mass madness over Diana. But I would certainly want to recommend psychiatric treatment for all such people, including some in our country who stayed glued to television for days on end, wallowing in Diana's tragic saga, and those who wasted huge amounts of newspaper space to give us detailed glimpses of that fairly flimsy life.

Needless to say, we wouldn't be allowed the right to rectify the world views of Diana devotees. But the rest of the world thinks it has the right to 'educate', to 'civilize', to 'modernize' those who consider Charan Shah praiseworthy.

Secular Icons More Sacred?

Some 'rationalists' might well argue that the exaltation of Diana or Marilyn Monroe is secular whereas Charan Shah has become a religious icon. There are serious flaws in this line of argument. Are we concerned about potentially harmful icons and role models or about whether they come with religious or secular connotations? Why should only religious icons be banned and why not secular ones as well? What is so sacred about the secular domain?

Commercializing Sati

An additional concern voiced by our reformers is that the villagers of Satpura have started propagating a mystique about Charan Shah 'in order to translate the alleged sati into a money-spinning enterprise'. It has also been said that villagers are keen on converting that immolation site into a pilgrimage spot, since they expect many visitors after the interest generated by the event. This in turn may lead to some increased income for to the community.

First, most of this is in the realm of speculation. Both the NCW and AIDWA reports have emphasized that media reports about 'devotees' thronging at the cremation site are highly exaggerated and irresponsible. Pressmen took photographs of a couple of family members of Charan Shah performing the usual post-funeral rituals to build a case that they were promoting a sati cult.

Even if it were true that by romanticizing the death of one Charan Shah this horribly neglected and poverty stricken village hopes to receive a little cash flow, I find it a more understandable venture than other more modern and socially approved forms of commercialization. Today, thanks to generous grants available from international aid organizations, a whole slew of educated, 'enlightened' people are making a living from writing about atrocities on Indian women, organizing seminars on the theme, and filming the subject. There won't be any dearth of people likely to want to make documentaries on the Satpura sati; any number of research grants will be proposed to discuss the misery and cultural backwardness of this region where a few sati temples already exist. Myriad careers will be enhanced as people suddenly become experts on the culture of sati. Even those who would never subject themselves to the inconvenience of making a trip to Satpura village and spending a couple of days there, will organize glamorous conferences in foreign universities, write glamorous treatises on the subject, construct and deconstruct Charan Shah's life until it becomes unrecognizable to even her own children. These will be important additions to various CVs, but there is not a faint chance that even one rupee from all the thousands of dollars or lakhs of rupees thus earned would reach those miserable creatures upon whose lives we castigate and pontificate.

What if Satpura villagers were to demand the enactment of a law which stipulates that anyone making money by writing about or filming a sati case should be declared a criminal? How about a law which lays down that getting hefty grants to produce 'research' for foreign universities and international aid agencies will invite life imprisonment? Or those making films on the real or imagined miseries of Indian women will be subjected to punitive fines if they make any money for it?

Today, these activities documenting the event fetch far more money, name, and fame than running a sati temple in India. Those who disapprove of commercializing Roop Kanwar or Charan Shah's sati cults by people of their respective communities, ought to be willing to have similar curbs put on the commercialization of social concern, whereby a whole tribe of people have made hi-fi, jet-set careers out of peddling the poverty and misery of Indian women in the international arena—of making a lucrative profession of defaming and condemning people with whom they have no relationship. More often than not, these commentators do not even embrace the ethical responsibility which calls for accuracy in their facts and credibility in their interpretations. Information is disseminated to the world on BBC, CNN, and ABC—not to those people whose lives are to be critiqued and presumably reformed. If a money-making scheme in the name of various Charan Shahs and Roop Kanwars is a condemnable practice when done by their own communities, how does it become a respectable moral intervention when taken up by total strangers?

All this however is not in support of a culture that encourages women to devalue their own being and adjudge their own worth only as *suhagin*s. There is an urgent need to combat actively all those received notions which condition women to act in destructive ways. To do that effectively we need to learn to distinguish between crime and culture. For example, if honest and judicious investigations reveal that Charan had been goaded into killing herself, the act can be legitimately classified as murder—in which case the Indian Penal Code can be justifiably invoked. Even calling it 'sati murder' as some reformers have done is absurd because two words are mutually contradictory. Even supporters of sati cults would be able to make common cause in preventing such acts because according to the logic of their own value system, they cannot possibly apotheosize a murdered woman as a sati. However, if Charan Shah's devotion to her spouse and unwillingness to live without him leads to a whole heroic cult emerging around her, this falls in the realm of culture, not crime.

In such situations, there is need for not only a dialogue, for understanding the mainsprings of such ideologies, but also for channelling the idealism that sustains them into more creative expressions. We have to approach people as caring insiders rather than as attacking outsiders if we want their cooperation in building a new, life-affirming culture of respect for women. By refusing to draw a distinction between coerced immolation and a voluntary act of Charan Shah's, we are needlessly lending respectability to criminal acts of violence against women.

Notes

[1] Kishwar, Madhu, 'Deadly Laws and Zealous Reformers: The Conflicting Interpretatious and Politics of Sati', in *Manushi*, No. 115, November–December 1999.

[2] 'Sati' really means a 'woman of chastity', a woman 'devoted to her husband'. 'Sati' does not mean, a woman who burns herself on her dead husband's funeral pyre. The practice of widow-burning was termed 'satidaha', meaning 'burning of a devoted wife'. Form this, the term 'sati' got the extended meaning of 'a widow who burns herself on her husband's funeral pyre'.

[3] Investigative reports by women's organizations came several days later. All India Democratic Women's Association [AIDWA] released its reports on 16 November 1999 followed by another one by National Commission for Women [NCW]. Since AIDWA's findings went contrary to the demand for stringent action by several women activists, yet another multi-organization team went and made their own enquiry. As is evident, there are substantial differences in their 'factual narration' as also in their interpretation of events.

[4] What is meant here is Commission of Sati (Prevention) Act, 1987.

21

Secondary Sources

Romila Thapar, 'In History'[1]

Romila Thapar's article on sati, produced in response to the burning of Roop
Kanwar, provides an excellent overview of the origins of sati, and its historical development. She deals with both textual authorities and social issues,
debunking some older explanations of the custom's development (e.g. Muslim invasions) and contextualizing the issues involved for contemporary audience.

PERSPECTIVE IN HISTORY

P.V. Kane in his monumental work, *History of Dharmasastra*, starts
his brief chapter on sati with what can only be described now as
a quotable quote. He states: 'This subject is now of academic
interest in India since for over a hundred years (i.e. from 1829)
self-immolation of widows has been prohibited by law in British
India and has been declared to be a crime.'

What is of significance today is not just the incidence of widows
becoming satis but the attempt to justify a custom at a particular
historical juncture, a justification which involves more than merely
a custom for it also symbolizes an attitude towards women as
well as a view of what is regarded as 'tradition'. It is defended as
being a recognized symbol of Hindu values especially those concerning the idealized relationship between husband and wife,
the assumption being that it was therefore required in theory of all
Hindu women. Another prevalent view is that it was necessitated
by the 'Muslim invasions' when upper-caste Hindu women resorted

to it to defend their honour from Muslim marauders, a view which was propagated in the nineteenth century. Neither of these is supported by historical evidence. The defence of sati today is a deliberate attempt at justifying an act for reasons quite other than the preservation of Hindu values and the assumptions which accompany the revival of sati require investigation.

It is easy enough to take the stand that those who do not accept sati as part of the Hindu tradition are westernized Indians deracinated from the mainsprings of the Hindu ethos and therefore unable to understand either the Rajput concept of honour or to appreciate the idealized relationship between a Hindu husband and wife, such, that it is sought to be perpetuated to eternity through sati; or to see that sati is a pure act of the ultimate in sacrifice (even if such an act is reduced to a public spectacle with a variety of entrepreneurs literally cashing in on it). Such arguments deny a discussion on the subject and the latter is necessary if we are to attempt an understanding of our traditions. Traditions in any case often arise out of contemporary needs but seek legitimation from the past. Therefore, the past has to be brought into play where such legitimation is sought.

There is no simple explanation for the origin of the custom of burning widows on the pyres of their dead husbands. It is said to be a symbol of aristocratic status associated with many early societies such as those of the Greeks and the Scythians. There is, however, no other society where it was practised by variant social groups for different reasons at various points in time and where the controversy over whether or not it should be practised was so clearly articulated over many centuries. Because of this, in India it underwent changes of meaning as well as degrees of acceptance.

Its origin is generally traced to the subordination of women in patriarchal society and this seems to be the form it takes in more recent times. But in searching for origins it might be as well to consider other situations which prevailed in India. The notion of bride-price for example, can suggest in some situations the purchase of a woman, the logical termination of which may have been the requirement of her dying together with her husband, although this is not typical of bride-price. But perhaps a more acceptable explanation may relate to societies changing their systems of kinship and inheritance. In some circumstances the wife would be an alien in the early stages of change. Control over female sexuality would be a further reason. The practice may have originated among societies in flux and become customary among those holding property such as the families of chiefs and Kshatriyas. Once it was established as a custom associated with the Kshatriyas it would continue to be so among those claiming Kshatriya status as well.

The earliest hint comes from the *Rig Veda* of the second millennium BC although the text does not provide evidence of the act. The Vedic texts on the contrary endorse the system of niyoga or levirate where a widow is permitted to marry her husband's brother if she has not borne a son to her husband. Levirate in patrilineal clans is often intended to consolidate property. In the *Rig Veda* the act was only a mimetic ceremony. The widow lay on her husband's funeral pyre before it was lit but was raised from it by a male relative of her dead husband. Attempts were made, probably in the sixteenth century, to seek Vedic sanction for the act by changing the word *agre*, to go forth into *agneh*, to the fire, in the specific verse. But since the widow is not meant to immolate herself this change is spurious. The Vedic act, referring to families of high status, may encapsulate the termination of an earlier practice or the symbolic death of the wife.

The act of immolation is first described in Greek texts of the first century BC quoting from earlier accounts referring to incidents of the fourth century. Widows are burnt on the funeral pyres of their dead husbands among the Katheae (Kshatriya/Khattiya) in the Punjab. Unable to explain this practice the author remarks that it was an attempt to prevent wives from poisoning their husbands! According to the same sources bride-price was the prevalent custom in the Punjab. If bride-price was a factor, one would expect it to encourage the legitimacy of sati in other parts of India as well where the Kshatriya ethos combined with this form of marriage. Bride-price incidentally is objected to in the early dharmashastras as being degrading whereas the giving of a dowry is favoured. The Mahabharata has references to some widows becoming satis such as Madri the wife of Pandu or the wives of Krishna. Curiously, the custom is not generally observed among other Pandavas or by the wives of those Kauravas who died in the battle at Kurukshetra. It was obviously not required of all Kshatriyas. It has been argued that these references to sati are late interpolations. Madri however was from the Punjab. Krishna's marriage to Rukmani was said to be unorthodox as he had abducted her. Kidnapping and the paying of bride-price were ranked as low among the eight forms of marriage listed in the dharmashastras.

The dharmashastras seem to hold contradictory views on sati. The Munoo Dharamashastra dating to the turn of the Christian era requires the widow to live a chaste life and if she has no son, then alone is she permitted to obtain one through niyoga. The later Vishnu Dharmashastra allows an option to the widow: she can either be celibate and live like an ascetic or else can become a sati. Medhatithi, the major commentator on Munoo, writing in about the tenth century AD is strongly opposed to widows becoming satis. He argues that the practice is *adharma* and *ashastriya*, against the laws of dharma and not conceded by the shastras. He maintains that it amounts to suicide which is forbidden and that each person must live his allotted span of life. He even urges that in some situations a widow should be permitted to remarry. Medhatithi's position was not unique and the discussion was controversial and continued to be so over the centuries. That Medhatithi felt it necessary to comment forcefully on sati whereas Munoo does not even refer to it, indicates its wider prevalence during the later period. Nevertheless, there are also inscriptions from these times which record widows from royal families donating property to religious beneficiaries.

This change is reflected in other sources as well. The *Hitopadesha*, a collection of stories dating to the early first millennium AD glorifies the act of becoming a sati with the theory that it ensures for the wife and the husband an eternity of living together after death. The act is described in various texts as *sahamarana* (dying together), *sahagamana* (going together) and *anuvarohana* (ascending the pyre). More precisely dateable evidence comes from inscriptions. An inscription of AD 510 at Eran in central India refers to the wife of Goparaja who immolated herself when her husband died in battle. The practice was by now well known in this area. Similar inscriptions from Rajasthan and Nepal date to the seventh and eighth centuries AD. This evidence predates even the emergence of Islam let alone its arrival in India. Banabhatta writing the *Harshacharita* in the seventh century AD does not condemn the mother of king Harshavardhana for becoming a sati, perhaps because the book was an official biography. But in his other work, the *Kadambari*, he objects strongly to the practice and lists many women of high status who did not become satis.

Inscriptions from the peninsula refer to women becoming satis when their husbands died in battles fought between and among Hindu rulers such as the Chalukyas, Yadavas, and Hoysalas, in the period from the tenth to the fourteenth centuries AD. Many of these inscriptions are located in Maharashtra and Karnataka. The peak period of sati in these areas was pre-Islamic in that Muslim invasions were not the cause. However, when faced by Turkish armies from the end of the thirteenth century, the earlier ritual would have continued. The other interesting feature is that most of these inscriptions refer either to families of Kshatriya status or those seeking such a status. One oft-quoted inscription of the eleventh century refers to a Shudra woman whose husband died in battle against the Ganga ruler and who, in spite of the opposition from her parents became a sati. Her husband held a high military position under Chola control. Her insistence may have been occasioned, among other things, by the wish to establish status. The custom, it would seem, was prevalent at this time among those who held high administrative and military positions generally associated with Kshatriyas. Therefore, it is likely that members of lower castes holding similar positions emulated the style of the Kshatriyas.

Another indication of the existence of satis are the sati memorial stones. These have been recorded and studied in some detail only in recent years. The location, numbers, chronology and the statements both inscriptional and visual, of the hero-stones and the associated sati-stones have provided new insights into the history of these areas (S. Setter and G. D. Sontheimer, *Memorial Stones*, Dharwad, 1982). Some of these areas were subject to raids by kingdoms in the vicinity, contesting this territory. The sati-stones generally occur in the same locality as the hero-stones which commemorated death in the course of a heroic act of either defending the village or a herd of cattle or of killing predatory wild animals and so on. Sometimes the sati-stone and the hero-stone are on the same slab. The sati-stone has a standard set of symbols: the sun and the moon indicating eternity, an upright, open, right arm and hand, bent at the elbow and clearly showing bangles intact (a woman's bangles being broken when she is widowed, the bangles being intact would be an indication of her continuing marital status); a lime held in the hand to ward off evil. On occasion a sati is indicated by a single standing female figure or a couple, where generally the right arm of the woman has the same features as above.

Sati-stones like hero-stones occur more often, not in fertile agricultural mainlands but in ecologically marginal areas, where local conflicts and skirmishes would be frequent. Possibly in marginal areas, the process of transition from tribe to jati may have required an underlining of the new norms which would have implications for the inheritance and status of women. Tribal chiefs are also memorialized in hero-stones and this was part of the process of kshatriya-ization, assimilation into the Sanskritic tradition. Doubtless by now, sati would also have played a part in the adoption of a Kshatriya lifestyle.

Inscriptional and archaeological evidence suggests that greater occurrence of immolation seems to date to the end of the first and the early second millennium AD. This was a time of new areas being opened up to settlement by caste-based society and encroachments on a larger scale into tribal areas. New castes emerged in this background of a changing economy, some with antecedents in the earlier pre-caste society. In the competition for status various observances of upper-caste society became current. Why the immolation of widows was introduced requires explanation. Apart from other things it may relate to a deliberate subordination of women who had earlier had an important role. As a ritual it was the most traumatic in underlining the subordination of women. Or, it could have been a reaction against the many growing socio-religious movements some of which disapproved of caste differentiations and supported the continuing participation of women in social roles whether as wives or widows, and which movements were not always regarded with favour by the upper castes. The immolation of widows may have been seen as a method of demarcating status.

It is interesting that there is little reference to the deification of the woman at this time. The incentive to becoming a sati is accompanied by a listing of rewards for the woman. She will dwell in heaven for as many years as there are hairs on the human body and will dwell with her husband served by *apsaras*. (In some Kannada texts the wife is said to be jealous of the apsaras and therefore insistent on dying with her husband). Her act will purify of all sins, not only her husband but also her parents and of course herself. The inclusion of her parents was a shrewd move appealing to her filial emotions. The ultimate threat is that if she does not burn she will be reborn as a woman in many successive births. The package of rewards is based quite clearly on the Kshatriya view of the afterlife. Only the hero went to Indraloka (or to Shivaloka as in the Kerala tradition), and lived eternally in heaven. The other view of afterlife, as developed in the theory of karma and *sansara*, action and rebirth, did not necessarily apply to the hero. Heaven for the hero is a paradise land. The notion of sati therefore is tied to the heroic ideal of the Kshatriya and it is not surprising that up to this point in history it is not permitted to other castes and specifically not to Brahman women as is stated in the *Padma Purana*. But this was soon to change. In the early second millennium AD, the *Mitakshara*, a legal text treating of family law, argued that all women be permitted to become satis and that niyoga be prohibited.

A very different point of view emerges from another category of people and texts. The followers of the Shakta sects were opposed to it even from the religious point of view. The *Mahanirvana Tantra* states, 'A wife should not be burnt with her dead husband. Every woman is the embodiment of the goddess. That woman who in her delusion ascends the funeral pyre of her husband, shall go to hell.' This contradiction of the Kshatriya ethic has its own interest as a statement of opposition particularly as it comes from those who were initially regarded as being of lesser status but constituting the larger percentage of people. Possibly, this kind of opposition nurtured the compensatory notion of a sati being converted into a goddess, a notion which seems to have gained currency in the later second millennium AD. Madri in the Mahabharata for instance, is not deified.

As the idea developed it was said that the goddess entered the body of the woman when she resolved to become a sati. Deification was a compensation for suicide and acted as an incentive as well as an attempt to take the act onto another plane, where mundane considerations would not apply. But the deification was not individualized, for the women are not worshipped as goddesses in their own name but as part of the generalized sati goddess. There was less emphasis now on the continuity of living with the husband after death in heaven. Was this due to non-Kshatriya women, especially Brahmans being encouraged to become satis?

It is also worth remembering that Buddhist texts did not support sati and widows were instead welcomed as nuns if they so chose. Some of the votive inscriptions at Buddhist stupas record donations by widows. The later Jaina texts conceded that in special circumstances a Jaina muni could die by slow starvation. This concession prevented the Jainas from opposing other forms of suicide. However, judging by the large number of Jaina widows who became nuns, it is evident that although some might have become satis, this was not the prevailing custom.

It has been stated that there was an epidemic of satis in south India at the time when the Vijayanagara kingdom was collapsing. In 1420, Nicolo dei Conti visited Vijayanagara well before its peak period in the early sixteenth century and left an account which survives only through a series of translations. He describes the ritual of self-immolation and adds that three thousand wives and concubines of the king of Vijayanagara had pledged to burn themselves on the death of the king. We have only Conti's word for the pledge and there is no other evidence to prove that it was carried out. Nor did the neighbouring Muslim Bahmani kingdom have to do with such a pledge since the princess of Vijayanagara had been married with great pomp and splendour to the Bahmani Sultan, Barbosa, and Nuniz visiting in the early sixteenth century also refer to the ritual but again in general terms.

There was a spate of European traders after the Portuguese established settlements on the coast. These visitors found the custom new and strange and described it at length. This perhaps gives the impression that it was more prevalent in Vijayanagara than elsewhere. There is in fact little evidence to suggest that there was a substantial increase to epidemic proportions in self-immolation in the south at the time of the collapse of the Vijayanagara kingdom in the late sixteenth century.

State intervention to try and control incidents of widow immolation begins during the time of the Sultans and the Mughals. They could not prohibit it but indirectly attempted to reduce the numbers by insisting that it should not be forced on the woman. We are told that those wishing to become satis had to obtain a special licence from the governors of the Mughal provinces. If this was actually so it might have acted as a deterrent. That the need for permission became part of the procedure seems evident from incidents occurring even among Indian communities living outside India. 'In 1723, the widow of an Indian merchant in Moscow asked permission to be burned alive alongside her husband on his funeral pyre. Her request was refused. At once all the Indian factors disgusted by this act, decided to leave Russia, taking their wealth with them. Faced with this threat the authorities gave in. The incident was repeated in 1767.'[2]

That families of wealthy traders took to this practice in the eighteenth century was doubtless due to their close proximity to political power and Kshatriya practice. This was particularly the case in regions such as Rajasthan where many kingdoms derived substantial revenue from the traders. Possibly, this association with commercial groups encouraged the emergence of the sati temples. Sati memorials in the past were simple memorial stones, but the more recent temples are vast enterprises such as the one at Jhunjhunu, where the Marwari talent for finance has combined with Rajput notions of honour, to the material benefit of both. There is a continuing link between sati temples and the Marwari community elsewhere, too. The appropriation of the custom by other upper castes was known in the eighteenth century, although there was no uniformity of attitude towards it within the caste or even within the extended family. Thus whereas one Peshwa was opposed to it, the wife of another became a sati in 1772.

The practice of immolating widows took a turn in a new direction from the seventeenth century in eastern India. The overwhelming incidence was among the Brahmans of this area and particularly in Bengal. The major cause for this unprecedented rise in widow immolation, particularly in the early nineteenth century has been attributed to the legal system relating to inheritance. In areas where the Dayabhaga system prevailed, as in eastern India, women were entitled to a share in the inheritance of immovable property on the death of their husbands. Sati became a means of removing one among the claimants to inheritance. It is interesting that during the second millennium AD. when Brahman widows were permitted to become satis, this was also the time when Brahman property holders increased both in numbers owing to the land grants which they received from royalty. Thus what was in origin a custom associated with Kshatriya notions of heroism and honour was now converted into a convenient way of eliminating an inheritor. It has been suggested that the largest occurrence was among *kulin* Brahman families for the ratio of male to female seems to have been severely out of balance, requiring that the kulin marry many wives from several families. The effect of this on the ritual of widow immolation was self-evident.

The movement for the abolition of widow self-immolation was hesitatingly taken up by the British Indian government and was supported by Rammohan Roy. Eventually in 1829, a law was passed prohibiting the practice in territories held by the British Indian government. The figures given for registered cases of sati in the early nineteenth century in the Bengal Presidency are quite staggering. In 1815 there were 378 cases. In 1818 the figure rose to 839 and in 1828 there were 463 cases. These figures make an interesting parallel to those of dowry deaths in recent years. If widow immolation is to be seen as significant to Hindu values it would seem that Hindu culture has a propensity to burn its women. A magistrate of Hooghly describes the practice in 1818 as a religious act but also a choice entertainment for the neighbourhood. In areas where the Dayabhaga did not prevail and there was also an absence of kulin custom, the figures are substantially lower. The Madras Presidency in 1818 registers about 170 cases and the Bombay Presidency over the period from 1819–27, about fifty. Here it was largely among the families of chiefs and rajas.

This sharp variation in figures suggests that the appalling frequency of widow immolation, was, for various reasons endemic to Bengal at this time and its occurrence cannot be attributed only to the disjuncture in society caused by British colonial domination. Given the wide popularity of Shakta and Tantric sects in eastern India it is possible that the deliberate subordination of upper-caste widows was also a reaction to the more equitable status of women in these sects. The Shakta sects which, more than most, emphasized the androgynous both in belief and deity, were opposed to the self-immolation of widows.

Viewed over time, the justification for widows becoming satis moved from the initial explanation that it was the faithful wife following her husband into death to one which included the idea of the sati becoming a goddess. In some cases the faithful wife followed her husband irrespective of how he died, as in the case of Madri. Here the question of honour was not centrally involved as Pandu, if anything, died an ignoble death, unable to contain his lust for Madri. And Madri gives this as one of the reasons why she should follow her husband into the realms of Yama. Faithfulness in this situation seems theoretical, since both Pandu's wives had conceived sons from various other males, albeit deities, Pandu not being in a position to father a child.

The memorial stones suggest a different situation, where the husband dies a hero's death and the self-immolation of the wife is also memorialized. It is possible that immolation could have been enforced as a requirement to enhance the glory of the hero's death. The question of honour becomes central to the explanation where there is the possible violation of the wife by the enemy. The third situation relates to that of elimination of a competitor for inheritance where both faithfulness and deification are emphasized. These situations relate to families of the upper castes and of high status and wealth. The act is supported by some persons of the upper castes, condemned by others of the same castes, but prohibited among those whose beliefs and values are said to have prevailed to a larger extent among the lower castes and persons of lesser status. The degree to which the motives conformed to the explanation given or arose from other factors needs to be analysed.

This is not to deny that on rare occasions it may have been an act of genuine grief and the desire to follow a husband into death. That the act of immolation is a form of sacrifice seems to be a more recent interpretation. The widow's life was not an offering or *bali* for the motivation of the act in theory is that she continues to live after death with her husband in heaven. Furthermore, it can only be an act of self-sacrifice if it is not enforced.

It is argued that sati involves the question of Rajput honour and is deeply ingrained in all Rajputs. It is surely rather dishonourable that a society's honour should be dependent on women having to immolate themselves. The frequency of female infanticide in these areas makes one suspect that it was less a matter of honour and more a matter of other concerns. The custom has not been limited to Rajputs alone in the past, as has been claimed by various recently organized Rajput associations.

It is also quoted as a symbol of an idealized husband–wife relationship. If so, it has an unbalanced manifestation for, as has often been remarked, there is never any question of the husband immolating himself on the pyre of his wife. Nor is the immolation of the widow invariably voluntary. The widows of Bengal had to be tied to the pyre and kept down by bamboo staffs and there is little certainty that recent acts of immolation were also not enforced.

When it is stated that sati is a revival or continuation of a tradition, the particular tradition and the particular social group professing it needs to be ascertained. An attempt is being made to transfer a ritual associated with a small segment of upper-caste society to the entire society with the claim that it is the rite/right of the Hindu community. It was never regarded as universally applicable to all Hindus and even its limited applicability has always been controversial. Neither among Kshatriyas nor among Brahmans was there a universal adherence to the custom. When it is taken up arbitrarily by some members of castes other than the Kshatriyas, it is in the context of demonstrating status or linked to property inheritance. Thus, in spite of the disapproval of the act in their own religious texts it was observed on occasion by the wives of certain Sikh chiefs and of Maharaja Ranjit Singh. The justification incorrectly sought from Hindu dharma is an attempt to legitimize it so that it can be treated as universally applicable.

To argue that the abolition of sati is a deliberately anti-Hindu act is to replay the debate of the nineteenth century where Rammohan Roy had maintained correctly that it does not carry the sanction of the Vedas and Mrityunjaya Vidyalankar maintained that it was not enjoined by the shastras. If status has to be demonstrated today there are other ways of doing it than by burning wives.

That sati is being claimed as a Rajput ritual links it to the present-day concerns of the Rajputs. They were earlier the dominant caste both in terms of social status and access to economic resources not only in Rajasthan but in many parts of northern India. That dominance is now being eroded by new political groups. The Rajputs therefore seek to demonstrate their solidarity and status through other kinds of actions. One mechanism is to choose a ritual which is controversial and insist on supporting it. This is also one way of testing strength.

The choice of sati ties in with what is seen as a major threat to traditional authority, the changing role and status of women. The questioning of the earlier subordinate status of women is perceived as a loss of face for a male-dominated society. This reflects a social crisis but nevertheless, the reason why it results in the burning of widows cannot be explained merely by the existence of a social crisis. Apart from this, by demonstrating solidarity on an issue such as sati there is a covert attempt to mobilize Rajputs and to undermine the perceived changes. This is in turn linked to political faction fights where those claiming to belong to Rajput castes can use this issue either way to consolidate their factions.

The notion of sati has moved a long way from questions of honour, the faithfulness of the wife and the deification of the widow. The particular social groups, supporting sati have changed over time and this change has had to do with the role, function, and rights of women in social relations, property relations, and rituals. Some social crisis may have enhanced the ideal of sati but significantly this idea was also endorsed by upper castes in situations where those of lesser standing argued for a better status for women. The extension of the symbolism of sati from the faithful wife to the goddess was not unrelated to the purposes of the social group endorsing the act. What is being objected to now by many is not merely the act of suicide, or when it is as in most cases enforced, the act of murder, but also the context of the act. This endorses an inconsequential existence for a woman and the subordination of her being to the vulgarity of a public spectacle and to the manipulation of those claiming to be acting in defence of traditional values.

Sporadic references for or against the ritual do not tell us much. If sati is to be properly understood it would require a tracking down of information on widow self-immolation involving a number of sources, pertaining to a range of social groups and with reference to various regions at different points in time. Only when we examine the juxtaposition of kinship, property relations, rights of inheritance, the approach to sexuality, the ethic of the hero, attitudes to deity, and adjustments to social change in the context of our history, will we begin perhaps to understand why and how women were encouraged or forced to become satis.

Notes

[1]   Thapar, Romila, 'In History' in 'Symposium on Sati', *Seminar*, vol. 342, February 1988.

[2]   F. Braudel, *The Wheels of Commerce*, New York, 1979. My attention was drawn to this statement by Nitin Desai.